A CENTURY OF THE

ALL BLACKS

IN BRITAIN AND IRELAND

A CENTURY OF THE

ALL BLACKS

IN BRITAIN AND IRELAND

DAVE FOX, KEN BOGLE & MARK HOSKINS

TEMPUS

Frontispiece: *The All Blacks walk out onto the pitch against Yorkshire & Cumberland in September 1935.*

First published 2006

Tempus Publishing Limited
The Mill, Brimscombe Port,
Stroud, Gloucestershire, GL5 2QG
www.tempus-publishing.com

British Library Cataloguing in Publication Data.
A catalogue record for this book is available from the British Library.

ISBN 0 7524 3355 5

Typesetting and origination by Tempus Publishing Limited
Printed in Great Britain

CONTENTS

FOREWORD

'The All Blacks are coming! The All Blacks are coming!' When I was a young lad and living in the western valleys of South Wales, the thought of an impending All Blacks tour brought visions of excitement and great expectations to the people. The mighty, all-powerful, unbeatable rugby team from the other side of the world was visiting, once again, these shores of Great Britain. Their reputation was immense – their rugby to match – and we were soon to see them on our own playing fields. There were magical qualities to New Zealand rugby, which boasted an amazing seventy-two per cent success rate in Test match rugby, and they have won more Test matches than lost against every nation in the world.

In the days before the World Cup, the Home International Championship and visits by New Zealand and South Africa (Australia came later) were the pinnacles of international rugby for players and supporters alike. But it was the All Blacks' tour that set the rugby world alight. These giant men – kitted out in all-black kit and with their ferocious 'Haka', which was a prelude to every game – became the focus of attention everywhere they visited. To think of actually defeating these giants from the Southern Hemisphere was merely wishful thinking. Yet it did happen!

To play in a side that actually beat the All Blacks was like acquiring a place in rugby folklore. Great victories that spring to mind are Cardiff's famous win in 1953 and Wales's effort to emulate it only a few weeks later. This latter victory was the third defeat for the All Blacks at Cardiff Arms Park. They had previously lost a still-disputed game in 1905 (Wales 3 New Zealand 0), although Deans' 'try' is still claimed by New Zealand!

A game against the All Blacks brought a new dimension to rugby football. Everything seemed so much faster, harder, skilful and committed, yet they were a joy and privilege to be part of, almost irrespective of the result! Everyone who did play will remember 'the day I tackled an All Black!'

The games discussed in this book are those featuring the All Blacks in the UK and Ireland. One thing common to them all, whether in Wales, Ireland, Scotland or England, is that those people who played against these mighty rugby warriors will remember it forever, because it was that special! For me, I played in a game now revered as one of the greatest games ever: Barbarians 23 New Zealand 11. It was as near to perfection as international rugby football could hope to get. It wouldn't have mattered if the All Blacks had won.

John Dawes
Cardiff, March 2005

John Dawes's Barbarians team that defeated New Zealand 23-11 at Cardiff in January 1973. From left to right, back row: E. Lewis (touch judge), G. Windsor Lewis (secretary), J. Pullin, W.J. McBride, R. Wilkinson, D. Quinnell, A. Carmichael, D. Duckham, G. Domercq (referee), D. Spyer (touch judge). Seated: G. Edwards, M. Gibson, G. Hughes (president), J. Dawes (captain), H. Waddell (vice-president), J. Bevan, R. McLoughlin. In front: F. Slattery, T. David, P. Bennett, J.P.R. Williams.

INTRODUCTION AND ACKNOWLEDGEMENTS

There's something special about the New Zealand All Blacks: the raw power and directness; the constant air of invincibility; that indefinable aura that makes them rugby union's biggest attraction. There's also something special when the All Blacks tour, travelling up and down the land and pitting their strength, wits and reputation against local sides, spreading the gospel of rugby in the process.

2005 marks the centenary of the first full New Zealand tour to Great Britain and Ireland. To celebrate the event, we have compiled this book as a record of every game that the All Blacks have played in these islands, beginning with their very first match on British soil against Devon at the County Ground, Exeter, on 16 September 1905. The book includes a handful of 'unofficial' matches when these were tour games in all but name. We have also referred to matches in other countries, such as France or Canada, when these were part of a tour involving at least one of the four home unions, and provided details of New Zealand's matches in the World Cups hosted by England and Wales, although these games were not tours in the traditional sense. The book also includes a review of the 2005 Centenary tour when the All Blacks played all four home nations and achieved their second 'Grand Slam' of victories.

Writing this book has certainly been a challenge and we owe an enormous debt to many people who have been generous with their time and assistance. Our good friend Roger Harris of Cardiff kicked us off with the suggestion that the centenary of the 1905 tour be commemorated with a book. From this came the idea of covering every tour game that the All Blacks have played in Britain and Ireland, but looking at them from a home point of view. Our intention was to have at least one photograph or item of memorabilia to illustrate each game. Thanks to contacts made through the Rugby Memorabilia Society, doors have opened and people have been extraordinarily kind. This book contains many rare illustrations and we are grateful to those who provided them.

Inevitably, we have found conflicts of information in our research. Newspaper reports didn't always match the descriptions in books, particularly regarding the home teams. We spent many hours checking original source material to get as accurate a record as possible. But despite our best efforts, the book may well contain errors and we apologise for our own fallibility.

We would like to thank John Dawes, a man with a unique place in the history of rugby, and New Zealand rugby in particular, for writing his superb foreword. John not only captained the British Lions to their historic win in the Test series of 1971, but also led the Barbarians to their remarkable win over the All Blacks in Cardiff in 1973. There are few British players who can say that they led two sides to victory over the All Blacks.

We would also like to thank the following people: Phil Atkinson, Geoff Austin, Bob Baker, Steve Bennett, Paddy Bradley, David Bridges, Mark 'Semtex' Buchanan, Treve Chesterfield, Jeff Coveney, Willie Darcy, Brian Gillespie, Ron Hall, Paul Harris, Roger Harris, Ann-Rachael Harwood of Cheltenham Art Gallery & Museum, John Hood, Roy Hough, Kevin Jarvis, John Jenkins, Ian Landles of Hawick, Bob Luxford, Bryan Lyons, John Mace, John Methven, Pauline Mills, Ian Mitchell, Ellis Morgan-Thornton, Mike O'Reilly of the Scottish Rugby Union, Feargal O'Rourke, Dave Parfitt, Steve Parrett, Phil Price, Tony Price of Lord Price Pictures, Dai Richards of the World Rugby Museum, Derek Robinson, Andy Shorney, Jed Smith and staff at the Museum of Rugby, John Sullivan, John Treleven, Stan Whitehead, John Whittaker and Les Williams. Special thanks must go to Timothy Auty, Jeff Kemp and Willow Murray who have given immeasurable help. Thanks also to Holly and James at Tempus for giving us the chance to publish this book. We would also like to thank Ray Ruddick, who would have been part of the writing team had it not been for a family bereavement, but who helped greatly with resolving queries and proof-reading.

We would like to thank the *Daily Mail* for permission to publish 'The Whistling Fantasia' and International Artistes Ltd for permission to publish extracts from the work of Max Boyce. Thanks also go to the Alexander Turnbull Library for the Crown Studios images used. Also to *The Yorkshire Post* and *The Daily Telegraph* for permission to use images. The authors have made every effort to identify and trace copyright holders and we apologise in advance if we have inadvertently broken copyright.

Finally, we must thank our families, who have put up with us being away from home, heads buried in old rugby books, or surfing the Internet trying to find answers to obscure questions. Without the patience and support of Bunty and Alison in particular, this book would not have been produced.

DF, KB, MH
March 2005

EXPLANATORY NOTE

The line-ups of the teams listed in this book follow positional rather than numerical sequences. At varying times sides have played with and without numbers or letters, and have been numbered with the full-back wearing 1 or 15. Some superstitious sides have excluded a player wearing 13 but have fielded one wearing 16. The All Blacks have, occasionally, chosen players wearing squad numbers. We felt use of numbers would be very confusing. Broadly speaking, the domestic sides' backs line up as follows: full-back, wing, centre, centre, wing, outside half, scrum-half. The New Zealand backs are listed thus: full-back, wing, centre, wing, second five-eighth, first five-eighth, half-back, with the forwards for both sides the same: prop, hooker, prop, lock, lock, flanker, flanker, number eight. On the early tours, the British and Irish sides tended not to select forwards with specialist positional skills. In 1905 the approach was 'first up, first down' whereas the All Blacks were better organised. New Zealand also had a seven-man scrum plus a wing-forward at this time. He appears as the last man in the list of forwards. The diamond scrum formation they adopted had a two-man front row, and these are the first two forwards appearing on the list. Several home teams opted for the seven-man scrum too, with the spare player frequently utilised as a rover or wing-forward, an extra three-quarter or half-back.

Replacements first appeared in representative rugby in the late 1960s. Initially only used for injury, they were later permitted to be used for tactical purposes.

The point-scoring values have changed over the last 100 years. Conversions and penalties have remained constant at 2 and 3 points respectively but the drop goal value was 4 points until 1948, when it was reduced to 3. The value of the try was 3 points until 1971, when it was increased to 4 points, eventually reaching its current value of 5 in 1992. There was a further method of scoring available to players in the early days – a goal from a mark, made when a clean catch was awarded, and the catcher dropped a goal for 3 points. Changes to the laws have effectively made the goal from a mark impossible since 1977.

Wherever possible, we have used the full initials and correct spelling of the players' names. Some players have rarely had their name spelt properly. Dicky Owen of Swansea and Wales, for example, was actually called Owens. We recognise that there will be occasions where initials are missing, but we have used the information we have. There is one notable exception in David Gallaher, captain of the original All Blacks of 1905. His birth certificate quite clearly states his surname as Gallagher. Whether the loss of the second 'g' was of his choice or not is unknown, but we have used the more familiar spelling of his name throughout this book.

1905/06
NEW ZEALAND TO BRITAIN, FRANCE & NORTH AMERICA

THE MATCHES

Devon	16 September 1905	Exeter	won 55-4
Cornwall	21 September 1905	Camborne	won 41-0
Bristol	23 September 1905	Bristol	won 41-0
Northampton	28 September 1905	Northampton	won 32-0
Leicester	30 September 1905	Leicester	won 28-0
Middlesex	4 October 1905	London	won 34-0
Durham	7 October 1905	Durham	won 16-3
Hartlepool Clubs	11 October 1905	West Hartlepool	won 63-0
Northumberland	14 October 1905	North Shields	won 31-0
Gloucester	19 October 1905	Gloucester	won 44-0
Somerset	21 October 1905	Taunton	won 23-0
Devonport Albion	25 October 1905	Devonport	won 21-3
Midland Counties	28 October 1905	Leicester	won 21-5
Surrey	1 November 1905	Richmond	won 11-0
Blackheath	4 November 1905	Blackheath	won 32-0
Oxford University	7 November 1905	Oxford	won 47-0
Cambridge University	9 November 1905	Cambridge	won 14-0
Richmond	11 November 1905	Richmond	won 17-0
Bedford XV	15 November 1905	Bedford	won 41-0
SCOTLAND	18 November 1905	Edinburgh	won 12-7
West of Scotland	22 November 1905	Glasgow	won 22-0
IRELAND	25 November 1905	Dublin	won 15-0
Munster	28 November 1905	Limerick	won 33-0
ENGLAND	2 December 1905	London	won 15-0
Cheltenham	6 December 1905	Cheltenham	won 18-0
Cheshire	9 December 1905	Birkenhead	won 34-0
Yorkshire	13 December 1905	Leeds	won 40-0
WALES	16 December 1905	Cardiff	lost 3-0
Glamorgan	21 December 1905	Swansea	won 9-0
Newport	23 December 1905	Newport	won 6-3
Cardiff	26 December 1905	Cardiff	won 10-8
Swansea	30 December 1905	Swansea	won 4-3
FRANCE	1 January 1906	Paris	won 38-8
New York	1 February 1906	New York	won 46-13 (unofficial game)
British Columbia	10 February 1906	Berkeley	won 43-6
British Columbia	13 February 1906	San Francisco	won 65-6

Played 36, Won 35, Drew 0, Lost 1. Scored: 1,022 points, Conceded: 72.
In Britain & Ireland: Played 32, Won 31, Drew 0, Lost 1. Scored: 830 points, Conceded: 39.

The New Zealand Tour Party:

G.A. Gillett (Canterbury), W.J. Wallace (Wellington), H.L. Abbott (Taranaki), E.E. Booth (Otago), D. McGregor (Wellington), G.W. Smith (Auckland), H.J. Mynott (Taranaki), R.G. Deans (Canterbury), J. Hunter (Taranaki), J.W. Stead (Southland), H.D. Thomson (Wanganui), F. Roberts (Wellington), S.T. Casey (Otago), G.A. Tyler (Auckland), G.W. Nicholson (Auckland), W. Cunningham (Auckland), F.T. Glasgow (Taranaki), W.H.C. Mackrell (Auckland), W.S. Glenn (Taranaki), C.E. Seeling (Auckland), J.M. O'Sullivan (Taranaki), E.T. Harper (Canterbury), J. Corbett (West Coast), A. McDonald (Otago), W. Johnston (Otago), F. Newton (Canterbury), D. Gallaher (Auckland).

Captain: D. Gallaher. Vice-Captain: J.W. Stead. Manager: G.H. Dixon. Coach: J. Duncan.
Leading points scorer: W.J. Wallace – 246 points (230 in Britain & Ireland).
Leading try-scorer: J. Hunter – 44 tries (39 in Britain & Ireland).
Most appearances: F. Roberts – 30 games (29 in Britain & Ireland).

Saturday 16 September 1905
County Ground, Exeter
Won 55-4

DEVON	NEW ZEALAND
F.J. Lillicrap (Devonport Albion)	G.A. Gillett
F. Dean (Devonport Albion)	W.J. Wallace
A.J.R. Roberts (Barnstaple)	G.W. Smith
E.J. Vivyan (Devonport Albion)	H.D. Thomson
D. Moir (Devonport Albion)	J. Hunter
J. Peters (Plymouth)	J.W. Stead
R.A. Jago (Devonport Albion)	F. Roberts
Forwards:	Forwards:
W. Spiers (Devonport Albion, Capt.)	S.T. Casey
W.A. Mills (Devonport Albion)	G.A. Tyler
J. Huggins (Paignton)	W. Cunningham
D. Gordon (Devonport Albion)	G.W. Nicholson
T.S. Kelly (Exeter)	J.M. O'Sullivan
J. Tucker (Torquay Athletic)	C.E. Seeling
T. Willocks (Plymouth)	F.T. Glasgow
W.A. Knight (Plymouth)	D. Gallaher (Capt.)

Scorers:
Exeter: DG: Lillicrap.
New Zealand: Tries: Smith (4), Wallace (3), Hunter (2), Nicholson, Glasgow, Stead. Cons: Wallace (8). PG: Wallace.

Referee: P. Coles (RFU).
Attendance: 10,500.

After a tortuous sea trip, which took forty days to complete, the New Zealand team disembarked from the *Rimutaka* at Plymouth excited at the prospect of a first rugby tour of Britain. They were not the first New Zealanders to undertake such a tour; the NZ Natives had played on British soil during their remarkable fourteen-month expedition, which took in 107 games throughout the world, in 1888/89. However, this was the first fully representative New Zealand side to tour.

They established themselves at the Globe Hotel in the quiet Devon town of Newton Abbot and addressed concerns over fitness that had arisen at sea. They trained daily and attended a match between Devonport Albion and Torquay – a typical early season affair which failed to impress the tourists. They eventually took to the field at Exeter against a Devon side who wore the Exeter club shirts rather than their usual colours as they had mislaid their kit. New Zealand captain David Gallaher led the team onto the pitch and the side entertained the crowd with the Haka. Then the referee, RFU secretary Percy Coles, blew the whistle and the tour began in earnest.

It took three minutes for the first score to come, second five-eighth Jimmy Hunter racing in for a try converted by Billy Wallace. It was immediately clear that the tourists were a focused outfit determined to exploit their opponents' weaknesses. In Devon they found many. Their passing was poor, support non-existent and the defensive play particularly feeble. With the exception of full-back Lillicrap and wings Dean and Moir there appeared a reluctance to tackle or to fall on the loose ball. New Zealand were 27-0 ahead at half-time. A second try for Hunter, plus four from George Smith, three from Wallace and further tries from George Nicholson, Frank Glasgow and Billy Stead saw New Zealand home by the remarkable score of 55-4. Wallace, who wore a sun hat during the match, had a fine game. His 28 points from 3 tries, a penalty and 8 conversions was a record for a New Zealand representative player that stood until 1951. Devon scored through a dropped goal from Lillicrap late in the game. Elliott Vivyan had dropped the ball with the line at his mercy following good play by Dean and Roberts in the first half, but the home side failed to pose any other threat to New Zealand during the game. The Devon side included James 'Darkie' Peters, who later became the first black player to play for England and was at the centre of controversial team selections during the 1906 South African tour to Britain.

Sitting in the stand, all togged up in their kit, were the Exeter side who

The New Zealand squad before the first game of the tour.

Billy Wallace, resplendent in a sun hat, kicks for goal in the opening game of the tour.

were due to play 'A Next XVIII' in a trial match immediately after the game with New Zealand. The game was so early in the season that the Exeter club, who had turned down the chance to play the tourists in their own right, were unprepared for the rigours ahead. The trial match must have been an absurd anticlimax to the fare served up by New Zealand.

Home players and onlookers alike were bemused at the New Zealand formation. They had a full-back, three three-quarters, two five-eighths, a half-back, seven forwards who scrummaged in a 2-3-2 diamond formation and a wing-forward, Gallaher, who fed the New Zealand scrum then immediately assumed a position adjacent to its back row, perfectly placed to deny the opposition easy access to his half-back. One Devon official described Gallaher as 'A sort of blooming hermaphrodite, forward and half-back too!' Arguments began in Exeter and continued throughout the tour and afterwards as to whether the positioning of the wing-forward was legal. Gallaher, like many fine New Zealand forwards after him, played on the limit and to the referee.

The result was stunning. Devon had not played well, although their subsequent form was good enough to win them the County Championship. But, in reality, they had not encountered a side with the pace and organisation of the New Zealanders before. There was also considerable confusion at first over the scoreline. Had New Zealand won 5-4 and there had been a copying error? Had Devon won 5-4, or indeed had the powerful Devon side won 55-4? Surely the Devon team could not have been defeated by a scoreline of such magnitude! The reality that New Zealand were playing rugby in a manner not seen in Britain before would dawn over the coming weeks. The date, 16 September 1905, became a seminal one in the history of sport.

CORNWALL 1905/06

Thurdsay 21 September 1905
Recreation Ground, Camborne
Won 41-0

New Zealand moved Billy Wallace from wing to full-back and introduced 5 new players. Cornwall included three sets of brothers: the Jacketts, Bennettses and Miltons.

Playing into the sun and wind in the first half, Wallace again donned a hat which he managed to keep on his head when scoring a try after five minutes. He appeared outside wing 'Bunny' Abbott at top speed to cross in the corner after some crisp passing inside. He failed with the conversion, and missed again when attempting the conversion of Hunter's first try, scored after a drop-out had been

CORNWALL	NEW ZEALAND
E.J. Jackett (Falmouth & Leicester, Capt.)	W.J. Wallace
E. Bennetts (Camborne)	H.L. Abbott
C.H. Milton (Camborne School of Mines)	G.W. Smith
H. Bodilly (Camborne)	R.G. Deans
B.B. Bennetts (Penzance)	J. Hunter
F. Carter (Exeter)	H.J. Mynott
T.G. Wedge (St Ives)	F. Roberts
Forwards:	Forwards:
J.G. Milton (Camborne School of Mines)	S.T. Casey
N.N. Gore (Camborne School of Mines)	G.A. Tyler
E. Edmonds (Camborne School of Mines)	W. Cunningham
R. Jackett (Falmouth)	G.W. Nicholson
J. Bishop (Falmouth)	A. McDonald
J. Trevaskis (St Ives)	C.E. Seeling
N. Tregurtha (St Ives)	W. Johnston
T. Peters (Camborne)	D. Gallaher (Capt.)

Scorers:
New Zealand: Tries: Abbott, Deans, Hunter (3), McDonald, Mynott, Nicholson, Smith (2), Wallace. Cons: Wallace (4).

Referee: C.T.W. Finch (Devon).
Attendance: 7,000.

gathered by New Zealand and run back at Cornwall. George Smith then outstripped the defence to score a try and 'Simon' Mynott scored later in the first half. Wallace could convert neither, but New Zealand arrived at the interval 12-0 ahead.

The New Zealand Team which faced Cornwall.

With the conditions behind them, New Zealand attacked from the resumption of play. Smith nearly scored before George Nicholson was awarded a try, closely followed by touchdowns from Abbott, Bob Deans and a second for Hunter, converted from the touchline by Wallace, who had earlier converted Abbott's score. Hunter completed his hat-trick before Alex McDonald crashed over from a lineout and Smith then scored the final try of the match when his pace was again too much for the Cornish defence.

The Cornwall forwards were robust but they were worn down through constantly tackling and chasing the black jerseys. They matched the New Zealanders in the lineout but the two-man front row acted as a wedge, driving into the Cornish scrum and causing difficulty in securing clean ball. With Gallaher causing further disruption the Cornish backs seldom had the ball.

At this time British teams employed the 'first up, first down' formation of the scrum, whereby it formed largely based on who was there first. By contrast New Zealand formed their scrum deliberately, with each player taking up a specific position. This cohesiveness, matched with technique meant the seven-man scrum held the upper hand over most eight-man formations. This also caused comment and criticism.

John Jackett made his debut for England in the international against New Zealand. A fine footballer, he later represented Great Britain in the 1908 Olympic Games rugby union final and toured New Zealand and Australia with the Anglo-Welsh side in the same year. He later played rugby league for Dewsbury.

BRISTOL 1905/06

Saturday 23 September 1905
County Cricket Ground, Bristol
Won 41-0

New Zealand marched on to their next game with satisfaction and confidence. Their opponents were Bristol, a leading English club at the time, who were expected to provide tougher opposition for the tourists. However, Lloyd Mathias, their international forward, later admitted that before the match the team was mainly concerned about how many points they would lose by.

The game was played in gloomy conditions at the County Ground in the Horfield district of Bristol. The venue was the home of Gloucestershire County Cricket Club, where Bristol were tenants until the outbreak of the First World War.

BRISTOL	NEW ZEALAND
J. Oates (Capt.)	E.E. Booth
F.S. Scott	W.J. Wallace
H.E. Shewring	H.D. Thomson
C. Phillips	G.W. Smith
T. Leonard	J. Hunter
J.A. Spoors	J.W. Stead
J. Larcombe	F. Roberts
Forwards:	Forwards:
J.L. Mathias	S.T. Casey
H. T. Webb	F. Glasgow
N.J.H. Moore	W. Cunningham
A. Manning	W. Johnston
W.H. Thomas	C.E. Seeling
W. Cooper	G.W. Nicholson
W.H. Needs	J. Corbett
W.W.A. Hoskin	D. Gallaher (Capt.)

Scorers:
New Zealand: Tries: Thomson (2), Hunter (2), Smith (2), Roberts, Seeling, Stead. Cons: Wallace (7).

Referee: D.H. Bowen (WRU).
Attendance: 6,000.

The crowd of 6,000 was stunned at the pace and creativity of the passing movements and the energy of the New Zealanders, who would have scored several early tries but for forward passes. After ten minutes George Smith scored with his first touch of the ball. He scored a second later in the half and tries from Hunter and Fred Roberts saw the New Zealanders 18-0 ahead at the break. Jimmy Hunter's try was a spectacular score initiated by Stead from a scrum on halfway. The first five-eighth evaded the tackle of Jack Spoors before passing to Hunter and Smith, who exchanged passes before Hunter touched down between the posts for a glorious try which was greeted by rapturous applause.

Bristol had barely time to draw breath at half-time before the second half began with New Zealand on the attack. Hunter scored a second try early on and, following a period when Bristol held their own, 'Mona' Thomson crossed for 2 tries, one of which followed a cross-kick from forward Frank Glasgow, and further scores came from 'Bronco' Seeling and Stead. The goal-kicking of Billy Wallace was of the highest order; he only missed two of his nine conversion attempts.

Referee Harry Bowen, a Welsh international from the 1880s, struggled to deal with the scrummaging.

New Zealand's two-man front row adopted techniques that were unfamiliar to him. Consequently the three-man Bristol unit, attempting to deny New Zealand, frustrated the tourists as well as referee, who called for the scrums to be reformed on countless occasions. The ball, Bowen later explained, needed to go past the second man in the front row – in today's terminology the hooker – but as New Zealand only had two front-rowers this was hard to comprehend. Bowen also regularly penalised New Zealand for forward passes.

The crowd included the NZRFU president, Francis Logan of Hawke's Bay, and several New Zealand supporters who had recently arrived from home to watch their first game of the tour. Also observing were several leading Welsh players, including Rhys Gabe and Willie Llewellyn, and WRU secretary Walter Rees. They were impressed with the tourists' play and also the creative work of Gallaher, whose unusual stance at the scrum continued to be questioned as being obstructive.

The New Zealand team that played Bristol, photographed at the County Cricket Ground.

Bristol were playing only their second game of the season, an unimpressive 3-3 draw with local side Lydney being their previous result. Despite this, Gallaher had been impressed with the Bristol pack: 'I thought Bristol a good side, especially in the front rank, and I think this is our best win to date.' Harry Shewring and Mathias later played for England in the international with New Zealand. Norman Moore had played for England in 1904, and Frank Scott was later capped by England. Spoors, who was one of five brothers who played for Bristol, was the hero of the 1910 British Isles tour in South Africa, scoring a try in each Test match, a record that still stands. Curiously, he was never capped by England.

NORTHAMPTON   1905/06

Thursday 28 September 1905
Franklin's Gardens, Northampton
Won 32-0

NORTHAMPTON	NEW ZEALAND
C. Leigh	W.J. Wallace
J.H. Miles	H.L. Abbott
H.C. Palmer (Capt.)	J.W. Stead (Capt.)
F. Coles	E.T. Harper
J.L. Malkin	J. Hunter
T.H. Preston	H.J. Mynott
C.F. Malkin	F. Roberts
Forwards:	Forwards:
H.B. Follitt	G.A. Tyler
A.J. Hobbs	F.T. Glasgow
L. Johnson	W. Cunningham
C. Franklin	G.W. Nicholson
H.B. Grandidge	J. Corbett
G. Burke	C.E. Seeling
A. Chalmers	J.M. O'Sullivan
J. Warren	G.A. Gillett

Scorers:
New Zealand: Tries: Harper (2), Hunter (2), Mynott (2), Stead, Tyler. Cons: Wallace (4).

Referee: F.W. Nicholls (Midlands).
Attendance: 5,000.

Captain David Gallaher took a rest from the rigours of play and ran the touchline for the New Zealanders in this match. His place in the controversial position of wing-forward was taken by George Gillett, who had moved up from full-back. Billy Wallace played in Gillett's normal position with Billy Stead leading the side from centre. There were several other changes to the side. The Northampton team selection was interesting in that several leading players were left out in favour of some guest players, including, J.L. and C.F. Malkin who were drafted in from the Civil Service club.

Northampton started the match in determined fashion and applied pressure to New Zealand. However, their backs conviction and pace to penetrate the visitors' defence, although wing Jack Miles impressed the tourists with his swerve and strong running in the second half.

After weathering the early storm, the New Zealanders began to take control. They began to dominate the home pack and Gillett proved an able deputy for Gallaher on the fringes of the scrum. Once more the question of obstruction was raised but, again, the home team didn't possess the means to deal with the wing-forward. Mynott opened the scoring with a try from a scrum after the seven-man unit had disintegrated the home formation. A sidestepping Hunter then scored a try and this was closely followed by one from Stead, the latter being converted by Wallace. Hunter scored again and Eric Harper raced in for a fine try following some accurate passing in the three-quarters. Wallace converted and New Zealand were 21-0 ahead at the break, although there were more handling errors from the tourists in this half than in all the previous matches combined.

New Zealand also squandered a couple of opportunities to score early in the second half before Gillett kicked ahead and athletically regathered the ball for George Tyler to score a try. Tyler was one of the five tourists to have represented New Zealand in their first international match, against Australia in 1903, when he also scored a try. Mynott scored the next try for New Zealand following a quick break by half-back Roberts, before a dropped pass in midfield handed possession to Northampton. However, the tourists won the scrum and swift passing gave Harper the space to score his second try.

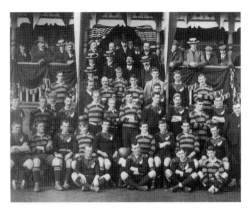

Northampton and New Zealand players before the match at Franklin's Gardens.

This was another resounding win for the New Zealanders and it provided food for thought for future opponents. How were they to counter the athleticism, cohesiveness and power of the tourists' pack and their rapid transfer of ball?

The 1905/06 campaign was the first season in which the Northampton club wore its now familiar black, green and gold-hooped jerseys. 'Saints' captain Claude Palmer later became club secretary and was instrumental in the rebuilding of the ground after the First World War. In the club's first match of the season they played Olney, who had a wing who caught the eye. Edgar Mobbs joined Northampton shortly after and played for them in the match immediately prior to their encounter with New Zealand – against Bedford. Although making an impact, he was dropped for the game against the tourists. Curiously, the iconic Mobbs, whose contribution to rugby is today commemorated in an annual match between the East Midlands and the Barbarians, did play against New Zealand – as a guest player for Bedford forty-eight days later.

LEICESTER   1905/06

Saturday 30 September 1905
Welford Road, Leicester
Won 28-0

The Leicester club was thought likely to provide one of the toughest tests for the New Zealanders in England. They prepared well for the game and attended the tourists' match against Northampton, and were unbeaten in their 3 games played before the match. Interest in the game was considerable and Welford Road was full. Leicester considered several options to counter the New Zealand forwards and experimented with the diamond scrum formation of seven players with a roving wing-forward. Although their defence improved with the extra man, he proved something of a hindrance in attack by getting in the way of his teammates.

LEICESTER	NEW ZEALAND
A.O. Jones	G.A. Gillett
A.O. Parsons	H.L. Abbott
N. McFarlane	G.W. Smith
J.W. Bainbridge	W.J. Wallace
A.E. Hind	H.J. Mynott
B. Hills	J.W. Stead
J. Braithwaite	F. Roberts
Forwards:	Forwards:
S. Matthews (Capt.)	S.T. Casey
S.H. Penny	G.A. Tyler
T. Goodrich	W. Cunningham
A. Goodrich	G.W. Nicholson
R.F. Russell	F.T. Glasgow
F.S. Jackson	C.E. Seeling
D.B. Atkins	J.M. O'Sullivan
H.P. Atkins	D. Gallaher (Capt.)

Scorers:
New Zealand: Tries: Abbott, Mynott, Nicholson, Smith, Tyler, Wallace. Cons: Wallace (5).

Referee: P. Coles (RFU).
Attendance: 16,000.

The Tigers were able to pressurise New Zealand early on and the home forwards nearly scored from a forward rush. New Zealand were matched for the first half hour or so and the kicking of the tourists, excellent so far on tour, was strangely indifferent. However, after twenty-eight minutes, a ball won in a lineout was moved to Smith, who hurdled over an opponent to escape the defence on his way to a spectacular try. Further tries by Wallace and Abbott, the latter converted by Wallace, saw New Zealand race to a 13-0 lead at the interval.

The Leicester defence was excellent in the second half, repelling wave after wave of attacks. Even so, the defence was breached on three occasions. Mynott dummied and sidestepped his way through to score a fine try then Nicholson and Tyler crossed for less extravagant scores late in the match. Wallace converted all three.

After the game Gallaher complimented the Leicester side: 'When we were down south we were told that when we got to Leicester we should know about it. Well, we do know about it. You gave us one of the hardest games

Action from the match with Leicester. (Museum of Rugby)

I've ever played in.' The pace of the New Zealand side prevented the Tigers' backs getting into the game. However, Ernest Hind, Jacky Braithwaite and forward Richard Russell were later selected to play for England against New Zealand. Leicester full-back Arthur Jones commented: 'We have not the same class players as the New Zealanders, and if they played us at our own game they would beat us just as easily.' Jones, an England trialist and later an international referee, achieved greater fame as a cricketer. He was one of the leading fielders of his time, captained Nottinghamshire and England, and is regarded as being the inventor of the gully fielding position. He also played soccer for Notts County.

MIDDLESEX   1905/06

Wednesday 4 October 1905
Stamford Bridge, London
Won 34-0

New Zealand returned south and made their first visit to London for a game at Stamford Bridge, the home of the recently formed Chelsea Football Club. They were impressed with the large stadium, a venue eventually agreed upon after lengthy debate by the Middlesex committee. In fact Chelsea had only played on the surface twice before this match. Middlesex selected a strong team that included tough Welsh forwards Arthur 'Boxer' Harding, Jack Jenkins and John 'Scethrog' Williams, all of whom toured New Zealand with Harding's Anglo-Welsh side of 1908. They were led by 'Curly' Hammond, and the backs included the inspirational Harlequin

MIDDLESEX	NEW ZEALAND
E.M. Harrison (Guy's Hospital)	G.A. Gillett
H. Hosken (Old Leysians)	R.G. Deans
H.T. Maddock (London Welsh)	G.W. Smith
R.E. Godfray (Richmond)	W.J. Wallace
F.H. Palmer (Richmond)	J. Hunter
A.L. Wade (London Scottish)	J.W. Stead
A.D. Stoop (Harlequins)	F. Roberts
Forwards:	Forwards:
C.E.L. Hammond (Harlequins, Capt.)	S.T. Casey
H. Alexander (Richmond)	F.T. Glasgow
F.H. Turner (Richmond)	W. Cunningham
A.F. Harding (London Welsh)	W.S. Glenn
J.F. Williams (London Welsh)	A. McDonald
J.C. Jenkins (London Welsh)	C.E. Seeling
W.B. Grandage (St Bart's Hospital)	W. Johnston
R.O.C. Ward (Harlequins)	D. Gallaher (Capt.)

Scorers:
New Zealand: Tries: Hunter (2), Smith (2), Deans, Johnston, Seeling, Wallace. Cons: Wallace (5).

Referee: P. Coles (RFU).
Attendance: 11,000.

Adrian Stoop. Yet, despite their undoubted quality, Middlesex were poorly organised and could not handle the tourists' speed and accurate handling.

The writing was on the wall for Middlesex after three minutes when Smith made a telling break and passed inside to Johnston for the loose forward to score. Wallace added the conversion. Hunter opened his try account next, a score that Wallace converted, before Smith, renowned for his subtle play, barged his way through the Middlesex defence after Deans had confused them by dummying

The sides battle for the ball at Stamford Bridge. (World Rugby Museum)

to drop a goal. Wallace again converted, then scored a try himself when his speed took him past several bemused defenders on his way to the line. He missed the conversion but added the extra points to Smith's second try shortly afterwards to see New Zealand ahead 23-0 at the interval.

Middlesex started the second half with renewed confidence, but this was broken when Charlie Seeling forced his way through the home forwards to score. A try by Deans almost immediately from the restart destroyed any hope of a home recovery and the game was over as a contest. New Zealand eased off but the final score, including another try for Hunter, condemned Middlesex to a comprehensive defeat.

The match saw the first organised attempt to counter the New Zealand scrum. As the packs engaged their two-man front row veered to one side or the other, thus binding either side of a home prop rather than the hooker. Hence the other prop, as it were, had nothing to push against and the scrum was rendered lop-sided. Middlesex attempted to counter this by having the redundant prop detach himself and run around to the other side of the scrum. Sadly for them it rarely worked, such was the speed of Gallaher's put-in and the New Zealand heel.

Two of the international players in the Middlesex side were to lose their lives during the First World War. Harry Alexander in 1915 and Albert Wade at Arras in 1917. R.O.C. 'Roc' Ward also died on active service and 'Hop' Maddock died in 1921 of wounds sustained in battle. George Smith and 'Massa' Johnston played at Stamford Bridge once more but this time in the New Zealand rugby league 'All Golds' team that defeated the Northern Union international side 18-6 in February 1908. Both players scored tries on that occasion too.

DURHAM 1905/06

Saturday 7 October 1905
Hollow Drift, Durham
Won 16-3

Gallaher stood down for this match against Durham, the English County Champions, his place at wing-forward once more being filled by Gillett. Booth took over at full-back and Stead took up the reins of leadership.

There was a bizarre start to the game. The New Zealand team took to the field only to discover that the home side was without Jack Knaggs and Frank Boylen, who had missed a train connection and had not yet arrived at the ground. It was agreed the match be delayed and it duly kicked-off twenty minutes later with Durham fielding fourteen players, Robert Elliott replacing Boylen. Fortunately the missing players arrived shortly after kick-off and Knaggs was permitted to play.

DURHAM	NEW ZEALAND
S. Horsley (Hartlepool Rovers)	E.E. Booth
P. Clarkson (Sunderland)	H.D. Thomson
J.T. Taylor (West Hartlepool, Capt.)	G.W. Smith
C.Y. Adamson (Durham City)	W.J. Wallace
H.M. Imrie (Durham City)	J. Hunter
J. Knaggs (Hartlepool Rovers)	J.W. Stead (Capt.)
H. Wallace (West Hartlepool)	F. Roberts
Forwards:	Forwards:
R. Elliott (Durham City)	S.T. Casey
H. Havelock (Hartlepool Old Boys)	F.T. Glasgow
C.J.H. Stock (Sunderland)	W. Cunningham
G.E. Carter (Hartlepool Rovers)	W. Johnston
T.B. Hogarth (Hartlepool Rovers)	G.W. Nicholson
J. Elliott (Durham City)	A. McDonald
G.E. Summerscales (Durham City)	W.S. Glenn
L. West (West Hartlepool)	G.A. Gillett

Scorers:
Durham: Try: Clarkson.
New Zealand: Tries: Wallace (2), Hunter, Stead.
Cons: Wallace (2).

Referee: A Turnbull (Hawick).
Attendance: 8,000.

Boylen remained a spectator. To add to the comedy, full-back Sid Horsley mislaid his boots and initially played in shoes.

The absentees arrived just in time to see Roberts break from a scrum and feed Wallace who drew the defence before passing to Hunter for a try. Durham settled down but the tourists showed their ability to capitalise on half-chances and Wallace was at hand to score following quick passing within the backs after Nicholson had won a lineout. Durham again pressurised the visitors and their pack took temporary control. Quick ball was moved from a scrum to centre Charles Adamson, who threw out a long pass to Phil Clarkson to run in for the first try conceded by New Zealand on tour. The crowd went wild but their cheers turned to groans as Adamson's conversion rebounded off the post. New Zealand remained ahead 6-3 at the break.

Billy 'Carbine' Wallace. He was the leading scorer on ther tour with 230, including 10 against Durham.

The New Zealanders eased further ahead after the restart when Roberts again broke quickly from a scrum for his captain to score. Durham tried to regain the initiative but loose play saw the ball lost and Stead and Johnston created an opportunity for Wallace to cross for another try. The Wellington wing converted both scores. The Durham pack remained difficult to overcome and in the dying minutes the other home wing, Harry Imrie, was tackled into touch at the corner flag. Referee Adam Turnbull blew for time shortly afterwards and New Zealand had survived the toughest game of the tour so far. They later complained that Durham had been regularly offside and criticised Turnbull for not pulling them up for this. Billy Wallace continued his scoring feats with a further 10 points. He amassed 230 in Britain on this tour. He was predominantly a winger but he also played full-back, and played in every position behind the scrum except half-back in his career for New Zealand. He is justifiably regarded as one of the greatest of all New Zealand rugby players. Dr Leonard West went on to play for the Hartlepool Clubs and Scotland against New Zealand. Harry Imrie later made his debut for England against the tourists, accompanied by George Summerscales. Thomas Hogarth made a try-scoring debut for England against France later in the season. Adamson and Robert Elliott were killed in the First World War.

HARTLEPOOL CLUBS 1905/06

Wednesday 11 October 1905
The Friarage, West Hartlepool
Won 63-0

There was great interest in the game locally with schools and factories closing so that people could attend the match. Consequently, the small Hartlepool Rovers Ground was full to capacity. Frank Boylen, the Hartlepool Rovers forward who had arrived too late to face the tourists for Durham, was this time able to play. New Zealand selected a pack based around their largest forwards. Gallaher stood down and Gillett again assumed the tour captain's position of wing-forward, with Stead leading the side again. The Hartlepool team was comprised of players from West Hartlepool and Hartlepool Rovers and used a diamond scrum formation.

HARTLEPOOL CLUBS	NEW ZEALAND
D.E. Ellwood (Hartlepool Rovers)	W.J. Wallace
J.T. Taylor (West Hartlepool)	H.L. Abbott
J. Wass (West Hartlepool)	R.G. Deans
B.S. Wellock (West Hartlepool)	G.W. Smith
H. Wallace (West Hartlepool)	J. Hunter
J. Knaggs (Hartlepool Rovers)	J.W. Stead (Capt.)
J. Thompson (Hartlepool Rovers)	F. Roberts
Forwards:	Forwards:
S. Brittain (Hartlepool Rovers)	A. McDonald
T.B. Hogarth (Hartlepool Rovers)	F.T. Glasgow
F. Boylen (Hartlepool Rovers)	W. Cunningham
G.E. Carter (Hartlepool Rovers, Capt.)	F. Newton
A. Scott (West Hartlepool)	J.M. O'Sullivan
R. Moule (West Hartlepool)	C.E. Seeling
H. Metcalfe (West Hartlepool)	W. Johnston
L. West (West Hartlepool)	G.A. Gillett

Scorers:
New Zealand: Tries: Hunter (4), Abbott (3), Roberts (2), Smith (2), Deans, O'Sullivan, Stead, Wallace. Cons: Wallace (8), Glasgow.

Referee: R. Welsh (Scotland).
Attendance: 13,000.

Results of tour of New Zealand Rugby Team in Great Britain

The original owner of this card poignantly wrote 'Poor Rovers' in recognition of the drubbing the Hartlepool clubs received.

The 'scratch' home team lacked cohesiveness and the tourists were ahead 33-0 at half-time through tries from, in order, Smith, Deans, Roberts, Stead, Hunter, Smith and Abbott. Full-back Wallace converted six.

New Zealand started the second half playing uphill and into the stong wind but it was an equally demoralising period for the home side with further scores from Hunter, Abbott, Abbott again, Hunter, O'Sullivan, Roberts and Wallace, and finally Hunter crossed for his fourth and New Zealand's fifteenth try of the game. Wallace kicked two more conversions with Glasgow chipping in with one. The match became a demonstration of running rugby. The home crowd was stunned that such big forwards could run and pass like three-quarters, and the backs seemed to possess winged feet as they raced up the field with barely a hand laid on them. At a time when scores were rarely in double figures such a crushing defeat was remarkable.

It had been claimed that this game created the name 'All Blacks'. The popular myth was that *Daily Mail* reporter J.A. Buttery had described the complete team as playing like 'all backs' against Hartlepool and that this was used in posters advertising the game against Somerset ten days later. The printer had, in fact, inserted a 'l' into 'backs' to form 'blacks'. However, recent research has proved that a local Exeter newspaper made reference to 'All Blacks' in the report of the opening game against Devon. Tour manager George Dixon referred to the squad as 'All Blacks' in his diary. Certainly Buttery, who reported on the tour with considerable artistry, used the term 'All Blacks' in reference to 'their sombre football garb' from the Hartlepool game onwards, and other newspapers quickly followed suit.

During the 1980s future New Zealand internationals Gary and Allan Whetton played for West Hartlepool and All Black Mike Brewer later coached the team.

NORTHUMBERLAND   1905/06

Saturday 14 October 1905
Preston Avenue, North Shields
Won 31-0

Billy Stead skippered the tourists in the absence of Gallaher. With Gillett still occupying the wing-forward position, Ernest 'General' Booth played at full-back. This match was staged at the home of the Percy Park club. Northumberland full-back Christopher Stanger-Leathes played for the British Isles on their 1904 tour to New Zealand and Australia before being capped by England the following season. Wing James Hutchinson played for England later in the season, remarkably so, after an injury as a child had badly damaged his hand.

The New Zealanders kicked off down a significant slope with strong wind and

NORTHUMBERLAND	NEW ZEALAND
C.F. Stanger-Leathes (Northern)	E.E. Booth
J.E. Hutchinson (Durham City)	E.T. Harper
J.E. Scott (Percy Park)	R.G. Deans
J. Harrison (Rockcliff)	G.W. Smith
T. Simpson (Rockcliff)	J. Hunter
W. Maddison (Percy Park)	J.W. Stead (Capt.)
C. Russell (Percy Park)	F. Roberts
Forwards:	Forwards:
W. Steadman (Percy Park)	W.S. Glenn
J. Kyle (Rockliff)	F.T. Glasgow
A.L. Kewney (Rockliff)	W. Cunningham
W.G. Heppel (Northern)	F. Newton
A. Emerson (Tynedale)	J.M. O'Sullivan
R.F. Cumberledge (Northern)	C.E. Seeling
H. Beckerson (Percy Park)	J. Corbett
E. Averill (Rockliff)	G.A. Gillett

Scorers:
New Zealand: Tries: Hunter (5), Deans, Gillett, Harper, Seeling.
Cons: Cunningham (2).

Referee: F.W. Nicholls (Midlands).
Attendance: 11,000.

rain at their backs and immediately pressurised Northumberland. Although the weather played a part in the game, most notably making goal-kicking especially challenging, the crowd was impressed with the handling of the tourists, which was skilful and precise. Gillett opened the scoring by kicking ahead and diving on the ball ahead of the covering defence before Jimmy Hunter scored 2 tries in quick succession. Then Bob Deans collected a loose pass and using power and pace scored a try, closely followed by Hunter's third, which was made by some good passing and running by the New Zealand backs. Pressure on the Northumberland defence was intense and a misfielded kick bounced kindly for Harper, who set up Seeling to cross for another try. With only two of the tries converted by Bill Cunningham, the All Blacks were 22-0 ahead at half-time.

Jimmy Hunter, scorer of 5 tries against Northumberland and 44 on the complete tour.

The All Blacks turned around to face the gale for the second half and, despite the dreadful weather, they managed to score three more tries. Hunter crossed for two and Eric Harper scored after a passing movement that defied the elements. New Zealand were happy enough with a 31-0 victory.

Hunter, scorer of 5 tries, was a superb second five-eighth. Possessing the speed of a wing and the guile of a first five-eighth, he was described by British rugby writer E.H.D. Sewell as 'one of the most sinuous runners' he had seen play. Hunter and Stead formed a remarkable partnership, with both players able to create opportunities for each other. Hunter scored a stunning 44 tries in the 25 games he played on tour, 10 in the 3 games the All Blacks played in the North-East of England. He later captained New Zealand. Eric Harper, scorer of the ninth New Zealand try of the game, was a considerable athlete, a one-time national champion at 880 yards and 440 yards hurdles. He was plagued by injuries on this tour and the crowds who flocked to see the All Blacks rarely saw the best of him. He played little rugby after he returned home. Trooper Harper served with the Canterbury Mounted Rifles, NZEF, in Palestine, where he was killed in action in April 1918.

GLOUCESTER 1905/06

Thursday 19 October 1905
Kingsholm, Gloucester
Won 44-0

The All Blacks returned to the West Country for a game against Gloucester. Kingsholm was packed with a crowd inflated by Welsh supporters, who had made their way to see the team that was causing such a stir throughout England. The entire Welsh Rugby Union committee was also in attendance. Gallaher returned to the fray having missed the last 3 games. The match was Gloucester's fifth game of the season. They had enjoyed good wins over Clifton and Bristol but had suffered a 3-0 defeat at Swansea.

New Zealand started on the attack but stout defence from the home side kept them out. Once again, the pace of the New Zealand

GLOUCESTER	NEW ZEALAND
L. Vears	G.A. Gillett
C. Smith	G.W. Smith
E. Hall	R.G. Deans
J. Harrison	W.J. Wallace
A. Hudson	J. Hunter
D.R. Gent	J.W. Stead
J. Stephens	F. Roberts
A. Wood	Forwards:
Forwards:	W.S. Glenn
W. Johns (Capt.)	F.T. Glasgow
A. Hawker	W. Cunningham
F. Pegler	J.M. O'Sullivan
G. Vears	G.W. Nicholson
B. Parham	C.E. Seeling
H. Collins	W. Johnston
G. Matthews	D. Gallaher (Capt.)

Scorers:
New Zealand: Tries: Deans (3), Hunter (2), Wallace (2), Glasgow, Seeling, Smith. Cons: Wallace (6), Gillett.

Referee: F.W. Nicholls (Midlands).
Attendance: 15,000.

New Zealand forwards Charlie Seeling (left) and William 'Massa' Johnstone photographed at Gloucester.

backs caused problems for their opponents and they applied pressure in both attack and defence. The first score of the match followed a heavy tackle by Gillett on Arthur Hudson who was bundled into touch, and from the lineout, which was taken quickly, Hunter was at hand to burst through for his customary try. Smith, Deans and Glasgow then scored before Wallace scored a spectacular try close to the break. The All Blacks moved the ball quickly across the three-quarter line to Wallace, who had space to move. With blistering pace he rounded his immediate opponent then completely outstriped the covering defence to score. The crowd, vociferous in their encouragement of the home side throughout, cheered as though it was their own player who had scored. The buzz from Wallace's score had barely died down when Hunter scored his second. New Zealand led 26-0 at the break.

The Gloucester defence was tested again straight from the kick-off but it was twenty-five minutes before it cracked again when Deans scored his second try. Gloucester played far better than the score suggested, but their cause was hampered when scrum-half Wood was injured and had to leave the field. While he was being attended to, Wallace scored again, and Charlie Seeling crashed over from a lineout shortly afterwards. With the match drawing to its end, Roberts gathered the ball and cross-kicked for Deans to gather and score his hat-trick try. Wallace and Gillett converted seven of the All Blacks' 10 tries for a 44-0 win. It was hard on Gloucester who contributed much to the game.

'Dai' Gent had a trial for Wales but played outside half for England against New Zealand later in the tour. He was a Barbarians committeeman and later became rugby correspondent of the *Sunday Times*. Hudson, who was concussed early in the game went on to score 4 tries for England in the first international with France. Through Hudson's encouragement, Duncan McGregor and Simon Mynott, played briefly for Gloucester after the tour. McGregor later returned to the city and opened a sports shop with Hudson.

SOMERSET   1905/06

Saturday 21 October 1905
Jarvis's Field, Taunton
Won 23-0

The All Blacks were a little surprised at the size of the Taunton ground, a small, ramshackle venue that barely contained the sizeable crowd. Suggestions were made that the Somerset County Cricket ground or the Wellington RFC ground would be more suitable but the Taunton club provided temporary stands from overturned wagons and the match went ahead on their pitch. The playing surface was uneven and slightly narrower than normal, and there were occasions during the game when the tourists ran out of space and were called back because they had ventured into touch. The Somerset side included Bristol centre Harry

SOMERSET	NEW ZEALAND
A. Mead (Bridgwater Albion)	G.A. Gillett
W.M. Penny (Taunton & London Welsh)	E.E. Booth
J.T. Timmins (Bath & London Welsh, Capt.)	E.T. Harper
H.E. Shewring (Bristol)	W.J. Wallace
R. Meister (Bath)	R.G. Deans
C. Kingston (Bridgwater Albion)	H.J. Mynott
H.C. Jackson (Bridgwater Albion)	J.W. Stead
Forwards:	Forwards:
A. Vickary (Aberavon)	S.T. Casey
R. Dibble (Bridgwater Albion)	G.A. Tyler
H. Winter (Taunton)	J.M. O'Sullivan
G.V. Kyrke (Marlborough Nomads)	W.S. Glenn
W.H. Needs (Bristol)	G.W. Nicholson
N.J.H. Moore (Bristol)	C.E. Seeling
W. Archer (Bridgwater Albion)	J. Corbett
A. Manning (Taunton Albion & Bristol)	D. Gallaher (Capt.)

Scorers:
New Zealand: Tries: Mynott (2), Seeling (2), Wallace. Cons: Wallace (2). DG: Wallace.

Referee: A.J. Davies (Cardiff).
Attendance: 9,000.

Shewring and forwards Billy Needs, Norman Moore and A. Manning, who had all played against New Zealand in the third match of the tour. The side, captained by James Timmins, was bolstered by the inclusion of London Welsh three-quarter W.M. Penny, who was selected because first-choice wing Ralph Thomas was playing for his club, Penarth. Penny later played for Cambridge University against New Zealand. Several of the All Blacks were suffering from colds. Fred Roberts stepped down for the first time on tour, and without another specialist half-back in the tour party Billy Stead took over. Stead was inexperienced at playing in this position and the move was not a great success. The passing from set-piece and loose play was less accurate and slower. This pressurised his outside backs into hasty passing, which although usually going to hand didn't give them the opportunity to attack at pace. If nothing else it proved the worth of Roberts.

Nevertheless, New Zealand attacked whenever they could, Booth being close to scoring on several occasions. Gallaher prowled the pitch with his commanding presence and had it not been for the defensive play of Mead and Shewring the New Zealand score would have been greater. New Zealand were also hampered by injuries to Deans and Tyler, who remained on the field but were largely ineffective. Deans swapped with Gillett and suffered behind his three-quarters for the remainder of the match. Tyler's injury meant that the All Blacks effectively only had six forwards. This, coupled with the team selection, and being faced by a fiercely passionate and powerful Somerset team, meant the All Blacks had a match more difficult than anticipated.

Despite these problems, New Zealand still managed to run in 5 tries. Mynott opened the scoring with a try converted by Wallace, before Seeling touched down after some loose play. Wallace dropped a goal and Seeling scored again direct from a lineout before Wallace scored a try himself. Mynott completed the scoring with another try late in the game. Wallace helped himself to 12 points in a slightly flattering 23-0 win.

DEVONPORT ALBION 1905/06

Wednesday 25 October 1905
The Rectory Ground, Devonport
Won 21-3

For the first time on tour New Zealand faced a club side that had managed to get some rugby under its belt and had resisted the temptation to supplement its team with imports. A successful side – they had not lost at home for two years – Devonport Albion's player combinations were sound and provided a tough proposition for the All Blacks.

This seemed far from the case to start with. The home team appeared very nervous and after several close shaves, which included Hunter dropping the ball with the line at his mercy, Roberts ran down the blind side of a scrum and fed Thomson, who easily beat two defenders

DEVONPORT ALBION	NEW ZEALAND
F.J. Lillicrap	G.A. Gillett
C. Hosking	H.D. Thomson
S.H. Irvin	J.W. Stead
W. Jackman	G.W. Smith
D. Moir	J. Hunter
F. Dean	H.J. Mynott
R.A. Jago	F. Roberts
Forwards:	Forwards:
W. Spiers	F.T. Glasgow
J. Cummings	G.A. Tyler
S.G. Williams	W. Cunningham
W.A. Mills	G.W. Nicholson
C. Edwards	J.M. O'Sullivan
H. Harris	C.E. Seeling
A.C. Campbell	W. Johnston
W. Rooks	D. Gallaher (Capt.)

Scorers:
Devonport Albion: PG: Spiers.
New Zealand: Tries: Thomson (2), Roberts, Nicholson, Gallaher.
Cons: Gillett (2), Cunningham.

Referee: F.W. Nicholls (Midlands).
Attendance: 19,000.

A postcard showing the kick-off of the Devonport Albion match.

to score. In the absence of Wallace, who withdrew on the morning of the match, Gillett converted. From this point Albion seemed to start playing. They had adopted the diamond scrum formation but developed an interesting tactical variation that wheeled the scrum, allowing their pack to burst away with the ball in a series of foot-rushes, which were only repelled by stout defence, particularly from Stead and Gillett. The bustling Raphael Jago harried Roberts and Albion attacked incessantly. New Zealand were fortunate to arrive at the interval 5-0 ahead.

The second half was a different story with the All Blacks at their exhilarating best. They had seen that their tactics of the first half were not working so they adopted a more open approach and were confident of their own abilities to change tactics as and when appropriate. Albion, on the other hand, were one-dimensional, and once New Zealand worked out how to deal with that the home side lost its momentum and the opportunity to win. Thomson ran in for his second try before Roberts spotted a gap close to the scrum and scored himself. Then Nicholson crashed through a lineout for a try. Gallaher scored next after Stead had shown the Albion defence what a clever footballer he was by creating a gap for the elusive Hunter to race through from the New Zealand half of the field. Hunter had Glasgow and Nicholson in support and they carried the ball on into the home 25 before passing to the captain, who raced in between the posts for a magnificent try. Albion never gave up. They tacked robustly and late in the game Gallaher was penalised on the New Zealand 25 and Spiers kicked a penalty goal. Even after that Bill Mills and George Smith raced for a ball that was bouncing near the New Zealand line but the wing beat the forward to the ball and it was cleared. It was a terrific game of rugby and the crowd cheered and applauded for some time after the final whistle was blown.

Despite their efforts not one Albion player was selected to play for England against the All Blacks, although Mills and Jago were capped by England later in the season. Devonport Albion merged with Plymouth after the First World War to form the Plymouth Albion club.

Saturday 28 October 1905
Welford Road, Leicester
Won 21-5

MIDLAND COUNTIES	NEW ZEALAND
G.H. Rose (Stratford-on-Avon)	G.A. Gillett
A.E. Hind (Leicester)	D. McGregor
A.G. Neilson (Notts)	J.W. Stead
J.G. Cooper (Moseley)	G.W. Smith
J.H. Miles (Northampton)	J. Hunter
L. Kirk (Notts)	H.J. Mynott
J. Braithwaite (Leicester)	F. Roberts
Forwards:	Forwards:
V.H. Cartwright (Notts, Capt.)	W.S. Glenn
S. Matthews (Leicester)	G.A. Tyler
R.F. Russell (Leicester)	W. Cunningham
H.P. Atkins (Leicester)	F. Newton
D.B. Atkins (Leicester)	J.M. O'Sullivan
A. Goodrich (Leicester)	C.E. Seeling
C.H. Shaw (Moseley)	W. Johnston
W.L. Oldham (Coventry)	D. Gallaher (Capt.)

Scorers:
Midland Counties: Try: Shaw. Con: Cooper.
New Zealand: Tries: Hunter, Mynott, Roberts, Smith, Stead.
Cons: Cunningham (3).

Referee: G. Evans (Midlands).
Attendance: 17,000.

With the All Blacks' visit to Leicester four weeks previously still fresh in their minds, the Midlands' selectors looked hard at the make-up of their side. Basing their team around the Leicester side that had performed well against New Zealand, they took the opportunity to strengthen key positions. In the pack the side was bolstered by England captain Harry 'Lump' Cartwright. Leicester forward Percy Atkins was given the task of dealing with Gallaher. He had only limited success. Although he was able to subdue the All Blacks' captain at first, the resourceful Gallaher called upon his own troops to protect him and Atkins's threat was eventually nullified. New Zealand wing Duncan McGregor took to the field for the first time on tour, having recovered from a serious muscle injury.

The match started at a furious pace and the local press described 'electrical bouts of passing', which led up to Smith's try after two minutes. Cunningham converted and shortly after that the All Blacks scored again when Mynott put Hunter in for a try. Then Seeling cleverly cross-kicked and pressurised winger Ernest Hind, who delayed his clearance kick. Stead charged it down and scored. New Zealand were 13-0 up at the break. Hind later made amends by making a try-saving tackle on McGregor.

Early in the second half the Midlands team built up a head of steam and put New Zealand under pressure. Following an error by Gillett, when he failed to deal with a difficult kick, Miles, Cartwright, Goodrich and Russell combined to put forward Cecil Shaw in for a try that John Cooper converted. Roberts and Mynott combined from a scrum for the half-back to score, then they repeated the move for Mynott to go over, despite the efforts of Cooper. The latter try was converted and New Zealand won 21-5.

New Zealand secure lineout possession. (Museum of Rugby)

Fred Roberts was the star for New Zealand. Given extra space through the attention Midlands gave to Gallaher, Roberts was able to do largely as he pleased. A late convert to rugby from soccer, he was described by a contemporary as having 'a rugged physique and a tremendous capacity for taking punishment'. Remarkably, he played in 29 of the 32 matches the All Blacks played on the 1905/06 tour and in 1910 became New Zealand captain.

Wednesday 1 November 1905
Athletic Ground, Richmond
Won 11-0

SURREY	NEW ZEALAND
D.G. Schulze (London Scottish)	E.E. Booth
C.H. Grenfell (United Services)	E.T. Harper
J.E. Raphael (Old Merchant Taylors, Capt.)	G.W. Smith
J.G.G. Birkett (Harlequins)	D. McGregor
W.C. Wilson (Richmond)	J.W. Stead (Capt.)
C.F. Malkin (Civil Service)	H.J. Mynott
S.P. Start (United Services)	F. Roberts
Forwards:	Forwards:
J.F. Shaw (United Services)	S.T. Casey
A.L. Picton (United Services)	G.A. Tyler
J.G. Bussell (Harlequins)	F. Newton
G. Fraser (Richmond)	G.W. Nicholson
J. Ross (London Scottish)	J.M. O'Sullivan
C. Bourns (Old Merchant Taylors)	J. Corbett
S.N. Crowther (Lennox)	W. Johnston
F.C. Pheysey (Richmond)	G.A. Gillett

Scorers:
New Zealand: Tries: Roberts, Johnston, McGregor. Con: Gillett.

Referee: W. Williams (RFU).
Attendance: 11,000.

The Surrey game was an extraordinary affair. For reasons best known to himself, referee Billy Williams blew the whistle at every conceivable opportunity and destroyed the match as a spectacle. This was wonderfully recorded by the *Daily Mail*'s J.A. Buttery, in a report entitled *A Whistling Fantasia*:

In face of the lowering clouds, which threatened every minute to burst – which, in fact, did eventually drench the great majority of the spectators – over 10,000 people, many of them ladies, made their way from various parts of the metropolis to see the 'All Blacks' that everybody is talking about. They expected to see some wonderful football, but they had reckoned without one factor – the referee.

This gentleman – a Londoner, and a member of the Rugby Union Committee – was evidently under the impression that everybody had come to hear him perform on the whistle, and as he was in charge of the stage, so to speak, he was enabled to indulge his fancy to his heart's content. The finest artists are said to shut their eyes when whistling their hardest, and, judged on that hypothesis, the referee must have had his eyes closed on and off for the greater part of the game.

The fantasia commenced in the first minute, and continued, with brief intervals for respiration, throughout the game. As one of the rules of Rugby is that you may not kick or handle the ball while the whistle is blowing, it is obvious that there was very little actual football. Directly someone got the ball, and there was a prospect of a bit of play worth seeing, the referee would recommence his fascinating solo.

A Scottish young lady, whose first football match this was, and evidently with literary recollections of the efficacy of the pibroch in clan warfare, asked her escort, after one particularly dangerous 'All Black' movement had been stopped at the referee's musical behest: 'Why aren't the New Zealanders allowed to have a man to whistle for them, too?'

The rain came down in torrents, and between the bars of the referee's interminable selection the players flipped and flopped about the slippery ground like seals on an ice floe. A confused, entangled mass of legs and arms and black and red-and-white jerseys danced in rhythm to the referee's music in various corners of the field. But there was no football.

'When are they going to begin?' inquired a 'Soccer' enthusiast, who had come many miles because a Rugby friend had assured him that he would see something in the way of football he would remember all his life. It was then closely approaching half-time.

Twenty-five minutes from the start, however, the referee showed signs of fatigue whereupon the 'All Blacks,' quickly seizing their opportunity – and the ball – crossed the Surrey line and kicked a goal. Several explanations were advanced for the referee's extraordinary lapse, but the two more generally accepted were that he had either dropped his whistle or that the pea in it had stuck. Unabashed by his temporary eclipse, however, he blew harder than ever, and for the remainder of the first half football was again out of the question.

During the interval the referee was the recipient of many congratulations from musical friends on his magnificently sustained effort, though fears were expressed that the severe exertions he had undergone would tell on him in the second half. And this proved to be only too true. His whistle failed him on at least two other occasions. The line was crossed twice more.

To their credit be it said, the crowd had by this time realised the mistake they had made in supposing that the affair would be an athletic display. Some whistled obbligatos to the shrill music that rose from the middle of the field. Others, with their sodden coats over their ears and their dripping umbrellas in front of their faces, beat time to the pulsating notes that indicated the whereabouts of the referee's triumphant march 'What an awful day for an open-air concert!' shivered a young lady in the grand stand, as she gathered up her skirts to depart.

As for the game – there was no game. It was an exposition of the power of music to tame even the New Zealand Rugby footballers.

Though unnoticed by the crowd, there were some highly interesting interludes to some of the referee's most brilliant flights. The 'All Blacks' 'captain, who evidently has no ear for music, desired enlightenment on more than one, to him, discordant passage. He is still pondering over the answers. It is understood that Mr Dixon, the New Zealand manager, is also dubious as to the correctness of many of the notes, and that he intends to take the earliest opportunity of interviewing the president of the English Musical Union on the matter.

Everybody went away whistling – except the New Zealanders. 'No wonder it rained!' they said.
At the end of these games there is usually a rush for the jersey of the man who has scored, so that it may be kept as a trophy. On this occasion there was a wild scramble for the referee's whistle.

Referee Williams later organised the purchase and development of a rugby ground for the RFU. The ten acres of market garden purchased for £5,572 12s 6d, affectionately known as 'Billy Williams's Cabbage Patch', became the Twickenham ground.

As far as the rugby was concerned, the combination of the conditions and the curious eye of the referee meant the match was even as a contest and mediocre as a spectacle. It poured with rain throughout, having been raining all morning. To make matters worse a gale blew as strongly as the referee's whistle.

In the first half New Zealand played into the wind but their running and passing skills made light of this. John Raphael missed a straightforward penalty with the wind behind him before Duncan McGregor ran in for a try, but was called back, and later Tyler crossed but the referee had spotted a forward pass. Half-back Fred Roberts then broke from a scrum and was able to scamper over for a try that Gillett converted and New Zealand led 5-0 at half-time.

In the second half New Zealand changed tactics and opted not to challenge the Surrey pack at the scrum. This had been one of the areas the referee had taken exception to in the first half. Instead they played a very physical game to secure possession and relied on their defence to tackle the ball carrier and the weather to influence what Surrey did. Douglas Schulze, the London Scottish and Scotland full-back, failed to retain possession when driven over his own line and dropped the slippery ball. The energetic Johnston followed up and dived on the ball for a try. Then McGregor ran in but with the line at his mercy he lost control of the ball as he was about to score. Later, Mynott picked up a loose ball at top speed and passed to Smith, who made ground before passing to McGregor, who this time held onto the ball and skimmed over puddles to score the third try. Surrey later made a dash for the line and the ball was kicked ahead, but Smith won the race to the ball for what was the only serious attempt the home side made to score a try. The final blast on the referee's whistle signalled the end of a game, much to the relief of all concerned. New Zealand had won 11-0.

James Ross, a forward who served the Surrey cause from the London Scottish club, died at Messines in the autumn of 1914. A Scottish international, he was one of over 100 members of London Scottish who perished during the First World War, including forty-five of their sixty playing members. The name of Ross, and most of the others, can be seen on the London Scottish memorial at the Richmond Athletic Ground.

BLACKHEATH   1905/06

Saturday 4 November 1905
Rectory Field, Blackheath
Won 32-0

BLACKHEATH	NEW ZEALAND
H. Lee	G.A. Gillett
S.F. Coopper	W.J. Wallace
H.J. Anderson	G.W. Smith
B. MacLear	D. McGregor
W.H. Newton	J. Hunter
J.C. Joughlin	J.W. Stead
C.T. Robson	F. Roberts
Forwards:	Forwards:
B.C. Hartley (Capt.)	S.T. Casey
B.A. Hill	G.A. Tyler
C.J. Newbold	W. Cunningham
W.L. Rogers	F.T. Glasgow
W.T. Cave	J.M. O'Sullivan
C.G. Liddell	C.E. Seeling
W.S.D. Craven	W. Johnston
J.E.C. Partridge	D. Gallaher (Capt.)

Scorers:
New Zealand: Tries: Wallace (3), McGregor (2), Glasgow, Stead. Cons: Wallace (4). PG: Wallace.

Referee: P. Coles (RFU).
Attendance: 15,000.

Dave Gallaher returned to the starting line-up for this game which was regarded as a potential banana skin for the All Blacks. The Blackheath side had eight international players, including talented Irish centre Basil MacLear. They had only lost once during the season before this match. The large crowd included Lord Ranfurly, the former Governor of New Zealand who four years previously had presented the NZRFU with the Ranfurly Shield for its inter-provincial rugby.

The All Blacks performed the Haka before the match and there were 'three cheers' from the Blackheath team at its conclusion. These cheers had barely died down when Johnston gathered a loose ball and made an excellent pass to Smith, who promptly kicked over the Blackheath defence for the alert Wallace to collect the ball and score a try that he also converted. Wallace scored again after Hunter charged down a clearing kick from Lee, and he completed his hat-trick before half-time and also kicked a penalty. McGregor crossed for a try late in the half to put the All Blacks ahead 17-0 at the interval.

It was one-way traffic in the second half too, with Glasgow, McGregor and Stead crossing for tries, all of which were converted by Wallace. A couple of runs from MacLear and Anderson, and a foot-rush by Hartley were the only threats Blackheath offered but the New Zealand line was never in danger. The All Blacks completely dominated the game. Blackheath were a major club side at the time but had no answer to the organisation, power and handling

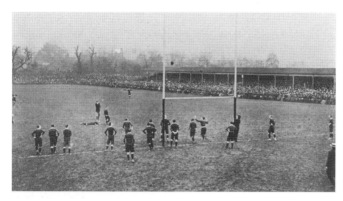

Wallace kicks a goal against Blackheath.

skills of the New Zealand pack. Both sets of backs were of similar pace but the awareness and creativity of the All Blacks was far greater. The home half-backs had not encountered a game played at such pace before and were hopelessly outplayed.

Forward Basil Hill played for England against New Zealand, and following a successful military career that saw him attain the rank of major-general and win the DSO he became president of the RFU for the 1937/38 season. He was later knighted. His captain, Bernard Hartley, was also elected RFU president, gaining that honour in 1947/48. Wing Sydney Coopper was first capped by England in 1900, one of thirteen new caps in a disastrous match against Wales played at Gloucester. He served as an engineer in the Royal Navy and upon retiring from the service in 1924 he was appointed secretary of the RFU, a position he held until 1947. He has been described as 'the founder of modern Twickenham.'

OXFORD UNIVERSITY   1905/06

Tuesday 7 November 1905
Iffley Road, Oxford
Won 47-0

The All Blacks made a couple of changes for the visit to Iffley Road, where they anticipated an open game. They could never have imagined just how open the game would be. The students offered very little resistance to the waves of attacks from the tourists.

The match was played at a frantic pace right from the kick-off and New Zealand would have scored several early tries had it not been for some uncharacteristic handling errors. However, they were not to be denied and Wallace eventually scored a try that opened the floodgates. The Oxford pack was overwhelmed by the

OXFORD UNIVERSITY	NEW ZEALAND
D.B. Davies (Jesus)	G.A. Gillett
A.A. Lawrie (Trinity)	E.E. Booth
A.E. Wood (University)	W.J. Wallace
L. Parker (Christ Church)	D. McGregor
A.M.P. Lyle (Lyle)	J. Hunter
P. Munro (Christ Church, Capt.)	H.J. Mynott
H.C. Jackson (Exeter)	F. Roberts
Forwards:	Forwards:
W.W. Hoskin (Trinity)	S.T. Casey
R.S. Wix (BNC)	G.A. Tyler
C.J. Gardner (Trinity)	F. Newton
H.A. Hodges (Trinity)	G.W. Nicholson
N.R.F.G. Howe-Browne (Oriel)	W. Johnston
N.T. White (Trinity)	F.T. Glasgow
A.A. Hoadley (Keble)	J. Corbett
G.D. Roberts (St John's)	D. Gallaher (Capt.)

Scorers:
New Zealand: Tries: Hunter (5), Booth (2), Wallace (2), Glasgow, Johnston, McGregor, Roberts. Cons: Wallace (3), Tyler.

Referee: A.L. Soper (London).
Attendance: 6,000.

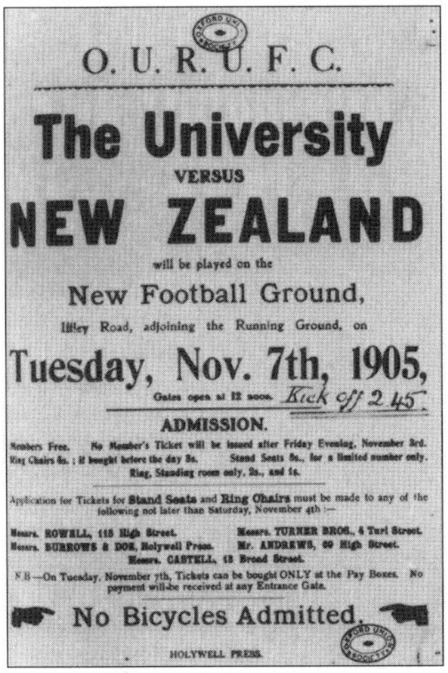

A handbill produced to advertise the students' game with the All Blacks.

All Blacks forwards. They completely dominated every facet of play and denied the students chance to launch an attack, let alone score. While the Oxford forwards seemed to have forgotten how to win the ball, their outside backs appeared to have forgotten how to tackle, yet the handling of the All Blacks backs was poor at times. However, New Zealand ran in tries almost at will and the remarkable Hunter helped himself to five. Booth and Wallace crossed for a brace each and in the end 11 of the 13 tries were scored by the backs. Had the kicking of Wallace been more accurate, the score would undoubtedly have been even more of a humiliation for Oxford. This was, in any case, the biggest defeat suffered by the Oxford University club at that time.

Having reached the halfway point of the tour the All Blacks were able to reflect on unparalleled success and development. However, they could not have been impressed with the standard of English rugby thus far. Levels of fitness, speed and basic handling skills were below expectation.

Military service subsequently took its toll on the Oxford side. Harold Hodges, also a Nottinghamshire County cricketer, was capped by England later in the season and served with distinction for the 3rd Monmouthshire Regiment, and latterly the 11th South Lancashires, but was killed in action at Mons in March 1918. Leonard Parker served in the Royal Flying Corps but was shot down in 1917. Archibald Lyle, also a regular half-back for the university, won the Military Cross in 1918, as did David Davies and Charles Gardner, all of whom survived the First World War. Patrick Munro later became MP for Llandaff & Barry but lost his life while on duty with the Home Guard in 1942. Geoffrey 'Khaki' Roberts, an England international, was later a prosecutor at the Nuremberg Trials. Rhodes Scholar Noel Howe-Browne later represented South Africa against the 1910 Great Britain tourists.

CAMBRIDGE UNIVERSITY 1905/06

Thursday 9 November 1905
Grange Road, Cambridge
Won 14-0

CAMBRIDGE UNIVERSITY	NEW ZEALAND
J.G. Scoular (St John's)	E.E. Booth
J. Burt-Marshall (Clare)	H.D. Thomson
K.G. MacLeod (Pembroke)	G.W. Smith
W.M. Penny (Jesus)	D. McGregor
L.M. MacLeod (Pembroke, Capt.)	R.G. Deans
H.F.P. Hearson (King's)	W.J. Wallace
T.G. Pitt (Emmanuel)	F. Roberts
J.V. Young (Emmanuel)	Forwards:
Forwards:	S.T. Casey
H.G. Monteith (Pembroke)	G.A. Tyler
B.G. Harris (Pembroke)	W. Cunningham
F.J.V. Hopley (Pembroke)	G.W. Nicholson
R. McCosh (Trinity)	J.M. O'Sullivan
J.W. Alexander (Clare)	W.S. Glenn
R.B. Gibbins (King's)	F.T. Glasgow
W.C. Currie (Trinity)	D. Gallaher (Capt.)

Scorers:
New Zealand: Tries: Deans (2), McGregor (2).
Cons: Cunningham.

Referee: J.C. Findlay (SRU).
Attendance: 7,000.

Cambridge was regarded as being the stronger of the Universities at the time and was expected to offer a stiffer challenge than Oxford had two days previously. The All Blacks made six changes and a couple of positional switches. Gillett stood down and Booth moved from wing to full-back with Wallace having a run out at five-eighth. Cambridge selected five three-quarters, including W.M. Penny, the London Welshman who had played for Somerset earlier in the tour. Also included were the MacLeod brothers, Lewis and Kenneth, who formed the centre partnership for Scotland against

New Zealand ten days later. The seventeen-year-old Kenneth had won the freshman's 100-yards race two days earlier.

It was an even game played between two teams committed to playing rugby with the ball in their hands. The game was thirty minutes old before the first score. Roberts kicked ahead and Smith chased the ball, causing panic in the students' defence. Burt-Marshall failed to deal with the situation and the alert Wallace gathered the loose ball and passed to Deans, who scored. Shortly afterwards McGregor crossed for a try in the corner. Wallace failed to convert either try, but New Zealand were 6-0 ahead at the break.

The second half was a hard battle for both sides and the All Blacks were impressed with the strength and fitness of the students, who were superior in every way to the Oxford players. However, New Zealand pressure increased and it was inevitable that McGregor should score again, following good play by Wallace. The match had featured attack and counter-attack. Then Deans scored after a back move had created space for him. He showed good pace and power to clear the first line of defence before swerving past the last to score a fine try. Cunningham converted.

It was the hardest game of the tour so far and a good

Duncan McGregor, who scored two tries against Cambridge University and later scored a record four in the victory over England.

examination for the All Blacks with the international with the Scots looming. Thomson and McGregor both suffered injuries during the game but played on. Several of the Cambridge players were or became internationals: Monteith, Scoular and the MacLeod brothers played for Scotland, and Hopley for England. Twelve of the Cambridge team were in the XV which defeated Oxford 15-13 in the Varsity match at Queen's Club the following month.

RICHMOND   1905/06

Saturday 11 November 1905
Athletic Ground, Richmond
Won 17-0

Fred Roberts stood down for only the second time on tour. This time his place at half-back was taken by Hunter. As this was a week before the Scotland international, New Zealand selected a weaker side for the game. Heavy overnight rain, which had carried on into the morning, left the surface of the pitch slippery and the ball greasy. The conditions made play very difficult.

In the first half-hour both sides missed a penalty goal, and Richmond wing Wilson failed to take a chance when a big gap appeared in front of him. Hunter opened the scoring after thirty minutes when he

RICHMOND	NEW ZEALAND
G.H. Glover	E.E. Booth
W.C. Wilson	W.J. Wallace
R.E. Godfray	R.G. Deans
H. Morley-Lawson	E.T. Harper
B.B. Bennetts	J.W. Stead
H.G. Aveling	H.J. Mynott
L.C. Smith	J. Hunter
Forwards:	Forwards:
H. Alexander (Capt.)	F.T. Glasgow
G . Fraser	G.A. Tyler
C.B. Smith	F. Newton
R.C. Grellett	J. Corbett
F.T. Turner	A. McDonald
F.C. Pheysey	W.S. Glenn
C.E. Chase	W. Johnston
W. Blake-Odgers	D. Gallaher (Capt.)

Scorers:
New Zealand: Tries: Wallace (2), Deans, Hunter, Stead.
Cons: Wallace.

Referee: E.J. Andrews (Middlesex).
Attendance: 7,000.

Richmond captain Harry Alexander.

picked his way through the puddles and, so it appeared, the Richmond defence to score a try between the posts. Wallace missed the simple conversion but the crowd loudly cheered the try. He was then on the end of a three-quarter move that defied the conditions to score a try, but the kick was too difficult for him. New Zealand led 6-0 at half-time.

Early in the second half the ball was moved to Wallace, who kicked over the Richmond defence. Stead showed commendable speed to run around the Richmond players and beat the cover to the ball to score a further try. Shortly afterwards Deans dummied and swerved his way through the Richmond defence to score close to the posts. Wallace converted and then rounded off a move to score his second try of the game. Richmond centre Reginald Godfray scarcely had the ball to show his attacking skills but was required to tackle constantly to repel the All Black attackers. He performed well enough to win a place in the England XV that played New Zealand later in the tour. The rest of the Richmond team had played well and given the All Blacks a tough game.

Tour vice-captain Billy Stead was the captain of the first New Zealand international side to play at home when they defeated the British team in 1904. He later captained the All Blacks again and, by the time he retired, he had represented New Zealand on forty-two occasions and was never on the losing side. Home captain Harry Alexander, a lieutenant in the Grenadier Guards, died on active service in Hulluch, France, in 1915. C.E. Chase also lost his life in battle in 1918.

BEDFORD XV   1905/06

Wednesday 15 November 1905
Goldington Road, Bedford
Won 41-0

Interest was great and the crowd was a record for Goldington Road, its number including the Duke and Duchess of Manchester. Fearing the prospect of a humiliating defeat, Bedford bolstered their team with several guest players. 'Bedford were appalled at what they had taken on. So they went out into the highways and byeways and collected a pretty hot side', wrote old Bedfordian Brigadier M.C.T. Gompertz. Only Finlinson was a regular in the Bedford back division. The lack of familiarity and random field positions of the five three-quarters probably worked against them, for Bedford conceded 10 tries. Roberts returned to the

BEDFORD XV	NEW ZEALAND
G. Romans	G.A. Gillett
E.R. Mobbs	E.T. Harper
B. MacLear	R.G. Deans
M.E. Finlinson	D. McGregor
H.J. Anderson	J. Hunter
A. Hudson	H.J. Mynott
H.C. Palmer	F. Roberts
T.H. Preston	Forwards:
Forwards:	S.T. Casey
A.L. Rogers	G.A. Tyler
R.B. Campbell	F. Newton
H.B. Follitt	G.W. Nicholson
W. Johns	J. Corbett
J. Mason	C.E. Seeling
R. MacLear (Capt.)	A. McDonald
A.V. Manton	D. Gallaher (Capt.)

Scorers:
New Zealand: Tries: Hunter (4), Roberts, Seeling, Deans, McDonald, McGregor, Mynott. Cons: Gillett (2), Tyler (2). Goal from mark: Gillett.

Referee: F.W. Nicholls (Leicester).
Attendance: 8,000.

New Zealand XV, and despite a wet surface and slippery ball, his handling was exemplary.

Jimmy Hunter crossed for 4 tries, one of which stirred a reporter to write: 'it is next to impossible to describe Hunter's zigzag, eel-like bursts for the goal line... They are quite unlike anything ever seen on a rugby field... Hunter... carves his way through not one, but three or four lines of defence, and, instead of losing speed in the avoidance of obstacles, seems to gain increased momentum at every stride.' Hunter scored the first two New Zealand tries before Roberts nipped in for the third. Then Seeling scored after Gallaher made a break. Gillett converted and New Zealand were 14-0 ahead at half-time.

It was one-way traffic in the second half. The All Blacks ran in six more tries and Gillett kicked a goal from a mark. Deans raced in after Roberts and Hunter had given him a gap. The next try came from McDonald after a forward rush, then McGregor ran in for a try before Hunter scored twice and Mynott rounded things off with the tenth try. Harper, McGregor, Gillett and Tyler attempted goal kicks in the absence of Wallace but only the latter two were successful. The Bedford pack fought manfully but, Basil MacLear apart, the backs failed to threaten the New Zealand defence.

Lieutenant-Colonel Edgar Mobbs achieved considerable fame from his exploits with Northampton and England but this war hero played against the All Blacks for Bedford.

Edgar Mobbs, dropped from the Northampton side to play the All Blacks, was selected on the wing as a guest in the Bedford team. He failed to impress but subsequently played with distinction for Northampton and England, and later worked on various committees for the Barbarians and the RFU. He formed a Sportsman's Battalion during the First World War and rose to the rank of lieutenant-colonel in the 7th Battalion, the Northamptonshire Regiment. He was awarded the DSO but was killed in action at Zillebeke, Passchendaele, nine weeks before Dave Gallaher died on the same Belgian battlefield in 1917.

SCOTLAND   1905/06

Saturday 18 November 1905
Inverleith, Edinburgh
Won 12-7

This was New Zealand's first Test match in the Northern Hemisphere. Having swept through England, the tourists faced their sternest examination so far, although the Scottish Football Union, rather ungraciously, did not consider this a full international and did not award caps. Caps were, however, awarded retrospectively. Reflecting their lukewarm approach, the Scottish selectors only finalised their team shortly before kick-off. Their preparations had been upset by the withdrawal of Nolan Fell from the original selection. A New Zealand student undertaking a postgraduate medical course at Edinburgh University, Fell had already made 7 appearances for Scotland, but

SCOTLAND	NEW ZEALAND
J.G. Scoular (Cambridge University)	G.A. Gillett
J.T. Simson (Watsonians)	W.J. Wallace
K.G. MacLeod (Cambridge University)	R.G. Deans
L.M. MacLeod (Cambridge University)	G.W. Smith
T. Sloan (Glasgow Acads)	J.W. Stead
L.L. Greig (United Services)	J. Hunter
E.D. Simson (Edinburgh University)	F. Roberts
P. Munro (London Scottish)	Forwards:
Forwards:	S.T. Casey
D.R. Bedell-Sivright	G.A. Tyler
(Edinburgh University, Capt.)	W. Cunningham
W.E. Kyle (Hawick)	F.T. Glasgow
J.C. MacCallum (Watsonians)	J.M. O'Sullivan
J.M. Mackenzie (Edinburgh University)	A. McDonald
W.L. Russell (Glasgow University)	C.E. Seeling
L. West (Carlisle)	D. Gallaher (Capt.)
W.P. Scott (West of Scotland)	

Scorers:
Scotland: Try: MacCallum. DG: Simson.
New Zealand: Tries: Smith (2), Glasgow, Cunningham.

Referee: W. Kennedy (Ireland).
Attendance: 21,000.

decided not to play against his fellow countrymen, much to the annoyance of the selection committee who never selected him again. Fell was replaced by Louis Greig, a fine all-rounder, who played as a third half-back outside 'Kemo' Simson and Pat Munro, a move that was designed to counter the New Zealanders' unusual formation. Making his debut in the Scottish centre was Ken 'Grunt' MacLeod, a brilliant runner and kicker who was still aged under eighteen.

The match had been in some doubt because of a harsh overnight frost, and the pitch was very slippery and hard underneath. In an engrossing and exciting encounter, the two sides presented a contrast of styles. Scotland's main attacking weapon was the traditional forward rush while the back division, lying up close, concentrated on spoiling work. By contrast, the New Zealanders were more enterprising and tried to play their famed attacking game, although the conditions were very difficult.

Several opportunities were wasted because of poor handling and a lack of composure. Scotland opened the scoring when Simson dropped a goal from a close scrum. New Zealand replied with tries from Frank Glasgow and George Smith, the first from a forward charge and the second after a good passing movement. Shortly before half-time, the Scottish forwards made another devastating rush and John MacCallum was on hand to score. This was the first try that the tourists had conceded in 8 matches and the first time on the tour that any side had managed to score twice against them. Scotland led 7-6 at the interval.

The second half was closely fought, New Zealand making most of the chances but unable to score because of unforced errors and the stout Scottish defence. Unluckily, Lewis MacLeod, Kenneth's brother, suffered a serious ankle injury and could only play with a limp, which was to be an important factor in the closing stages of the match. For New Zealand, Wallace hit an upright with a penalty attempt. With a few minutes remaining, it seemed that the tourists were about to lose their unbeaten record. Amid great excitement, a quick passing movement on the Scottish 25 saw George Smith take the ball at full speed, round 'Dan' Scoular and score at the corner. The New Zealanders were overjoyed and Smith was warmly embraced by his team mates, breaking the unwritten rule that rugby players were not supposed to show their emotions. Wallace missed the awkward conversion attempt, but a few minutes later Cunningham latched on to a long kick over the Scottish line to seal the New Zealanders' victory. Although limping heavily because of a leg injury, their captain, David Gallaher, was delighted at this first international win. The Scots did not take their defeat very well and the final whistle was greeted in stony silence, apart from some visiting colonial students, who were ecstatic. Likewise, in the evening, the New Zealanders received no hospitality from their hosts, as was customary after an international match, but instead they were honoured guests of the local Australasian club. There was further controversy when it was revealed that the visitors would receive a substantial share of the gate money, as per a previous agreement. For the Scottish authorities, this raised questions about their amateur status, the long-term consequence being that the Scots refused to play the New Zealanders when they next toured in 1924/25. Problems aside, this was an historic rugby encounter. The New Zealanders had been pushed all the way by a determined Scottish side, and it was to their credit that they had been able to hold their nerve when facing defeat. The Scottish forward drives and tight defensive play had upset the tourists who, perhaps affected by nerves at the sense of occasion, did not perform up to expectations. Nevertheless, it was New Zealand's first international victory in the British Isles.

**Wednesday 22 November 1905
Hampden Park, Glasgow
Won 22-0**

After the excitement of their first international, the New Zealanders continued their winning ways against a Glasgow XV, usually described as 'West of Scotland' (not to be confused with the local club of the same name). The tourists rested six of their first-choice team, including the injured captain Dave Gallaher. The West of Scotland fielded four players from Saturday's international and a few up-and-comers, but not too much was expected them. The home side played with seven forwards and eight backs, but unlike Scotland the extra man performed as an additional three-quarter. The match was played at Hampden Park

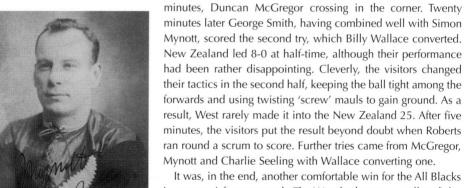

WEST OF SCOTLAND	NEW ZEALAND
H.N. Tennant (West of Scotland)	W.J. Wallace
W. Church (Glasgow Acads)	E.T. Harper
T. Sloan (Glasgow Acads)	G.W. Smith
C.W. Stewart (West of Scotland)	D. McGregor
C.C. Fitzgerald (West of Scotland)	H.J. Mynott
J.A. Finlay (Kelvinside Acads)	J.W. Stead (Capt.)
L.L. Greig (Glasgow Acads)	F. Roberts
A.C. Frame (Glasgow Acads)	Forwards:
Forwards:	G.A. Tyler
W.L. Russell (Glasgow Acads)	W. Johnston
W.P. Scott (West of Scotland, Capt.)	F. Newton
R.B. Waddell (Glasgow Acads)	A. McDonald
H. Wilson (Glasgow University)	W.S. Glenn
G.M. Frew (Glasgow HSFP)	C.E. Seeling
W. Law (Kelvinside Acads)	F.T. Glasgow
E.G. Copestake (Clydesdale)	G.A. Gillett

Scorers:
New Zealand: Tries: McGregor (2), Smith, Roberts, Mynott, Seeling. Cons: Wallace (2).

Referee: J.T. Gillespie (Edinburgh Acads).
Attendance: 10,000.

football ground, then the largest stadium in the world and a marvel of its age. Local schoolchildren were given a half-holiday to attend, but unfortunately heavy rain and a strong wind blowing down the pitch ruined much of the spectacle. To make matters worse, the game, according to the *Scotsman*, 'was contested in anything but a pleasant spirit'. Some sections of the crowd were displeased at the New Zealanders' rough tactics and matters reached a head when one of the visiting forwards was lectured by the referee, something that was almost unheard of in rugby at the time.

In a scrappy encounter New Zealand, as expected, dominated the game, although stout home defence kept the score respectable. Playing with the wind, the tourists opened the scoring after ten

Harry Mynott, the Taranaki five-eighth known as 'Simon', had a fine game for New Zealand and scored a try.

minutes, Duncan McGregor crossing in the corner. Twenty minutes later George Smith, having combined well with Simon Mynott, scored the second try, which Billy Wallace converted. New Zealand led 8-0 at half-time, although their performance had been rather disappointing. Cleverly, the visitors changed their tactics in the second half, keeping the ball tight among the forwards and using twisting 'screw' mauls to gain ground. As a result, West rarely made it into the New Zealand 25. After five minutes, the visitors put the result beyond doubt when Roberts ran round a scrum to score. Further tries came from McGregor, Mynott and Charlie Seeling with Wallace converting one.

It was, in the end, another comfortable win for the All Blacks in an unsatisfactory match. The West had put up a gallant fight, but there was no doubt that the visitors were the better side, having more power in the forwards, and speed and penetration in the backs. Mynott had a particularly fine game, given the conditions, breaking through repeatedly and showing a rare turn of speed. George Gillett was described as a 'sore thorn in the flesh' of the West half-backs, although Will Russell fought hard for the home side.

Saturday 25 November 1905
Lansdowne Road, Dublin
Won 15-0

IRELAND	NEW ZEALAND
M.F. Landers (Cork Constitution)	W.J. Wallace
H.B. Thrift (Dublin University)	G.W. Smith
B. MacLear (Cork County)	R.G. Deans
J.C. Parke (Dublin University)	H.J. Mynott
C.G. Robb (Queen's University, Belfast)	J. Hunter
T.T.H. Robinson (Dublin University)	J.W. Stead (Capt.)
E.D. Caddell (Dublin University)	F. Roberts
J. Wallace (Wanderers)	Forwards:
Forwards:	G.A. Tyler
C.E. Allen (City of Derry, Capt.)	S.T. Casey
J.J. Coffey (Lansdowne)	W. Cunningham
G.T. Hamlet (Old Wesley)	J.M. O'Sullivan
H.J.B. Knox (Lansdowne)	A. McDonald
H.S. Sugars (Dublin University)	C.E. Seeling
A.D. Tedford (Malone)	F.T. Glasgow
H.G. Wilson (Malone)	G.A. Gillett

Scorers: Tries: Deans (2), McDonald. Cons: Wallace (3).

Referee: J.C. Findlay (SFU).
Attendance: 12,000.

Gallaher's leg injury prevented him being considered for the game and so his place was again taken by Gillett, with Wallace reverting to full-back and Mynott coming in on the wing, a rather surprising selection as the usual wings were ignored. Stead captained the side from first five-eighth. These were the only changes to the side that played Scotland. Ireland had played an inconclusive trial match earlier in the month in torrential rain and were a little undecided about their line-up. Harold Sugars was given his international debut but the Trinity College forward was not presented with a cap as these were not awarded by the IRFU against 'colonial' sides. Two years later, when he played against Scotland, he was eventually able to wear his international cap. Interest was great for the first All Blacks match in Ireland and, as a consequence, the IRFU made it an all-ticket affair, the first such arrangement for a rugby international. The crowd witnessed a magnificent struggle played in poor light and drizzle.

Ireland began on the attack when Knox burst away from the first lineout. He was tackled and the danger diminished, but it showed the All Blacks that they would have their hands full dealing with the Irish pack. The home forwards put New Zealand under great pressure during the first half. Despite the talents of MacLear and Thrift outside, Ireland chose to keep the ball among the forwards. This tactic proved wise as Ireland squandered several opportunities to score using their backs. There was an interlude early on when the ball was lost behind the stand and the players had to wait while a replacement was found. Sadly, it burst shortly afterwards. Rather than huddling together to discuss tactics during these stoppages, the players mingled together and chatted. It was thirty-two minutes before the first score. The Irish lost the ball deep in New Zealand territory and the All Blacks counter-attacked at great pace, Deans eventually looping outside his wing for the try. Wallace converted for the only score of the half. Then Allen and Tedford led a drive through Roberts and Hunter and only good

The Ireland side that faced the All Blacks.

defence by Deans and Mynott stopped them. It was thrust and counter-thrust.

Ireland lost Thomas Robinson with an injury just before the interval but he returned early in the second half. Deans scored his second try and Alex McDonald also touched down. Both tries were converted by Wallace to see the All Blacks home 15-0. At the end of the exciting game there was great cheering for both sides. It was acknowledged that the match had been greatest international game ever played in Ireland.

The match was the first all-ticket international.

MUNSTER   1905/06

Tuesday 28 November 1905
Market's Field, Limerick
Won 33-0

New Zealand headed south to Limerick for their second and last game in Ireland. There was great interest in the province and special arrangements were made to squeeze a record crowd into the small ground. The band of the 5th Northumberland Fusiliers entertained the crowd, many of whom had greeted the All Blacks when they arrived at Limerick station and accompanied them to their hotel the previous evening. David Gallaher was still injured and thus unable to play on the island of his birth. A native of Ramelton in County Donegal, Gallaher emigrated to New Zealand aged five. He played for Auckland and New Zealand on the first fully representative tour to Australia

MUNSTER	NEW ZEALAND
A. Quillinan (Garryowen)	E.E. Booth
A. Newton (Cork County)	H.L. Abbott
B. MacLear (Cork County, Capt.)	G.W. Smith
W.O. Stokes (Garryowen)	D. McGregor
R.M. McGrath (Cork Constitution)	J.W. Stead (Capt.)
F. McQueen (Queen's College, Cork)	H.J. Mynott
J. O'Connor (Garryowen)	F. Roberts
Forwards:	Forwards:
J. Wallace (Garryowen)	W.H.C. Mackrell
W. Parker (Cork County)	F. Newton
A. Acheson (Garryowen)	W. Cunningham
T.S. Reeves (Garryowen)	A. McDonald
T. Churchward (Cork County)	G.W. Nicholson
M. White (Queen's College, Cork)	J. Corbett
S.K. Hosford (Cork County)	F.T. Glasgow
R. Welply (Queen's College, Cork)	G.A. Gillett

Scorers:
New Zealand: Tries: Abbott (3), Roberts, Glasgow, McGregor, Booth, Stead. Cons: Glasgow (3). PG: Glasgow.

Referee: J.M. Magee (Bective).
Attendance: 3,500.

in 1903. He retired after the 1905/06 tour but still played occasionally for the Ponsonby club. A military man, Gallaher served in the Boer War in 1901 and then during the First World War, when he fought in the 21st Reinforcements, Auckland Regiment of the NZ Expeditionary Force. He lost his life in the muddy hell of Passchendaele in 1917. Billy Mackrell had recovered from a serious injury and infection and played his first game of the tour. Gillett continued in the wing-forward role with Booth at full-back. Munster lost the services of the injured 'Mossie' Landers following the international and the full-back was replaced by Quillinan of Garryowen. Several of the home side were carrying minor injuries and there was some consternation that they may suffer as a consequence.

Overnight heavy rain had left the pitch boggy and uneven in places, making playing conditions difficult. However, these had little effect on the All Blacks. They started the match at top speed and Abbott was soon over the line for a try after Gillett and Smith opened up the Munster defence. Glasgow missed the conversion but kicked a penalty goal shortly afterwards. Roberts then scored a try supporting a forward drive, which Glasgow converted before scoring a try himself. Smith bruised his shoulder and struggled with the injury, eventually leaving the field shortly after half-time. McGregor then scored following another break by Roberts from a scrum, and a fine movement involving

Far left: *One of Irish rugby's true greats, Basil MacLear, who faced the All Blacks four times during the tour.*

Left: *Captain of 'The Originals', Irishman Dave Gallaher.*

forwards and backs was finished off by Abbott close to half-time. The heavy ball made kicking difficult but the All Blacks were content with a 20-0 half-time lead.

Booth crossed for a fine try early in the second half and further tries were scored by Abbott and Stead, Glasgow converting two. The loss of Smith disrupted the three-quarters but the forwards denied the Munster team the ball, and despite a couple of runs from MacLear and McGrath they rarely threatened to score. The crowd cheered the New Zealanders as if they were their own side, such was the quality of rugby the tourists displayed. When the final whistle went they cheered loudly for five minutes even though the home side had been soundly beaten 33-0.

Home captain Basil MacLear faced the All Blacks for the fourth time on tour and was again left unrewarded. A fine footballer and rugby icon of his time, MacLear scored a magnificent try for Ireland against South Africa in 1906. When serving as a captain in the Royal Dublin Fusiliers, he was killed in action at Ypres in 1915.

ENGLAND   1905/06

**Saturday 2 December 1905
Crystal Palace, London
Won 15-0**

Gallaher returned for this match, although he had not completely recovered from injury. The injured George Smith stood down, allowing Duncan McGregor to play. McGregor took his chance with both hands and scored a record 4 tries for New Zealand in an international. England opted for a seven-man scrum and selected John Raphael as an extra back. It was not a great success. They selected an inexperienced side with eight players new to international rugby. Remarkably, only Raphael and Harry Shewring of the backs had played for England before.

ENGLAND	NEW ZEALAND
E.J. Jackett (Falmouth)	G.A. Gillett
H.M. Imrie (Durham City)	W.J. Wallace
R.E. Godfray (Richmond)	R.G. Deans
H.E. Shewring (Bristol)	D. McGregor
A.E. Hind (Leicester)	J. Hunter
J.E. Raphael (OMT's)	J.W. Stead
D.R. Gent (Gloucester)	F. Roberts
J. Braithwaite (Leicester)	Forwards:
Forwards:	S.T. Casey
C.E.L. Hammond (Harlequins)	G.A. Tyler
V.H. Cartwright (Notts, Capt.)	F. Newton
B.A. Hill (Blackheath)	J.M. O'Sullivan
J.L. Mathias (Bristol)	F.T. Glasgow
E.W. Roberts (RNE College)	A. McDonald
R.F. Russell (Leicester)	C.E. Seeling
G.E. Summerscales (Durham City)	D. Gallaher (Capt.)

Scorers:
New Zealand: Tries: McGregor (4), Newton.

Referee: G. Evans (Midlands).
Attendance: 45,000.

The England team that faced New Zealand at Crystal Palace. From left to right: Gil Evans (referee), H.M. Imrie, H.E. Shewring, D.R. Gent, J. Braithwaite, A.E. Hind, C.E.L. Hammond, B.A. Hill, R.F. Russell, V.H. Cartwright (captain), J.L. Mathias, E.W. Roberts, G.E. Summerscales, E.J. Jackett, R.E. Godfray, J.E. Raphael.

The trees around the ground were full of spectators, raising speculation that the actual attendance was nearer to 75,000 than to the official figure of 45,000. England kicked off on a heavy pitch and were behind after five minutes. Fred Roberts made a break down the blind side of a scrum and opened the defence up for McGregor to score. The Wellington wing scored again ten minutes later and the match was effectively over when McGregor scored his third try after a similar move to opening score. Wallace had three very difficult kicks to add the extra points and missed them all. It was 9-0 to New Zealand at half-time.

The England pack struggled to deal with the power and pace of the New Zealand forwards and the All Blacks' fourth try came from the forwards, who burst away from a lineout for Fred Newton to score. Gillett took over the kicking, but with the same lack of success as Wallace. England managed to repel the New Zealand attacks until five minutes from time, when the All Blacks made the most of quick ball from a ruck and McGregor showed his tremendous pace to run in and score his fourth try. England's only opportunity to score occurred in the dying seconds when the ball was kicked ahead over the goal line. Ernest Hind and McGregor raced to get to the ball first, with the New Zealander just getting his boot to the ball and kicking it dead.

The New Zealand pack dominated possession and Roberts and Stead had time and plenty of opportunity to launch attacks. Once again, the superior teamwork of the New Zealanders was a decisive factor. The All Blacks attacked constantly, and had it not been for the remarkable performance of John Jackett at full-back, New Zealand would have scored more than 5 tries. Duncan McGregor's 4 tries in an international was a New Zealand record that was equalled in the 1987 World Cup before being overtaken by Marc Ellis's six against Japan in the 1995 tournament. McGregor played briefly for Gloucester after the tour before returning to New Zealand. He later turned professional and was part of the 'All Golds' rugby league tour of 1907/08. He opened a sports shop in Gloucester with Arthur Hudson after he retired from playing. England captain 'Lump' Cartwright later became an international referee and served in both World Wars, winning the DSO and the Croix de Guerre. He was elected RFU president for the 1928/29 season. Raphael, who also played for Surrey against the New Zealanders and captained an English team on tour to Argentina in 1910, was an elegant three-quarter. He later served in the Duke of Wellington's West Riding Regiment and died of wounds sustained at Messines Ridge in 1917.

Wednesday 6 December 1905
Athletic and Recreation Ground,
Cheltenham
Won 18-0

CHELTENHAM	NEW ZEALAND
B. Davey	E.E. Booth
L.W. Hayward	H.L. Abbott
F.H.B. Champain	D. McGregor
G.T. Cottrell	E.T. Harper
C. Clifford	R.G. Deans
A. Goddard	H.J. Mynott
R.P. Burn	F. Roberts
G.T. Unwin (Capt.)	Forwards:
Forwards:	S.T. Casey
L. Cook	F.T. Glasgow
G. Cossens	F. Newton
F. Jacob	J. Corbett
F. Goulding	G.W. Nicholson
H. Pike	W.S. Glenn
J.V. Bedell-Sivright	W.H.C. Mackrell
W.N. Unwin	D. Gallaher (Capt.)

Scorers:
New Zealand: Tries: Abbott (3), Roberts. Cons: Harper (3).

Referee: P. Coles (RFU).
Attendance: 12,000.

After their success at the Crystal Palace, New Zealand headed west to the attractive town of Cheltenham for a game with the local rugby team, at that time a significant club side in English rugby. Cheltenham had recently beaten local rivals Gloucester. Their captain, Geoffrey Unwin, won a solitary England cap in 1898 against Scotland when a Blackheath player. All Blacks' wing Duncan McGregor found himself at centre for this game with Abbott and Harper, fine wings themselves, outside him.

The match proved to be an open game in which both sides adopted a positive approach. Although this made for a fast, entertaining game, Cheltenham's tactics played into the hands of the All Blacks who were accomplished at capitalising on opponents' errors. Roberts opened the scoring with a try when he charged down a clearing kick and gathered the loose ball to score. Harper converted. Then Abbott raced in for 2 tries, both of which Harper was able to convert, and New Zealand were ahead 15-0 at the interval.

The only score of the second half, a period in which Cheltenham were able to disrupt New Zealand's possession, was the third try for Abbott. Both wings, Abbott and Harper, had outstanding games for New Zealand. They ran hard and fast at the Cheltenham defence, in which Leslie Hayward and Bert Davey were outstanding. However, as with so many other games New Zealand played in on this tour, their line was scarcely threatened. One foot-rush involving Cook and Pike took Cheltenham close to the All Blacks' line but Booth was able to gather the ball and clear to touch. The hat-trick of tries scored by Harold 'Bunny' Abbott was one of three he achieved on tour. Unfortunately he suffered from injuries, a poisoned leg following the game at Hartlepool preventing him from playing for some time. However, he played in the international against France and had the unusual distinction of playing for New York, in an exhibition game, and British Columbia against New Zealand on the

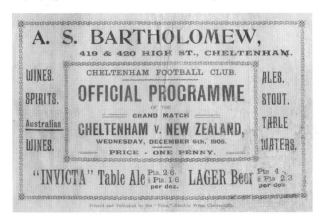

All Blacks' way home when the local side was short of players. He scored a try in both games. The Cheltenham pack included John Bedell-Sivright, who was capped by Scotland against Wales in 1902 when a Cambridge student. He was the brother of David 'Darkie' Bedell-Sivright who captained Scotland against New Zealand and led the British tour to New Zealand and Australia in 1904.

Saturday 9 December 1905
Upper Park, Birkenhead
Won 34-0

CHESHIRE	NEW ZEALAND
G.F. Tomes (New Brighton)	G.A. Gillett
E.S. Ashcroft (Birkenhead Park)	H.D. Thomson
T.C. Clarke (New Brighton)	R.G. Deans
A.S. Anderson (Birkenhead Park)	H.L. Abbott
A. Hartley (Sale)	J. Hunter
P.D. Kendall (Birkenhead Park, Capt.)	J.W. Stead
F.C. Hulme (Birkenhead Park)	F. Roberts
Forwards:	Forwards:
E. Herschell (Birkenhead Park)	S.T. Casey
J.S. Francomb (Sale)	G.A. Tyler
E.A. Weir (New Brighton)	W. Cunningham
A.M. Johnstone (Birkenhead Park)	J.M. O'Sullivan
H.J.M. Edgar (Birkenhead Park)	J. Corbett
A. McM. Taylor (Birkenhead Park)	G.W. Nicholson
S. Richardson (Birkenhead Park)	C.E. Seeling
G.C. Sanderson (Birkenhead Park)	D. Gallaher (Capt.)

Scorers:
New Zealand: Tries: Hunter (3), Thomson (3), Nicholson, Abbott, Deans, Roberts. Cons: Cunningham, Tyler.

Referee: F.W. Nicholls (Midlands).
Attendance: 8,000.

There was considerable interest in this match in the North-West of England. The Lancashire Rugby Union had turned down the chance to play the All Blacks due to the poor state of their finances, and thus the Cheshire game attracted spectators from beyond the county boundaries. Cheshire had narrowly lost two and won one of their preceding games and were quietly confident of doing themselves justice. However, a series of problems denuded Cheshire of several players through injury, work commitments and, in the case of the two MacLeod brothers who had faced the All Blacks for Scotland and Cambridge, commitments to the Varsity match the following Tuesday.

The large crowd, which wedged itself into the ground, was instantly impressed by the play of the All Blacks, especially the power of the forwards in the loose. This gave Roberts plenty of ball and the time to distribute it to his backs. Hunter was at his exuberant best and he raced in for another hat-trick of tries. Thomson also scored three and in total the tourists crossed for 10. Only two were converted. The first score came after eight minutes when an attempted clearance was charged down and Nicholson and O'Sullivan dived on the ball, the score being awarded to Nicholson. Hunter then embarked on

a sinuous run that ended with Thomson scoring his first try. Hunter then scored himself before Thomson scored again and Abbott dashed in to see the All Blacks 17-0 up at half-time.

Deans crossed soon after the restart before Thomson completed his trio. Hunter then scored a further 2 tries in quick succession before Roberts scored the final try, from a scrum. Cunningham converted Roberts' try, but Gillett, Thomson and Abbot all failed with attempted kicks at goal. Tyler converted Hunter's first try.

The match featured great running from Bob Deans. A tall, powerful centre, he possessed good pace and footballing skills that thrilled the crowd. Home captain Percy Kendall had led England against Scotland in 1903. A solicitor, he later served as a lieutenant in the King's Liverpool Regiment but was killed in action in January 1915 at Ypres. The same fate befell Ashcroft, Anderson, Herschell, Edgar and Taylor, all fellow players with the Birkenhead Park club.

Cheshire captain Percy 'Toggie' Kendall, in the uniform of the 10th Battalion, King's Liverpool Regiment (the Liverpool Scottish).

Wednesday 13 December 1905
Headingley, Leeds
Won 40-0

YORKSHIRE	NEW ZEALAND
J.S. Auty (Headingley)	W.J. Wallace
R.C. Dobson (Headingley)	E.E. Booth
A.S. Pickering (Harrogate)	R.G. Deans
W. Lynch (Castleford)	D. McGregor
B. Dalton (Castleford)	J.W. Stead
T. Orton (Harrogate)	H.J. Mynott
B. Oughtred (Barrow-in-Furness, Capt.)	J. Hunter
B. Moss-Blundell (Harrogate)	Forwards:
Forwards:	G.A. Tyler
J. Green (Skipton)	W. Cunningham
R. Duckett (Skipton)	F. Newton
W. Knox (Skipton)	J. Corbett
T. Chapman (Harrogate)	G.W. Nicholson
W. Smith (Harrogate)	A. McDonald
W.H. Hutchinson (Hull & East Riding)	W.H.C. Mackrell
J. Dobson (Wakefield Balne Lane)	D. Gallaher (Capt.)

Scorers:
New Zealand: Tries: Booth (2), Deans (2), Hunter (2), McGregor (2), Mynott (2). Cons: Wallace (4), Tyler.

Referee: P. Coles (RFU).
Attendance: 24,000.

This match proved that English rugby had not recovered from the upheaval of the schism that had seen clubs break from the Rugby Union to form the Northern Union, in 1895. Yorkshire were a poor side and looked under-prepared.

The home side had won two of their 4 matches played earlier in the season, including an 11-3 win over Northern Universities a week before the match with New Zealand. They included future international Arthur Pickering, and Joe Auty, uncle of 1930s England international Dick Auty. They were captained by England international, Bernard Oughtred.

This was another crushing win, although the New Zealand side made mistakes and lacked the togetherness of previous games. Despite this, the All Blacks still ran in 10 tries. Fred Roberts took a well-earned rest and his place at half-back was taken by Hunter for the first half with Stead, initially at first five-eighth, fulfilling the role in the second half. Yorkshire were on the back foot from kick-off but kept their line intact until the tenth minute when Booth crossed for a try. It was then one-way traffic for the rest of the half with tries coming from, in order, Mynott, Hunter, Deans, Deans again, and Mynott. With three converted, the All Blacks were 24-0 ahead at the break.

Booth and Hunter scored their second tries early in the second half before the pace of McGregor took him clear of the Yorkshire defence for two further scores. Wallace converted two and New Zealand had won their last game in England 40-0.

After the game, several of the All Blacks were approached by officials of the Northern Union clubs with a view to switching to the professional code. Four of the squad, Smith, Mackrell, Johnston and McGregor returned to Britain as paid players with the 1907/08 'All Golds' side. Referee Percy Coles was an original member of the Barbarians Football Club and played for them in that club's first encounter with Cardiff. A former Oxford University captain and Blackheath forward, he became the RFU's first full-time secretary in 1904 and refereed the New Zealanders on six occasions during this tour. Centre Billy Lynch later joined Wakefield Trinity and became a leading rugby league international. Remarkably, three of the Yorkshire side were to win Military Crosses in the First World War: R.C. Dobson, a lieutenant in the RGA, Will Hutchinson, a major in the Royal Field Artillery and R. Duckett, second lieutenant in the West Yorkshire Regiment. All three survived the war.

Saturday 16 December 1905
Cardiff Arms Park, Cardiff
Lost 3-0

WALES	NEW ZEALAND
H.B. Winfield (Cardiff)	G.A. Gillett
W. Llewellyn (Penygraig)	W.J. Wallace
E.G. Nicholls (Cardiff, Capt.)	R.G. Deans
R.T. Gabe (Cardiff)	D. McGregor
C.C. Pritchard (Pontypool)	J. Hunter
E. Morgan (London Welsh)	H.J. Mynott
P.F. Bush (Cardiff)	F. Roberts
R.M. Owens (Swansea)	Forwards:
Forwards:	G.A. Tyler
D. Jones (Aberdare)	S.T. Casey
G. Travers (Pill Harriers)	F. Newton
C.M. Pritchard (Newport)	F.T. Glasgow
J.J. Hodges (Newport)	J.M. O'Sullivan
W. Joseph (Swansea)	C.E. Seeling
J.F. Williams (London Welsh)	A. McDonald
A.F. Harding (London Welsh)	D. Gallaher (Capt.)

Scorers:
Wales: Try: Morgan.

Referee: J.D. Dallas (Scotland).
Attendance: 40,000.

Welsh international rugby was in the middle of what is now known as the first golden era. Wales had won the Triple Crown in the previous season and were unbeaten at home since 1899. Percy Bush was the only new cap in the home side, although he had tasted international rugby before as a member of the British tour of Australia and New Zealand in 1904. Cliff Pritchard, who had played for Wales as a centre, was chosen as the extra back-cum-rover to counter the threat of Dave Gallaher. There was some concern over the fitness of Welsh captain Gwyn Nicholls – he had injured his shoulder playing for Cardiff at Blackheath – but he recovered in time to lead his side in this seminal encounter.

The All Blacks retained the side that had beaten England in the previous international with the exception of Billy Stead. Sources differ as to why Stead was unavailable, but it seems probable that he was ill rather than injured. His place in the side went to 'Simon' Mynott. George Smith and Bill Cunningham were also unfit and not considered for selection – had they been fit they would both have played. Visiting the tourists in their hotel on the morning of the match, Welsh centre Rhys Gabe found them 'keyed-up and ill at ease, with the thought of a possible defeat.'

There was a dispute over the appointment of the match referee, George Dixon objecting to the four names submitted by the WFU, and the WFU in turn rejecting the New Zealand manager's four suggestions. In the circumstances, under International Board rules, a neutral country was asked to supply the referee. Consequently, Scotland appointed John Dallas, a former international cap who was only in his second season as a match official. At twenty-seven years of age he was younger than both the captains.

Crowds started arriving at the ground long before kick-off time, and a terrific atmosphere was created by the time the gates were closed at 1.30 p.m. Journalist J.A. Buttery described the pre-match sound as 'a continuous crackle of ardent Celtic chatter, broken every now and again by the deep, harmonious resonance of some patriotic refrain.' Jehoida Hodges kicked off for Wales, and Gallaher soon found himself falling foul of Mr Dallas, who continually penalised him when he fed the scrum. Eventually, the New Zealand captain instructed his hooker not to strike for the ball, thus eliminating the risk of penalties, yet giving extra possession to the Welsh forwards. The All Blacks struggled to contain the speed and strength of the Welsh pack, and Mynott seemed very nervous, dropping or knocking on a series of passes from Fred Roberts as Cliff Pritchard bore down on him. Nicholls, Cliff Pritchard and Dicky Owens all put in excellent tackles to disrupt the New Zealand backs, and the tourists had great difficulty mounting any effective three-quarter moves. Jimmy Hunter and Bob Deans both made handling errors, and Gallaher was constantly barracked by the crowd. The New Zealand backs often kicked straight down the field, where their efforts were returned with interest by Welsh full-back Bert Winfield. Willie Llewellyn should have scored a try for Wales, dropping the ball when he had nobody left to beat, but soon the home side created what was to be the only score of the game. The move had been planned in advance, and was based on the theory that the All Blacks viewed

43

Far left: *The official match programme, arguably the most sought-after piece of rugby memorabilia.*

Left: *An unofficial programme from the match.*

Percy Bush as the chief source of danger in the Welsh backs. For the first quarter, Owens deliberately fed Bush, knowing that the All Black defenders would get into the habit of tracking him. Then, after twenty-three minutes, Owens ran to the right with Bush, Nicholls and Llewellyn in support, but changed direction after a couple of paces, moving back to the left and sending a long pass out to Cliff Pritchard. This move successfully wrong-footed the defence, and Pritchard, taking the ball off his toes, handed on to Gabe who gave the scoring pass to Teddy Morgan. Morgan raced twenty yards down the left touchline and George Gillett was unable to catch him as he scored in the corner. Winfield's conversion attempt fell just to the left of the posts.

The All Blacks mounted numerous attacks in the second half, prompted by the excellent Roberts, who himself was held up inches short of the line. Wales had their own chances to increase the lead, one run by Nicholls nearly bringing a try for Arthur Harding, but as the end of the game drew closer, the tourists made a supreme effort to score. The defining incident in the second half occurred about ten minutes from the end, with accounts varying as to what exactly happened. Billy Wallace, according to his own version of the story, caught a Welsh kick-ahead following a lineout inside the New Zealand half. He cut across in front of the forwards and ran diagonally into the Welsh half, sidestepping Nicholls and running between Nicholls and Gabe as he approached Winfield. As Wallace neared Winfield he was intent on either dummying him or chipping over the full-back's head when he heard Bob Deans calling for the ball. Winfield came in to make the tackle and Wallace threw a long pass to Deans, who veered towards the posts, but changed direction as he saw Morgan coming across to tackle him. Deans grounded the ball six inches over the line as Morgan tackled him, but as he got off the ball to receive the congratulations of his teammates, Owens placed the ball down short of the line. Mr Dallas had not kept up with the move and accepted Owens's word that 'he forced the ball here', awarding a scrum instead of a try. Bush cleared the ball from the ensuing scrummage, but further New Zealand pressure saw Mynott held up over the line and another Deans run halted by Nicholls. At the very end of the game Roberts sent Duncan McGregor over the line, but the pass was forward. Shortly afterwards the final whistle heralded the end of a proud unbeaten record and scenes of triumphant Welsh rejoicing.

The above report quotes Billy Wallace's view of the Deans incident, but other versions contradict this. Rhys Gabe later claimed that it was he, rather than Morgan who tackled Deans, stating that he thought at first that Deans had scored, but realised that Deans was still wriggling towards the line. Consequently, Gabe and Cliff Pritchard pulled him back into play. Llewellyn added to the confusion by claiming that he, rather than Winfield, had tackled Wallace, and that as they had been on the ground Wallace could not have seen what happened next. A spectator, quoted by David Parry-Jones in his recent biography of Nicholls, claimed: 'Deans did not score. And he knew it as he lay there.' Mr Dallas insisted that he had made the correct decision, but Teddy Morgan always asserted that Deans had scored. Deans himself,

The victorious Welsh XV.

who was to die of peritonitis only three years later, was certain that the try was good, sending a telegram to the *Daily Mail* to back up his claims. All Black coach Jimmy Duncan, and at least two newspapers, further clouded the issue by attributing the whole incident to Hunter rather than Deans.

Whatever the truth is behind the Deans 'try', the All Blacks accepted defeat gracefully, although George Dixon remarked on the unsuitability of Mr Dallas's 'ordinary' boots and clothing, implying that he did not always keep up with play. Such attire, however, would have been the accepted dress for many referees of the period. Gallaher's post-match view was totally diplomatic and sporting: 'It was a rattling good game, played out to the bitter end, with the result that the better team won, and I am content. I have always made it a point never to express a view regarding the referee in any match in which I have played.'

The fact that Wales won what many consider to be the greatest international game of all time, plus the controversy surrounding the Deans incident, has forged a special bond between New Zealanders and the Welsh. While rivalry is fierce on the field of play, a mutual love of the game has ensured a lasting respect between two nations that view rugby football as the finest of sports.

GLAMORGAN   1905/06

Wednesday 20 December 1905
St Helen's, Swansea
Won 9-0

Six of the backs who participated in the historic Welsh victory over the All Blacks were originally selected for the Glamorgan team, but Bert Winfield, Teddy Morgan, Gwyn Nicholls, Rhys Gabe, Percy Bush and Dicky Owens, along with another established international, Billy Trew, all withdrew for a variety of reasons. The side that eventually took the field at St Helen's to defend Glamorgan's five-year unbeaten record included three of the victorious Welsh pack in Will Joseph, David 'Dai Tarw' Jones and 'Scethrog' Williams, but the backs looked a scratch outfit. One of

GLAMORGAN	NEW ZEALAND
J.C.M. Dyke (Penarth)	E.E. Booth
J.L. Williams (Cardiff)	W.J. Wallace
H. Jones (Neath)	G.W. Smith
W. Pullen (Cardiff)	H.L. Abbot
R.A. Gibbs (Cardiff)	J.W. Stead
W.R. Arnold (Swansea)	H.J. Mynott
P. Hopkins (Swansea)	F. Roberts
J. Jones (Aberavon)	Forwards:
Forwards:	F.T. Glasgow
W. Joseph (Swansea, Capt.)	S.T. Casey
E.J. Thomas (Mountain Ash)	W. Cunningham
W.H. Hunt (Swansea)	J.M. O'Sullivan
D. Jones (Aberdare)	F. Newton
J.A. Powell (Cardiff)	C.E. Seeling
D. Westacott (Cardiff)	A. McDonald
J.F. Williams (London Welsh)	D. Gallaher (Capt.)

Scorers:
New Zealand: Tries: Smith, McDonald, Wallace.

Referee: J. Games (Aberearn).
Attendance: 20,000.

Above: *The matches in Wales were eagerly anticipated. This souvenir previews the games.*

Left: *George Smith, a try-scorer against Glamorgan. Smith returned as a member of the professional 'All Golds' team two seasons later.*

the centres, Billy Pullen, was a Cardiff reserve player, while his co-centre, Howell Jones of Neath, was actually a Welsh international forward. The half-backs had never played together before, though at least the scrum-half, John 'Bala' Jones, had played once for Wales. Willie Arnold had also represented his country, while Phil Hopkins, along with John Dyke, Johnnie Williams, Reggie Gibbs, Jack Powell, Dick Thomas and Dai Westacott would do so in the future. The tactic of playing an extra back which had been used by Wales against the tourists was repeated in this match, Gibbs taking this position. For New Zealand, everybody who had appeared against Wales played again apart from Jimmy Hunter, Bob Deans, George Gillett, Duncan McGregor and 'Bubs' Tyler.

There was a major row between the WFU and New Zealand manager George Dixon before the game went ahead. Dixon objected to the appointment of Jack Games of Abercarn as referee, having heard that he was on a blacklist in England for disallowing a Leicester try against Swansea. He also took exception to the fact that the referee had been chosen without consultation. This lack of consultation and mutual agreement was contrary to the laws of the game and Dixon cabled his home union to get advice. Dixon wanted Gil Evans as referee, and his return cable instructed him to cancel the game if necessary, but the WFU called his bluff and insisted on using Games. Dixon finally agreed to play on the eve of the match, though he was at pains to point out that this was only because there was no time to cancel existing arrangements. In the event, Games had a fine match and there were no complaints from the tourists over the way he handled the game.

Both sides missed scoring chances in the first half. 'Bunny' Abbott dropped a pass from George Smith when an All Black try seemed likely, while Pullen was tackled before he could get the ball out to an unmarked Johnnie Williams. Both Johnnie Williams and Gibbs were held up close to the line, but the only score of the first half went to New Zealand, Smith running through a hesitant defence to touch down. There was some suspicion that the ball might have been knocked on, but the score stood, although Wallace failed to add the conversion.

The half-time score of 3-0 was unaltered for most of the second half, a half dominated for long periods by the home side. Glamorgan missed numerous chances, starting with a penalty from Joseph that dropped just under the bar. Dai Jones punted the ball over Wallace but Pullen failed to gather, Jones himself was stopped just short of the line and a break from Arnold nearly led to a try, Abbott managing to tackle the winger in the corner. Having withstood the siege, the All Blacks scored 2 tries in the final five minutes, through Alex McDonald, following a good break, and Wallace, who gathered a Smith cross-kick. This was Smith's final action of the tour as he had aggravated his shoulder injury during the first half. Wallace failed with both conversions, but along with Fred Roberts he had the best game for the visitors.

The British press took the view that New Zealand were certainly not 3 tries better than their hosts and that the win was rather lucky. The Glamorgan pack had competed well in the scrums and it was felt that a pair of quality centres might have made a big difference to the result. There was certainly every reason for the tourists to view their remaining games with some apprehension.

George Smith, normally a wing but selected at centre for this game, was a magnificent athlete. He won fourteen New Zealand national titles at hurdling and sprinting, and was the 1902 British AAA 440-yard hurdles champion. It is rumoured he was the jockey on the horse that won the New Zealand Cup in 1894. As a thirty-three-year old he was omitted from the All Blacks' 1907 tour to Australia, and shortly afterwards he turned to rugby league. He toured Britain with the 'All Golds' and remained in Britain after the tour, playing for Oldham until he was in his forties.

NEWPORT 1905/06

Saturday 23 December 1905
Rodney Parade, Newport
Won 6-3

Newport were not having a particularly good season, having lost four and drawn two of their previous 11 games. When Harry Uzzell, later a Welsh international forward but then a fledgling centre, withdrew from the side with a shoulder injury, the club asked Pontypool to lend them their former player Cliff Pritchard, one of the heroes of the Welsh victory. Pontypool were due to play Pontnewydd in a Monmouthshire League match, a game they subsequently lost 6-0, but they agreed to release Pritchard, who went on to have an outstanding game against the All Blacks. Rowland Griffiths, later to tour Australia and New Zealand with the

NEWPORT	NEW ZEALAND
R.B. Griffiths	W.J. Wallace
W.R. Thomas	H.D. Thomson
C.C. Pritchard	R.G. Deans
S. Adams	E.T. Harper
G. Jones	J.W. Stead (Capt.)
A. Davies	H.J. Mynott
W.J. Martin	F. Roberts
T.H. Vile	Forwards:
Forwards:	G.A. Tyler
J.J. Hodges	S.T. Casey
W.H. Williams	W. Cunningham
W.H. Dowell	J.M. O'Sullivan
C.M. Pritchard (Capt.)	A. McDonald
J.G. Boots	C.E. Seeling
E. 'Beddoe' Thomas	W.S. Glenn
E. Jenkins	G.A. Gillett

Scorers:
Newport: PG: Griffiths.
New Zealand: Try: Harper. PG: Wallace.

Referee: G. Evans (Birmingham).
Attendance: 12,000.

1908 Anglo-Welsh party but never a Welsh international, was selected at full-back, despite the fact that he was a winger. At scrum-half was Tommy Vile, who had played Test rugby on the British tour to Australia and New Zealand in 1904 but was yet to win the first of his eventual eight Welsh caps. Walter Martin, Ernie Jenkins and William Dowell were also capped later, George Boots and 'Beddoe' Thomas were capped players, while Jehoida Hodges and skipper Charlie Pritchard had played in the Welsh triumph. Dave Gallaher did not play for New Zealand as his finger had been bitten in the Glamorgan match.

NEWPORT ATHLETIC CLUB.

NEW ZEALAND

Newport,

On Saturday, December 23rd, 1905.

Kick off at 2.30 p.m.

26 Seat Inside Ropes, 1/-

This Ticket does not include admission to the Ground.

This was a game of two halves, with New Zealand dominating the first period. 'Mona' Thomson was tackled into touch in the corner after a fine move, and Billy Wallace was just short of the target when he attempted a goal from a mark. The home line was finally crossed when Fred Roberts fed Billy Stead from a scrum. Bob Deans continued the move before Eric Harper scored near the posts. Wallace missed the conversion, but was soon successful with

an excellent penalty goal. Newport's only real chance in their indifferent first-half showing came when Willie Thomas was stopped five yards from the line.

The second half saw a complete reversal of form, with the home side dominating without quite being able to cross the line. Griffiths kicked a good penalty early in the half but, well though Cliff Pritchard, Vile and Martin played, they were unable to break down the tourists' defence. A break from Cliff Pritchard nearly led to a try from Willie Thomas, but Wallace tackled him just in time. Then Dowell put in a good run, but again the move was halted when a try seemed likely. The half was full of thrilling rugby, but New Zealand held on to record a narrow victory.

Suggestions were made after the game that the All Blacks were getting stale, an allegation refuted by the watching Gallaher. Referee Gil Evans felt that Newport could have won, while Vile later recalled that the playing of Griffiths at full-back was a mistake, contrasting the play of the Newport man with the brilliant performance of Wallace for the tourists. Charlie Pritchard led his pack well and Hodges, Boots and 'Beddoe' Thomas all had impressive games. The All Blacks were hampered by an ankle injury to 'Bubs' Tyler, an injury that kept him out of the remaining games in Wales.

Charlie Pritchard, captain of Newport in this match and for three consecutive seasons from 1906-1909, became Captain Pritchard of the 12th Battalion, South Wales Borderers. In August 1916 he was badly wounded leading a raiding party at the Somme, later dying of his injuries.

CARDIFF   1905/06

Tuesday 26 December 1905
Cardiff Arms Park, Cardiff
Won 10-8

The Cardiff club was enjoying a brilliant season and remained unbeaten throughout, with the exception of the New Zealand match. Four of the backs had played for Wales against the All Blacks, while a further two, plus Jack Powell in the pack, had featured in the Glamorgan game. Scrum-half Dicky David was a future international, as was forward Jack Brown. None of the Cardiff pack had played international rugby at the time of the match, and future cap Dai Westacott missed the match because he had injured his shoulder against London Welsh the previous Saturday. Dave Gallaher's finger

CARDIFF	NEW ZEALAND
H.B. Winfield	W.J. Wallace
J.L. Williams	E.E. Booth
E.G. Nicholls	R.G. Deans
R.T. Gabe	H.D. Thomson
R.A. Gibbs	J. Hunter
R. Thomas	J.W. Stead
P.F. Bush (Capt.)	F. Roberts
R.J. David	Forwards:
Forwards:	F.T. Glasgow
W. Neill	S.T. Casey
G. Northmore	F. Newton
J.A. Powell	J.M. O'Sullivan
F. Smith	G.W. Nicholson
J.A. Brown	C.E. Seeling
L. George	A. McDonald
E. Rumbelow	D. Gallaher (Capt.)

Scorers:
Cardiff: Tries: Nicholls, Thomas. Con: Winfield.
New Zealand: Tries: Thomson, Nicholson. Cons: Wallace (2).

Referee: G. Evans (Birmingham).
Attendance: 50,000.

had recovered sufficiently for him to reclaim his place in the New Zealand side.

This was a memorable game of rugby, considered by journalist J.A. Buttery, who followed the tour for the *Daily Mail*, to be a better game to watch than the recent international. It will forever be remembered for the error of judgement by Cardiff captain Percy Bush, which resulted in what proved to be the winning All Black try. Bush, a hugely talented footballer at the peak of his game, was ever afterwards haunted by his momentary lapse, although he did his utmost in the closing stages of the game to atone for his error.

Cardiff opened the scoring in the first half when Brown passed to Bush from a lineout. The ball went via Reggie Gibbs and Rhys Gabe to Gwyn Nicholls, who touched down wide out. The conversion attempt of Bert Winfield struck a post before crossing the bar and Cardiff led 5-0. After this, New Zealand suffered a major blow when forward Jim O'Sullivan left the field with a broken collarbone, an injury which was to end his playing involvement in the tour. Gallaher was forced to abandon his role as a rover, playing the rest of the game in the pack as his side faced the remainder of the match with just fourteen men. This handicap did not stop the tourists

attacking, and after Charlie Seeling had knocked on when a try was possible, Fred Roberts, who had an outstanding game for the visitors, started a move that involved Jimmy Hunter and Bob Deans, before 'Mona' Thomson beat Winfield to score in the corner. As Wallace attempted the conversion, the Cardiff players charged too early. 'No charge' was signalled by the referee and Wallace kicked the goal to level the scores at 5-5 at half-time.

Early in the second half Nicholls halted a dangerous New Zealand attack by intercepting, and then Bush came close to scoring for Cardiff. The defining moment of the match came when Seeling fly-kicked towards the Cardiff line. The ball appeared to have gone too far and Winfield and Bush had plenty of time to deal with the situation. However, Winfield slipped as he turned to reach the ball, leaving Bush with the task of touching down as the ball crossed the Cardiff line. Unaccountably, the Cardiff skipper delayed, and as All Black forward George Nicholson approached he was forced to kick the ball dead. To the horror of the crowd he missed his kick, leaving the surprised Nicholson with the simple task of touching down for a try, which Wallace converted. Stunned silence greeted the score, but the crowd soon got behind their team as Cardiff, with the unfortunate Bush to the fore, made a great effort to rescue the game. Bush himself put in a great run but Gabe passed the wrong way, then in the final minutes Cardiff managed a brilliant try when David, Bush, Gibbs and Nicholls all handled before Ralph Thomas crossed in the corner. All now hinged on the conversion attempt, but although the crowd roared with initial optimism, Winfield's kick was just wide. The game ended shortly afterwards.

Bush was distraught after the match, knowing that he had let his side down. He later explained that he had seen Nicholson approaching and decided to delay touching down so that Nicholson would waste some energy. 'As he came near, I stooped to pick up the ball, but just then it bounced awkwardly off one of its points. It rolled out of my reach and I tried to kick it, but missed.' Despite Bush's error, it should be remembered that New Zealand played a man short for much of the game. Would they have won more comfortably with a full side? George Dixon certainly felt that in the circumstances his team's victory was well deserved.

Saturday 30 December 1905
St Helen's, Swansea
Won 4-3

SWANSEA	NEW ZEALAND
G. Davies	W.J. Wallace
W. R. Arnold	H.D. Thomson
F. Gordon (Capt.)	R.G. Deans
F. Scale	D. McGregor
W.J. Trew	J.W. Stead
P. Hopkins	H.J. Mynott
R.M. Owens	F. Roberts
Forwards:	Forwards:
W. Parker	S.T. Casey
D.J. Thomas	D. Gallaher (Capt.)
W. Cole	W. Cunningham
W.H. Hunt	F.T. Glasgow
W.I. Joseph	J. Corbett
A. Smith	C.E. Seeling
I. Morgan	W.S. Glenn
F.G. Scrine	G.A. Gillett

Scorers:
Swansea: Try: Scrine.
New Zealand: DG: Wallace.

Referee: G. Evans (Birmingham).
Attendance: 20,000.

Swansea had enjoyed an invincible season but the club had surrendered its unbeaten record to Cardiff in October and was to lose all 4 games against its East Wales rivals. Two of the side, Owens and Joseph, had played for Wales against the tourists, while Joseph, along with Arnold, Hopkins and Hunt, had appeared in the Glamorgan match. Of the side that faced the All Blacks in the final British game of the tour, only Hunt, skipper Gordon, Scale, Cole, and Smith would never play international rugby. Scrine was selected to play as a rover, although he found himself up against George Gillett rather than Dave Gallaher, the New Zealand captain electing to play in place of the injured 'Bubs' Tyler.

A strong wind blew straight down the pitch throughout the match. Swansea began with the wind behind them and their forwards made life difficult for the tourists, electing to take scrums rather than lineouts. Davies was just wide with a penalty, and a run by Hopkins was only just stopped by Deans. With the home pack dominating, Scrine scored after twenty-five minutes, with a charge over after a bout of passing, to the delight of the huge crowd. Davies missed the conversion and Swansea led 3-0 at the break.

With the wind blowing at strength, the Swansea pack now faced the elements. New Zealand began to create chances, and a try seemed certain when Gillett dived for the line, but as he was in the act of scoring Owens managed to knock the ball from his hands. However, the decisive score came after thirty minutes when Billy Wallace picked up the ball in the face of a Swansea forward rush. He was 40 yards from the posts and kicking at a wide angle, but dropped a fantastic left-footed goal. It appeared that a friendly blast of wind took it between the posts. With drop goals valued at 4 points, New Zealand now held the lead.

Swansea made frantic efforts to score in the closing stages of the match. Davies missed another penalty, Owens had a try disallowed when referee Gil Evans ordered a scrum to be re-formed, and Arnold failed to take Owens's pass when a score seemed likely. Hard though the home side tried the All Blacks were victorious, despite failing to score a try for only the second time on tour.

The original Swansea programme from 1905.

There was much debate in the press after the game concerning Wallace's amazing drop goal, the *Western Mail* correspondent even wondering whether Wallace had intended to go for goal at all. A draw would perhaps have been a fairer result to a match that New Zealand five-eighth 'Simon' Mynott described as 'A very dirty game. I think it was the dirtiest we have played.'

Thus ended the historic first All Blacks tour of Britain. There is no doubt that the tourists faced their toughest opposition in Wales, although the All Blacks were nearing the end of a long trip and were inevitably tired. In the circumstances, to win even by such narrow margins was a fine achievement for these pioneers. The tour also highlighted the poor state of English rugby following the schism which led to the formation of the Northern Union in the previous decade.

1924/25
NEW ZEALAND TO BRITAIN, FRANCE & CANADA

THE MATCHES

Devon	13 September 1924	Devonport	won 11-0
Cornwall	18 September 1924	Camborne	won 29-0
Somerset	20 September 1924	Weston-super-Mare	won 6-0
Gloucestershire	25 September 1924	Gloucester	won 6-0
Swansea	27 September 1924	Swansea	won 39-3
Newport	2 October 1924	Newport	won 13-10
Leicester	4 October 1924	Leicester	won 27-0
North Midlands	8 October 1924	Birmingham	won 40-3
Cheshire	11 October 1924	Birkenhead	won 18-5
Durham	15 October 1924	Sunderland	won 43-7
Yorkshire	18 October 1924	Bradford	won 42-4
Lancashire	22 October 1924	Manchester	won 23-0
Cumberland	25 October 1924	Carlisle	won 41-0
IRELAND	1 November 1924	Dublin	won 6-0
Ulster	5 November 1924	Belfast	won 28-6
Northumberland	8 November 1924	Newcastle	won 27-4
Cambridge University	12 November 1924	Cambridge	won 5-0
London Counties	15 November 1924	Twickenham	won 31-6
Oxford University	20 November 1924	Oxford	won 33-15
Cardiff	22 November 1924	Cardiff	won 16-8
WALES	29 November 1924	Swansea	won 19-0
Llanelly	2 December 1924	Llanelly	won 8-3
East Midlands	6 December 1924	Northampton	won 31-7
Warwickshire	11 December 1924	Coventry	won 20-0
Combined Services	13 December 1924	Twickenham	won 25-3
Hampshire	17 December 1924	Portsmouth	won 22-0
London Counties	27 December 1924	Blackheath	won 28-3
ENGLAND	3 January 1925	Twickenham	won 17-11
French Selection	11 January 1925	Paris	won 37-8
FRANCE	18 January 1925	Toulouse	won 30-6
Vancouver	14 February 1925	Vancouver	won 49-0
Victoria (British Columbia)	18 February 1925	Victoria	won 68-4

Played 32, Won 32, Drew 0, Lost 0. Scored: 838 points, Conceded: 116.
In Britain & Ireland: Played 28, Won 28, Drew 0, Lost 0. Scored: 654 points, Conceded: 98.

The New Zealand Tour Party:
G. Nepia (Hawke's Bay), A.H. Hart (Taranaki), J. Steel (West Coast), A.C.C. Robilliard (Canterbury), K.S. Svenson (Wellington), F.W. Lucas (Auckland), H.W. Brown (Taranaki), A.E. Cooke (Auckland),

L. Paewai (Hawke's Bay), N.P. McGregor (Canterbury), C.E.O. Badeley (Auckland), M.F. Nicholls (Wellington), W.C. Dalley (Canterbury), J.J. Mill (Hawke's Bay), H.G. Munro (Otago), B.V. McCleary (Canterbury), Q. Donald (Wairarapa), W.R. Irvine (Hawke's Bay), L.F. Cupples (Bay of Plenty), I.H. Harvey (Wairarapa), M.J. Brownlie (Hawke's Bay), C.J. Brownlie (Hawke's Bay), R.R. Masters (Canterbury), J. Richardson (Southland), A.H. West (Taranaki), C.G. Porter (Wellington), R.T. Stewart (South Canterbury), J.H. Parker (Canterbury), A. White (Southland).

Captain: C.G. Porter. Vice-Captain: J. Richardson. Manager: S.S.M. Dean.

Leading points scorer: M.F. Nicholls – 109 points (97 in Britain & Ireland).
Leading try-scorer: A.E. Cooke – 23 tries (A.H. Hart 18 and A.E. Cooke 16 in Britain & Ireland).
Most appearances: G. Nepia – 32 games (28 in Britain & Ireland).

Saturday 13 September 1924
Rectory Ground, Devonport
Won 11-0

DEVON	NEW ZEALAND
G. Baker (Devonport Services)	G. Nepia
W.B. Syms (Plymouth Albion)	F.W. Lucas
T. Lee (Devonport Services)	H.W. Brown
C. Garrett (Devonport Services)	K.S. Svenson
A. Hugo (Newton Abbot)	A.E. Cooke
J. Hanley (Plymouth Albion)	M.F. Nicholls
W. Douglas (Tiverton)	W.C. Dalley
C.R. Knapman (Devonport Services)	Forwards:
Forwards:	H.G. Munro
F.W. Sanders (Plymouth Albion, Capt.)	Q. Donald
L.R. Stephens (Plymouth Albion)	R.R. Masters
J.C.R. Buchanan (Exeter)	R.T. Stewart
T.R. Jones (Exeter)	M.J. Brownlie
H. Rew (Exeter)	J. Richardson
D. Mole (Newton Abbot	A.H. West
J. Boddy (Plymouth Albion)	C.G. Porter (Capt.)

Scorers:
New Zealand: Tries: Svenson, Cooke, Brown. Cons: Nepia.

Referee: R.A. Roberts (Gloucester).
Attendance: 18,000.

New Zealand prepared for the tour by playing 4 matches in Australia and 2 games against New Zealand provinces, losing to New South Wales and Auckland. The captain was Ces Badeley, the Auckland five-eighth, but when the squad to tour Britain was announced the identity of the captain was initially kept secret. Badeley was in pole position but, controversially, the captaincy was awarded to Cliff Porter, the Wellington loose forward. Whether it was felt a niggling knee injury that had recently plagued Badeley would render him ineffective, or whether Porter's leadership skills were superior, is not known. There were other selections that caused debate in New Zealand and serious doubts were expressed about the quality of the squad with full-back and half-back the areas of greatest concern.

The All Blacks docked in Plymouth in early September and based themselves in Newton Abbot, as the 1905 team had done. Ten days later the tour opened against Devon in a rematch of the opening game of the previous tour. This time the match and result was not so one-sided.

Porter led the tourists onto Devonport's Rectory Ground to a magnificent reception from an excited crowd. Full-back George Nepia, a Maori, led the Haka to great encouragement and cheering. The All Blacks had been forced to make a change to their planned side, when William 'Bull' Irvine withdrew from the pack with a foot injury, but the selected fifteen remained strong. Devon, who adopted the diamond scrummaging formation for the game with future international loose forward Joe Hanley as an extra back, began the game well and the rusty New Zealanders took a while to get into their stride. The home defence was committed and it took thirty minutes before the tour account was opened. A missed clearance kick was fielded by Bert Cooke, who kicked over the advancing Devon defence, regathered and passed to Kenneth 'Snowy' Svenson, who beat the full-back to score the first try of the tour. Then, shortly after a missed penalty kick from Hanley, Svenson raced down the wing, creating

George Nepia leads the Haka for the opening match of the Invincibles' tour.

space inside for the supporting Cooke to cross for a second try. Nepia converted Cooke's try, having missed his earlier attempt. New Zealand were ahead 8-0 at half-time.

A substantial downpour hampered both sides during the second half. Handling became difficult and the match degenerated into a forward struggle. However, Svenson made another dash down the touchline and this time centre Handley Brown was on hand to accept the scoring pass and touch down. The conversion was missed but New Zealand had won a close game. The forward exchanges were even and it was only outside the darkened recesses of the pack that the tourists had any superiority.

Devon captain Frank Sanders had played for England in 1923. The team also featured John Buchanan, the former Scottish captain, who had left Edinburgh to work in England. Forward Henry Rew was later capped by England and toured with the 1930 British Lions. He served as a major in the Royal Tank Corps during the Second World War and died of wounds in May 1940.

CORNWALL   1924/25

Thursday 18 September 1924
Recreation Ground, Camborne
Won 29-0

The All Blacks ventured further west to Camborne for their game against Cornwall, a match played in glorious sunshine. They made several changes to the side and Jock Richardson, the Southland loose forward, took over the captaincy. Cornwall had only won one competitive match since the First World War. Their cause against New Zealand was not helped when fifteen minutes before kick-off they were instructed to change their scrum formation from 3-4-1 to 2-3-2, with Roy Jennings acting as a rover to match the All Blacks. The twenty-year-old Jennings, a tough Redruth player, was removed from the pack during the game to strengthen the defence of the backs. He later toured New Zealand with the 1930 British Lions as a three-quarter, and also played against the 1935 All Blacks, although he never played for England.

The match was five minutes old when good close passing under pressure by the New Zealand forwards saw Jim Parker score the opening try. Five minutes later the All Blacks scored again when Neil McGregor broke clear and gave a scoring

CORNWALL	NEW ZEALAND
H. Ham (Redruth)	G. Nepia
G. Jago (Penryn)	A.C.C. Robilliard
P.A. Collins (Camborne)	H.W. Brown
F. Barnard (Camborne)	K.S. Svenson
E.L. Rees (Newlyn)	A.E. Cooke
R. Hamblin (Camborne)	N.P. McGregor
A. Gibson (Hayle)	J.J. Mill
Forwards:	Forwards:
G. Thomas (Camborne)	H.G. Munro
S.H. Wakeham (Camborne)	W.R. Irvine
W. Mayne (Camborne)	I.H. Harvey
W.T. Biddick (Camborne)	L.F. Cupples
G.P. Rust (Camborne School of Mines)	M.J. Brownlie
J.F. Richards (Redruth, Capt.)	J. Richardson (Capt.)
G.D. Young (Army)	A. White
R. Jennings (Redruth)	J.H. Parker

Scorers:
New Zealand: Tries: Parker (3), Cooke, Brownlie, Irvine, Mill. Cons: Brown (2), Nepia (2).

Referee: F.W. Jeffery (Plymouth).
Attendance: 19,000.

Munro and Brownlie scramble for the ball on the Cornish line.

pass to Cooke. Nepia converted both tries but failed to convert the third New Zealand try of the half when Parker crashed over from a scrum on the Cornish line just before half-time. The All Blacks were 13-0 ahead at the break.

The All Blacks' momentum continued in the second half, although Cornwall were hampered by the loss through injury of Herbert Wakeham, an influential forward from the host club. 'Rafie'

The New Zealand and Cornwall teams together before the match.

Hamblin was affected by a knee injury, but stayed on the field. Maurice Brownlie scored the next try after a break by Cooke was carried on by Brown, Brown himself converting. 'Snowy' Svenson then made good ground before passing to Parker, who scored his third try of the match. Almost directly from the restart, New Zealand attacked again and 'Bull' Irvine scored a try when he capitalised on some loose Cornish play. Brown converted again but missed adding the extra points to the final All Black try, scored by half-back Jimmy Mill. It was a pleasing if not entirely satisfying win.

SOMERSET 1924/25

Saturday 20 September 1924
Recreation Ground,
Weston-super-Mare
Won 6-0

SOMERSET	NEW ZEALAND
A.E. Thompson (Royal Navy)	G. Nepia
R.G.B. Quick (Bristol, Capt.)	A.C.C. Robilliard
E.L. Stinchcombe (Bristol)	F.W. Lucas
S.G.U. Considine (Bath)	K.S. Svenson
W.J. Gibbs (Bath)	A.E. Cooke
J.C. Russell (RAF)	L. Paewai
W.R. Collins (Taunton School)	J.J. Mill
Forwards:	Forwards:
J. Hawkins (Bridgwater)	H.G. Munro
E. Meakin (Weston-super-Mare)	W.R. Irvine
R.S. Chaddock (Bath)	I.H. Harvey
C.R. Wordsworth (Oxford University)	L.F. Cupples
L.W. Bisgrove (Bath)	M.J. Brownlie
A.J. Spriggs (Bridgwater)	J. Richardson (Capt.)
T. Rose (Bath)	A. White
H.B.L. Wake (Bath)	J.H. Parker

Scorers:
New Zealand: Tries: Cooke, Mill.

Referee: W.H. Jackson (Camborne).
Attendance: 12,000.

The tourists headed to the popular seaside town of Weston-super-Mare for the next game. They were unable to appreciate the delights of the town due to the torrential rain that had greeted them when they arrived on the Friday and continued to lash down. The pitch was a quagmire and very heavy.

The first half was little more than a series of scrums and lineouts, interspersed with handling errors and kicks to touch. Handling was virtually impossible and it became a dour forward battle and New Zealand met a strong unit in the Somerset pack. The score was 0-0 at half-time.

The second half began in a similar vein and the tight forward encounter continued. With fifteen minutes to go the New Zealand pack kicked the ball into the Somerset half of the field. They chased the ball and were joined by the speedy Bert Cooke who picked up the ball with great dexterity and kicked it over the last line of the Somerset defence to beat Reg Quick to the ball for the opening try. Shortly afterwards, a neat break by Jim Mill from a scrum in the Somerset 25 enabled him to score a second try. Neither try was converted and New Zealand won 6-0.

The selection of Mill was heavily criticised in New Zealand. Many critics felt he was not a leading half-back and should not have been chosen to tour. However, by the time the tour ended he justified his

selection by returning home as the senior half-back. William Collins, one of the Somerset halves, was still a pupil at Taunton School at the time of the match. He later played County rugby for Surrey. Somerset captain Reg Quick was a prolific try-scorer. He scored a then-record 33 tries for Bristol in the 1920/21 season. He captained his club in the early 1920s and after he stopped playing served as an administrator with Bristol and Somerset until the early 1960s. He won the Croix de Guerre for bravery in the First World War, played in a trial match for England and was regarded as being particularly unfortunate not to play international rugby.

GLOUCESTERSHIRE   1924/25

Thursday 25 September 1924
Kingsholm, Gloucester
Won 6-0

GLOUCESTERSHIRE	NEW ZEALAND
T. Millington (Gloucester)	G. Nepia
S.A. Brown (Gloucester)	F.W. Lucas
L.J. Corbett (Bristol, Capt.)	H.W. Brown
R.C.W. Pickles (Bristol)	A.H. Hart
T.G. Spoors (Bristol)	M.F. Nicholls
G.C. Taylor (Gloucester)	N.P. McGregor
G. Thomas (Gloucester)	W.C. Dalley
C.B. Carter (Bristol)	Forwards:
Forwards:	W.R. Irvine
O.M.V. Shaw (Bristol)	Q. Donald
A.S. Prowse (Bristol)	I.H. Harvey
A.T. Hore (Bristol)	L.F. Cupples
A.R. Rickards (Cardiff)	M.J. Brownlie
S. Bayliss (Gloucester)	J. Richardson
W. Preece (Bream)	R.T. Stewart
S. Dubberley (Cinderford)	C.G. Porter (Capt.)

Scorers:
New Zealand: Tries: Donald (2).

Referee: R. Fear (Somerset).
Attendance: 12,000.

The weather was little better when the All Blacks crossed the county border. Rain made the pitch heavy and the ball slippery amounting to another forward struggle. Gloucestershire were without leading forwards Tom Voyce, yet to return from the Lions' tour of South Africa, and Sam Tucker. They were captained by Len Corbett, who possessed remarkable running, kicking and handling skills. (In 1921 on his debut England appearance when players were given the rose badge but had to provide their own shirt, Corbett appeared in a white PT vest as he could not afford to buy a shirt.) New Zealand made wholesale changes to the backs but individually and collectively, they had an off day – no doubt thanks in part to the weather.

The only score of the first half was one typical of the conditions. Tom Spoors, whose brother Jack had faced the original All Blacks for Bristol, missed a clearing kick to touch. The ball was gathered by the New Zealand forwards who, in a furious foot-rush dribbled the ball over the line for Quentin Donald score. Nepia's conversion failed to threaten the posts and the All Blacks were 3-0 ahead at half-time.

Gloucestershire's reputation for fielding tough forwards was demonstrated during the second half, however the home side were unable to capitalise on their superiority largely due to George Nepia, who had an outstanding game in defence and unquestionably saved his side from certain scores on several occasions. Fred Lucas dropped the ball with the line at his mercy before New Zealand ventured into Gloucestershire territory and the forwards set up camp on the home line. Eventually Donald scored his second try and New Zealand won 6-0.

There was considerable concern among the tour party that the pack had not been more dominant. As with 1905, they adopted the diamond scrum formation, but they were not able to monopolise possession.

The home side included tough prop Mervyn Shaw, who came close to playing for England at several points in his career and later captained the county, and the combined Gloucestershire and Somerset side that lost to the Waratahs in 1927. Shaw was joined by club mate Cecil Carter, a diminutive scrum-half with a magnificent pass. He was a very unlucky player as on three occasions he had to withdraw from England trials due to injury and never played for his country. He was a popular hero locally and he played in the county's three successive championship final victories in the early 1930s.

Above: *The Gloucestershire side, led by the great Len Corbett, that played the All Blacks.*

Below: *The New Zealand team at Gloucester.*

SWANSEA   1924/25

Saturday 27 September 1924
St Helen's, Swansea
Won 39-3

Cliff Porter's All Blacks ventured into Wales for the first time to take on Swansea, where the 1905 side had narrowly avoided defeat. They were able to choose from a full squad and duly selected a strong side for the game. Cyril Brownlie and Jack Steel played their first games on British soil. Welsh rugby had struggled after the ravages of the First World War and it was suffering generally from a dearth of creative backs. There were concerns about Swansea's prospects, with most predicting a narrow defeat. The Whites included internationals Tom Evans, Dai Parker, Ivor Morris and Scottish international David Bertram. They were captained by Jack John, who later played for Wales. Later in the season

SWANSEA	NEW ZEALAND
P. Lloyd	G. Nepia
J.E. Watkins	F.W. Lucas
T.D. Evans	H.W. Brown
M. Evans	J. Steel
D. Jenkins	A.E. Cooke
R. Smitham	M.F. Nicholls
E. Rees	W.C. Dalley
Forwards:	Forwards:
D.S. Parker	Q. Donald
D.M. Bertram	W.R. Irvine
J.H. John (Capt.)	I.H. Harvey
G. White	C.J. Brownlie
I. Morris	M.J. Brownlie
E. Thomas	A.H. West
H. Rees	A. White
I. Thomas	C.G. Porter (Capt.)

Scorers:
Swansea: PG: Parker.
New Zealand: Tries: Steel (3), Brown (2), M Brownlie, Lucas, Irvine, Cooke. Cons: Nicholls (4). DG: Nicholls.

Referee: W.J. Llewellyn (Bridgend).
Attendance: 45,000.

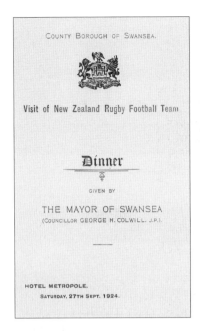

Swansea changed their playing kit, discarding their blue shorts to become 'all white'.

The match started with both sets of forwards squaring up to each other before eventually settling down and getting on with the game. Midway through the first half Mark Nicholls dropped a goal to open the scoring, and then the New Zealand forwards started to dominate the phases. Shortly before half-time, the tourists moved the ball through several pairs of hands for Fred Lucas to score a fine try. Swansea had made a contest of the match until this point but, almost immediately afterwards, 'Bull' Irvine scored from a lineout on the home line. Both tries were unconverted and the All Blacks held a 10-0 interval lead.

Five minutes into the second half, Handley Brown scored the third New Zealand try. Nicholls took over kicking duties from George Nepia and converted. Future British Lion Dai Parker then kicked a fine penalty for Swansea from close to halfway, the first points conceded by the All Blacks on tour. This seemed to spur the New Zealanders into greater action and their backs cut loose. In a blistering final quarter of the game they ran in tries from Jack Steel, Brown, Maurice Brownlie and Steel again. Steel then scored his third try before Bert Cooke rounded off the win with the tourists' eighth try. Nicholls converted three.

It had been a fine win for New Zealand. For the first time on tour they had played without inhibition and, although their team was badly beaten, the Swansea crowd cheered the play of Brownlie, Cooke and Steel in particular.

NEWPORT
1924/25

Thursday 2 October 1924
Rodney Parade, Newport
Won 13-10

The All Blacks were based in Newport for their early visit to Wales. They made three changes to their side and welcomed back Read Masters, who had not played since the Devon game.

NEWPORT	NEW ZEALAND
F. Baker	G. Nepia
G.E. Andrews	J. Steel
E. Kitson	H.W. Brown
W. Jones	K.S. Svenson
A. Stock	A.E. Cooke
J.J. Wetter	M.F. Nicholls
E. Dowdall	J.J. Mill
Forwards:	Forwards:
J. Whitfield	Q. Donald
G.F. Hathway	W.R. Irvine
R. Edwards (Capt.)	R.R. Masters
V. Waite	C.J. Brownlie
T. Roberts	M.J. Brownlie
J. Collins	A.H. West
W. Friend	A. White
T. Jones	C.G. Porter (Capt.)

Scorers:
Newport: Tries: Friend, Andrews. Cons: Wetter, Baker.
New Zealand: Tries: Mill, Svenson. Cons: Nicholls (2).
PG: Nicholls.

Referee: A.E. Freethy (Neath).
Attendance: 25,000.

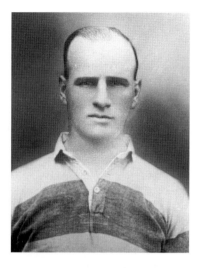

Jack Wetter, who had a fine game for Newport in the close match with the All Blacks. He later captained Wales against the tourists.

Unbeaten Newport selected eight forwards for the game, and included seven internationals, plus George Andrews, who was later capped by Wales. They were unable to select injured Scottish international Neil McPherson. The month after this game the 'McPherson affair' blew up when the Scottish Rugby Union suspended the forward for receiving a gold watch valued at £21 in recognition of being a Newport player in the club's invincible season of 1922/23. The acceptance of such a high-value gift contravened the regulations of payments to players, but after the WRU had been admonished for sanctioning the gift, the suspension was lifted. Nevertheless, McPherson never played for Scotland again.

Newport attacked from the kick-off and New Zealand were forced to defend for most of the game. The physical approach of the home forwards unsettled the tourists, who were denied the possession, time and space they had enjoyed at Swansea. There were occasionally fierce forward exchanges and Newport captain, prop Reg Edwards, was able to disrupt the All Blacks' scrum through methods that, the tourists claimed, were illegal. New Zealand defended stoically until thirty minutes had been played when Bill Friend scored a try for Newport after a fine passing movement involving several players. Jack Wetter, who won the DCM in the First World War, converted the first try New Zealand conceded on tour, and Newport led 5-0 at half-time.

Shortly after the second half started, Bert Cooke was knocked unconscious by a late tackle from Tom 'Cooking' Jones, who was fortunate to remain on the field. Cooke was stretchered off but returned fifteen minutes later, although obviously concussed. Midway through the second period Jimmy Mill scored from a scrum close to the Newport posts and Nicholls's conversion tied the scores. The play flowed from end to end in an exciting contest that thrilled the big crowd. Both sides attempted and missed penalties before Nicholls was eventually successful with one that put New Zealand into the lead. Then Wetter attempted a drop goal. It narrowly missed but Kenneth 'Snowy' Svenson slipped as he tried to gather the ball and Andrews dived on it for Newport's second try. Fred Baker converted and, with time running out, Newport were back in front. However, Baker then made an error that cost Newport the match. With little more than a minute to go, he kicked poorly and missed touch. The ball was caught by Maurice Brownlie who passed to Svenson, who redeemed himself by racing down the touchline and scoring a super try. Nicholls converted and New Zealand had won a wonderfully exciting game.

It was a bitter pill for the home side to swallow. They had been superior in virtually every facet of play. It was the closest New Zealand were to come to defeat on tour. This was recognised by the tourists, who admitted they were extremely lucky. Mysteriously, the Welsh selectors ignored the fine display of the Newport pack when later choosing their side for the international with New Zealand. Backs Albert Stock and Wetter were the only Newport players selected, although Edwards renewed acquaintance with New Zealand later in the tour when he played against them for England.

Saturday 4 October 1924
Welford Road, Leicester
Won 27-0

LEICESTER	NEW ZEALAND
L.C. Sambrook	G. Nepia
O.C. Bryson	F.W. Lucas
M.S. Holden	K.S. Svenson
P.G. Scott	J. Steel
A.M. Smallwood	M.F. Nicholls
H.L. Price	N.P. McGregor
E.J. Massey	W.C. Dalley
J.C. Russell	Forwards:
Forwards:	W.R. Irvine
W.B.N. Roderick	H.G. Munro
H. Sharratt	R.R. Masters
J.E. Davis	J. Richardson
G. Ward	M.J. Brownlie
F.D. Prentice	L.F. Cupples
J.R.C. Buchanan	A. White
J.R. Lawrie	C.G. Porter (Capt.)

Scorers:
New Zealand: Tries: Cupples, Richardson, Steel, Lucas, White, Svenson. Cons: Nicholls (3). PG: Nicholls.

Referee: A.E. Freethy (Neath).
Attendance: 35,000.

After the All Blacks' close shave at Newport and concerns about indifferent form, Leicester went into the game with confidence. The local press predicted a home win, since the club's only defeat of the season to date had been a narrow loss to Plymouth Albion, and they had John Buchanan in the side, the Scottish international who had faced the All Blacks in the opening game of the tour, plus fellow Scot Jock Lawrie with many of the other players were at the top of their game. Although mindful that New Zealand could turn in a mesmerising performance, as they had against Swansea, it was believed that the tourists' colours would be lowered. Leicester adopted the diamond scrum formation with an extra five-eighth for the game.

The match started with New Zealand on the attack and it was only good defence that kept the tourists out. Eventually their resilience cracked, and after fifteen minutes Les Cupples picked up a loose ball to score a try. Two minutes later Richardson charged over for Mark Nicholls to convert, and New Zealand were 8-0 ahead. Then Jack Steel scored a try after a dazzling run in which he beat four would-be tacklers to touch down between the posts. The Leicester defence seemed to give up and an orthodox three-quarter move across the backline saw Lucas score in the corner. Nicholls converted Steel's try and New Zealand looked good with an 18-0 lead at half-time.

Leicester regained their composure for the second half and Herbert Sharratt was narrowly beaten by Nepia to a ball that bounced over the New Zealand line. However, play returned to the Leicester half where Cliff Porter broke through a weak tackle in midfield and passed to Richardson, who in turn passed to Andrew White, for the Southland loose forward to score. Nicholls's conversion put the match beyond doubt. Ten minutes into the second half All Black forward 'Abe' Munro severely damaged knee ligaments and never played again in Britain. He remained with the tour party and managed to play in the very last game, in Canada, on his way home. Despite the retirement of Munro, the All Blacks' pack was now totally in control. Svenson scored another try and, in the dying minutes, Nicholls kicked a penalty goal after Leicester were spotted offside by referee Albert Freethy.

At 27-0 the All Blacks had at last shown English spectators what they could do. Their support play was first class and their aggressive defence pressurised the Tigers into mistakes. Newport had been a tough game against a good side. Leicester, also a good side, were outplayed in every aspect of the game. The All Blacks appeared to have turned a corner. Despite this result, Leicestershire won the County Championship later in the season with a team made up of fifteen Leicester players. Smallwood, Price, Massey, Prentice and Ward played for England, the latter having previously played for Midlands against South Africa in 1912. No Leicester players were selected for England in the international against New Zealand.

LEICESTER FOOTBALL CLUB.

DINNER

In honour of the New Zealand R.F.U.

CHAIRMAN :
KENNETH McALPIN, Esq.,
President Leicester Football Club.

LEICESTER.
SATURDAY, OCTOBER 4TH, 1924.

Wednesday 8 October 1924
Villa Park, Birmingham
Won 40-3

NORTH MIDLANDS	NEW ZEALAND
J.A. Pritchard (Moseley)	G. Nepia
R.H. Orcutt (Moseley)	K.S. Svenson
W.S. Shaw (Birmingham University)	A.E. Cooke
R. Baker (Aston Old Edwardians)	J. Steel
L.S. Hammer (Birmingham)	N.P. McGregor
S.J. Huins (Moseley)	C.E.O. Badeley
W.H. Hill (Moseley)	W.C. Dalley
G. German (Burton)	Forwards:
Forwards:	B.V. McCleary
A. Woodward (Moseley, Capt.)	Q. Donald
J.C. Timmis (Wolverhampton)	R.R. Masters
R.S. Symons (Moseley)	C.J. Brownlie
J.R. McDowell (Moseley)	J. Richardson (Capt.)
W.E. Richardson (Kidderminster)	R.T. Stewart
C.G. Stanley (Moseley)	A. White
K.B. Smith (Burton)	J.H. Parker

Scorers:
North Midlands: Try: Orcutt.
New Zealand: Tries: Parker (5), Cooke (2), Donald, Brownlie, Stewart. Cons: Nepia (5).

Referee: T.H. Vile (Newport).
Attendance: 22,000.

The next match was a spectacular game staged on the smooth surface of Villa Park, home of Aston Villa Football Club. It was a game that New Zealand dominated but the home side contributed greatly to the fare with some stout defence and good runs. It is a tribute to New Zealand rather than a criticism of North Midlands that so many tries were scored. Ces Badeley played his first game of the tour. The Midlands selectors chose several players who had never played for the county before, and several never played for them again. They selected seven forwards, with Hammer chosen as a sort of rover-cum-centre. The disorganisation meant that the All Blacks had a field day.

The first score came after a period of pressure from the All Blacks, Jim Parker crossing for a try from a forward rush. Nepia converted but failed to add the extra points to a further try scored by Donald and a spectacular score from Bert Cooke, following a move that featured all of the New Zealand backs. Parker then scored his second try following some loose play and New Zealand were out of sight. However, this did not daunt the North Midlands team who battled away and were rewarded when Ralph Orcutt scored a fine try in which some good play by his inside backs created space for him. The Moseley wing, who also played football for Aston Villa, showed admirable speed in escaping his opponent, then he kicked ahead and beat the New Zealand cover to the ball. Although the conversion was missed, the cheering of the crowd went on for some time.

Turning round at the interval 14-3 ahead, the All Blacks started the second period in determined fashion and after a couple of minutes Cyril Brownlie scored a try that Nepia converted. This was quickly followed by a try from Cooke after Parker had made a spectacular break. Parker then scored his third try, this time from a lineout, and his fourth and fifth shortly afterwards. He left the field with a leg injury late in the game, no doubt to the relief of the home side. Badeley's troublesome knee injury also recurred. Ron Stewart gathered a loose ball and drove through the dispirited Midlands defence for the final All Blacks' try. It was an excellent

October 8, 1924.   THE VILLA NEWS AND RECORD.   97

NEW ZEALAND (ALL BLACKS)
v.
NORTH MIDLANDS R.U.
At Villa Park, Birmingham, Wednesday, October 8th, 1924.
KICK-OFF 3 15 p.m.

NEW ZEALAND.

Full Back :
(1) G. NEPIA
Hawkes Bay

Right Wing.   Left Wing.
(2) J. STEEL   Three-Quarters :   (6) K. S. SVENSON
West Coast   (11) A. E. COOKE   Wellington
                      Auckland
       (9) N. P. McGREGOR   Five-Eighths   (10) C. BADELEY
          Canterbury   Auckland
       (13) W. C. DALLEY   Half-Backs   (15) J. H. PARKER
          Canterbury   Canterbury
                          Forwards :
                                         (17) B. McCLEARY
                                            Canterbury
(23) J. RICHARDSON (Capt.)   (26) R. R. MASTERS   (27) C. BROWNLIE
       Otago   Canterbury   Canterbury
(22) A. WHITE   (24) R. T. STEWART
   Southland   South Canterbury

The "Daily Chronicle," London's Best
for Rugby Football.

Forwards :
(16) K. R. SMITH   (11) J. C. TIMMIS   (14) C. G. STANLEY   (15) W. E. RICHARDSON
    Burton   Wolverhampton   Moseley & London Irquine   Kidderminster
     (9) A. WOODWARD (Capt.)   (10) R. S. SYMONS   (12) J. S. McDOWELL
          Moseley   Moseley   Moseley
                 Half-backs :
       (7) G. GERMAN (Scrum)   (8) W. H. HILL (Stand-off)
          Burton   Moseley
                 Five-eight :
              (4) LEN HAMMER
                 Birmingham
                 Three-quarters :
(2) R. A. ORCOTT   (3) W. S. SHAW   (5) R. BAKER   (6) J. HUINS
   Moseley   Birmingham   Aston O.E.   Moseley
Left Wing.   Right Wing.
                    Full Back :
                  (1) J. PRITCHARD
                       Moseley

NORTH MIDLANDS R.U.

Referee: Mr. T. H. VILE, Welsh Rugby F.U.

performance by New Zealand, well refereed by Tommy Vile, the former Welsh international who played for Newport against the 1905 tourists.

Wing-forward Parker made the headlines with his 5 tries. A winner of the Military Medal in the First World War, his rugby career suffered as a result of attacks of malaria contracted during the war. However, he was a great success on this tour, his terrific speed and footballing talents being such that he also played in the backs. He later served the NZRFU with distinction and managed the 1949 All Blacks tour to South Africa.

CHESHIRE   1924/25

Saturday 11 October 1924
Upper Park, Birkenhead
Won 18-5

Cheshire selected a powerful eight-man scrum for the game with the intention of restricting All Black possession. The side included Leslie 'Bill' Gracie, the former Harlequins and Scotland player, who was regarded as being one of the greatest exponents of the tactical kick at this time. Several of the All Blacks were unwell with stomach upsets. The local press sensationally announced this as 'All Blacks Poisoned!' This meant New Zealand had to make several changes to the team, but they fielded a strong side nevertheless.

It took New Zealand the first quarter of the game to gain supremacy over the

CHESHIRE	NEW ZEALAND
R.D. Green (Birkenhead Park)	G. Nepia
H.W. Douglass (New Brighton)	A.H. Hart
J.V. Richardson (Birkenhead Park)	H.W. Brown
H.M. Locke (Birkenhead Park)	J. Steel
M.G.C. Hobday (New Brighton)	N.P. McGregor
A.L. Gracie (Manchester)	L. Paewai
O.W. Roberts (Birkenhead Park)	J.J. Mill
Forwards:	Forwards:
W.H. Taylor (Birkenhead Park, Capt.)	B.V. McCleary
J.R. Paterson (Birkenhead Park)	W.R. Irvine
P. Paxton Harding (Birkenhead Park)	R.R. Masters
J.B. Oldham (Birkenhead Park)	C.J. Brownlie
D.T. Raikes (Birkenhead Park)	J. Richardson
P.H. Davies (Sale)	R.T. Stewart
R.L. Holmes (New Brighton)	A.H. West
G.H. Williams (Sale)	C.G. Porter (Capt.)

Scorers:
Cheshire: Try: Locke. Con: Richardson.
New Zealand: Tries: Hart (4), Porter, Steel.

Referee: D. Helliwell (Yorkshire).
Attendance: 16,000.

Cheshire forwards. It was a physical encounter but, as the game progressed, the All Blacks' forwards began to take control. The only score of the first half came from Gus Hart, who finished off a good move by the tourists' three-quarters. Nepia was unable to convert and the half ended with the visitors 3-0 ahead.

Hart scored his second try shortly after the second half kicked off and then crossed for a fine try directly from the restart, when the All Blacks ran the ball back at Cheshire. Hart was involved in the next New Zealand try when he and Steel created a try for Porter in the corner. Steel was next on

The Cheshire forwards burst away.

the scoresheet with a fine try, in which he beat four Cheshire defenders before crossing in the corner. Nepia's goal-kicking was indifferent so Steel attempted the conversion, but his kick was charged down. Cheshire then scored a fine try themselves when Harold Locke made a break and swerved past several New Zealanders to score. It was a memorable try, talked about on Merseyside for many years. The try was converted by John Richardson. With the New Zealand pack having to battle hard to subdue the

Cheshire forwards, it was again left to their backs to dazzle the crowd. Some clever handling by the backs created space for Hart to run through and outstrip the defence for his fourth try. Cheshire never gave up and their forwards were excellent, but the New Zealand backs stole the show with their speed and creativity.

The Cheshire side included David Raikes, who won four rowing Blues for Oxford, and Paxton Harding, who was killed during the Second World War. Locke and Richardson were capped by England while John Paterson later won twenty-one caps in the Scottish pack.

DURHAM   1924/25

Wednesday 15 October 1924
Roker Park, Sunderland
Won 43-7

DURHAM	NEW ZEALAND
H.L. Lister (Hartlepool Rovers)	G. Nepia
L. Chiverton (Hartlepool Rovers)	A.H. Hart
V.G. Davies (Harlequins)	F.W. Lucas
W.H.R. Alderson (Hartlepool Rovers)	K.S. Svenson
J. Webster (Hartlepool Rovers)	C.E.O. Badeley
J. McNall (North Durham, Capt.)	N.P. McGregor
T.S. Short (Hartlepool Rovers)	J.J. Mill
Forwards:	Forwards:
G.S. Conway (Rugby)	B.V. McCleary
R.J. Hillard (Oxford University)	W.R. Irvine
H. Dawes (Ryton)	R.R. Masters
W. Carroll (Hartlepool Rovers)	L.F. Cupples
R.L. Clarke (Darlington)	R.T. Stewart
R. Hymers (Blaydon)	A.H. West
H.A. Eccles (Sunderland)	A. White
J. Middlemass (Houghton)	C.G. Porter (Capt.)

Scorers:
Durham: DG: Alderson. GM: Alderson.
New Zealand: Tries: Hart (3), Svenson (3), Lucas, Mill, West, Masters. Cons: White (3), Nepia (2). PG: Nepia.

Referee: J. Brunton (Northumberland).
Attendance: 15,000.

The All Blacks headed to the North-East to play Durham. The venue for the match was Roker Park, the home of Sunderland Football Club. As with the game against the Midlands, the teams benefited from the level and well-drained playing surface. Durham were the weakest of the northern counties, and despite improved results later in the season, their progress of rebuilding after the First World War was very slow. This was the highest score New Zealand achieved on tour.

After a close opening ten minutes, the scoring opened with a try from Hart after a break by Lucas. Hart scored a second shortly afterwards when Neil McGregor made a break. Nepia kicked a penalty but failed to add the extra points to Hart's third try of the half. Later, a misdirected kick was fielded by Rudd Alderson in the New Zealand 25. He called for a mark and kicked a goal to put Durham on the scoresheet. Finally, Lucas scored a try after the Durham defence was cut to shreds by a glorious handling move. Nepia converted from close to the posts to see New Zealand ahead 19-3 at the interval.

Jimmy Mill scored the first try of the second period shortly after the game recommenced. From the restart, New Zealand attacked and quickly moved the ball to Svenson, who scored the sixth All Black try. Svenson scored again following a break by Nepia, and then came a glorious try from Alf West, which involved most of his teammates in a passing movement. Svenson then scored his third try of the match before Alderson dropped a goal for Durham. The final score of the match came from Read Masters, seconds before time. New Zealand had won by the convincing score of 43-7 and the total of 10 tries emphasised their dominance. Forwards and backs had played well and Durham were outclassed in every facet of play. However, forwards Geoff

Durham County Rugby Union.

Mr. _W.C. Dalley_

is a Member of the

NEW ZEALAND
RUGBY TEAM.

Grand Hotel, Sunderland,
Oct. 13th—17th, 1924.

Bill Dalley's itinerary for the match with Durham. (World Rugby Museum)

Conway and Ronald Hillard had fine games and were selected for England to play against New Zealand.

Ces Badeley, the man tipped to be the tour captain, played his last game on tour. His troublesome knee injury ended his participation as a player but he helped coach the backs for the rest of the tour. Injuries plagued him throughout his rugby career to the extent that, when he retired in the late 1920s, he had only played forty-seven first-class matches. 'Bobby' Davies, a guest in the Durham side, also played for London and England against the All Blacks. A soldier who served with distinction in the First World War and with the Royal Artillery in the Second World War, he was killed by a bomb in December 1941.

Powerful lock Read Masters, who later published an invaluable record of the tour.

YORKSHIRE   1924/25

Saturday 18 October 1924
Lidget Green, Bradford
Won 42-4

The tour continued apace when the All Blacks headed for Bradford to play Yorkshire, who were widely expected to offer the tourists a stern challenge. The match was staged at Lidget Green, a ground opened when Yorkshire played the New Zealand Services side that toured after the First World War in 1919. The home side relied greatly on their talented outside half and captain, Eddie Myers, as team leader and major attacking weapon. A late injury to Ben Stokes, the Wakefield wing, saw Herbert Fletcher of Bramley step up to play. The Brownlie brothers played their first game together in England and Svenson was chosen at centre. With Hart and Steel he formed a pacey three-quarter line and the match became very open.

YORKSHIRE	NEW ZEALAND
S. Walker (Barnsley)	G. Nepia
F.A. Adams (Halifax)	A.H. Hart
W. Smith (Halifax)	K.S. Svenson
F.W. Roberts (Bradford)	J. Steel
H.T. Fletcher (Bramley Old Boys)	N.P. McGregor
E. Myers (Bradford, Capt.)	L. Paewai
J. Haigh-Lumby (Bradford)	W.C. Dalley
Forwards:	Forwards:
G. Scarth (Bradford)	B.V. McCleary
C.H. Wrighton (Bradford)	W.R. Irvine
H.H. deB. Monk (Bradford)	R.R. Masters
D.S. Smith (Bradford)	M.J. Brownlie
H. Eastwood (Halifax)	J. Richardson (Capt.)
H. Wilkinson (Halifax)	R.T. Stewart
S.R. Whitfield (Batley)	C.J. Brownlie
E. Winkley (Hull & East Riding)	J.H. Parker

Scorers:
Yorkshire: DG: Myers.
New Zealand: Tries: Hart (4), McGregor (2), Richardson, Svenson. Cons: Nepia (6). PG: Nepia (2).

Referee: J.T. Bradburn (Lancashire).
Attendance: 15,000.

After eleven minutes of play Lui Paewai created a try for Jock Richardson when he received quick ball from a scrum and beat four Yorkshire defenders. Nepia missed the conversion but was more successful with a long-range penalty some time later. He also added the conversion to a try by Gus Hart, who managed to squeeze past Walker, the Yorkshire full-back, to score. Myers dropped a goal after half an hour to put Yorkshire on the board before Svenson restored the New Zealand momentum with a try after he gathered a loose ball. Then, pressure on the Yorkshire defence close to their line saw the ball go loose and McGregor score. Nepia converted and kicked another long-range penalty and the All Blacks turned around 22-4 ahead at half-time.

Having witnessed the original All Blacks thrash their side, the Yorkshire crowd was again treated to a spectacular display of attacking rugby. McGregor scored his second try early in the second half and then Hart crossed for his second. The Taranaki wing then scored two more tries, the first of which came from a superb break by half-back Bill Dalley. Although the All Blacks lost Steel with an injury, they were in effervescent form and there was nothing Yorkshire could do to stop them. The New Zealand forwards were powerful, quick and athletic, with Maurice Brownlie, Masters and Richardson monopolising possession.

Yorkshire's forwards played well, but their backs were hopelessly outclassed by the tourists, a situation not helped when Wilson Smith left the field with a leg injury. The vision, speed, running lines and moves of the New Zealanders were well thought-out and well executed, with Gus Hart outstanding.

The diminutive Hart was converted by his province Taranaki into a wing, having originally been a five-eighth. He was probably the fastest runner in the tour party and ended the tour as top try-scorer with 20, 15 of which were scored in 5 consecutive games. Three of the four Yorkshire three-quarters, Fletcher, Adams and Smith, later enjoyed successful rugby league careers with Halifax.

LANCASHIRE   1924/25

**Wednesday 22 October 1924
Old Trafford, Manchester
Won 23-0**

LANCASHIRE	NEW ZEALAND
R.K. Mellhuish (Fylde)	G. Nepia
G.P. Lammert (Fylde)	A.H. Hart
S.R. Jackson (Broughton Park)	A.E. Cooke
A.R. Aslett (Richmond)	K.S. Svenson
J.C. Samuels (Manchester)	N.P. McGregor
E.J. Massey (Liverpool)	L. Paewai
S.B. McQueen (Waterloo)	W.C. Dalley
Forwards:	Forwards:
G.L. Wood (Manchester)	A. White
A.F. Blakiston (Liverpool)	W.R. Irvine
H.G. Periton (Waterloo)	R.R. Masters
S. Brown (Birkenhead Park)	J. Richardson
A.H. Goold (Liverpool)	M.J. Brownlie
G.A. Rutter (Liverpool)	R.T. Stewart
P.H. Wooler (Sale)	L.F. Cupples
M. Robinson (Manchester University)	C.G. Porter (Capt.)

Scorers:
New Zealand: Tries: Cooke (2), Porter (2), Richardson, Svenson, Masters. Con: Nepia.

Referee: D. Helliwell (Yorkshire).
Attendance: 35,000.

The All Blacks crossed the Pennines to Manchester for a game with Lancashire at the Manchester United Football Club ground at Old Trafford. Unfortunately, rain during the week had made the pitch very heavy. After several years in the doldrums, Lancashire had started to improve. They based their substantial pack around Arthur Blakiston and Joe Periton, international forwards and leaders of men, and it was these players that helped develop Lancashire into the side that reached the County Championship final in 1929. New Zealand selected Andrew 'Son' White in the front row.

The game started and soon became a scrappy affair dominated by the forwards. Lancashire pressurised in the early stages before the New Zealand forwards began to take control. It was entirely appropriate that the opening try should come from a forward – skipper Cliff Porter crossing

after some good close passing among the All Blacks' pack. Nepia converted. Richardson then scored a good try after a fine run by Gus Hart from within his own half, and Svenson scored the next after the ball rebounded off a Lancashire defender. Porter ran in for his second try and then a good Svenson break created space for Cooke to score. The crowd was then entertained by Richardson attempting the conversion, which failed.

Leading 17-0 at half-time, New Zealand continued to dominate the forward exchanges. Direct from the restart, the Lancashire forwards nearly dribbled the ball over the line, with only the courageous Nepia keeping them out, but shortly afterwards Read Masters finished off a forward rush to score for New Zealand. Thereafter the game degenerated into an error-strewn affair. Midway through the half, Cooke scored his second try, but Nepia's conversion attempt hit the post. There was no further score and New Zealand won 23-0.

Above right: Cliff Porter, scorer of two tries. The All Blacks' unfortunate tour captain missed all the internationals in Britain, but played against France.

It was a disappointing game all round. Lancashire were unhappy they had not had more of the ball, particularly as their scrum had gone very well, and New Zealand felt that they should have scored more points from the possession they had secured.

CUMBERLAND   1924/25

Saturday 25 October 1924
Brunton Park, Carlisle
Won 41-0

New Zealand headed north to play Cumberland at another football stadium, Brunton Park, home of Carlisle United FC. Cumberland were the reigning County Champions, with tough forwards and a strong defence. They included the Little and Lawson brothers from Workington, the latter of whom later played in the back row for England. The All Blacks had injury problems in their backline and consequently the versatile Jim Parker was selected on the wing. It was Parker himself who opened the scoring after a three-quarter move gave him space to run in. Then a poor pass and a dropped ball under pressure gave Mill the opportunity to score in the corner. His second try came after

CUMBERLAND	NEW ZEALAND
J.W. Brough (Silloth)	G. Nepia
W. Johnston (Kendal)	A.H. Hart
R.E.E. Cass (Rhine Army)	A.E. Cooke
T. Fletcher (Workington)	J.H. Parker
J.W. Burrows (Workington)	M.F. Nicholls
J. Little (Workington)	L. Paewai
T. Little (Workington)	J.J. Mill
Forwards:	Forwards:
W.H. Walling (Kirkby Lonsdale)	W.R. Irvine
R. Hanvey (Aspatria)	Q. Donald
T. Cavanagh (Carlisle)	R.R. Masters
H. Wills (Kendal)	J. Richardson
J. Ward (Aspatria)	M.J. Brownlie
T.M. Lawson (Workington, Capt.)	R.T. Stewart
R.G. Lawson (Workington)	A. White
J. McCade (Keswick)	C.G. Porter (Capt.)

Scorers:
New Zealand: Tries: Hart (4), Cooke (2), Mill (2), Parker, Stewart, Nicholls. Cons: White (3), Nepia.

Referee: R.A. Lloyd (Lancashire).
Attendance: 17,000.

the New Zealand pack had taken play up to the Cumberland line. Then the All Blacks scored a try of the tour. Maurice Brownlie broke away with the ball and passed to the supporting Porter. The ball was moved

to Hart, who made good ground and veered inside before a beautifully executed scissors move put Cooke clear. He confused the remaining Cumberland defence to score. The final try of the half went to Hart. Nicholls failed to convert but New Zealand were 15-0 ahead at half-time.

Cumberland started the second half by appliying pressure on the All Blacks but the tourists' defence held. A run from Burrows was stopped by Nepia, and Porter stopped a dangerous foot-rush. However, the resurgence of the home side was ended after twenty minutes when a move involving most of the New Zealand team ended with a try by Hart. Porter injured his knee and was forced to leave the field. Cooke then opened the defence for Hart to score again and, after a spectacular run, Hart scored his fourth try.

The New Zealand pack dominated the home forwards and a break by Brownlie was finished off by Stewart. New Zealand were almost scoring at will. A clever run by Lui Paewai created the opportunity for Cooke to score. Finally, Cooke received the ball in space and kicked ahead. Full-back Jim Brough gathered the ball but received the New Zealand pack at the same time. They stripped him of the ball and moved it to Mark Nicholls for a final try. The All Blacks had scored 11 tries but Nepia and Nicholls had difficulty in kicking goals. In the end it was Andrew White who had the success.

Brough was outstanding in defence, despite the heavy defeat. He was later capped by England in the international with New Zealand before turning to rugby league and joining Leeds at the end of the season. He went on to become one of the professional code's all-time greats, captaining the England side. He was a Rugby League Challenge Cup winner and in his seventies he presented Silloth, his home rugby union club, with the jersey he wore against the All Blacks. Unfortunately, the RFU instructed Silloth to remove it from display because Brough had become a professional.

IRELAND   1924/25

Saturday 1 November 1924
Lansdowne Road, Dublin
Won 6-0

IRELAND	NEW ZEALAND
W.E. Crawford (Malone)	G. Nepia
H.W.V. Stephenson (United Services, Capt.)	A.H. Hart
J.B. Gardiner (NIFC)	F.W. Lucas
G.V. Stephenson (Queen's University, Belfast)	K.S. Svenson
T.R. Hewitt (Queen's University, Belfast)	A.E. Cooke
F.S. Hewitt (Instonians)	M.F. Nicholls
J.C. McDowell (Instonians)	W.C. Dalley
Forwards:	Forwards:
A.W. Spain (U.C. Dublin)	W.R. Irvine
R.J. Collopy (Bective Rangers)	Q. Donald
T.N. Brand (NIFC)	R.R. Masters
J. McVicker (Collegians)	M.J. Brownlie
T.A. McClelland (Queen's University, Belfast)	J. Richardson (Capt.)
J.D. Clinch (Dublin University)	L.F. Cupples
R.Y. Crichton (Dublin University)	A. White
W.R.F. Collis (Wanderers)	J.H. Parker

Scorers:
New Zealand: Try: Svenson. PG: Nicholls.

Referee: A.E. Freethy (Wales).
Attendance: 25,000.

The injury Cliff Porter sustained in Carlisle prevented him from leading the team in the first international of the tour. With Badeley also nursing a knee injury, it was left to Jock Richardson to captain the side. Ron Stewart was suffering from pleurisy and was replaced by Les Cupples. Dalley was chosen at half-back and Jim Parker joined the pack. Twelve of the tourists made their international debuts, with only Nicholls, White and Richardson having played international rugby before. There was considerable debate as to whether Ireland should include an eighth forward or back. Unfortunately, their plans were affected by a series of injuries to their original selection. Joe Clarke of Bective Rangers had to withdraw, replaced by John McDowell. Charles Hallaran was replaced by Bob Collis. There were new caps for Alexander Spain and Tom Brand, although neither

Above: The New Zealand team that defeated Ireland.

was actually presented as caps were not awarded by the IRFU for games with colonial sides. 'Jammie' Clinch came into the side later in the week. By the day of the match the entire back division was supplied by Ulster.

Both sides struggled with the heavy pitch and wet ball, following a morning of torrential rain. Then it began to rain again making handling difficult. The first half was forward-dominated and neither side was able to score, although Ernie Crawford missed a penalty goal from in front of the posts when Ireland were in the ascendancy. However, he regularly saved the day with magnificent tackles when New Zealand seemed certain to score. His opposing full-back, Nepia, was also busy in defence and tackled well and kicked accurately.

The wind picked up in the second half and New Zealand played into the gale. Cooke kicked ahead but was beaten to the ball by an Irish defender. Then outside half Frank Hewitt was injured stopping a rush. Spain covered for him until he limped back on as a wing. Then only try of the game came when with Ireland trying to run out of defence, Harry Stephenson was tackled and the ball went loose. Parker gathered the ball and passed it to Brownlie, who moved it out to Svenson to score out wide. Although the try was awarded, many felt the pass from Brownlie was forward. Shortly after Nicholls kicked a penalty from in front of the posts. It had been a fine contest between two good teams in difficult conditions, something the record crowd recognised in their extended applause at the final whistle.

ULSTER   1924/25

Wednesday 5 November 1924
Ravenhill, Belfast
Won 28-6

There had been disappointment in Ulster that the original All Blacks had not played in the province, but at last the New Zealanders were there. The match was staged at the new Ravenhill ground and the weather was glorious. The Ulster side included eight players who had represented Ireland against New Zealand the previous weekend. Even so, their side was hit by injuries. Bill Hall replaced Frank Hewitt, and G. Caruth stood in for Tom McCleland, who had himself replaced the ill Hugh McVicker. The crowd included the Prime Minister.

The All Blacks again discovered the ferocity of Irish packs. The Ulster forwards played well and put New Zealand under pressure. The Irish team came close to

ULSTER	NEW ZEALAND
W.E. Crawford (Malone)	G. Nepia
H.W.V. Stephenson (United Services)	J. Steel
J.B. Gardiner (NIFC)	F.W. Lucas
G.V. Stephenson	K.S. Svenson
(Queen's University, Belfast, Capt.)	
T.R. Hewitt (Queen's University, Belfast)	A.E. Cooke
W.H. Hall (Instonians)	M.F. Nicholls
J.C. McDowell (Instonians)	J.J. Mill
Forwards:	Forwards:
J. Campbell (Instonians)	W.R. Irvine
W.F. Browne (NIFC & Army)	Q. Donald
T.N. Brand (NIFC)	R.R. Masters
H. Copeland (Instonians)	M.J. Brownlie
G. Caruth (Queen's University, Belfast)	J. Richardson (Capt.)
J. McDowell (Instonians)	L.F. Cupples
J.T. Smyth (Knock)	A. White
J. McVicker (Collegians)	J.H. Parker

Scorers:
Ulster: Try: H Stephenson. PG: Crawford.
New Zealand: Tries: Svenson (2), Parker (2), Irvine, Steel.
Cons: Nicholls (5).

Referee: J.H. Miles (Leicester).
Attendance: 16,000.

scoring early in the game but the tourists' gradually subdued the home forwards. Play moved into Ulster territory and Richardson tore away from a lineout. Although he was tackled, the ball was moved through the backs at pace for Svenson to score in the corner, with Nicholls converting. Then a good cross-kick by Cooke was gathered by 'Bull' Irvine, who scored the second try. Nicholls then set up a try for Parker, which he converted, before Ernie Crawford kicked a penalty. Crawford, who was outstanding against the All Blacks the previous weekend, also had a fine game for Ulster.

Leading 15-3 at the break, the All Blacks started the second half at top speed. Mill made several breaks from the fringes of the scrum, which regularly confused the Ulster defence. He broke twice in the second half to set up a try for Steel and a second score for Parker. Then George Nepia ran hard down the touchline, drew the defence and passed inside to Lucas for Svenson to score. As the match approached its conclusion, Ireland captain Harry Stephenson scored after beating three New Zealanders in a fine run. The cheering from the crowd was intense but it was too little too late for Ulster and New Zealand won 28-6. After the game Nepia declined £1,200 in cash to turn professional and play rugby league.

Referee Jack Miles annoyed the tourists with his interpretation of the scrummaging laws. The first England international from the Leicester club, Miles refereed three internationals before the First World War. He had played on the wing for Northampton against the 1905 All Blacks.

Above: *The New Zealand side that faced Ulster.*

Right: *Ulster's full-back Ernie Crawford. He had fine games for Ulster and Ireland against the All Blacks.*

NORTHUMBERLAND 1924/25

Saturday 8 November 1924
County Ground, Gosforth
Won 27-4

New Zealand faced another difficult side in Northumberland when they moved on to Newcastle. Local interest and excitement were high and there was some difficulty in getting the crowd into the Gosforth ground, which was full over an hour before kick-off. Northumberland were led by Carston Catcheside, the local three-quarter who had played for England the previous season and scored a remarkable try against France, in which he jumped over the French full-back. That season he became the first English player to score a try in each game in the Home International championship. Richardson continued in his role of captain of the All Blacks, while

NORTHUMBERLAND	NEW ZEALAND
G. Wilkinson (Gosforth Nomads)	G. Nepia
W. Wallace (Percy Park)	A.H. Hart
H.C. Catcheside (Percy Park, Capt.)	H.W. Brown
L. Trotter (Armstrong College)	J. Steel
J.C. Yeoman (Gosforth Nomads)	A.E. Cooke
L. Cartmel (Gosforth Nomads)	N.P. McGregor
H. Whitley (Northern)	J.J. Mill
Forwards:	Forwards:
R. Armstrong (Northern)	B.V. McCleary
W.R. Arkless (Northern)	Q. Donald
O. Kaiser (Seghill)	R.R. Masters
H. Davidson (Rockliff)	C.J. Brownlie
M. Lambert (Percy Park)	J. Richardson (Capt.)
C. Lister (Percy Park)	L.F. Cupples
J. Punshon (Gateshed Fell)	A.H. West
G. Nicholson (Tynedale)	J.H. Parker

Scorers:
Northumberland: DG: Catcheside.
New Zealand: Tries: Mill (2), Hart, Cooke, Brown, Richardson, Steel. Cons: Mill (3).

Referee: R.O. Jenkins.
Attendance: 15,000.

Northumberland Rugby Union.

Patron : Brig. Gen.
Sir J. F. Laycock,
K.C.M.G., D.S.O.

President :
H. O. Robinson, Esq.

Official Programme

NORTHUMBERLAND

versus

NEW ZEALAND

SATURDAY, NOVEMBER 8TH.

KICK OFF 3 p.m.

County Ground Gosforth.

REFEREE : MR. R. O. JENKINS.
(Durham Rugby Union)

Northumberland had recently been frustratingly inconsistent but possessed a set of backs that tackled ferociously and had the ability to counter-attack at pace.

Although the New Zealand forwards were superior to their opponents, the first half was a tough encounter and the rain made handling difficult. The Northumberland side played with great commitment and tenacity, and their tackles were potent. They also possessed forwards who were capable dribblers and New Zealand frequently had to deal with the ball on the floor. Close to half-time, Gus Hart finished off a three-quarter movement that defied the elements. The conversion was missed but New Zealand finished the half 3-0 ahead.

Shortly after the teams turned around at the break, a kick ahead by Jim Parker was gathered by Bert Cooke for a try that Jim Mill converted. Then the Northumberland forwards took the initiative, and, using fine footwork, kicked and dribbled the ball into New Zealand territory where Catcheside dropped a goal. The All Blacks became more dominant and put pressure on Northumberland. Had it not been for good defence, the tourists would have scored several tries. Under great pressure, Catcheside dropped the slippery ball and the athletic Mill gratefully gathered it and scored a try. It was one-way traffic from this point and soon afterwards a break by McGregor resulted in a try from Brown. Mill scored and converted his second try shortly after this, following good play by Cooke, before Richardson scored after some excellent close passing within the forwards. The final try came from Steel, who was on the end of a smooth back movement.

At 27-4 New Zealand were happy with their win but the scoreline did little to reflect the contribution of the home side, whose pack gave their visitors a difficult afternoon. Hawke's Bay half-back Jimmy Mill was outstanding. Having lost out to Bill Dalley for the Ireland international, Mill put in several excellent performances. He leap-frogged the Canterbury player and was selected for the remaining Tests of the tour.

CAMBRIDGE UNIVERSITY   1924/25

**Wednesday 12 November 1924
Grange Road, Cambridge
Won 5-0**

The All Blacks resisted the temptation to make many changes for the game with the students at Cambridge, reflecting on their tough encounter in 1905. The 1924 match was also a hard game of rugby, even though Cambridge had been beaten 39-3 by Leicester the previous weekend. Cambridge opted to field five three-quarters for the game with a seven-man pack. The athletic David MacMyn, later a Scottish international lock, played in the centre. It had rained hard before the match and Grange Road was saturated. The pitch had developed swamp-like qualities and the

CAMBRIDGE UNIVERSITY	NEW ZEALAND
P.S. Doughty (Pembroke)	G. Nepia
Sir T.G. Devitt (Corpus)	A.H. Hart
B.R. Turnbull (Christ's)	H.W. Brown
W.R. Harding (Pembroke)	A.C.C. Robilliard
D.J. MacMyn (Pembroke)	M.F. Nicholls
J.H. Bordass (Caius)	N.P. McGregor
T.E.S. Francis (Pembroke)	J.J. Mill
A.T. Young (Caius, Capt.)	Forwards:
Forwards:	B.V. McCleary
W.E. Tucker (Caius)	W.R. Irvine
W.I. Jones (Caius)	J. Richardson (Capt.)
D.C. Cumming (Caius)	C.J. Brownlie
W.B. Scott (Pembroke)	L.F. Cupples
C.S. Barlow (Caius)	A. White
R.G. Howell (Caius)	A.H. West
W. Ross-Skinner (Trinity Hall)	J.H. Parker

Scorers:
New Zealand: Try: Mill. Con: Nicholls.

Referee: T.H. Vile (Newport).
Attendance: 8,000.

ball was particularly difficult to handle. It was therefore always going to be a tight affair dominated by forward exchanges.

New Zealand were in control for most of the game and spent long periods in the Cambridge half of the field, but they met with stern resistance from the students. The Varsity side was very committed, matched the tourists in the scrum, and had the edge over them in the lineout. Where New Zealand excelled was in loose play and in foraging for the ball on the floor. There was no score during the first half. The few attacks New Zealand were able to mount which threatened the line were repelled by the students. In the second half Cambridge posed more of a threat, but were beaten back by good tackling and defensive organisation, although Rowe Harding was close to scoring on one occasion.

The Cambridge forwards dribble the ball away from a scrum.

The one score of the game came midway through the second half when the home captain, Arthur Young, threw a long, risky pass that was difficult for his centres to gather. The dropped ball was collected by Jimmy Mill with great dexterity, who then evaded some desperate tackles on a mazy run to score. Mark Nicholls converted.

The previous day the All Blacks were represented at Whitehall, London, for the Armistice Day commemorations. New Zealand team manager Stan Dean laid a wreath on behalf of the tour party. The same Cambridge XV later played Oxford in the Varsity match, but was defeated 11-6 in a fine game. This time MacMyn played in his more accustomed position in the forwards.

LONDON COUNTIES   1924/25

Saturday 15 November 1924
Twickenham, London
Won 31-6

This was the first time a New Zealand side played at Twickenham. The tour schedule included 2 matches with London, the second game being staged at Blackheath at the end of the year. By the end of the tour the All Blacks had played at Twickenham three times, including games with Combined Services and England. London were led by Wavell Wakefield. The versatile Harlequins forward, who had served in the Royal Flying Corps in the First World War, played a loose role similar to that of a rover. The side also included Tom Lawton, who later played for Australia and appeared in each international of the Waratahs' 1927/28 tour. He later captained his country.

The weather was fine and the pitch excellent providing for an attractive opening exchange between the forwards.

LONDON COUNTIES	NEW ZEALAND
H.W.F. Franklin	G. Nepia
(Old Blues & Eastern Counties)	
R.H. Hamilton-Wickes	A.H. Hart
(Harlequins & Middlesex)	
A.R. Aslett (Richmond)	A.E. Cooke
J.V. Richardson (Richmond)	K.S. Svenson
R.K. Millar (London Scottish & Kent)	M.F. Nicholls
A.T. Lawton (Blackheath)	N.P. McGregor
A.P. Guthrie (Blackheath & Kent)	J.J. Mill
Forwards:	Forwards:
W.F. Browne (Harlequins & Surrey)	W.R. Irvine
J.S.H. Drysdale (Blackheath & Kent)	Q. Donald
A.W.L. Row (Barts Hospital & Middlesex)	R.R. Masters
D.C.D. Ryder (Blackheath)	M.J. Brownlie
B.G. Scholefield (Guy's Hospital & Kent)	J. Richardson (Capt.)
R. Cove-Smith	A. White
(Old Merchant Taylors & Middlesex)	
R.R. Stokes (Harlequins & Middlesex)	R.T. Stewart
W.W. Wakefield	J.H. Parker
(Harlequins & Middlesex, Capt.)	

Scorers:
London Counties: Tries: Millar (2).
New Zealand: Tries: Brownlie (2), Cooke (2), Parker (2), Richardson. Cons: Nicholls (5).

Referee: R.A. Lloyd (Lancashire).
Attendance: 50,000.

Jimmy Mill launches a New Zealand back move.

Maurice Brownlie opened the scoring with a try after Hart had kicked ahead and the London defence had failed to deal with the ball. Nicholls converted. Midway through the first half, good passing by London created space for Robert Millar to score a try in the corner. The conversion was missed, but shortly afterwards Wakefield set the three-quarters away and Millar ran in for his second try. The Scot proved to be a handful for the New Zealand defence. Neither try was converted, but London were 6-5 ahead to the vociferous delight of the crowd. The All Blacks won back the lead on the stroke of half-time when Brownlie raced away from a lineout in the London 25 to score between the posts. Nicholls' conversion was the last act of the half and saw New Zealand leading 10-6.

Parker retired to the backs, having incurred the displeasure of the referee during the first period. Three minutes after the restart he deftly kicked the ball into midfield. Cooke gathered and exchanged passes with Svenson to score a fine try. The All Blacks then threatened to break loose. Shortly after Nicholls missed converting Cooke's try, he missed again, this time after a score by Parker following accurate passing in the backs. Then Mill made a break and found his loose forwards in support. They carried the ball on and Richardson crashed over for another try. A fine break by Mark Nicholls took play up to the London goal line and Cooke scored. The final score came following a kick ahead by Lawton which was collected by Parker on halfway, who showed great pace for a forward, to run in the seventh try. Nicholls converted the last three tries.

There was some concern over the tackling of the New Zealanders. The press claimed that they were too physical, but on the positive side they also received many plaudits for their fine running.

OXFORD UNIVERSITY 1924/25

Thursday 20 November 1924
Iffley Road, Oxford
Won 33-15

The All Blacks picked a strong side for what was anticipated to be a tough game. Oxford possessed an outstanding three-quarter line, with Wallace, George Aitken and MacPherson all capped by Scotland. Aitken had also played international rugby for New Zealand prior to attending the university, and 'Johnny' Wallace later returned to Britain as the captain of the New South Wales Waratahs in 1927. Ian Smith, the other first-choice wing, who scored a remarkable 24 tries in 32 internationals for Scotland, was unable to play.

Oxford nearly scored from the kick-off, and after early exchanges, which were quite even, they took the lead. A clearance kick by Cooke was so badly sliced it went over the New Zealand goal line and Herbert Jacob,

OXFORD UNIVERSITY	NEW ZEALAND
R.L. Raymond (New College)	G. Nepia
A.C. Wallace (New College)	J. Steel
G.G. Aitken (St John's)	A.E. Cooke
G.P.S. MacPherson (Oriel)	A.C.C. Robilliard
H.P. Jacob (Christ Church)	M.F. Nicholls
H.J. Kittermaster (University)	N.P. McGregor
W.I.N. Strong (Brasenose)	W.C. Dalley
Forwards:	Forwards:
A.C. Valentine (Balliol)	W.R. Irvine
G.E.B. Abell (Corpus Christi)	Q. Donald
R.J. Hillard (Christ Church)	R.R. Masters
C.R. Wordsworth (Balliol, Capt.)	C.J. Brownlie
W.N. Roughead (Oriel)	M.J. Brownlie
V.G. Wesche (New College)	A. White
A. deH. Boyd (Trinity)	L.F. Cupples
W.V. Berkeley (Hertford)	C.G. Porter (Capt.)

Scorers:
Oxford University: Tries: Jacob, MacPherson, Wallace.
Cons: Berkeley (3).
New Zealand: Tries: White, Cooke, M Brownlie, Steel, Robilliard. Cons: Nicholls (5). DG: Nicholls (2).

Referee: A.E. Freethy (Neath).
Attendance: 15,000.

the Oxford wing, won the race to the ball. Berkeley converted the try. Nicholls opened the visitors' account with a drop goal before converting a try by Andrew White. Then came one of the tries of the tour. Dalley gathered the ball from a scrum and passed quickly to McGregor, who beat one man. The ball then moved to Bert Cooke, who swerved and sidestepped through the Oxford defence to score a spectacular try, which was loudly applauded by the crowd. Nicholls converted. Oxford showed they were still in the game by pressing the All Blacks' line.

The Oxford backs attack from a scrum.

Then a cross-kick by Wallace was caught by Phil MacPherson, who beat Nepia for a converted try. New Zealand were ahead 14-10 at half-time.

Oxford rearranged their line-up after half-time with Venn Wesche being withdrawn from the pack to play full-back and fellow Australian Roland 'Pup' Raymond moving forward to join the three-quarters. Running by McGregor opened up the Oxford defence for the forwards to race through and 'Morrie' Brownlie scored. Oxford then scored a magnificent third try. With New Zealand on the attack, Steel was tackled on the Oxford line by Wallace, who somehow stripped the ball off him and raced up the touchline. He passed inside to Raymond, who took play up to halfway. He drew Nepia and then passed back to Wallace, who sprinted in for the try. Berkeley converted, although he also missed several kickable penalties. Jack Steel made amends by scoring after an orthodox three-quarter move. The try was converted by Nicholls, who then dropped another goal and converted a try by Alan Robilliard after a clever move in the backs.

Aside from the result, this was a magnificent game of rugby, a game of thrust and counter-thrust between two fine sides intent on attack. Among many remarkable players who featured in the game was Alan Valentine, captain of the USA's 1924 Olympic rugby champions. Oxford went on to win the Varsity match 11-6, fielding the same side as played New Zealand.

CARDIFF 1924/25

Saturday 22 November 1924
Cardiff Arms Park, Cardiff
Won 16-8

The All Blacks returned to Wales for a match with a powerful Cardiff side. The home team had been enjoying a successful season, winning ten of their first 11 games including a 19-0 win over Gloucester. They then lost 3 games in succession, a poor run that ended with a win over United Services at Portsmouth the previous weekend. Cardiff's plans for the match with New Zealand were hampered by an injury to outside half Danny Davies, but he recovered to play. Bernard Turnbull was unable to leave Cambridge to play so was replaced by international Arthur Cornish. Cardiff were captained by fellow capped player Tom 'Codger' Johnson and coached by Gwyn Nicholls, who had led the Wales side that beat the All Blacks in 1905. They also included internationals Jack Powell, Bobby Delahay

CARDIFF	NEW ZEALAND
T. Wallace	G. Nepia
T.A.W. Johnson (Capt.)	F.W. Lucas
R.A. Cornish	H.W. Brown
J. Powell	K.S. Svenson
P. Rayer	A.E. Cooke
D.E. Davies	M.F. Nicholls
W.J. Delahay	J.J. Mill
Forwards:	Forwards:
W. Ireson	Q. Donald
I. Richards	W.R. Irvine
T.W. Lewis	R.R. Masters
J. Brown	M.J. Brownlie
S. Hinam	J. Richardson
C. O'Leary	J.H. Parker
F. Stephens	A. White
W.J. Ould	C.G. Porter (Capt.)

Scorers:
Cardiff: Try: Delahay. Con: Wallace. PG: Wallace.
New Zealand: Tries: Lucas, White, Porter. Cons: Nicholls (2). PG: Nicholls.

Referee: Capt. A.S. Burge (Penarth).
Attendance: 45,000.

and Billy Ould. Idris Richards, Sid Hinam, Jim Brown and Tom Lewis were later capped by Wales. A week before the international with Wales, the All Blacks chose a strong side but but not their international team. Late in the game, it looked as though this may have been a mistake.

The gates were closed half an hour before kick-off, and many thousands were locked out in the adjoining streets, but 45,000 were packed into Cardiff Arms Park. Those in the ground witnessed a tough forward battle in which the play was vigorous but fair. In Cardiff, the All Blacks met the most difficult pack of forwards they had encountered thus far on tour.

Cardiff attacked from the kick-off, and while both sides attempted to attack, the opposing defences cancelled each other out. The Welsh club made the most of the freedom referee Burge allowed and they pressurised the opposition's backs into errors. However, Mark Nicholls opened the scoring when he kicked a long-range penalty after the Cardiff half-backs were caught offside. Then Jock Richardson won the ball at a lineout and it was moved quickly through the back division for Fred Lucas to score a try, which Nicholls converted. Close to half-time, the All Black forwards broke away in a passing rush and Andrew 'Son' White scored between the posts for Nicholls to convert. The tourists went into the interval with an 11-0 lead.

With the wind at their backs in the second half, Cardiff dominated the territory and regularly threatened. Their forwards created opportunities but their backs were unable to capitalise on them. New Zealand, however, made the most of their chances and, shortly after the restart, Cliff Porter picked up the ball after a forward rush to score their third try, which the accurate Nicholls converted. Eventually, Cardiff's territorial dominance bore fruit when Tom Wallace kicked a penalty goal. A few minutes later, Bobby Delahay dummied his way through the New Zealand defence for a fine try that Wallace converted. There was no further score and New Zealand had come through a tough match to win.

Later in the evening several All Blacks, including Porter, were invited to a radio studio. After being interviewed and singing some New Zealand songs, they performed the Haka in the studio.

WALES   1924/25

Saturday 29 November 1924
St Helen's, Swansea
Won 19-0

The All Blacks prepared for this match, which Read Masters described in his valuable tour record as: 'the one match of the tour we wanted to win', in Tenby, where they trained on the beach and had a relaxing time. 'Son' White was not considered following his injury against Cardiff, and they delayed choosing the half-back until the weather conditions were known on the morning of the match. It was a fine day and Jimmy Mill took the field to win his first cap. Cyril Brownlie also made his international debut. Cliff Porter was fit to play but the tour management preferred to retain Jim Parker. Porter accepted this decision in the interests of the team, but was deeply upset at being

WALES	NEW ZEALAND
T.A.W. Johnson (Cardiff)	G. Nepia
E. Finch (Llanelly)	J. Steel
A.E. Jenkins (Llanelly)	A.E. Cooke
A. Stock (Newport)	K.S. Svenson
R. Harding (Swansea)	M.F. Nicholls
J.J. Wetter (Newport, Capt.)	N.P. McGregor
E. Williams (Neath)	J.J. Mill
W.J. Delahay (Newport)	Forwards:
Forwards:	Q. Donald
D.S. Parker (Swansea)	W.R. Irvine
J.H. Gore (Blaina)	R.R. Masters
C.H. Pugh (Maesteg)	C.J. Brownlie
S. Morris (Cross Keys)	M.J. Brownlie
C. Williams (Llanelly)	L.F. Cupples
D.M. Jones (London Welsh)	J. Richardson (Capt.)
D.D. Hiddlestone (Neath)	J.H. Parker

Scorers:
New Zealand: Tries: Irvine (2), M. Brownlie, Svenson.
Cons: Nicholls (2). PG: Nicholls.

Referee: Col J.S. Brunton (England).
Attendance: 50,000.

left out. Wales selected a seven-forward pack to match the tourists, with captain Jack Wetter and new cap Eddie Williams as five-eighths playing outside scrum-half Bobby Delahay. This put the lighter Welsh pack at an immediate disadvantage. Aberavon's Bob Randall withdrew from the chosen side to be replaced by

Above left: *The Zealand team which faced Wales.*

Left: *Nineteen-year-old George Nepia played in every tour game. Undoubtedly his greatest performance was against Wales.*

Cliff Williams, who also made his debut. There was some concern about the choice of backs in the local press. The WRU seemed uncertain as to who should play full-back, eventually choosing Tom Johnson, who had never played there before. Captain Jack Wetter played his last game for Wales, ten years after his first. After Mill led the Haka, the tourists were entertained by a strange parody of their war-dance undertaken by the Welsh side.

Wales threatened from the start of the match but New Zealand counter-attacked and Jack Steel was tackled when a try looked a distinct possibility. Mark Nicholls opened the scoring with a penalty goal after ten minutes, before Wales launched an attack that caused momentary panic in the New Zealand defence. George Nepia made a fine tackle on Ernie Finch after a dangerous run by Albert Jenkins. 'Snowy' Svenson was twice close to scoring for the All Blacks, and the match was played at pace with good attacks and hard tackles on both sides. Eventually, Maurice Brownlie scored the first try, using his enormous strength to force his way over the Welsh line. Nicholls converted. Then Welsh captain Jack Wetter was forced to leave the field with a serious leg injury after a collision with Nepia, and although he returned later he was scarcely able to walk and joined the pack. The All Blacks pressed the Welsh line but eventually the home team's excellent defence cracked again and 'Bull' Irvine scored a try. The conversion missed but New Zealand led by the handsome margin of 11-0 at half-time.

Wales pressed early in the second half but the New Zealand defence was well organised and the attacks were repelled. The All Blacks looked dangerous every time they ran the ball and Steel had a try disallowed after he put a foot in touch. Shortly afterwards Mill sent Svenson in for a try from an attacking scrum, which put the game out of the reach of the Welshmen. Close to full time, New Zealand scored again following an extraordinary dribbling rush by the forwards which travelled most of the length of the field. Irvine touched the ball down for Nicholls to convert.

New Zealand had won largely through the greater pace of their backs and their superior lineout play. They had also kept Wales out when they attacked. Neil McGregor had a fine game in defence, but it was Nepia who received the plaudits, including this glowing reference from the *Western Mail*: 'There were times when it appeared that nothing would stay the fierce rushes of the Welsh pack. By sheer strength they barged their way through with the ball, and there stood Nepia alone between them and their desired objective... His judgement is uncanny and his pluck magnificent... Nepia was a stone wall which the Welshmen hurled themselves against in vain.' The celebrations of the victors were lengthy and well deserved.

Welsh and All Black forwards battle for supremacy.

LLANELLY   1924/25

Tuesday 2 December 1924
Stradey Park, Llanelly
Won 8-3

The All Blacks were suffering from some severe bumps and bruises after their match with Wales but still included nine players from the Test match, including six forwards, for their first visit to Stradey Park. Neil McGregor dropped out shortly before kick-off to be replaced by Lui Paewai. Mark Nicholls was also injured, but Bert Cooke played, although against the instructions of his doctor. Brian McCleary played for the first time since the match at Cambridge. Llanelly chose an eight-man pack and included internationals Ernie Finch, Albert Jenkins and Cliff Williams, who had played in the international three days earlier, plus Dai John, Gwyn Francis and William Jones, who were also capped players. Arthur John and Will Lewis later played for Wales. They had won 13 of their 17 games to date.

LLANELLY	NEW ZEALAND
E. Thomas	G. Nepia
E. Finch	A.H. Hart
A.E. Jenkins (Capt.)	H.W. Brown
W.J. Davies	K.S. Svenson
E. Evans	A.E. Cooke
D.E. John	L. Paewai
A. John	W.C. Dalley
Forwards:	Forwards:
W. Hopkins	W.R. Irvine
W.J. Jones	B.V. McCleary
F. Harries	R.R. Masters
E. Phillips	C.J. Brownlie
C. Williams	M.J. Brownlie
R. Evans	L.F. Cupples
G. Francis	J. Richardson
W. Lewis	C.G. Porter (Capt.)

Scorers:
Llanelli: Try: Finch.
New Zealand: Hart, Svenson. Con: Nepia.

Referee: W.J. Llewellyn (Bridgend).
Attendance: 20,000.

Despite their sore bodies, the All Blacks attacked from the kick-off and in the initial stages looked as though they would overrun Llanelly. The All Blacks laid siege to the Llanelly goal line and eventually a hurried touch-kick was gathered by Gus Hart who burst through the first line of defence and sprinted sixty yards for the opening try. George Nepia converted from in front of the posts. Then, after a period of defensive duties, New Zealand scored again. Maurice Brownlie, 'Bull' Irvine, Lui Paewai and Bill Dalley created an opening for 'Snowy' Svenson to score a fine try in the corner. The conversion failed. Llanelly had the best of the rest of the half and close to the break Ernie Finch took a quick lineout in the New Zealand 25 and scored an unconverted try, brilliantly escaping the clutches of Nepia in the process. It was 8-3 to New Zealand at half-time.

Llanelly pressed constantly during the second half but the New Zealand defence held out. The partisan crowd cheered and shouted loudly but, despite this encouragement, Llanelly were unable to score. It was a fine second-half performance by the Welsh club but the New Zealand defence was equal to anything they threw at it. Paewai and Read Masters were magnificent for the All Blacks. There was no further score and New Zealand became the first touring side to emerge from Wales with their unbeaten record intact.

Bert Cooke received a presentation recognising his Welsh heritage – his parents came from Llanelly.

EAST MIDLANDS   1924/25

Saturday 6 December 1924
County Cricket Ground,
Northampton
Won 31-7

The All Blacks returned to England to take on the East Midlands. The home side was not considered strong, but the All Blacks believed they would provide a difficult challenge. Their suspisions were confirmed when East Midlands scored first. New Zealand attacked from the kick-off, but a move broke down and the Midlands counter-attacked, culminating in outside half Bobby Jones scoring a try. The conversion attempt from full-back Charles Churchill missed. New Zealand responded with a try from Steel after a move in which the All Blacks' backs passed accurately and at pace. Nepia converted but failed to

EAST MIDLANDS	NEW ZEALAND
C.J. Churchill (Bedford)	G. Nepia
L.A.R. Fensome (Bedford)	F.W. Lucas
D. Williams (Northampton)	H.W. Brown
W.R.B. Dodgson (Northampton)	J. Steel
P. Johnstone (Bedford)	A.E. Cooke
R. Jones (Northampton)	N.P. McGregor
S.H. Townell (Harlequins, Capt.)	J.J. Mill
W.H. Weston (Northampton)	Forwards:
Forwards:	W.R. Irvine
A.E. Luck (Northampton)	Q. Donald
R. Webb (Northampton)	C.J. Brownlie
T. Harris (Northampton)	R.R. Masters
J.C. Benyon (Northampton)	J. Richardson
E. Coley (Northampton)	J.H. Parker
A.H. Greenwood (Bedford)	L.F. Cupples
L.H. Nicholson (Bedford)	C.G. Porter (Capt.)

Scorers:
East Midlands: Try: Jones. DG: Jones.
New Zealand: Tries: Steel (3), Brownlie (2), Brown, Cooke.
Cons: Nepia (5).

Referee: A.E. Freethy (Neath).
Attendance: 16,000.

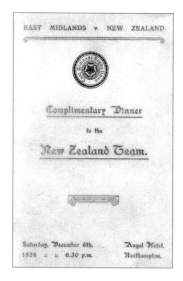

convert the second New Zealand try, scored by Cyril Brownlie after Porter had broken away from a loose maul. The tourists were ahead 8-3 at the break.

After six minutes of the second half, Brownlie scored his second try from a forward rush, then McGregor carved a hole in the Midlands' defence for Brown to score. Nepia converted both scores and, as their pace and fitness told, the All Blacks threatened to cut loose. Jones, who had a fine game for the Midlands, dropped a goal to stem the flow of points. Unconcerned by this, the All Blacks attacked furiously again and Cooke scored another try. This was shortly followed by a second try from Steel who rode two tackles on his way to the line. Desperate to attack, the Midlands ran the ball from within their 25, but the ball went loose and Steel gratefully collected it, scoring his third try of the match. Nepia converted and New Zealand won the game with a scoreline that failed to reflect the contribution of the East Midlands and the tenacity of their tackling.

This match emphasised the fitness of the All Blacks, who scored many of their points in the last quarter of games when their opponents' fitness levels were waning.

WARWICKSHIRE   1924/25

Thursday 11 December 1924
Highfield Road, Coventry
Won 20-0

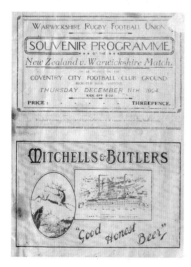

WARWICKSHIRE	NEW ZEALAND
O. Hicks (Coventry)	G. Nepia
J.M. Wale (Coventry)	A.H. Hart
H.J. Pemberton (Coventry, Capt.)	H.W. Brown
F. Wood (Nuneaton)	J. Steel
I. Davies (Nuneaton)	L. Paewai
A.P. Wayte (Richmond)	N.P. McGregor
G.W. Wood (Nuneaton)	W.C. Dalley
Forwards:	Forwards:
T. Carter (Coventry)	W.R. Irvine
T. Coulson (Coventry)	Q. Donald
A.H. Evans (Coventry)	I.H. Harvey
R.V. Howell (Coventry)	C.J. Brownlie
N.J. Pugh (Coventry)	M.J. Brownlie
E.H. Coleman (Nuneaton)	A. White
W.J. Streather (Nuneaton)	A.H. West
C.W. Streather (Nuneaton)	C.G. Porter (Capt.)

Scorers:
New Zealand: Tries: Steel (3), Paewai, Hart, McGregor.
Con: Nepia.

Referee: T. Bradburn (Lancashire).
Attendance: 25,000.

New Zealand took to the field of an association football ground for the fifth time on tour. This time the hosts were Coventry City FC, and the tourists considered it the best pitch they had played on to date. Warwickshire were at something of a low ebb, largely because the Coventry club was particularly weak at the time. The county had struggled to win a match for some time. They included the Wood brothers, 'Pedlar' and Frank, from the Nuneaton club.

The opening exchanges were close and tight and Warwickshire were close to scoring, but Steel broke the deadlock after thirteen minutes when some confident passing in the New Zealand backs created space for the West Coast wing to score a try. Nepia converted. The second New Zealand try came after McGregor broke through the Warwickshire defence and linked with Brown to put Hart in. Nepia missed the conversion. At half-time it was 8-0 to the All Blacks.

Paewai was the next try-scorer after Dalley had made a run from a scrum. The Hawke's Bay five-eighth touched down between the posts, but the erratic kicking form that had periodically plagued Nepia during the tour returned and he missed the conversion. He also missed converting the next try, scored by Steel after the sharp-eyed wing gathered a loose ball near the Warwickshire goal line. Dalley and McGregor interpassed for the latter to score the next try, and finally Steel scored again close to the end of the match after the New Zealand backs had handled at pace. Steel attempted the conversion but suffered the same luck as Nepia and missed. Steel's second successive hat-trick of tries was a fine achievement and New Zealand won without being overstretched. Warwickshire battled hard but never threatened the New Zealand line.

The following day the tourists headed to London again and met Lord Ranfurly, who in 1901 had donated the famous Ranfurly Shield for New Zealand provincial rugby. Ranfurly had seen the 1905 team play at Blackheath.

COMBINED SERVICES 1924/25

Saturday 13 December 1924
Twickenham, London
Won 25-3

The sides were presented to King George V prior to the match. A strong Services team included Robert Millar, the Scottish wing who had scored twice against the All Blacks for London Counties the previous month. Also included was Irish captain Harry Stephenson. Ernest Gardner, Bill Luddington, Alfred Aslett, John Worton and John Forrest were, or later became, England internationals. William 'Horsey' Browne played for Ireland later in the season.

New Zealand opened the scoring with a try after five minutes when Steel touched down between the posts for White to convert. The New Zealand forwards took control, and following a period where they were close to the Services line, McGregor

COMBINED SERVICES	NEW ZEALAND
Lt-Commdr A.E. Thomson (Royal Navy)	G. Nepia
Lieut H.W.V. Stephenson (Royal Navy)	K.S. Svenson
Lieut A.R. Aslett (Army)	F.W. Lucas
S/Lieut J.A.S. Coutts (Army)	J. Steel
Lieut R.K. Millar (Army)	A.E. Cooke
Lieut J.R.B. Worton (Army)	N.P. McGregor
Sq. Ldr J.C. Russell (RAF, Capt.)	J.J. Mill
Forwards:	Forwards:
R/P/O W.E.G. Luddington (Royal Navy)	W.R. Irvine
Marine E.R. Gardner (Royal Navy)	Q. Donald
Lieut J.A. Ross (Army)	R.R. Masters
Lieut G.N. Loriston-Clarke (Royal Navy)	J. Richardson
Lieut J.W. Forrest (Royal Navy)	M.J. Brownlie
F/L J.S. Chick (RAF)	A. White
Lieut T.G. Rennie (Army)	A.H. West
S/Lieut W.F. Browne (Army)	C.G. Porter (Capt.)

Scorers:
Combined Services: PG: Forrest.
New Zealand: Tries: Lucas (3), Steel (2), Masters, Richardson.
Cons: Nepia, White.

Referee: F.C. Potter-Irwin (London).
Attendance: 25,000.

and Cooke combined to create a chance for Fred Lucas. The Auckland centre scored close to the corner and the conversion attempt hit the crossbar. The Combined Services trimmed the lead when Forrest kicked a penalty from halfway into a strong wind but they then lost the influential Geoffrey Loriston-Clarke with a serious injury. New Zealand went in at the break 8-3 ahead.

Whereas the first half was close, the second period was dominated by New Zealand. Brownlie gathered the kick-off at top speed and passed to Richardson. He threw a long pass to his backs, each of whom drew his man to give Lucas space to run in for his second try of the match. It was a fine try and drew loud applause from the crowd. The Services hung on for a few minutes then, as the All Blacks applied pressure, the home side made mistakes. A poor clearance kick was well fielded by Read Masters, who scored. The desire to run the ball was strong; another long pass from Richardson to McGregor was capitalised upon and through good passing, Steel was able to score a further try. Nepia converted. The

Right: *Cliff Porter is presented to King George V. Jock Richardson is to Porter's right.*

next New Zealand try was scored when the ball was moved to Svenson. He ran outside his opposing wing and made good ground before drawing the cover and passing inside to Lucas for a fine try. Svenson and Lucas combined well for the final try of the match, scored by the supporting Richardson.

New Zealand scored 7 tries against a tough side. There was considerable satisfaction and the All Blacks' management felt it was one of the best wins of the tour. Royal Navy and Devon forward Luddington scored the first points in an international at Murrayfield when he kicked a penalty for England later in the season. He was killed on active service in the Mediterranean in June 1940. Tom Rennie, an Army Major-General who had trials for Scotland, was killed in action March 1945. Geoffrey Loriston-Clarke, known as 'Lorriker', was forced to withdraw from the forthcoming England trial as a result of the three broken ribs and broken colar bone he suffered during the game. He later captained HMS *Wellington*.

HAMPSHIRE   1924/25

Wednesday 17 December 1924
Fratton Park, Portsmouth
Won 22-0

HAMPSHIRE	NEW ZEALAND
C.M. Evan-Thomas (Richmond)	G. Nepia
H.W.V. Stephenson (United Services)	A.H. Hart
R. Hamilton-Wickes (Harlequins)	F.W. Lucas
J.A.S. Coutts (Army)	K.S. Svenson
W.H. Wood (United Services)	A.E. Cooke
D. MacDonald (London Scottish)	N.P. McGregor
C.A. Kershaw (RNC)	J.J. Mill
Forwards:	Forwards:
P.B.R.W. William-Powlett (Navy)	W.R. Irvine
T.G. Rennie (Army)	Q. Donald
K.L. Herbert (Army)	I.H. Harvey
W.G. Agnew (United Services, Capt.)	M.J. Brownlie
D. Orr-Ewing (United Services)	A.H. West
J.W. Forrest (United Services)	A. White (Capt.)
J.S. Chick (RAF)	L.F. Cupples
J.A. Ross (Army)	J.H. Parker

Scorers:
New Zealand: Tries: McGregor (2), Donald, Cooke, Svenson. Cons: Nepia, White. PG: Nepia.

Referee: H.E.B. Wilkins (Kent).
Attendance: 13,000.

Due the enormous demand for tickets the match was switched from the United Services ground to Fratton Park, home of Portsmouth Football Club, who were paid the princely sum of £75 for its use.

Early fog cleared but, although it was football pitch, the ground was very heavy after torrential rain earlier in the week. Six of the players put through the mill by the All Blacks for the Combined Services were selected for Hampshire, with Irishman Harry Stephenson also having another go. The county side had enjoyed a 23-0 win over Eastern Counties the previous week and had lost only one game in the season.

It was honours even at first, but David Orr-Ewing, a lieutenant in the Royal Navy, dislocated a shoulder in the first half and had to be carried off. Outside half Donald MacDonald badly bruised a knee but carried on. Five minutes before half-time, Cooke was given space and interpassed with Svenson. Their attack went close to the Hampshire line when the ball was passed to Quentin Donald, who barged over for the opening try. Soon afterwards Cooke scored a try that White converted. New Zealand were 8-0 ahead at half-time.

In the second half Cecil Kershaw, whose quick passing had impressed the tourists, came close to scoring, but the New Zealand defence refused to yield. Instead, New Zealand attacked and Cooke and Parker created an opportunity for McGregor to score, his momentum taking him through a tackle. Nepia missed the conversion but later kicked a penalty. The fog, which had caused concern before the game, began to descend again and shortly before the end of the match the referee spoke to both captains but play continued. In the gloom Svenson and McGregor scored tries, the latter converted by Nepia. In the dying minutes Andrew 'Son' White, the acting All Blacks' captain, damaged his shoulder and left the field.

Scrum-half Kershaw, known as 'K', won sixteen caps for England. A submariner during the First World War, he later became a captain in the Royal Navy and was involved in planning the D-Day landings of 1944. He also fenced for Britain in the 1920 Olympic Games. 'Big hearted Dave' Orr-Ewing later served on HMS *Hood* and after the war was influential in establishing rugby in Malta. The All Blacks took time out to enjoy a well-deserved break after this match, which included Christmas at the Royal Hotel in Deal.

LONDON COUNTIES 1924/25

Saturday 27 December 1924
Rectory Field, Blackheath
Won 28-3

LONDON COUNTIES	NEW ZEALAND
R.K. Mellhuish (OMT)	G. Nepia
R.H. Hamilton-Wickes (Harlequins)	K.S. Svenson
H.P. Jacob (Harlequins)	A.E. Cooke
V.G. Davies (Harlequins)	J. Steel
J.C. Gibbs (Harlequins)	M.F. Nicholls
A.L. Gracie	N.P. McGregor
(Manchester & Harlequins, Capt.)	J.J. Mill
W.I.N. Strong (Blackheath)	Forwards:
Forwards:	W.R. Irvine
F.W.R. Douglas (Richmond)	Q. Donald
J.H.F. Edminston (Blackheath)	R.R. Masters
R.J. Hillard (Old Paulines)	C.J. Brownlie
R.G. Howell (Harlequins)	M.J. Brownlie
R.C. Hare (Old Blues)	L.F. Cupples
H.P. Marshall (Harlequins)	J. Richardson (Capt.)
W.F. Browne (Army)	J.H. Parker
H.L. Price (Harlequins)	

Scorers:
London Counties: Try: Gibbs.
New Zealand: Tries: C Brownlie (3), M. Brownlie, Donald, Irvine, Parker, Richardson. Cons: Nicholls (2).

Referee: T.J. Bradburn (Lancashire).
Attendance: 15,000.

This match was a triumph for the will of the rugby player to play open rugby when the conditions up against him. The match was played in pouring rain and a gale, with the pitch best described as a quagmire at kick-off, from which point it deteriorated. Despite this, both the London Counties and New Zealand teams took to the Rectory Field with the intention of moving the ball whenever the opportunity presented itself. Only Dickie Hamilton-Wickes in the backs and forward 'Horsey' Browne, a late replacement for Ronald Cove-Smith, remained in the side that had faced New Zealand at Twickenham earlier in the tour. Browne was facing the All Blacks for the fourth time.

The teamwork of the New Zealanders was immediately apparent, in contrast to that of the scratch London side. The All Blacks' pack took control and after fifteen minutes Cyril Brownlie opened the scoring, after Cooke had dislodged the ball when tackling Mellhuish, the London full-back, who gathered his own kick ahead. Nicholls converted. Then the New Zealand forwards passed among themselves in a movement that began close to halfway, and Donald crossed the line for a fine forward try. London were hampered by a leg injury to Leo Price, but they responded to the All Blacks' score in style. The ball was moved to John Gibbs, who had the space and speed to round Svenson. He then sped away and, when faced with the last line of defence in Nepia, he kicked over his head and won the race to the ball for a fine try. Nepia was then seen in attack, making a break that was carried on by the forwards for Maurice Brownlie to score. The score was 11-3 to New Zealand at half-time.

The big New Zealand forwards used their physique to pressurise their opponents in the second half and dominated the game. The outstanding forward was Cyril Brownlie, who crossed for two more tries in the early stages of the period. The Hawke's Bay forward, the biggest player in the tour party, was in the thick of the forward battle, whether in the tight or the loose. Parker was next on the scoresheet when he supported a break by Mill and skidded over for the try. Then the All Blacks' backs made ground with a passing movement that culminated in Richardson scoring another try. Nicholls converted, but conditions were not ideal for goal-kicking and he missed converting the final try of the match, scored by 'Bull' Irvine late in the game after the New Zealand pack pushed the London forwards over their own line.

Despite all the New Zealand tries being scored by the forwards, the backs contributed greatly. Nepia in particular was heroic, as he had been all tour, and his trademark crash tackling had to be utilised on many occasions.

ENGLAND   1924/25

Saturday 3 January 1925
Twickenham, London
Won 17-11

England were regarded as being the All Blacks' biggest challenge on tour. Brough, Gibbs, Kittermaster and Hillard all made their international debuts for England. Excitement was intense and at dawn the queue to pay at the gate was considerable. Despite the return to full fitness of Porter, Richardson remained the New Zealand captain. Parker was in such a rich vein of form the management felt there was no need to change the side. The teams were presented to the Prince of Wales before kick-off.

The match started at pace with fierce clashes between the forwards. Reg Edwards, the Newport prop was again causing difficulties for the tourists. He cleverly moved the England front row one step to the left at engagement which meant the two-man New Zealand front row was under

ENGLAND	NEW ZEALAND
J.W. Brough (Silloth)	G. Nepia
R.H. Hamilton-Wickes (Harlequins)	J. Steel
L.J. Corbett (Bristol)	A.E. Cooke
V.G. Davies (Harlequins)	K.S. Svenson
J.C. Gibbs (Harlequins)	M.F. Nicholls
H.J. Kittermaster (Oxford University)	N.P. McGregor
A.T. Young (Cambridge University)	J.J. Mill
Forwards:	Forwards:
R. Edwards (Newport)	W.R. Irvine
J.S. Tucker (Bristol)	Q. Donald
A.F. Blakiston (Liverpool)	R.R. Masters
R. Cove-Smith (OMT)	C.J. Brownlie
W.W. Wakefield (Harlequins, Capt.)	M.J. Brownlie
R.J. Hillard (Oxford University)	J. Richardson (Capt.)
G.S. Conway (Rugby)	A. White
A.T. Voyce (Gloucester)	J.H. Parker

Scorers:
England: Tries: Cove-Smith, Kittermaster. Con: Conway.
PG: Corbett.
New Zealand: Tries: Svenson, Steel, M. Brownlie, Parker.
Con: Nicholls. PG: Nicholls.

Referee: A.E. Freethy (WRU).
Attendance: 60,000.

severe pressure. Edwards was rarely far away from any skirmishes. He was censured by the RFU after the game for rough play and was not selected for England again. The referee, had warned both sides about their play but, after eight minutes, the ball went loose at a lineout and he spotted something, called over Cyril Brownlie and sent him off the field. Horrified, Richardson protested but Brownlie took the long trudge into the record books as the first player to be sent off in an international. His walk was undertaken in total silence from the 60,000 crowd. There were no boos nor jeers. Freethy later explained he had seen him kick an England player. After the sending-off, the match settled down. New Zealand, incensed at Brownlie's dismissal, increased their determination to win and the other Brownlie, Maurice, was outstanding for the visitors. However, it was England who scored first when Tom Voyce created the opportunity for Ronald Cove-Smith to score a try. English tails were up and they attacked incessantly, but it was Nepia who saved the day for New Zealand, frequently diving on the ball at the feet of the England forwards with total disregard for his own safety. After half an hour, New Zealand opened their account when Svenson touched down and tie the scores. Five minutes later, Mill nipped down the blind side of a scrum and fed Steel for another try. Nicholls missed both conversions but kicked a penalty when Hillard was caught offside and New Zealand ended the half 9-3 ahead.

England began the second half confidently but the New Zealand defence prevented further scoring. Morrie Brownlie collected a loose ball and barged his way over the line for a try that Nicholls converted. Brownlie was a constant threat to England, Jim Parker went over for a try in the corner and at 17-3 New Zealand seemed home and dry. Then England began to come back. Len Corbett kicked a penalty, electing to drop-kick it. Shortly afterwards, England scored their second try. Dickie Hamilton-Wickes rounded Svenson, drew Nepia and passed to Kittermaster in support, who had enough pace to beat the cover to score a fine try. Conway converted. It was the last score of the game and New Zealand hung on to win. All Black forward Read Masters described it as 'the hardest and most gruelling game I have ever played'.

The match was over and the tour to Britain and Ireland completed. The All Blacks were due to fly to Paris from Croydon Aerodrome after the game for the French matches but bad weather meant they adopted more conventional means and crossed the English Channel by ship. They played twice in France before heading home via British Columbia.

Their legacy was remarkable. In total they played thirty-two matches on tour and were victorious in every game. They also had the extraordinary George Nepia at full-back, who played in every match. Given that he also played on a short six-match tour of Australia and New Zealand before embarking for Britain, his achievement of playing all thirty-eight games is astonishing. They were called 'The Invincibles', and rightly so. Unfortunately, they were not able to become the first New Zealand side to achieve a Grand Slam of victories over the home unions. The Scottish Football Union, still concerned over the financial arrangements of the 1905 tour, had made an agreement with the other home unions that incoming tours would take place under the auspices of the International Rugby Board. When it became clear the RFU was organising the 1924/25 tour they concluded the agreement had been broken and declined the RFU's offer of two games against New Zealand. Scotland, who won the Grand Slam later that season, would have been New Zealand's toughest challenge. It would be over fifty years before a New Zealand side could claim the honour of being 'Grand Slam All Blacks'.

Jim Mill gathers the ball. In the background, referee Albert Freethy is distracted by a squabble between the forwards.

1935/36
NEW ZEALAND TO BRITAIN, FRANCE & CANADA

THE MATCHES

Devon & Cornwall	14 September 1935	Devonport	won 35-6
Midland Counties	19 September 1935	Coventry	won 9-3
Yorkshire & Cumberland	21 September 1935	Bradford	won 14-3
Abertillery & Cross Keys	25 September 1935	Abertillery	won 31-6
Swansea	28 September 1935	Swansea	lost 11-3
Gloucestershire & Somerset	3 October 1935	Bristol	won 23-3
Cheshire & Lancashire	5 October 1935	Birkenhead	won 21-8
Northumberland & Durham	9 October 1935	Gosforth	won 10-6
South of Scotland	12 October 1935	Hawick	won 11-8
Glasgow & Edinburgh	16 October 1935	Glasgow	won 9-8
Combined Services	19 October 1935	Aldershot	won 6-5
Llanelly	22 October 1935	Llanelly	won 16-8
Cardiff	26 October 1935	Cardiff	won 20-5
Newport	31 October 1935	Newport	won 17-5
London Counties	2 November 1935	Twickenham	won 11-0
Oxford University	6 November 1935	Oxford	won 10-9
Hampshire & Sussex	9 November 1935	Bournemouth	won 14-8
Cambridge University	14 November 1935	Cambridge	won 25-5
Leicestershire & East Midlands	16 November 1935	Leicester	won 16-3
SCOTLAND	23 November 1935	Murrayfield	won 18-8
North of Scotland	27 November 1935	Aberdeen	won 12-6
Ulster	30 November 1935	Belfast	drawn 3-3
IRELAND	7 December 1935	Dublin	won 17-9
Mid Districts	12 December 1935	Aberdare	won 31-10
Aberavon & Neath	14 December 1935	Port Talbot	won 13-3
WALES	21 December 1935	Cardiff	lost 13-12
London Counties	26 December 1935	Twickenham	won 24-5
ENGLAND	4 January 1936	Twickenham	lost 13-0
Vancouver	25 January 1936	Vancouver	won 32-0
Victoria (British Columbia)	29 January 1936	Victoria	won 27-3

Played 30, Won 26, Drew 1, Lost 3. Scored: 490 points, Conceded: 183.
In Britain & Ireland: Played 28, Won 24, Drew 1, Lost 3. Scored: 431 points, Conceded: 180.

The New Zealand Tour Party:
G.D.M. Gilbert (West Coast), D. Solomon (Auckland), G.F. Hart (Canterbury), N.A. Mitchell (Southland), N. Ball (Wellington), H.M. Brown (Auckland), C.J. Oliver (Canterbury), J.R. Page (Wellington), T.H.C. Caughey (Auckland), E.W.T. Tindill (Wellington), J.L. Griffiths (Wellington), B.S. Sadler (Wellington), M.M.N. Corner (Auckland), C.S. Pepper (Auckland), D. Dalton (Hawke's Bay),

J. Hore (Otago), G.T.A. Adkins (South Canterbury), W.E. Hadley (Auckland), A. Lambourn (Wellington), W.R. Collins (Hawke's Bay), R.M. McKenzie (Manawatu), R.R. King (West Coast), S.T. Reid (Hawke's Bay), H.F. McLean (Auckland), J.G. Wynyard (Waikato), J.J. Best (Marlborough), A. Mahoney (Bush Districts), J.E. Manchester (Canterbury), F.H. Vorrath (Otago).

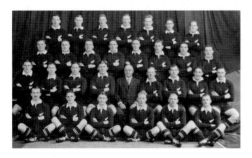

Captain: J.E. Manchester. Vice-Captain: C.J. Oliver. Manager: V.R.S. Meredith.

Leading points scorer: G.D.M. Gilbert – 125 points (116 in Britain & Ireland).
Leading try-scorer: T.H.C. Caughey – 18 tries (14 in Britain & Ireland).
Most appearances: G.D.M. Gilbert – 27 games (26 in Britain & Ireland).

DEVON & CORNWALL   1935/36

Saturday 14 September 1935
Rectory Ground, Devonport
Won 35-6

New Zealand toured Australia in 1934, then waited over a year before they next got together to tour Britain, Ireland and Canada. The 1935/36 tour was managed by the dictatorial Vincent Meredith, and he had a major influence on the make-up of his squad. Meredith ignored several leading players who were known for their forthright views, including half-back Frank Kilby, who had successfully captained New Zealand on tours to Australia in 1932 and 1934. Kilby's omission was all the more remarkable as there didn't appear to be a natural successor and captaincy was thus given to Jack Manchester, a high-class loose forward but one who had little experience of the role. Only eight of the side that drew their last international with

DEVON & CORNWALL	NEW ZEALAND
C.R. Knapman (Devonport Services)	G.D.M. Gilbert
G.R. Matthews (Torquay Athletic)	G.F. Hart
C.W. Ford (St Luke's College, Exeter)	C.J. Oliver
R. Jennings (Redruth, Capt.)	N. Ball
R.S. Hurdon (Plymouth Albion)	T.H.C. Caughey
D.T. Jones (Redruth)	J.R. Page
F. Bone (Redruth)	M.M.N. Corner
Forwards:	Forwards:
C.L. Ashford (Exeter & Richmond)	J. Hore
A.H. Brigstocke (Plymouth Albion)	W.E. Hadley
C.S.H. Webb (Devonport Services)	A. Lambourn
R. Matthews (Penzance)	S.T. Reid
C.S. Scott (Torquay Athletic)	R.R. King
F. Gregory (Redruth)	A. Mahoney
J.R. Spear (Plymouth Albion)	J.E. Manchester (Capt.)
P. Rogers (Redruth)	H.F. McLean

Scorers:
Devon & Cornwall: Try: R. Matthews. PG: Jennings.
New Zealand: Tries: King, Hart, Manchester, Caughey, Ball, Reid. Cons: Gilbert (2). PG: Gilbert (3). DG: Gilbert.

Referee: J. Hughes (London).
Attendance: 20,000.

Australia in 1934 were chosen and only fourteen of that tour party were included. Instead, the selectors searched New Zealand for players who met the management's criteria and consequently the squad included fourteen players who had never represented New Zealand before, and was roundly criticised.

The tour party, after arriving in early September, initially based themselves in Newton Abbot, the Devon town used by the 1905 and 1924 squads. After two weeks' preparation they took the field against a combined Devon & Cornwall side led by centre Roy Jennings, who had been a thorn in the side of New Zealand on the 1930 British Lions tour and had played at loose forward for Cornwall against the Invincibles. Another opponent of the previous New Zealand tourists was Reg Knapman who had played at scrum-half for Devon in 1924. The teams were introduced to Lord Bledisloe, who, when Governor General of New Zealand, had presented the cup for which New Zealand and Australia have since competed. The All Blacks did not to perform the Haka on tour but Devon & Cornwall started the game and the tour got underway.

The first points were scored when full-back Mike Gilbert kicked a penalty goal from close to halfway. He added to this ten minutes later with a drop goal that drew applause from the crowd. The home side attacked and, after being initially repelled, Dick Matthews scored a try. The conversion was missed but Jennings kicked a penalty to keep them within striking distance. To have conceded a try before scoring one themselves was a blow to New Zealand pride. They went directly onto the attack and crisp passing led to the opening try of the tour, second row Ron King scoring for Gilbert to convert. Then five-eighth Pat Caughey made a try for wing George Hart, and Manchester scored close to half-time to see New Zealand 18-6 ahead at the break.

Gilbert kicked two more penalties early in the second half before Caughey broke through the stout Devon & Cornwall defence to score a fine solo try. Charlie Oliver then created an opening for Nelson 'Kelly' Ball to score. New Zealand missed a chance to increase their lead before a home team attack broke down and Tori Reid scored from turned-over ball. Gilbert's conversion concluded the scoring, with the All Blacks winning by the satisfactory scoreline of 35-6, despite hooker Bill Hadley breaking his jaw late in the game.

Although the score was pleasing, it didn't reflect the contribution from the home side, who attacked whenever they had the opportunity, and it masked a problem the All Blacks had in the forwards. Three years previously New Zealand were forced to adopt a three-man front row and the eight-man 3-4-1 scrum formation, but they were still largely unfamiliar with it, although it had been employed in Britain for many years. However, they started the tour with a seven-man scrum with a wing-forward. At the first scrum the home pack pushed the All Blacks' pack back six yards. This continued and, as a consequence, 'loosie' Hugh McLean, who began the match feeding the scrum, was required to join the pack for the scrum. The New Zealand forwards weren't helped by a leg injury to Athol 'Tonk' Mahoney, which restricted his play and also ruled him out for several weeks.

MIDLAND COUNTIES   1935/36

Thursday 19 September 1935
Coundon Road, Coventry
Won 9-3

The All Blacks moved on to Coventry for a match with a Midlands selection at the Coventry club ground. The All Blacks had beaten Warwickshire in 1924 at Highfield Road, the home of the city's soccer club. A Midlands XV had defeated the South Africans four years earlier but that side was based around the Leicester club. The 1935 side that was built around the Coventry team, a club with a substantial forward unit. Ten of the Coventry side had been in the Warwickshire side that lost the semi-final of the County Championship the previous season. The Midlands' side included Prince Alexander Obolensky, in the first of 3 games he played against the tourists, and

MIDLAND COUNTIES	NEW ZEALAND
R.A. Harris (Coventry)	G.D.M. Gilbert
Prince A. Obolensky (Oxford University)	G.F. Hart
H. Kenyon	C.J. Oliver
(Birmingham University & Coventry)	
S.G. Walker (Derby)	N.A. Mitchell
C.K. Thacker (Walsall)	D. Solomon
G. Bayliss (Wolverhampton)	J.R. Page
J.L. Giles (Coventry)	B.S. Sadler
Forwards:	Forwards:
A. Walker (Coventry)	G.T.A. Adkins
A.A. Wyman (Coventry)	D. Dalton
H. Wheatley (Coventry)	A. Lambourn
A.J. Clarke (Coventry)	R.M. McKenzie
P.E. Dunkley (Harlequins, Capt.)	R.R. King
C.E. StG. Beamish (Leicester & RAF)	J.J. Best
S.E.A. Anthony (Old Edwardians)	J.E. Manchester (Capt.)
A.H.G. Purchas (Coventry)	C.S. Pepper

Scorers:
Midlands Counties: PG: Harris.
New Zealand: Tries: Mitchell (2), McKenzie.

Referee: R.J. Hanvey (Cumberland).
Attendance: 15,000.

former Wales full-back Gwyn Bayliss. New Zealand made eight changes to their side and chose Cyril Pepper at number eight. He was to make the rest of his appearances on tour as a prop. Pepper served during the Second World War, was awarded the Military Cross but died at home of wounds in 1943.

This match turned out to be surprisingly difficult for New Zealand. The early part of the game was a close affair before 'Brushy' Mitchell scored his first try of the tour after twenty-five minutes. The conversion was missed but then, late in the half, he charged down a clearance kick and scored a second. This conversion was also awry but New Zealand led 6-0 at half-time. The Midlands' only threat had been a fine run from speedy wing Charles 'C.K.' Thacker.

The second half was another tight affair and, as the game went into its closing minutes, no further score looked likely. Then Mitchell gathered the ball and sped down the touchline, drew the home full-back and passed to the supporting Rod McKenzie for the Manawatu forward to score the third try. The conversion was again missed, but on the stroke of full time, Coventry full-back Harris kicked a penalty to put the Midlands on the scoreboard. New Zealand had won but it had been a difficult game. They also lost 'Rusty' Page during the match with a knee injury, which effectively ruled him out of the rest of the tour, the Wellington five-eighth only playing once more and being forced to retire from the game when he returned home.

New Zealand's problem was the formation of their forwards for set-piece play. On their previous tours they had adopted a seven-man diamond scrum with a wing-forward, but there had been some difficult games on the Invincibles' tour, Now, a decade on, the All Blacks struggled to adopt the the eight-man scrum that was the norm elsewhere.

YORKSHIRE & CUMBERLAND 1935/36

Saturday 21 September 1935
Lidget Green, Bradford
Won 14-3

It was a wet and miserable day and anticipating one of their easier games the All Blacks took the opportunity to field an eight-man scrum.

The home players had played little rugby before the match but proved to be committed even without Maurice Bullus, the injured Headingley forward. After an initial quarter during which New Zealand gradually took control, Eric Tindill broke from a scrum and passed to Cyril Pepper to score. Mike Gilbert failed to convert. This spurred the home side into action and they dominated the remainder of the half, captain Dick Kingswell exhorting his troops to score. New Zealand just held out under pressure to reach the break 3-0 ahead.

Early in the second half All Blacks' half-

YORKSHIRE & CUMBERLAND	NEW ZEALAND
T. Kilmartin (Otley)	G.D.M. Gilbert
L.A. Booth (Headingley)	N. Ball
J.C. Boyce (Bradford)	J.L. Griffiths
A. Bush (Kendal)	N.A. Mitchell
B. Hooton (Kendal)	T.H.C. Caughey
E.F. Simpson (Bradford)	E.W.T. Tindill
R.M.A. Kingswell (Headingley, Capt.)	M.M.N. Corner
Forwards:	Forwards:
P.E. Hepworth (Wakefield)	G.T.A. Adkins
G.S. Cottington (Headingley)	A. Lambourn
A. Horner (Skipton)	C.S. Pepper
R. Messenger (Silloth)	S.T. Reid
J.S. Mellor (Huddersfield Old Boys)	W.R. Collins
R. Leigh (Otley)	F.H. Vorrath
W. McC. Ross (Millom & Instonians)	J.E. Manchester (Capt.)
J. Back (Kendal)	H.F. McLean

Scorers:
Yorkshire & Cumberland: Try: Boyce.
New Zealand: Tries: Caughey (2), Pepper. Cons: Corner.
PG: Gilbert.

Referee: J.W. Lock (Somerset).
Attendance: 16,000.

back Merv Corner raced away from a scrum, showing the defence a clean pair of heels before the cover came across. By then he had covered thirty yards and had Pat Caughey in support, to whom he passed for the Auckland five-eighth to score a further try. Gilbert missed the conversion but added a penalty shortly afterwards before pressure on the Counties' backs forced a handling error. Mitchell collected the loose ball and quickly passed to Caughey, who scored the try. Corner enjoyed

more success by adding the conversion. New Zealand were dominant. Close to full time Jack Boyce gathered a bouncing ball at pace and ran in for a home try, which was not converted.

New Zealand won a game in which they failed to impress, but their experiment with the eight-man scrum meant this was to be the preferred option from this point onward. Yorkshire and Cumberland had contrasting success in the County Championship. Cumberland only won one game, a close win over Cheshire, while Yorkshire's narrow defeat to eventual Championship runners-up Northumberland denied them the chance to play in the final. England international Lewis Booth, who played on the wing, later joined the Royal Air Force but lost his life in June 1942.

Jack Manchester leads the All Blacks onto the pitch at Bradford.

ABERTILLERY & CROSS KEYS   1935/36

**Wednesday 25 September 1935
Abertillery Park, Abertillery
Won 31-6**

New Zealand ventured into Wales for the first time on tour to take on the combined Monmouthshire valley clubs. At the time both sides had tough packs of forwards and the combined unit was thought likely to provide the tourists with a challenge in tight play. There was great interest in the match, the first time the All Blacks had played in Wales away from the coastal clubs. Kick-off was scheduled to at 4 p.m. to allow miners to finish the day shift and get to the ground, and two of the home team played in the game having toiled underground earlier in the day. Abertillery & Cross Keys were forced to make a late change when Rees Fildes of Abertillery withdrew with illness and Hector Berrow was brought into the

ABERTILLERY & CROSS KEYS	NEW ZEALAND
R.G. Brown (Cross Keys)	G.D.M. Gilbert
T. Jones (Cross Keys)	H.M. Brown
I. Jones (Cross Keys)	C.J. Oliver (Capt.)
I. Richards (Abertillery)	G.F. Hart
B. George (Abertillery)	T.H.C. Caughey
H. Richardson (Abertillery, Capt.)	E.W.T. Tindill
C. Thornbury (Cross Keys)	B.S. Sadler
Forwards:	Forwards:
E. Jones (Abertillery)	G.T.A. Adkins
G. Morgan (Abertillery)	A. Lambourn
V. Yearsley (Cross Keys)	C.S. Pepper
T.G. Williams (Cross Keys)	W.R. Collins
W.S. Ward (Cross Keys)	R.R. King
K. Jones (Cross Keys)	R.M. McKenzie
H. Norster (Abertillery)	J.G. Wynyard
H. Berrow (Abertillery)	H.F. McLean

Scorers:
Abertillery & Cross Keys: PGs: Brown (2).
New Zealand: Tries: Brown (2), Caughey (2), Hart, McKenzie, King. Cons: Oliver (4), Gilbert.

Referee: J.W. Faull (Swansea).
Attendance: 20,000.

side. They included internationals Trevor 'Tabber' Williams and Bill Ward in the second row. Back-row forward Harold Norster's great-nephew Robert played for Cardiff against the All Blacks in 1978 and 1980, and captained Wales against New Zealand in Christchurch in 1988. There were seven changes to the All Blacks' side from the game in Bradford, with Jim Wynyard and Henry Brown making their debuts.

The New Zealand pack had a fine afternoon against a disjointed home selection. Behind the forwards, half-back Joey Sadler was outstanding. Eight minutes into the game, he made a dash from a lineout close to halfway, which led to George Hart scoring the opening try following a break by Pat Caughey. Then Rod McKenzie scored after the New Zealand pack had controlled a foot-rush from the halfway line. Charlie Oliver converted, and then was on hand to continue another Caughey break and put Henry Brown in for a try. Caughey himself scored the fourth New Zealand try after a rebounded fly-kick was recovered. The All Blacks' second five-eighth then scored again in support of Brown, with Oliver converting both. At the end of a stunning first half, New Zealand led 21-0.

The New Zealand backs were far superior to their sluggish opponents who had only had one training session. The All Blacks also tackled ferociously and on several occasions the Welsh side was repelled. Home full-back Reg Brown eventually kicked 2 penalty goals either side of a try by Ron King, which was created by Mike Gilbert and Oliver. Henry Brown scored his second try for New Zealand. Oliver and Gilbert converted for a satisfying win.

Abertillery & Cross Keys battled hard and their

The Abertillery & Cross Keys XV. From left to right, back row: C. Berrow, W. Ward, T. Williams, C. Veysey, H. Norster, C. Morgan. Seated: R. Brown, E. Berrow, B. George, H. Richardson (captain), G. Woodhouse, K. Jones, I. Jones. In front: C. Thornbury, I. Griffiths. Inset: T. Jones.

loose forwards played well, but the difference was behind the scrum. The All Blacks had been able to win sufficient ball for Sadler to dictate play. Cross Keys went on to win the Welsh club championship the same season.

SWANSEA 1935/36

Saturday 28 September 1935
St Helen's, Swansea
Lost 11-3

Swansea had won their first 3 games of the season before losing 3-0 at Cardiff. Colin Davies and Welsh international Tom Day were injured in this defeat, and did not recover in time to face the All Blacks. The Swansea selectors employed their customary policy of the time, inviting 'exiled' players back for important matches. Thus, Edryd Jones played at full-back and international centre Claud Davey, then a Sale player, was also included. The half-backs, Davies and Tanner, both destined to play for Wales, were still school pupils. Davey was the only current Welsh cap in the side. Tanner and forwards Tarr and Payne were to make their Welsh debuts against the All Blacks later in the tour, while skipper Edgar Long was also a future international. The All Blacks altered their original selection on the morning of the match, Charlie Oliver pulling out with a torn thigh muscle. His place went to Mike Gilbert, while David Solomon was full-back.

SWANSEA	NEW ZEALAND
E. Jones	D. Solomon
G. Davies	N. Ball
C. Davey	G.D.M. Gilbert
R. Williams	N.A. Mitchell
G. Griffiths	T.H.C. Caughey
W.T.H. Davies	E.W.T. Tindill
H. Tanner	M.M.N. Corner
Forwards:	Forwards:
H. Payne	G.T.A. Adkins
D.J. Tarr	A. Lambourn
G. Taylor	C.S. Pepper
D. Hunt	W.R. Collins
J. White	R.R. King
D. White	J.E. Manchester (Capt.)
W. Harris	J.G. Wynyard
E.C. Long (Capt.)	H.F. McLean

Scorers:
Swansea: Tries: Davey (2), Hunt. Con: Harris.
New Zealand: Try: Ball.

Referee: F.J. Phillips (Pontardulais).
Attendance: 30,000.

Although the Swansea pack was lighter, the home forwards won a lot of ball from set pieces. This allowed the young half-backs to settle into their normal pattern of play and the New Zealand line was soon under threat. Wilf Harris was short with a penalty attempt, and Tanner narrowly wide with a drop goal, before Gilbert attempted a huge penalty from inside his own half, that only just missed the target. Ball put in a good run, before a dropped pass halted the move, Caughey came close to scoring and Gilbert missed a long-range shot, but Swansea scored first when Hunt forced his way

Willie Davies attacks, with his cousin Haydn Tanner inside. Davies and Tanner were instrumental in inflicting defeat upon New Zealand.

over for a try following a lineout. Harris missed the conversion, but Swansea scored again almost immediately. Tanner sent a long, fast pass out to Davies, who swerved past Tindill and, faced with only Solomon to beat, sent a lovely pass to Davey who scored. This time Harris converted and Swansea led 8-0 after half an hour. After these setbacks, the New Zealand forwards raised their game and attacked the Swansea line. Gilbert burst through the defence after a lineout, passing to Ball who had an easy run to the line. Gilbert failed to convert. A third Swansea try followed before half-time. Davies made another exciting break after Swansea had won a lineout, before handing on to Ron Williams, who sent Davey in for a brilliant try. Harris missed another easy conversion, but the All Whites led the All Blacks 11-3 at the break.

Rain made handling difficult in the second half, and the tourists' forwards tried in vain to break through the defence, which was well organised by the strong-tackling Davey. The visitors rearranged their back division but still the home defence held firm. Play moved from end to end, but there was no further scoring and on the final whistle Swansea to celebrated the first victory by a club side over New Zealand.

Much was made after the match of the outstanding play of the young Swansea half-backs. Tanner had tormented New Zealand half-back Merv Corner with his darting runs, and Davies had shown many touches of brilliance that belied his tender years. Edgar Long had led his forwards superbly and Joe and Dai White gave Jack Manchester and James Wynyard a difficult time. Writing in their book of the tour, Oliver and Tindill referred to the referee, Mr Phillips of Pontardulais, as 'shocking' and 'very weak'. In general though, the All Blacks accepted this shock defeat gracefully, although Manchester famously stated: 'Don't tell them at home that we were beaten by a pair of schoolboys.'

GLOUCESTERSHIRE & SOMERSET 1935/36

Thursday 3 October 1935
Memorial Ground, Bristol
Won 23-3

New Zealand desperately needed to get the tour back on the road after the defeat at Swansea and the home combination feared a backlash, even though Gloucestershire had won the County Championship three times in the early 1930s and were runners-up in 1934, while Somerset were runners-up the previous season. They were captained by Ronald 'Gerry' Gerrard, the Bath and England centre who was killed in Libya in 1943 when serving with the Royal Engineers. The All Blacks made the most of the extra day given to them by the schedule, which meant this

GLOUCESTERSHIRE & SOMERSET	NEW ZEALAND
H. Broughton (Gloucester & Gloucestershire)	G.D.M. Gilbert
W.V. Shepherd (Leicester & Gloucestershire)	G.F. Hart
F.C. Edwards (Gloucester & Gloucestershire)	C.J. Oliver
R.A. Gerrard (Bath & Somerset, Capt.)	N.A. Mitchell
H. Sherman (Bristol & Somerset)	T.H.C. Caughey
R.R. Morris (Bristol & Gloucestershire)	J.L. Griffiths
M.S. Hobbs (Bristol & Gloucestershire)	B.S. Sadler
Forwards:	Forwards:
F.W. Williams (Weston & Somerset)	J. Hore
F.W. Tucker (Bristol & Gloucestershire)	A. Lambourn
A.D. Carpenter (Gloucester & Gloucestershire)	C.S. Pepper
P.Z. Henderson (Bristol & Somerset)	R.R. King
R.G. Hurrell (Bristol & Gloucestershire)	W.R. Collins
G. Maunder (Wellington & Somerset)	S.T. Reid
J.K. Watkins (Devonport Services & Somerset)	J.E. Manchester (Capt.)
J. Price (Taunton & Somerset)	F.H. Vorrath

Scorers:
Gloucestershire & Somerset: Try: Watkins
New Zealand: Tries: Hore, Manchester, Hart, Mitchell, Caughey.
Cons: Gilbert (2). DG: Caughey.

Referee: E. Holmes (Durham).
Attendance: 20,000.

game was played on a Thursday. They licked their wounds and trained especially hard to improve the play of their forwards and they chose a substantial pack for the game.

It was one of the forwards who opened the scoring when Bill Hore touched down after a scramble on the home line. Shortly after, a fine break by 'Did' Vorrath led to a try by skipper Manchester, which was converted by Gilbert. Pat Caughey then dropped a goal for the All Blacks before a slick three-quarter move put Hart into space and his pace took him past the defence to score a fine try in the corner. The conversion was missed but New Zealand were 15-0 ahead at the break and the home side feared a hiding in the second half. Gloucester forward 'Bumps' Carpenter later said: 'at half-time we thought we were going to be badly beaten.'

The home pack was more competitive in the second half but despite this Mitchell scored another try after an orthodox three-quarter movement was completed accurately and at pace. Gilbert converted from the touchline. Then the Gloucestershire & Somerset pack burst through and, after a foot-rush in which they displayed fine dribbling skills, John 'Watty' Watkins scored an unconverted try. Once again the All Blacks, backs showed how dangerous they were when Caughey broke through and beat several players on a spectacular run for a superb individual try, which brought great applause from the crowd. Oliver attempted the conversion, but missed, and Gilbert later missed a penalty, but it was a satisfying return to winning ways for the tourists. They didn't have things entirely their own way up front but the backs were outstanding.

The Gloucestershire & Somerset side included Ronnie Morris, a former Wales international. Morris was a fine player who later won a further cap and became the first Bristol player to play for Wales. He captained Gloucestershire to the County Championship title in 1937 and after his playing days were over he became a leading administrator with his club until the mid-1960s.

From this point onwards, New Zealand had a tendency to select the strongest available side for their games, no doubt fuelled by criticism from home and a determination to ensure they didn't suffer the ignominy of defeat again. This also caused some staleness in leading players in the last weeks of the tour.

LANCASHIRE & CHESHIRE   1935/36

Saturday 5 October 1935
Upper Park, Birkenhead
Won 21-8

Lancashire were the reigning County Champions and, with that side enhanced with the leading Cheshire players, the combined counties were expected to present the All Blacks with one of their toughest games in England. The XV included many current or future internationals: Watcyn Thomas and Claud Davey of Wales, plus England players Jack Heaton, Roy 'Bus' Leyland, Joe Mycock, Bert Toft, Henry Fry and Hal Sever, who made a try-scoring debut for England against New Zealand at the end of the tour. The threat was partially recognised by the All Blacks, who shuffled their pack for the game but rested Jack Manchester.

LANCASHIRE & CHESHIRE	NEW ZEALAND
R. Horne (Furness)	G.D.M. Gilbert
C. Davey (Sale)	G.F. Hart
J. Heaton (Liverpool University)	C.J. Oliver (Capt.)
R. Leyland (Waterloo)	H.M. Brown
H.S. Sever (Sale)	T.H.C. Caughey
J .Bowker (Furness)	J.L. Griffiths
J.C. Pank (Furness)	B.S. Sadler
Forwards:	Forwards:
J.A. Cooper (Rosslyn Park)	J. Hore
H.B. Toft (Waterloo, Capt.)	A. Lambourn
R.U. Reynolds (Sale)	G.T.A. Adkins
G.P.C. Vallance (Leicester)	R.R. King
E.K. Ashworth (Birkenhead Park)	R.M. McKenzie
J. Mycock (Sale)	S.T. Reid
H.A. Fry (Liverpool)	J.J. Best
W.G. Thomas (Waterloo)	F.H. Vorrath

Scorers:
Lancashire & Cheshire: Try: Sever. Con: Mycock. PG: Mycock.
New Zealand: Tries: Adkins (2), Vorrath, Oliver, Hart.
Cons: Gilbert (3).

Referee: J.H. Holder (Gloucester).
Attendance: 18,000.

They also experimented with a 3-2-3 scrum formation with the flankers packing down against the locks rather than the props. They didn't use this again but concentrated on the 3-4-1 formation for the rest of the tour, and by the end of the tour this practice began to yield good results.

The power of the home side was prevalent early on and, when Sever beat Brown with consummate ease to score a try after five minutes, the All Blacks must have felt they were in for a long afternoon. However, five minutes later the New Zealand forwards powered through the home defence and 'Did' Vorrath scored a try that Mike Gilbert converted. Then acting skipper Charlie Oliver made a break through the centre and passed to Brown, before looping around the wing to score a well-worked try. The confident Oliver then broke through again and created an opportunity for George Hart to score a further try. Gilbert's conversion from the touchline was roundly cheered by the crowd and New Zealand were 13-5 ahead at half-time.

The All Blacks scored another fine try in the second half when Sadler nipped down the blind side of a scrum and passed to Hart. He then swerved inside and found his forwards in support, who passed among themselves before George Adkins scored near the posts for Gilbert to convert. The South Canterbury prop then scored again when collecting a loose ball on the Lancashire & Cheshire 25 and showed outstanding speed to race in for the try. The conversion was missed but the only further score was a penalty from the nineteen-year-old Mycock, who was to earn his England caps after the Second World War.

Lancashire failed to reach the final stages of the County Championship later in the season, losing to Northumberland and Yorkshire. Cheshire were indifferent, but suffered the ignominy of losing 36-3 to Lancashire.

NORTHUMBERLAND & DURHAM   1935/36

Wednesday 9 October 1935
County Ground, Gosforth
Won 10-6

The Counties played 2 trial matches to gain familiarity, but the selection that took the field against the All Blacks was roundly criticised, with each observer noting the absence of one player or another. While recognising that there was a paucity of good backs in this part of England, there was agreement that the pack was big enough to trouble the tourists, whose forwards had so far failed to impress. Commentators from further afield expected New Zealand to win well. Although played on a midweek afternoon, there was considerable interest in the match and the crowds gathered at the Gosforth ground several hours before kick-off.

NORTHUMBERLAND & DURHAM	NEW ZEALAND
E.R. Blench (Tynedale)	D. Solomon
A.C. Harrrison (Hartlepool Rovers)	N. Ball
G.H. Bailey (Old Novos)	C.J. Oliver (Capt.)
T.B. Bland (Tynedale)	H.M. Brown
J.C. Oldroyd (Northern)	T.H.C. Caughey
I.H. McLaren (Durham City)	J.L. Griffiths
C.P.B. Goldson (Northern)	M.M.N. Corner
Forwards:	Forwards:
W. Smith (Ryton)	J. Hore
J.C. Suddes (Tynedale)	A. Lambourn
J.T. Roddham (Gateshead Fell)	C.S. Pepper
A.H. Spence (Sunderland)	W.R. Collins
E. Paulin (Old Novos)	R.M. McKenzie
F. Nicholson (Durham City)	S.T. Reid
J.McD. Hodgson (Northern)	H.F. McLean
A. McLaren (Durham City, Capt.)	J.G. Wynyard

Scorers:
Northumberland & Durham: Tries: Oldroyd, McLaren.
New Zealand: Tries: Ball (2). DG: Griffiths.

Referee: C.H. Gadney (London).
Attendance: 12,000.

In the first half New Zealand took a quick lineout and Nelson Ball ran in for a try. Henry Brown, younger brother of Handley (who toured with the Invincibles), missed the conversion. Shortly after this, the New Zealand pack won loose ball and Corner threw a long pass to Jack Griffiths who dropped a goal. New Zealand were 7-3 ahead at half-time.

In the second half Corner made another blind-side break from a scrum and kicked ahead. Ball followed up and beat full-back Blench to score a try, but the conversion failed. The Counties tried to attack whenever they had good ball and after a good back movement, Jimmy Oldroyd went outside Ball and scored in the corner. The conversion narrowly missed. Unfortunately Oldroyd, who was very quick, rarely saw the ball. Late in the match, Ian McLaren used a dummy and then commendable strength to force his way over for the second home try. Northumberland & Durham finished the game on top but the New Zealand defence was good enough to protect their lead and secure the win.

The All Blacks seemed unimaginative when compared to their predecessors and they appeared to be preoccupied with winning and going through set moves, rather than with the more instinctive play that previous New Zealanders seemed to adopt. It was generally felt this was the worst performance of the tour to date.

SOUTH OF SCOTLAND 1935/36

Saturday 12 October 1935
Mansfield Park, Hawick
Won 11-8

The New Zealanders moved north for their first visit to Scotland for twenty years. Setting up camp at the famous Hydropathic Hotel at Peebles, the tourists were given a civic reception by the local provost and taken on a visit to Sir Walter Scott's house at Abbotsford. For the match against the South of Scotland, the New Zealanders made eight changes from the previous game against Northumberland & Durham, including the return of Jack Manchester. The South of Scotland fielded the best side available, including three internationals, Jock Beattie the captain, Gordon Cottington and Bob Grieve. So far New Zealand's form on tour had been less

SOUTH OF SCOTLAND	NEW ZEALAND
A. Clark (Hawick)	G. Gilbert
A. McKie (Hawick)	G.H. Hart
J. Breckenridge (Hawick)	N.A. Mitchell
W. Fairbairn (Jed-Forest)	N.J. Ball
R.B. Thomson (Gala)	J.L. Griffiths
J. Peden (Hawick)	D. Solomon
T.F. Dorward (Gala)	B.S. Sadler
Forwards:	Forwards:
R.M. Grieve (Kelso)	C.S. Pepper
G.L. Gray (Gala)	J. Hore
G.S. Cottington (Kelso)	G.T. Adkins
J. Beattie (Hawick, Capt.)	R.R. King
R. Cowe (Melrose)	R.M. McKenzie
R.W. Barrie (Hawick)	S.T. Reid
H.S. Aitchison (Kelso)	J.E. Manchester (Capt.)
G.D. Shaw (Gala)	F. Vorrath

Scorers:
South of Scotland: Tries: McKie, Shaw. Con: Shaw.
New Zealand: Tries: Hart, Vorrath. Cons: Gilbert. PG: Gilbert.

Referee: M.A. Allan (Scotland).
Attendance: 10,892.

than impressive and it was felt that the South of Scotland could take them on in the forwards. Four years earlier, the South of Scotland had fought out a stirring 0-0 draw with the touring South Africans and, if they could repeat that performance, then they would have a good chance.

On a fine but overcast afternoon, New Zealand played into a strong wind. After nine minutes, Tommy Dorward flashed the ball from a scrum to Tony McKie, who scored amid great cheering from the large crowd. The lead was short-lived however, and a few minutes later the South defence got into difficulties and George Hart dribbled the ball over the line to score. 'Mike' Gilbert converted from in front of the posts. The South of Scotland forwards took control and brought out some good defensive play from Gilbert, who fell courageously at the feet of the Border forwards. Johnny Breckenridge hit the post from a free kick while 'Brushy' Mitchell, making a rare New Zealand attack, was caught at the

last moment by Fairbairn. There was no further scoring and the visitors led 5-3 at half-time.

With the wind at their backs, the New Zealanders became more involved in the game, although Solomon kept play tight. The South of Scotland broke away and, after hammering on the line for several minutes, the ball was taken over in a forward rush for a score by Duncan Shaw. The same player converted to put his side 8-5 ahead. The All Blacks battled hard and began to win more ball in the loose, but could not make any impact in the scrums. Five minutes from the end, Gilbert kicked a forty-yard penalty to level the scores. Then, with a couple of minutes remaining, Nelson Ball made a good run down the touchline and passed to 'Did' Vorrath for a try wide out. Just before the end, Shaw missed an easy penalty chance and New Zealand escaped.

It was hard on the South of Scotland, who matched the visitors in all aspects and did not deserve to lose. The Border forwards played magnificently, especially in their footwork and also in the scrums, which they dominated. Beattie was an inspiring leader who was ably supported by Shaw, Robert Barrie and Aitchison. The backs were solid enough, but lacked sufficient pace and subtlety to beat the defence. In retrospect, the South of Scotland did not make enough use of the wind in the first half and tried to handle the ball too much instead of keeping it among the forwards. For New Zealand, Gilbert was outstanding in his fielding and kicking, but the visiting backs were rarely seen in attack. The New Zealand forwards appeared rather cumbersome and they were unable to master their lighter opponents, although Vorrath was prominent in the loose. After the match, both teams dined at the Crown Hotel, Hawick, where the visitors watched wide-eyed as the haggis was piped in in traditional style.

GLASGOW & EDINBURGH   1935/36

**Wednesday 16 October 1935
Old Anniesland, Glasgow
Won 9-8**

This was a fast and exciting game that the New Zealanders were again lucky to win, having to rely on their opportunism to see them through. The Combined Cities fielded a strong side with seven international players, including the brilliant half-back pairing of Wilson Shaw and Ross Logan. Played in midweek, the match created great interest and the crowd was estimated at around 11,000 people, with many others locked outside before the kick-off.

The pitch at Anniesland was in excellent condition and the weather was favourable, although there was a strong wind. The visitors opened the scoring after four minutes with a penalty goal by Mike Gilbert. The

GLASGOW & EDINBURGH	NEW ZEALAND
J.M. Kerr (Heriot's FP)	G.D.M. Gilbert
J.E. Forrest (Glasgow Acads)	G.F. Hart
W.C.W. Murdoch (Hillhead HSFP)	N.A. Mitchell
E.C. Hunter (Watsonians)	H.M. Brown
R.N.M. Robertson (Glasgow University)	J.L. Griffiths
R.W. Shaw (Glasgow HSFP, Capt.)	D. Solomon
W.R. Logan (Edinburgh Wanderers)	M.M.N. Corner
Forwards:	Forwards:
H.B. Johnston (Stewart's FP)	J. Hore
P.W. Tait (Royal HSFP)	A. Lambourn
E.J. Oxley (Heriot's FP)	C.S. Pepper
J.D. Lowe (Heriot's FP)	R.R. King
E.F. Hill (Glasgow University)	W.R. Collins
I. MacLachlan (Kelvinside Acads)	H.F. McLean
L.B. Lambie (Glasgow HSFP)	J.E. Manchester (Capt.)
P.L. Duff (Glasgow Acads)	A. Mahoney

Scorers:
Glasgow & Edinburgh: Try: Shaw. Con: Murdoch. PG: Murdoch.
New Zealand: Try: Solomon. PGs: Gilbert (2).

Referee: R.A. Beattie (Watsonians).
Attendance: 11,000.

Cities responded with a series of attacks, but on twenty minutes came a decisive score against the run of play. 'Copey' Murdoch cut through and was almost at the corner flag when he slipped a reverse pass inside for his wing Jimmy Forrest, who unfortunately was not expecting it. 'Brushy' Mitchell intercepted and broke away. Challenged by Jimmy Kerr near the midfield, Mitchell kicked ahead and David Solomon won the ensuing race for the try-line. Gilbert missed the conversion, but it was a bitter blow for the Cities, who did not deserve to go further behind. On thirty minutes, Murdoch drew back 3 points with a penalty goal, but New Zealand led 6-3 at half-time.

In the second half, the Cities took the lead with a superb try. Taking a pass from Logan, Shaw, going at full pace, cut between the New Zealand five-eighths and around Gilbert in a swerving run. Mitchell just managed to tap Shaw's ankles, but he recovered to score between the posts. Murdoch converted to put the Cities 8-6 ahead with fifteen minutes to play. Almost immediately, the Cities infringed and Gilbert kicked a great penalty against the wind to regain the lead. Both sides fought hard in the closing stages, but there was no further scoring.

This was a fine match that could have gone either way. The Cities' back division was in sparkling form and made the New Zealanders work very hard. However, they often lacked composure at crucial moments and threw away three try-scoring opportunities by over-eagerness. Shaw was always dangerous, quick off his mark and made ground with his accurate kicking. His partner Logan had a good game, despite the attentions of the All Blacks forwards. By contrast, the visiting backs were disappointing and showed little determination in their running,

The outstanding Wilson Shaw, regarded by many as the leading Scottish rugby player of the 1930s. Predominantly an outside half, he achieved everlasting fame following his almost single-handed destruction of England in 1938 at Twickenham, which saw Scotland win the Triple Crown.

although they did play well in defence. Gilbert had another solid display at full-back. The New Zealand forwards were much livelier than in previous matches, showing better mobility in the open, but again they were unable to dominate. For the Cities, 'Sam' Oxley was an inspiring pack-leader.

COMBINED SERVICES 1935/36

Saturday 19 October 1935
Command Central Ground,
Aldershot
Won 6-5

A strong Services side, ably led by Tony Novis of the Leicestershire Regiment, was expected to provide the All Blacks with a tough match. The team had 2 warm up games and was well prepared. The weather was appalling, with pouring rain and a very strong wind. This was more likely to hamper the All Blacks than the Combined Services. In the end it ruined the game as a spectacle. The All Blacks welcomed back Bill Hadley and faced Reg Knapman, who had played in the opening match of this and the previous tour.

The match proved to be a dour affair. A sliced clearance kick to touch was deftly

COMBINED SERVICES	NEW ZEALAND
A/B C.R. Knapman (Royal Navy)	G.D.M. Gilbert
Lieut E.J. Unwin (Army)	G.F. Hart
Lieut R. Leyland (Army)	C.J. Oliver (Capt.)
L/S C.Criddle (Royal Navy)	N.A. Mitchell
Lieut A.L. Novis (Army, Capt.)	T.H.C. Caughey
P/O G.A. Walker (RAF)	E.W.T. Tindill
Lieut G.J. Dean (Army)	M.M.N. Corner
Forwards:	Forwards:
Lieut D.A. Kendrew (Army)	J. Hore
Schoolmaster D.J. Tarr (Royal Navy)	W.E. Hadley
Lieut C. O'N. Wallis (Army)	C.S. Pepper
Marine C.S.H. Webb (Royal Navy)	F.H. Vorrath
Lieut N.L. Evans (Royal Navy)	R.R. King
L.A.C. J. Holland (RAF)	J.J. Best
Paymr Lieut J.K. Watkins (Royal Navy)	R.M. McKenzie
Sgt A. Boast (Army)	A. Mahoney

Scorers:
Combined Services: Try: Unwin. Con: Knapman.
New Zealand: Tries: Mitchell, Caughey.

Referee: J.G. Bott (London)
Attendance: 12,000.

caught by 'Brushy' Mitchell, who was running at top speed, and the Southland wing scored wide out. Gilbert, who had missed several earlier penalty kicks at goal, despite the wind behind his back, missed

again. Following a forward rush Caughey scored, but this try also remained unconverted and the All Blacks led 6-0 at half-time.

The Combined Services had the better of exchanges in the second half but the only score came when 'Tinny' Dean nipped away from a scrum and passed to Jim Unwin in support for the try. Knapman's conversion made the final stages close and tense, but the All Blacks hung on to win 6-5.

In a largely forgettable game, the All Blacks were criticised for their uninspired performance and lack of imagination and commitment. Their forwards struggled with the abrasive Combined Services pack and failed to win enough good ball for the backs to run with.

LLANELLY

1935/36

Tuesday 22 October 1935
Stradey Park, Llanelly
Won 16-8

LLANELLY	NEW ZEALAND
G. Bayliss	G.D.M. Gilbert
W.H. Clement	G.F. Hart
E. Davies	C.J. Oliver
R. Jones	N.A. Mitchell
E.L. Jones	T.H.C. Caughey
D.E. John	J.L. Griffiths
R. Smith	B.S. Sadler
Forwards:	Forwards:
E. Evans	J. Hore
B. Evans	W.E. Hadley
W. Williams	A. Lambourn
T.R.F. Harries	R.R. King
J.L. Morgan	F.H. Vorrath
J. Lang	J.E. Manchester (Capt.)
G. Lewis	J.G. Wynyard
I.E. Jones (Capt.)	A. Mahoney

Scorers:
Llanelli: Try: Davies. Con: I. Jones. PG: I. Jones.
New Zealand: Tries: Oliver (2), Caughey, Sadler. Cons: Gilbert (2).

Referee: T.H. Phillips (Pontypridd).
Attendance: 20,000.

Llanelly had only lost one and drawn one of the 9 games they had played during the season, and they were expected to give the tourists a tough game. The Llanelly selectors sprang a surprise by including former Pontypool and Wales player Gwyn Bayliss at full-back. Although he had appeared in some matches for the Scarlets, he was currently living in Wolverhampton and playing his rugby for the Wolverhampton club. He had already faced the All Blacks as an outside half for the Midland Counties in the second game of the tour. Other capped players in the home side were Dai John, who had played against the tourists for Llanelly in 1924, Bryn Evans, Jim Lang, Llanelly skipper Ivor Jones, a 1930 British Lion. Of the remaining players, Bill Clement, Elvet Jones and Emrys Evans were future caps. Clement later served the WRU for many years as its secretary. For New Zealand, Bill Hadley played his first match since fracturing his jaw in the opening game of the tour.

A wet, dismal afternoon greeted the visitors, but they took an early lead when Pat Caughey scored a try after just three minutes. Joey Sadler, who was the outstanding player for the All Blacks, sent out a pass to Jack Griffiths, who handed on to Caughey for the try, which Mike Gilbert converted. Prompted by Sadler's excellent handling of the greasy ball, the tourists' backs produced some attractive rugby, but Llanelly came close to claiming the next score when Elvet Jones put in a good run, only to lose the ball as he was tackled near the line. As the half wore on, the home pack increased in strength, dominating the scrums and lineouts, and a series of forward drives nearly brought a try. However, the New Zealand defence remained impregnable and the half-time score was 5-0 to the visitors. The home side had one chance to score from a penalty, the kick from Ivor Jones falling just under the bar from twenty-five yards.

Three minutes into the second half, Jack Manchester was penalised for offside and Ivor Jones kicked a superb penalty from fifty yards. Then Sadler scored a marvellous individual try for the All Blacks following a clever jinking run. Gilbert could not convert, and the game then degenerated as a series of brawls led to both captains being cautioned by the referee. The next score came from one of several handling errors by Dai John. 'Brushy' Mitchell picked up the loose ball and set off on a run before passing to Manchester. Athol Mahoney and Caughey then continued the move and Charlie Oliver crossed the line for an excellent try, which Gilbert converted. The tourists grew in confidence after this score, and another try soon followed when Caughey drew the defence before passing to Mitchell, who sent Oliver over for his second score of the match. Gilbert missed the conversion, but the All Blacks now led 16-3 and the game was safe. In a frantic final few minutes, a scramble at the other end resulted in a try for Emrys Davies that Ivor Jones converted. Jones missed a late penalty and Oliver came close to scoring his hat-trick just before the end of the game.

This was a hard-earned but well-deserved victory for the tourists, in a game marred by bouts of fighting. Along with Sadler, the undisputed star of the match, Griffiths, Ron King, 'Did' Vorrath and Jack Hore all had good games for the All Blacks, while Elvet Jones was the best player in a rather disappointing Llanelly backline. The tour party could now look forward to the next Welsh challenge, at the Arms Park against Cardiff.

CARDIFF 1935/36

Saturday 26 October 1935
Cardiff Arms Park, Cardiff
Won 20-5

CARDIFF	NEW ZEALAND
T. Stone (Capt.)	G.D.M. Gilbert
A. Bassett	N. Ball
R.W. Boon	C.J. Oliver
H. Edwards	N.A. Mitchell
A.H. Jones	T.H.C. Caughey
H.M. Bowcott	J.L. Griffiths
J. Bowcott	B.S. Sadler
Forwards:	Forwards:
R. Bale	G.T.A. Adkins
J. Regan	W.E. Hadley
V. Osmond	A. Lambourn
N. Rees	R.R. King
H.T. Rees	J.E. Manchester (Capt.)
G. Williams	A. Mahoney
E.V. Watkins	S.T. Reid
L. Spence	H.F. McLean

Scorers:
Cardiff: Try: Osmond. Con: Boon.
New Zealand: Tries: Caughey (2), Mitchell, Reid. Cons: Gilbert (2). DG: Gilbert.

Referee: G. Goldsworthy (Newport).
Attendance: 35,000.

Cardiff had lost 3 and drawn 2 of their previous 12 matches. The side to face the tourists included 1930 British Lion Harry Bowcott, who partnered his brother Jackie at half-back. Harry Bowcott was already a Welsh international, as were Bassett, Boon and Jones. Teenager Eddie Watkins was to make his Welsh debut against New Zealand in December, while Harry Rees received his first cap in 1937. Gwyn Williams was the eldest brother of Bleddyn, a major star of post-war Welsh rugby.

New Zealand took the lead after just three minutes when Cardiff full-back Tommy Stone failed to hold a high kick from Pat Caughey. Tori Reid hacked the loose ball over the line and Caughey followed up his kick to touch down under the posts. Mike Gilbert missed the easiest of conversion attempts, but the tourists gained confidence and continued to attack. Joey Sadler passed to Caughey, who set off on a dangerous run, and then Caughey secured the ball again, putting 'Brushy' Mitchell clear for a thirty-yard run to the line. Gilbert again missed the conversion, but New Zealand led 6-0 after less than ten minutes. Next it was Cardiff's turn to attack, as Jackie Bowcott set off on a long run from a scrum. He tried to chip the ball over Gilbert, but the ploy failed and New Zealand

Autographed centre pages from the match programme.

retrieved the ball. The game continued at great pace, Jones putting in a good run for Cardiff and Bassett preventing a try for Mitchell by bundling him into touch after a good break from Sadler. Gilbert missed a penalty, but another score came soon afterwards when Ball intercepted a wild pass from Boon to Edwards. Ball jinked past three defenders and put Caughey in the clear for his second try, Gilbert at last managing a conversion. Cardiff continued to have as much of the game as the All Blacks, but just before half-time Gilbert collected a loose kick from Harry Bowcott and kicked a drop goal from forty yards giving New Zealand a 15-0 lead at half-time.

New Zealand started the second half with another entertaining attack, but Cardiff got the try their enterprising play deserved when Jackie Bowcott collected a New Zealand fumble and sent Bassett away on a run. As Bassett reached the covering Gilbert he passed to Vic Osmond, who stormed over the line. This was converted by Boon and the Cardiff pack began to dominate. It was Sadler who initiated the final score handing the perfect scoring pass to Reid. Gilbert converted, but even after this Cardiff continued to press for a score. The closest they came to adding further points was when Boon missed a late penalty.

This was a thoroughly entertaining match in which both sides strove to play attacking rugby. Harry Bowcott struggled because of an early knee injury, but his brother played well, as did Edwards. Both George Adkins and Bill Hadley suffered back injuries and were unable to control the New Zealand scrum, but Caughey and Jack Griffiths were always a danger for the visitors, while Ron King and Athol Mahoney were the outstanding All Black forwards. The press was lavish in its praise for this fine New Zealand victory.

NEWPORT   1935/36

Thursday 31 October 1935
Rodney Parade, Newport
Won 17-5

Newport had only lost twice prior to their meeting with the All Blacks, and the club was unbeaten at home. Only two of the side that faced the tourists, Rees and Evans, were Welsh internationals, although Walter Legge, Billy Hopkin, 'Bunner' Travers and Viv Law would all win caps. Wing-forward Jack Wright, an England international, had only made his Newport debut the previous Saturday and was preferred to Welsh international Albert Fear for this game. Scrum-half Jim Hawkins was still in the Newport side after the war. Newport vice-captain and outside half Joe Dunn was unable to face the All Blacks because of injury, as was referee Albert Freethy, who had a twisted knee.

This was an exciting match, played on a pitch that was soaking from the rain that did not stop until just before kick-off. The poor weather had a bad effect

NEWPORT	NEW ZEALAND
W.S.G. Legge	G.D.M. Gilbert
W.H. Hopkin	N. Ball
R. Allen	N.A. Mitchell
A. Gear	G.F. Hart
J. Knowles	J.L. Griffiths
K. Squire	E.W.T. Tindill
J. Hawkins	M.M.N. Corner
Forwards:	Forwards:
T.J. Rees	A. Lambourn
W.H. Travers	J. Hore
V.J. Law	C.S. Pepper
J. Jerman	R.R. King
R. Williams	J.E. Manchester (Capt.)
J.R. Evans (Capt.)	R.M. McKenzie
E. Wright	S.T. Reid
J. Wright	A. Mahoney

Scorers:
Newport: Try: Knowles. Con: J.R. Evans.
New Zealand: Try: Ball. PG: Gilbert. DG: Tindill (2). GFM: McKenzie.

Referee: R.W. Barry (Cardiff).
Attendance: 18,000.

on the attendance, which was only half the number expected. Newport pressed early, but a fine run from Eric Tindill set up the first All Black attack. George Hart came close to scoring but an excellent tackle from Hopkin prevented him. Shortly afterwards, the ball came to Tindill, who dropped a goal. The home pack then took control for a while with Hawkins and Knowles both coming close to scoring, but the only other points in the first half came from a Gilbert penalty, making the half-time score 7-0 to the All Blacks.

The second half began with Hopkin again preventing a possible try, this time by tackling Nelson Ball after good work by Merv Corner. 'Brushy' Mitchell nearly put Ball in the clear, before Tindill dropped his second goal. A brilliant seventy-yard move nearly brought a try for Hart, but Legge cut him off. Unfortunately, Legge was involved in the next New Zealand score, his kick out of defence being claimed as a mark by Rod McKenzie. Although he had never kicked a goal before, McKenzie chose to go for the posts from forty yards out which gave his side a 14-0 lead. Afterwards, Evans missed with a penalty for Newport, and then the All Blacks finally scored a try. The move, started on the New Zealand line, saw Mitchell break up the middle of the field passing to Ball on halfway, and the winger swerved his way to the line. Manchester missed the conversion. Newport finally got some points in the last minute. After Hawkins had missed a penalty, a cross-kick from Squire was collected by Knowles, who scored under the posts, Evans adding the extra points.

New Zealand were worthy winners of the match, despite the fact that they only scored one try. Tori Reid and Athol Mahoney excelled in the pack, while Tindill was also impressive. For Newport, Travers out-hooked Jack Hore in the scrums, while young Ron Williams had a fine game.

LONDON COUNTIES   1935/36

Saturday 2 November 1935
Twickenham, London
Won 11-0

Rugby Football Union
Twickenham

OFFICIAL 2D PROGRAMME

London Counties v. New Zealand
SATURDAY, 2nd NOVEMBER, 1935
Kick-off 3 p.m.
PRICE TWOPENCE

LONDON COUNTIES

V.G.J. Jenkins (London Welsh & Kent)
E.J. Unwin (Rosslyn Park & Army & Eastern Counties)
G.E.C. Hudson (Harlequins & Middlesex)
R.C.S. Dick (Guy's Hospital & Kent)
H.L.V. Faviell (Redruth & Eastern Counties)
P.L. Candler (St Bartholomew's Hospital & Middlesex)
L.B. Bok (Guy's Hospital & Middlesex)
Forwards:
D.A. Kendrew (Leicester & Army & Eastern Counties, Capt.)
D. John (Metropolitan Police & Middlesex)
D.G.H. Gordon (London Scottish & Kent)
D.E. Pratten (Blackheath & Kent)
J.P. Reidy (London Irish & Eastern Counties)
D.H. Swayne (Harlequins & Middlesex)
D.A. Thom (London Scottish & Middlesex)
P.W.P. Brook (Harlequins & Eastern Counties)

NEW ZEALAND

D. Solomon
G.F. Hart

N.A. Mitchell
H.M. Brown
T.H.C. Caughey
E.W.T. Tindill

M.M.N. Corner
Forwards:
J. Hore

W.E. Hadley
C.S. Pepper
R.R. King
J.E. Manchester (Capt.)
S.T. Reid
J.G. Wynyard
A. Mahoney

Scorers:
New Zealand: Tries: Pepper, Caughey, Mitchell. Cons: Corner.

Referee: C.R. Browne (Devon).
Attendance: 30,000.

The London selectors chose a team from a cross-section of county players. They resisted the temptation to base their side on the Harlequins team, which had lost only seven of its 30 games played the previous season. They did include England's Kendrew and Candler, Scotland's Thom and Dick, and Jenkins of Wales who all played for their countries against New Zealand. The All Blacks selected a strong forward unit but were without Oliver and Griffiths. They were, however, in a better frame of mind returning from Wales than they had been going to the Principality. However, they failed to lift themselves again, causing *Daily Telegraph* writer Howard Marshall to write: 'The All Blacks, playing like somewhat elderly gentlemen, scrambled home'.

Midway through a scrappy first half Peter Candler retired with concussion, forcing David Thom to relocate to the wing, with Charles Dick moving to Candler's position of outside half and Jim Unwin filling Dick's place. Nevertheless, the seven London forwards were largely able to match the New Zealand eight, and regularly took the scrum ball. However, New Zealand dominated the territory but the backs, the saviours of several close encounters already on tour, seemed to be lacking the inspiration to break through the London defence, particularly after Candler's departure. It was 0-0 at half-time.

Things looked up in the second half, but Vivian Jenkins narrowly missed a long-range penalty and Thom dropped a scoring pass following a break by Unwin. Shortly after this, Unwin dived for the line but the ball was dislodged by a tackle from Corner. Fortunate not to be behind, the All Blacks took play back into the London half and, after Reid broke from a lineout, the supporting Pepper kicked ahead and scored. London tried to hit back but several scoring chances were squandered either by mistakes or scrambling New Zealand defence. As the game progressed the All Blacks took the steam out of the London side and, after King had nearly scored, Caughey raced in through a defence that was static – the home players reacting to a perceived knock-on rather than the silence of the referee's whistle. Corner converted but missed adding the points to a scruffy late try from Mitchell.

New Zealand won 11-0 and this time it was the forwards who won them the game, albeit against only seven Londoners. Marshall was at a loss to suggest why the All Blacks were so ordinary, but surmised: 'They need the stimulus of Welsh aggression to bring out the best in them.'

OXFORD UNIVERSITY   1935/36

Wednesday 6 November 1935
Iffley Road, Oxford
Won 10-9

Oxford were captained by 'Mac' Cooper, who took over the captaincy of the university when Kenneth Jackson was injured at the start of the season. A New Zealander, Cooper later played for Scotland and became captain of the Wellington province before becoming a senior academic on the subject of agriculture.

In a keen game played in torrential rain, the Oxford pack stood up well to the All Blacks, and their backs tackled ferociously. A blistering run by Alexander Obolensky early on served warning to the All Blacks of his qualities. Then, from a steady scrum in front of the All Blacks'

OXFORD UNIVERSITY	NEW ZEALAND
J.L. Stuart-Watson (Brasenose)	G.D.M. Gilbert
Prince A. Obolensky (Brasenose)	N. Ball
M.M. Walford (Trinity)	C.J. Oliver (Capt.)
R.F. Harding (Brasenose)	N.A. Mitchell
G.R. Rees-Jones (University)	T.H.C. Caughey
C.F. Grieve (Christ Church)	J.L. Griffiths
J.M.S. McShane (New College)	B.S. Sadler
Forwards:	Forwards:
J.A. Brett (St Edmund Hall)	A. Lambourn
N.F. McGrath (University)	W.E. Hadley
J.H. Pienaar (Worcester)	C.S. Pepper
G.A. Reid (University)	F.H. Vorrath
G.D. Roos (University)	R.M. McKenzie
M.McG. Cooper (University, Capt.)	S.T. Reid
H.M. Hughes (University)	A. Mahoney
C.T. Bloxham (Oriel)	J.J. Best

Scorers:
Oxford University: Try: Obolensky. Con: Brett. DG: Grieve.
New Zealand: Tries: McKenzie, Sadler. Cons: Gilbert (2).

Referee: R.B. Hunt (Eastern Counties).
Attendance: 16,000.

posts, Australian Jan McShane passed quickly to Charles Grieve, who dropped a neat goal to open the scoring. This inspired the All Blacks into action and, after a determined forward rush, Rod McKenzie crashed over for a try that Gilbert, who had been unsuccessful with previous penalty attempts, converted. New Zealand led 5-4 at half-time.

In the second half the students regained the lead. Although deep in his own half, 'Micky' Walford spotted a gap in the New Zealand defence. He passed to Obolensky and the Russian prince set off on a run down the touchline with too much pace for the New Zealanders. He raced around and touched down between the posts. It was a seventy-five-yard run and the cheering was still ringing around Iffley Road when John Brett converted, although many thought the Russian had put a foot in touch at one point. Oxford protected their lead and it looked as though the All Blacks were about to suffer their second defeat until, in the closing stages, 'Joey' Sadler broke down the blind side to score a try inches from the corner flag. As if to confound the critics, Mike Gilbert converted majestically from the touchline to win the game for New Zealand.

Russian Prince Alexander Obolensky first came to prominence with a dazzling performance against the All Blacks for Oxford University.

It had been a tough game and New Zealand declared the Oxford pack one of the best they had met on tour. They were extremely lucky to get away with a win.

Full-back John Stuart-Wilson was killed in action in November 1944, while RAF Officer Prince Alexander Obolensky crashed his Hurricane and was killed in 1940. Oxford forward Gideon Roos was the son of Paul Roos, the 1906 South African captain.

HAMPSHIRE & SUSSEX   1935/36

Saturday 9 November 1935
Dean Court, Bournemouth
Won 14-8

New Zealand changed several players and welcomed back Jack Manchester, who was rested at Oxford. 'Rusty' Page, who had not played since the second game of the tour, was selected to play but his knee injury flared up again and he was replaced at the last minute by Eric Tindill. There were some familiar faces in the opposing side, including Wallis, Tarr and captain 'Tinny' Dean from the Combined Services match. Early rain had left the surface of the pitch, normally played upon by Bournemouth & Boscombe Athletic, greasy and slippery. The sun shone but there was a stiff breeze behind the All Blacks in the first half.

After a scrappy opening twenty minutes

HAMPSHIRE & SUSSEX	NEW ZEALAND
J.D. Ronald (Harlequins)	G.D.M. Gilbert
R.J.E. Whitworth (London Scottish)	N. Ball
I.D.M. Wilson (Blackheath)	C.J. Oliver
A.D. Hodges (King's College)	G.F. Hart
G.D.A. Lundon (Harlequins)	T.H.C. Caughey
W.T. Anderson (Harlequins)	E.W.T. Tindill
G.J. Dean (Harlequins & Army, Capt.)	M.M.N. Corner
Forwards:	Forwards:
C.R. Owen (Army)	J. Hore
D.J. Tarr (Swansea & Royal Navy)	D. Dalton
V.J. Pike (Army)	A. Lambourn
A. Boast (Salisbury & Army)	W.R. Collins
C.O'N. Wallis (Wanderers & Army)	R.R. King
D.T. Kemp (Trojans)	R.M. McKenzie
N.J. Newton (Bournemouth)	J.E. Manchester (Capt.)
P.C. Horden (Gloucester)	H.F. McLean

Scorers:
Hampshire & Sussex: Try: Newton. Con: Owen. PG: Owen.
New Zealand: Tries: McKenzie (2), Hart, Corner. Con: Gilbert.

Referee: R.G. Langham (Leicester).
Attendance: 14,000.

played exclusively in the Hampshire & Sussex half, the tourists opened the scoring when Rod McKenzie crossed for a try at the end of a forward passing movement. Gilbert failed to convert. The home side ventured into New Zealand territory soon afterwards but the ball went loose when a try looked

a distinct possibility. Oliver gathered the ball and, after some fine close passing under pressure in a move that swept downfield, Hart broke clear to score a spectacular try. Hart had come close to scoring twice earlier. With All Black tails up, a forward rush was finished off by McKenzie again to see New Zealand 9-0 ahead at half-time.

With the wind at their backs the home side started the second half with some determined runs that were stopped by the good defending of the All Blacks. Then a clever kick into the corner was fielded by Gilbert but run into touch close to the corner flag. A quick lineout was taken, with the ball lobbed in to N.J. Newton for a try. This was converted by C.R. Owen, the tough Welsh Regiment soldier, with a fine kick. The All Blacks scored again in the closing stages when a clean break by Caughey was finished off by Corner for a try, which Gilbert was able to convert. Close to full-time Owen kicked a penalty from halfway to conclude the scoring.

The All Blacks had won but had encountered a torrid battle up front. Don Tarr caused them serious trouble at the scrum, winning several tight-heads and completely outplaying Doug Dalton in the tight exchanges. The New Zealand loose play was superior to the Combined Counties and their backs were something near their best.

Hampshire enjoyed a successful campaign and won the County Championship for the second time in three years. Wing Robert Whitworth later became a Scottish international. Gordon Lundon DFC was killed in the Second World War.

CAMBRIDGE UNIVERSITY   1935/36

Thursday 14 November 1935
Grange Road, Cambridge
Won 25-5

CAMBRIDGE UNIVERSITY	NEW ZEALAND
G.W. Parker (Selwyn)	G.D.M. Gilbert
J.R. Rawlence (Pembroke)	G.F. Hart
J.A. McDonald (Clare)	C.J. Oliver
W. Wooller (Christ's)	N.A. Mitchell
K.C. Fyfe (Clare, Capt.)	T.H.C. Caughey
C.W. Jones (Clare)	J.L. Griffiths
J.D. Low (Jesus)	B.S. Sadler
Forwards:	Forwards:
C.D. Laborde (St Catherine's)	J. Hore
J.R.C. Lord (Christ's)	W.E. Hadley
H.P. Dinwiddy (Pembroke)	D. Dalton
J.S. Young (St Catherine's)	R.M. McKenzie
K.G. Irving (Jesus)	R.R. King
B.C. Smith (Emmanuel)	S.T. Reid
J.M. Hunter (Christ's)	J.E. Manchester (Capt.)
W.B. Young (St Catherine's)	A. Mahoney

Scorers:
Cambridge University: Try: Low. Con: Parker.
New Zealand: Tries: Sadler (2), Mitchell (2), King, Hart, Oliver. Cons: Gilbert (2).

Referee: C.H. Gadney (London).
Attendance: 12,000.

Cambridge had won the previous season's Varsity match with some ease and there was considerable confidence that, given sufficient possession, the Cambridge backs could run New Zealand close. There were, however, concerns that the forwards may not be up to the mark and that the silky skills of Welsh internationals Cliff Jones and Wilf Wooller might be seen in defence rather than attack. New Zealand selected a strong side, conscious of the international with Scotland on the horizon.

The apprehension over the home forwards proved justified as the New Zealand pack took control early on, and when Charles Laborde had to leave the field injured midway through the first half, the students' problems mounted. Played in drizzle, the match was a fine display of running rugby from New Zealand, while Cambridge made many mistakes with ball in hand, particularly Wooller who had an off day in attack. His defence, however, was exemplary and he repelled several All Blacks' attacks single-handedly. Midway through the first half Wooller scrambled a kick away, having expected to be awarded a mark, but it failed to find touch. The All Blacks ran it back and Ron King scored. Shortly after this, 'Brushy' Mitchell scored a second try after good play by Sadler and Jack Griffiths, which Mike Gilbert converted. Then Mitchell scored again after Wooller and John Rawlence had got themselves in a mess, and then Ray Lord passed to nobody in particular and Pat Caughey picked up to put Hart in for the fourth try. It was 14-0 to New Zealand at the break and, for once, the All Black pack had totally dominated their opponents.

In the second half the Cambridge backs were starved of possession. Mistakes continued and poor passing under pressure let in Charlie Oliver for a try, and then the cool Sadler spotted a gap in the defence to score another. It was the half-back who concluded the scoring with a further try a few minutes later following good passing from forwards and backs. Late in the game, Wooller and John McDonald were close to scoring before Cambridge eventually got on the scoresheet when Douglas Low kicked the ball out of Sadler's hands and dribbled the ball over the line for a try that Grahame Parker converted. It was too little too late for the disappointed and disappointing students. Wooller later claimed that he

Cliff Jones, outside half for Cambridge and Wales. He became president of the Welsh Rugby Union in their centenary season.

and Jones had spotted weaknesses in the New Zealand defence during the game. Despite his 'curate's egg' of a game Wooller, and Cliff Jones, played for Wales against New Zealand, and Ken Fyfe played for Scotland. Centre McDonald was killed during the Second World War.

The following month the Universities battled out a 0-0 draw in the Varsity match at Twickenham, a result no-one would have predicted having seen the respective sides play New Zealand. Observant journalist Howard Marshall was more complimentary to the tourists this time, writing: 'I have never seen the All Blacks play better'.

LEICESTERSHIRE & EAST MIDLANDS 1935/36

Saturday 16 November 1935
Welford Road, Leicester
Won 16-3

The home selectors based their team around the Leicester club side that had enjoyed success in recent seasons, although they had been defeated by both Oxford and Cambridge Universities in the lead up to the All Blacks' visit to Welford Road. The All Blacks had a free week after this game, allowing them to prepare for the first international.

In glorious sunshine the home side nearly scored after Manchester dropped the ball directly from the kick-off. England captain Bernard Gadney was stopped just inches from the New Zealand line and the visitors were able to clear. Tindill and Gilbert missed penalty attempts at goal before the All Blacks opened their account

LEICESTERSHIRE & EAST MIDLANDS	NEW ZEALAND
R.J. Barr (Leicester)	G.D.M. Gilbert
J.B. Charles (Leicester)	G.F. Hart
M.P. Crowe (Leicester)	N.A. Mitchell
J.B.S. Fox (Leicester)	N. Ball
T.D. Thevenard (Bedford)	T.H.C. Caughey
C.F. Slow (Leicester)	E.W.T. Tindill
B.C. Gadney (Leicester, Capt.)	B.S. Sadler
Forwards:	Forwards:
R.J. Longland (Northampton)	C.S. Pepper
E.S. Nicholson (Leicester)	W.E. Hadley
G.T. Dancer (Bedford)	D. Dalton
J. Dicks (Northampton)	R.M. McKenzie
M.A. Robinson (Leicester)	R.R. King
R. Willsher (Bedford)	J.G. Wynyard
W.H. Weston (Northampton)	J.E. Manchester (Capt.)
D.L.K. Milman (Bedford)	A. Mahoney

Scorers:
Leicestershire & East Midlands: Try: Longland.
New Zealand: Hart (2), Wynyard (2). Cons: Gilbert (2).

Referee: J. Hughes (London).
Attendance: 29,000.

LEICESTERSHIRE & EAST MIDLANDS COMBINED XV
NEW ZEALAND TOURING XV

IRISH TWEED OVERCOATS FROM 3½ GNS.
Knights of Leicester · UNIVERSITY OUTFITTERS

when Tindill made a break and passed inside to his forwards. Ron King drove on and was tackled short but slipped a pass to the supporting Jim Wynyard for the try. Gilbert converted and Wynyard scored again when he and the rest of the pack chased a high kick from Hart, which full-back Barr failed to gather. The Waikato loose forward, the youngest man in the tour party, touched the ball down and Gilbert kicked his second conversion. In-between these tries, the home side launched several exciting attacks that were repelled by good defence. In one first-half move the home team lost the services of Charlie Slow with an injury.

Leading 10-0 at half-time, the All Blacks had to deal with several dangerous home attacks early in the second half. But Sadler broke from a scrum and passed to Tindill, who worked a fine scissors movement with Hart that deceived the opposition defence, Hart sprinting clear to score a glorious try. Then the livewire Gadney broke clear in the New Zealand 25 and, when stopped close to the goal line, he passed to the powerful Northampton and England prop Ray Longland who drove through for the try. On the stroke of full-time the ball went loose and was kicked ahead by Hart, who beat the defence and gathered the ball to dash in and dive over the line for the try.

George Hart was a fine rugby player. A regular try-scorer since his international debut against the British Lions in 1930, he retired from representative rugby in 1936. He played in several services matches in the Mediterranean theatre during the Second World War before being killed at Monte Cassino in 1944. His try-scoring compatriot, Wynyard, suffered injuries that plagued his career after the tour but he was back at top form when the Second World War intervened. Wynyard also served in the war but was killed in action at the Battle of El Alamein in 1941. East Midlands wing Theodore Thevenard also died on active duty, with the Royal Naval Volunteer Reserve in March 1942.

SCOTLAND 1935/36

Saturday 23 November 1935
Murrayfield, Edinburgh
Won 18-8

After two good displays by the Scottish district teams earlier in the tour, it was expected that this would be a very close international and that home advantage might be decisive. The Combined Cities XV, who had lost by a single point to New Zealand, supplied five of the Scottish back division while the South of Scotland provided four of the forwards. There were three new caps in full-back Jimmy Kerr, hooker Dod Gray and wing-forward Duncan Shaw. New Zealand, meanwhile, were strengthened by the return of centre Charlie Oliver, the vice-captain, Pat Caughey at five-eighth, and Bill Hadley at hooker. Mike Gilbert, Brushy

SCOTLAND	NEW ZEALAND
J.M. Kerr (Heriot's FP)	G.D.M. Gilbert
J.E. Forrest (Glasgow Acads)	G.F. Hart
R.C.S. Dick (Guy's Hospital)	C.J. Oliver
W.C.W. Murdoch (Hillhead HSFP)	N.A. Mitchell
K.C. Fyfe (Cambridge University)	T.H.C. Caughey
R.W. Shaw (Glasgow HSFP, Capt.)	J.L. Griffiths
W.R. Logan (Edinburgh Wanderers)	B.S. Sadler
Forwards:	Forwards:
D.A. Thom (London Scottish)	J. Hore
J.A. Waters (Selkirk)	W.E. Hadley
L.B. Lambie (Glasgow HSFP)	A. Lambourn
J. Beattie (Hawick)	R.R. King
W.A. Burnet (West of Scotland)	R.M. McKenzie
G.D. Shaw (Gala and Sale)	S.T. Reid
R.M. Grieve (Kelso)	J.E. Manchester (Capt.)
G.L. Gray (Gala)	A. Mahoney

Scorers:
Scotland: Tries: Fyfe, Dick. Con: Murdoch.
New Zealand: Tries: Caughey (3), Hadley. Cons: Gilbert (3).

Referee: C.H. Gadney (England).
Attendance: 60,000.

Mitchell, Joey Sadler, Tori Reid and Tonk Mahoney all made their international debuts. Conditions were near-perfect with bright sunshine, no wind and a firm pitch that had been protected by straw.

New Zealand rose to the occasion and produced their best rugby of the tour for a handsome victory. This was a thrilling, open game played at great pace. The surprising feature was the transformation in the play of the visiting forwards. Jack Manchester gave an outstanding lead and he was well supported by Hore, Hadley, King and McKenzie. The match was a personal triumph for Caughey, who scored 3 of his side's 4 tries. The Scots competed well, but it was clear that the New Zealanders were the better side and had more speed, power and decisiveness. Scotland opened the scoring after ten minutes. Wilson Shaw and Charlie Dick made a good break and Ken Fyfe finished off with a strong run to the corner. 'Copey' Murdoch was forced to leave the field for six or seven minutes, during which time Caughey raced straight through for his first try. Gilbert easily converted. In the second quarter, New Zealand hammered on the Scottish line and Hadley picked up and forced his way over from a scramble in front of the posts. Gilbert converted again. Play swung from end to end before Caughey scored his second in the corner and New Zealand were 13-3 ahead at half-time.

Action from the New Zealanders' first visit to Murrayfield, November 1935. (Scottish Rugby Union)

There was a Scottish revival after the restart and Wilson Shaw cut through to send Dick racing in at the posts. Murdoch's conversion brought Scotland back into the game, but a great opportunity was lost when Fyfe dropped a scoring pass after Murdoch had broken through the defence. The visitors clinched the game when Sadler, playing a fine game at half-back, went blind and fed Mitchell, who threw out a long pass. Caughey caught the ball at speed and was in at the posts. The conversion was a formality for Gilbert. A convincing win for New Zealand, who played some top-quality football with some outstanding teamwork. Caughey was quick to seize any openings and thoroughly deserved his 3 tries. For Scotland, Dick and Shaw were good in attack while Jock Beattie and Bill Burnet were the best of the forwards.

NORTH OF SCOTLAND 1935/36

**Wednesday 27 November 1935
Pittodrie Park, Aberdeen
Won 12-6**

Their first visit to the north of Scotland, New Zealand made ten changes from the side that had beaten Scotland four days earlier. Not too much was expected from the North, although the side had several prominent players. At stand-off, the veteran international Harry Lind of Dunfermline and London Scottish was a fine attacking player, but perhaps too much of an individual. The right-winger Charles Brown had won a single cap in 1929. At centre, Ronnie Boon had played for Cardiff and Wales before moving north of the border.

The match was played in near-perfect conditions at Pittodrie Park, the home of

NORTH OF SCOTLAND	NEW ZEALAND
J.A. Innes (Aberdeen GSFP)	G.D.M. Gilbert
C.H.C. Brown (Dunfermline)	N. Ball
J.A.K. Hunter (Gordonians)	C.J. Oliver (Capt.)
R.W. Boon (Dunfermline)	H.M. Brown
R.S. Lind (Dunfermline)	D. Solomon
H. Lind (Dunfermline)	J.R. Page
A.I. Dickie (Gordonians)	M.M.N. Corner
Forwards:	Forwards:
G.D.W. Stroud (Aberdeenshire)	G.T. Adkins
G.F. Ritchie (Dundee HSFP)	W.E. Hadley
J.R. Ness (Dunfermline, Capt.)	C.S. Pepper
P.S. Morris (Perthshire)	S.T. Reid
J.I. Morrice (Aberdeen GSFP)	F.H. Vorrath
J.W. Hall (Highland)	H.F. McLean
J. Bald (Dunfermline)	J.G. Wynyard
R.D. Bain (Aberdeen GSFP)	A. Mahoney

Scorers:
North of Scotland: Tries: Bain, Hunter.
New Zealand: Try: Oliver. PG: Gilbert (3).

Referee: W. Burnet (Hawick).
Attendance: 8,000.

Aberdeen Football Club, but the attendance was disappointing, reflecting that the area was something of a rugby desert. To everyone's surprise, the North put on a great show and outscored the visitors by 2 tries to 1, and once again New Zealand had to rely on Mike Gilbert's powerful goal-kicking to get them out of trouble. Within ten minutes, Gilbert opened the scoring with a long-range penalty. Play was very ragged, but the pace was fast and the game swung from end to end. After twenty minutes, Harry Lind picked up a loose ball, flashed down the centre of the field and passed on to Boon, who in turn fed Ronald Bain, who dived across near the corner flag. Gilbert kicked a fine penalty from forty yards after a lineout infringement, but a minute later the North scored their second try. Stroud broke away from a loose scrum and passed to Hunter, who scored in the corner. Innes failed with the conversion to leave the half-time score tied at 6-6.

New Zealand dominated most of the second period, their forwards winning the lion's share of the scrums and lineouts, but the backs did little with their possession, partly because of courageous tackling by the North. Five minutes after the restart, Gilbert kicked his third penalty, a monster effort from halfway that just cleared the bar. Moving into the final quarter, Charlie Oliver went blind and raced forty yards through the defence for the clinching try. The North rallied towards the end and several times came close to another score.

In a rousing tussle, Gilbert was once again the New Zealand trump card. He was solid in defence and made a vital contribution with his kicking. The New Zealand back play was very lacklustre and ridden with errors, in part because Rusty Page, at five-eighth, had just returned from a leg injury and was still a little off the pace. Hugh McLean played a great game among the forwards and was always in the thick of the action. For the North, Harry Lind was in tremendous form with his swift running and resolute tackling. He was well supported by his centres while the North forwards, although beaten in the tight, could take pride in their sterling efforts.

ULSTER   1935/36

Saturday 30 November 1935
Ravenhill, Belfast
Drawn 3-3

ULSTER	NEW ZEALAND
R.R. Davey (Queen's University)	G.D.M. Gilbert
S. Dobbin (Queen's University)	G.F. Hart
S.J.M. Cole (Queen's University)	N.A. Mitchell
L.M. Malcolmson (NIFC)	N. Ball
V.J. Lyttle (Collegians)	T.H.C. Caughey
V.A. Hewitt (Instonians)	E.W.T. Tindill
A.F. Turner (Instonians)	B.S. Sadler
Forwards:	Forwards:
R. Alexander (NIFC)	C.S. Pepper
T.B. Dunn (NIFC)	D. Dalton
D.A. Kendrew (Derry & Army)	A. Lambourn
C.E. St J. Beamish (NIFC & RAF)	S.T. Reid
S.K. Neill (Instonians)	R.R. King
W.McC. Ross (Instonians)	H.F. McLean
J.A.E. Siggins (Collegians, Capt.)	J.E. Manchester (Capt.)
S. Walker (Instonians)	F.H. Vorrath

Scorers:
Ulster: Try: Dunn.
New Zealand: Try: Hart.

Referee: F.W. Haslett (Ulster).
Attendance: 12,000.

The All Blacks' visit to Belfast coincided with the arrival of monsoon-like conditions that rendered the Ravenhill pitch a muddy swamp. Facing an Ulster side famous for its tough forwards on such a surface was a daunting task. The home pack was bolstered by the considerable presence of Douglas 'Joe' Kendrew who was selected because the Leicestershire Regiment was based in the province at that time. The home pack also included 1938 Lions captain Sammy Walker, Jack Siggins and Charles Beamish, and all except Neill played international rugby at some time. New Zealand struggled up front. They were out-scrummaged and had problems in the lineout, but they used their physique in loose play and several of the tight five showed up well running with the ball. It was a different approach from the All Blacks.

After half an hour Tindill cut through and kicked ahead over the Ulster defence. George Hart showed commendable pace to skim the surface of the pitch and outstrip the cover to score. Three minutes later Ulster equalised when Thomas Dunn scored after the Ulster forwards had set up a good attacking position and dribbled the ball over the line. Neither try was converted.

With the scores tied at 3-3 the second half became an absorbing contest and both sides served up hard forward rugby. Ulster had the greater share of possession and threatened to score but the New Zealand defence held out. Mike Gilbert, New Zealand's West Coast full-back, was outstanding in defence and Tori Reid, whose full name was Sana Torium Reid, tackled Jack Siggins when a second Ulster try looked likely. New Zealand were close on several occasions but seemed incapable of scoring. Gilbert missed a simple penalty, and a drop goal from Tindill was disallowed because it was touched in flight by an opponent. The second half concluded without any further scoring with a draw, arguably, the right result.

Five of the heroic Ulster pack, Siggins, Walker, Beamish, Dunn and Ross were selected for the international with New Zealand.

IRELAND   1935/36

**Saturday 7 December 1935
Lansdowne Road, Dublin
Won 17-9**

The Irish and New Zealand teams together before the international.

The All Blacks had a free week to prepare for the game and trained at several grounds in Dublin. Ireland awarded international debuts to Charles Boyle, Leslie Malcolmson, Thomas Dunn and

IRELAND	NEW ZEALAND
D.P. Morris (Bective Rangers)	G.D.M. Gilbert
C.V. Boyle (Dublin University)	G.F. Hart
G.L. Malcolmson (NIFC)	C.J. Oliver
A.H. Bailey (University College, Dublin)	N.A. Mitchell
J.J. O'Connor (University College, Cork)	T.H.C. Caughey
V.A. Hewitt (Instonians)	J.L. Griffiths
G.J. Morgan (Clontarf)	B.S. Sadler
Forwards:	Forwards:
S.J. Deering (Bective Rangers)	A. Lambourn
T.B. Dunn (NIFC)	W.E. Hadley
C.E. St J. Beamish (NIFC & RAF)	D. Dalton
C.R. Graves (Wanderers)	S.T. Reid
W.McC. Ross (Instonians & Millom)	R.R. King
J.A.E. Siggins (Collegians, Capt.)	H.F. McLean
C.O'N. Wallis (Wanderers)	J.E. Manchester (Capt.)
S. Walker (Instonians)	A. Mahoney

Scorers:
Ireland: Try: Beamish. PGs: Bailey, Siggins.
New Zealand: Tries: Mitchell, Oliver, Hart. Con: Gilbert. PGs: Gilbert (2).

Referee: R.W. Jeffares (Ireland).
Attendance: 30,000.

Clive Wallis. The side also included Seamus Deering, whose son, Shay, captained Ireland against New Zealand forty-three years later. All Black Jack Hore had not recovered from his injury at Murrayfield so Doug Dalton played in his place and made his international debut. There was an unusual incident just before the match started, when it was discovered that the referee had not arrived. Mr M.A. Allen, of Scotland, had elected to come to Dublin on the Friday evening but poor weather in the Irish Sea delayed the arrival of the boat to the extent that Billy Jeffares, a Dublin referee who was the son of the IRFU Secretary and had intended to watch the game from the comfort of the stand, was asked to officiate.

The match was three minutes old when Caughey sped through a hole in the Ireland defence. His pass went astray but was kicked on by Oliver for Mitchell to pick up and score in the corner. It was not long before the next All Blacks' try. A miskick by full-back Morris in front of the Irish posts presented Oliver with a gift try, which Gilbert converted. New Zealand had scored 8 points in ten minutes. Aiden Bailey hit the crossbar with a penalty kick before opening the Irish account with a successful penalty shortly after. Then Hart scored a fine try for New Zealand in which every three-quarter touched the ball and moved it at pace, Mitchell coming in off his wing to create the overlap. As the match progressed so the Irish forwards became more prominent. They embarked on a forward rush up the field and Charles Beamish scored a try close to the posts. Unfortunately Bailey was unable to convert. The score was 11-6 at half-time.

It rained throughout the second half, which meant the game degenerated into a vigorous forward battle. After another frantic forward rush Jack Siggins, the Irish captain, scored but the referee disallowed it. However, Siggins kicked a penalty shortly afterwards to cut the New Zealand lead to 2 points with thirty minutes to go. Gilbert kicked a penalty goal and a second late in the game to make the tourists' victory safe.

The Irish pack was magnificent but the biggest difference between the sides was in the backs, where New Zealand were far superior on the day. The IRFU did not award caps to players making their international debuts against Dominion teams. Thus Dunn and Wallis, who were not selected again, never received the ultimate recognition of their status.

MID-DISTRICT 1935/36

Thursday 12 December 1935
Ynys Park, Aberdare
Won 31-10

Having missed the opportunity to officiate at the Newport match because of injury, Albert Freethy, the man who had sent All Black forward Cyril Brownlie off at Twickenham in 1925, finally caught up with the tourists. There was much criticism of the WRU's decision to give a fixture to a side made up of players from junior clubs, and with only a small crowd turning up to watch in what was chiefly a soccer area, the venture was not a financial success. Captain Glan James of Treorchy had appeared in a Welsh trial, but none of the other players had played representative rugby.

In the event, the local side gave a good account of itself, none more so than scrum-half Luther Davies, who outplayed his opposite number Merv Corner, earning personal praise

MID-DISTRICT	NEW ZEALAND
T. Williams (Pontypridd)	G.D.M. Gilbert
T. Keegan (Pontypridd)	H.M. Brown
T. le Clare (Cilfynydd)	C.J. Oliver
G. James (Treorchy, Capt.)	N.A. Mitchell
E. Phillips (Pontypridd)	T.H.C. Caughey
E. Tucker (Pontypridd)	E.W.T. Tindill
L. Davies (Cilfynydd)	M.M.N. Corner
Forwards:	Forwards:
A. Thomas (Aberaman)	A. Lambourn
W. Francis (Cilfynydd)	D. Dalton
R. Leyshon (Merthyr)	C.S. Pepper
B. Davies (Ystrad Rhondda)	R.R. King
T.E. James (Treorchy)	R.M. McKenzie
L. Rees (Cilfynydd)	J.J. Best
E. Carter (Penygraig)	J.E. Manchester (Capt.)
F. Harding (Treorchy)	F.H. Vorrath

Scorers:
Mid Districts: Tries: G. James, Phillips. Cons: le Clare (2).
New Zealand: Tries: Brown (2), King, Pepper, Oliver, Mitchell. Cons: Gilbert (2), Corner. PG: Gilbert. DG: Tindill.

Referee: A.E. Freethy (Neath).
Attendance: 6,000.

from his opponent after the game. Davies was prominent in the early exchanges, working the blind side, and the home forwards surprised the All Blacks with their attacks. One particularly promising move resulted in Tommy le Clare having a thirty-yard run to the line, but 'Brushy' Mitchell cut him off. Having survived this early scare, New Zealand took the lead when Mike Gilbert kicked a penalty from near the halfway line, and shortly afterwards Pat Caughey lost the ball over the line after a brilliant handling move. Then Tindill set up a try for King, which Gilbert converted to bring up his century of points for the tour. James missed with a drop goal for Mid-District, and then New Zealand scored their second try when Best kicked over the home line. Best and Pepper followed up the kick, Pepper getting to the ball first for a try that Gilbert could not convert. The half-time score was 11-0 to New Zealand.

The Mid-District XV, made up of players from junior Welsh clubs.

Caughey, having injured a leg, limped back to play at full-back for the second half, with Gilbert moving to the centre and Charlie Oliver going to second five-eighth. Oliver scored the next try after a superb solo run that took him past nearly all the home team. Corner kicked the conversion and then, following a good bout of passing, Mitchell was held up just short by a Tom Williams tackle. At the ensuing scrum, New Zealand won the ball and Tindill dropped a goal. Much to the delight of the home crowd Mid-District scored next, Phillips, having been initially stopped by Henry Brown's tackle, regaining his feet and sending a long, possibly forward scoring pass to James. Le Clare converted, but New Zealand scored again when Oliver set up a try for Mitchell, Gilbert converting. The All Blacks appeared to slacken off towards the end and Phillips beat the struggling Caughey to the ball following a kick over the tourists' line. Once again le Clare converted taking the home score into double figures, but as they began to tire the All Blacks added two late unconverted tries. First, Gilbert and Oliver set up a try for Henry Brown and then Brown scored again, running in a try from the halfway line. Gilbert missed the first conversion attempt, Tindill the second.

Walt Francis won his hooking duel with Doug Dalton, although this was partly due to Dalton's injury. Brown, Pepper, King and Jack Manchester all played well for the visitors in this unusual tour fixture.

ABERAVON & NEATH   1935/36

**Saturday 14 December 1935
Talbot Athletic Ground,
Port Talbot
Won 13-3**

This match was considered to be one of the hardest the All Blacks were likely to encounter outside the internationals. Neath were the previous season's leading Welsh club, with Aberavon not far behind them. Their combined team, selected to ensure both sides had an equal representation, was less than the sum of its constituent parts. Although the forwards were a hard bunch of individuals, the backs failed to make the best of the possession they were given. Outside half Gwyn Moore was injured and withdrew, forcing captain Gwyn Thomas to move from his more familiar position of centre. The Aberavon & Neath side included current Welsh international Glyn Prosser, who joined Huddersfield rugby league club a few days afterwards. Full-back

ABERAVON & NEATH	NEW ZEALAND
T.O. James (Aberavon)	G.D.M. Gilbert
H. Powell (Neath)	N. Ball
R. Lewis (Aberavon)	C.J. Oliver (Capt.)
J. Thomas (Aberavon)	N.A. Mitchell
J. Bevan (Neath)	J.L. Griffiths
G. Thomas (Neath, Capt.)	E.W.T. Tindill
M. Baker (Aberavon)	B.S. Sadler
Forwards:	Forwards:
D.M. Evans (Neath)	G.T.A. Adkins
T. Morgan (Neath)	W.E. Hadley
I. Bennett (Aberavon)	A. Lambourn
G.M. Williams (Aberavon)	R.R. King
H.W. Thomas (Neath)	S.T. Reid
H. Matthews (Aberavon)	H.F. McLean
W.E. Vickery (Aberavon)	R.M. McKenzie
I.G. Prosser (Neath)	A. Mahoney

Scorers:
Aberavon & Neath: PG: James.
New Zealand: Tries: Oliver, Griffiths, McLean.
Cons: Gilbert (2).

Referee: D.D. Hiddlestone (Pontardulais).
Attendance: 20,000.

Tommy James had also played for Wales, and Bennett, Williams, Thomas and Vickery were later capped. New Zealand picked a strong side but rested captain Manchester ahead of the international with Wales. Prop George Adkins made his first appearance since the South of Scotland game, but was not selected to play in Europe on tour again.

The match turned out to be a thoroughly unpleasant affair. Both sides infringed and incurred the displeasure of referee Dai Hiddlestone, who had played for Wales against the 1924/25 All Blacks. There were sporadic outbursts of fighting, and the partisan crowd irritated the tourists by jeering whenever a New Zealander was penalised or made an error. The first score came after five minutes when Charlie Oliver looped outside Brushy Mitchell to score a try close to the corner flag. The conversion was missed, but Mike Gilbert converted the second New Zealand try, scored by Jack Griffiths after a fine passing rush started in their own 25, ten minutes later. Later in the half James, who played with considerable aplomb, kicked a penalty goal for the home team, but New Zealand led 8-3 at the interval.

The second half was a torrid affair with both packs getting angry. The home side was over-physical and several of the forwards were admonished. However, Reid and King were in outstanding form for New Zealand. Hugh McLean scored by driving through the home defence from a scrum, Gilbert converting.

Aberavon & Neath pushed the All Blacks to the limit, and although the tourists deserved their win, it gave them food for thought ahead of the match with Wales.

WALES   1935/36

Saturday 21 December 1935
Cardiff Arms Park, Cardiff
Lost 13-12

The All Blacks made the most of the week allowed to prepare for the third international of the tour. Unbeaten in the Test matches thus far, they trained in Porthcawl but were forced to leave out the injured Pat Caughey. A reshuffle saw Charlie Oliver take his place. Brushy Mitchell moved from wing to Oliver's position of centre and Nelson Ball came in onto the wing. Wales selected three new caps in Don Tarr, Eddie Watkins, and scrum-half Haydn Tanner. Tanner, still not nineteen, was not joined by his cousin and Swansea club-mate Willie Davies, the selectors opting instead for Cambridge student Cliff Jones at outside half. Jones's fellow Cantabrigian, Wilf Wooller, was chosen on the wing, a largely unfamiliar

WALES	NEW ZEALAND
V.G.J. Jenkins (London Welsh)	G.D.M. Gilbert
G.R. Rees-Jones (Oxford University)	N. Ball
J.I. Rees	N.A. Mitchell
(Edinburgh Wanderers & Swansea)	
C. Davey (Sale & Swansea, Capt.)	G.F. Hart
W. Wooller (Cambridge University)	C.J. Oliver
C.W. Jones (Cambridge University)	J.L. Griffiths
H. Tanner (Swansea)	B.S. Sadler
Forwards:	Forwards:
T.J. Rees (Newport)	D. Dalton
D.J. Tarr (Swansea & Royal Navy)	W.E. Hadley
H. Payne (Swansea)	A. Lambourn
T.G. Williams (Cross Keys)	R.R. King
E.V. Watkins (Cardiff)	S.T. Reid
I.G. Prosser (Neath)	H.F. McLean
J. Lang (Llanelly)	J.E. Manchester (Capt.)
A.M. Rees (London Welsh)	A. Mahoney

Scorers:
Wales: Tries: G. Rees-Jones (2), Davey. Cons: Jenkins (2).
New Zealand: Tries: Ball (2). Con: Gilbert. DG: Gilbert.

Referee: B.C. Gadney (England).
Attendance: 50,000.

position for him. The thinking was that Wooller would be able to deal with George Hart, but this view ignored his primary skills as an attacker. Wales were captained by Claud Davey.

On an icy day, New Zealand started better and Vivian Jenkins was forced to bring off a try-saving tackle on Hart. Cliff Jones played ten-man rugby, kicking for field position unless the opportunity presented itself to run. Athol Mahoney nearly scored for the All Blacks before Cliff Jones scythed through the New Zealand defence, only to be stopped inches from the line. Eventually a score came. Quick passing from Joey Sadler and a fine Jack Griffiths break gave Ball the space to run in for a good try. Mike Gilbert missed the conversion, but an action-packed half ended with New Zealand ahead 3-0.

Wilfred Wooller, scourge of the All Blacks in a remarkable game of rugby football.

At half-time, Wooller and Idwal Rees swapped positions at Davey's behest. Wales opted to run the ball and, within a few minutes of the restart, they were ahead. Cliff Jones kicked ahead but Gilbert failed to gather. Davey chased the ball, deftly kicked ahead, gathered and scored. Jenkins converted. With the crowd roaring their approval, Wales attacked again. Five minutes later, Cliff Jones put Wooller into a gap and the tall centre raced through. As he approached Gilbert he kicked over the full-back's head but, just as he was about to gather the ball and score, it bounced away. Not to be denied, the supporting Geoffrey Rees-Jones dived on the ball for the second Welsh try. Jenkins converted again and stretched the Welsh lead to 7 points. Desperate to score, the All Blacks threw everything at Wales. Then, under pressure, Cliff Jones miscued a clearance kick, which Gilbert gathered. He composed himself, and coolly dropped a fine goal. Gilbert missed a penalty goal shortly afterwards, but then attempted a further drop goal. This time he sliced it badly, but communication between Davey and Rees-Jones was poor and, while they hesitated, Ball raced up, kicked ahead, gathered and scored his second try. With the scores tied, Gilbert's conversion put New Zealand back into the lead. Wooller and Cliff Jones were prominent in further attacks but they were unable to score. Then disaster hit the home side when Tarr broke his neck and was carefully carried from the field. The popular hooker never played rugby again. Down to fourteen men and with ten minutes left, it seemed all over for Wales. Then Tanner quickly fed Cliff Jones in the Welsh half from a scrum. Jones veered across field and employed a Cambridge move, which saw Wooller come up and take the ball in a scissors movement. Once more he kicked over the defence and tore after the ball. Then, just as Wooller was about to regather the ball it changed direction and bounced over his head. His momentum propelled him into the straw used to protect the pitch, piled up behind the posts. Wooller was buried there when he heard the cheers: the ball was once more gathered by Rees-Jones who touched down for the winning try. As the mist descended, referee Gadney blew for time and Wales began to celebrate.

It had been a desperately exciting match, a game that had everything. Even the critical Howard Marshall, writing in the *Daily Telegraph*, observed: 'I never saw a more splendid match or one played in finer spirit.'

The hero of the day was Wilf Wooller. A tall, long-striding centre, he earned Blues at Cambridge in rugby and cricket, and was a regular player with Glamorgan CCC before the Second World War. Wooller later joined Cardiff and captained Wales. A multi-talented sportsman, he occasionally played soccer for Cardiff City. In 1943 he was captured by the Japanese and spent the rest of the Second World War in a prisoner-of-war camp. He played a little rugby afterwards but devoted his time to cricket and played for Glamorgan until 1962. He was an England cricket selector and a leading broadcaster and journalist on cricket and rugby. He was outspoken in his views on South African sport and was seen as a controversial character. However, there can be no doubt that the pinnacle of Wilf Wooller's rugby career was this win over the All Blacks. Writing about the match in later years, Wooller quoted the sporting reaction at the final whistle of Jack Manchester: 'A great game. It did not matter who won it.'

Thursday 26 December 1935
Twickenham, London
Won 24-5

LONDON COUNTIES	NEW ZEALAND
V.G.J. Jenkins (London Welsh & Kent)	G.D.M. Gilbert
E.J. Unwin	G.F. Hart
(Rosslyn Park & Army, & Eastern Counties)	
R.F. Harding (Oxford University & Kent)	N.A. Mitchell
R.C.S. Dick (Guy's Hospital & Kent)	N. Ball
G.R. Rees-Jones	J.L. Griffiths
(Oxford University, & Eastern Counties)	
P.L. Candler	E.W.T. Tindill
(St Bartholomew's Hospital & Middlesex)	
L.B. Bok (Guy's Hospital & Middlesex)	M.M.N. Corner (Capt.)
Forwards:	Forwards:
D.A. Kendrew	J. Hore
(Leicester & Army & Eastern Counties, Capt.)	
D. John (Metropolitan Police & Middlesex)	W.E. Hadley
H.G. Bailey (Metropolitan Police & Surrey)	A. Lambourn
W.M. Allen (Rosslyn Park & Surrey)	S.T. Reid
S.R. Couchman (Old Cranleighans & Surrey)	R.R. King
W.B. Young (Cambridge University)	R.M. McKenzie
E.A. Hamilton-Hill (Harlequins & Surrey)	F.H. Vorrath
P.W.P. Brook (Harlequins & Eastern Counties)	J.G. Wynyard

Scorers:
London Counties: Try: Dick. Con: Jenkins.
New Zealand: Tries: Mitchell (2). PGs: Gilbert (2). DGs: Tindill (2), Ball.

Referee: J. Hughes (London).
Attendance: 20,000.

Five days after the defeat in Cardiff, the All Blacks faced two of the Welsh heroes again as London Counties included Vivian Jenkins and Geoffrey Rees-Jones for the return fixture between the sides on Boxing Day. Charles Dick was in the three-quarter line, as he was for Scotland against New Zealand earlier in the tour, and Peter Candler and 'Joe' Kendrew were to play for England against New Zealand in nine days' time. New Zealand made several changes and rested Manchester and Oliver, so the responsibility of leading the side went to Merv Corner.

The All Blacks' forwards started well and won sufficient ball for the backs to stretch the London defence. After fifteen minutes Eric Tindill dropped a goal before the tourists launched several back moves. There was a rash of infringements for which penalties were awarded with Mike Gilbert kicking a fine forty-yard penalty to see New Zealand ahead 7-0 at the break.

New Zealand attacked incessantly in the second half. Shortly after the restart a clearance kick to touch was gathered by Mitchell close to the touchline who, with the balancing skills of a tightrope walker, stayed in field and beat his opponent before racing past Jenkins to score a fine try. The conversion was missed but, shortly afterwards, Nelson Ball dropped a goal to extend the New Zealand lead to 13-0. Then the London forwards won the ball and released it to the backs. It came to Charles Dick, who punted over the New Zealand defence and dribbled the ball over the line for the try. Jenkins converted. New Zealand went back onto the attack and Tindill dropped the third All Blacks' goal of the match. The scorer then made a clean break and fed Mitchell who had come off his wing. The Southland speedster made good ground before veering to one side and rounding the defence to score. Gilbert added the final nail in the London coffin by kicking a penalty late in the match. The final score failed to recognise the contribution of London but reflected the superiority of the New Zealand backs.

Lock forward Stanley Couchman was never capped by England but toured South Africa with the British Lions in 1938. In 1972 he was the RFU's liaison officer who had the unenviable task of seeing the expelled Keith Murdoch onto the plane for his return to New Zealand.

London put pressure on the All Blacks.

Saturday 4 January 1936
Twickenham, London
Lost 13-0

RUGBY FOOTBALL UNION

ENGLAND v. Saturday, January 4th, 1936
AT TWICKENHAM.
NEW ZEALAND Kick-off **2.15** p.m.

EAST ENTRANCE Row Seat
Upper Stand **Y H** 102

IMPORTANT.– Kindly occupy your Seat by **2** p.m.

PRICE TEN
SHILLINGS
(including Tax and
Admission to Ground)

S.F. Cooper.
Engineer Commander, R.N. Secretary, R.F.U.

N.B.—OFFICIAL PROGRAMMES INSIDE THE GROUND ONLY

ENGLAND	NEW ZEALAND
H.G.Owen-Smith (St Mary's Hospital)	G.D.M. Gilbert
Prince A. Obolensky (Oxford University)	N.A. Mitchell
R.A. Gerrard (Bath)	C.J. Oliver
P. Cranmer (Richmond)	N. Ball
H.S. Sever (Sale)	T.H.C. Caughey
P.L. Candler (St Bartholomew's Hospital)	E.W.T. Tindill
B.C. Gadney (Leicester, Capt.)	M.M.N. Corner
Forwards:	Forwards:
R.J. Longland (Northampton)	J. Hore
E.S. Nicholson (Leicester)	W.E. Hadley
D.A. Kendrew (Leicester & Army)	A. Lambourn
A.J. Clarke (Coventry)	S.T. Reid
C.S.H. Webb	R.R. King
(Devonport Services & Royal Navy)	
E.A. Hamilton-Hill (Harlequins)	H.F. McLean
P.E. Dunkley (Harlequins)	J.E. Manchester (Capt.)
W.H. Weston (Northampton)	A. Mahoney

Scorers:
England: Tries: Obolensky (2), Sever. DG: Cranmer.

Referee: J.W. Faull (Wales).
Attendance: 72,000.

England awarded new caps to Prince Alexander Obolensky, Hal Sever and Edward 'Ham' Hamilton-Hill. New Zealand made several changes to their Test side with the inclusion of Mitchell for Hart, Corner for Sadler and Tindill, who made his international debut for Griffiths.

The first score of the game came when some sloppy passing gave Obolensky the ball with little space. However, he veered outside Ball and sprinted from his own half to score. Dunkley's conversion hit the post. Then Cranmer and Candler carved an opening for Obolensky again. This time 'Obo' cut inside and ran diagonally through the retreating All Blacks to score in the 'opposite' corner. The conversion was missed but England turned around 6-0 in the lead.

New Zealand attacked in the early stages of the second half. Then from a scrum in front of the New Zealand posts, Candler and Cranmer combined for the latter to drop a goal to put England 10 points ahead. The ecstatic crowd believed the game was won. It effectively was after England's third try, scored by Sever after Cranmer had cut another hole in the New Zealand defence. His pass to Sever was high, but the Sale wing gathered the ball and outstripped the defence to score. The conversion was missed again. New Zealand attacked incessantly. Gilbert missed two late penalty attempts but they would have been little more than a consolation.

England thus defeated New Zealand for the first time, a victory achieved through the remarkable England pack and the play of Bernard Gadney, the captain, who dictated the course of the game.

Rugby Football Union
Twickenham

OFFICIAL PROGRAMME

ENGLAND v. NEW ZEALAND
SATURDAY, 4th JANUARY, 1936
Kick-off 2.15 p.m.
PRICE TWOPENCE

Obolensky got the headlines for his remarkable tries but the victory was due to a complete team performance. This was New Zealand's heaviest defeat since losing 17-0 to South Africa in 1928.

The All Blacks returned to New Zealand via Canada, where they won two games and took part in an exhibition match. When they returned to New Zealand they were well received, but the statistics showed that they had lost three games and drawn one, and this added fuel to the criticism from before the tour. However, both the 1905 and 1924 sides probably met teams that were weaker than those Jack Manchester's side encountered. Where New Zealand came unstuck was in tight forward play, where they suffered from the unfamiliarity of an eight-man scrum, small props and opposition who were experts after years of fine-tuned scrummaging. Many of the tourists never wore the black jersey of New Zealand again.

NEW ZEALAND TO BRITAIN, FRANCE & CANADA

THE MATCHES

Southern Counties	31 October 1953	Hove	won 24-0
Cambridge University	4 November 1953	Cambridge	won 22-11
London Counties	7 November 1953	Twickenham	won 11-0
Oxford University	11 November 1953	Oxford	won 14-5
Western Counties	14 November 1953	Bristol	won 11-0
Llanelly	17 November 1953	Llanelly	won 17-3
Cardiff	21 November 1953	Cardiff	lost 8-3
Glasgow & Edinburgh	25 November 1953	Glasgow	won 23-3
South of Scotland	28 November 1953	Galashiels	won 32-0
North of Scotland	2 December 1953	Aberdeen	won 28-3
Leicestershire & East Midlands	5 December 1953	Leicester	won 3-0
Devon & Cornwall	9 December 1953	Camborne	won 9-0
Swansea	12 December 1953	Swansea	drew 6-6
WALES	19 December 1953	Cardiff	lost 13-8
Abertillery & Ebbw Vale	23 December 1953	Abertillery	won 22-3
Combined Services	26 December 1953	Twickenham	won 40-8
Midland Counties	30 December 1953	Birmingham	won 18-3
Ulster	2 January 1954	Belfast	drew 5-5
IRELAND	9 January 1954	Dublin	won 14-3
Munster	13 January 1954	Cork	won 6-3
Pontypool & Cross Keys	16 January 1954	Pontypool	won 19-6
Newport	21 January 1954	Newport	won 11-6
Neath & Aberavon	23 January 1954	Neath	won 11-5
ENGLAND	30 January 1954	Twickenham	won 5-0
North-Eastern Counties	6 February 1954	Bradford	won 16-0
SCOTLAND	13 February 1954	Murrayfield	won 3-0
North-Western Counties	17 February 1954	Manchester	won 17-3
Barbarians	20 February 1954	Cardiff	won 19-5
South-West France	24 February 1954	Bordeaux	lost 11-8
FRANCE	27 February 1954	Stade Colombes, Paris	lost 3-0
South-Eastern Counties (Unofficial fixture)	1 March 1954	Ipswich	won 21-13
Victoria (British Columbia)	9 March 1954	Victoria	won 39-3
British Columbia University	11 March 1954	Vancouver	won 42-3
British Columbia Mainland	13 March 1954	Vancouver	won 37-11
California University	17 March 1954	Berkeley	won 14-6
California All-Stars	20 March 1954	San Francisco	won 20-0

Played 36, Won 30, Drew 2, Lost 4. Scored: 598 points, Conceded: 152.

In Britain & Ireland: Played 29, Won 25, Drew 2, Lost 2. Scored: 438 points, Conceded: 115. These figures include the unofficial match.

The New Zealand Tour Party:
J.W. Kelly (Auckland), R.W.H. Scott (Auckland), M.J. Dixon (Canterbury), A.E.G. Elsom (Canterbury), W.S.S. Freebairn (Manawatu), R.A. Jarden (Wellington), R.G. Bowers (Wellington), L.S. Haig (Otago), J.T. Fitzgerald (Wellington), B.B.J. Fitzpatrick (Wellington), C.J. Loader (Wellington), J.M. Tanner (Auckland), D.D. Wilson (Canterbury), V.D. Bevan (Wellington), K. Davis (Auckland), I.J. Clarke (Waikato), B.P. Eastgate (Canterbury), K.L. Skinner (Otago), H.L. White (Auckland), R.C. Hemi (Waikato), C.A. Woods (Southland), K.P. Bagley (Manawatu), W.H. Clark (Wellington), G.N. Dalzell (Canterbury), P.F.H. Jones (North Auckland), W.A. McCaw (Southland), R.J. O'Dea (Thames Valley), D.O. Oliver (Otago), R.C. Stuart (Canterbury), R.A. White (Poverty Bay).

Captain: R.C. Stuart. Vice-Captain: L.S. Haig. Manager: J.N. Millard. Assistant Manager: A.E. Marslin.

Leading points scorer: R.A. Jarden – 94 points (73 in Britain & Ireland).
Leading try-scorer: R.A. Jarden – 15 tries (10 in Britain & Ireland).
Most appearances: R.A. White – 30 games (24 in Britain & Ireland).

SOUTHERN COUNTIES   1953/54

Saturday 31 October 1953
Greyhound Stadium, Hove
Won 24-0

New Zealand had toured Australia in 1951 and hosted a tour by Australia the following year, but had not played as a side in 1953. They held a series of trial matches and announced a fresh squad for the tour, which was largely accepted by critics in New Zealand, although there were many claims for the inclusion of outstanding Taranaki lock Peter Burke, who remained at home. Bob Stuart received unanimous approval in his selection as captain, and the squad flew to England.

Eleven days after their arrival, Bob Stuart's All Blacks played the first match of their tour against a Southern Counties side. Although most of the Southern Counties players were attached to senior sides, it looked an easy first run for the visitors.

SOUTHERN COUNTIES	NEW ZEALAND
J.C. Marshall	J.W. Kelly
(London Scottish & Oxfordshire)	
J.S. Swan (London Scottish & Berkshire)	A.E.G. Elsom
W.P.C. Davies (Harlequins & Sussex)	J.T. Fitzgerald
S.J. McDermott	R.A. Jarden
(London Irish & Hertfordshire)	
D.S. Rosborough	C.J. Loader
(Old Southfieldians & Oxfordshire)	
J.B. Graham (Bedford & Hertfordshire)	L.S. Haig
G.N. Peters (Richmond & Hertfordshire)	K. Davis
Forwards:	Forwards:
A.L. Canham	B.P. Eastgate
(Rosslyn Park & Dorset & Wilts)	
J.C. Chadwick (Salisbury & Dorset & Wilts)	C.A. Woods
P.D. Strang (Harlequins & Berkshire)	K.L. Skinner
D.W. Mattingley (Bath & Berkshire)	R.A. White
C. Pickford (Northampton & Oxfordshire)	K. Bagley
L.H. Webb (Bedford & Hertfordshire)	R.C. Stuart (Capt.)
C.D. Williams (Cardiff & Berkshire)	W.H. Clark
N.G. Davies (Blackheath & Sussex, Capt.)	W.A. McCaw

Scorers:
New Zealand: Tries: Haig, Fitzgerald, Clark, Jarden. Cons: Kelly (3). PG: Kelly. DG: Kelly.

Referee: Dr B.S. Mills (Northumberland).
Attendance: 12,000.

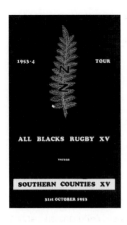

1953·4 TOUR

N Z

ALL BLACKS RUGBY XV

versus

SOUTHERN COUNTIES XV

31st OCTOBER 1953

The New Zealanders had been training for several days at Eastbourne College and planned to give the entire tour party a tryout during the opening 2 games of the tour. As the game approached the weather deteriorated and the match day was cold, wet and windy. The waiting crowd had to endure driving sleet and rain during the introduction of the teams to the Duke of Norfolk and the New Zealand High Commissioner.

Glyn Davies, the Counties captain, promptly handed the All Blacks first use of the wind. The offer was gratefully received and by half-time the contest was effectively over. Full-back Jack Kelly, who was destined to play second fiddle to the great Bob Scott on this tour, kicked the first points of the tour with a fourth-minute penalty and, soon afterwards, first five-eighth Laurie Haig crossed between the posts for the opening try. Kelly converted this score and added the extra points when centre Jim Fitzgerald scored.

At 13-0 a heavy defeat loomed for the Southern Counties, but errors crept into the New Zealanders' play. Kelly dropped a goal after a Counties forward had hacked the ball straight into his hands and Bill Clark scored the third try following a scrum pick-up by Bill McCaw, but the home side refused to crumble despite a half-time score of 21-0. With the wind at their backs in the second half the Counties pack played much better. The All Blacks continued to attack, but only one try was added, a late score from winger Ron Jarden.

Press comment was generally positive, although J.B.G. Thomas of the *Western Mail* perceptively stated that the side was 'not unbeatable'. Clark, McCaw and Richard 'Tiny' White all received glowing reports while Glyn Davies of the home side atoned for his blunder over the wind by impressing in the lineouts. He was selected to make his debut for Wales against New Zealand later in the tour but had to withdraw through injury. Davies eventually gained a solitary cap against England in 1955. Three of the Southern Counties side went on to meet the visitors in internationals during the tour. Phil Davies, one of the finest centres of his day, was in the England team, while Marshall and Swan both played for Scotland.

CAMBRIDGE UNIVERSITY   1953/54

Wednesday 4 November 1953
Grange Road, Cambridge
Won 22-11

Bright sunshine and a record Grange Road crowd greeted the New Zealanders for their second tour match. The tourists' intention to use all the playing squad in the opening 2 games was thwarted, partly by the reputation of a Cambridge XV containing nine Blues, and partly by an injury to scrum-half Vince Bevan. Despite scoring 6 tries, New Zealand were given a testing workout by the students. Cambridge had a fine pair of flankers in Ian Beer and Peter Ryan, and Ryan in particular had an excellent game, constantly harrying scrum-half Keith Davis and deservedly scoring both the Cambridge tries by capitalising on errors.

CAMBRIDGE UNIVERSITY	NEW ZEALAND
P.M. Davies (Trinity Hall)	R.W.H. Scott
H.B. Griffiths (Christ's)	W.S.S. Freebairn
K.J. Dalgleish (St Catharine's)	J.M. Tanner
H.S. Cormack (St John's)	R.A. Jarden
R.W.W. Dawe (St Catharine's)	D.D. Wilson
H.P. Morgan (St John's)	L.S. Haig
T.C. Pearson (Clare)	K. Davis
Forwards:	Forwards:
M.J.O. Massey (St John's)	H.L. White
R. McEwen (St Catharine's)	R.C. Hemi
D.G. Massey (Christ's)	I.J. Clarke
P.J.F. Wheeler (Magdalene, Capt.)	G.N. Dalzell
J.P.K. Asquith (Pembroke)	R.A White
I.D.S. Beer (St Catharine's)	O.D. Oliver
P.H. Ryan (Caius)	P.F. Jones
J.W. Clements (Trinity Hall)	R.C. Stuart (Capt.)

Scorers:
Cambridge University: Tries: Ryan (2). Con: Davies. PG: Davies.
New Zealand: Tries: Jarden (2), Oliver, Tanner, H.L. White, Jones.
Cons: Jarden (2).

Referee: A.E. Padfield (Somerset).
Attendance: 10,000.

New Zealand scored first through flanker Des Oliver. Ron Jarden converted this try, and then scored a gem of his own, twice swinging his body to confuse opponents, before dashing for the corner. Then Ryan scored the first of his tries, kicking ahead after a wild Davis pass and winning the race to touch down. Full-back Peter Davies kicked the conversion and, with only 3 points separating the sides, the All Blacks knew they had to raise their game. Cue Bob Scott, as the full-back burst into the line at speed to put John Tanner in for the visitors' third try. Jarden's conversion attempt hit a post and the half ended with New Zealand by no means safe with a lead of 11-5.

This lead looked even less secure when Davies kicked an early second-half penalty, but with Bob Stuart calling for a concerted effort from his pack, Scott once again showed why he was the star of the side. Gathering the ball, he beat four men in a sprint up the right touchline before sending in a cross-kick from which 'Snow' White scored. Jarden converted, and 16-8 soon became 19-8 when Peter Jones scored the All Blacks' fifth try. Once again Jarden hit a post with his conversion attempt. The New Zealanders added one further try when a break from Doug Wilson gave Jarden his second touchdown of the game, but as the tourists' pack eased off Cambridge came back with a try of their own. Ryan, still the tormentor of Davis, made a head-high interception of a pass from the hapless scrum-half and sprinted over like a winger.

There was universal praise for Bob Scott after the game. He had already won the hearts of the British public when he toured in 1945 with the New Zealand Services side known as the Kiwis, and now he was back with his mighty kicking and his crucial ability to turn dogged defence into lethal attack. Thirteen of the Cambridge side went on to draw that season's Varsity match with Oxford. Peter Ryan eventually received the caps his fine play deserved, appearing twice for England in 1955. Strangely, he appeared against Wales and Ireland, while his old Cambridge teammate and co-flanker Ian Beer played against France and Scotland.

LONDON COUNTIES 1953/54

Saturday 7 November 1953
Twickenham, London
Won 11-0

Many people expected London Counties to defeat the All Blacks. The home side contained nine current internationals and had even managed the luxury of a warm-up match against Glamorgan. In addition to this, there was the chance of an historic hat-trick, for London Counties had beaten Australia in 1947 and had been the only side to defeat the 1951/52 South African tourists. None of the New Zealanders had played at Twickenham before – even Bob Scott, the Kiwi veteran of 1945, was new to the ground, and injuries kept both Bill McCaw and Laurie Haig out of the side for this match. However, scrum-half Vince Bevan was

LONDON COUNTIES	NEW ZEALAND
G. Williams (London Welsh & Middlesex)	R.W.H. Scott
C.E. Winn (Rosslyn Park & Surrey)	W.S.S. Freebairn
H.C. Forbes (Harlequins & Surrey)	J.T. Fitzgerald
D.G.S. Baker	R.A. Jarden
(Old Merchant Taylors & Middlesex)	
B.M. Gray (Richmond & Middlesex)	J.M. Tanner
N.M. Hall (Richmond & Middlesex, Capt.)	D.D. Wilson
P.W. Sykes (Wasps & Middlesex)	V.D. Bevan
Forwards:	Forwards:
J.H. Smith (London Irish & Middlesex)	H.L. White
N.A. Labuschagne (Harlequins & Middlesex)	R.C. Hemi
D.L. Sanders (Harlequins & Eastern Counties)	K.L. Skinner
B.A. Neale (Rosslyn Park & Surrey)	R.A. White
P.G. Yarranton (Wasps & Middlesex)	G.N. Dalzell
G.M.D. Archer (London Irish & Surrey)	P.F. Jones
D.S. Wilson	O.D. Oliver
(Metropolitan Police & Middlesex)	
P.W. Kininmonth (Richmond & Middlesex)	R.C. Stuart (Capt.)

Scorers:
New Zealand: Tries: Fitzgerald, Dalzell. Con: Jarden. PG: Jarden.

Referee: R.J. Todd (North Midlands).
Attendance: 50,000.

now fit and was selected for his first appearance of the tour. Sadly, as a spectacle the match was very dull, although in retrospect the tourists' victory turned out to be one of their finest achievements. The game was for the most part a forward battle, with many breaks for injury. Unfortunately the Counties' captain, outside half Nim Hall, decided to play an almost exclusively kicking game and this really killed the match as entertainment.

After nineteen minutes of untidy scrummaging and injury breaks, New Zealand scored their first points when Ron Jarden kicked a penalty. Another spate of dropped passes and interruptions followed before, deep into injury time, a try was finally scored. The London Counties full-back, Welsh international Gerwyn Williams, fumbled a punt from Jarden. John Tanner was there to gather the loose ball and he put Jim Fitzgerald in for the score, which Jarden converted. Jarden himself looked to have scored a try earlier, but Jack Kelly, acting as touch judge for New Zealand, decided that Jarden had hit the corner flag before he grounded the ball. Many thought otherwise.

With the tourists leading 8-0, the sides changed ends, but the second half was even less eventful than the first. Vince Bevan was constantly targeted by the opposition flankers, but he stood up to them bravely and enjoyed an impressive tour debut. Bob Scott lightened the gloom with his usual array of monster kicks and safe catching, but there was little else to enthuse over. The only other score was slightly controversial, in that Gerwyn Williams appeared to have claimed a mark fairly from a Stuart Freebairn kick, before he was bundled over the goal line. Mr Todd, the referee, thought differently and awarded a scrum, from which Nelson Dalzell scored a pushover try.

Some of the British press accused the All Blacks of using rough tactics in their victory, but they were probably justified in keeping the game tight in what was their first major game of the tour; the play was rugged rather than dirty. Of the London Counties players not capped at the time of the match, 'Sandy' Sanders and Peter Yarranton received England caps before the end of the season and centre Doug Baker was capped in 1955, prior to going on the British Lions tour to South Africa. To win against such a strong selection so early in the tour was a tremendous boost to the confidence of the All Blacks.

OXFORD UNIVERSITY 1953/54

Wednesday 11 November 1953
Iffley Road, Oxford
Won 14-5

This Oxford University XV relied heavily on its Rhodes scholars. There were five South Africans and two Rhodesians in the side and the university was often jokingly referred to as 'Springboxford'. For good measure, prop forward Jeffery Steel was a New Zealander. There were seven Blues in the team to face the All Blacks, but the visitors were expected to win easily. The tourists only retained three of the side that had defeated London Counties. Fitzpatrick, Dixon, Guy Bowers and O'Dea all made their first appearances. Dixon had been taken ill with a poisoned knee in Singapore and had missed the opening few days in England. Kevin Skinner led the team.

OXFORD UNIVERSITY	NEW ZEALAND
D.A.B. Robinson (Trinity)	J.W. Kelly
J.C. Baggaley (Trinity)	M.J. Dixon
P.G. Johnstone (St John's)	C.J. Loader
T.J. Fallon (Worcester)	A.E.G. Elsom
D.J. Skipper (Brasenose)	B.B.J. Fitzpatrick
R.R. Winn (Exeter)	R.G. Bowers
L.P. MacLachlan (Exeter)	K. Davis
Forwards:	Forwards:
J.J. Steel (New College)	B.P. Eastgate
R.C.P. Allaway (University)	C.A. Woods
J.P. Fellows-Smith (Brasenose)	K.L. Skinner (Capt.)
A.W. Boyce (St Edmund Hall)	K.P. Bagley
L.W. Bryer (University)	H.L. White
E.A.J. Ferguson (Oriel)	R.J. O'Dea
A.W. Ramsay (Brasenose, Capt.)	W.H. Clark
D.E. Wood (St Edmund Hall)	O.D. Oliver

Scorers:
Oxford University: Try: Fallon. Con: Robinson.
New Zealand: Tries: Dixon, Eastgate, Clark. Con: Kelly. PG: Kelly.

Referee: R.W. Foster (Durham).
Attendance: 9,000.

What followed was ranked by the great New Zealand journalist Terry McLean as the worst All Black display of all time. Unfancied Oxford were considered unlucky not to have won, and had their full-back Dennis Robinson not had an off day with his kicking the result might have been different. The New Zealanders dropped passes, kicked aimlessly and missed the leadership of Stuart. Ewen Ferguson had a field day in the lineouts and centre Paul Johnstone was always a threat. Johnstone, a South African who had toured with the 1951/52 Springboks, should not really have been playing as he had a torn thigh muscle. It was Johnstone, in fact, who very nearly put the students ahead early when a drop goal narrowly missed. Oxford's forwards began impressively and loose forwards Dudley Wood, a future RFU secretary, and his captain Alec Ramsay, whose father was the current RFU treasurer and future president, gave Keith Davis a difficult time. Unfortunately for Oxford, Robinson missed three penalties. The opening try came after just ten minutes and was scored by Morrie Dixon. Peter Eastgate increased the

Kevin Skinner, who stood in as captain in the absence of Bob Stuart and Laurie Haig. (Rugby Museum of New Zealand)

lead when he touched down and Jack Kelly converted this try for an 8-0 lead. Then, with Johnstone looking dangerous, Oxford got the try they deserved. Johnstone kicked ahead, and centre Terry Fallon pinched the ball out of the air before Jack Kelly could reach it. Fallon crossed the line and Robinson converted, leaving a worried New Zealand only 3 points ahead at half-time.

During the second half, Bill Clark relieved the pressure for the visitors by running through to score, following his own charge down of a kick. Oxford continued to attack, but Kelly had the last word, kicking a penalty at the very end of a long half to give New Zealand a flattering winning margin.

Of the Oxford side, only David Skipper, a Blue in 1952, did not appear in the subsequent Varsity match. Despite his Rhodesian origins, Lachlan MacLachlan played for Scotland against the tourists, while 'Pom-Pom' Fellows-Smith became a prominent Test cricketer, touring England with the 1960 South Africans. Ricky Winn was the younger brother of Chris Winn, who had appeared in the London Counties XV in the previous match of the tour.

WESTERN COUNTIES 1953/54

**Saturday 14 November 1953
Memorial Ground, Bristol
Won 11-0**

A sell-out crowd of 21,000 came to Bristol to see the All Blacks. Among the throng was a contingent from Wales, including officials from Cardiff, New Zealand's opponents on the following Saturday. The Western Counties team had five capped players, including winger and captain Jack Gregory. The Counties hooker Dai Davies, a Welsh international, had toured New Zealand with the British Lions in 1950.

Everyone had now played at least one game for the tourists and the selected side was a strong one. Right at the start

WESTERN COUNTIES	NEW ZEALAND
R. Challis (Bristol & Somerset)	R.W.H. Scott
C.G. Woodruff (Cheltenham & Gloucestershire)	M.J. Dixon
J.E. Taylor (Gloucester & Gloucestershire)	J.T. Fitzgerald
D.T. Williams (Bridgwater & Albion & Somerset)	R.A. Jarden
J.A. Gregory (Bristol & Gloucestershire, Capt.)	B.B.J. Fitzpatrick
G. Davies (Bristol & Gloucestershire)	D.D. Wilson
B.A. Tuttiett (Clifton & Somerset)	V.D. Bevan
Forwards:	Forwards:
G.W. Hastings (Gloucester & Gloucestershire)	I.J. Clarke
D.M. Davies (Somerset Police & Somerset)	R.C. Hemi
H.R. Bastable (Bridgwater & Albion & Somerset)	B.P. Eastgate
E.G. Hopton (Bath & Somerset)	G.N. Dalzell
P.D. Young (Dublin Wanderers & Gloucestershire)	R.A. White
A.C. Lewis (Bath & Somerset)	P.F. Jones
D. Ibbotson (Gloucester & Gloucestershire)	W.H. Clark
R.C. Hodge (Gloucester & Gloucestershire)	R.C. Stuart (Capt.)

Scorers:
New Zealand: Tries: Clark, Jones. Con: Scott. DG: Scott.

Referee: Dr P.F. Cooper (London).
Attendance: 21,000.

Ron Jarden was narrowly wide with a penalty attempt, but the first score was a try from Bill Clark. Bob Scott sent a kick towards Jarden's wing, where Jarden forced Counties' centre John Taylor to rush his pass to Bob Challis at full-back. Challis was hit by Clark and Peter Jones, and Clark picked up the loose ball and scored in the corner. To the disappointment of the crowd, the Western Counties' outside half, Glyn Davies, elected to play a kicking game. He had a fine understanding at club level with his fellow Bristol player Gregory, and frequently directed kicks to Gregory's wing that resulted in tries. Sadly, this tactic failed to work against Ron Jarden. Just before half-time an error by Davies led to New Zealand's second score. He sent a relieving kick from his 25, but failed to find touch. Instead, he found Bob Scott waiting for the ball just inside the touchline on halfway. Scott proceeded to drop a magnificent goal. New Zealand led 6-0 at half-time.

Davies was harried throughout by Clark and Jones, and he was again at fault in the second half when he dropped a pass from a lineout. Bill Clark grabbed the loose ball and put Jones in for a try that Scott converted. This was the only score of a disappointing half, during which the New Zealand backs played very poorly. Vince Bevan and Doug Wilson had a difficult afternoon, with Counties flankers Alec Lewis and Denis Ibbotson being particularly severe on Bevan. Counties number eight Bob Hodge also played well, as did scrum-half Ben Tuttiett of Clifton, who came as close as anyone to scoring for the home side when his attempted drop goal went just wide.

Local journalist Tony Reed felt that the crowd deserved more entertainment and the New Zealanders were frequently booed by sections of the crowd who became frustrated at their play.

Of the Western Counties side, only second-row Peter Young played for England against the All Blacks later in the tour. Bristol player Bob Challis, the Western Counties full-back, found fame four years later as a member of England's 1957 Grand Slam side. He was not, however, a member of the 1957 Western Counties side that defeated Australia in Bristol. Only Harlequins and England winger 'Peter' Woodruff and prop George Hastings survived from the 1953 team for this match.

LLANELLY   1953/54

Tuesday 17 November 1953
Stradey Park, Llanelly
Won 17-3

The All Blacks ventured into Wales for the first time and faced 'the Scarlets' of Llanelly. After a few indifferent years, the home side had enjoyed an improved season. They had won thirteen of their 17 games to date, including an 8-3 win over Cardiff. The famous the 'Tanner Bank' terrace had been opened in early September. RAF lock Rhys 'R.H.' Williams rejoined Llanelly from Bristol in time for the game and also played against New Zealand for Combined Services. He was later capped by Wales and toured with the British Lions in 1955 and 1959. After the latter tour he was declared one of the five 'Players of the Year'

LLANELLY	NEW ZEALAND
L. Phillips	R.W.H. Scott
R. Thomas	R.A. Jarden
D. Thomas	J.T. Fitzgerald
H.R. Williams	A.E.G. Elsom
J.H. Daniels	J.M. Tanner
G.R. Tucker	L.S. Haig
W. Evans	V.D. Bevan
Forwards:	Forwards:
H. Morgan	I.J. Clarke
C. Higgins	R.C. Hemi
D. Clarke	K.L. Skinner
R.H. Williams	G.N. Dalzell
G. Hughes	R.A. White
L. Davies	W.H. Clark
D.G. Sanders	R.C. Stuart (Capt.)
P.D. Evans (Capt.)	W.A. McCaw

Scorers:
Llanelli: Try: Tucker.
New Zealand: Tries: Elsom (3), White. Con: Scott. PG: Jarden.

Referee: D.C. Joynson (Rogerstone).
Attendance: 18,000.

by the *New Zealand Rugby Almanack*. Llanelly were led by Peter Evans, a former Welsh international, who later emigrated to New Zealand. The All Blacks made several changes to their side and welcomed back Bill McCaw, playing in his first game since the opening match.

The tourists opened the scoring after seven minutes when Rhys Williams was penalised for being offside and Ron Jarden kicked a fine penalty from close to halfway. Shortly after this the scores were level when John Tanner was heavily tackled by Ray Williams just outside the Llanelly 25. The ball went loose and Denzil Thomas kicked ahead. He gathered the ball and passed outside to wing Ron Thomas, who made good ground before feeding the ball to Geoff Tucker for a spectacular try that brought deafening cheers from the capacity crowd. Full-back Les Phillips missed the conversion. The match was very tight and the home pack disrupted the All Blacks, with forwards Williams, Len Davies, Derek Sanders and skipper Evans outstanding. It was 3-3 at half-time.

Shortly after the restart, Bill Clark charged down a clearance kick and 'Tiny' White gathered the ball to score an unconverted try. Then, crucially, Llanelly wing Ron Thomas was injured and had to leave the field. The All Blacks made the most of their numerical advantage and exploited the weakness in the Llanelly backs. They scored 11 points in the last fifteen minutes. Bob Scott joined the three-quarters to make an overlap for Allan Elsom to score, and then converted a fine second try from Elsom in the dying minutes. Then the Canterbury three-quarter scored his hat-trick try on the stroke of full-time to see New Zealand home by a margin that failed to reflect Llanelly's contribution. It had been a fine, hard game of rugby that raised some unnecessary criticism of the All Blacks for over-vigorous play. It did, however, show that the tourists' backs were something to behold.

CARDIFF 1953/54

Saturday 21 November 1953
Cardiff Arms Park, Cardiff
Lost 8-3

Cardiff was unquestionably the leading club side in Britain, possessing good forwards and highly talented, fast, creative backs. They had defeated the Australians in 1947 and, although they lost to South Africa four years later, the Springboks were so relieved to get away with a win that they presented Cardiff with a mounted Springbok head that was otherwise only awarded to the first side to defeat them on tour. Cardiff had lost only three of their 17 games played before this match, and scored nearly 50 tries in the process. There was a belief that if the Cardiff pack could win enough ball the backs were good enough to score the points. New Zealand recognised the threat and selected their strongest side. Bob Stuart was originally chosen for the game but had to withdraw when a cut on his leg sustained in the match at Bristol became infected, and

CARDIFF	NEW ZEALAND
J.E.L. Llewellyn	R.W.H. Scott
G. Rowlands	R.A. Jarden
B.L. Williams (Capt.)	J.T. Fitzgerald
A.G. Thomas	A.E.G. Elsom
G.M. Griffiths	D.D. Wilson
C.I. Morgan	L.S. Haig (Capt.)
W.R. Willis	V.D. Bevan
Forwards:	Forwards:
A.D.S. Bowes	H.L. White
G.T. Beckingham	R.C. Hemi
J.D. Evans	K.L. Skinner
M. Collins	G.N. Dalzell
E. Thomas	R.A. White
C.D. Williams	W.H. Clark
J.D. Nelson	W.A. McCaw
S. Judd	D.O. Oliver

Scorers:
Cardiff: Tries: Judd, Rowlands. Con: Rowlands.
New Zealand: PG: Jarden.

Referee: V.S. Llewellyn (Llansamlett).
Attendance: 56,000.

the captain was prescribed penicillin and rest. His place was taken by Bill McCaw, who had expected to run the line for New Zealand, with Laurie Haig taking over as captain.

After several days of intense anticipation, the match eventually started. After two minutes Bob Scott attempted a penalty from halfway but it fell short into the arms of Cliff Morgan. Instead of clearing to touch the outside half ran the ball back at the All Blacks, cutting through the centre before kicking ahead into space and pressurising the tourists' defence into clearing to touch. A small incident, but an early

The Cardiff team that defeated New Zealand in 1953. From left to right, back row: Gareth Griffiths, John Llewellyn, Eddie Thomas, Malcolm Collins, John Nelson, J.D. Evans. Front row: C.D. Williams, Stan Bowes, Rex Willis, Sid Judd, Bleddyn Williams (captain), Cliff Morgan, Alun Thomas, Gwyn Rowlands, Geoff Beckingham.

illustration as to how Cardiff were going to approach the game. They played attacking rugby without inhibition. Then, after New Zealand had come close to scoring, Cardiff gained scrum possession and Morgan, at the end of Rex Willis's long pass, made a half break before kicking into space behind the defence. The ball rebounded off an All Black into his arms and he made ground before passing to Alun Thomas who fed Gwyn Rowlands. As the New Zealand cover closed him down he kicked across towards the posts, where Cardiff's vice-captain Sid Judd reached the ball first and dived over the line for the try. Eight minutes had gone and the crowd bellowed their approval. Rowlands converted. Five minutes later New Zealand were on the board. Cardiff were caught offside and Ron Jarden kicked a fine penalty from close to touch. Cardiff scored again shortly afterwards. Quick ball from a scrum was moved to Bleddyn Williams, who deftly punted the ball over the New Zealand defence. Alun Thomas was perfectly placed to gather the bouncing ball at pace, ran at Scott and, having committed the full-back, passed outside to Rowlands who sprinted in from thirty yards to score by the corner flag. The conversion was missed and, remarkably, with less than twenty minutes gone the scoring was complete at 8-3. From this point onwards the All Blacks threw everything at Cardiff but the home defence managed to keep them out.

In the second half New Zealand tried everything to score, but kept the ball tight, opting to win the game through their forwards. Although the All Blacks' forwards had the lion's share of possession, the lighter Cardiff eight disrupted and confounded their moves and plans. Richard 'Tiny' White and Bill McCaw were tackled on the line but once Cardiff got the ball they counter-attacked at pace and Rowlands was close to scoring again. It was thrust and counter-thrust, and every time the Cardiff backs broke through, the magnificent All Blacks back row would cover the break and make a tackle: then the All Blacks' pack was nearly over, then Bleddyn Williams was through but Bill Clark tackled him. It was wonderful rugby and Morgan was at his effervescent best. The main Cardiff tactics were continuity and movement at pace – to try and run the All Blacks off their feet. But to do that they needed the ball. In the Cardiff pack Stan Bowes was immense. Although in his mid-thirties, the charismatic prop shored up the scrum and used his extraordinary strength seemingly to hold up the All Blacks on his own. Cardiff tried to tie up the back row by throwing to the back of the lineout, a successful ploy which helped them win plenty of ball. It was an heroic performance by the Cardiff forwards as New Zealand pressed and pressed. As the match neared its conclusion, Scott kept missing drop goal attempts. The crowd cheered incessantly and, after an All Blacks tight head was lost, Cliff Morgan kicked the ball to touch and the final whistle went shortly after. Cardiff had won a breathlessly exciting game.

New Zealand's legendary rugby writer, Terry McLean, in his role as the All Blacks' press representative, said: 'You had more speed, more resource, and a spirit that I feel sure can never have been excelled in all your glorious history.'

Derek 'C.D.' Williams had played for Southern Counties against the All Blacks in the opening match of the tour. Judd played in the Wales pack that later played the All Blacks. He was joined by all the Cardiff backs except John Llewellyn and Alun Thomas. Thomas later toured South Africa with the British Lions in 1955 and returned there in 1974 as the victorious British Lions' manager.

GLASGOW & EDINBURGH   1953/54

Wednesday 25 November 1953
Old Anniesland, Glasgow
Won 23-3

GLASGOW & EDINBURGH	NEW ZEALAND
D.H. Crighton (Watsonians)	R.W.H. Scott
W.H. Clephan (Watsonians)	W.S.S. Freebairn
A. Cameron (Glasgow HSFP)	C.J. Loader
D.M. Scott (Watsonians)	M.J. Dixon
A.D. Cameron (Hillhead HSFP)	B.B.J. Fitzpatrick
J.N.G. Davidson (Edinburgh University)	R.G. Bowers
A.A.W. Waddell (Glasgow Acads)	V.D. Bevan
Forwards:	Forwards:
S.T.H. Wright (Stewart's FP)	B.P. Eastgate
N.G.R. Mair (Edinburgh University, Capt.)	C.A. Woods
J.C. Dawson (Glasgow Acads)	K.L. Skinner (Capt.)
J.W.Y. Kemp (Glasgow HSFP)	R.A. White
V.H. Leadbetter (Edinburgh Wanderers)	K.P. Bagley
J.S. Ure (Edinburgh Wanderers)	R.J. O'Dea
W.S. Glen (Edinburgh Wanderers)	P.F.H. Jones
R.A. Cadzow (Edinburgh Wanderers)	W.A. McCaw

Scorers:
Glasgow & Edinburgh: Try: Clephan.
New Zealand: Tries: Freebairn (2), Jones, Loader. Cons: Scott (4). PG: Scott.

Referee: A.I. Dickie (Gala).
Attendance: 9,000.

The New Zealanders arrived in Scotland, where many of them had family connections, not really knowing what to expect. The reports suggested that Scottish rugby was at a low ebb, but the tourists were wary enough not to take their fixtures north of the border too lightly. For the match against the combined cities of Glasgow & Edinburgh, the New Zealanders rested many of their first-choice players and fielded an understrength side. Nevertheless, the forward pack was big and powerful, and the Wellington half-back pairing of Guy Bowers, a shy twenty-year-old, and Vince Bevan, a milkman and a chainsmoker, was full of promise. The Cities were weakened by the withdrawal of the Scotland back-row player Douglas Elliot because of a leg injury, but the forwards, with four players from Edinburgh Wanderers, looked strong while the back division had four internationals.

In near-perfect conditions, the first half was a comedy of errors, with both sides making many mistakes. The Cities dropped passes, kicked aimlessly and used the ball poorly, while the New Zealanders were disjointed and lacking in fire. However, it was clear that the visiting forwards were superior, Tiny White and

Under the auspices of the Scottish Rugby Union

Glasgow and Edinburgh
v.
New Zealand
at
Old Anniesland, Glasgow
Wednesday, 25th November, 1953
Kick-off 2.15 p.m.
PRICE   SIXPENCE
Printed by the Scottish Rugby Union
by
Rowans, 70 Buchanan Street, Glasgow, C.1.

Keith Bagley dominating the lineouts and Arthur Woods doing well in the scrums. There was no score at half-time, but during the interval Bob Scott could be seen exhorting his players to much greater efforts. Predictably, the New Zealanders raised their game and opened the scoring within three minutes of the restart. Scott came into the line and kicked to the corner where Stu Freebairn, following-up at speed, beat Bill Clephan to the ball. Scott added the conversion and a few minutes later kicked a penalty after Alan Waddell had been caught offside at a scrum. There was joy for the Cities when Norman Davidson, a medical student from Hawick, made a superb break from his own half, kicking ahead for Clephan, an Englishman, to flash past Scott for the touchdown. Hamish Kemp made a poor effort of the conversion attempt and this was the last time that the Cities threatened. New Zealand responded with a powerful forward rush from a scrum and Peter Jones forced his way over. In the final quarter, as the Cities began to fade, the visitors had a good passing movement with Brian

Fitzpatrick and Colin Loader making ground before sending Freebairn away. Finally, Scott sped into the backline and fed Loader, who beat several defenders to score. Scott converted all of the tries as a matter of course. In contrast, the Cities missed four penalty attempts during the match.

This was a fairly routine win for New Zealand, who performed only in fits and starts. According to the *Scotsman*, they 'gave no glimmerings of being world beaters'. The pack was physically superior with Skinner, O'Dea, White and Jones all prominent. Bill McCaw covered the ground hungrily and was a constant menace. Once again, Bob Scott showed that he was the ideal full-back with his impeccable catching, gigantic touch kicks, uncanny positional sense and readiness to join the attack. For the Cities, Ure and Bill Glen defended well and Norman Mair, Ralph Cadzow and Kemp showed plenty of fighting spirit.

SOUTH OF SCOTLAND   1953/54

Saturday 28 November 1953
Netherdale, Galashiels
Won 32-0

SOUTH OF SCOTLAND	NEW ZEALAND
J.R. McCredie (Hawick)	R.W.H. Scott
W.R. Scott (Hawick)	R.A. Jarden
J.L. Allan (Melrose)	A.E.G. Elsom
R.G. Charters (Hawick)	M.J. Dixon
S.S. Cowan (Selkirk)	B.B.J. Fitzpatrick
J.M. Maxwell (Langholm)	L.S. Haig (Capt.)
A.F. Dorward (Gala)	K. Davis
Forwards:	Forwards:
H.F. McLeod (Hawick)	K.L. Skinner
J.H. King (Selkirk)	R.C. Hemi
R.L. Wilson (Gala, Capt.)	I.J. Clarke
T. Elliot (Gala)	G.N. Dalzell
J.J. Hegarty (Hawick)	K.P. Bagley
A. Robson (Hawick)	W.H. Clark
G.K. Smith (Kelso)	D.O. Oliver
J. Grant (Hawick)	W.A. McCaw

Scorers:
New Zealand: Tries: Jarden (3), Dixon (2), Dalzell, Clarke. Cons: Jarden (2), Scott (2). PG: Jarden.

Referee: A.W.G. Austin (Glasgow HSFP).
Attendance: 12,000.

New Zealand turned on the style in a high-scoring and controversial display. The visitors fielded a strong fifteen with ten of the players who had lost at Cardiff the previous Saturday. Allan Elsom, the determined Canterbury winger, was moved into the centre to stiffen the defence while the forwards were nearly the strongest available. The South's best chance, it was felt, was to take on the visitors up front. The home forwards were smaller and lighter, but they were sturdy and battle-hardened with three international players and several others pressing for recognition. Looking on among the large crowd was octogenarian Tom Riddle, who had played for Hawick against the New Zealand Natives way back in 1888.

In soft and slippery conditions, the first half was marred by an unsavoury undercurrent, which threatened to erupt on several occasions. On eleven minutes, the South captain Bob Wilson was penalised for throwing a punch, although he claimed that he had been held back illegally. Ron Jarden kicked the goal from about thirty yards out. Both sides were fired up and handed out some abrasive treatment to each other, earning strong rebukes from the referee. The crowd took exception to some of the New Zealand tactics, responding with a chorus of booing and badgering of individual players, something almost unheard of in rugby at the time and forcing some spectators to leave the ground in disgust. Fortunately, the atmosphere cooled in the second half as the visitors took firm control. Despite these incidents New Zealand played an open and attractive game, with 5 of their 7 tries scored by their wingers Ron Jarden (3) and Maurice Dixon (2). A beautiful fast runner with a devastating body swerve, Jarden was a constant threat to the South defence and gave his opposite number Cowan an uncomfortable afternoon. At full-back, Bob Scott turned in another good display, making frequent intrusions into the line and kicking and fielding in fine style, despite the difficult conditions. However, it was the forwards who laid the foundations, slowly wearing their opponents down with their bulldozing drives. Kevin Skinner, Keith Bagley and Bill McCaw were very prominent, although the South forwards stuck manfully to their task and deserved better reward for their efforts, several playing themselves to a

The All Blacks perform their traditional Haka before demolishing the South of Scotland in 1953. (Robert D. Clapperton Photographic Trust)

standstill. Arthur Dorward had a good game at scrum-half and Les Allan tried his best in the centre, but the South back division made little use of the ball they received, their tackling was fatally weak and in general they lacked pace and guile. Their cause was not helped by the loss of full-back Jim McCredie through injury in the second half. The home side never stopped trying, but fell far short of expectations. This was an impressive and decisive win for New Zealand, the nature of which sent a shudder through Scottish rugby.

NORTH OF SCOTLAND   1953/54

Wednesday 2 December 1953
Linksfield Stadium, Aberdeen
Won 28-3

The New Zealanders travelled north to the Granite City of Aberdeen, where they were warmly welcomed. The North of Scotland was the weakest of the four Scottish district sides, drawing players from a huge geographical area, which did little to help the side's cohesiveness. New Zealand were firm favourites and fielded their midweek side, including four players making their debut in Scotland. It was predicted that the visiting forwards would be too powerful and the North could only hope to keep the score respectable. Despite being written off, the North included several talented players, including the thirty-four-year-old William Allardice, who had won eight Scottish caps in the 1940s,

NORTH OF SCOTLAND	NEW ZEALAND
W. Thomson (St Andrews University)	J.W. Kelly
E.H. Cruickshank (Aberdeen GSFP)	J.M. Tanner
J. Sabin (Highland)	J.T. Fitzgerald
A.M. Nicoll (Harris Academy FP)	W.S.S. Fairbairn
D.J. McPherson (Gordonians)	D.D. Wilson
J.A. Murray (Panmure)	R.G. Bowers
W.D. Allardice (Aberdeen GSFP, Capt.)	K. Davis
Forwards:	Forwards:
A. Tullet (Gordonians)	B.P. Eastgate
W. Bravin (Dunfermline)	C.A. Woods
F.J. Moore (Perthshire Acads)	I.J. Clarke
E.J.S. Michie (Aberdeen University)	K.P. Bagley
C.D. Mowat (Aberdeen GSFP)	R.A. White
J.A. Blake (Panmure)	R.J. O'Dea
J. Greenwood (Dunfermline)	P.F.H. Jones
N.Z. Sacks (Aberdeen Wanderers)	W.A. McCaw (Capt.)

Scorers:
North of Scotland: Try: Sabin.
New Zealand: Tries: Freebairn (3), Jones (2), Fitzgerald.
Cons: Kelly (5).

Referee: W.C.W. Murdoch (Hillhead HSFP).
Attendance: 6,000.

and the dynamic back-row forward Jim Greenwood, a future Scottish captain and one of the stars of the 1955 British Lions tour to South Africa. The match was played in front of about 6,000 people, the smallest crowd of the tour, and refereed by former international 'Copey' Murdoch.

Typically, New Zealand started slowly and with the wind behind them the North stormed into the lead. Eric Cruickshank hit the post with a penalty, but almost immediately Guy Bowers was firmly tackled by Allardice. John Murray kicked the loose ball across the field diagonally and Jack Sabin, a strong-running centre who had previously played for Notts, Lincs and Derbys, raced up to score. The North dominated for the first fifteen minutes, but gradually the visitors began to settle. Keith Davis broke away from a scrum and fed Peter Jones, who crossed for a try converted by Jack Kelly. Normally a wonderful place-kicker, the New Zealand full-back missed an easy penalty in front of the posts, but he made no mistake towards the end of the half when he converted a try by Stu Freebairn. The credit for the score went to Bowers, who had made a devastating thirty-yard dash around the blind side. The All Blacks led 10-3 at half-time.

In the second half, the New Zealand forwards got on top and the backs began to throw the ball around, despite valiant defence from the North. Jones, McCaw and Bagley led some furious assaults and Doug Wilson, playing at second five-eighth, began to find his form. Kelly made his presence felt by cutting clean through and presenting Freebairn with an easy try. Some crisp handling led to further tries by Jim Fitzgerald, Jones and Freebairn. The victory had been emphatic and complete, undertaken with characteristic New Zealand efficiency. As expected, the forwards had dominated and only in loose play did the North eight have a chance. Of the New Zealand backs, Davis and Bowers had played strongly, and Fitzgerald showed himself a straight and determined runner. Clearly outclassed, the North had put up a spirited resistance, all of the backs tackling firmly and Neville Sacks, Ernie Michie and Jimmy Blake playing well at forward. Thus, the tourists successfully completed their third and final game against the Scottish district teams, having scored 83 points and conceded only 6. Curiously, both Scottish scores were by Englishmen, Clephan for the Combined Cities and Sabin for the North.

LEICESTERSHIRE & EAST MIDLANDS   1953/54

Saturday 5 December 1953
Welford Road, Leicester
Won 3-0

This was a tremendous game of rugby and a match that the All Blacks were fortunate to win. Leicestershire & East Midlands had a reputation for doing well against touring sides. The combined fifteen had inflicted the only defeat on the great South African side of 1931/32, and more recently had lost to the fourth Springboks just 3-0. Unfortunately for the home side, three of its best players, England internationals Don White, Lewis Cannell and John Hyde withdrew through injury prior to the game. Also missing was outside half Ray Williams of Northampton. Williams was involved in a Welsh trial so Alan Towell was moved from the centre. As it happened, Towell

LEICESTERSHIRE & EAST MIDLANDS	NEW ZEALAND
J. Hodgkins (Northampton)	R.W.H. Scott
G.H. Cullen (Leicester)	W.S.S. Freebairn
J. Elders (Leicester)	A.E.G. Elsom
R.W. Hosen (Loughborough Colleges)	R.A. Jarden
D. Macnally (Northampton)	B.B.J. Fitzpatrick
A.C. Towell (Bedford)	L.S. Haig (Capt.)
J.W. Hobbs (Gloucester)	V.D. Bevan
Forwards:	Forwards:
C.R. Jacobs (Northampton)	B.P. Eastgate
T.H. Smith (Northampton)	R.C. Hemi
D.St G. Hazell (Leicester)	K.L. Skinner
J.M. Jenkins (Leicester)	R.A. White
V.H. Leadbetter (Edinburgh Wanderers)	G.N. Dalzell
P.S. Collingridge (Bedford, Capt.)	O.D. Oliver
T. Bleasdale (Leicester)	W.H. Clark
R.C. Hawkes (Northampton)	W.A. McCaw

Scorers:
New Zealand: PG: Jarden.

Referee: T.E. Priest (London).
Attendance: 22,000.

had a superb game and must have greatly impressed the watching England selectors, although he was not destined to add to the two England caps he had already received. Future England full-back Roger Hosen was selected in the centre. New Zealand arrived without their captain Bob Stuart, who was in London receiving treatment for his injured knee. The All Blacks missed his leadership and for the only time in the tour their pack was outlasted by the opposition eight and appeared tired towards the end.

The only score of the game came after just five minutes when Jarden kicked a penalty. Several All Black tries went a-begging, notably when Stuart Freebairn knocked-on on the try line. Later in the game Freebairn elected to pass when he had only the full-back to beat and again the ball was dropped. Bill McCaw did cross the line for the All Blacks, but he was recalled for a forward pass. The tourists' backs had a poor afternoon, but Bob Scott came close to scoring with two drop goals. Despite the brilliant tactical kicking and running of Towell, the Counties rarely looked like scoring a try. They attacked very strongly in the dying minutes of the game, by which time their pack was well on top, but the nearest they got to a score was when Towell's attempted drop goal was narrowly wide. Dick Hawkes gave a superb display in the lineouts. The New Zealanders were so impressed with Hawkes that when he was chosen as an uncapped player in the Barbarian XV for the final game of the tour, 'Tiny' White was given the specific job of marking him and ensuring that New Zealand had some lineout ball.

Modern rugby players at the top level are more than used to the hazards of booing and jeering during the taking of place kicks. This was most certainly not the case in 1953, and there was much enraged comment in the press about the unsporting behaviour of the home crowd. Towards the end of the match, Scott had to suffer boos and then slow handclapping as he prepared to take a penalty. The referee, Mr Priest, suggested to Scott that he sit down and wait until the noise subsided, but Scott continued with the kick, which missed the target. Terry Mclean was incensed, writing in his book on the tour: 'It is almost impossible to say a good word for Leicester. If this were to be the behaviour associated with rugby, I do not think the game would last for more than a few years.'

It is unfortunate that the behaviour of the crowd spoiled such a tense, close struggle, although it must have encouraged everyone to see such a large gathering on the day, particularly with Leicester City playing a home Second Division game just down the road.

LEICESTERSHIRE & EAST MIDLANDS
COMBINED XV. v.
NEW ZEALAND TOURING XV.
SATURDAY, DECEMBER 5th, 1953

SOUTH-WESTERN COUNTIES 1953/54

Wednesday 9 December 1953
Recreation Ground, Camborne
Won 9-0

The home side included a number of internationals for this game. John Williams, the centre, had won two England caps in 1951, while forwards Vic Roberts, a 1950 British Lion, Eddie Woodgate and captain John Kendall-Carpenter were all England players. Eddie Woodgate was the only player to be capped from the Paignton club and his fellow prop in this match was his twin brother Bill. Hooking between them in the front row was a young student at St Luke's College, Exeter who was destined to become one of the giants of Welsh rugby. Bryn Meredith won thirty-four Welsh caps and toured

SOUTH-WESTERN COUNTIES	NEW ZEALAND
C.T. Bowen (Newton Abbot & Devon)	J.W. Kelly
H. Stevens (Redruth & Cornwall)	M.J. Dixon
J.M. Williams (Penzance & Newlyn & Cornwall)	J.M. Tanner
C.M. Terry (Penzance & Newlyn & Cornwall)	R.A. Jarden
J.L. Stark (Exeter & Devon)	C.J. Loader
H. Oliver (St Ives & Cornwall)	L.S. Haig (Capt.)
R.F.G. Meadows (Devonport Services & Devon)	K. Davis
Forwards:	Forwards:
E.E. Woodgate (Paignton & Devon)	H.L. White
B.V. Meredith (St Luke's College & Devon)	C.A. Woods
W. Woodgate (Paignton & Devon)	K.L. Skinner
I. Zaidman (St Luke's College & Devon)	K.P. Bagley
T.K. Vivian (Camborne & Cornwall)	G.N. Dalzell
V.G. Roberts (Penryn & Cornwall)	P.F. Jones
A. Bone (St Ives & Cornwall)	W.H. Clark
J. MacG. K. Kendall-Carpenter	I.J. Clarke
(Penzance & Newlyn & Cornwall, Capt.)	

Scorers:
New Zealand: Try: Davis. PG: Jarden. DG: Haig.

Referee: H.B. Elliott (Durham).
Attendance: 18,000.

three times with the British Lions. Bob Stuart was still in London and missed out on the lavish hospitality provided by the people of Cornwall. He also missed the first playing before the game of *God Defend New Zealand*, courtesy of the band of the First Battalion, Duke of Cornwall's Light Infantry. Among the crowd at Camborne were the Lord Lieutenant of Cornwall and the Bishop of Truro.

The game itself was not especially memorable, although the All Blacks had to work hard for victory, especially when Nelson Dalzell left the field after ten minutes with an eye injury. He did not return until the

second half. Kendall-Carpenter and Roberts made life very difficult for the New Zealand midfield, while Ian Clarke put in a tremendous effort for the visitors, especially while Dalzell was absent. New Zealand gained the upper hand in the lineouts thanks to Keith Bagley and Kevin Skinner. Ron Jarden, who hit the post with a goal-kick in each half, opened the scoring with a penalty after thirteen minutes. That was the only score of the first half, although a penalty from Cornish winger Harold Stevens fell just under the bar. Both sides had difficulty controlling the greasy ball on a surface that was slippery after a heavy dew, but Keith Davis managed a second half blind-side try following a forward surge. Right on time Laurie Haig completed the scoring with a well-struck drop goal.

The game was played in an excellent spirit, and Kendall-Carpenter made a valuable sporting contribution to the day when he gestured and shouted to a section of the crowd to 'shut up' after an outbreak of booing. He was also very complimentary to the All Blacks at the after-match dinner held at the Queen's Hotel in Penzance, thanking the visitors for the game and declaring that they were the better side. This dinner was followed by a civic ball at St John's Hall, attended by 500 guests. The hall had been set out as a rugby pitch for the event, complete with posts. On one of these posts was suspended a stuffed kiwi that had been borrowed for the occasion from the New Zealand High Commission in London. There was also a map of New Zealand hanging up, showing the towns of all the members of the tour party. Among the guests was one of Cornwall's greatest sportsmen, Roy Jennings. He was one of a select group who had toured with the British Lions, but never played for his country. Jennings, a Redruth player who learned his rugby at Taunton School, went to Australia and New Zealand with the Lions in 1930, although he did not appear in a Test match. He played in the pack for Cornwall against the 1924/25 All Blacks, and captained Devon & Cornwall as a centre against the All Blacks of 1935.

SWANSEA   1953/54

Saturday 12 December 1953
St Helen's, Swansea
Drawn 6-6

Swansea had defeated the 1935 All Blacks, becoming the first non-international side to do so in Britain and France. Although rebuilding, they were a good side and still posed a threat to the All Blacks, even though leading backs Terry Davies and Handel Greville were injured. Their injury situation was so bad that John Faull was selected at centre, although he had only played for Swansea once before, and that at full-back. However, Swansea were in inconsistent form. They had defeated Cardiff but lost to Richmond in the preceding weeks. Dil Johnson was a hard-working captain, whilst W.O.G. 'Stoker' Williams was a powerful prop who played in each Test with the 1955 Lions in South Africa. Horace Phillips and Len Blyth played for Wales during their careers, as did Blyth's son Roger, in the 1970s and 1980s. Clem Thomas became one of Welsh rugby's all-time greats, toured as a Lion in 1955 and later became a leading rugby journalist. The nineteen-year-old Faull later played

SWANSEA	NEW ZEALAND
W. Bratton	R.W.H. Scott
T. Williams	R.A. Jarden
J. Faull	A.E.G. Elsom
B. Jenkins	M.J. Dixon
D.H. Phillips	B.B.J. Fitzpatrick
J. Marker	L.S. Haig (Capt.)
G. Morgan	V.D. Bevan
Forwards:	Forwards:
W.O.G. Williams	B.P. Eastgate
T. Petherbridge	R.C. Hemi
D. Jones	K.L. Skinner
D. Bruce-Thomas	K.P. Bagley
W.D. Johnson (Capt.)	R.A. White
E.J. Rees	P.F.H. Jones
R.C.C. Thomas	D.O. Oliver
L. Blyth	W.A. McCaw

Scorers:
Swansea: PGs: Faull (2).
New Zealand: Tries: Elsom (2).

Referee: V. Parfitt (Newport).
Attendance: 40,000.

for Wales and the British Lions in the back row. His father refereed England's victory over New Zealand in 1936. New Zealand changed two-thirds of the side for this game, welcoming back 'Tiny' White and Bob Scott, among others. Bob Stuart was still unfit so Laurie Haig continued to lead the team.

The match was a terrific forward battle in which both packs played with great ferocity. The All Blacks again based their play around the pack, while Haig failed to get the best out of his outside backs. Against the odds Swansea majestically rose to the occasion. The match was five minutes old when Faull kicked a long-range penalty goal to put Swansea into the lead. New Zealand equalised when Peter Jones picked up the loose ball for Brian Fitzpatrick to put centre Allan Elsom in for a try. Ron Jarden's goal-kick missed, as did a penalty a few minutes later, but shortly afterwards, Faull was more successful and put the home side back into the lead with another penalty, this time from halfway. Close to half-time Brian Fitzpatrick kicked out from his 25, but full-back Wyn Bratton, who had replaced the injured Davies, misfielded and Elsom collected the loose ball just inside the Swansea half and raced in for his second try. Jarden's conversion narrowly missed.

With the score 6-6 at the break, the second half was similar to the first, an absorbing forward battle in which the Swansea pack matched the All Blacks' pack and their backs tackled like demons. New Zealand dominated the game but seemed reluctant to move it through the backs. Despite several long-range kicks by Bob Scott, there was no further score and the match ended in a disappointing draw for the All Blacks, but an ecstatic draw for Swansea.

WALES   1953/54

Saturday 19 December 1953
Cardiff Arms Park, Cardiff
Lost 13-8

Rival captains Bleddyn Williams and Bob Stuart. Williams also captained Cardiff to victory over New Zealand.

WALES	NEW ZEALAND
G. Williams (London Welsh)	R.W.H. Scott
K.J. Jones (Newport)	R.A. Jarden
B.L. Williams (Cardiff, Capt.)	J.M. Tanner
G.M. Griffiths (Cardiff)	A.E.G. Elsom
G. Rowlands (Cardiff)	B.B.J. Fitzpatrick
C.I. Morgan (Cardiff)	L.S. Haig
W.R. Willis (Cardiff)	K. Davis
Forwards:	Forwards:
W.O.G. Williams (Swansea)	I.J. Clarke
D.M. Davies (Somerset Police)	R.C. Hemi
C.C. Meredith (Neath)	K.L. Skinner
E.R. John (Neath)	G.N. Dalzell
J.R.G. Stephens (Neath)	R.A. White
S. Judd (Cardiff)	W.H. Clark
J.A. Gwilliam (Gloucester)	R.C. Stuart (Capt.)
R.C.C. Thomas (Swansea)	W.A. McCaw

Scorers:
Wales: Tries: Judd, Jones. Cons: Rowlands (2). PG: Rowlands.
New Zealand: Try: Clark. Con: Jarden. PG: Jarden.

Referee: P.F. Cooper (RFU).
Attendance: 56,000.

Wales were confident of victory. They fielded five backs from Cardiff, including the captain Bleddyn Williams. Southern Counties captain Glyn Davies of London Welsh withdrew, Sid Judd replacing him. Clem Thomas was involved in a fatal road accident on the day before the game but chose to play. Having had a week to prepare for the game, the All Blacks were confident that Bob Stuart had recovered sufficiently from his leg infection and was selected to play. They awarded first international caps to

Clarke, Hemi, Dalzell, Clark and Fitzpatrick. They initially announced a side with both half-backs included, the final decision between Bevan and Davis to be made when the weather was known. It was cold but sunny, with a light breeze, and Davis played.

After initial hard exchanges Davis made a fine break for New Zealand and linked with his backs but Laurie Haig made a bad pass and a scoring opportunity had gone. Then came the first score. At a New Zealand scrum Rex Willis harassed Davis and pinched the ball before finding Judd in support. He kicked ahead, then Ken Jones reached the ball first and also kicked ahead. Bob Scott gathered the ball but Jones tackled him and the full-back's pass went loose for Judd to pick up and score. Gwyn Rowlands converted. The Welsh pack was then put under great pressure by New Zealand. The All Blacks' forwards could be covered by a small blanket. The tight play was complemented by almost constant kicking by the New Zealand backs. It was inevitable that Wales would infringe and Ron Jarden kicked a penalty after Wales were penalised at a scrum. Then a garryowen from Scott brought confusion in the Welsh defence. Defenders collided and the ball went loose for the speedy Bill Clark to dive on and score. Jarden converted, and shortly afterwards, the referee blew for half-time with New Zealand 8-5 in the lead.

The second half was dominated by New Zealand. 'Tiny' White went close to scoring. Bill Clark had the task of subduing Cliff Morgan, which he largely achieved. Then Gareth Griffiths dislocated his shoulder and left the field. With Wales down to fourteen men and Thomas withdrawn from the pack to play on the wing it would surely only be a matter of time before New Zealand scored. But they were unable to capitalise on their possession and countless chances were squandered by the backs. Against doctor's orders Griffiths returned to the field, his arm strapped to his body. His heroic action seemed to inspire the Welsh pack. Play moved into the New Zealand half and when McCaw was penalised at a ruck, Rowlands kicked a goal to tie the scores. The All Blacks ran the ball and Allan Isom was tackled by Rowlands. Thomas was first to the breakdown and suddenly, finding his path blocked, cross-kicked towards the posts. Ken Jones was alert to what was going on and followed up, caught the ball and side-stepped Jarden to score for Rowlands to convert. The Welsh held out and scrambled a famous win. Wales and New Zealand had now played each other on four occasions, and Wales were ahead 3-1.

ABERTILLERY & EBBW VALE   1953/54

Wednesday 23 December 1953
Abertillery Park, Abertillery
Won 22-3

The All Blacks made several changes for the match against this combined clubs selection from the top of the Monmouthshire valleys. The home selectors picked club partnerships for key positions to attempt to offset the lack of familiarity that affects scratch sides. Nevertheless, as both clubs were playing well at the time, they were thought capable of a decent challenge.

After an initial period in which the forwards struggled down, the All Blacks' backs started to move the ball. Laurie Haig came out of his shell and regularly brought his outside backs into the game. The visitors took the lead when Jack Kelly

ABERTILLERY & EBBW VALE	NEW ZEALAND
G. Tovey (Abertillery)	J.W. Kelly
J. Pugh (Ebbw Vale)	M.J. Dixon
R. Cecil (Abertillery)	C.J. Loader
M. Davies (Abertillery)	W.S.S. Freebairn
J.B. Williams (Ebbw Vale)	D.D. Wilson
E.M. Lewis (Abertillery)	L.S. Haig
D. Wilcox (Abertillery)	V.D. Bevan
Forwards:	Forwards:
L. Coldrick (Ebbw Vale)	H.L. White
A. Jackson (Ebbw Vale)	R.C. Hemi
B. Jones (Abertillery)	K.L. Skinner
L. Harris (Ebbw Vale)	K.P. Bagley
B.O. Edwards (Ebbw Vale)	R.A. White
H. Matthews (Ebbw Vale)	D.O. Oliver
K. Morley (Abertillery)	W.A. McCaw
L.E.T. Jones (Abertillery, Capt.)	R.C. Stuart (Capt.)

Scorers:
Abertillery & Ebbw Vale: PG: Edwards.
New Zealand: Tries: Oliver (2), Dixon, Loader, Freebairn.
Cons: Haig (2). PG: Kelly.

Referee: D.O.H. Davies (Carmarthen).
Attendance: 12,000.

kicked an awkward penalty goal, but the match was thirty minutes old before the first try came. The New Zealand forwards quickly released the ball from a ruck in the Abertillery & Ebbw Vale 25 and moved it to Stu Freebairn, who scored between the posts. Kelly's conversion was charged down. The second New Zealand try came soon after this when clever play by the forwards created space for Des Oliver to score. Kelly missed the conversion from alongside the posts, but New Zealand led 9-0 at half-time.

The restart was quickly followed by a third try when Kelly joined the line to create space for wing Morrie Dixon to score. Kelly missed this conversion as well. Then a penalty goal was kicked by home second row Ben Edwards, a powerful factory foreman who had played for Newport against South Africa in 1951 with a broken and dislocated shoulder, and kicked a goal in his only appearance for Wales in 1951. The All Blacks dominated the match and scored two further tries that were good team efforts. Colin Loader finished off a move he had earlier been involved in for a fine try and, after a move in which forwards and backs had combined on several occasions, Oliver scored again. Haig converted both tries and, had it not been for stout defence, he may have had more to convert. New Zealand played within themselves but at last showed what their backs could do.

The All Blacks pack was a fine unit superbly led by Bob Stuart. The tour captain had served in the Royal Navy Corvettes during the Second World War and began playing for Canterbury when he returned to New Zealand. He was first capped by New Zealand against Australia in 1949. As Canterbury's successful captain he was a surprise but inspired choice to lead the All Blacks. An agricultural economist, he later became an All Blacks' coach and served for many years on the executive of the NZRFU. He was awarded an OBE in 1974.

COMBINED SERVICES   1953/54

Saturday 26 December 1953
Twickenham, London
Won 40-8

Less than a fortnight after they had defeated the All Blacks, a slightly weaker Cardiff team had lost 18-9 to the Combined Services. Since then the Services had also beaten a strong Irish XV in Dublin. Of the team to play New Zealand at Twickenham on Boxing Day, seven were internationals and a further three were capped before the end of the season. Gus Black, a 1950 Lion, 'Ian' Swan, Ian Thomson and Alec Valentine had all played for Scotland, while skipper Bob Stirling, Vic Tindall and Reg Bazley were all England caps. Peter Yarranton and Reg Higgins were less than a month away from their England debuts, and Rhys Williams was on the brink of

COMBINED SERVICES	NEW ZEALAND
2/Lt I.H.M. Thomson (Army)	R.W.H. Scott
O/Cdt R.C. Bazley (Army)	W.S.S. Freebairn
F/Lt V.R. Tindall (RAF)	J.T. Fitzgerald
F/Lt T.R. Beatson (RAF)	R.A. Jarden
2/Lt J.S. Swan (Army)	B.B.J. Fitzpatrick
Lieut G.H. Sullivan (Army)	R.G. Bowers
F/O A.W. Black (RAF)	K. Davis
Forwards:	Forwards:
P/O B.S. Lilley (RAF)	B.P. Eastgate
A/C M.U. Hughes (RAF)	C.A. Woods
F/Lt R.V. Stirling (RAF, Capt.)	K.L. Skinner
F/Lt P.G. Yarranton (RAF)	R.A. White
F/O P.S. Collingridge (RAF)	G.N. Dalzell
F/O R.H. Williams (RAF)	P.F. Jones
L/Cpl R. Higgins (Army)	W.H. Clark
A/A/3 A.R. Valentine (Royal Navy)	R.C. Stuart (Capt.)

Scorers:
Combined Services: Tries: Collingridge, Beatson. Con: Thomson.
Tries: Fitzpatrick (2), Freebairn, Fitzgerald, Jarden, Jones, Bowers, Clark, White. Cons: Scott (2), Fitzgerald (2), Jarden. PG: Scott.

Referee: Dr P.F. Cooper (London).
Attendance: 20,000.

Bob Stuart's men that took on the Combined Services at Twickenham.

a distinguished international career that included twenty-three Welsh caps and two Lions tours. It is hardly surprising that many people regarded the Combined Services as favourites to win their encounter with New Zealand.

The ease of the tourists' victory was remarkable, particularly in view of the fact that Ron Jarden was a passenger for much of the game due to an injured knee. Peter Jones was forced to play as an emergency left wing, yet the All Blacks scored 21 points in the final rousing fifteen minutes, and Jones himself stormed up the wing to score a memorable try. Towards the end of the game the home pack was completely swamped and the visitors clearly enjoyed what was the biggest victory of the British section of their tour. The match was also a personal triumph for the young first five-eighth Guy Bowers. He had been constantly overlooked by the selectors because they were reluctant to risk his more adventurous approach in important matches and this was only his fourth game of the tour. Bowers enjoyed a dream game, impressing everyone with his skilful runs and clever passing. From then on he had a much fairer deal in terms of games played and appeared in the Irish and French internationals.

The afternoon began sombrely. On Christmas Eve, 151 people had died in a rail disaster at Tangiwai, North Island, and the crowd stood in silence to remember and reflect with their New Zealand visitors. The game then started with a bang and 13 points were scored in as many minutes. First Jim Fitzgerald picked up a loose Services' pass to send Stuart Freebairn over in the corner. Then Fitzgerald exchanged passes with Jarden before scoring himself for Bob Scott to convert. Jarden ended the early scoring rush by sprinting in under the posts and kicking his own conversion. After that the All Blacks eased off, and after Jarden missed a tackle, Peter Collingridge scored a try for the Services, which Thomson converted. Scott kicked a penalty just before half-time, leaving the interval score at 16-5.

Combined Services were the first to score in the second half when Terry Beatson touched down following a run from Swan, but thereafter it was all New Zealand. Jones made his great thirty-yard run for the next score and then the riot really began. The gem among the final 5 tries was a brilliant individual score from Bowers. Brian Fitzpatrick twice and Bill Clark also crossed the line and the final try was a real team effort, involving a great run from Scott and finished off by a galloping 'Tiny' White. Scott converted one of these tries and Fitzgerald two.

For the Combined Services, Vic Tindall had put in some good runs and Gus Black had played well behind a beaten pack, while Yarranton and Williams had both won some useful lineout ball. Overall though, the Services had been run ragged by a happy All Black XV playing carefree, entertaining rugby and giving the watching Twickenham crowd a Boxing Day to remember.

Wednesday 30 December 1953
Villa Park, Birmingham
Won 18-3

MIDLAND COUNTIES	NEW ZEALAND
J.D. Young	J.W. Kelly
(Birmingham University & N Midlands)	
P.B. Jackson (Old Edwardians & N Midlands)	M.J. Dixon
A.R. Corley (Old Edwardians & N Midlands)	C.J. Loader
A. Sabin (Notts & Notts, Lincs & Derbys)	J.M. Tanner
H.F. Greasley (Coventry & Warwickshire)	D.D. Wilson
M.R. Channer	R.G. Bowers
(Leicester & Notts, Lincs & Derbys)	
A.W. Black	V.D. Bevan
(Leicester & Notts, Lincs & Derbys)	
Forwards:	Forwards:
W.A. Holmes (Nuneaton & Warwickshire)	H.L. White
E. Robinson (Coventry & Warwickshire)	R.C. Hemi
R.V. Stirling	I.J. Clarke
(RAF & Notts, Lincs & Derbys, Capt.)	
M. Hutt (Nuneaton & Warwickshire)	R.A. White
S.J. Adkins (Coventry & Warwickshire)	K.P. Bagley
N.G. Naylor (Coventry & Warwickshire)	O.D. Oliver
J. Gardiner (Coventry & Warwickshire)	R.J. O'Dea
D.E. Davies (Moseley & N Midlands)	R.C. Stuart (Capt.)

Scorers:
Midland Counties: PG: Channer.
New Zealand: Tries: Bagley, Clarke, Wilson. Cons: Kelly (3).
PG: Kelly.

Referee: R.W. Forster (Durham).
Attendance: 25,000.

This was another very satisfying victory for the All Blacks. Midland Counties was a strong side, yet the visitors only picked three of the team that had trounced Combined Services the previous Saturday. Significantly, Guy Bowers was retained and again played well, although the short grass of Aston Villa's soccer ground was slippery after prolonged rain. Bob O'Dea was selected for only the fourth time. Two of the home players, Gus Black and Bob Stirling, had faced the All Blacks in the Combined Services game, and Stirling was again captain. He and his fellow prop Wally Holmes had played for England in the previous season, as had second-row forward Stan Adkins. Ernie Robinson, the hooker, was capped by England later in the season and then had to wait seven years before he was capped again. On the right wing was Peter Jackson, then an Old Edwardians player but later to become one of the most entertaining of wingers for Coventry, Warwickshire, England and the 1959 British Lions.

During their stay in the area the tourists had trained at Rugby School, the founding home of the game, and they took the field at Villa Park to a rapturous welcome. The behaviour of the crowd throughout was in stark contrast to that experienced at Leicester in the other Midlands match and the visitors were sportingly applauded at every opportunity. The All Blacks faced a stiff breeze in the first half and, despite a good showing from their pack, could only manage a Jack Kelly penalty before half-time. This was cancelled out just before the interval when South African outside half Mel Channer, Gus Black's half-back partner at Leicester, was successful with a penalty.

After half-time, Keith Bagley scored the opening try, his first in all senior rugby. He picked up a loose ball when Ian Clarke and Counties full-back John Young collided. Jack Kelly, who had an excellent

New Zealand Rugby Football Tour · 1953-4

NEW ZEALAND
(All Blacks)
v.

MIDLAND COUNTIES
(North Midland, Notts., Lincs. & Derbyshire and Warwickshire)

at

Villa Park, Birmingham

on

Wednesday, December 30, 1953

Kick-off 2·30 p.m.

Official Programme - 6d.

all-round game despite the problems caused by the greasy ball, converted this and the other 2 tries scored in the second period. The first of these was a pushover try accredited to Clarke, although it was also claimed by 'Tiny' White. Then, with the game apparently safe, Bob Stuart instructed second five-eighth Doug Wilson to be a little more adventurous. The result was a series of exciting movements and a good try from Wilson himself following a clever reverse pass from Colin Loader. Towards the end of the match Bowers put in some exciting runs, but there was no further scoring.

Victory had been based on the forward superiority of New Zealand. Stirling, Holmes, Adkins and Robinson all played well for the home side, but they had to give second best to the likes of 'Tiny' White. Bowers and Wilson both received complimentary write-ups for their exciting approach in tricky conditions and in all it was a very satisfying afternoon for the All Blacks.

Before the match the rugby correspondent of the *Birmingham Post* had bemoaned the fact that despite the size of the city and its rugby following there was not a suitable rugby ground to stage the game. The 1923/24 All Blacks had also used Villa Park and it was not until 1972 that a New Zealand team actually played at a rugby ground in Birmingham.

The Midlands XV at Villa Park.

ULSTER   1953/54

Saturday 2 January 1954
Ravenhill, Belfast
Drawn 5-5

ULSTER	NEW ZEALAND
J.G.M.W. Murphy (Lurgan)	R.W.H. Scott
W.J. Hewitt (Instonians)	W.S.S. Freebairn
A.C. Pedlow (Queen's University)	J.T. Fitzgerald
N.J. Henderson (NIFC)	A.E.G. Elsom
J.T. Gaston (Dublin University)	B.B.J. Fitzpatrick
J.W. Kyle (NIFC, Capt.)	L.S. Haig
H. McCracken (NIFC)	V.D. Bevan
Forwards:	Forwards:
F.E. Anderson (Queen's University)	B.P. Eastgate
E.S. Wilson (NIFC)	R.C. Hemi
J.H. Smith (London Irish & Collegians)	K.L. Skinner
R.H. Thompson (Instonians)	G.N. Dalzell
J.R. Brady (CIYMS)	R.A. White
J.S. Ritchie (London Irish & Collegians)	W.H. Clark
A.G. Kennedy (Queen's University)	W.A. McCaw
J.E. Nelson (Malone)	R.C. Stuart (Capt.)

Scorers:
Ulster: Try: Gaston. Con: Murphy.
New Zealand: Try: Hemi. Con: Fitzgerald.

Referee: M.J. Dowling (Munster).
Attendance: 15,000.

Ulster were given little chance against a strong All Blacks' side but those prophets of doom who forecast a big win for the tourists were left to eat their words at the end of a pulsating game at Ravenhill. From kick-off to final whistle, the Ulster pack ripped into the New Zealanders with a ferocity that disrupted them and pressurised the backs into uncharacteristic errors. Ulster had injury scares before the match and there was considerable doubt whether Robin Thompson, the Instonians lock who was to captain the British Lions to South Africa at the end of the following season, would be able to play. He passed himself fit and led the pack with an energy suggesting his life depended on it. It was similar for the other forwards, including veteran hooker Jim Nelson who had an outstanding match although selected out of position at number eight.

The match started at a frantic pace with an Ulster forward rush nearly creating an opening for wing Joe Gaston. It soon became clear the match would be predominantly a forward battle. However, after fifteen minutes Cecil Pedlow tackled Bob Scott with such ferocity that the ball bounced clear. Noel Henderson, at Pedlow's side, kicked the ball ahead. Gaston chased and saw the ball bounce into his hands before outstripping Allan Elsom to score a try ten yards from the corner. Gerry Murphy converted to put the home side 5-0 ahead. This stung the All Blacks into even greater action, yet whatever the tourists tried to do Ulster had a counter-plan. However, they were guilty of giving away penalties, but the usually reliable Scott had a shocking day with the boot, missing five penalties that he would normally have converted with ease. Two of these hit the posts and he was close with two drop goals, one from the halfway line. Centres Henderson and Pedlow never missed a tackle, and they had plenty of work to do, particularly with Jim Fitzgerald running dangerous lines. After the game Henderson was taken to hospital suffering with concussion. He was accompanied by Ritchie with a similar complaint. While the forwards battled for possession, the halves efficiently dictated moves. Vince Bevan played well for the All Blacks, as did McCracken for the home side, but it was the artistry of Jackie Kyle that illuminated the gloomy afternoon. During the second half his tactical kicking was immaculate and he caused major problems for the New Zealand defence.

Ten minutes into the second half, a clever kick by Fitzgerald was gathered by Bill Clark, who passed to the supporting Ron Hemi who crossed for a try. Fitzgerald converted and everyone expected the All Blacks to take control and pull away, but they hadn't allowed for the tenacity of the Ulster pack, who never showed signs of tiredness and kept spoiling New Zealand plans until the end of the match. Haig crossed for a try but was called back due to a New Zealand infringement, and Kyle seemed to pop up at the most inconvenient times for the All Blacks and clear his lines. New Zealand felt they had deserved to win but in the end were fortunate to escape Belfast without defeat.

IRELAND   1953/54

Saturday 9 January 1954
Lansdowne Road, Dublin
Won 14-3

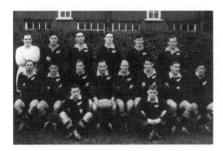

The New Zealand team which defeated Ireland.

IRELAND	NEW ZEALAND
J.G.M.W. Murphy (Lurgan & London Irish)	R.W.H. Scott
M. Mortel (Bective Rangers)	M.J. Dixon
A.C. Pedlow (Queen's University)	C.J. Loader
N.J. Henderson (NIFC)	R.A. Jarden
J.T. Gaston (Dublin University)	B.B.J. Fitzpatrick
J.W. Kyle (NIFC, Capt.)	R.G. Bowers
J.A. O'Meara (Dolphin)	K. Davis
Forwards:	Forwards:
J.H. Smith (London Irish)	H.L. White
F.E. Anderson (Queen's University)	R.C. Hemi
W.A. O'Neill (Wanderers)	K.L. Skinner
R.H. Thompson (Instonians)	G.N. Dalzell
P.J. Lawler (Clontarf)	R.A. White
J.S. McCarthy (Dolphin)	W.H. Clark
J.R. Kavanagh (Wanderers)	R.C. Stuart (Capt.)
T.E. Reid (Garryowen)	D.O. Oliver

Scorers:
Ireland: PG: Henderson.
New Zealand: Tries: Clark, Stuart. Con: Scott. PG: Scott. DG: Scott.

Referee: P.F. Cooper (RFU).
Attendance: 45,000.

Having lost one international and only managed a draw against Ulster, the All Blacks were even more determined to beat Ireland. They trained with great concentration at Trinity College and announced a side with Laurie Haig or Guy Bowers to play at first five-eighth. On the morning of the match Bowers got the nod. The weather was dry but breezy. Ireland prepared with a trial match against the Combined Services, after which the selectors made six changes to the side, four in the pack, with wing Joe Gaston the only new cap. Tom Reid usually a lock, was selected at number eight. John Smith played his third game against New Zealand and later played a fourth as a Barbarian. Ireland were captained by Jackie Kyle.

Kyle won the toss but chose to play into the wind in the first half. With the wind at their backs the All Blacks immediately pressurised the Irish line. The New Zealand forwards demonstrated their mobility and power, yet the ferocity of the Irish defence kept them at bay. 'Tiny' White made a great run but was cut down and other forwards were close to scoring. The first score came when Keith Davis chipped back over the forwards and Bill Clark, aided by a slightly fortuitous bounce, gathered the ball and crashed over by the corner flag. The conversion missed and, after a brief relief for the Irish defence when Gaston was bundled into touch in the New Zealand 25, the play swung back deep into Irish territory.

As the forwards rumbled towards the Irish posts the ball went loose and was kicked out of defence. Unfortunately, it landed in the arms of Scott, who dropped a goal. From the restart, play went back upfield and when Ireland were penalised for offside, Scott kicked a magnificent penalty from halfway. It was 9-0 to New Zealand at half-time, a score that failed to reflect their dominance and the effect of the wind. Ireland were still in the match when New Zealand should have been out of sight.

Five minutes into the second period Bowers made a clean break through an uncharacteristically weak defence and made good ground before linking with hooker Ron Hemi, who in turn fed skipper Bob Stuart to score a try close to the posts that Scott converted. With the wind behind their backs, Ireland picked up momentum and their forwards, with renewed energy, took the game to New Zealand. This time it was New Zealand who demonstrated the quality of their defence and everything Ireland threw at them was repelled. Scott, in particular, was magnificent and the thirty-two-year-old used all his experience to anticipate what Ireland were planning to do. Jim McCarthy went over but was beaten by the bounce of the ball and Gerry Murphy was unable to convert two penalties because he was suffering from double vision. Eventually Noel Henderson kicked a goal, which was scant reward for the way Ireland played in the latter stages. It was, however, a thoroughly deserved win for New Zealand.

MUNSTER   1953/54

Wednesday 13 January 1954
The Mardyke, Cork
Won 6-3

The All Blacks made eleven changes from the side that was victorious in Dublin, including the entire back division. The forwards selected were heavy and ideal for the soft ground of the Mardyke pitch. It was bitterly cold, with snow and sleet showers and a strong wind that made it tough going for both sides. The Munster pack included the substantial props of Tom Clifford and Gordon Wood. The robust Clifford had played for Munster since 1943 and was a member of the 1949 Irish Triple Crown side. He also toured New Zealand with the Lions the following year. Wood propped for the British Lions in 1959 and won twenty-nine caps for

MUNSTER	NEW ZEALAND
P.J. Berkery (Old Crescent & Lansdowne)	J.W. Kelly
G. Kenny (Sunday's Well)	W.S.S. Freebairn
R.P. Godfrey (UCD)	J.T. Fitzgerald
N. Coleman (Dolphin)	J.M. Tanner
B. Mullen (Cork Constitution)	D.D. Wilson
D. Daly (Sunday's Well)	L.S. Haig
J.A. O'Meara (Dolphin)	V.D. Bevan
Forwards:	Forwards:
B.G.M. Wood (Garryowen)	I.J. Clarke
D. Crowley (Cork Constitution)	C.A. Woods
J.T. Clifford (Young Munster)	K.L. Skinner
T.E. Reid (Garryowen)	G.N. Dalzell
M.N. Madden (Sunday's Well)	K.P. Bagley
B. Cussen (UCC)	D.O. Oliver
J.S. McCarthy (Dolphin, Capt.)	R.C. Stuart (Capt.)
G.F. Reidy (Dolphin & Lansdowne)	P.F.H. Jones

Scorers:
Munster: Try: Kenny.
New Zealand: Tries: Tanner, Wilson.

Referee: N.H. Lambert (Leinster).
Attendance: 7,500.

Ireland in a long international career that started later this season. His son, Keith, later became a British Lion and captain of his country. Tom Reid, the 1950 Lion who was chosen in the back row for Ireland the previous weekend, assumed his normal place in the second row. Skipper Jim McCarthy won twenty-eight caps for Ireland and was one of the key players in the 1948 Grand Slam success. He also toured New Zealand with the Lions in 1950. John O'Meara, Madden, Reidy, Godfrey and full-back Paddy Berkery also played for Ireland.

Munster started the match well and after three minutes Clifford attempted a long-range penalty, but the conditions were not conducive to goal-kicking. Rugby in any form, was difficult, although the foot-rush was executed with considerable aplomb by the Munster pack. However, both sides tried to play open rugby and a break by All Blacks' half-back Vince Bevan was continued by Jim Fitzgerald for John Tanner to put Doug Wilson in for a fine try wide out. Although the conversion was missed, the All Blacks attacked again and again, but outstanding defence, with Berkery and McCarthy to the fore, kept the tourists out. Then, close to half-time, the ball went loose and was kicked up field by Dan Daly. Gerry Kenny hared after it and kicked it ahead once more. Wilson covered but fumbled the ball. He was immediately tackled by the Munster back row and although Stuart tried to tidy up for New Zealand, the ball went loose again for Kenny to dive on it for an equalising score. The conversion missed and the scores were 3-3 at the interval.

The second half was all New Zealand but try as they might the Munster defence held out. Kenny was close to a second try for the home side but a draw looked the likely outcome. Then, as full time approached, Bevan fed Wilson down the narrow side of a scrum. It was done at such pace there was enough space to draw Kenny and pass outside to Tanner for the winning try. The conversion missed and the referee's whistle went for time. It was hard for Munster, who had lost to Australia and South Africa through last-minute scores in recent years.

PONTYPOOL & CROSS KEYS 1953/54

Saturday 16 January 1954
Pontypool Park, Pontypool
Won 19-6

PONTYPOOL & CROSS KEYS	NEW ZEALAND
N. Allsop (Cross Keys)	R.W.H. Scott
A. Williams (Cross Keys)	R.A. Jarden
B. Jones (Pontypool)	C.J. Loader
D. Prosser (Pontypool)	A.E.G. Elsom
J. Williams (Pontypool)	B.B.J. Fitzpatrick
J. Hurrell (Cross Keys)	L.S. Haig
W.A. Williams (Pontypool)	K. Davis
Forwards:	Forwards:
R. Beechey (Cross Keys)	H.L. White
H. Pugh (Pontypool)	R.C. Hemi
T.R. Prosser (Pontypool)	B.P. Eastgate
R. Greenway (Pontypool)	K.P. Bagley
J. Hancock (Cross Keys)	R.A. White
A. Forward (Pontypool, Capt.)	R.J. O'Dea
B. Padfield (Cross Keys)	W.A. McCaw
D. Preece (Cross Keys)	R.C. Stuart (Capt.)

Scorers:
Pontypool & Cross Keys: Try: J Williams. PG: Hancock.
New Zealand: Tries: Elsom (2), Jarden, H.L. White.
Cons: Jarden (2). DG: Scott.

Referee: W.J. Evans (Cardiff).
Attendance: 20,000.

The All Blacks changed the majority of their side for this game at Pontypool. It was considered one of the easier games of the tour but the New Zealanders hadn't reckoned on the tenacity of the home side and their tight forward play. The combined clubs were led by Allen Forward, a Welsh international flank forward who was the Pontypool club captain. The side also included the formidable Ray Prosser, second row for his club but prop for this combination, Wales and the British Lions, with whom he toured in 1959. He later coached Pontypool to greatness between 1969 and 1987.

Despite the clash between this match and the England v. Wales game at Twickenham, Pontypool Park was packed with local supporters. Jack Hancock kicked an early penalty from thirty-five yards. New Zealand hit back with several fine runs but were unable to score, then Brian Fitzpatrick burst through Don Prosser in the centre and linked with Colin Loader, who put Allan Elsom into space. The Canterbury wing raced down the touchline for a spectacular try. The conversion missed but Elsom scored again after a blistering sixty-yard run only to be called back due to a foot in

touch. After half an hour Bob O'Dea badly injured his knee and left the field, never to play again on tour. Half-time arrived with the score at 3-3, and the home side was regretting several missed penalty kicks.

Shortly after the restart, the home forwards raced up field but Forward knocked-on in the act of scoring. However, they were not to be denied and immediately after this, a cross-kick from Don Prosser confused Elsom, the ball went over the line and Bob Scott and wing Jack Williams dived on the ball. The former came up with the ball but the latter was awarded the try. Hancock missed the conversion but Pontypool & Cross Keys were back ahead. This seemed to fuel the All Blacks and, although a man down, they ran fast and hard. Elsom nearly scored after fine play by Ron Jarden, but he was more successful shortly afterwards when Jarden appeared between the five-eighths and made a half break from which Elsom scored. The conversion was missed but then Scott nearly scored.

Shortly afterwards the full-back, who had been in the stand watching his fellow 'Kiwis' lose to Monmouthshire on the same ground in 1946, dropped a sublime goal from close to halfway. The All Blacks were now showing they were stronger and fitter than their opponents. The ball went to Elsom who kicked towards the posts for prop 'Snow' White to gather the ball and score. Jarden converted and close to full time he scored a try himself after a kick ahead by Fitzpatrick bounced his way. He converted his own try and New Zealand had won with something to spare.

NEWPORT 1953/54

Thursday 21 January 1954
Rodney Parade, Newport
Won 11-6

With Stuart and Haig taking a rest, Kevin Skinner captained the tourists in their absence. It was a confident if risky approach to a match that promised to be a tough encounter. Several previous tourists had found Newport a hard team to beat. Newport were led by 1948 Olympic 4x100m relay silver medallist Ken Jones. A prolific try-scorer and eventual record Welsh cap holder, Jones was the Test wing on the 1950 Lions tour. Also in the side was eighteen-year-old centre Brian Jones, who later played for Wales and became a leading rugby administrator. Roy Burnett was a doubt for the match with an Achilles injury but played. He

NEWPORT	NEW ZEALAND
P. Smith	J.W. Kelly
K.J. Jones (Capt.)	M.J. Dixon
B.J. Jones	J.T. Fitzgerald
M.C. Thomas	J.M. Tanner
J. Lane	D.D. Wilson
R. Burnett	R.G. Bowers
D.O. Brace	V.D. Bevan
Forwards:	Forwards:
B.V. Meredith	I.J. Clarke
L. Davies	C.A. Woods
H.A. Davies	K.L. Skinner (Capt.)
A. Morris	G.N. Dalzell
J. Herrera	K.P. Bagley
D.A.G. Ackerman	W.H. Clark
M. Quargley	W.A. McCaw
L.H. Jenkins	P.F.H. Jones

Scorers:
Newport: Try: Lane. PG: B. Jones.
New Zealand: Try: Dixon. Con: Kelly. PG: Kelly. DG: Wilson.

Referee: E.D. Williams (Clydach).
Attendance: 20,000.

and half-back partner Onllwyn Brace also played for Wales, and in a big, powerful pack several internationals were joined by Doug Ackerman, who served the Newport club for many years as a committeeman and administrator. Ackerman's son, Robert, played for Wales in the 1980s. The pack also included St Luke's College student Bryn Meredith, who earlier played for Cornwall & Devon against the tourists. Normally a hooker, he propped in this game. He was first capped for Wales later in the season before touring with the British Lions in 1955, 1959 and 1962.

The first half began as many of the other matches had, with New Zealand on the attack but being kept out by resolute defence. Then, after nearly forty minutes of attacking, the ball came quickly back from a ruck and was moved to Doug Wilson who kicked for Morrie Dixon to gather the bouncing ball and score. John Kelly converted and New Zealand went into the break 5-0 ahead.

With Burnett struggling, Malcolm Thomas started the second half and kicked deep to Dixon. The ball was stripped off him and Brace ran down the narrow side and fed John Lane. He found lock Gordon Morris inside and they exchanged passes for Lane to break clear and run in for a try. Future Lion Thomas missed the straightforward conversion. Then All Black Peter Jones burst away from inside his own half, only to be hauled down close to the Newport line. Brace was penalised and Kelly kicked the penalty. While the forwards knocked lumps out of each other, the backs moved play from one end to the other without further score, until Newport were awarded a penalty just outside the New Zealand 25. Brian Jones kicked the goal and with fifteen minutes to go it was anybody's game. Unfortunately for the Black and Ambers it was the All Blacks', and late in the game a clearance kick from Brace went straight to Wilson, who coolly dropped the winning goal.

NEATH & ABERAVON   1953/54

Saturday 23 January 1954
The Gnoll, Neath
Won 11-5

The clubs of Neath and Aberavon had previously combined to play the 1935 All Blacks. They had individually played the New Zealand Army side, 'The Kiwis', in 1945/46 when both sides were defeated. They had both faced Bob Scott in those early post-war games, while home captain Rees Stephens had played in the Neath pack. They were forced to make a change to the side originally selected. Neath full-back Viv Evans withdrew and Ross Richards played in his place. Given the problems of fielding combined club XVs, it was felt these players would function well together and this might be the hardest of the combined sides the All Blacks were to

NEATH & ABERAVON	NEW ZEALAND
R. Richards (Aberavon)	R.W.H. Scott
K. Thomas (Aberavon)	R.A. Jarden
B. Phillips (Neath)	C.J. Loader
R. Bish (Aberavon)	W.S.S. Freebairn
K. Maddocks (Neath)	B.B.J. Fitzpatrick
G. John (Aberavon)	L.S. Haig
G. Thomas (Neath)	K. Davis
Forwards:	Forwards:
C.C. Meredith (Neath)	P. Eastgate
D. Davies (Aberavon)	R.C. Hemi
L.J. Cunningham (Aberavon)	K.L. Skinner
E.R. John (Neath)	G.N. Dalzell
D. Thomas (Aberavon)	R.A. White
J. Evans (Aberavon)	W.H. Clark
J.R.G. Stephens (Neath, Capt.)	D.O. Oliver
B.A. Sparkes (Neath)	R.C. Stuart (Capt.)

Scorers:
Neath & Aberavon: Try: Meredith. Con: Richards.
New Zealand: Tries: Jarden, Freebairn. Con: Scott. DG: Scott.

Referee: L. Griffin (Blaina).
Attendance: 17,000.

face in Wales. The All Blacks completely changed their backline for the game and only retained three forwards. However, they welcomed back Bob Stuart and most of the Test pack for the game.

The match started with some fierce forward exchanges, but the first score came after fifteen minutes when a scruffy clearance by Richards went to Scott, who dropped a goal. The rest of the half was a tight affair in which each side cancelled the other out. New Zealand led 3-0 at half-time.

Early in the second half New Zealand attacked at pace and, from second-phase possession, moved the ball quickly along the three-quarters. Colin Loader's pass to Ron Jarden was timed to perfection and the wing ran flat-out around the defence and scored in the corner. Scott converted with ease from the

touchline. Later, the tourists scored again after a kick ahead confused the home defence and an improvised pass from Loader sent Stu Freebairn in for an unconverted try. The home team had threatened occasionally during the game and outside half Glyn John had shown good running and passing skills. The side didn't give up and late in the game Roy John broke away and slipped the ball to Brian Sparkes. The future Welsh international forward raced forty yards before being caught. The ball went inside to Glyn John who passed to Courtenay Meredith for the 1955 Lions prop to score. Richards converted for the last score of the match and New Zealand held out to win.

Aberavon prop Len Cunningham later played for Wales, as did Keith Maddocks and Glyn John. Their centre colleague, Roy Bish, later became a leading coach and had a major influence on the development of rugby in Italy.

ENGLAND   1953/54

Saturday 30 January 1954
Twickenham, London
Won 5-0

A fortnight before they met New Zealand, England, with six new caps, had defeated Wales 9-6 at Twickenham. Logic suggested that since Wales had already beaten the All Blacks, England, who were the reigning Five Nations champions, should be too good for New Zealand. During the week leading up to the match the weather turned very cold. The tourists were back where their British tour had started, in Eastbourne, but they were unable to train due to frozen pitches. Skipper Bob Stuart used the situation to his and the team's advantage and ensured that his players were kept active while at the same time able to relax before the tough

ENGLAND	NEW ZEALAND
I. King (Harrogate)	R.W.H. Scott
J.E. Woodward (Wasps)	M.J. Dixon
J.P. Quinn (New Brighton)	C.J. Loader
J. Butterfield (Northampton)	R.A. Jarden
W.P.C. Davies (Harlequins)	D.D. Wilson
M. Regan (Liverpool)	L.S. Haig
G. Rimmer (Waterloo)	K. Davis
Forwards:	Forwards:
R.V. Stirling (Wasps, Capt.)	K.L. Skinner
E. Evans (Sale)	R.C. Hemi
D.L. Sanders (Harlequins)	H.L. White
P.D. Young (Wanderers)	R.A. White
P.G. Yarranton (Wasps)	G.N. Dalzell
D.S. Wilson (Metropolitan Police)	P.F. Jones
R. Higgins (Liverpool)	W.H. Clark
J. MacG. K. Kendall-Carpenter (Bath)	R.C. Stuart (Capt.)

Scorers:
New Zealand: Try: Dalzell. Con: Scott.

Referee: I. David (Wales).
Attendance: 72,000.

game ahead. Veteran New Zealand journalist Winston McCarthy described the week thus in his book of the tour: 'They wallowed in snowdrifts; they chased foxes; they snowballed each other, they rolled each other in the snow; and they walked in the cold air, limbering themselves up for the great game. You couldn't keep them away from it. They skated up and down the road, the icy road, outside the hotel. They went for more hikes. They laughed and they enjoyed themselves.'

Seventeen tons of straw had been placed on the Twickenham surface, weighed down by tarpaulins. Despite the continuing bad weather – snow fell during the second half of the match – the precautions left the playing surface in excellent condition, and this was one of very few games played that day.

England made only one change from the side that beat Wales, bringing in Phil Davies on the wing in place of Chris Winn, and retaining all the new players. Bob Stirling captained a team against the tourists for the third time. The All Black selectors decided to go for Laurie Haig rather than Guy Bowers, and this suggested that they planned a safety-first approach. They also handed an international debut to Peter Jones. The referee, the popular Ivor David of Neath, was officiating on the tour for the first time; he had taken the whistle for several of the Kiwis' games in 1945/46.

Soon after the start Ron Jarden missed a penalty. New Zealand were very wary of the big England winger Ted Woodward, and were only just able to cut off one of his powerful runs in the first half. The only try of the game came after nineteen minutes when hooker Ron Hemi who, along with 'Snow' White, had an outstanding match, dribbled the ball before Clark picked up and passed to the waiting Dalzell. Dalzell crashed Woodward out of the way and touched down. Woodward was knocked out for a short while but recovered sufficiently to continue the game. Bob Scott, another tourist who enjoyed a good afternoon, converted the try from near touch. Before the break England full-back Ian King went off with an injury. Fortunately, he returned for the second half.

Although this was a low-scoring game it was full of excellent rugby. There was plenty of excitement during the second half, including a further Woodward run that nearly resulted in a try, but New Zealand deserved their victory. The win meant a great deal and at the final whistle Bob Scott flung himself onto the ground in elation.

NORTH-EASTERN COUNTIES 1953/54

Saturday 6 February 1954
Lidget Green, Bradford
Won 16-0

NORTH-EASTERN COUNTIES	NEW ZEALAND
I. King (Harrogate)	J.W. Kelly
A.G.L. Wood (Headingley)	A.E.G. Elsom
D. Freeman (Darlington Grammar School OB)	J.T. Fitzgerald
J. Butterfield (Northampton, Capt.)	J.M. Tanner
F.D. Sykes (Huddersfield)	B.B.J. Fitzpatrick
D.C. Hopper (Harrogate)	R.G. Bowers
R. Green (Durham City)	V.D. Bevan
Forwards:	Forwards:
R. Sutherland	I.D. Clarke
(Darlington Grammar School OB)	
R. Coe (Westoe)	C.A. Woods
R.G. Porisse (Sale)	K.L. Skinner
B.A. Neale (Billingham)	R.A. White
R.A. Cadzow (Edinburgh Wanderers)	K.P. Bagley
R. Cross (Headingley)	R.C. Stuart (Capt.)
J.E. Frater (Northern)	O.D. Oliver
G. Mitchell (Halifax)	W.A. McCaw

Scorers:
New Zealand: Tries: Tanner, Oliver, Elsom, Bowers.
Cons: Fitzgerald (2).

Referee: L.M. Bowdy (London).
Attendance: 17,500.

Following the game with England, the All Blacks were due to play South-Eastern Counties at Ipswich, but this match fell victim to the severe frost that now gripped the country. Conditions had not improved by the following Saturday, and Bradford's Lidget Green was bone hard, despite the presence of twenty-five tons of straw. Winston McCarthy's description of the efforts to make the pitch playable is worth recording: 'You can't beat these Yorkshire men for grit. Out they went armed with pitchforks and gardening forks and prodded the surface. Then salt was spread over the pitch to counteract the frost. Not content with this as the ground was still frozen they procured a steamroller and sent the driver careering around the ground followed by a tractor with a roller attached, a jeep with harrows and another jeep with a spiked roller.'

Terry McLean, in his book of the tour, referred to the equipment being used as 'medieval-looking' but, although the ground remained very hard, a pre-booked sell-out crowd was desperate to see the All Blacks play and Bob Stuart agreed to allow the match to go ahead. Only three of the New Zealanders who had beaten England were retained for this game, while North-Eastern Counties included Ian King and skipper Jeff Butterfield. One of the home pack, Robert Porisse of Sale, was of French origin, and Ralph Cadzow had played for Glasgow & Edinburgh against the All Blacks earlier in the tour.

The game began with King missing a long-range penalty kick. His opposite number Jack Kelly fared no better and, despite chances for both sides, the first score of the game did not occur until just

North-Eastern Counties and New Zealand pictured in front of the main stand at Lidget Green.

before half-time. Guy Bowers was the provider, John Tanner the finisher, of a try that Jim Fitzgerald converted.

The second half contained numerous thrilling moments. Having scored the opening try, Tanner made the second, sending over a cross-kick that Ian Clarke caught before handing on to the scorer, Des Oliver. Jack Kelly made the third and best try of the match, running the ball from close to his own line and then setting up Bowers, who sent Allan Elsom away on a thrilling sixty-five yard dash to the line. Bowers himself scored a deserved try of his own at the end of the game, kicking a loose ball over the line before touching down. Fitzgerald could only convert Oliver's score, and his missed conversion of the final try was the last act of this entertaining game.

SCOTLAND   1953/54

Saturday 13 February 1954
Murrayfield, Edinburgh
Won 3-0

Scottish rugby was still in a state of shock after the catastrophic 44-0 defeat by the South Africans three years earlier. It was feared that the New Zealanders might inflict another humiliation. The visitors had spent the week at North Berwick preparing for the game and selected fourteen of the side that had beaten England, the only change being the introduction of the fair-headed Peter Eastgate in the front row. Scotland fielded three new caps in Elgie, Ross and MacLachlan. However, the main talking point was the inclusion of Douglas Elliot as captain. Elliot had returned after a year's lay-off because of injury and there were serious concerns about his fitness.

SCOTLAND	NEW ZEALAND
J.C. Marshall (London Scottish)	R.W.H. Scott
J.S. Swan (London Scottish)	R.A. Jarden
M.K. Elgie (London Scottish)	C.J. Loader
D. Cameron (Glasgow HSFP)	M.J. Dixon
T.G. Weatherstone (Stewart's FP)	D.D. Wilson
G.T. Ross (Watsonians)	L.S. Haig
L.P. MacLachlan (London Scottish)	K. Davis
Forwards:	Forwards:
T.P.L. McGlashan (Royal HSFP)	K.L. Skinner
R.K.G. MacEwan (Cambridge University)	R.C. Hemi
H.F. McLeod (Hawick)	B.P. Eastgate
E.A.J. Fergusson (Oxford University)	R.A. White
E.J.S. Michie (Aberdeen University)	G.N. Dalzell
W.I.D. Elliot (Edinburgh Acads, Capt.)	W.H. Clark
J.H. Henderson (Richmond)	P.F.H. Jones
P.W. Kininmonth (Richmond)	R.C. Stuart (Capt.)

Scorers:
New Zealand: PG: Scott.

Referee: I. David (Wales).
Attendance: 40,000.

New Zealand won with the only score of the game, a penalty goal by Bob Scott after forty-seven minutes, but the Scots produced a stirring performance that merited at least a draw. In the first half, a reverse pass from Weatherstone to Elgie put 'Ian' Swan away, but he was held short of the line. Near the interval, John Marshall failed with a penalty attempt. Scott fielded and found touch ten yards inside the Scottish half, a

The All Blacks team that defeated Scotland in 1954.

SCOTLAND
v
NEW ZEALAND

Murrayfield, Edinburgh
SATURDAY, 13th FEBRUARY
1954

Official Programme One Shilling

remarkable kick with a wet and heavy ball. After Scott's winning penalty, the New Zealanders lifted their efforts, calling for some desperate defence from the Scots. To everyone's surprise, Scotland hit back with some spirited attacking play. New Zealand ended with a fighting finish and Haig came close on two occasions. At the final whistle, the crowd surged onto the pitch to give both sides a deserved ovation.

Bob Scott made a huge contribution to his side's victory, proving himself the best New Zealander in that position since George Nepia. At scrum-half, Keith Davis had a good all-round game, while winger Maurice Dixon was solid in defence. Of the forwards, 'Tiny' White and Bob Stuart were outstanding, but the New Zealanders were unable to dominate. For Scotland, Douglas Elliot was an inspirational leader, tackling with relish and always at the front of a forward rush. The new half-backs Ross and MacLachlan played very well, the former showing a cool head and good hands while his partner was sharp enough to beat the All Black back row. At full-back, Marshall was excellent and Swan never slackened his grip on Ron Jarden. It was a truly memorable rugby occasion that neither side deserved to lose.

NORTH-WESTERN COUNTIES 1953/54

Wednesday 17 February 1954
Maine Road, Manchester
Won 17-3

North-Western Counties fielded a side that looked to be capable of giving the tourists a strong challenge. The side was built principally around the Lancashire team that was to reach (and lose) the final of the County Championship to Middlesex later in the season. Five of the players – Gordon Rimmer, Martin Regan, Pat Quinn, Eric Evans and Reg Higgins – had faced New Zealand in the England match. Reg Bazley was also an England player and Alec Valentine had played for Scotland in 1953. The chosen venue, until 2003 the home of Manchester City Football Club, was not ideal for a rugby match. The in-goal area was very small, the pitch was too short and

NORTH-WESTERN COUNTIES	NEW ZEALAND
H. Scott (Manchester & Lancashire)	J.W. Kelly
R.C. Bazley (Waterloo & Lancashire)	A.E.G. Elsom
J.P. Quinn (New Brighton & Lancashire)	J.T. Fitzgerald
F.G. Griffiths (Sale & Lancashire)	W.S.S. Freebairn
K. Smith (Preston Grasshoppers & Lancashire)	B.B.J. Fitzpatrick
M. Regan (Liverpool & Lancashire)	R.G. Bowers
G. Rimmer (Waterloo & Lancashire, Capt.)	V.D. Bevan
Forwards:	Forwards:
D. Chapman (Broughton Park & Lancashire)	H.L. White
E. Evans (Sale & Lancashire)	C.A. Woods
D.G. Massey	I.J. Clarke
(Wilmslow, Cambridge University & Cheshire)	
W. Hosker (Birkenhead Park & Cheshire)	R.A. White
J. Sewell	K.P. Bagley
(Old Creightonians & Cumberland-Westmorland)	
A.R. Valentine	R.C. Stuart (Capt.)
(RNAS Anthorn & Cumberland-Westmorland)	
R. Higgins (Army, Liverpool & Lancashire)	O.D. Oliver
T. Barker (Sale & Lancashire)	W.A. McCaw

Scorers:
North-Western Counties: PG: Griffiths.
New Zealand: Tries: McCaw, Bevan, Kelly, Fitzgerald.
Con: Kelly. PG: Kelly.

Referee: T.E. Priest (London).
Attendance: 25,000.

it was covered in sand in an attempt to combat bad weather. The All Blacks had a surprisingly comfortable victory, partly because they played so well themselves, and partly because a number of the home stars had off days. The Counties' half-backs, in particular 1950 British Lion Gordon Rimmer, looked badly off form. Rimmer passed poorly and was constantly outshone by his opposite number Vince Bevan. In fact, Bevan was the outstanding New Zealand player, always busy and eager to get his line moving. Jack Kelly also stood out for the tourists, playing what was generally considered to be his best game of the tour, while Guy Bowers, Jim Fitzgerald and Brian Fitzpatrick all caught the eye. The pack subdued their much-vaunted opponents and Des Oliver forced Martin Regan into many errors. Bob Stuart, led his side superbly, and 'Tiny' White had an excellent match.

Bill McCaw scored the opening try of the game, being pushed over the line following a mistake by Rimmer. Kelly kicked a penalty and then, after Stuart Freebairn had a try ludicrously disallowed due to a Counties infringement, Bevan crossed the line from a scrum to make the half-time score 9-0. In an entertaining second half, Fitzgerald set up Kelly's first try of the tour and then scored himself after Fitzpatrick had intercepted a pass from the unfortunate Rimmer. Kelly converted the last score, and there could well have been further tries. Kelly himself lost the ball over the line following a brilliant handling move, 'Snow' White marred a fine performance by dropping the ball in a scoring position and Allan Elsom put a foot in touch before crossing. Right on time Freddie Griffiths, an England trialist, kicked a consolation penalty for the Counties. The nearest the home side came to a try was from a fine run by Valentine, but he spoiled this with a forward pass. The home side was at a disadvantage for part of the second half because Scott had to leave the field injured.

Despite the poor showing from the opposition, this was a satisfying New Zealand victory. The All Blacks certainly impressed the large crowd with their willingness to handle the ball in difficult conditions and the side looked good as it moved on to face the challenge of the Barbarians.

BARBARIANS 1953/54

Saturday 20 February 1954
Cardiff Arms Park, Cardiff
Won 19-5

The Barbarians selected a strong side for their first encounter with New Zealand. It featured seven Welshmen, seven English and John Smith of Ireland. The backs were regarded as very strong but there were some concerns over the choice of forwards. There was great pressure on the uncapped Hawkes and Ron Jacobs, and the six others to win ball for the backs. It was hoped that they could, at least, hold their own. The All Blacks selected a strong side, with Bowers chosen at first five-eighth. It was a magnificent contest.

The All Blacks' forwards immediately put the scratch Barbarians pack under pressure and it was clear they were going to struggle. However, they battled manfully and were

BARBARIANS	NEW ZEALAND
I. King (Harrogate)	R.W.H. Scott
K.J. Jones (Newport)	R.A. Jarden
J. Butterfield (Northampton)	J.T. Fitzgerald
W.P.C. Davies (Harlequins)	M.J. Dixon
G.M. Griffiths (Cardiff)	B.B.J. Fitzpatrick
C.I. Morgan (Cardiff)	R.G. Bowers
W.R. Willis (Cardiff)	K. Davis
Forwards:	Forwards:
C.R. Jacobs (Northampton)	H.L. White
E. Evans (Sale)	R.C. Hemi
J.H. Smith (London Irish)	K.L. Skinner
R.C. Hawkes (Northampton)	G.N. Dalzell
J.R.G. Stephens (Neath)	R.A. White
S. Judd (Cardiff)	D.O. Oliver
D.F. White (Northampton)	W.A. McCaw
R.C.C. Thomas (Swansea)	R.C. Stuart (Capt.)

Scorers:
Barbarians: Try: Griffiths. Con: King.
New Zealand: Tries: Jarden, Dixon, Davis, R.A. White.
Cons: Jarden (2). DG: Scott.

Referee: I. David (Neath).
Attendance: 56,000.

never completely subdued. What they lacked was neither ability nor power, but cohesive teamwork achieved from playing games together. Against the run of play, it was the Barbarians who opened the scoring when Gareth Griffiths followed up Ian King's kick ahead, gathered the ball as Bob Scott slipped, and ran through the covering defence to score a brilliant try between the posts. King converted. Both sides attacked with pace and it was good defence that stopped the score changing. Then, close to half-time, Rees Stephens kicked the ball into space. It was quickly filled by Scott, who turned and dropped another goal. The Barbarians remained ahead 5-3 at half-time.

Having adopted a win-at-all-costs approach in previous games, which was reflected in the conservative approach of the midfield backs, the All Blacks went into this game with the intention of playing open rugby. Their forwards, with 'Tiny' White outstanding at the lineout, provided sufficient ball for them to show what they could do. The second half was one-way traffic with New Zealand dominant. As impressive as the Barbarians backs had appeared with ball in hand during the first half, they were required to tackle almost constantly in the second. Even then, Cliff Morgan ran in a wonderful 'try', only to find he had put a foot in touch when veering outside the All Blacks' defence. The second half was minutes old when a kick ahead by Keith Davis was misfielded by King and Davis followed up to score, Ron Jarden converting. Bob Scott joined the All Blacks' line shortly afterwards and, finding space in front of him, raced for the try line. Although tackled short he passed to the supporting Jarden for another try, which Jarden converted. He missed the conversion of a try wide out from Morrie Dixon and also missed converting 'Tiny' White's late try.

The final whistle went and the crowd burst into a rendition of *Now is the Hour*, followed by *Auld Lang Syne*. Bob Stuart and Scott were carried off the field. Both sides had served up a rugby feast. It would be nearly twenty years before it was bettered.

SOUTH-EASTERN COUNTIES 1953/54

**Monday 1 March 1954
Portman Road, Ipswich
Won 21-13**

The original fixture with South-Eastern Counties, on 3 February, was cancelled due to a frozen pitch. The venue, Ipswich Town Football Club, was governed by Football Association regulations, which forbade the covering of pitches with straw as protection against winter weather. This was very much a football area and there was a great desire locally to bring the All Blacks to East Anglia so that the profile of rugby in the region could be raised. Cyril Gadney, the Middlesex representative of the RFU, led requests for a game to be fitted

SOUTH-EASTERN COUNTIES	NEW ZEALAND
N. Gibbs (Harlequins & Surrey, Capt.)	J.W. Kelly
J.E. Boothman (Harlequins, RAF & Surrey)	A.E.G. Elsom
D. Fothergill (Richmond & Eastern Counties)	J.M. Tanner
P.C. Delight	W.S.S. Freebairn
(Loughborough Colleges, Old Blues & Middlesex)	
T.J. Brewer (London Welsh & Hampshire)	D.D. Wilson
D.G.S. Baker (Old Merchant Taylors & Middlesex)	R.G. Bowers
J.E. Williams (Old Millhillians & Middlesex)	K. Davis
Forwards:	Forwards:
D.L. Sanders	R.C. Stuart (Capt.)
(Ipswich YMCA, Harlequins & Eastern Counties)	
H.D. Doherty (London Irish & Kent)	C.A. Woods
E.V.J. Hammond (Blackheath & Middlesex)	I.J. Clarke
H.B. Neely (Blackheath & Kent)	R.A. White
R.E. Syrett (Wasps & Middlesex)	K.P. Bagley
I.T. Jenkins	O.D. Oliver
(United Services Portsmouth, Royal Navy & Hampshire)	
D.A. Emms	W.A. McCaw
(Lowestoft & Yarmouth, Northampton & Eastern Counties)	
K.J.H. Mallett (St Mary's Hospital & Surrey)	G.N. Dalzell

Scorers:
South-Eastern Counties: Tries: Brewer, Delight, Hammond. Cons: Gibbs (2).
New Zealand: Tries: Dalzell (2), Wilson, McCaw, Kelly. Cons: Kelly (3).

Referee: A.E. Brough (Northumberland).
Attendance: 6,000.

in at the end of the tour, following the All Blacks' return from France. The New Zealand RU was not particularly helpful in this matter, leaving cables unanswered and putting the onus for the decision on the tour manager Norman Millard. Time was in short supply, and the tourists would have to give up a day of sightseeing and shopping in London, but Mr Millard agreed to have the game played, although it does not count in the official record of the tour. This last point seems strange, and rugby historians have tended to give the match its proper place among the official games. Writing in his book of the tour, New Zealand journalist Winston McCarthy stated: 'The match was played under official control, the All Blacks appearing in the correct regalia, so it is difficult to believe that history will not always regard it as a first-class fixture.'

Following a spate of injuries, a tired and rather stale side of volunteer New Zealanders travelled to Ipswich. Skipper Bob Stuart had to play at prop and, although he changed places with Keith Bagley during the match, second row Nelson Dalzell started at number eight. The home side, although not particularly strong up front, contained a number of well-known players. The half-backs, John Williams and Doug Baker, were to become England players and 1955 British Lions, 'Sandy' Sanders had played for England against the tourists and full-back and captain Nigel Gibbs was capped by England against Scotland later in the month. Winger Trevor Brewer had played for Wales.

The game turned out to be a hard-fought and entertaining encounter that the All Blacks only won in the last ten minutes. The tourists were behind as early as the fourth minute, trailed 13-3 at half-time and 13-11 before their late rally. The Counties' backs were in superb form in the first half, with Brewer scoring early try from a Baker cross-kick, despite initially over-running the ball. Williams, Baker and centre Paul Delight all stood out, with Baker's sidestepping causing Guy Bowers plenty of problems. A further try followed from Delight when Doug Wilson missed a tackle. Gibbs converted this for a lead of 8-0 and, although Wilson soon made amends by scoring himself, Counties scored their third try when Hammond crossed from a lineout, Gibbs again converting. Hammond's try came at a time when Delight was off the field due to injury, but despite their healthy half-time advantage, that was the end of the home side's scoring.

The All Blacks recovered from their mediocre showing in the first half, scoring straight after the break when Dalzell finished off a break from halfway by Keith Davis and Wilson. Jack Kelly converted this try, but could not add the extra points when Bill McCaw scored following good work from Dalzell and Bagley. Dalzell finally gave New Zealand the lead with his second try after a break from a lineout and Kelly finished off a good performance at full-back by scoring the final try, finishing off a run by John Tanner. Kelly converted both the late tries, thus claiming the honour of scoring the first and last points of the European section of the tour. The people of Ipswich, not least the many children in the crowd, certainly appreciated the fact that the All Blacks took the trouble to play this extra game at the end of an exhausting schedule. That evening, back in London, Cyril Gadney threw a party in honour of the tourists, and each player who turned out at Ipswich was presented with a London Counties blazer badge.

The popular tourists departed British shores and headed to North America, as their predecessors had done. They played 3 games in British Columbia and two more in California, enjoying comfortable wins in all the games except against California University when the students held New Zealand to a 14-6 score.

Bob Stuart's All Blacks were excellent ambassadors for the sport and their country. They possessed athletic forwards and exciting backs, although it was a regret felt by many that they had not made more of their talented runners.

NEW ZEALAND TO BRITAIN, FRANCE & CANADA

THE MATCHES

Oxford University	23 October 1963	Oxford	won 19-3
Southern Counties	26 October 1963	Hove	won 32-3
Newport	30 October 1963	Newport	lost 3-0
Aberavon & Neath	2 November 1963	Port Talbot	won 11-6
Abertillery & Ebbw Vale	6 November 1963	Abertillery	won 13-0
London Counties	9 November 1963	Twickenham	won 27-0
Cambridge University	13 November 1963	Cambridge	won 20-6
South of Scotland	16 November 1963	Hawick	won 8-0
Glasgow & Edinburgh	20 November 1963	Glasgow	won 33-3
Cardiff	23 November 1963	Cardiff	won 6-5
Pontypool & Cross Keys	27 November 1963	Pontypool	won 11-0
South-Western Counties	30 November 1963	Exeter	won 38-6
Midland Counties	3 December 1963	Coventry	won 37-9
IRELAND	7 December 1963	Dublin	won 6-5
Munster	11 December 1963	Limerick	won 6-3
Swansea	14 December 1963	Swansea	won 16-9
Western Counties	17 December 1963	Bristol	won 22-14
WALES	21 December 1963	Cardiff	won 6-0
Combined Services	26 December 1963	Twickenham	won 23-9
Midland Counties	28 December 1963	Leicester	won 14-6
Llanelly	31 December 1963	Llanelly	won 22-8
ENGLAND	4 January 1964	Twickenham	won 14-0
North-Western Counties	8 January 1964	Manchester	won 12-3
North-Eastern Counties	11 January 1964	Harrogate	won 17-11
North of Scotland	14 January 1964	Aberdeen	won 15-3
SCOTLAND	18 January 1964	Murrayfield	drew 0-0
Leinster	22 January 1964	Dublin	won 11-8
Ulster	25 January 1964	Belfast	won 24-5
South-Eastern Counties	29 January 1964	Bournemouth	won 9-6
France B	1 February 1964	Toulouse	won 17-8
South-West France	5 February 1964	Bordeaux	won 23-0
FRANCE	8 February 1964	Paris	won 12-3
South-Eastern France	12 February 1964	Lyon	won 8-5
Barbarians	15 February 1964	Cardiff	won 36-3
British Columbia Under 25 XV	22 February 1964	Vancouver	won 6-3
British Columbia	24 February 1964	Vancouver	won 39-3

Played 36, Won 34, Drew 1, Lost 1. Scored: 613 points, Conceded: 159.

In Britain & Ireland: Played 30, Won 28, Drew 1, Lost 1. Scored: 508 points, Conceded: 137.

The New Zealand Tour Party:

D.B. Clarke (Waikato), R.W. Caulton (Wellington), W.L. Davis (Hawke's Bay), M.J. Dick (Auckland), I.S.T. Smith (Otago), P.F. Little (Auckland), I.R. MacRae (Hawke's Bay), D.A. Arnold (Canterbury), M.A. Herewini (Auckland), E.W. Kirton (Otago), P.T. Walsh (Counties), B.A. Watt (Canterbury), K.C. Briscoe (Taranaki), C.R. Laidlaw (Otago), I.J. Clarke (Waikato), K.F. Gray (Wellington), J.M. Le Lievre (Canterbury), W.J. Whineray (Auckland), J. Major (Taranaki), D. Young (Canterbury), R.H. Horsley (Manawatu), C.E. Meads (King Country), A.J. Stewart (Canterbury), K.E. Barry (Thames Valley), D.J. Graham (Canterbury), W.J. Nathan (Auckland), K.A. Nelson (Otago), K.R. Tremain (Hawke's Bay), B.J. Lochore (Wairarapa), S.T. Meads (King Country).

Captain: W.J. Whineray. Vice-Captain: K.C. Briscoe. Manager: F.D. Kilby. Assistant Manager: N.J. McPhail.

Leading points scorer: D.B. Clarke – 149 points (129 in Britain & Ireland).

Leading try-scorer: M.J. Dick – 19 tries (18 in Britain & Ireland).

Most appearances: D.B. Clarke – 26 games (D.B. Clarke & W.J. Whineray 21 in Britain & Ireland).

OXFORD UNIVERSITY 1963/64

Wednesday 23 October 1963
Iffley Road, Oxford
Won 19-3

During the previous summer, England had undertaken a tour that included 5 games in New Zealand. The English found how tough New Zealand rugby was, only managing to defeat Wellington and losing both internationals. With no other international rugby for New Zealand prior to their tour, the NZRFU held a series of trial matches from which they selected a squad that, in general, was well received. There were several new players and they were led by the Auckland prop Wilson Whineray.

The All Blacks commenced their tour at Iffley Road, Oxford against a student side playing only its third game of the season, having defeated Guy's Hospital and losing

OXFORD UNIVERSITY	NEW ZEALAND
J.T. Reid (University)	D.B. Clarke
E.L. Rudd (Wadham)	M.J. Dick
D.K. Jones (Merton)	P.F. Little
M.S. Cunningham (Lincoln)	R.W. Caulton
A.K. Morgan (Brasenose)	P.T. Walsh
R.H. Lamb (St Edmund Hall)	M.A. Herewini
A.J.A. Lewin (St Edmund Hall)	K.C. Briscoe
Forwards:	Forwards:
E.G.H. Gould (St Edmund Hall)	W.J. Whineray (Capt.)
A.G.D. Whyte (St Edmund Hall)	D. Young
R.M. Wilcock (St Edmund Hall)	K.F. Gray
F.J.R. Craig (Balliol)	C.E. Meads
I.C. Jones (Queen's)	A.J. Stewart
N. Silk (Merton, Capt.)	D.J. Graham
B.B. King (Exeter)	K.R. Tremain
E.P. Gush (St Edmund Hall)	B.J. Lochore

Scorers:
Oxford University: Try: Rudd.
New Zealand: Tries: Dick, Tremain. Cons: Clarke (2). PGs: Clarke (3).

Referee: A.C. Luff (Notts, Lincs & Derby).
Attendance: 12,000.

heavily to Richmond. There were five old Blues in the Oxford side, including the captain and future England cap Nick Silk, but injuries deprived the team of full-back Stewart Wilson and centre David Whyte, both of whom went on to play for Scotland. Wilson's replacement, John Reid, was a New Zealander. The only international in the student line-up was Ken Jones, a Welsh cap who had toured

South Africa with the 1962 British Lions and who would be a Lion again in New Zealand in 1966. Second row Ian Jones gained a Welsh cap in 1968. The All Blacks had all their squad available except Stan Meads, who had been to hospital to have a boil pierced.

This was undoubtedly Don Clarke's match. He scored 13 of his side's points and the game would have been much closer but for his kicking. He kicked the first points of the tour with a penalty after nineteen minutes and then converted the opening try, scored by Malcolm Dick after Reid had fumbled a kick ahead. A further penalty was added to make the half-time score 11-0.

The Oxford side played with great enthusiasm throughout the game, with the back row of Silk,

The Oxford University and New Zealand teams before the opening game. Standing tall and prominent in black in the back row is Colin Meads.

Brian King and Edwin Gush constantly harrying their opponents. Due reward came after fifteen minutes of the second half when a pass by Ken Jones sent winger Ed Rudd off on a seventy-yard run. Rudd swerved to avoid the tackle of Don Clarke and scored a superb try. This was only Rudd's second first-class match in a career that eventually brought him six England caps. After the euphoria had died down, Kel Tremain restored the All Blacks' advantage by galloping over for a try from a lineout. Clarke converted this score and then added a late penalty to complete an excellent afternoon's work. It had been a reasonable start for Whineray's side, although there was concern that the pack had tired towards the end. Whineray himself had played well, but the half-back partnership of Kevin Briscoe and Mac Herewini had not really worked, with Briscoe guilty of some wayward passing.

SOUTHERN COUNTIES 1963/64

Saturday 26 October 1963
Greyhound Stadium, Hove
Won 32-3

The Southern Counties side that took on the All Blacks at the Hove Greyhound Stadium was very much a scratch selection, some of the players meeting each other for the first time on the day before the match. Two of the side, the captain, Geoff Windsor Lewis and Leighton Jenkins, were Welsh internationals and Australian-born Larry Webb was an England cap, but the team as a whole was not expected to cause the tourists too many problems. The All Black selectors, anxious to give everyone a run-out, made thirteen changes from the side that had won at Oxford, although Stan Meads was still on the injured list. With Wilson

SOUTHERN COUNTIES	NEW ZEALAND
H.H. Bain (Worthing & Sussex)	D.B. Clarke
L.P.F. L'Estrange (London Irish & Sussex)	W.L. Davis
G. Windsor Lewis	I.R. MacRae
(Richmond & Oxfordshire, Capt.)	
I.P. Reid (London Scottish & Dorset & Wilts)	I.S.T. Smith
P.C. Sibley (Black Heath & Oxfordshire)	D.A. Arnold
L. Tatham (Bedford & Hertfordshire)	B.A. Watt
F. Booth (Saracens & Berkshire)	C.R. Laidlaw
Forwards:	Forwards:
St L. H. Webb (Bedford & Hertfordshire)	I.J. Clarke (Capt.)
J. Bazalgette (Harlequins & Hertfordshire)	J. Major
S.T. Jones (London Irish & Sussex)	J.M. Le Lievre
J.R.L. Adcock (Harlequins & Berkshire)	A.J. Stewart
S.K. Mulligan (London Irish & Oxfordshire)	R.H. Horsley
K.J.H. Mallett (RAF & Hertfordshire)	W.J. Nathan
A.J.S. Todman (Harlequins & Sussex)	K.E. Barry
L.H. Jenkins (Bath & Dorset & Wilts)	K.A. Nelson

Scorers:
Southern Counties: Try: Mallett.
New Zealand: Tries: Nelson, Davis, Smith, Arnold, MacRae.
Con: D. Clarke. PGs: D. Clarke (3). DGs: D Clarke (2).

Referee: H. Keenen (Durham).
Attendance: 8,000.

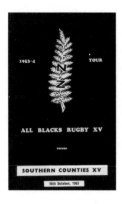

1963-4 TOUR

ALL BLACKS RUGBY XV

versus

SOUTHERN COUNTIES XV

26th October, 1963

Whineray and vice-captain Briscoe both standing down, the captaincy was given to Don Clarke's brother Ian.

Don Clarke once again dominated proceedings, scoring a total of 17 points, despite converting only one of the five All Black tries. He also missed two penalties and had an attempted drop goal charged down, but the two drop goals he kicked were both enormous efforts. This was a great afternoon for the New Zealand backs, who between them accounted for all but one of the tries. The backs were well marshalled by scrum-half Chris Laidlaw, at nineteen years of age the youngest player in the tour party. Despite being outplayed in the loose, the Counties did well in the scrums and won some good lineout ball through John Adcock.

The tourists were 12-0 ahead within twenty minutes through two early Clarke penalties, the first of his drop goals and a try scored by Nelson. Bill Davis added a second try later in the half and the score at the break was 15-0. Shortly after the restart the Counties had their moment of glory when Webb initiated a move that resulted in John Mallett crossing the line. Thereafter it was all New Zealand. Ian Smith scored the next try following a break from MacRae, and although Clarke missed the conversion he was successful with a penalty and then caught a clearance on the touchline and dropped a goal. Derek Arnold was the next to score with a try in the corner, and then MacRae rounded things off with a try that Clarke converted. Try scorer John 'Chopper' Mallett had faced the previous All Black tourists as a student. An amateur boxer, he became a highly regarded surgeon. His son John propped for Bath and England.

NEWPORT

1963/64

Wednesday 30 October 1963
Rodney Parade, Newport
Lost 3-0

The All Blacks ventured into Wales for the first time on tour on a miserable Wednesday afternoon for a match with Newport which was regarded as being a tougher prospect than their first 2 games. The All Blacks changed eight players and Earle Kirton made his first start of the tour. Prop Ian Clarke played in the 1954 match between the sides. The only home survivor of the previous game was centre Brian Jones. Newport were coached by former Wales and Lions hooker Bryn Meredith, who had faced Bob Stuart's side for Newport as a prop, and were led by Brian Price, a powerful second row who dominated the lineout for Newport, Wales and the British Lions throughout the 1960s. He had a substantial pack around him, with Glyn Davidge and Ian Ford

NEWPORT	NEW ZEALAND
R. Cheney	D.B. Clarke
S.J. Watkins	R.W. Caulton
J. Uzzell	I.R. MacRae
B.J. Jones	W.L. Davis
D.J. Perrott	P.T. Walsh
D. Watkins	E.W. Kirton
W.R. Prosser	K.C. Briscoe
Forwards:	Forwards:
N. Johnson	W.J. Whineray (Capt.)
G. Bevan	J. Major
D. Jones	I.J. Clarke
B. Price (Capt.)	C.E. Meads
I.R. Ford	R.H. Horsley
A.R.F. Thomas	K.R. Tremain
K.W. Poole	W.J. Nathan
G.D. Davidge	B.J. Lochore

Scorers:
Newport: DG: Uzzell.

Referee: D.G. Walters (Gowerton).
Attendance: 25,000.

international players, and Alan Thomas, who played for Wales later in the season. It was this pack that dominated the game. They won eight scrum heels against the head and Price drove the pack with relentless passion. In Davidge they had a forward who typified the commitment of the home side by diving on the ball and putting his body at the feet of the New Zealand forwards with almost reckless disregard for his own safety. The ball the Newport forwards won was used with skill by David Watkins. He kicked into space with unerring accuracy, forcing Don Clarke to cover every inch of the pitch.

Above: *The ball clears the crossbar for the only points of the game. Dick Uzzell, kicker of the drop goal, quickly entered Welsh folklore.*

Below: *The winning Newport team.*

The conditions demanded that the game would be a tight and low-scoring affair, and it fell to centre 'Dick' Uzzell to write his name into the history books with the only score of the game. When David and Stuart Watkins set up a good position the young centre coolly dropped a goal after seventeen minutes. Uzzell had managed to get time off from his studies to visit his supposedly sick father in hospital. His father apparently made a remarkable recovery and assisted his son from the field at the end of the game!

There were some dangerous runs from New Zealand but they were infrequent. With the forwards eclipsed by the Newport eight and back moves stopped at source by their back row, New Zealand threatened little. It was the commitment of the Newport side, epitomised by Davidge, that won the day. They played percentage rugby, having the confidence in each other that they would beat New Zealand. When Gwynne Walters blew the whistle for time, the pitch was invaded by thousands of exuberant Welshmen. Newport had delivered a perfect present for their captain, it being Brian Price's twenty-sixth birthday.

New Zealand manager Frank Kilby made no excuses: 'It was Newport all the way. They were the better side and we did not look like scoring,' he commented to journalist J.B.G. Thomas. Newport were able to add the scalp of New Zealand to those of Australia and South Africa and join Swansea and Cardiff as a club that had beaten all three major Southern Hemisphere nations.

ABERAVON & NEATH 1963/64

Saturday 2 November 1963
Talbot Athletic Ground,
Port Talbot
Won 11-6

The wounded All Blacks moved further along the South Wales coast to Port Talbot to face Aberavon & Neath. The weather was wet and they set about the home side in determined fashion. Late changes to the All Blacks saw the inclusion of Chris Laidlaw for Briscoe, Pat Walsh for Arnold and Waka Nathan for Nelson. The home side was captained by Aberavon prop Phil Morgan, a steelworker who had won three caps for Wales in 1961. He was joined in the front row by fellow international Len Cunningham, the only survivor from the 1954 encounter. Elsewhere in the pack were second row Brian Thomas,

ABERAVON & NEATH	NEW ZEALAND
G.T.R. Hodgson (Neath)	D.B. Clarke
R. Staddon (Aberavon)	M.J. Dick
B. Jones (Aberavon)	P.F. Little
D. Thomas (Aberavon)	I.S.T. Smith
H. Rees (Neath)	P.T. Walsh
C. Jones (Aberavon)	M.A. Herewini
A. O'Connor (Aberavon)	C.R. Laidlaw
Forwards:	Forwards:
L.J. Cunningham (Aberavon)	W.J. Whineray (Capt.)
M. Williams (Neath)	D. Young
P.E.J. Morgan (Aberavon, Capt.)	K.F. Gray
B.E. Thomas (Neath)	C.E. Meads
D. Davies (Neath)	A.J. Stewart
A. Butler (Neath)	D.J. Graham
P. Jones (Aberavon)	W.J. Nathan
W.D. Morris (Neath)	S.T. Meads

Scorers:
Aberavon & Neath: Try: Cunningham. PG: Hodgson.
New Zealand: Tries: Smith, Little, Gray. Con: D. Clarke.

Referee: F.G. Price (Blaenavon).
Attendance: 21,000.

a current international, and back-row forward Dai Morris, who went on to become a Welsh rugby folk hero.

Aberavon & Neath offered stubborn resistance for half an hour. Then the home side attacked. The ball was kicked ahead and Mac Herewini was tackled by Peter Jones as he gathered the ball. It then went loose and Cunningham dived on it to score. Welsh full-back Grahame Hodgson missed the conversion. Shortly afterwards, the try-scorer received a head injury that caused him to leave the field and Walsh damaged his knee, which forced him off as well. Although both returned, the injury to Walsh was serious and he did not play again until close to Christmas. Laidlaw then broke down the blind side of a scrum and beat the first line of defence, drew Hodgson and passed to Ian Smith for the equalising try. Clarke's conversion missed and the sides were tied 3-3 at the interval.

The rain increased as the second half started, which made open play difficult. It became a forward battle and, fifteen minutes into the second half, the home side eased ahead again when Hodgson kicked a penalty. This inspired the All Blacks and a kick from Herewini was followed up by Paul Little, who caught the ball and scored. With the score level again the impetus was with New Zealand and, with five minutes remaining, Herewini kicked over the defence. The ball was gathered by Gray who crashed over, even though there was some doubt about it as O'Connor was underneath him. Clarke converted and the match was won.

ABERTILLERY & EBBW VALE   1963/64

Wednesday 6 November 1963
Abertillery Park, Abertillery
Won 13-0

ABERTILLERY & EBBW VALE	NEW ZEALAND
I.M. James (Abertillery)	D.B. Clarke
M. Williams (Ebbw Vale)	W.L. Davis
K. Westwood (Ebbw Vale)	I.R. MacRae
R. Howell (Abertillery)	R.W. Caulton
R.S. Cecil (Abertillery)	D.A. Arnold
W. Hunt (Ebbw Vale)	B.A. Watt
R. Evans (Ebbw Vale)	K.C. Briscoe (Capt.)
Forwards:	Forwards:
J.M. Hurn (Abertillery)	J.M. Le Lievre
M. Preece (Ebbw Vale)	D. Young
D. Winters (Ebbw Vale)	I.J. Clarke
R.L. Gladwyn (Abertillery)	C.E. Meads
D. Williams (Ebbw Vale)	A.J. Stewart
G. Jones (Ebbw Vale)	K.R. Tremain
H.J. Morgan (Abertillery, Capt.)	K.A. Nelson
A.E.I. Pask (Abertillery)	K.E. Barry

Scorers:
New Zealand: Tries: MacRae (2). Cons: D. Clarke (2). DG: Watt.

Referee: G.J. Treharne (Port Talbot).
Attendance: 18,000.

Abertillery and Ebbw Vale had combined to play South Africa three years previously and had put in a tremendous display that nearly won them the game. So far in 1963 neither club side had played particularly well and and it was expected that the All Blacks should win without too much difficulty. Abertillery captain Haydn Morgan led the side, with Ebbw Vale skipper Graham Jones, a Welsh international, joining him in the back row. The third loose forward was Alun Pask, a tremendous footballing number eight who was unquestionably a player ahead of his time. Morgan and Pask were also stalwarts for Wales and the British Lions. Also in the pack was Denzil Williams, second row for Ebbw Vale and this combination, but a prop for Wales with a reputation as one of the strongest forwards to have played postwar international rugby. The All Blacks made wholesale changes and there was a doubt about the fitness of Derek Arnold, but the Canterbury five-eighth shook off his injury to play.

The first score came after eight minutes when New Zealand created space for Bruce Watt to drop a goal. The All Blacks dominated from this point and it was only strong defence which kept them out. However, close to half-time they scored again when Watt hoisted a high garryowen that bounced badly for the defence and careered into the in-goal area. Ian MacRae was up in a flash and dived on the ball as it approached the dead-ball line. Despite the protests of the home players the try was awarded and Don Clarke converted superbly from the touchline. New Zealand were 8-0 up at the break.

MacRae scored his second try later in the game when another kick to the corner bounced awkwardly and MacRae just placed it down before it went out of the field of play. Clarke converted again from wide out.

The All Blacks played within themselves and seemed reluctant to move the ball when opportunities presented themselves. It was a disappointing game, marred by constant infringements by New Zealand as they struggled to come to terms with British refereeing interpretations.

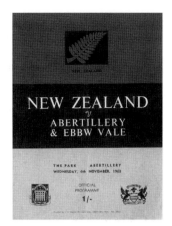

LONDON COUNTIES   1963/64

Saturday 9 November 1963
Twickenham, London
Won 27-0

The London Counties selectors caused a sensation by picking seven members of the London Scottish pack in their side to face New Zealand at Twickenham. The inclusion of scrum-half Tremayne Rodd meant that eight London Scottish players faced the tourists. London Scottish was undoubtedly the strongest side in the capital, only surrendering its undefeated tag a week after the All Blacks game when losing to Richmond. The only non-London Scot in the Counties pack was the captain, England international David Perry. Scrum-half Rodd, later Lord Rennell, was a Scottish cap, as were Frans ten Bos, Mike Campbell-Lamerton, Rory Watherston and Norman Bruce, while flanker 'Chilla' Wilson had played for Australia. Andy Hurst and Jim

LONDON COUNTIES	NEW ZEALAND
S.A. Morris (Newton Abbot & Hampshire)	D.B. Clarke
A.C.B. Hurst (Wasps & Middlesex)	M.J. Dick
J.C. Gibson	P.F. Little
(United Services, Portsmouth & Hampshire)	
D.J.J. Allanson (Rosslyn Park & Kent)	I.S.T. Smith
J. Roberts (Sale & Middlesex)	B.A. Watt
R.F. Read (Harlequins & Surrey)	M.A. Herewini
J.A.T. Rodd (London Scottish & Hampshire)	C.R. Laidlaw
Forwards:	Forwards:
J.D. Macdonald	W.J. Whineray (Capt.)
(London Scottish & Hampshire)	
N.S. Bruce (London Scottish & Hampshire)	D. Young
R.L. Challis (London Scottish & Kent)	K.F. Gray
M.J. Campbell-Lamerton	C.E. Meads
(London Scottish & Surrey)	
F.H. ten Bos (London Scottish & Surrey)	R.H. Horsley
C.R. Wilson (London Scottish & Surrey)	D.J. Graham
W.R.A. Watherston	W.J. Nathan
(London Scottish & Middlesex)	
D.G. Perry (Bedford & Surrey, Capt.)	K.E. Barry

Scorers:
New Zealand: Tries: Dick (2), Nathan (2), Smith, Barry, Clarke.
Cons: Clarke (3).

Referee: P.G. Brook (Yorkshire).
Attendance: 40,000.

Roberts, both England players, brought the total of capped players in the side to nine, while prop forward John Macdonald was to represent Scotland later in his playing career. Campbell-Lamerton had played for the British Lions in South Africa in 1962, and would go on to captain the 1966 Lions in New Zealand. It was anticipated that this team would run the tourists close.

What followed was arguably the All Blacks' finest display of the tour, with many commentators declaring that their play featured the best teamwork ever seen at Twickenham. In a magnificent performance, flank forward Waka Nathan, dubbed 'The Black Panther', stood out with his superb running and there were also memorable displays from Don Clarke, Kevin Barry, Paul Little, Malcolm Dick, Ian Smith and skipper Wilson Whineray.

RUGBY FOOTBALL UNION

LONDON COUNTIES V NEW ZEALAND

TWICKENHAM
SATURDAY NOVEMBER 9th
1963
OFFICIAL PROGRAMME
ONE SHILLING

Ian Smith scored the opening try following a break from Herewini. Clarke converted and then Barry pounced on a loose ball to score following a poor pass from Rodd that his outside half Bob Read fumbled. The score at half-time was 8-0.

Early in the second half Colin Gibson mishandled and Graham and Colin Meads set up the first of Dick's tries. With victory secure, Whineray instructed his side to throw the ball around. Some fantastic rugby ensued, starting with a try from Dick. Clarke converted and then scored himself. The full-back added a conversion, but could not add the extra points to the final two scores. Both tries came from Nathan, the first an individual one, the second a team effort that really brought the house down. It was started and finished by Nathan, but involved most of the side as backs and forwards combined in a superb bout of passing. Journalist Richard Evans described the try in his book on the tour: *Everything they touched turned to gold, and Whineray, of course, bent fifteen stone of muscle and bone with the ease of a ballet dancer, and scooped the ball delicately off his toes to keep the action flowing. Two more passes and Nathan appeared on the scene again to finish off what he had started by diving over the line as the crowd roared with incredulous delight.*

CAMBRIDGE UNIVERSITY 1963/64

Wednesday 13 November 1963
Grange Road, Cambridge
Won 20-6

The University included seven Blues in their side to face New Zealand at Grange Road, but the extraordinary decision was taken to drop the team's only reliable goal-kicker, Jonathan Harvey. This selectorial blunder certainly put the home side at a disadvantage and no Cambridge goals were kicked in the match. Of the side that encountered the All Blacks, scrum-half Simon Clarke and prop Nick Drake-Lee were England caps, while skipper Dick Greenwood and centres David Rosser and Geoff Frankcom would play for England in future years. Hooker Brian Rees was a future Welsh international, and full-back Denis Gethin later became secretary of the WRU. However, the star of the side

CAMBRIDGE UNIVERSITY	NEW ZEALAND
D. Gethin (Selwyn)	D.B. Clarke
S.A. Martin (Christ's)	M.J. Dick
D.W.A. Rosser (Christ's)	I.R. MacRae
G.P. Frankcom (Queens')	R.W. Caulton
B.J. Hewett (Trinity)	B.A. Watt
C.M.H. Gibson (Queens')	E.W. Kirton
S.J.S. Clarke (Downing)	K.C. Briscoe
Forwards:	Forwards:
N.J. Drake-Lee (Downing)	W.J. Whineray (Capt.)
B.I. Rees (Christ's)	J. Major
A.R. Pender (Queens')	J.M. Le Lievre
C.S. Dutson (St Catharine's)	A.J. Stewart
L.J. McMorris (Christ's)	R.H. Horsley
J.H.H. James (Christ's)	K.R. Tremain
J.R.H. Greenwood (Emmanuel, Capt.)	K.A. Nelson
R.J. Phillips (Downing)	B.J. Lochore

Scorers:
Cambridge University: Tries: Gibson, Frankcom.
New Zealand: Tries: Tremain (2), Dick, Caulton. Con: Clarke.
PG: Clarke. DG: Clarke.

Referee: R.A.B. Crowe (London).
Attendance: 8,000.

was outside half Mike Gibson, who was at the start of a glittering rugby career that would encompass sixty-nine Irish caps and an incredible five British Lions tours.

Just as the London Counties game had brought the very best out of Waka Nathan, so this match showed Wilson Whineray at his finest. New Zealand journalist Terry McLean called the game Whineray's 'greatest in an All Black uniform'. The New Zealand skipper was a constant threat at the lineout, regularly pinching the ball. He also excelled in the loose and set up three All Black tries, one of them even involving the sort of tactical kick not normally associated with prop forwards.

New Zealand took an early lead when Don Clarke thumped over a penalty after just three minutes, but the University drew level when the brilliant Gibson, who had already caused problems to the All Blacks' defence with his sidestepping runs, cut through from his own half and exchanged passes with Rosser before scoring an excellent try. Unfortunately for Cambridge, Gethin missed the conversion, and this was followed by more ill luck for the home team when the referee, Mr Crowe, awarded a drop goal to Don Clarke when most of the crowd and players thought the kick had fallen just under the bar. In fact, the Cambridge side lined up on the 25-yard line expecting a drop out, although Rosser confirmed to journalists after the game that he thought the kick was a good one. There was no further score in the first half, which finished with the University trailing 6-3.

CAMBRIDGE
UNIVERSITY

versus

NEW ZEALAND

GRANGE ROAD, CAMBRIDGE
WEDNESDAY, NOVEMBER 13th
1963

Three minutes into the second half, Whineray cut between the Cambridge halves and put Kel Tremain in for a try. Clarke's conversion went over, but was disallowed because Gibson had charged and touched the ball in flight. Shortly afterwards Gibson looked to have landed a drop goal, but Mr Crowe did not award it. The All Blacks stretched their lead to 12-3 when Whineray broke and then sent a high kick towards Malcolm Dick's wing. Dick scored the try, but Clarke failed to add the extra points. For the next thirty minutes the home side strove hard to reduce the deficit. Eventually, Frankcom capitalised on a bad pass from Don Clarke and ran half the length of the field to score a try. Sadly for Cambridge, Gethin failed with the kick, as did winger Alan Martin with a penalty shortly afterwards. Then Whineray instigated another attack, from which Tremain scored his second try, and a cross-kick from Dick led to a final score from Ralph Caulton that Clarke converted.

Earle Kirton at outside half had not had a particularly happy game, being forced to kick too much due to the attentions of the Cambridge pack. Thirteen of the Cambridge side, along with the restored Harvey, went on to defeat Oxford in the Varsity match in December.

SOUTH OF SCOTLAND   1963/64

Saturday 16 November 1963
Mansfield Park, Hawick
Won 8-0

The New Zealanders expected a hard game against the South of Scotland and fielded almost their strongest side, including thirteen of the team that had demolished London Counties the previous weekend. Built around the successful Hawick team of the early 1960s, the South boasted three international players and several others pressing for recognition. It was felt that if the South could hold the visitors in the frontal battle, then they had an outside chance of causing an upset.

There had been heavy rain during the week and the pitch was very soft in places. In front of the largest crowd ever seen at

SOUTH OF SCOTLAND	NEW ZEALAND
J.H. Gray (Hawick)	D.B. Clarke
A.S. Amos (Gala)	W.L. Davis
C. Elliot (Langholm)	P.F. Little
E.W. Broatch (Hawick)	I.S.T. Smith
W.D. Jackson (Hawick)	B.A. Watt
D.H. Chisholm (Melrose, Capt.)	M.A. Herewini
A.J. Hastie (Melrose)	C.R. Laidlaw
Forwards:	Forwards:
R.M. Paterson (Gala)	W.J. Whineray (Capt.)
R.J. Grieve (Hawick)	D. Young
N. Suddon (Hawick)	K.F. Gray
W.J. Hunter (Hawick)	C.E. Meads
J.W. Telfer (Melrose)	R.H. Horsley
R. Valentine (Hawick)	D.J. Graham
D. Grant (Hawick)	K.R. Tremain
T.O. Grant (Hawick)	K.E. Barry

Scorers:
New Zealand: Try: Barry. Con: Clarke. DG: Laidlaw.

Referee: A.C. Luff (Notts., Lincs. & Derbys.).
Attendance: 15,000.

Mansfield Park, the visitors did most of the pressing in the first half, but were held for twenty-five minutes until Kevin Barry crashed over for a try that Don Clarke converted. Five points down at half-time, the

South fought back splendidly. The forwards were gloriously aggressive, playing with fire and spirit, while Dougie Jackson on the wing came near to scoring after a good handling movement. The New Zealanders struggled to cope with the referee's interpretation of the lineout laws, losing out heavily in the penalty count. To make matters worse, the celebrated Don Clarke had a rare off day with his place-kicking, missing three penalties and a mammoth drop goal effort. Gradually, the visitors got their second wind and began to dictate the pace, but it was not until the closing minutes that Chris Laidlaw, celebrating his twentieth birthday, sealed the win with a drop goal. Despite the defeat, the crowd gave the South a heartfelt ovation as they left the field. The New Zealanders had deserved their win, but there was not 8 points between the teams.

This was a great rugby match that has gone down in Border folklore. Jim Telfer gave his forwards a magnificent lead and the Grant brothers, Oliver and Derrick, caused Mac Herewini all kinds of problems. Arthur Hastie proved an excellent link player and was full of virility, bursting through in an exciting fashion and coming close on several occasions. In the centre, Christie Elliot was solid and pulled off some memorable tackles, but the real hero for the South was Jim Gray at full-back. Gray's fielding of the greasy ball was impeccable and his kicking even outmatched his opposite number Clarke. For New Zealand, Dennis Young was in good form in the scrums, taking eight strikes against the head, and Barry had his best game on the tour so far. Colin Meads and Kel Tremain were also very prominent, especially in the first half. The South had exposed some of the tourists' limitations: a dislike of heavy conditions, hesitancy when faced with a rolling ball and suspect technique in the lineout. The South's downfall had been the lack of a player with enough speed to make the final breakthrough.

GLASGOW & EDINBURGH 1963/64

Wednesday 20 November 1963
Hughenden, Glasgow
Won 33-3

The New Zealanders retained only four players who had taken part in the match against the South of Scotland, but were still able to field twelve internationals. Don Clarke was rested for the first time on the tour but his brother Ian played in front row. Wilson Whineray also stood down, allowing scrum-half Kevin Briscoe to captain the side. The New Zealanders presented a formidable challenge to the Combined Cities, thirteen of whom were drawn from Edinburgh, but the home side could boast several international players, including the captain Brian Neill and British Lion John Douglas.

On a sunny but cool day, New Zealand enjoyed their most polished victory of the tour to date, running in 8 tries. Technically and physically superior, the visiting forwards dominated all aspects of the game, securing an endless supply of ball for their backs to exploit, the whole team regularly

GLASGOW & EDINBURGH	NEW ZEALAND
C.F. Blaikie (Heriot's FP)	M.A. Herewini
A.J.W. Hinshelwood (Stewart's FP)	M.J. Dick
B.C. Henderson (Edinburgh Wanderers)	P.F. Little
G.R. Craig (Glasgow HSFP)	R.W. Caulton
J.D. Jardine (Edinburgh Acads)	D.A. Arnold
B.M. Simmers (Glasgow Acads)	B.A. Watt
G.F. Goddard (Heriot's FP)	K.C. Briscoe (Capt.)
Forwards:	Forwards:
W.A.M. Crow (Edinburgh Wanderers)	I.J. Clarke
G. Grahamslaw (Royal HSFP)	J. Major
J.B. Neill (Edinburgh Acads, Capt.)	J.M. Le Lievre
J. Douglas (Stewart's FP)	S.T. Meads
J.K. Millar (Edinburgh Acads)	A.J. Stewart
J.P. Fisher (Royal HSFP)	K.R. Tremain
K.I. Ross (Boroughmuir FP)	W.J. Nathan
A.C. McNish (Watsonians)	K.A. Nelson

Scorers:
Glasgow & Edinburgh: PG: Blaikie.
New Zealand: Tries: Arnold (3), Dick (2), Major, Nathan, Caulton. Cons: Herewini (3). DG: Herewini.

Referee: P.G. Brook (Yorkshire).
Attendance: 8,000.

combining with some fine handling and support play. By contrast, the Cities never looked like scoring a try and spent most of the match defending.

From the kick-off, New Zealand set about pounding their smaller and lighter opponents into submission. John Major, the only uncapped player in the pack, opened the scoring with a try following Kel Tremain's lineout take. Thirteen minutes later, Tremain took advantage of a defensive error to score his side's second try, which Mac Herewini converted. Malcolm Dick and Derek Arnold added further scores and Herewini converted one to put the visitors 16-0 ahead at the interval. By this stage, the Cities had long forgotten about victory and were only concerned about keeping the score down. In the second half, the visitors turned up the heat. Dick, Ralph Caulton and Arnold, with two, scored tries, Herewini converted one and dropped a goal from thirty yards to complete a very emphatic victory. The only crumb of comfort for the Cities was a penalty goal by Colin Blaikie.

In a one-sided match, the New Zealand forwards had laid the foundations with their irresistible power play. They kept up pressure in the scrums and lineouts and were superior in the loose. At hooker, Major gave his side a monopoly of ball. Playing their first match together in the second row, Stan Meads and Allan Stewart were in fine form, but the outstanding player was Waka Nathan, who made life extremely difficult for the opposition half-backs. Despite a greasy ball, the New Zealand backs handled beautifully and showed great strength in the middle, even when Arnold was moved to the wing in the second half because of an injury. For the Cities, Brian Henderson defended very well, but it was largely a lost cause.

CARDIFF   1963/64

Saturday 23 November 1963
Cardiff Arms Park, Cardiff
Won 6-5

New Zealand had famously lost to Cardiff ten years before and were determined to seek revenge. They won, but it was mighty close and had Alun Priday, Cardiff's record-breaking goal-kicker, managed to convert one of several penalty attempts New Zealand would have lost again. The 1963/64 season had been disappointing for Cardiff so far, and the prospect of a win over New Zealand was very unlikely, particularly as the All Blacks chose what looked like a Test XV for the match. Cardiff, however, had underachieved and had nine internationals in the starting line-up plus Maurice Richards, who was later capped by Wales and the British Lions. They were captained by Dai Hayward and included Lloyd Williams, whose brother Bleddyn had led the Cardiff side in 1953.

CARDIFF	NEW ZEALAND
A.J. Priday	D.B. Clarke
S. Hughes	M.J. Dick
M.C.R. Richards	P.F. Little
H.M. Roberts	R.W. Caulton
R. Wills	B.A. Watt
C. Ashton	M.A. Herewini
L.H. Williams	C.R. Laidlaw
Forwards:	Forwards:
C.H. Norris	W.J. Whineray (Capt.)
W.J. Thomas	D. Young
K.D. Jones	K.F. Gray
K.A. Rowlands	C.E. Meads
W.G. Davies	A.J. Stewart
E.R. Williams	D.J. Graham
D.J. Hayward (Capt.)	W.J. Nathan
C. Howe	K.R. Tremain

Scorers:
Cardiff: Try: Howe. Con: Priday.
New Zealand: PG: Clarke. DG: Herewini.

Referee: D.M. Hughes (Llanelly).
Attendance: 45,000.

Cardiff started confidently and with purpose. Their forwards played with a fire that had been missing so far that season. However, Lloyd Williams conceded a penalty fifty yards out that Don Clarke kicked to open the scoring eleven minutes into the game. It was a fine kick into the strong breeze.

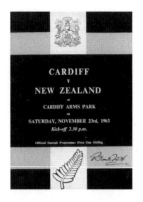

Undaunted, the Cardiff forwards caused trouble for the New Zealand forwards and the back row disrupted the backs. They put pressure on Laidlaw and Herewini and forced them into errors. After twenty-eight minutes Herewini failed to hold a rushed pass, the ball went loose and Cliff Howe dived on the ball for the only try of the game. Priday converted and Cardiff went in to the break 5-3 ahead. The success of the home forwards would prove their undoing. They played a tight game and elected not to use their backs. Their lead, gained with the wind at their back, wasn't sufficient.

After close exchanges early in the second half, Herewini dropped a neat goal to put New Zealand back into the lead after twelve minutes. The All Blacks' forwards began to improve and soon dominated in a way Cardiff had done in the first half. The battle remained ferocious but New Zealand held on to their lead and denied the home side possession. Cardiff were left to rue the missed penalties of the first half when they had dominated New Zealand.

Alun Priday, villain of the day for leaving his kicking boots at home, had set a club scoring record the previous season. His ability was undoubted, and as an international full-back he had experience of big matches too. Every player has an off day now and again and unfortunately for Priday, and Cardiff, this was to be his.

PONTYPOOL & CROSS KEYS   1963/64

Wednesday 27 November 1963
Pontypool Park, Pontypool
Won 11-0

The fortunes of both Pontypool and Cross Keys were at something of a low ebb. Neither club was playing well and both sides had forwards who struggled in club matches. This was anticipated to be the easiest game for the All Blacks in Wales. It was reflected in their team selection, which had a distinctly 'Second XV' feel about it. The home combination patched together a pack and was led by Clive Rowlands, current Welsh captain and an inspirational leader. But those anticipating a heavy defeat failed to consider the Welsh, the importance of rugby to them, and 'valley spirit' that combined to make the team play

PONTYPOOL & CROSS KEYS	NEW ZEALAND
B. Anthony (Cross Keys)	D.B. Clarke
R. Beese (Cross Keys)	I.S.T. Smith
D. Hardacre (Cross Keys)	I.R. MacRae
M. Cooper (Pontypool)	W.L. Davis
W.J. Morris (Pontypool)	M.J. Dick
G. Musto (Cross Keys)	E.W. Kirton
D.C.T. Rowlands (Pontypool, Capt.)	K.C. Briscoe (Capt.)
Forwards:	Forwards:
C. Cobley (Pontypool)	J.M. Le Lievre
A. Talbot (Cross Keys)	J. Major
G. Regan (Cross Keys)	I.J. Clarke
G. Bishop (Pontypool)	R.H. Horsley
M. Panter (Pontypool)	S.T. Meads
B. Powell (Cross Keys)	K.E. Barry
M. Edwards (Cross Keys)	K.A. Nelson
J. Jarrett (Pontypool)	B.J. Lochore

Scorers:
New Zealand: Tries: Briscoe, Horsley, Smith. Con: D. Clarke.

Referee: I. Matthews (Swansea).
Attendance: 18,000.

above itself and confound those critics without local knowledge. The New Zealand pack, considerably bigger and heavier than their hosts' unit, dominated possession but the Pontypool & Cross Keys team's determination to hinder their plans worked perfectly.

Kevin Briscoe opened the scoring when the All Blacks disrupted a scrum close to the home goal line. Rowlands was unable to secure the ball and his opposing half-back dived on the loose ball. The conversion missed and it was to be the only score of the first half, New Zealand turning round 3-0 ahead.

The second New Zealand try was initiated by a Briscoe break on the home 25, and he passed to Brian Lochore in support, who put Ron Horsley in for a try wide out that Don Clarke, who had an uncharacteristically poor game with the boot, couldn't convert. The All Blacks then scored at the death. Wing Ian Smith rounded off a rare passing movement to score a try that Clarke converted.

There were some criticisms levied at the All Blacks for not making better use of their possession but Rowlands had his charges well focussed on the task of containing the opponents.

SOUTH-WESTERN COUNTIES   1963/64

Saturday 30 November 1963
County Ground, Exeter
Won 38-6

SOUTH-WESTERN COUNTIES	NEW ZEALAND
R.W. Hosen (Northampton & Cornwall)	D.B. Clarke
P. Thorning (Richmond & Devon)	W.L. Davis
J. Glover (Bristol & Cornwall)	P.F. Little
A.M. Underwood (Exeter & Devon)	R.W. Caulton
P.S. Lewis (Torquay Athletic & Devon)	D.A. Arnold
R.A.W. Sharp (Wasps & Cornwall, Capt.)	M.R. Herewini
P.J.B. Michell (Penzance & Newlyn & Cornwall)	K.C. Briscoe
Forwards:	Forwards:
C.R. Johns (Redruth & Cornwall)	J.M. Le Lievre
T.L. Scott (Devonport Services & Devon)	D. Young
R.G. Smerdon (St Luke's College & Devon)	W.J. Whineray (Capt.)
W.N. Southern (Plymouth Albion & Devon)	C.E. Meads
A.M. Davis (St Luke's College & Devon)	A.J. Stewart
D.C. Manley (Exeter & Devon)	D.J. Graham
P.E. McGovan (Redruth & Cornwall)	K.A. Nelson
R. Glazsher (Plymouth Albion & Cornwall)	S.T. Meads

Scorers:
South-Western Countes: PG: Hosen (2).
New Zealand: Tries: Briscoe (3), Davis (2), S. Meads (2), Arnold, Herewini. Cons: Clarke (4). PG: Clarke.

Referee: Dr N.M. Parkes (London).
Attendance: 20,000.

With the first Test of the tour approaching, the New Zealand selectors decided to give Kevin Briscoe a run at scrum-half to see if his steadier game was sound enough to oust Chris Laidlaw from the side to face Ireland. Briscoe certainly grabbed his chance, scoring a hat-trick of tries in this comfortable victory and gaining the berth. Well though Briscoe played, the All Blacks' victory was achieved by the forwards, with the pack once again dominating an English counties selection, running away with the game in the second half as the home forwards tired. South-Western Counties was not considered a particularly strong side, but it did include the great Richard Sharp at outside half. Sharp, a 1962 British Lion who had captained England the previous season, was much respected by the tourists and Wilson Whineray had already stated that he was the back they most feared. Two England selectors came to watch Sharp at Exeter, but they left disappointed. John Graham had been given the job of snuffing out the threat of Sharp, a task he performed superbly. The outside half's game was not helped by the wayward passing of his half-back partner Peter Michell, and he failed to leave any mark on the match. When the England side to play New Zealand was announced, Phil Horrocks-Taylor of Leicester was the chosen outside half. In addition to Sharp, the home side fielded four other England caps in Martin Underwood, Dick Manley, Mike Davis and Roger Hosen, of whom the latter two had impressed on England's tour to Australia and New Zealand the previous summer. Hosen had caused such an impression that he was named one of the five players of the year in New Zealand – a rare accolade for a visiting player. Strangely, despite playing a good game at Exeter, he too was overlooked for the international against New Zealand.

The first half was close, with Mike Davis, Terry Scott and 'Bonzo' Johns all standing out for the home team. Hosen kicked a penalty to give the Counties the lead, but this was overhauled when Michell made a hash of a clearance kick and Briscoe pounced for his first try, which Don Clarke converted. Tempers boiled over during the half, with the referee Norman Parkes, a renowned disciplinarian, lecturing both captains and then speaking severely to Stan Meads about rough play. Hosen restored the Counties' lead with a further penalty when Stan Meads transgressed at a lineout, but New Zealand led 8-6 at half-time thanks to a Derek Arnold try, scored after Clarke had come into the line.

The game turned irrevocably in the All Blacks' favour just two minutes into the second half when Michell sent out a wild pass that went nowhere near Sharp. Bill Davis gratefully dribbled the ball over

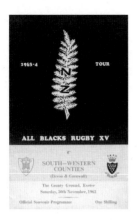

the line and touched down for a try that Clarke converted. Then a Ralph Caulton run sent Stan Meads over in the corner to put the visitors 16-6 up. Clarke missed the conversion, and a stir was caused when Briscoe was handed the ball for New Zealand's next penalty. He missed, and it was Clarke who converted the next try, Briscoe's second. Clarke kicked a penalty to make it 24-6, then Briscoe completed his hat-trick. A brilliant run from Paul Little gave Davis his second try and Clarke his fourth conversion, Stan Meads completed his brace, and the final try went to Herewini following a clever blind-side run. The only chance of a home try came when Peter Lewis ran sixty yards, but he was caught by Davis just short of the line. There was some criticism afterwards about Herewini's over-reliance on the high kick, Clarke's fallibility as a goal-kicker and the rough play of Stan Meads, but this was a satisfying victory for the tourists.

MIDLAND COUNTIES   1963/64

Tuesday 3 December 1963
Coundon Road, Coventry
Won 37-9

The Midland Counties side was based around the great Warwickshire county team, which was in turn founded on the might of the Coventry club. England hooker Bert Godwin and promising Moseley number eight David Ramsbottom had to withdraw from the selected team due to a bout of flu, but the side was still a strong one, with England players Mike Gavins, Peter Robbins, Phil Judd, John Owen, Stan Purdy and the brilliant Peter Jackson, a 1959 British Lion. The sell-out crowd arrived expecting a close match.

For once, New Zealand did most of their scoring in the first half. The game was already won by the interval, with the tourists leading 26-3, and there was little the Counties could do against the superb rucking of the All Black

MIDLAND COUNTIES	NEW ZEALAND
M.N. Gavins (Moseley)	D.B. Clarke
P.B. Jackson (Coventry)	M.J. Dick
R.G. Reynolds (Rosslyn Park)	I.R. MacRae
D.K. Hill (Moseley)	I.S.T. Smith
J.R. Melville (Coventry)	D.A. Arnold
T.J. Dalton (Coventry)	B.A. Watt
G.H. Cole (Coventry)	C.R. Laidlaw
Forwards:	Forwards:
M.R. McLean (Coventry)	W.J. Whineray (Capt.)
D.E. Lane (Moseley)	J. Major
P.E. Judd (Coventry)	K.F. Gray
C.M. Payne (Harlequins, Capt.)	C.E. Meads
J.E. Owen (Coventry)	R.H. Horsley
S.J. Purdy (Rugby)	K.R. Tremain
P.G.D. Robbins (Coventry)	K.E Barry
A. Fraser (Scunthorpe)	S.T. Meads

Scorers:
Midland Counties: Try: Jackson. PG: Cole (2).
New Zealand: Tries: Tremain (2), Dick (2), MacRae, Laidlaw, C. Meads. Cons: Clarke (5). DGs: Watt, Clarke.

Referee: H.B. Laidlaw (Hawick).
Attendance: 16,000.

pack. Kel Tremain was outstanding for the visitors, scoring the first 2 tries and setting up two of the others. George Cole missed an early penalty for Midland Counties – the highly regarded Coventry scrum-half had an unhappy time with the boot, missing four penalties and a conversion – then Tremain burst through some weak defence to score under the posts. Don Clarke converted the try, and added the points again when Kevin Barry set up Tremain's second score. In between these scores Cole managed to find the target with a penalty, but a Bruce Watt drop goal took the score to 13-3, before Derek Arnold charged down a kick from outside half Tim Dalton and sent Ian MacRae over by the posts, Clarke converting. The ubiquitous Tremain charged down a kick from a scrum to give Chris Laidlaw a try and the half ended with the flanker passing to Malcolm Dick for a corner try, which Clarke goaled beautifully. The All Blacks' open play had cut the home side to pieces.

The tourists relaxed a little after half-time, but achieved further scores without greatly exerting themselves. Clarke kicked one of his trademark long-range drop goals and then added an excellent

Above: 1 Bristol on the attack against New Zealand in 1905, a rare event for the 6,000 crowd to cheer at the Gloucestershire County Cricket Ground.

Right: 2 An artist's impression of the 1905 England and New Zealand international played at the Crystal Palace, from *The Book of Football*. (Museum of Rugby)

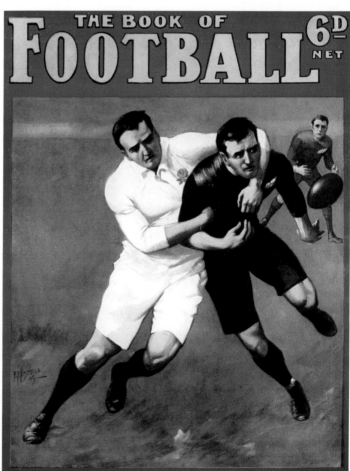

THE BOOK OF FOOTBALL 6D NET

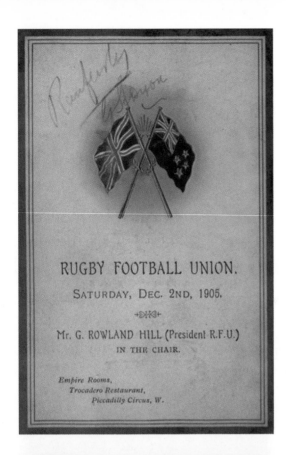

RUGBY FOOTBALL UNION.

SATURDAY, DEC. 2ND, 1905.

Mr. G. ROWLAND HILL (President R.F.U.)
IN THE CHAIR.

Empire Rooms,
Trocadero Restaurant,
Piccadilly Circus, W.

Left: 3 England *v.* New Zealand, 1905. The lavish menu from the post-match banquet at the Trocadero restaurant in Piccadilly Circus, autographed by Lord Ranfurly, the former Governor of New Zealand, who four years previously presented the NZRFU with the Ranfurly Shield as a trophy for its inter-provincial rugby. (Museum of Rugby)

Below left: 4 The ornate dinner menu for the 1905 Wales match. The All Blacks had ample opportunity to drown their sorrows. The match programme is now the 'penny black' among memorabilia collectors, while the dinner menu from the most famous of matches is even rarer.

Below right: 5 The menu for the post-match 'high tea' held in the honour of the 1905 All Blacks at Cheltenham Town Hall. (Cheltenham Art Gallery & Museum)

WELSH FOOTBALL UNION.

New Zealand v. Wales.

MENU

Complimentary

DINNER

Saturday,
Dec. 16th,
1905.

In honour of the

New Zealand Team.

Queen's Hotel
Cardiff

President:
Sir J. T. D. LLEWELYN, Bart.

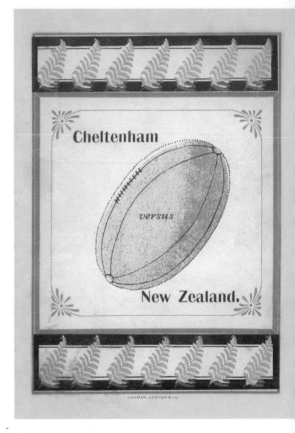

Cheltenham

versus

New Zealand.

Above: 6 The match programme from the 'Invincible' All Blacks' game against a strong Swansea team. The match saw New Zealand hit top form for the first time on tour.

Right: 7 Cardiff provided Porter's All Blacks with one of the hardest games outside the internationals. After the game, several players performed the Haka in a local radio studio.

Above: 8 The 1905 Wales and New Zealand game was remembered at a reunion dinner for the survivors of the victorious Welsh team held on the eve on the 1935 encounter between the sides.

Left: 9 The attractive programme from the opening game of the Third All Blacks' tour – against Devon & Cornwall at Devonport.

10 The cover for the British Sportsman's Club dinner in the All Blacks' honour. A popular dinner across all sports, the menu has the autographs of All Blacks captain Bob Stuart and England cricket and football player Denis Compton on the cover.

SCOTTISH RUGBY UNION

DINNER

IN HONOUR OF

THE
NEW ZEALAND FIFTEEN

THE CHARLOTTE ROOMS
SATURDAY, 18th JANUARY 1964

CHAIRMAN:
MR H. WADDELL, PRESIDENT, S.R.U.

11 The Scottish Rugby Union hosted a fine dinner in honour of New Zealand after their scoreless draw at Murrayfield. This is the banquet menu.

Ireland v. New Zealand

20th January, 1973.

BARBARIAN FOOTBALL CLUB

Dinner

IN HONOUR OF

The
New Zealand Rugby Touring Team
1972-73

CHAIRMAN

H. L. GLYN HUGHES

Royal Hotel, Cardiff
Saturday, January 27th, 1973

Above: 12 The dinner menu for the post-match banquet for the drawn game with Ireland in 1973, which denied New Zealand a 'Grand Slam' of victories over the home unions.

Left: 13 Frequently described as the greatest rugby match played, the players of the Barbarians and New Zealand encounter of 1973 enjoyed a lavish dinner and celebrated long into the night.

Right: 14 A poster advertising Ireland's international with New Zealand, as part of the centenary celebrations of the IRFU.

Below: 15 New Zealand loose forward Ian Kirkpatrick is tackled by Roger Uttley in the drawn game with the Barbarians at Twickenham in 1974. In support of the two forwards are, from left, Mervyn Davies, Sid Going, Andy Leslie, Fran Cotton and Hamish Macdonald, who is partially obscured by referee George Domercq.

16 Graham Mourie's All Blacks of 1979.

17 First five-eighth Eddie Dunn attempts to escape the attentions of Leicester's Clive Woodward in the 1979 match between the Midlands and New Zealand at Woodward's home ground of Welford Road. Supporting Dunn is full-back Richard Wilson.

18 Peter Winterbottom passes to the supporting Nick Youngs as England attack New Zealand during their win over the All Blacks in 1983. Supporting the move is Paul Simpson (with bandaged head) and captain Peter Wheeler (extreme left). The All Black attempting to halt the move is half-back Andrew Donald. Referee Alan Hosie is extreme right.

19 All Black prop Steve McDowell leads the Haka against Pontypool at picturesque Pontypool Park in 1989. Opposing him, wearing 3, is veteran Graham Price, McDowell's childhood rugby hero. McDowell's side were convincing winners 47-6.

The Daily Telegraph

WILL CARLING

Right: 20 Will Carling, captain of the England side that defeated New Zealand in 1993, as a caricature on a card produced by the *Daily Telegraph* for the 1995 Rugby World Cup.

Below: 21 England players celebrate their victory over New Zealand in 1993. From the left: Rory Underwood, Ben Clarke, Kyran Bracken, Jon Callard, Rob Andrew, Phil de Glanville, Dean Richards and Tony Underwood.

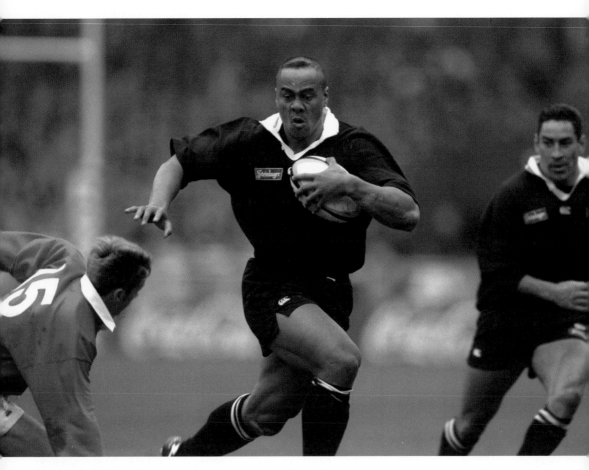

22 Jonah Lomu evades the tackle of Kevin Morgan in New Zealand's 42-7 win over Wales at Wembley Stadium in 1997. To Lomu's left is centre Frank Bunce.

23 The Wales A forwards feed the ball back to scrum half Andy Moore in the 1997 match with the All Blacks at Pontypridd. The New Zealand players are Todd Blackadder, left, and Anton Oliver, right. In front of Oliver is Welsh hooker Garin Jenkins.

24 England captain Lawrence Dallaglio races away from the New Zealand defence, pursued by All Blacks Frank Bunce, Andrew Mehrtens and Zinzan Brooke, during the unusual tour schedule of the 1997 tourists that included two Tests with England.

25 Powerful All Black prop
Greg Feek exhorts his troops
when leading the Haka
against Scotland in 2001. New
Zealanders responding to his
calls are, from the left, Norm
Maxwell, Caleb Ralph, Greg
Somerville and Reuben Thorne.

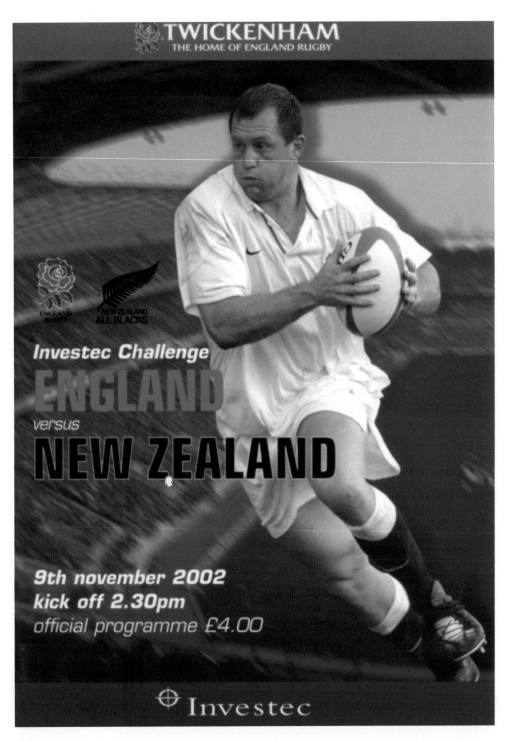

26 The programme cover from England's famous victory over New Zealand in 2002. Appropriately, the cover features England loose forward Richard Hill who had a fine game in a superb game of rugby football.

conversion to a corner try from Colin Meads. Midland Counties gained some respectability when Cole kicked a second penalty and Jackson scored the only home try from a position achieved by a great run from future England cap Dalton. Peter Robbins did some fine covering work and full-back Gavins was very steady, but nobody could do anything about the final try, a fantastic effort from Dick involving a kick ahead and a fifty-yard run. Clarke's conversion would have given the All Blacks one more point than they had scored in their previous game, but the kick was off-target. Nevertheless, this had been one of Clarke's best games of the tour.

Midland Counties skipper Colin Payne, who would later win 10 England caps, had done his best to combat the threat of the New Zealand lineout, but the All Blacks took great heart from their domination of what was expected to be a top-quality home pack. The tourists travelled to Ireland in confident mood.

IRELAND 1963/64

Saturday 7 December 1963
Lansdowne Road, Dublin
Won 6-5

The New Zealand team which narrowly defeated Ireland.

IRELAND	NEW ZEALAND
T.J. Kiernan (Cork Constitution)	D.B. Clarke
J.J. Fortune (Clontarf)	M.J. Dick
J.C. Walsh (U.C. Cork)	P.F. Little
P.J. Casey (U.C. Dublin)	R.W. Caulton
A.T.A. Duggan (Lansdowne)	D.A. Arnold
M.A.F. English (Lansdowne)	M.A. Herewini
J.C. Kelly (U.C. Dublin, Capt.)	K.C. Briscoe
Forwards:	Forwards:
R.J. McLoughlin (Gosforth)	W.J. Whineray (Capt.)
A.R. Dawson (Wanderers)	D. Young
P.J. Dwyer (U.C. Dublin)	K.F. Gray
W.A. Mulcahy (Bective Rangers)	A.J. Stewart
W.J. McBride (Ballymena)	C.E. Meads
N.A.A. Murphy (Cork Constitution)	K.R. Tremain
P.J.A. O'Sullivan (Galwegians)	D.J. Graham
E.P. McGuire (U.C. Galway)	S.T. Meads

Scorers:
Ireland: Try: Fortune. Con: Kiernan.
New Zealand: Try: Tremain. PG: Clarke.

Referee: H. Keenan (England).
Attendance: 32,000.

After the dazzling displays of the last 2 games, the All Blacks went to Ireland supremely confident. They awarded first international caps to Ken Gray and Malcolm Dick. Ireland made a couple of changes from the side that had last played – a 14-6 win in Cardiff the previous season – and selected new wings Alan Duggan and John Fortune for their first caps. Noel Murphy was recalled to the back row having missed the previous season. The pack also included Ray McLoughlin and Bill Mulcahy, plus Ronnie Dawson and Willie John McBride, who both captained the Lions during their careers, and at full-back was 1968 Lions captain Tom Kiernan.

Ireland took the game to New Zealand and a fierce battle ensued. New Zealand attacked constantly but the Irish defence was tight and Kiernan regularly kicked clear into the New Zealand half of the field. Ireland never gave an inch and Duggan came off his wing to make the extra man, Jerry Walsh made a break and Fortune ran in for a fine opening try. Kiernan converted. The All Blacks returned to the attack and close to half-time Stan Meads broke through from a scrum and passed to Kel Tremain, who burst through the Irish defence for a try that Clarke couldn't convert. Ireland were 5-3 ahead at the interval.

In a close second half, Herewini and Briscoe made good use of the wind to set up attacking positions, but the only score was a penalty from Clarke. It was sufficient to win the game for the tourists, but it was a game that Ireland could well have won. They attacked whenever they had good ball and regularly stretched the New Zealand defence. At one point a fine run by Pat Casey ended with a cross-kick that John Graham gathered close to his own line. He was tackled immediately and the ball went loose over the New Zealand line. Tony O'Sullivan dived on the ball for the try but the referee, who was fifteen yards away, ruled a knock-on by the Irish. However, in the latter stages of the match the All Blacks began to dominate and they created several opportunities to score through their forwards but were unable to convert these opportunities to points. Had they used their backs they may well have done so.

MUNSTER 1963/64

Wednesday 11 December 1963
Thomond Park, Limerick
Won 6-3

MUNSTER	NEW ZEALAND
T.J. Kiernan (Cork Constitution, Capt.)	M.A. Herewini
M. Lucey (U.C. Cork)	I.S.T. Smith
J.C. Walsh (U.C. Cork)	I.R. MacRae
B. O'Brien (Shannon)	W.L. Davis
P. McGrath (U.C. Cork)	B.A. Watt
M.A.F. English (Lansdowne)	E.W. Kirton
N. Kavanagh (Dolphin)	C.R. Laidlaw
Forwards:	Forwards:
M. O'Callaghan (Sunday's Well)	J.M. Le Lievre
P. Lane (Old Crescent)	J. Major
M. Carey (U.C. Dublin)	I.J. Clarke
J. Murray (Cork Constitution)	R.H. Horsley
M. Spillane (Old Crescent)	A.J. Stewart
M.D. Kiely (Lansdowne)	K.E. Barry
N.A.A. Murphy (Cork Constitution)	K.R. Tremain (Capt.)
H. Wall (Dolphin)	B.J. Lochore

Scorers:
Munster: Try: Wall.
New Zealand: Try: MacRae. PG: Herewini.

Referee: R.C. Williams (Ulster).
Attendance: 11,500.

The All Blacks made several changes for the mid-week match with Munster, one which the tourists anticipated would be a hard game. They were not wrong. Their plans were hampered when Don Clarke dropped out with a groin injury shortly before kick-off and Mac Herewini stepped up to take his place. Munster had several players who had played for Ireland a few days previously, including their captain Tom Kiernan. They possessed a small but skilful and highly motivated pack in which Noel Murphy was prominent.

With the wind and rain in their faces, the All Blacks attacked from the kick-off but they met stern resistance from the Munster side, particularly their pack. The home forwards played with a fanatical determination to disrupt and harry their opponents, and prevented New Zealand from getting the degree of control up front that they needed. Nevertheless, midway through the first half Herewini, who had a fine game, kicked a penalty to open the scoring. Shortly afterwards, the Munster defence, for once, let Earle Kirton break through and he kicked ahead for Ian Smith to gather and feed Tremain, who timed his pass to Ian MacRae perfectly

for the Hawke's Bay centre to score in the corner. The conversion was missed but New Zealand remained in the lead, 6-0, at half-time.

The second half was all Munster. Their smaller pack played with such spirit and energy that they had the upper hand, putting New Zealand onto the back foot in a way they had not experienced since the match at Newport. Herewini was put under constant pressure with a barrage of garryowens to deal with, but he coped with the ploy admirably. However, on one occasion he was unable to gather the ball and it bounced into touch close to the corner flag. The touch judge awarded the throw-in to Munster, and wing Mick Lucey quickly threw the ball in to Henry Hall, who crashed over for a try. Kiernan missed the conversion and missed several other attempts at goal, any one of which would have given the Munster team a draw that was the least they deserved. Their bizarre run of bad luck against touring sides continued. Once again Munster were heroic but ultimately beaten.

Saturday 14 December 1963
St Helen's, Swansea
Won 16-9

SWANSEA	NEW ZEALAND
D. Parkhouse	M.A. Herewini
D.I.E. Bebb (Capt.)	M.J. Dick
W. Upton	I.R. MacRae
J. Simonson	R.W. Caulton
D. Weaver	D.A. Arnold
G. Thomas	B.A. Watt
E. Lewis	K.C. Briscoe
Forwards:	Forwards:
G. Thomas	W.J. Whineray (Capt.)
J. Isaacs	D. Young
W. Jenkins	K.F. Gray
J. Clifford	R.H. Horsley
G. Morgan	C.E. Meads
M. Evans	K.R. Tremain
M. Thomas	D.J. Graham
R. Jones	K.E. Barry

Scorers:
Swansea: PG: Parkhouse (2). DG: Parkhouse.
New Zealand: Tries: Dick (2), Graham (2). Cons: Herewini (2).

Referee: M. Joseph (Cwnavon).
Attendance: 20,000.

In Swansea, New Zealand faced a side against whom they had widely differing results. It was therefore targeted as a key game. Herewini continued at full-back as the All Blacks made wholesale changes to their side and fielded a strong team. Stan Meads had a hip problem and was briefly hospitalised, but brother Colin returned. With the match against Wales the following Saturday a good win was essential. Swansea were led by Dewi Bebb, a North-Walian with blistering pace and swerve. He won thirty-four caps for Wales on the wing and toured with the British Lions in 1962 and 1966. He later became a broadcaster and television producer. The side also included talented centre Billy Upton and the robust Morrie Evans in the back row, a player with a reputation for his tough, uncompromising style. At full-back was David Parkhouse, who had had a metal pin inserted in his leg to repair a break, which his admirers believed to be 'the golden pin', such were his talents. The crowd included Sir Thomas McDonald, High Commissioner of New Zealand. They all stood and shivered in the bitterly cold wind as the preliminaries were conducted, including a minute's silence for a recently deceased former player. The Swansea side wore tracksuits until kick-off, and everyone was thankful when the game started as the opening exchanges took their minds off the freezing conditions.

Midway through the first half a poor pass from scrum-half Eiryn Lewis was misfielded by Parkhouse, who was unable to secure it before John Graham raced up and pounced on the ball for the opening try. Herewini converted. Playing with purpose, the All Blacks scored again shortly after. The ball was moved to Malcolm Dick, who rounded Bebb and raced away. When faced with Parkhouse he kicked

SWANSEA RUGBY FOOTBALL CLUB
Capt. 1963-64—Dewi Bebb

ST. HELEN'S GROUND, SWANSEA — Souvenir Programme

SWANSEA
V
NEW ZEALAND

SATURDAY, DECEMBER 14th, 1963
KICK - OFF 2.30 P.M.   1/-

ahead and won the race to the ball for a well-finished try. The conversion went wide. Swansea hit back with a Parkhouse penalty soon afterwards, when the All Blacks were penalised at a lineout, then he dropped a fine goal. The match continued as a close, hard-fought affair without further score during the rest of the half, at the end of which New Zealand led 8-6.

During the second half Swansea carried the ball over their own line and kicked clear. The kick was sliced and caught by Graham, who scored his second try of the match. This fired up the Swansea forwards who were all over New Zealand and pressurised the tourists into errors. Parkhouse kicked a further penalty and with the score at 11-9 it was anybody's game. Unfortunately for the 'All Whites', it was the All Blacks who won the game. New Zealand got back into Swansea territory and a well-executed quick passing back movement put Dick in for his second try close to full time, which Herewini converted. Although satisfied with the win, New Zealand had not made the most of their chances.

Tuesday 17 December 1963
Memorial Ground, Bristol
Won 22-14

WESTERN COUNTIES	NEW ZEALAND
P.J. Colston (Bristol & Gloucestershire)	M.A. Herewini
M.R. Collins (Bristol & Gloucestershire)	W.L. Davis
C.W. McFadyean (Bristol & Somerset)	P.T. Walsh (Capt.)
R.C. Collard (Bridgwater & Albion & Somerset)	I.S.T. Smith
J. Lewis (Bridgwater & Albion & Somerset)	P.F. Little
J.T. Hopson (Gloucester & Gloucestershire)	E.W. Kirton
M. Booth (Gloucester & Gloucestershire)	C.R. Laidlaw
Forwards:	Forwards:
D.StG. Hazell (Bristol & Somerset, Capt.)	J.M. Le Lievre
J.D. Thorne (Bristol & Gloucestershire)	J. Major
B.A. Dovey (Rosslyn Park & Gloucestershire)	I.J. Clarke
D.W. Neate (Bristol & Gloucestershire)	R.H. Horsley
J.D. Currie (Bristol & Somerset)	A.J. Stewart
P. Ford (Gloucester & Gloucestershire)	K.E. Barry
D. Smith (Gloucester & Gloucestershire)	W.J. Nathan
D.M. Rollitt (Bristol University & Gloucestershire)	B.L. Lochore

Scorers:
Western Counties: Tries: Lewis, Collins. Con: Hazell.
PGs: Hazell (2).
New Zealand: Tries: Davis, Nathan, Little, Smith.
Cons: Herewini (2). PGs: Herewini (2).

Referee: D.C.J. McMahon (Scotland).
Attendance: 18,000.

This was a magnificent game of rugby, certainly one of the most exciting of the tour. The home side took the positive decision to run the ball at the All Blacks and in doing so became the first team to score 2 tries against the tourists. The Western Counties' back row of Peter Ford – who gained 4 England caps later in the season – Dick Smith and Bristol University student Dave Rollitt performed brilliantly. Rollitt, a great forward, was at the start of a distinguished playing career that brought him 11 England caps, although most good judges felt he deserved far more. The Gloucester half-back pairing of Terry Hopson and Mickey Booth worked fluently together and the side was superbly led by prop forward and Taunton schoolmaster David Hazell, winner of 4 England caps back in 1955. The entire front row of Hazell, John Thorne and Bev Dovey were England players, as was second-row forward John Currie. Of the backs, Colin McFadyean was another player with a great future, culminating in a place on the 1966 British Lions tour to New Zealand. Two All Blacks returned from injury for this game. Pat Walsh had been out of action with a knee ligament problem since early in the tour. He was not really match fit, but was anxious to play and was given the captaincy. Also returning was Waka Nathan, who had missed the Irish Test with a broken little finger. He elected to play against doctors' advice as he was desperate to prove his fitness before the game with Wales. Don Clarke was injured – he sat in the stand booming encouragement to his teammates – and Mac Herewini took his place at full-back.

MEMORIAL GROUND, FILTON AVENUE, BRISTOL
TUESDAY, DECEMBER 17th, 1963

Western Counties v. New Zealand
SOMERSET — GLOUCESTERSHIRE

THE NEW ZEALAND TOURING TEAM

OFFICIAL PROGRAMME - - - SIXPENCE

Western Counties produced a sensational start, scoring a try in the first minute. Peter Ford charged down a Herewini clearance and toed the ball over the line for winger John Lewis to score. Skipper Hazell converted and added a penalty to stretch the lead to 8-0 after just eight minutes. Herewini endured a miserable half of goal-kicking, missing three penalties. He did, however, come into the line just before half-time as part of a move that saw Paul Little – who had an outstanding match – put Bill Davis over for the first New Zealand try. The conversion missed and the home side led 8-3 at the break.

Good work from Little gave Nathan a twenty-yard run to the line soon after the restart, Herewini at last finding the target with the conversion to bring the scores level. However, Hazell kicked another penalty to restore Western Counties' lead with seventeen minutes remaining. The scores were level once again when Herewini was successful with a penalty, then with time running out the All Black backs moved into top gear. Davis made a break and passed to Ian Smith, who created an overlap, allowing Little to run in for a good try. Herewini converted and added a second penalty to leave the All Blacks looking relatively safe at 19-11. Even then the Counties did not throw in the towel, and they were rewarded with their second try. Rollitt made a break and Hopson and Booth carried the move on, Hopson eventually passing to Bristol winger Mike Collins. Collins burst through the tackle of Herewini to score, but Hazell's conversion drifted wide. The game ended with another New Zealand score, this time from a sprint by Smith, who had been put in the clear by Davis. It had been a memorable afternoon of rugby, an honourable defeat for the home team and a treat for the crowd.

WALES   1963/64

Saturday 21 December 1963
Cardiff Arms Park, Cardiff
Won 6-0

Wales were forced to make a late change when Denzil Williams dropped out and was replaced at prop by Kingsley Jones. New caps were awarded to John 'Dick' Uzzell and Alan Thomas, and the pack was generally well-received by the Welsh public. The All Blacks were forced to make a change from the side that played Ireland, with Stan Meads still unfit. His place was taken by Waka Nathan, and Herewini was replaced by Bruce Watt at first five-eighth. Don Clarke was fit enough to play. History dictated that this would be the match the All Blacks most wanted to win.

They started with conviction and when Wales were penalised at the first lineout, Clarke attempted a kick at goal from inside his own half. He hit the woodwork. Then, after five minutes, Clarke kicked a goal after Dai Hayward was penalised at a scrum. Clarke hit the post again with a long-range kick and Welsh confidence was low. However, New Zealand failed to make the most of their possession and Wales began to get into the game. Close to half-

WALES	NEW ZEALAND
G.T.R. Hodgson (Neath)	D.B. Clarke
D.R.R. Morgan (Llanelly)	M.J. Dick
D.K. Jones (Oxford University & Llanelly)	P.F. Little
J.R. Uzzell (Newport)	R.W. Caulton
D.I.E. Bebb (Swansea)	D.A. Arnold
D. Watkins (Newport)	B.A. Watt
D.C.T. Rowlands (Pontypool, Capt.)	K.C. Briscoe
Forwards:	Forwards:
L.J. Cunningham (Aberavon)	W.J. Whineray (Capt.)
N.R. Gale (Llanelly)	D. Young
K.D. Jones (Cardiff)	K.F. Gray
B.E. Thomas (Neath)	A.J. Stewart
B. Price (Newport)	C.E. Meads
D.J. Hayward (Cardiff)	D.J. Graham
A.R.F. Thomas (Newport)	W.J. Nathan
A.E.I. Pask (Abertillery)	K.R. Tremain

Scorers:
New Zealand: PG: Clarke. DG: Watt.

Referee: R.C. Williams (IRFU).
Attendance: 58,000.

time they moved ball quickly and when Uzzell cut inside the New Zealand defence he passed to Brian Price. Unfortunately the second row knocked-on with the line at his mercy. New Zealand went into the break leading 3-0 when, potentially, they could have been behind.

Midway through the second period Kel Tremain and Kevin Briscoe created space for Watt to drop a goal from just outside the Welsh 25. New Zealand protected their lead superbly and the back row was marvellous in attack and defence. Late in the game Clive Rowlands caught a high kick in the Welsh 25. As he called for the mark he was hit with such power by Colin Meads that he had to be carried off with a spinal injury. It was a disappointing end to a largely disappointing game that New Zealand deserved to win. Whineray was frustrated that New Zealand had not scored a try, but stated at the post-match dinner: 'I would have liked us to have scored a try. We will try to do so when we come back to Cardiff to face the Barbarians… It is an omission we want to remedy.'

Thursday 26 December 1963
Twickenham, London
Won 23-9

COMBINED SERVICES	NEW ZEALAND
Surgeon Lt P.L. Golding (Royal Navy)	M.A. Herewini
Cadet C.P. Simpson (Army)	R.W. Caulton
E/A J.C. Gibson (Royal Navy)	P.T. Walsh
Flg. Off. H.J.C. Brown (RAF)	W.L. Davis
Lt I.F. Duckworth (Royal Marines)	I.R. MacRae
Flg. Off. R.H. Palin (RAF)	E.W. Kirton
P/O J.R.L. Thomas (RAF)	C.R. Laidlaw
Forwards:	Forwards:
Flg. Off. M.J.D. Stear (RAF)	I.J. Clarke
Capt. N.S. Bruce (Army)	J. Major
Lt J.D. MacDonald (Army)	J.M. Le Lievre
Sgt P.A. Eastwood (Army)	C.E. Meads (Capt.)
Lt T.C. Jones (Royal Navy)	R.H. Horsley
Flt Lt K.J.H. Mallett (RAF)	K.A. Nelson
Lt A.R. Godfrey (Royal Navy, Capt.)	W.J. Nathan
Jnr-Tech R. Glazsher (RAF)	B.J. Lochore

Scorers:
Combined Services: Try: Brown. PG: MacDonald (2).
New Zealand: Tries: Davis, Meads, Caulton, MacRae.
Con: Herewini. PGs: Herewini (3).

Referee: M.F. Turner (London).
Attendance: 18,000.

British Lion Mike Campbell-Lamerton was due to play for the Combined Services, but he withdrew through injury. This meant that Scottish hooker Norman Bruce was the only international in the Services XV, although Colin Simpson of England and John MacDonald of Scotland would gain caps later. Centre John Brown had joined the 1962 British Lions in South Africa as a replacement, but he never won an international cap. The All Blacks received bad news on Christmas Eve when the luckless Stan Meads was taken into St Mary's Hospital to have his appendix removed, but they approached this match in a festive manner and both sides endeavoured to move the ball and entertain the crowd.

Colin Meads was named captain for the day and he certainly led by example, playing a superb game that included a fine individual try. Writing in his tour book, Andrew Mulligan stated: 'We are unlikely to see a greater all round second row in these islands, and certainly no greater runner with the ball in his hands. For a second row forward who was doing the grafting as well, his feats were gargantuan.'

This carefree game started with an early try by Bill Davis following a break from Waka Nathan. Mac Herewini missed the conversion, but soon added a penalty to give the tourists a 6-0 lead. A further score was prevented when centre Colin Gibson brought off a brilliant tackle on Ralph Caulton. Peter Golding played bravely at full-back, but he was off target with a penalty kick and the kicking duties were handed to MacDonald who managed to cut the deficit to 3 points. Then Meads scored his wonderful try, sprinting for the line and selling a dummy worthy of the finest three-quarter. The half-time score was 9-3.

Soon after the break, Herewini created an overlap and his well-timed pass sent Caulton over in the left corner. Nothing daunted, the Services replied with an excellent try of their own. The move was started by the skipper Tony Godfrey and involved most of the backs before Brown crossed the line. Godfrey had to

leave the field for a while during the half, but even in his absence the Services' back row of John Mallett and Ron Glazsher covered well. Peter Eastwood, Campbell-Lamerton's replacement in the second row, won plenty of ball in the lineouts, but it was the All Blacks who scored next when Herewini landed a forty-yard penalty. After that, Caulton kicked ahead for Ian MacRae to score wide out and Herewini converted from the touchline. A further Herewini penalty took New Zealand clear at 23-6, but the Services continued to attack and gained their reward when MacDonald landed a further penalty.

Besides the inspirational Meads, Brian Lochore and Keith Nelson stood out in the tourists' pack, while Chris Laidlaw, Herewini and Davis all provided entertaining moments. Boxing Day is a traditional day for festive rugby, and both sides gave the crowd plenty to cheer about on a grey afternoon at Twickenham.

Saturday 28 December 1963
Welford Road, Leicester
Won 14-6

MIDLAND COUNTIES	NEW ZEALAND
J. Smith (Bedford)	P.T. Walsh
D.W. Bird (Leicester)	I.S.T. Smith
R. Leslie (Northampton)	M.J. Dick
L.H. Drury (Bedford)	W.L. Davis
M.R. Wade (Leicester)	I.R. MacRae
F.E.J. Hawkins (Wasps)	E.W. Kirton
R.C. Ashby (Wasps)	K.C. Briscoe
Forwards:	Forwards:
C.R. Jacobs (Northampton, Capt.)	W.J. Whineray (Capt.)
A.G. Johnson (Northampton)	D. Young
N.J. Drake-Lee (Leicester)	J.M. Le Lievre
R. Rowell (Leicester)	R.H. Horsley
C.P. Daniels (Northampton)	A.J. Stewart
D.J. Coley (Bedford)	K.A. Nelson
D.P. Rogers (Bedford)	K.R. Tremain
C.G. Martin (Leicester)	K.E. Barry

Scorers:
Midland Counties: Try: Hawkins. PG: Coley.
New Zealand: Tries: Dick, Stewart. Con: Briscoe. PGs: Briscoe (2).

Referee: H.B. Laidlaw (Hawick).
Attendance: 30,000.

Scottish international centre, Ian Laughland was due to captain the Midland Counties in their clash with the All Blacks, but he was required for a trial at Murrayfield and had to withdraw. The Counties XV still fielded four internationals in skipper Ron Jacobs, Nick Drake-Lee, Michael Wade and 'Budge' Rogers. All these were England players, while Clive Ashby and Bob Rowell were future English caps. Colin Martin, who had captained the Midland Counties side that drew with the 1960 South African tourists, was a New Zealander. The All Blacks entered the game with an experimental backline, using Pat Walsh at full-back and Malcolm Dick in the centre. They also took the field without a recognised goal-kicker. This was a tough match for New Zealand and the final score flattered them. The home pack competed well and Budge Rogers gave Earle Kirton a difficult afternoon. Ron Horsley attempted to stamp his authority on the game by pushing the balding Bob Rowell out of a lineout, but Rowell thumped him at the next one and stood no more nonsense. The Wasps club pairing of Ashby and Hawkins combined well together, and it was Hawkins who was the real star for the Midlands. He scored a memorable try and regularly caused problems for the visitors with his jinking runs. It was unfortunate for the home side that their goal-kicker David Coley had an off day, landing only one of his five attempts. In contrast, Kevin Briscoe had a great afternoon as makeshift kicker for the All Blacks, landing two superb penalties and a late conversion.

Briscoe's penalties were the only scores of a hectic first half that had begun with a sensational run from Hawkins, which nearly brought a try. Coley missed an easy penalty after just five minutes

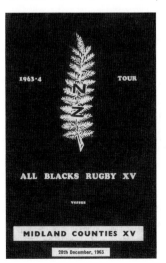

and this seemed to affect his confidence. The tourists led 6-0 at half-time thanks to Briscoe's kicking. At the start of the second half the Midlands looked to be on their way to a try when winger David Bird intercepted a pass, but the referee called play back. Coley finally managed a successful kick after ten minutes, but Michael Wade made the mistake of cutting inside straight into a tackle when he was put in the clear, and from this move Kel Tremain set up a try for Dick. Then followed the try of the match, scored by Hawkins after an amazing run. In the words of Terry McLean, 'one All Black after another bought his dummy' during a run of thirty yards. Unfortunately for the Counties, Coley could not convert, but at 9-6 the All Blacks were not yet home and dry. Had the score remained that way it would perhaps have been a fair reflection of the play, but a late charge from a lineout by Allan Stewart brought a further score and Briscoe's conversion gave the New Zealanders a more comfortable winning margin than they deserved.

Kel Tremain was the outstanding All Black in this game, while Briscoe had surprised everybody with the quality of his goal-kicking. Walsh had looked sound at full-back, but Dick was uncertain in the unfamiliar surroundings of centre. The All Blacks were relieved to gain this victory over a competitive side in a game that was thoroughly enjoyed by a sporting and appreciative crowd.

LLANELLY   1963/64

Tuesday 31 December 1963
Stradey Park, Llanelly
Won 22-8

LLANELLY	NEW ZEALAND
I. Jones	M.A. Herewini
D.R.R. Morgan	M.J. Dick
J. Butt	I.R. MacRae
C. Evans	R.W. Caulton
T.E. Price	P.T. Walsh
B. Davies	B.A. Watt
D. Thomas	C.R. Laidlaw
Forwards:	Forwards:
A. Gale	W.J. Whineray (Capt.)
N.R. Gale	D. Young
C. Jones	K.F. Gray
H. Jones	C.E. Meads
W.D. Thomas	K.E. Barry
M. Morgan (Capt.)	D.J. Graham
J. Leleu	W.J. Nathan
D. Lloyd	B.J. Lochore

Scorers:
Llanelly: Try: Evans. Con: I. Jones. PG: I. Jones.
New Zealand: Tries: Dick (2), Caulton, Meads, Nathan.
Cons: Herewini (2). PG: Herewini.

Referee: W. Thomas (Clydach).
Attendance: 28,000.

Llanelly had had an indifferent season thus far, enjoying good wins over Swansea and Neath and a cricket score against Bath, but had lost heavily to Newport and been defeated by Cardiff. A comfortable New Zealand victory was predicted. Llanelly's captain was Marlston Morgan, an inspirational flank forward who took over captaincy midway through the previous season. A prolific try-scorer, he was the club's leading scorer the previous season, repeating this feat in 1963/64. He later served the club with distinction as an administrator. The pack included the Gale brothers, Aubrey and Norman, in the front row plus international John Leleu at number eight. The forwards also included twenty-one-year-old Delme Thomas, who was to tour New Zealand with the British Lions in 1966 before being capped by Wales. He also toured with the Lions in 1971 and captained Llanelli and Wales in their matches against the All Blacks in 1972. The back division included eighteen-year-old schoolboy Terry Price, who later played for Wales as a full-back, in only his second game of senior rugby. New Zealand chose a strong side with Brian Lochore at number eight. Chris Laidlaw was preferred at half-back. Don Clarke was a doubt so Mac Herewini was chosen at full-back while Clarke ran the line.

STRADEY PARK, LLANELLY

LLANELLY
v
NEW ZEALAND
TUESDAY, DECEMBER 31st, 1963
Kick-off 2.15 p.m.
SOUVENIR PROGRAMME
PRICE 6d

The 'Scarlets' started the game at a terrific pace and after eight minutes were awarded a penalty which full-back Ieuan Jones converted. The home pack played with great determination and midway through the half Jeff Butt tackled Herewini running out of defence. The ball went loose and skipper Morgan kicked the ball ahead and was chased by Cyril Evans. The centre kicked ahead again but MacRae failed to clear, allowing Evans to regather the ball and score a try. Jones converted and Llanelly were 8-0 ahead. This spurred New Zealand into action, and when Butt had his clearance kick charged down Malcolm Dick dived on the ball for the try. The home side went into the break 8-3 ahead.

The second half was all New Zealand with Llanelly defending heroically. Meads nearly scored before John Graham created space for Ralph Caulton to score an unconverted try. Then Llanelly outside half Beverley Davies was knocked unconscious and as he left the field the match swung from scarlet to black. Immediately after, Herewini kicked a penalty to take his side into a lead which they never surrendered. The All Blacks then had a penalty close to the Llanelly goal line and took a quick tapped kick for Meads to score near the corner. Shortly afterwards, Dick scored again when Ieuan Jones failed to deal with a kick ahead. Herewini converted. Llanelly wing Robert Morgan pulled a hamstring and went off and, with Llanelly down to thirteen, they had little chance of holding out. Their forwards battled away against the All Blacks but it was only a matter of time before New Zealand scored again, Nathan touching down after a clever change of direction by Watt. In scoring, Nathan managed to break his jaw. Herewini converted again and New Zealand ran out convincing winners, although the score didn't reflect the part the home side played in a fine game.

ENGLAND   1963/64

Saturday 4 January 1964
Twickenham, London
Won 14-0

Ten of the England side had faced New Zealand during the Australasian tour in 1963 and there was only one new cap, Roger Sangwin of Hull & East Riding. However, there were some surprise choices in the selected XV, particularly since a number of the summer tour party had been off-form during the early part of the season. Vic Marriott of Harlequins had been rested by his club and dropped from the Surrey county side, yet he retained his international place, despite the claims of Gloucester's Peter Ford, who had played so well against the tourists at Bristol. Ron Jacobs and Bob Rowell were also strange

ENGLAND	NEW ZEALAND
J.G. Willcox (Harlequins, Capt.)	D.B. Clarke
M.S. Phillips (Fylde)	M.J. Dick
M.P. Weston (Durham City)	P.F. Little
R.D. Sangwin (Hull & East Riding)	R.W. Caulton
J. Roberts (Sale)	D.A. Arnold
J.P. Horrocks-Taylor (Middlesbrough)	B.A. Watt
S.J. S Clarke (Cambridge University)	K.C. Briscoe
Forwards:	Forwards:
P.E. Judd (Coventry)	K.F. Gray
H.O. Godwin (Coventry)	D. Young
N. Drake-Lee (Cambridge University)	W.J. Whineray (Capt.)
A.M. Davis (Torquay Athletic)	A.J. Stewart
J.E. Owen (Coventry)	C.E. Meads
V.R. Marriott (Harlequins)	D.J. Graham
D.P. Rogers (Bedford)	K.R. Tremain
D.G. Perry (Bedford)	B.J. Lochore

Scorers:
New Zealand: Tries: Caulton, Meads. Con: Clarke. PGs: Clarke (2).

Referee: D.C.J. McMahon (Scotland).
Attendance: 65,000.

omissions, while many were surprised that John Owen was preferred to Colin Payne in the second row. Wingers Peter Jackson and Martin Underwood were both injured and the selectors chose Malcolm Phillips on the right wing. Phillips was probably England's best centre at the time and had performed well with Sangwin, in the final England trial, so a promising partnership was broken up. The New Zealand selection problems centred around Don Clarke, who had a leg injury, and Waka Nathan, who had broken his jaw at Llanelly. In the event, both were selected and listed in the match programme, but Nathan was withdrawn on the morning of the game and replaced by Brian Lochore, who thus won his first Test cap. There was some debate about whether Lochore or Keith Nelson should come in for Nathan, but in the event Lochore had an excellent match.

The result of this game was never in doubt. The England pack could not compete with the power of the All Blacks, and the only surprise was that New Zealand did not win by more. As it stood, the final score was the biggest margin of defeat suffered by England at Twickenham since the ground opened in 1910, but the tourists were criticised in the press for their lack of imagination and for their continuous obstruction in the lineouts. John Willcox, the England captain, played a brave game at full-back, but overall this was a poor performance by the home side.

On a misty afternoon at a less than full Twickenham, Don Clarke kicked the first points after five minutes with a forty-six-yard penalty. He added a simpler one after twenty-two minutes, but failed to convert Ralph Caulton's try, set up by Wilson Whineray after a lineout break by the ever-impressive

Kel Tremain. The half-time score was 9-0, and two minutes after the restart the All Blacks scored again. England outside half Phil Horrocks-Taylor made a good break but lost his supporting runners. Caulton intercepted his desperate pass and John Graham sent Colin Meads away on a storming run that even the gallant Willcox could not stop. Meads scored under the posts, Clarke converted and, despite dominating the rest of the

The New Zealand team which defeated England.

game, New Zealand did not add to the score. Willcox missed three penalties in a ten-minute spell, one of them hitting the crossbar, but England never looked like getting a try.

The British press tended to take the view that the All Blacks had a duty to entertain since it was gate money that allowed tours like theirs to take place. They had certainly provided more memorable rugby in their previous two visits to Twickenham on the tour, but there was no denying the fact that England had been soundly beaten by a much stronger side.

NORTH-WESTERN COUNTIES 1963/64

**Wednesday 8 January 1964
White City Stadium,
Manchester
Won 12-3**

Malcolm Phillips and John Willcox faced the All Blacks for the second time in a week, although this time Phillips was captain and playing in his preferred position of centre. The Counties included England international Bill Patterson, a British Lion in 1959, and the side also featured future England caps in Ed Rudd, Tom Brophy, David Wrench and Barry Jackson, who was to become the first player ever capped from the Broughton Park club. Rudd, who had scored such a memorable try in the tourists' opening match at Oxford University, was called into the side on the morning of the game when England trialist M.F. Gibson of New Brighton withdrew. At scrum-

NORTH-WESTERN COUNTIES	NEW ZEALAND
J.G. Willcox (Harlequins & Lancashire)	P.T. Walsh
S.A. Martin	W.L. Davis
(Cambridge University, Old Birkonians & Cheshire)	
M.S. Phillips (Fylde & Lancashire, Capt.)	I.R. MacRae
W.M. Patterson (Sale & Cheshire)	I.S.T. Smith
E.L. Rudd (Liverpool & Oxford University)	M.J. Dick
T.J. Brophy	M.A. Herewini
(Liverpool, Loughborough Colleges & Lancashire)	
W.R. French (St Helen's & Lancashire)	C.R. Laidlaw
Forwards:	Forwards:
G. Johnston	I.J. Clarke (Capt.)
(Carlisle & Cumberland & Westmorland)	
D.L. Airey (Birkenhead Park & Cheshire)	J. Major
D.F.B. Wrench	J.M. Le Lievre
(Wilmslow, Harlequins & Cheshire)	
B.H. Kalvin	A.J. Stewart
(Whitehaven & Cumberland & Westmorland)	
B.S. Jackson (Broughton Park & Lancashire)	K.F. Gray
K.R.F. Bearne (Liverpool & Lancashire)	K.A. Nelson
J. Burgess (Broughton Park & Lancashire)	K.R. Tremain
D. Murray	K.E. Barry
(Workington & Cumberland & Westmorland)	

Scorers:
North-Western Counties: PG: Willcox.
New Zealand: Try: Laidlaw. PGs: Herewini (2). DG: Laidlaw.

Referee: W.J. Willeard (Kent).
Attendance: 16,000.

half, 1955 British Lion John Williams had a back injury and his place was taken by Billy French of St Helens. French, a regular Lancashire player, was a cousin of Ray French, dual rugby union and league international and now the BBC's rugby league commentator. Flanker Keith Bearne had played for Scotland, while John Burgess, a future president of the Rugby Football Union, would achieve fame in 1972 when he coached North-West Counties to their historic victory over New Zealand at Workington. Only Malcolm Dick, Allan Stewart, Kel Tremain and Ken Gray of the All Blacks who faced England played in this match.

Ron Horsley and Stan Meads were both unfit and Colin Meads was rested, so Gray played in the second row, a position he had occupied regularly at club level. This was a tough game for the All Blacks and many of them appeared stale. The home pack played with considerably more spirit than the England eight, with little-known number eight Dougie Murray putting in a lot of hard work. The Counties backs also shone, none more so than Brophy, who had recently impressed in an England trial at Bedford. He made several exciting breaks during the match and was rewarded with his England cap a month later.

Willcox missed an early long-range penalty, but put his side ahead with a goal after just seven minutes. Ian Smith was tackled into touch in the act of scoring for New Zealand, and the home side should have scored when Rudd was put clear, but he dropped the scoring pass. The Counties held their lead for most of the half, but a Mac Herewini penalty just before the break brought the tourists level at 3-3.

In the second half a late tackle gave Herewini a simple penalty to put New Zealand ahead, and the lead was stretched when Chris Laidlaw scored a try following a fifty-yard bout of passing. The score remained at 9-3 until just before the end when Laidlaw, who was the best New Zealand back on show, dropped a goal. Only Jules Le Lievre had impressed in the tourists' pack, while there was some outstanding tackling for North-Western Counties by Patterson and Brophy, who even managed to halt Kel Tremain. The home crowd had also enjoyed the foot-rushes of the thirty-nine-year-old Burgess. Burgess, who had played soccer for Blackburn Rovers, had recently taken up refereeing, but proved in this game that he was still a fine player. He and six of his teammates appeared for Lancashire in the county final later in the season, a game that his side narrowly lost to Warwickshire.

NORTH-EASTERN COUNTIES 1963/64

Saturday 11 January 1964
Show Ground, Harrogate
Won 17-11

Phil Horrocks-Taylor was injured and unable to play for North-Eastern Counties, so Mike Weston moved from centre to outside half. In addition to Weston, the home side included four English internationals in John Ranson, Roger Sangwin, Don Rutherford and Stan Hodgson, while Tony Peart was capped the following month. New Zealand fielded a strong side, but the All Blacks were taken all the way by a committed home team.

This was a great game of rugby with a sensational opening. Within eleven minutes the Counties led 11-0, the best start by any side against the tourists and they were still 11-3 up at half-time. In fairness to the All Blacks, the home side

NORTH-EASTERN COUNTIES	NEW ZEALAND
D. Rutherford (Percy Park & Northumberland)	D.B. Clarke
J.R. Donald (Northern & Northumberland)	R.W. Caulton
R.D. Sangwin (Hull & East Riding &Yorkshire)	P.F. Little
J. Rogan (Northern)	I.S.T. Smith
J.M. Ranson (Rosslyn Park & Durham)	B.A. Watt
M.P. Weston (Durham City & Durham, Capt.)	M.A. Herewini
P.M. Johnston (Headingley & Yorkshire)	K.C. Briscoe
Forwards:	Forwards:
R. Childs (Halifax & Yorkshire)	W.J. Whineray (Capt.)
S.A.M. Hodgson (Durham City & Durham)	D. Young
F.A. Whitcombe (Bradford & Yorkshire)	J.M. Le Lievre
J. Waind (Wakefield & Yorkshire)	C.E. Meads
I. Brown (Gillingham & Durham)	K.F. Gray
C. Heighton (Sheffield & Yorkshire)	D.J. Graham
T.G.A.H. Peart (Hartlepool Rovers & Durham)	K.A. Nelson
M.G. Forster (Durham City & Durham)	B.J. Lochore

Scorers:
North-Eastern Counties: Try: Forster. Con: Rutherford. PG: Rutherford. DG: Weston.
New Zealand: Tries: Graham, Smith. Con: Clarke. PG: Clarke (2). DG: Herewini.

Referee: J.M. Burgum (North Midlands).
Attendance: 20,000.

did have first use of a bitterly cold wind, but even so this was a tremendous effort. Rutherford kicked a forty-eight-yard penalty in the first minute following barging in the lineout, and then a high punt from Weston put Don Clarke under pressure. He was bundled over by Sangwin and John Rogan, and number eight Gordon Forster pounced on the loose ball to score under the posts, Rutherford converting. Clarke missed two penalties, one a relatively simple one, before Counties increased the lead to 11-0 with a

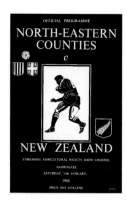

touchline drop goal from Weston. Clarke was finally successful with a penalty just before the break, passing 100 points for the tour in the process, but Rutherford was just wide with a kick.

During half-time Wilson Whineray gave his team a stern lecture and the All Blacks' play certainly improved in the second half. Clarke kicked a remarkable goal after just two minutes, the ball hitting both posts and the crossbar before dropping over, and as Whinerary, Colin Meads and John Graham began to take control of the game a New Zealand try looked likely. It came from Graham after a fine passing movement and Clarke's conversion brought the scores level. From then on the tourists got stronger and stronger, with Dennis Young outhooking Hodgson in the scrums. From one of Young's heels against the head Mac Herewini dropped a goal and the All Blacks were in front for the first time. Rutherford responded with a superb eighty-yard run, but no try ensued and he was also wide with an ambitious penalty kick. Finally, two minutes from the end, Graham drew a defender before giving a scoring pass to Ian Smith. Just before the close Weston was concussed and had to go to hospital, but he recovered in time to play well for England the following Saturday.

Many players stood out in the North-Eastern Counties team. Peart, Ian Brown and John Waind excelled in the lineouts, Forster covered a huge amount of ground during the match, and Peter Johnston and Mike Weston combined well at half-back. Both Rutherford and Weston kicked well in this brave home effort. John Graham was the star for New Zealand, playing his finest match of the tour, while Young won the tightheads 8-1 against Hodgson. There were also good performance from Herewini, Kevin Briscoe and Bruce Watt, but the tourists had certainly had a fright in this splendid game, a game perhaps best summed up by *Observer* correspondent Doddy Hay: 'What a match! What a roaring, tearing battle of fluctuating fortune, with the glorious impossible always on the cards but rugby justice done in the end.'

NORTH OF SCOTLAND   1963/64

Tuesday 14 January 1964
Linksfield, Aberdeen
Won 15-3

The New Zealanders arrived in Aberdeen to conditions of rain and sleet. With the Scotland match looming, the tourists played five of the Test side. Whineray was moved to number eight while Ken Gray, normally a prop, moved to the second row. Ian Clarke had played in the corresponding fixture in 1953/54. The North's most experienced player was Ken Scotland, who had toured with the 1959 Lions. Playing at stand-off, Scotland was partnered by Ian McCrae, who would become a legendary figure in rugby in the north of Scotland. Ronnie Glasgow had won his first international cap two years previously.

NORTH OF SCOTLAND	NEW ZEALAND
C.C. McLeod (Madras College FP)	D.B. Clarke
A.W. Sinclair (Perthshire Acads)	W.L. Davis
C.P. Carter (St Andrews University)	I.R. Macrae
B.W. Brown (St Andrews University)	M.J. Dick
D.A. Bryce (Dunfermline)	P.T. Walsh
K.J.F. Scotland (Aberdeenshire, Capt.)	E.W. Kirton
I.G. McCrae (Gordonians)	C.R. Laidlaw
Forwards:	Forwards:
G.P. Hill (Gordonians)	I.J. Clarke
A.G.D. Whyte (Gordonians)	J. Major
I.C. Spence (Gordonians)	J.M. Le Lievre
I.C. Wood (Gordonians)	K.F. Gray
M.G.H. Gibb (Aberdeen GSFP)	K.E. Barry
J.B. Steven (Madras College FP)	D.J. Graham
R.J.C. Glasgow (Dunfermline)	K.A. Nelson
J.P. Pashley (Perthshire Acads)	W.J. Whineray (Capt.)

Scorers:
North of Scotland: Try: Pashley.
New Zealand: Tries: Dick (3), Gray, Davis.

Referee: P.G. Brook (Yorkshire).
Attendance: 6,000.

Unexpectedly, the North raised their game and gave the New Zealanders a lot more than they bargained for. The visitors deserved to win, but the final score flattered them. Scotland's strategic kicking kept the New Zealanders pinned down in the first half until after twenty-two minutes, the New Zealanders gave a real glimpse of their physical power and pace, and excellent handling between backs and forwards resulted in a try for Gray. Soon after, Don Clarke missed a penalty attempt and also failed to convert a try by Dick. Playing into the wind in the second half, the North forwards showed immense spirit and for a period had their opponents on the retreat, much to the delight of the large crowd. Scotland's kicking was very astute, while Ron Glasgow was prominent with his venomous tackling. On fifty-eight minutes, the North gained their reward when McCrae broke away from a scrum and John Pashley was on hand to score. New Zealand replied with a try by Keith Davis after Billy Sinclair had unluckily slipped when going in for the tackle. Superior fitness started to tell and the visiting forwards finished strongly, the ever-willing Dick running in for a couple of tries.

Though beaten by 5 tries to one, the North had put up a great battle, which had been reminiscent of the South's stirring efforts the previous November. The New Zealand forwards held the advantage in the scrums, but they were unable to dominate other aspects of play. Ken Gray played intelligently and again showed that he was one of the stars of the tour. At full-back, Clarke was very disappointing, missing seven kicks at goal. The North forwards played a rare spoiling game, Gordon Hill, Ian Spence and Jock Steven were to the fore, but nobody performed better than Glasgow, who gave Earle Kirton an uncomfortable afternoon. At stand-off Ken Scotland revealed true generalship with some accurate kicking. Instead of trying to play his backs in difficult conditions, his cool and calculated tactics were correct against the fast following-up of the New Zealand forwards.

SCOTLAND

1963/64

Saturday 18 January 1964
Murrayfield, Edinburgh
Drawn 0-0

SCOTLAND	NEW ZEALAND
S. Wilson (Oxford University)	D.B. Clarke
C. Elliot (Langholm)	R.W. Caulton
J.A.P. Shackleton (London Scottish)	P.F. Little
I.H.P. Laughland (London Scottish)	M.J. Dick
R.H. Thomson (London Scottish)	M.A. Herewini
G. Sharp (Stewart's FP)	B.A. Watt
J.A.T. Rodd (London Scottish)	K.C. Briscoe
Forwards:	Forwards:
D.M.D. Rollo (Howe of Fife)	W.J. Whineray (Capt.)
N.S. Bruce (London Scottish)	D. Young
J.B. Neill (Edinburgh Acads, Capt.)	K.F. Gray
W.J. Hunter (Hawick)	A.J. Stewart
P.C. Brown (West of Scotland)	C.E. Meads
J.W. Telfer (Melrose)	K.R. Tremain
J.P. Fisher (Royal High School FP)	D.J. Graham
T.O. Grant (Hawick)	B.J. Lochore

Referee: R.C. Williams (Ireland).
Attendance: 70,000.

With the prospect of a firm and open pitch, the New Zealanders were optimistic about beating Scotland and completing their first-ever Grand Slam in the British Isles. New Zealand made one change from the side that had beaten England, Mac Herewini replacing Derek Arnold who was suffering from a leg injury and a general loss of form. Scotland retained almost the same side that had beaten France at Murrayfield a fortnight earlier, Jim Shackleton coming in at centre and Dave Rollo at prop.

In almost perfect conditions, both sides played it safe, keeping the ball among the forwards and the half-backs. In the first fifteen minutes, the powerful New Zealand forwards set about their usual tactics of softening up the opposition, but the Scots put up a completely successful resistance.

After twenty minutes, Colin Meads was given a stern warning for punching. The Scottish forwards were beaten in the scrums, but they performed miracles in the loose, and their cover defence and backing-up was exemplary. The New Zealand forwards looked increasingly frustrated, although the referee did not help by refusing to allow any protracted rucking. Scottish stand-off Gregor Sharp played a canny game, kicking for touch and reducing the tourists' attacking options. Scotland threatened the New Zealand line on at least three occasions. Likewise, Don Clarke missed several kicks at goal while Dick just failed to touch down as the ball slid into touch in-goal. In the second half, New Zealand made great use of high kicks, only to find that Stewart Wilson at full-back was dead safe. Visibly tiring, Scotland hung on for the last fifteen minutes thanks to fire and intelligence. In a heart-stopping conclusion, Clarke made a break that nearly brought the winning score.

At the end of an enthralling match, the crowd demanded a lap of honour from their heroes with shouts of 'We want Scotland, we want Scotland!', although the players were in their baths. Although this was the first no-scoring draw in the history of Murrayfield, Scotland had won a moral victory. It was the most unexpected result in international rugby since 1951, when a comparatively youthful Scottish team beat Wales, full of celebrities, 19-0. Playing their twenty-sixth match of the tour, there were signs of fatigue and mental tiredness about New Zealand. Whineray, Meads, Graham and Tremain were all prominent in the loose, and Young gave the visitors an advantage in the scrums, but the combined effort was not enough to quell the Scottish eight. Under the leadership of Brian Neill, the Scots had played the game of their lives. The back row was superb, Pringle Fisher doing tremendous work and producing a tackle on Meads that knocked the great All Black flat out. Sharp and Tremayne Rodd were a good pairing at half-back while Wilson was fearless under the high ball. It was a classic match that has gone down in Scottish rugby history.

LEINSTER   1963/64

Wednesday 22 January 1964
Lansdowne Road, Dublin
Won 11-8

The All Blacks returned to Dublin to play the province of Leinster. They looked to the game to restore their reputation, which had been tarnished in Scotland. Leinster picked a strong side with an international three-quarter line and a pack that included four internationals, including hooker Ronnie Dawson, who captained the 1959 British Lions in New Zealand. The back row included young veterinary student Mick Doyle, who subsequently played for Ireland and toured South Africa with the 1968 Lions. He later coached Ireland to the Triple Crown in 1985 and during the first Rugby World Cup in 1987.

LEINSTER	NEW ZEALAND
F.S. Keogh (Bective Rangers)	D.B. Clarke
J.J. Fortune (Clontarf)	I.S.T. Smith
M.K. Flynn (Wanderers)	P.F. Little
P.J. Casey (U.C. Dublin)	M.J. Dick
N.H. Brophy (Blackrock College)	E.W. Kirton
J. Murray (U.C. Dublin)	B.A. Watt
J.C. Kelly (U.C. Dublin, Capt.)	C.R. Laidlaw
Forwards:	Forwards:
A. Moroney (U.C. Dublin)	W.J. Whineray (Capt.)
A.R. Dawson (Wanderers)	J. Major
S. McHale (Lansdowne)	J.M. Le Lievre
W.A. Mulcahy (Bective Rangers)	A.J. Stewart
M.G. Culliton (Wanderers)	C.E. Meads
M.G. Doyle (U.C. Dublin)	K.R. Tremain
M. Hipwell (Terenure College)	K.A. Nelson
A. Bourke (Dublin University)	K.E. Barry

Scorers:
Leinster: Try: Casey. Con: Keogh. PG: Keogh.
New Zealand: Try: Tremain. Con: Clarke. PG: Clarke (2).

Referee: S.D. Wilson (Munster).
Attendance: 20,000.

New Zealand immediately took control and adopted a tight approach to the game, aiming to dominate through their forwards. It was a tactic that worked. The opening quarter was close with the home pack at its disruptive best, but they couldn't subdue the All Blacks forwards, who prevented the home backs getting the ball they needed to run at New Zealand. Chris Laidlaw played a masterly game at half-back, keeping the ball tight and working the touchlines. Midway through the half Don Clarke kicked a straightforward penalty before Fergus Keogh replied in kind. Then the All Blacks' forwards moved down the touchline in a passing rush before Laidlaw passed to Colin Meads running at pace. He burst through one tackle before passing to Kel Tremain, who scored. Clarke converted majestically from the touchline and New Zealand were 8-3 ahead at half-time.

In the second half, Clarke kicked a penalty and then later in the game home centre Pat Casey intercepted a pass from Earle Kirton as New Zealand ran the ball out of defence and raced in for a try that Keogh converted. There was no further scoring but the Leinster defence held out against constant pressure with great spirit and focus.

Meads was outstanding for New Zealand. He disrupted the Leinster lineout and was mobile and a threat in the loose. He gave everything from kick-off to final whistle. With their forwards so dominant, New Zealand should have won by a much bigger margin.

ULSTER 1963/64

Saturday 25 January 1964
Ravenhill, Belfast
Won 24-5

The Ulster side was not the power it had been when it drew with Bob Stuart's side ten years before. They were rebuilding their squad and had many young players in the side. The international forwards Millar, McBride and Donaldson were accompanied by youthful hooker Ken Kennedy, who later had a long career with Ireland and the British Lions. In the centre was silky-running Lion David Hewitt and at scrum-half Andy Mulligan, a controversial character, as he had become a journalist and was constantly questioned about whether he was a 'professional' because he wrote about the sport. Immediately

ULSTER	NEW ZEALAND
W.J. Hewitt (Instonians)	P.T. Walsh
K.N. Quinn (CIYMS)	W.L. Davis
D. Hewitt (Instonians)	I.R. MacRae
W.K. Armstrong (Dungannon, Capt.)	R.W. Caulton
K.J. Houston (Queen's University)	E.W. Kirton
C.M.H. Gibson (Cambridge University & NIFC)	M.A. Herewini
A.A. Mulligan (London Irish & Paris University)	C.R. Laidlaw
Forwards:	Forwards:
S. Millar (Ballymena)	W.J. Whineray (Capt.)
K.W. Kennedy (Queen's University)	J. Major
R.A. Jones (CIYMS)	I.J. Clarke
S.K. Mulligan (Malone & London Irish)	K.F. Gray
W.J. McBride (Ballymena)	A.J. Stewart
D.A. Crawford (Dungannon)	D.J. Graham
J.A. Donaldson (Collegians)	K.A. Nelson
J. Miller (NIFC)	B.J. Lochore

Scorers:
Ulster: Try: Houston. Con: Gibson.
New Zealand: Tries: Caulton (2), Davis, Stewart.
Cons: Herewini (3). DG: Herewini (2).

Referee: K.D. Kelleher (Leinster).
Attendance: 30,000.

outside Mulligan was Cambridge law student Mike Gibson. Then uncapped, Gibson became one of the greatest of all rugby players. He won his first international cap for Ireland later in the season and went on to win a record 69 in all in a career that ended in 1979. He made five Lions tours, but was at his best in 1971 when a Lions centre on their successful tour of New Zealand. New Zealand moved players around with Pat Walsh selected at full-back, Mac Herewini at first five-eighth and Earle Kirton at second five-eighth. Prop Ken Gray played at lock.

New Zealand started the game on the attack and were able to turn early possession into points when Herewini kicked 2 penalty goals. Ulster repelled the next All Blacks' attacks until Chris Laidlaw took a quick penalty close to the Ulster line and Allan Stewart scored the first try. Herewini converted from the touchline. The tourists had previously been criticised for not making the best of their backs but the critics were silenced when New Zealand scored a fine try. Walsh joined a three-quarter move at pace and created an overlap for Ralph Caulton to race in from thirty yards. Herewini's conversion saw New Zealand ahead 16-0 at half-time.

The second half was a closer affair. Ulster had to organise their backs when David Hewitt was injured but he continued, although limping, on the wing. But with New Zealand attacking, they conceded an interception try for the second game in succession, Ken Houston grabbing Kirton's pass and scoring by the posts for Gibson to convert. Both sides continued to attack but there was no further score until good passing by the All Blacks' backs put Ian MacRae into space. He raced away and timed his pass to Bill Davis to perfection and the Hawke's Bay wing sprinted away to score from forty yards out. Herewini converted and a few minutes later he kicked ahead for Caulton to gather the ball and score his second try. Herewini's conversion was good and New Zealand had won a game in fine style. They also saw the potential of Gibson, whose running was remarkable considering the lack of space he had to operate in. Those skills, honed by experience, would wreak havoc in New Zealand several years later.

SOUTH-EASTERN COUNTIES   1963/64

Wednesday 29 January 1964
King's Park, Bournemouth
Won 9-6

The attendance for this, the All Blacks' final game in England, was the highest for a match in Hampshire since the Second World War. Three internationals originally selected for the home side – winger Jim Roberts and scrum-half Steve Smith of England and Mike Campbell-Lamerton the Scottish forward – all withdrew through injury and it was felt that the Counties team was not particularly strong. The side contained only three capped players in 'Chilla' Wilson of Australia and Vic Harding and David Perry of England, although several would be capped later. John MacDonald was a future Scottish cap, while Bob Taylor, Bill Treadwell, Peter Cook and Andy Hancock would

SOUTH-EASTERN COUNTIES	NEW ZEALAND
S.A. Morris (Newton Abbot & Hampshire)	D.B. Clarke
A.W. Hancock (Cambridge & Eastern Counties)	M.J. Dick
H.J.C. Brown (RAF & Middlesex)	P.F. Little
J.C. Gibson (United Services Portsmouth & Hampshire)	I.S.T. Smith
P.W. Cook (Richmond & Surrey)	E.W. Kirton
P.E. Mettler (Wasps & Middlesex)	B.A. Watt
D.T. Stevens (Blackheath & Kent)	C.R. Laidlaw
Forwards:	Forwards:
J.D. MacDonald (London Scottish & Hampshire)	I.J. Clarke
W.T. Treadwell (Wasps & Surrey)	D. Young
R.L. Challis (London Scottish & Kent)	J.M. Le Lievre
P.A. Eastwood (Richmond & Hampshire)	C.E. Meads
V.S.J. Harding (Saracens & Middlesex)	B.J. Lochore
C.R. Wilson (London Scottish & Surrey)	D.J. Graham (Capt.)
R.B. Taylor (Northampton & Hampshire)	K.R. Tremain
D.G. Perry (Bedford & Surrey, Capt.)	K.E. Barry

Scorers:
South-Eastern Counties: Tries: Wilson, Hancock.
New Zealand: Tries: Dick, Smith. PG: Clarke.

Referee: T.F. Windridge (Warwickshire).
Attendance: 7,000.

all represent England, Hancock achieving lasting fame with his incredible try against Scotland at Twickenham in 1965. Kevin Briscoe was not considered for the All Blacks because of a neck injury, and in the absence of the resting Wilson Whineray, John Graham was given the captaincy. The game was much closer than had been anticipated. This was partly due to the tenacity of the home side – the tackling was excellent – and partly because the tourists played badly. They looked jaded and Don Clarke had a poor day with the boot, kicking just one penalty out of seven and missing both conversions.

The All Blacks scored first when a pass from Chris Laidlaw found Paul Little, who put Malcolm Dick away for a try. The Counties drew level when Colin Gibson and John Brown engineered a try for Wilson. MacDonald missed the conversion and the scores were level at half-time.

Colin Meads won a good lineout ball at the start of the second half and the resulting move led to a try for Ian Smith. Smith had exchanged passes with Dick on his way to the line, and many thought the final pass was forward, but at this stage the All Blacks were grateful to get any kind of score. Shortly afterwards Clarke managed his solitary successful penalty, but the Counties hit back with a great try involving a run and a perfectly timed pass from Brown. Brown's pass found Hancock who scored wide out, too wide for Stuart Morris to succeed with the conversion. Despite the usual strong finish from the visitors the home defence remained firm. Bob Taylor had enjoyed an excellent match, regularly causing problems for Laidlaw. The centres Gibson and Brown, together with outside half Peter Mettler, all tackled brilliantly and scrum-half David Stevens kicked intelligently. Near the end Cook brought off a superb tackle on Dick, which seemed to sum up the commitment of the South-Eastern Counties side.

Colin Meads and Kevin Barry were the most consistent players for the All Blacks. Afterwards Don Clarke admitted that he was embarrassed by his kicking and it was ironic his one successful goal should be the difference between the sides.

BARBARIANS   1963/64

Saturday 15 February 1964
Cardiff Arms Park, Cardiff
Won 36-3

After a successful four-match tour of France, which included a 12-3 win over the French national XV, the All Blacks returned to Wales for the last match of the tour in Britain. New Zealand announced their team including both half-backs and number eights. The final decision was made later and Chris Laidlaw and Kel Tremain played in a side as strong as could be chosen. Mac Herewini had returned home following a family bereavement so Bruce Watt played at first five-eighth. The Barbarians selected a team capable of playing open running rugby as its paramount criterion rather than a side who could beat New Zealand. This approach was criticised in the press as this precluded

BARBARIANS	NEW ZEALAND
S. Wilson (Oxford University)	D.B. Clarke
S.J. Watkins (Newport)	M.J. Dick
M.S. Phillips (Fylde)	P.F. Little
M.K. Flynn (Wanderers)	R.W. Caulton
C.P. Simpson (RMA Sandhurst)	D.A. Arnold
R.A.W. Sharp (Wasps)	B.A. Watt
S.J. Clarke (Blackheath)	C.R. Laidlaw
Forwards:	Forwards:
L.J. Cunningham (Aberavon)	W.J. Whineray (Capt.)
A.R. Dawson (Wanderers, Capt.)	D. Young
I.J. Clarke (Waikato)	K.F. Gray
E. Jones (Penarth)	C.E. Meads
B. Price (Newport)	A.J. Stewart
M.G. Culliton (Wanderers)	D.J. Graham
D.P. Rogers (Bedford)	W.J. Nathan
A.E.I. Pask (Abertillery)	K.R. Tremain

Scorers:
Barbarians: Goal from Mark: I. Clarke.
New Zealand: Tries: Nathan (2), Tremain, Meads, Graham, Dick, Caulton, Whineray. Cons: Clarke (6).

Referee: D.G. Walters (Gowerton).
Attendance: 58,000.

the game being staged as an international-standard match. There were two uncapped players in the Barbarians side: Penarth lock Elwyn Jones and Colin Simpson, an Army cadet from Sandhurst. Mike Gibson was chosen to face the All Blacks for the third time on tour but on the eve of the game the Irish

Barbarian Football Club

BARBARIANS
v
NEW ZEALAND

CARDIFF ARMS PARK
SATURDAY, 15th FEBRUARY
1964

Official Programme One Shilling

Ronnie Dawson's Barbarians side which lost heavily to New Zealand.

selectors asked him to withdraw to prepare for the international with Scotland the following week. He was replaced by Richard Sharp. The front row included veteran All Blacks' prop Ian Clarke, who was in the twilight of his representative career.

Both sides approached the game with the desire to play open rugby. They ran whenever they had the chance, but the New Zealand forwards took early control, winning a plethora of possession for their backs. However, the first points of the game were scored by the Barbarians. Prop Ian Clarke caught Don Clarke's kick out of defence, called for the mark and kicked a terrific drop goal from thirty-five yards. From then it was all New Zealand. Richard Sharp was tackled and robbed by Derek Arnold. The ball went to Colin Meads who raced away and passed to Kel Tremain to score the opening try. Shortly afterwards, Dennis Young charged down a kick and the forwards raced downfield in a forward rush finished off by Meads. Neither try was converted and New Zealand were ahead 6-3 at half-time.

The second half saw New Zealand play the best rugby of their tour. Shortly after the restart, they pressurised a scrum close to the Barbarians' goal line and, when the ball unexpectedly shot out the back of the scrum, John Graham dived on the ball to score. Clarke converted and then repeated the feat after a poor pass from Simon Clarke on the home goal line missed Sharp and Waka Nathan dived on the ball for another try. New Zealand then moved the ball at pace. Having adopted tactics earlier in the tour where the ball was only moved when scoring opportunities were created by the forwards, the All Blacks used their backs to create those scoring opportunities in this game. It was spectacular and a great thrill for the spectators. Every pass completed was greeted with loud cheers. They attacked incessantly and when Young was tackled on the line Malcolm Dick was in support to score. Nathan then scored his second when Tremain charged down a clearing kick. Later the All Blacks moved the ball to one wing and then back to the other culminating in a try for Ralph Caulton.

As the match approached its close, the Barbarians' defence was sliced open again. The ball was moved to Wilson Whineray. As the All Blacks' captain raced towards the last line of defence he had Caulton on his shoulder. He delivered the perfect dummy and raced in for a try that brought the house down. As Clarke prepared to convert the crowd erupted into a rendition of *For He's a Jolly Good Fellow*. The final whistle went with New Zealand having scored 20 points in the last twenty-five minutes. The pitch was invaded by countless spectators who chaired Whineray off the field shoulder high. The New Zealand captain later declared 'this has been the greatest day of my rugby career!'

The All Blacks returned to New Zealand via Canada where they played 2 games. They proved popular tourists with remarkable players, particularly in the pack, where the forwards were outstanding.

Whineray was a fabulous captain. He had the hardness of a prop but the footballing skills of a number eight, where as a young man he played. His handling was as good as a half-back's, where he once played a season. He captained New Zealand in 30 of his 32 internationals and was an accomplished boxer. On the 1963/64 tour, the All Blacks' pack created a move involving Whineray whereby he peeled off the back of a lineout. The move was called 'Willie Away', and it terrorised countless outside halves and back rows. Later a successful businessman, his contribution to sport and business was recognised in 1998 with a knighthood. He is still considered by many to be the greatest New Zealand captain.

1967

NEW ZEALAND TO BRITAIN, FRANCE & CANADA

THE MATCHES

British Columbia	14 October 1967	Vancouver	won 36-3
Eastern Canada	18 October 1967	Montreal	won 40-3
North of England	25 October 1967	Manchester	won 33-3
Midland, London & Home Counties	28 October 1967	Leicester	won 15-3
South of England	1 November 1967	Bristol	won 16-3
ENGLAND	4 November 1967	Twickenham	won 23-11
West Wales	8 November 1967	Swansea	won 21-14
WALES	11 November 1967	Cardiff	won 13-6
South-East France	15 November 1967	Lyon	won 16-3
France 'B'	18 November 1967	Toulouse	won 32-19
South-West France	21 November 1967	Bayonne	won 18-14
FRANCE	25 November 1967	Paris	won 21-15
Scottish Districts	29 November 1967	Melrose	won 35-14
SCOTLAND	2 December 1967	Murrayfield	won 14-3
Monmouthshire	6 December 1967	Newport	won 23-12
East Wales	13 December 1967	Cardiff	drew 3-3
Barbarians	16 December 1967	Twickenham	won 11-6

Played 17, Won 16, Drew 1, Lost 0. Scored: 370 points, Conceded: 135.
In Britain: Played 11, Won 10, Drew 1, Lost 0. Scored: 207 points, Conceded: 78.

The New Zealand Tour Party:
G.F. Kember (Wellington), W.F. McCormick (Canterbury), W.M. Birtwistle (Waikato), P.H. Clarke (Marlborough), W.L. Davis (Hawke's Bay), M.J. Dick (Auckland), I.R. MacRae (Hawke's Bay), A.G. Steel (Canterbury), G.S. Thorne (Auckland), W.D. Cottrell (Canterbury), M.A. Herewini (Auckland), E.W. Kirton (Otago), S.M. Going (North Auckland), C.R. Laidlaw (Otago), K.F. Gray (Wellington),

E.J. Hazlett (Southland), A.E. Hopkinson (Canterbury), B.L. Muller (Taranaki), J. Major (Taranaki), B.E. McLeod (Counties), A.G. Jennings (Bay of Plenty), C.E. Meads (King Country), A.E. Smith (Taranaki), S.C. Strahan (Manawatu), M.C. Wills (Taranaki), I.A. Kirkpatrick (Canterbury), B.J. Lochore (Wairarapa), W.J. Nathan (Auckland), K.R. Tremain (Hawke's Bay), G.C. Williams (Wellington).

Captain: B.J. Lochore. Vice-Captain: I.R. MacRae. Manager: C.K. Saxton. Assistant Manager: F.R. Allen.

Leading points scorer: W.F. McCormick – 118 points (77 in Britain).
Leading try-scorer: W.M. Birtwistle – 9 tries (8 in Britain).
Most appearances: B.J. Lochore – 14 games (10 in Britain).

NORTH OF ENGLAND   1967

Wednesday 25 October 1967
White City Stadium,
Manchester
Won 33-3

NORTH OF ENGLAND	NEW ZEALAND
M.P. Weston (Durham City & Durham, Capt.)	W.F. McCormick
E.L. Rudd (Liverpool & Lancashire)	W.M. Birtwistle
J.M. Dee (Durham City & Durham)	W.L. Davis
C.R. Jennins (Waterloo & Lancashire)	A.G. Steel
J.M. Ranson (Rosslyn Park & Durham)	W.D. Cottrell
A.E. Chapman (Rosslyn Park & Durham)	E.W. Kirton
R.D.A. Pickering (Bradford & Yorkshire)	S.M. Going
Forwards:	Forwards:
D.F.B. Wrench (Harlequins & Cheshire)	E.J. Hazlett
J.S. Lansbury (Sale & Cheshire)	B.E. McLeod
M.J. Coulman (Moseley & Staffordshire)	B.L. Muller
A.R. Trickey (Sale & Lancashire)	C.E. Meads
S.R. Hipps (Harrogate & Yorkshire)	S.C. Strahan
J.R.H. Greenwood (Waterloo & Lancashire)	W.J. Nathan
D.E. Barker (Wilmslow & Cheshire)	G.C. Williams
L.J. Rollinson (Coventry & Staffordshire)	B.J. Lochore (Capt.)

Scorers:
North of England: PG: Chapman.
New Zealand: Tries: Birtwistle (2), Williams (2), Going, McCormick. Cons: McCormick (3). PG: McCormick (3).

Referee: D.J.C. McMahon (Scotland).
Attendance: 12,000.

In 1967 New Zealand celebrated the seventy-fifth anniversary of the foundation of the NZRFU with a match against Australia. They won 29-9 and, following a resounding series win over the British Lions in 1966, they were justifiably described as the world's best. They were scheduled to tour South Africa in 1967 but the South Africans would not permit them to bring non-white players and the tour was cancelled. A tour to Europe was hastily arranged as a substitute.

Shortly after the start of the 1967/68 season, England toured Canada, playing and winning 5 matches. Before the tour party travelled, games were played against the three regions that were due to play the All Blacks. Thanks to a fine performance by its pack, the North of England defeated England 12-6, but in a final trial the plans of the North selectors for the All Blacks' game were thwarted by numerous withdrawals. The final selection to play New Zealand caused widespread criticism, partly because only three of the pack that had tamed England gained places in the side. An inexplicable omission was England international forward and Canada tourist John Pallant, while there was also concern about prop forward Mike Coulman. Coulman had played no rugby for any county affiliated to the northern region, and his selection was based on a letter he had sent declaring that he would be available for Staffordshire rather than his previous county North Midlands during the coming season. His selection would have been more palatable if the selectors had not chosen Arthur Chapman at outside half. Chapman, a Rosslyn Park player, had commuted to play for Durham for several seasons, but had indicated that he did not intend to do so this season. Despite this, the home side included nine capped players; Coulman, David Wrench and Dick Greenwood in the pack and all the backs except Chapman. Flanker David Barker had captained his club, Wilmslow, four years earlier at the age of twenty-one.

The White City Stadium was saturated by a heavy downpour shortly before kick-off. The rain stopped before the players emerged, but conditions were very difficult. Despite this, the All Blacks played a running game and totally outplayed their hosts. The score was 6-0 at half-time, but thereafter the tourists were unstoppable. Tony Steel set up the first try just before the break when he created an overlap for Bill Birtwhistle. Fergie McCormick missed the conversion, but added a penalty soon afterwards. Meanwhile, the North had missed five first-half penalties, despite trying Barker, Jennins and Weston as kickers.

Sid Going scored a try two minutes into the second half, then Graham Williams intercepted a pass from John Ranson and ran forty yards for a try that McCormick converted. Almost at once, Williams scored again. McCormick converted and soon added another penalty to take the score to 22-0. Kirton set up the next try with a great break that resulted in a second score for Birtwhistle. The North finally got on the scoresheet when Chapman kicked a penalty after twenty-nine minutes of the second half, but McCormick entered the line to score a try of his own, converted this and added a final penalty to complete the rout.

Along with Kirton and the prolific McCormick, Wayne Cottrell, Colin Meads, Sam Strahan, Jack Hazlett and skipper Brian Lochore all stood out in this stunning performance. The All Blacks looked in ominously good form.

MIDLANDS, LONDON & HOME COUNTIES   1967

Saturday 28 October 1967
Welford Road, Leicester
Won 15-3

The home side for this game was a strong one. All the pack were England internationals, including John Owen, who was a late replacement for another England man, John Barton. Of the backs, Danny Hearn and Rodney Webb had already played for England, Bill Gittings and Bob Lloyd would feature in the following Saturday's international against the tourists and Bob Hiller would get his first caps later in the season. Alan James had been on England's tour to Canada. The Counties side had lost 19-13 to England prior to this tour. Four players who went to Canada with England, Keith Savage, John Finlan, Jim Broderick and Steve Richards, were eligible, but not selected. Finlan and Savage both played in the forthcoming international. The All Blacks gave Herewini the opportunity to show what he could do in partnership with Laidlaw at half-back. In the event they did not combine well.

This game is remembered for the injury to Counties' centre Danny Hearn. Hearn, a renowned tackler, crash tackled Ian MacRae, fracturing his neck. He was paralysed and spent some time on

MIDLANDS, LONDON & HOME COUNTIES	NEW ZEALAND
R.B. Hiller (Harlequins & Surrey)	W.F. McCormick
J.T. Cox (Harlequins & Surrey)	M.J. Dick
R.D. Hearn (Bedford & Warwickshire)	G.S. Thorne
R.H. Lloyd (Harlequins & Surrey)	P.H. Clarke
R.E. Webb (Coventry & Warwickshire)	I.R. MacRae
A.J. James (Coventry & Warwickshire)	M.A. Herewini
W.I. Gittings (Coventry & Warwickshire)	C.R. Laidlaw
Forwards:	Forwards:
P.E. Judd (Coventry & Warwickshire, Capt.)	E.A. Hopkinson
H.O. Godwin (Coventry & Warwickshire)	J. Major
A.L. Horton (Blackheath & Surrey)	E.J. Hazlett
P.L. Larter (Northampton & Leicestershire)	C.E. Meads
J. Owen (Coventry & Warwickshire)	A.G. Jennings
D.P. Rogers (Bedford & East Midlands)	K.R. Tremain
R.B. Taylor (Northampton & East Midlands)	W.J. Nathan
G.A. Sherriff (Saracens & Middlesex)	B.J. Lochore (Capt.)

Scorers:
Midlands, London & Home Counties: Try: Lloyd.
New Zealand: Try: Dick. PG: McCormick (3). DG: Herewini.

Referee: D.P. D'Arcy (Ireland).
Attendance: 14,000.

the critical list. After nine months of courageous rehabilitation in Stoke Mandeville Hospital, Hearn was able to return home, having recovered some movement. He resumed his career in teaching and became a great example of triumph over adversity. Hearn wrote in his book *Crash Tackle*: 'I knew that I would be marking the All Blacks' powerful second five-eighth Ian MacRae, who was renowned for running straight into his opposite number so as to create a ruck for his forwards to heel the ball back. I thought I would spend most of the afternoon tackling the burly MacRae as the New Zealanders would win most of the ball. So I took the field determined to hit Ian with a crash tackle really early on; I would try and disrupt his game and show who was really the master.' Hearn did not time his tackle correctly and his head collided with MacRae's hip. It was an appalling accident.

Following Hearn's injury, the Counties took Bob Taylor out of the pack and the remaining seven forwards made a real fight of it. There was no score at half-time, although Peter Larter and Fergie McCormick both missed penalties for their sides. New Zealand took the lead shortly after the break when McCormick landed a forty-yard goal. This was followed by New Zealand's only try, scored by Dick. Herewini picked up a poor pass from Laidlaw and dropped a goal, then, when Gittings was ruled offside, McCormick kicked a penalty. To their credit, the Counties' players did not give up and scored an excellent try. Larter won a lineout, Taylor made a forty-yard run and handed on to John Cox. He gave a scoring pass to Lloyd who crossed the line. McCormick added a late penalty to the tourists' score, but at full time the crowd acclaimed the gallant effort of the home side, an effort good enough to earn the entire pack, plus Lloyd, Webb and Gittings a further tilt at New Zealand the following week.

Before they left the country, several New Zealanders, including MacRae, visited Danny Hearn in hospital. In years to come Hearn himself would visit New Zealand.

SOUTH OF ENGLAND 1967

**Wednesday 1 November 1967
Memorial Ground, Bristol
Won 16-3**

Following the game with Midlands, London & Home Counties it was discovered that Waka Nathan had broken his jaw. He had received a punch from 'Budge' Rogers and was now sidelined for 8 games. The South of England had played England prior to the tour of Canada, defeating the national side 13-8 at Exeter. The side selected to face New Zealand included seven capped players – skipper Bev Dovey, John Pullin, Dave Watt and Dave Rollitt in the pack and backs Don Rutherford, Colin McFadyean and Geoff Frankcom. Nigel Starmer-Smith, Derek Prout and Barry Nelmes were future England players. The South selectors

SOUTH OF ENGLAND	NEW ZEALAND
D. Rutherford (Gloucester & Gloucestershire)	G.F. Kember
M.R. Collins (Bristol & Gloucestershire)	W.M. Birtwhistle
C.W. McFadyean (Moseley & Somerset)	W.L. Davis
G.P. Frankcom (Bath & Somerset)	A.G. Steel
D.H. Prout (Northampton & Cornwall)	W.D. Cottrell
C.R. Tuffley	E.W. Kirton
(United Services Portsmouth & Hampshire)	
N.C. Starmer-Smith (Harlequins & Oxfordshire)	S.M. Going
Forwards:	Forwards:
B.A. Dovey (Bristol & Somerset, Capt.)	B.L. Muller
J.V. Pullin (Bristol & Gloucestershire)	B.E. McLeod
R.V. Grove (Leicester & Somerset)	A.E. Hopkinson
D.E.J. Watt (Bristol & Gloucestershire)	S.C. Strahan
B.G. Nelmes (Bristol & Gloucestershire)	A.E. Smith
B. Capaldi (Cheltenham & Gloucestershire)	G.C. Williams
R. Smith (Gloucester & Gloucestershire)	I.A. Kirkpatrick
D.M. Rollitt (Bristol & Gloucestershire)	B.J. Lochore (Capt.)

Scorers:
South of England: PG: Rutherford.
New Zealand: Tries: Steel, Kirton, Going, Birtwhistle.
Cons: Kember (2).

Referee: D.G. Walters (Wales).
Attendance: 16,000.

were uncertain who to play at outside half, and left the place vacant pending the Gloucestershire v. Devon match at Bristol on the Saturday before the New Zealand game. Unfortunately, this match fell victim to wet weather and the selectors sprang a surprise by choosing Chris Tuffley. Tuffley had only limited representative experience and had never partnered Starmer-Smith at half-back.

A capacity crowd filled the Memorial Ground. Rutherford opened the scoring with a penalty goal after ten minutes, but he was to miss a further three kicks during the half. The All Blacks took the lead when Brian Lochore stood off at the back of a scrum and worked a move involving Wayne Cottrell as a decoy. The tourists had a three-man overlap and Tony Steel crossed with Gerald Kember adding the conversion. There was no further score in the first half, which ended at 5-3 to the All Blacks. The home pack had given a good account of itself and Don Rutherford had impressed.

In the second half Rutherford made his only error of the game, slicing a kick straight to Earle Kirton. Kirton exchanged passes with Sid Going before scoring a try that Kember could not convert. Then Going scored himself, pouncing on a loose pass from a scrum by Starmer-Smith. In the final minutes, Bill Birtwhistle added a fourth try following a fine handling move. Kember converted this try to crown a good display, but Brian Lochore was outstanding. For the South, hooker John Pullin could look back on a successful afternoon – he comfortably out-hooked Bruce McLeod. There was some press criticism of referee Gwynne Walters after the game – he had stuck rigidly to the letter of the law and awarded around forty penalties. The South of England selectors had not helped their team with the strange selection of Chris Tuffley. However, Tuffley went on to serve Royal Navy rugby with distinction. In 2001 he was the Navy's representative on the RFU Council, and he was awarded life membership of the Royal Navy Rugby Union.

This copy of the match programme has been signed by the entire touring party.

ENGLAND 1967

Saturday 4 November 1967
Twickenham, London
Won 23-11

The inclusion of the entire pack from the Midland, London & Home Counties XV meant an international recall for hooker Bert Godwin, whose last England cap had been in 1964. Debuts were given to Bob Lloyd and Bill Gittings. Seven of the side had not toured Canada earlier in the season. New Zealand gave Test debuts to Earle Kirton and Graham Williams. The referee, Mr McMahon, had officiated on the last occasion the teams had met, at Twickenham in 1964. Both sides were presented to the Queen before the match.

The game was effectively over by half-time. Despite the slippery conditions, New Zealand produced a superb first half,

ENGLAND	NEW ZEALAND
D. Rutherford (Gloucester)	W.F. McCormick
K.F. Savage (Northampton)	M.J. Dick
C.W. McFadyean (Moseley)	W.L. Davis
R.H. Lloyd (Harlequins)	W.M. Birtwhistle
R.E. Webb (Coventry)	I.R. MacRae
J.F. Finlan (Moseley)	E.W. Kirton
W.J. Gittings (Coventry)	C.R. Laidlaw
Forwards:	Forwards:
A.L. Horton (Blackheath)	E.J. Hazlett
H.O. Godwin (Coventry)	B.E. McLeod
P.E. Judd (Coventry, Capt.)	B.L. Muller
P.J. Larter (Northampton)	C.E. Meads
J.E. Owen (Coventry)	S.C. Strahan
D.P. Rogers (Bedford)	G.C. Williams
R.B. Taylor (Northampton)	K.R. Tremain
G.A. Sherriff (Saracens)	B.J. Lochore (Capt.)

Scorers:
England: Tries: Lloyd (2). Con: Rutherford. PG: Larter.
New Zealand: Tries: Kirton (2), Birtwhistle, Laidlaw, Dick.
Cons: McCormick (4).

Referee: D.J.C. McMahon (Scotland).
Attendance: 74,000.

involving brilliant play by the backs and total domination by the forwards. The tourists took the lead after just six minutes when Bill Davis created an opening for debutant Kirton. He crossed near the posts and Fergie McCormick had no problem converting the try. The All Blacks' pack soon got on top in the forward exchanges, but the next score did not come until twenty-five minutes into the game. A kick ahead by Williams led to a try by Bill Birtwhistle and McCormick, who had earlier missed a simple penalty, converted from wide out. After that, the alert Chris Laidlaw pounced for a try when England messed up a scrummage heel on their own line. This took the score to 13-0 and then captain Brian Lochore set up a brilliant corner try for Kirton, which McCormick converted superbly. The England side battled hard towards the end of the half, and after Don Rutherford had missed a simple penalty, the backs set up an excellent try for Bob Lloyd. Rutherford converted what New Zealand coach Fred Allen later called the best try of the match, and an entertaining half ended with the visitors ahead 18-5.

The final All Black try came just three minutes after the restart. Once again Davis made the opening and this time Malcolm Dick was the scorer, McCormick converting via a post. Thereafter, with the game won, the All Blacks rather went off the boil. England gradually gained more territorial advantage and the only further chance of New Zealand points came when McCormick missed a penalty. Peter Larter was wide with a difficult kick for England, but then successfully goaled a penalty to take the score to 23-8. Just before time Lloyd scored his second try and his third in a week against New Zealand. He was the only Englishman to cross the line against the tourists.

This was a thoroughly entertaining international, memorable for the superb play of the All Blacks in the first half. Kirton had made an impressive Test debut, and Davis, Meads and Lochore all had outstanding matches. At the post-match dinner, England skipper Phil Judd urged the All Blacks to 'give the Welshmen hell.' It was a more than satisfactory start to the tourists' international campaign of 1967.

WEST WALES 1967

Wednesday 8 November 1967
St Helen's, Swansea
Won 21-14

The clubs of Neath, Aberavon, Llanelli and Swansea combined as West Wales to take on a touring side for the first time, playing at the latter club's home ground. They were led by Clive Rowlands, who had captained Wales and the combined Pontypool and Cross Keys team, against Whineray's All Blacks four years previously. West Wales were coached by Carwyn James. The home side included hooker Roy Thomas, who played with colleague Delme Thomas for Llanelli in their match with the All Blacks in 1972, international Dai Morris plus Bobby Wanbon, Doug Rees and Walter Williams, all of whom later played for Wales. Several of their strongest players

WEST WALES	NEW ZEALAND
D. Rees (Swansea)	G.F. Kember
H. Rees (Neath)	P.H. Clarke
J. Davies (Swansea)	G.S. Thorne
C. Jones (Aberavon)	A.G. Steel
H. Williams (Neath)	W.D. Cottrell
J.K. Evans (Neath)	M.A. Herewini
D.C.T. Rowlands (Swansea, Capt.)	S.M. Going
Forwards:	Forwards:
R.B. Gale (Llanelli)	K.F. Gray
E.R. Thomas (Swansea)	J. Major
W.P.J. Williams (Neath)	A.E. Hopkinson
B. Davies (Neath)	A.G. Jennings
W.D. Thomas (Llanelli)	C.E. Meads (Capt.)
W.D. Morris (Neath)	M.C. Wills
M. Evans (Swansea)	K.R. Tremain
R. Wanbon (Aberavon)	I.A. Kirkpatrick

Scorers:
West Wales: Try: H. Williams. Con: D. Rees. PG: D. Rees (3).
New Zealand: Tries: Thorne (2), Meads, Going. Cons: Kember (3). PG: Kember.

Referee: M.H. Titcomb (Bristol).
Attendance: 40,000.

were not considered due to the forthcoming international. The All Blacks rested virtually all their Test XV but made Colin Meads captain with Mac Herewini at first five-eighth and Grahame Thorne at centre. Ken Gray and Murray Wills played their first games on British soil. St Helens was a familiar ground to tour manager Charlie Saxton and coach Fred Allen. Saxton, the diminutive half-back who captained the New Zealand Army team, 'The Kiwis', which toured in 1945/46, had watched from the stand as his team, including Allen, beat Swansea 22-6 in the opening game of the British leg of that tour. Saxton later played for Swansea, against the Barbarians on Easter Monday 1946.

Once again, Rowlands proved a source of inspiration to his team, particularly the forwards, who disrupted the New Zealanders. Sid Going was deprived of the quantity of clean ball he normally expected and his back row was required to bale out the rest of the pack in tight play. The home side opened the scoring with a penalty from Doug Rees, who later added a second from close to halfway. Rees's successes contrasted with All Black Gerald Kember, who missed several early penalties. Then midway through the first half, the All Blacks ran the ball from deep in New Zealand territory. Thorne blasted through the Welsh defence and sprinted two-thirds the length of the field to score between the posts. This time Kember was successful, as he was later in the half when converting a try from Meads that Kirkpatrick had created. New Zealand led 10-6 at half-time.

In the second half Kember and Rees exchanged penalties and home centre Cyril Jones was close to scoring before Rowlands broke from a scrum and cross-kicked. Wing Haydn Williams reached the ball first to score a try that Rees converted superbly from wide out. West Wales were back in the lead and the crowd sensed a major shock. However, the All Blacks regained their composure and Herewini and Wayne Cottrell created space for Thorne to score again. Sid Going dived over for a late try and Kember's conversion made the game safe. It had been a terrific contest and a wake-up call for the All Blacks.

WALES   1967

Saturday 11 November 1967
Cardiff Arms Park, Cardiff
Won 13-6

Wales selected Neath lock Brian Thomas at prop for the first time, forming with skipper Norman Gale and Denzil Williams, the Ebbw Vale lock, a substantial front row. Barry John had moved from Llanelli to Cardiff during the summer, and played his first international with Gareth Edwards. His way into the side had been cleared when David Watkins joined Salford rugby league club at the start of the season. Keith Jarrett was injured but there were six new caps in Paul Wheeler, Ian Hall, Keri Jones, Max Wiltshire, Dennis Hughes and John Jeffrey. Ken Gray had done enough at Swansea to be included in the New Zealand pack at the expense of Jack Hazlett. This was the only

WALES	NEW ZEALAND
P.J. Wheeler (Aberavon)	W.F. McCormick
S.J. Watkins (Newport)	W.M. Birtwhistle
W.H. Raybould (London Welsh)	W.L. Davis
I. Hall (Aberavon)	M.J. Dick
W.K. Jones (Cardiff)	I.R. MacRae
B. John (Cardiff)	E.W. Kirton
G.O. Edwards (Cardiff)	C.R. Laidlaw
Forwards:	Forwards:
D. Williams (Ebbw Vale)	K.F. Gray
N.R. Gale (Llanelli, Capt.)	B.E. McLeod
B.E. Thomas (Neath)	B.L. Muller
W.T. Mainwaring (Aberavon)	S.C. Strahan
M.L. Wiltshire (Aberavon)	C.E. Meads
D. Hughes (Newbridge)	G.C. Williams
J. Taylor (London Welsh)	K.R. Tremain
J.J. Jeffrey (Newport)	B.J. Lochore (Capt.)

Scorers:
Wales: PG: Gale. DG: John.
New Zealand: Tries: Birtwhistle, Davis. Cons: McCormick (2). PG: McCormick.

Referee: M.H. Titcomb (RFU).
Attendance: 58,500.

change from the international with England, although McCormick, Laidlaw and Tremain were carrying injuries.

In a disappointing game, New Zealand capitalised on Welsh errors rather than creating opportunities themselves. Early in the game, Billy Raybould conceded a penalty that McCormick kicked and then Bill Davis created a try for Bill Birtwhistle, which McCormick converted from the touchline. It was 8-0 at the interval.

Shortly after the restart, Barry John dropped a goal to revive Welsh hopes but New Zealand extended their lead a few minutes later. A penalty from McCormick fell short to Jeffrey. He fumbled the ball but rather than taking the impending impact from the advancing All Blacks he threw wildly behind him where Davis gathered to score the second try. After several Welsh players had missed kicks at goal Norman Gale successfully kicked a penalty to conclude the scoring. New Zealand were deserved winners.

They were clinical and efficient, and in Fergie McCormick they had the outstanding player of the day. Nobody shone for Wales. Edwards was injured early on, John kicked aimlessly at times and Stuart Watkins lost the ball over the New Zealand line when tackled by McCormick. Jeffrey was pilloried for his mistake and although he was an accomplished number eight he never played in an international for Wales again.

SCOTTISH DISTRICTS   1967

Wednesday 29 November 1967
The Greenyards, Melrose
Won 35-14

The New Zealanders returned from the French leg of their tour and made twelve changes from the side that had beaten France. Colin Meads was ruled out because of a head wound sustained from a French boot, prompting one supporter to say: 'I hate to think what happened to the other fellow's toe-cap!' Brian Lochore played at lock. The Scottish Districts XV was essentially the Scottish Second XV, many of the side having played in the Scottish trial the previous Saturday. At lock, much was expected of Alastair McHarg, who became one of the most respected forwards of the 1970s.

On a fine winter day, spectators had to walk through disinfected sawdust to guard against the threat of foot-and-mouth disease. The pitch had been protected by straw. The

SCOTTISH DISTRICTS	NEW ZEALAND
C.F. Blaikie (Heriot's FP)	W.F. McCormick
A.D. Gill (Gala)	W.M. Birtwhistle
R.B. Welsh (Hawick)	G.S. Thorne
I. Davidson (Langholm)	M.J. Dick
G.J. Keith (Wasps)	G.F. Kember
B.M. Simmers (Glasgow Acads, Capt.)	W.D. Cottrell
R.C. Allan (Hutchison's GSFP)	C.R. Laidlaw
Forwards:	Forwards:
P.C. Robertson (Hawick)	E.J. Hazlett
D.T. Deans (Hawick)	J. Major
T.K. McDonald (London Scottish)	A.E. Hopkinson
W.J. Hunter (Hawick)	A.E. Smith
A.F. McHarg (West of Scotland)	B.J. Lochore (Capt.)
C.W. Thorburn (Guy's Hospital)	W.J. Nathan
T.G. Elliot (Langholm)	K.R. Tremain
R.J. Arneil (Edinburgh Acads)	M.C. Wills

Scorers:
Scottish Districts: Tries: Gill, Blaikie. Con: Blaikie.
PGs: Blaikie (2).
New Zealand: Tries: Birtwhistle (3), Thorne, Hopkinson, Laidlaw, Nathan. Cons: McCormick (4). PGs: McCormick (2).

Referee: M. Joseph (Wales).
Attendance: 7,000.

game followed the typical pattern: the New Zealanders gradually wearing their opponents down and scoring heavily in the closing stages. However, the Districts put up a better display than the final score suggested, especially with their stubborn tackling. It was collectively rather than individually that the Districts were outclassed and the visitors looked a superior combination from the start. Their handling movements were well planned and executed, their covering was splendid and they controlled the rucks with contemptuous ease. Despite their all-round brilliance, New Zealand led only 10-6 at half-time. Grahame Thorne and Bill Birtwhistle scored tries, both of which were converted by Fergie McCormick, while Colin Blaikie kicked two penalties for the Districts.

Shortly after the interval, the alert Brian Simmers hacked on and Drew Gill was on hand to score. Blaikie converted to put the Districts into an improbable lead. Unfortunately for the home side, the New Zealanders responded with an awesome display. The strain proved too much and as the Districts began to tire the visitors ran in 5 tries. The pick of the bunch was Waka Nathan's, who made an irresistible drive from twenty yards, leaving the defence burst asunder.

Several players distinguished themselves in the game. For New Zealand, Wayne Cottrell and Chris Laidlaw were clever and articulate while Nathan and Kel Tremain were the best of the forwards. On the right wing, Birtwhistle ran well for his 3 tries. Several Districts players also enhanced their reputations. Rodger Arneil was tireless in defence and pounded into the rucks with the determination of some of his opponents. Simmers had a very good game and the youthful Gill did the right thing in attack and defence. Despite their victory, Fred Allen, the New Zealand coach, was not too happy. 'I was disappointed at our handling,' he grumbled, prompting the British press to marvel at the super-high standards of New Zealand rugby.

SCOTLAND   1967

**Saturday 2 December 1967
Murrayfield, Edinburgh
Won 14-3**

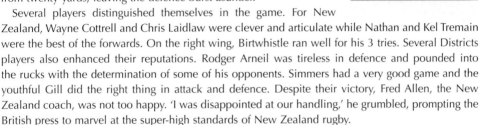

SCOTLAND	NEW ZEALAND
S. Wilson (London Scottish)	W.F. McCormick
A.J.W. Hinshelwood (London Scottish)	A.G. Steel
J.W.C. Turner (Gala)	W.L. Davis
J.N.M. Frame (Edinburgh University)	W.M. Birtwhistle
R.R. Keddie (Watsonians)	I.R. MacRae
D.H. Chisholm (Melrose)	E.W. Kirton
A.J. Hastie (Melrose)	C.R. Laidlaw
Forwards:	Forwards:
A.B. Carmichael (West of Scotland)	K.F. Gray
F.A.L. Laidlaw (Melrose)	B.E. McLeod
D.M.D. Rollo (Howe of Fife)	A.E. Hopkinson
P.K. Stagg (Sale, Capt.)	S.C. Strahan
G.W.E. Mitchell (Edinburgh Wanderers)	C.E. Meads
J.P. Fisher (London Scottish)	K.R. Tremain
D. Grant (Hawick)	G.C. Williams
A.H.W. Boyle (London Scottish)	B.J. Lochore (Capt.)

Scorers:
Scotland: DG: Chisholm.
New Zealand: Tries: MacRae, Davis. Con: McCormick.
PGs: McCormick (2).

Referee: K.D. Kelleher (Ireland).
Attendance: 60,000.

This match was overshadowed by the sending-off of Colin Meads, who became the first man to be ordered off in an international since Cyril Brownlie was dismissed in New Zealand's match against England in January 1925. Referee Kevin Kelleher had twice penalised Meads in the first half for treading on players in a loose maul and for obstructing an opponent as he was about to catch a long kick. Late in the second half, Meads took a reckless hack at the ball just as it had been gathered by Scottish scrum-half Dave Chisholm. Both players over-balanced, although neither was injured. The incident took place in front of Mr Kelleher, who in view of Meads's earlier indiscretions felt that he had no option but to send the New Zealander off the field. It was a brave and controversial decision against the most famous player in the world. Meads was undeniably guilty of dangerous play, but many felt that Kelleher had been unduly harsh. The incident looked worse than it really was and Chisholm was unhurt. Moreover, there were only three minutes left for play and the game

was already over as a contest. Ironically, the match was much cleaner than the very rough game against France the previous weekend, when Meads himself had his head cut open. The sending-off was a sad blight on the career of one of rugby's greatest forwards and also on a very successful and popular tour. Meads was admonished for his behaviour and suspended for the next 2 games. The game itself was hard and vigorous but rather unspectacular and New Zealand were less impressive than in their previous Test matches. The visitors made several changes from the side that had beaten France, including a first cap for Canterbury's Alister Hopkinson at prop. Scotland fielded three new caps in John Frame, Bob Keddie and Erle Mitchell as well as three players – Stewart Wilson, David Rollo and Pringle Fisher – who had played in the stirring no-scoring draw against the New Zealanders three years previously. The Scots also played four players from the British Lions tour the previous year. The home side did well against a much stronger side, but lacked sufficient resources of their own to pull off an upset. The Scottish tackling and covering was tight, especially Turner and Frame in the centres, while Pringle Fisher was prominent in the loose. The tactic of four-man lineouts was very successful, and hooker Frank Laidlaw took the only strike against the head. Deprived of their usual share of possession and in the face of a determined defence, the New Zealanders rarely produced the attacking flair that was their trademark.

After ten minutes Chisholm opened the scoring with a left-footed drop goal from an awkward angle. McCormack equalised with a penalty. From a lineout peel, Ken Gray made a storming charge and fed Ian MacRae, who dashed past the covering defenders for the first try. McCormick missed the conversion but later added a second penalty goal to give the visitors a 9-3 lead at the interval. The only score of the second half followed a lineout on the Scottish 25, when Kirton made a great break from a loop move with MacRae and sent Keith Davis over for a try. McCormick converted to seal New Zealand's win.

MONMOUTHSHIRE   1967

Wednesday 6 December 1967
Rodney Parade, Newport
Won 23-12

The home selectors chose a big pack to face the All Blacks, led by international Dennis Hughes, who was accompanied in the back row by his brother, Arthur. The side included Gareth Howls, a versatile forward from Ebbw Vale who was a regular Welsh squad member but was never capped; Brian Price, who captained Newport to victory over New Zealand in 1963; and future Welsh captain and 1971 Lion Arthur Lewis in the centre. Wing Laurie Daniel was capped for Wales against Scotland in 1970. The home team also included Glyn Turner, a fine scrum-half close to international honours, and Keith Jarrett, the young Newport

MONMOUTHSHIRE	NEW ZEALAND
B. Edwards (Ebbw Vale)	W.F. McCormick
L.T.D. Daniel (Pontypool)	A.G. Steel
K. Jones (Newbridge)	W.L. Davis
A.J.L. Lewis (Ebbw Vale)	G.S. Thorne
K.S. Jarrett (Newport)	W.D. Cottrell
M. Grindle (Ebbw Vale)	E.W. Kirton
G. Turner (Ebbw Vale)	S.M. Going
Forwards:	Forwards:
D. Williams (Ebbw Vale)	K.F. Gray
B. Wilkins (Abertillery)	J. Major
G. Howls (Ebbw Vale)	B.L. Muller
E. Phillips (Newbridge)	A.G. Jennings
B. Price (Newport)	S.C. Strahan
P. Watts (Newport)	W.J. Nathan
A. Hughes (Newbridge)	K.R. Tremain
D. Hughes (Newbridge, Capt.)	B.J. Lochore (Capt.)

Scorers:
Monmouthshire: PG: Jarrett (4).
New Zealand: Tries: Kirton, Steel, Tremain, Muller.
Con: McCormick. PG: McCormick (3).

Referee: G.C. Lamb (RFU).
Attendance: 20,000.

player who made a sensational debut for Wales against England the previous April, scoring 19 points when only a few months out of school. He had recovered from the injury that kept him out of the Wales side to face the tourists. New Zealand picked a strong side for the game but were not permitted to select the suspended Colin Meads.

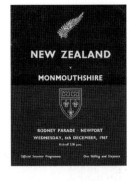

The first half was a tight affair in which both sides cancelled out their opponents. Jarrett and Fergie McCormick entered into an early goal-kicking contest in which the Welshman triumphed. Monmouthshire led 12-6 at half-time.

In the second half, New Zealand adopted a more expansive style with Earle Kirton at his best. He scored a fine early try himself and then created one for Tony Steel. Although McCormick failed with the conversions he kicked a penalty with ten minutes left to ease New Zealand into the lead. Two late tries from Kel Tremain and 'Jazz' Muller, the latter converted by McCormick, gave a false impression of the All Blacks' victory. They hadn't played that well and it hadn't been as good a game as the score suggested.

EAST WALES   1967

Wednesday 13 December 1967
Cardiff Arms Park, Cardiff
Drawn 3-3

EAST WALES	NEW ZEALAND
D. Griffiths	W.F. McCormick
(Bridgend & Cardiff College of Education)	
W.K. Jones (Cardiff)	A.G. Steel
T.G.R. Davies (Cardiff)	W.L. Davis
S.J. Dawes (London Welsh)	G.S. Thorne
F. Wilson (Cardiff)	G.F. Kember
B. John (Cardiff)	M.A. Herewini
G.O. Edwards (Cardiff, Capt.)	C.R. Laidlaw
Forwards:	Forwards:
B. James (Bridgend)	K.F. Gray
J. Young (Harrogate)	J. Major
J.P. O'Shea (Cardiff)	E.J. Hazlett
L. Baxter (Cardiff)	S.C. Strahan
I.C. Jones (London Welsh)	A.E. Smith
J. Hickey (Cardiff)	G.C. Williams
A.J. Gray (London Welsh)	I.A. Kirkpatrick
R.E. Jones (Coventry)	B.J. Lochore (Capt.)

Scorers:
East Wales: Try: Wilson.
New Zealand: Try: Steel.

Referee: F.B. Lovis (London).
Attendance: 40,000.

The match had been scheduled for the previous Saturday but heavy snow caused serious disruption and the sporting calendar was decimated. Fortunately, it was still possible to play the game on the following Wednesday. Cardiff may not have had a fixture against New Zealand on this tour but they had a major influence on the side selected for this match. With West Wales and Monmouthshire accounting for many Welsh clubs' players, East Wales effectively included all the rest, but in reality it was Cardiff with a few additions. John Dawes replaced shingles victim Billy Raybould the day before the match. The team was captained by twenty-year-old Gareth Edwards. The Welsh scrum-half was at the beginning of a career that brought him fame around the rugby world. His skills were such that more than twenty years after he retired he was declared the greatest rugby player of all time. Edwards and half-back partner Barry John later terrorised New Zealand teams on the 1971 Lions tour, where they were joined by East Wales centres Dawes, the tour captain, and Gerald Davies, by that time converted into a devastating wing. Colin Meads had been selected but had been forced to withdraw when the New Zealand protestations against the two-match ban imposed after his sending-off at Murrayfield were rejected. Otherwise it was a strong selection, although injuries meant Hazlett replaced Hopkinson and Major came in for McLeod from the original team.

The game was close and the forward contest was torrid, shaded by the home tight five. The New Zealand back row played well and dominated loose play. Both sides attempted to attack but the

The East Wales team, led by a youthful Gareth Edwards, that nearly beat New Zealand.

East Wales backs looked very dangerous and ran from every corner of the field. Their moves were stopped by a combination of sound tackling and the glutinous pitch. Midway through the first half John attempted a drop goal, but as it drifted wide, it was chased by Frank Wilson who beat Grahame Thorne to the ball for a try that Griffiths failed to convert. It was the only score of the first half.

With ten minutes to go the All Blacks quickly heeled the ball from a ruck. Bill Davis made a break and passed to Tony Steel who stepped out of a tackle and touched the ball down near the corner flag for a good try. The conversion missed. East Wales went back on the attack and wing Keri Jones raced away. He kicked ahead over McCormick but as he rounded the full-back, McCormick impeded him. Claims for a penalty try were dismissed by the referee, who was some distance away, struggling with an injury. Wilson was also denied when he dived on an Edwards chip to score but was penalised for offside. Four kickable penalties were missed. It was constant pressure from East Wales. With seconds remaining, Barry John missed a drop goal that would have won the match. It ended honours even but New Zealand should have lost. East Wales were superior but had no luck on the day.

BARBARIANS 1967

Saturday 16 December 1967
Twickenham, London
Won 11-6

The All Blacks' original tour schedule did not include this game as they were due to play 2 games, including an international, in Ireland. A virulent outbreak of foot-and-mouth disease in Britain was so serious the authorities in Northern Ireland and the Irish Republic requested that the tourists stay away. The Barbarians match was arranged as a substitute, but it also denied New Zealand the opportunity to achieve their first Grand Slam over the home union. The Barbarians' selection was well-balanced with a physical pack who could trouble New Zealand but had a back line capable of scoring tries, although no Irish

BARBARIANS	NEW ZEALAND
S. Wilson (London Scottish, Capt.)	W.F. McCormick
W.K. Jones (Cardiff)	M.J. Dick
T.G.R. Davies (Cardiff)	W.L. Davis
R.H. Lloyd (Harlequins)	A.G. Steel
R.E. Webb (Coventry)	I.R. MacRae
B. John (Cardiff)	E.W. Kirton
G.O. Edwards (Cardiff)	C.R. Laidlaw
Forwards:	Forwards:
A.L. Horton (Blackheath)	K.F. Gray
F.A.L. Laidlaw (Melrose)	B.E. McLeod
C.H. Norris (Cardiff)	B.L. Muller
M.L. Wiltshire (Aberavon)	S.C. Strahan
P.J. Larter (Northampton)	C.E. Meads
D. Grant (Hawick)	K.R. Tremain
R.B. Taylor (Northampton)	W.J. Nathan
G.A. Sherriff (Saracens)	B.J. Lochore (Capt.)

Scorers:
Barbarians: Try: Lloyd. DG: Wilson.
New Zealand: Tries: MacRae, Steel. Con: McCormick. DG: Kirton.

Referee: M. Joseph (WRU).
Attendance: 40,000.

The five Cardiff players in the Barbarians team. From left to right: Keri Jones, Gareth Edwards, Howard Norris, Gerald Davies, Barry John.

players were included due to the disease. They were captained by Scottish full-back Stewart Wilson and, on this occasion, no uncapped players were selected. New Zealand chose a very strong side that included Colin Meads, and the dynamic loose-forward unit of Lochore, Tremain and Nathan were together again. It was Waka Nathan's last game in a New Zealand jersey.

The Barbarians took an early lead when Wilson dropped a long-range goal that Earle Kirton matched shortly after. Despite some spectacular see-sawing of play there was no further score in the first half. It was 3-3 at the break.

Midway thought the second half, Barry John kicked cleverly behind the New Zealand defence into the corner for Bob Lloyd to score. Rather than sitting on their lead the Barbarians attacked, as did New Zealand. With eighty minutes up and the Barbarians seemingly home and dry New Zealand quickly moved the ball and Tony Steel popped up as the extra man and raced through a gap. He was tackled short of the line but was able to get the ball to Ian MacRae who scored. The conversion missed and the match seemed destined to end in a draw. Then, in the fifth minute of injury time, a poor kick from Wilson was fielded by Brian Lochore who immediately attacked up the touchline. He fed Kirton who passed to Steel who raced in for the winning try. It was a fine try at the end of a fine match, but quite different to the 1964 extravaganza.

New Zealand proved they were an excellent side with an outstanding pack of forwards but also with backs who could run and be creative. Many felt they were the best New Zealand side to visit Britain since the Second World War. They returned home unbeaten. However, they played less games than their predecessors and didn't play any of the individual Welsh clubs that had caused problems for other touring sides. Tour captain Brian Lochore was compared favourably with Wilson Whineray. They were both fine captains and leaders of men, earning enormous respect from their players and their opponents. As a tight forward, Whineray was always in the middle of the tight exchanges, but as a loose forward, Lochore was able to have a greater influence on open play. Lochore played in twenty-four internationals for New Zealand. He coached the New Zealand side that won the inaugural World Cup in 1987 and after that served in senior managerial positions in rugby, and other sports. In 1999, when a member of the Sports Foundation committee and chairman of the Hillary Commission, he was knighted for his outstanding services to sport.

NEW ZEALAND TO NORTH AMERICA & EUROPE

THE MATCHES

British Columbia	19 October 1972	Vancouver	won 31-3
New York Metropolitan	21 October 1972	New York	won 41-9
Western Counties	28 October 1972	Gloucester	won 39-12
Llanelli	31 October 1972	Llanelli	lost 9-3
Cardiff	4 November 1972	Cardiff	won 20-4
Cambridge University	8 November 1972	Cambridge	won 34-3
London Counties	11 November 1972	Twickenham	won 24-3
Leinster	15 November 1972	Dublin	won 17-9
Ulster	18 November 1972	Belfast	won 19-6
North-Western Counties	22 November 1972	Workington	lost 16-14
Scottish Districts	25 November 1972	Hawick	won 26-6
Gwent	28 November 1972	Ebbw Vale	won 16-7
WALES	2 December 1972	Cardiff	won 19-16
Midland Counties West	6 December 1972	Moseley	lost 16-8
North-Eastern Counties	9 December 1972	Bradford	won 9-3
Glasgow & Edinburgh	12 December 1972	Glasgow	won 16-10
SCOTLAND	16 December 1972	Murrayfield	won 14-9
Southern Counties	20 December 1972	Oxford	won 23-6
Combined Services	26 December 1972	Twickenham	won 31-10
East Glamorgan	30 December 1972	Cardiff	won 20-9
South-Western Counties	2 January 1973	Redruth	won 30-7
ENGLAND	6 January 1973	Twickenham	won 9-0
Newport	10 January 1973	Newport	won 20-15
Midland Counties East	13 January 1973	Leicester	won 43-12
Munster	16 January 1973	Cork	drew 3-3
IRELAND	20 January 1973	Dublin	drew 10-10
Neath & Aberavon	24 January 1973	Neath	won 43-3
Barbarians	27 January 1973	Cardiff	lost 23-11
South-West France	31 January 1973	Tarbes	won 12-3
France B	3 February 1973	Lyon	won 23-8
French Selection	7 February 1973	Clermont-Ferrand	won 6-3
FRANCE	10 February 1973	Paris	lost 13-6

Played 32, Won 25, Drew 2, Lost 5. Scored: 640 points, Conceded: 266.
In Britain & Ireland: Played 26, Won 20, Drew 2, Lost 4. Scored: 521 points, Conceded: 227.

The New Zealand Tour Party:
J.F. Karam (Wellington), T.J. Morris (Nelson Bays), G.B. Batty (Wellington), D.A. Hales (Canterbury), I.A. Hurst (Canterbury), B.J. Robertson (Counties), G.R. Skudder (Waikato), B.G. Williams (Auckland),

R.E. Burgess (Manawatu), R.M. Parkinson (Poverty Bay), M. Sayers (Wellington), I.N. Stevens (Wellington), G.L. Colling (Otago), S.M. Going (North Auckland), K.K. Lambert (Manawatu), J.D. Matheson (Otago), K. Murdoch (Otago), G.J Whiting (King Country), L.A. Clark (Otago)*, A.L.R. McNicol (Wanganui)*, R.W. Norton (Canterbury), R.A. Urlich (Auckland), I.M. Eliason (Taranaki), A.M. Haden (Auckland), H.H. Macdonald (Canterbury), P.J. Whiting (Auckland), I.A. Kirkpatrick (Poverty Bay), A.I. Scown (Taranaki), K.W. Stewart (Southland), A.J. Wyllie (Canterbury), B. Holmes (North Auckland), A.R. Sutherland (Marlborough). (*replacement on tour)

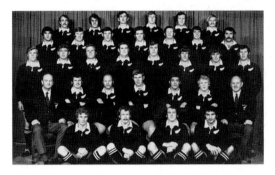

Captain: I.A. Kirkpatrick. Vice-Captain: S.M. Going. Manager: E.L. Todd. Assistant Manager: R.F. Duff.

Leading points scorer: J.F. Karam – 145 points (125 in Britain & Ireland). Leading try-scorer: G.B. Batty – 21 tries (17 in Britain & Ireland). Most appearances: I.A. Kirkpatrick – 24 games (20 in Britain & Ireland).

WESTERN COUNTIES   1972/73

Saturday 28 October 1972
Kingsholm, Gloucester
Won 39-12

WESTERN COUNTIES	NEW ZEALAND
P.E. Butler (Gloucester)	J.F. Karam
A.J. Morley (Bristol)	B.G. Williams
J.A. Bayliss (Gloucester)	B.J. Robertson
C.J. Williams (Bristol)	G.B. Batty
P.M. Knight (Bristol)	R.M. Parkinson
J.R. Gabitass (Bristol)	R.E. Burgess
J.A. Cannon (Clifton)	G.L. Colling
Forwards:	Forwards:
R.J. Cowling (Gloucester)	J.D. Matheson
J.V. Pullin (Bristol)	R.A. Urlich
M.A. Burton (Gloucester)	K. Murdoch
D.E.J. Watt (Bristol, Capt.)	H.H. Macdonald
A. Brinn (Gloucester)	P.J. Whiting
J.A. Watkins (Gloucester)	A.I. Scown
R. Smith (Gloucester)	I.A. Kirkpatrick (Capt.)
R.C. Hannaford (Bristol)	A.R. Sutherland

Scorers:
Western Counties: Try: Burton. Con: Butler. PGs: Butler (2).
New Zealand: Tries: Williams (3), Parkinson (2), Robertson, Colling. Cons: Karam (4). PG: Karam.

Referee: D.P. D'Arcy (Ireland).
Attendance: 16,000.

Having suffered the ignominy of losing a Test series at home to the British Lions the previous year, New Zealand began rebuilding in 1972 and undertook a nine-match internal tour before hosting Australia, destroying the Wallabies in all 3 Test matches. 2 trial matches were held after the final Test match and a squad to tour Europe and North America was announced that was generally accepted as being good but not brilliant, and there were some loudly voiced criticisms of the back selection. Under the leadership of magnificent loose forward Ian Kirkpatrick, the All Blacks played matches in Vancouver and New York on their way over. Comfortably winning both games, New Zealand arrived at Heathrow Airport with confidence and grim determination to avenge their defeat at the hands of the Lions.

The composition of the Western Counties side was only announced six days before the match, possibly to minimise criticism following the decision to exclude all Somerset players from the starting line-up. Western Counties traditionally featured players from both Gloucestershire and Somerset, but Gloucestershire had won the County Championship the previous season and the team chosen was a complete Gloucestershire XV, including eleven of the championship-winning side. There were Somerset players included on the replacements' bench, but one of these, Bob Orledge, a second-row forward from

Bryan Williams on the attack, with Bruce Robertson in support.

Bristol, withdrew in protest. 'It may not be the best way of making a protest, but that's the way I feel,' was the Orledge view. There was further confusion about the replacements when the selectors initially named only four, not realising that six were permitted, though this fault was rectified before the match. The side contained eight England capped players – Alan Morley and Peter Knight in the backs and all the pack except Robin Cowling and Dick Smith. Cowling would be capped later, as would full-back Peter Butler. A surprise omission from the team was Bristol and England back-row forward Dave Rollitt. The All Blacks fielded a strong side, with Joe Karam getting a chance at full-back because Trevor Morris had been injured playing against New York Metropolitan. It was a chance Karam was to grab with both hands, and he soon established himself as the number one full-back. Sid Going was picked at half-back, but withdrew on the morning of the game with a knee injury. The match, the first by an official All Black team at Kingsholm since 1924, was a sell-out.

The tourists enjoyed a perfect start to their British tour, scoring 7 tries, all through their backs, and playing exciting fifteen-man rugby. Bob Burgess outshone his opposite number Jon Gabitass at outside half, and New Zealand also gained superiority in the back row. Only in the front row, where Cowling, John Pullin and Mike Burton all excelled, was there a threat from the Counties team. Karam opened the scoring after seventeen minutes with a thirty-eight-yard penalty, and the first try was scored by Mike Parkinson, following a brilliant individual run. Karam converted this score, and also added the extra points after an overhead pass from Bryan Williams had put Bruce Robertson in under the posts. Just before half-time, a kick by Burgess was collected by Grant Batty who set Parkinson up for his second try. Karam's conversion brought the half-time score to 21-0.

Four minutes into the second period, Williams caught a poor clearance from Gabitass and gave a scoring pass to Lin Colling. Then came the only Counties try. After a lineout penalty Peter Whiting foolishly argued with the referee. The penalty was moved forward to the New Zealand line, scrum-half John Cannon tapped the ball and Burton powered over for the try, which Butler converted. Ten minutes later a high kick from Burgess was collected by Alan Sutherland who handed on for Williams to score. Two penalties from Butler brought some respectability to the scoreline, but Williams scored two further tries in the final minutes, the first from a great run and long pass by captain Ian Kirkpatrick and the second after a Burgess break.

The media was full of praise for the All Blacks and their style of rugby after this performance. All seemed set fair for an entertaining and successful tour, but a different fate awaited the tourists at Stradey Park.

Tuesday 31 October 1972
Stradey Park, Llanelli
Lost 9-3

LLANELLI	NEW ZEALAND
R. Davies	J.F. Karam
J.J. Williams	B.G. Williams
R.W.R. Gravell	B.J. Robertson
R.T.E. Bergiers	D. Sayers
A.F.G. Hill	D.A. Hales
P. Bennett	R.E. Burgess
R. Hopkins	G.L. Colling
Forwards:	Forwards:
A. Crocker	G.J. Whiting
E.R. Thomas	R.A. Urlich
D.B. Llewelyn	K. Murdoch
W.D. Thomas (Capt.)	A.M. Haden
D.L. Quinnell	P.J. Whiting
T. David	A.I. Scown
G. Jenkins	I.A. Kirkpatrick (Capt.)
H.W. Jenkins	A.R. Sutherland
	Replacement:
	G.B. Batty for Williams

Scorers:
Llanelli: Try: Bergiers. Con: Bennett. PG: Hill.
New Zealand: PG: Karam.

Referee: M.H. Titcomb (Bristol).
Attendance: 22,000.

'Twas on a dark and dismal day, in a week that had seen rain. When all roads led to Stradey Park with the All Blacks here again. They poured down from the valleys, they came from far and wide, there were 20,000 in the ground, and me and Dai outside.'

The opening lines of Welsh entertainer Max Boyce's humorous, but intensely moving poem *9-3* neatly summed up the expectation in Llanelli and the surrounding villages. Llanelli, 'the Scarlets', had a powerful and established squad that had been improved by the arrival of 'J.J.' Williams from Bridgend, Ray 'Chico' Hopkins from Maesteg and Tom David from Pontypridd at the start of the season. All were, or became British Lions. Llanelli had lost by a single point to South Africa in 1970 when their side was denuded of current Welsh players but this time the All Blacks met the full side. They also renewed their acquaintance with Carwyn James, the innovative coach of the 1971 British Lions. James, a former Scarlets' hero himself who had won two caps for Wales in the late 1950s, had taken his club to the final of the inaugural Welsh Cup the previous season and now, in the club's centenary season, he had the chance to prove once more that New Zealand were beatable. James had taken the Llanelli squad to Kingsholm for the All Blacks' first game in Europe and observed: 'When they are going forward, they are magnificent. When they're going backwards, they look quite ordinary.' James had an eye for detail and a fanatical passion that he imparted to his men. He was capable of getting

the best out of his players, and he had a plan to contain the All Blacks at the tail of the lineout, the platform from which he felt New Zealand built their play. The All Blacks themselves made only four changes from Gloucester for the game. In his pre-match talk, skipper Delme Thomas, who wore the red shirt of the Lions in 1966 before pulling on a Welsh jersey, told his players that he had travelled the world and won every honour rugby had to give but he would gladly give it all up for a win over the All Blacks. The emotional Phil Bennett later confessed to have been in tears. There were some concerns over the Llanelli line-up: Bennett had an injured shoulder, hooker Roy Thomas a damaged toe and Roy Bergiers was recovering from concussion. However, James prepared the side well and everyone knew exactly what they were expected to do.

Shortly after kick-off Bennett hoisted a garryowen that the usually secure Karam dropped in the face of the Llanelli pack, who welcomed him to Welsh Wales with

The Llanelli team that defeated New Zealand. From left to right, back row: S. Williams (replacement), P. Bennett, T. David, B. Peel (trainer), T. Crocker, D. Quinnell, Barry Llewelyn, G. Jenkins, R. Gravell, H. Jenkins, R. Thomas, A. James (replacement), C. Charles (replacement), Bryan Llewelyn (replacement). Seated: G. Ashby (replacement), R. Davies, A. Hill, R. Bergiers, N. Gale (assistant coach), D. Thomas (captain), C. James (coach), J. Williams, R. Hopkins, M. Davies (replacement).

the kind of treatment that he would have been more familiar with at home. The only try of the game was scored after three minutes of play. A penalty from Bennett wide out looked to be over but dipped at the last minute and bounced off the crossbar. Lin Colling took too long to clear and his kick was charged down by Bergiers, who dived on the ball for the try, which Bennett converted. Twenty minutes later Llanelli were penalised at a lineout and Joe Karam kicked a fine penalty which made the score 6-3 to Llanelli at half-time.

It was a fierce battle between the sides and the forward exchanges frequently erupted into fights. Referee Mike Titcomb had difficulty keeping control and there was later some press criticism of the ferocity of the All Blacks' rucking. Llanelli tied up the New Zealand back row and subdued the All Blacks. Andy Hill, narrowly missed a long-range drop goal but then kicked a penalty from a similar distance to increase the lead after Bennett and Karam had missed easier kicks. As the match neared its end the All Blacks piled on the pressure but not a single tackle was missed. New Zealand never looked like scoring – a run and kick ahead from Grant Batty, who had replaced the injured Bryan Williams, was the only threat and that was easily dealt with by J.J. Williams.

Terry McLean, writing for the *NZ Herald*, said: 'the better team, by a long, long margin, won the game. The All Blacks were out-thought and out-fought.' The All Blacks did not play badly, rather Llanelli were outstanding. Thomas inspired his side to heights never achieved before. Their pack took the game to New Zealand and the back row of Tom David, Gareth Jenkins and Hefin Jenkins eclipsed their opponents. Of these, David later played for Wales and toured South Africa with the Lions in 1974, Gareth Jenkins played for Wales in an uncapped international with Japan in 1975 and later became a leading coach, and Hefin Jenkins sat on the bench for Wales and was the carded replacement number eight for the 1974 Lions but, like his namesake Gareth, was never capped. For Llanelli the celebrations rightly went on for some time, many may say for several years. Their battle song *Sospan Fach* was amended to include a verse '*Who beat the All Blacks, but good old Sospan Fach?*' Bennett, Quinnell and David went on to enjoy success against the All Blacks for the Barbarians later in the tour. And as for Max Boyce: '*And when I'm old and my hair turns grey and they put me in a chair, I'll tell my great-grandchildren that their Datcu [Grandfather] was there. And they'll ask to hear the story of that damp October day, when I went down to Stradey, and I saw the Scarlets play.*'

Saturday 4 November 1972
Cardiff Arms Park, Cardiff
Won 20-4

CARDIFF	NEW ZEALAND
J. Davies	J.F. Karam
W. Lewis	B.G. Williams
N. Williams	B.J. Robertson
A.A.J. Finlayson	G.B. Batty
J.C. Bevan	M. Sayers
K. James	R.E. Burgess
G.O. Edwards	S.M. Going
Forwards:	Forwards:
F.M.D. Knill	J.D. Matheson
G. Davies	R.W. Norton
R. Beard	K. Murdoch
I.R. Robinson	H.H. Macdonald
L. Baxter	P.J. Whiting
R. Lane	A.J. Wyllie
M. John (Capt.)	I.A. Kirkpatrick (Capt.)
C. Smith	B. Holmes
	Replacement:
	G.J. Whiting for Matheson

Scorers:
Cardiff: Try: Edwards.
New Zealand: Tries: Kirkpatrick, Sayers, Batty.
Con: Karam. PG: Karam (2).

Referee: J. Young (SRU).
Attendance: 50,000.

Cardiff had lost three of the 16 games they had played before they took on the All Blacks. Their club captain, prop Gerry Wallace, was suffering from a broken thumb, but sat on the replacements' bench with his able deputy, Mervyn John, leading the 'Blue and Blacks'. Cardiff included future internationals Mike Knill, Ian Robinson and Alex Finlayson, plus current Welsh stars Gareth Edwards and John Bevan, both of whom had enjoyed successful tours of New Zealand with the 1971 Lions. Keith James had the unenviable task of filling the boots of the recently retired Barry John. The All Blacks changed half their wounded charges for the match. Sid Going, Alex Wyllie, Tane Norton and Bevan Holmes had recovered from injuries and played their first games in Britain. Trevor Morris was selected for the match but failed to recover from injury so Karam played again. In training, they pondered on their recent defeat and reviewed their approach to forthcoming games. It was a match they had to win at all costs.

What was served up by the two sides was dreadful. With both teams desperate to win for different reasons, the match quickly degenerated into an aggressive contest of constant niggle and violence. Referee Jake Young seemed reluctant to wield the ultimate penalty but several players received a ticking-off. The sides provoked each other and there were some public assaults. All Black prop Jeff Matheson was punched and taken from the field with concussion, Gareth Edwards received a karate chop that would have seriously injured a lesser player. There were off-the-ball incidents throughout the game and at one point three separate fights could be seen in different parts of the field. From a rugby point of view the New Zealanders were far superior. Their forwards were more together as a unit and, in Ian Kirkpatrick, they had the outstanding forward. His pack was able to win a

steady supply of ball that Going, although not completely fit, was able to distribute well. The half-back and vice-captain also had a fine game. Joe Karam kicked two penalties in the first half and Kirkpatrick scored a magnificent try for New Zealand, Grant Batty and Wyllie creating space for the captain to run in from forty yards. Cardiff had several scoring opportunities but squandered them all. New Zealand led 10-0 at half-time.

In the second half, Mark Sayers scored a try that Karam converted, then a break by Going was finished off by Batty for a third New Zealand try. Edwards scored a good try for Cardiff ten minutes from the end, receiving a blow in the act of scoring. After John Davies missed the conversion, the match restarted with a Davies penalty from halfway, which he also missed. The full-back had a disappointing day with his goal-kicking.

New Zealand thoroughly deserved their win but neither side could be proud of their performance. It was a game best forgotten, but there was a growing feeling within the New Zealand camp that the British press were 'out to get them'. As the tour progressed, the squad did little to make friends and developed a reputation for being aloof and occasionally rude.

CAMBRIDGE UNIVERSITY   1972/73

Wednesday 8 November 1972
Grange Road, Cambridge
Won 34-3

The University side was not an especially strong one, only two of the team, scrum-half Richard Harding and second row Bob Wilkinson, going on to play for England. Outside half Chris Williams was the brother of the great J.P.R. (John) Williams of Wales and British Lions fame, while the captain, John Howard, was the son of 1938 British Lion Bill Howard, one of a select band of players who never played for his country, yet appeared in a Lions test. The All Blacks gave first games in Britain to Ian Hurst, Ian Stevens, Ken Stewart, Ian Eliason and Kent Lambert. Despite the final scoreline, this was not that good a performance from the tourists and the students came out of the game with great credit, particularly since injuries reduced them to fourteen men for much

CAMBRIDGE UNIVERSITY	NEW ZEALAND
I.S. Williamson (Fitzwilliam)	J.F. Karam
G.P. Phillips (Queens')	G.B. Batty
J.M. Howard (Trinity, Capt.)	I.A. Hurst
N.W. Drummond (Fitzwilliam)	D.A. Hales
R.S. Page (Emmanuel)	R.M. Parkinson
C.R. Williams (Clare)	I.N. Stevens
R.M. Harding (St John's)	S.M. Going (Capt.)
Forwards:	Forwards:
G. Rees (Emmanuel)	K.K. Lambert
J.M. Smith (Selwyn)	R.A. Urlich
G.P. Goodall (St Catherine's)	G.J. Whiting
G.R. Thomas (Christ's)	I.A. Eliason
R.M. Wilkinson (Emmanuel)	A.M. Haden
A.D. Foley (Christ's)	A.J. Wyllie
W.A. Jones (Queens')	K.W. Stewart
J.P. Dickins (Corpus Christi)	A.R. Sutherland
Replacements:	Replacement:
T. Lintott (Christ's) for Goodall,	A.I. Scown for Sutherland
A. Walker (Emmanuel) for Williamson	

Scorers:
Cambridge University: PG: Howard.
New Zealand: Tries: Batty (4), Sutherland (2), Wylie.
Cons: Karam, Going (2).

Referee: G. Domercq (France).
Attendance: 8,000.

of the game. The star for the All Blacks was undoubtedly Grant Batty, who scored 4 tries, but Sid Going had an untidy game, sending out some poor passes to Stevens, while Joe Karam had a rare off day with the boot, missing four conversions and three penalties. Twenty-one-year-old Bob Wilkinson was the outstanding Cambridge player, winning fourteen lineouts and outplaying Eliason and Andy Haden.

After twenty-five minutes of play Batty scored his first try, finishing off a move involving Mike Parkinson and Karam. Charlie Goodall, the Cambridge prop, left the field with a fractured cheekbone and before his replacement Tim Lintott could join the action, Batty crossed the line again, this time taking a scoring pass from Karam after Going had started the move. With both conversions missed, the half-time score was 8-0.

As the second half wore on, the Cambridge pack began to tire, but despite this, most of the New Zealand scoring was achieved when Cambridge were a man short. Batty scored his third and best try after four minutes of the second half, sidestepping his way to the line. Shortly after this, Ian Williamson, the students' full-back, fractured a thumb and was replaced by Adrian Walker. No sooner had Walker come on than Cambridge lost another man when Richard Thomas had to leave the field temporarily for attention to a cut face. While Thomas was absent, Alan Sutherland broke from the back of a lineout and ran twenty yards to score. Howard was successful with his only penalty attempt, a good kick from a wide angle to bring the score to 16-3, but Sutherland then scored his second try, this time from a tap penalty. In scoring, he banged his knee on a post and was replaced by Alistair Scown. Karam finally managed the extra points, but Sid Going attempted and kicked the

CAMBRIDGE
UNIVERSITY
NEW ZEALAND

final two conversions. These followed Batty's fourth try when an overlap was worked and a score from Alex Wyllie after a forward move. Before the final 2 tries, Cambridge lost yet another man when Norman Drummond broke a thumb. Only two replacements were permitted, so the home side had to play the remainder of the game short of a player.

The lineout work of Wilkinson and the brave tackling of his teammates meant that the All Blacks had to work far harder for victory than they might have expected. In view of the number of injuries his side suffered, it is surprising to note that Cambridge captain John Howard referred to the match as 'a good clean game'.

LONDON COUNTIES   1972/73

Saturday 11 November 1972
Twickenham, London
Won 24-3

It was unfortunate for the home side that this game clashed with a Welsh trial. This deprived London Counties of the services of many of its London Welsh contingent, including J.P.R. Williams, Gerald Davies, Jeff Young, Geoff Evans, John Taylor and Mike Roberts. Of the side that took the field, Tony Jorden, Mike Bulpitt, Chris Ralston, Andy Ripley and skipper Tony Bucknall were England players, Mick Molloy was an Irish international and Billy Hullin and John Dawes had played for Wales. Dawes, the captain of the great 1971 British Lions side in New Zealand, coached the Counties team and played in the match despite receiving a recent eye injury. His co-centre David Cooke would later play for England, while prop forward

LONDON COUNTIES	NEW ZEALAND
A.M. Jorden (Blackheath & Eastern Counties)	J.F. Karam
A. Richards (London Welsh & Surrey)	B.G. Williams
S.J. Dawes (London Welsh & Middlesex)	I.A. Hurst
D.A. Cooke (Harlequins & Kent)	G.B. Batty
M.P. Bulpitt (Blackheath & Eastern Counties)	R.M. Parkinson
C.D. Saville (Blackheath & Surrey)	R.E. Burgess
W.G. Hullin (London Welsh & Surrey)	S.M. Going
Forwards:	Forwards:
R.L. Barlow (Rosslyn Park & Middlesex)	J.D. Matheson
A.V. Boddy (Metropolitan Police & Middlesex)	R.W. Norton
R.L. Challis (London Scottish & Kent)	K. Murdoch
C.W. Ralston (Richmond & Middlesex)	H.H. Macdonald
M.G. Molloy (London Irish & Surrey)	P.J. Whiting
A.L. Bucknall	K.W. Stewart
(Richmond & Eastern Counties, Capt.)	
S. James (London Welsh & Surrey)	I.A. Kirkpatrick (Capt.)
A.G. Ripley (Rosslyn Park & Middlesex)	A.R. Sutherland
	Replacement:
	M. Sayers (for Hurst)

Scorers:
London Counties: PG: Jordan.
New Zealand: Tries: Sutherland, Karam, Hurst, Williams, Batty. Cons: Karam (2).

Referee: G.A. Jamison (Ireland).
Attendance: 33,000.

Robin Challis had appeared in thee corresponding fixture nine years earlier. New Zealand selected from strength, but Trevor Morris was still unfit, allowing Joe Karam to continue his successful run at full-back. This was a competent New Zealand victory, and the game itself was often exciting, but there were too many All Black errors to allow the game to ranked with the great performance of Whineray's side in 1963. One of the tries was a classic, but there were doubts voiced in the press about the legality of two other All Black scores. London tackled well, particularly the back row of Bucknall, Ripley and Steffan James, and Chris Ralston excelled in the lineouts. The problems for the home side lay at half-back, where Hullin and his partner Chris Saville had a poor afternoon together. Many passes were dropped and, although Challis, Les Barlow, Tony Boddy gave Keith Murdoch and co. a difficult afternoon in the scrums, much possession was wasted.

There was no score until nearly half an hour had been played. Then Tane Norton won a strike against the head and Sid Going put Alan Sutherland in for the opening try. Shortly afterwards, Jorden scored London's only points, with a penalty awarded after Going was penalised at a scrum. Two minutes after this came a controversial try by Karam. New Zealand were awarded a penalty twenty yards out and Alf Jamison, the referee, assuming that Karam would go for goal, signalled to his touch judges to go behind the posts. Karam however, spotting that there were some home players attending to the injured Chris Saville, caught the everyone completely unawares and took a quick tap. He ran to the corner and just squeezed over, though he appeared to drop the ball rather than touch down cleanly. The try however was awarded, and just before half-time the visitors conjured a memorable score.

Going made a blind-side break and Ian Kirkpatrick, Bob Burgess, Ken Stewart, Hamish Macdonald and Mike Parkinson all handled, before Ian Hurst, with Grant Batty outside him, sold a dummy and scored a try described by New Zealand journalist Terry McLean as 'a sublime experience in sport.' Karam failed with all his first-half conversions, and the interval score was 12-3.

The All Blacks added two more tries in the second half, both converted by Karam, but their play often became scrappy and London continued to defend well. The first try, after twelve minutes, was scored by Bryan Williams following a Burgess cross-kick, although many felt Williams was offside. The final score, six minutes from the end, was achieved by the speed of Batty who crossed in the corner after Karam had come into the line.

There was much praise for Going after the game and Sutherland and Stewart stood out in the pack. Despite scoring a memorable try, Ian Hurst's first game at Twickenham was not to end happily. He dislocated his shoulder during the second half and was replaced by Alistair Scown.

LEINSTER 1972/73

Wednesday 15 November 1972
Lansdowne Road, Dublin
Won 17-9

The All Blacks made their first visit to Ireland for a match against confident opposition. They were led by the popular Sean Lynch, a 1971 Lions Test prop, and included many quality players such as future Lions scrum-half John Moloney and captivating back-row men Willie Duggan and Fergus Slattery. The All Blacks had renewed confidence from their wins in England and made wholesale changes to their line-up. With Trevor Morris still on the injured list, the All Blacks took the unusual step of selecting Sid Going at full-back so Karam could have a break. Waikato wing George Skudder made his first start since a hamstring injury sustained in Canada on the way over.

LEINSTER	NEW ZEALAND
A.H. Ensor (Wanderers)	S.M. Going (Capt.)
T.O. Grace (St Mary's College)	B.G. Williams
M.K. Flynn (Wanderers)	D.A. Hales
P. Andruchetti (St Mary's College)	G.R. Skudder
A.T.A. Duggan (Lansdowne)	M. Sayers
M. Quinn (Lansdowne)	I.N. Stevens
J.J. Moloney (St Mary's College)	G.L. Colling
Forwards:	Forwards:
J.F. Lynch (St Mary's College, Capt.)	K.K. Lambert
D.O. Barry (Wanderers)	R.A. Urlich
N. Dwyer (Lansdowne)	G.J. Whiting
K.M.A. Mays (University College, Dublin)	I.M. Eliason
C.F.P. Feighery (Wanderers)	P.J. Whiting
J. Craig (Lansdowne)	A.J. Wyllie
J.F. Slattery (Blackrock College)	A.I. Scown
W.P. Duggan (Blackrock College)	B. Holmes
Replacement:	
P. Inglis (Lansdowne) for Slattery	

Scorers:
Leinster: Try: W. Duggan. Con: Ensor. PG: Ensor.
New Zealand: Tries: Wyllie, Skudder, P. Whiting. Con: Going. PG: Williams.

Referee: M. Joseph (WRU).
Attendance: 25,000.

Leinster
New Zealand

Lansdowne Road
Wednesday 15th November 1972

Leinster Branch I.R.F.U.
Official Programme 10p

With typical Irish passion, the home pack set about the All Blacks in a physical game. Slattery suffered a head injury requiring stitches after twelve minutes and was replaced. However, it was an error-ridden half with the only score coming from a Bryan Williams penalty, which gave New Zealand a 3-0 lead at the break.

Tony Ensor equalised early in the second half with a penalty before New Zealand restored the lead when Alex Wyllie scored a try from a scrum on the Leinster line. The Irish side went back into the All Blacks' half and, shortly afterwards, Willie Duggan scored a try when the ball went loose at a lineout on the New Zealand goal line. Ensor converted and Leinster went into the lead. Leinster had the upper hand until they lost the ball at a ruck inside the tourists' half and it was kicked ahead by Lin Colling. He chased the ball and regathered expertly when the Leinster defence failed to control it. Mark Sayers took it on and put Skudder in for a try. Soon after this, Going launched a garryowen that Ensor inexplicably allowed to bounce. It shot away from the Wanderers' full-back and Peter Whiting won the race to the ball for another try. Going converted and New Zealand had won.

This had been a great chance for Leinster to gain a famous win, but when in command, they were careless and their errors cost them the match. Rugged Leinster try-scorer Duggan played for Ireland in forty-one internationals and toured New Zealand with the 1977 British Lions, playing in all 4 Test matches. A fine lineout jumper, he had a reputation for an intense dislike for training that was contrasted by an intense love of the social side of the sport.

ULSTER   1972/73

Saturday 18 November 1972
Ravenhill, Belfast
Won 19-6

Ulster had been starved of top-class rugby due to the political unrest and troubles that disrupted life in Northern Ireland. Australia were the last major tourists to play there in 1968. Security was paramount and the Army and Royal Ulster Constabulary were prominent. Everyone was searched on their way into the ground but the crowd gave both sides a massive cheer when they ran onto the field. Ulster had beaten Munster the previous weekend in the Inter-Provincial Championship. However, the key Ulster player, Mike Gibson, had injured his back and was not available to play. His place was taken

ULSTER	NEW ZEALAND
B.D.E. Marshall (CIYMS)	J.F. Karam
J. Myles (Malone)	B.G. Williams
R.A. Milliken (Bangor)	D.A. Hales
A. Goodrich (Queen's University, Belfast)	G.B. Batty
C.H. McKibbin (Instonians)	M. Sayers
A. Harrison (Collegians)	R.E. Burgess
W.R. Oakes (Instonians)	S.M. Going
Forwards:	Forwards:
P.J. Agnew (CIYMS)	J.D. Matheson
K.W. Kennedy (London Irish)	R.A. Urlich
R.J. Clegg (Bangor)	K. Murdoch
W.J. McBride (Ballymena, Capt.)	H.H. Macdonald
C.W. Murtagh (Portadown)	A.M. Haden
S.A. McKinney (Dungannon)	K.W. Stewart
J.C. Davidson (Dungannon)	I.A. Kirkpatrick (Capt.)
H.W. Steele (Queen's University, Belfast)	A.J. Wyllie
	Replacement:
	G.R. Skudder for Williams

Scorers:
Ulster: Try: Steele. Con: Marshall.
New Zealand: Tries: Burgess, Hales. Con: Karam. PGs: Karam (3).

Referee: R.F. Johnson (RFU).
Attendance: 25,000.

201

IRISH RUGBY FOOTBALL UNION
(Ulster Branch)
OFFICIAL PROGRAMME
ULSTER v.
NEW ZEALAND
AT RAVENHILL
SATURDAY, 18th NOVEMBER, 1972
at 2.30 p.m.
PRICE 5p
F. C. HUMPHREYS,
Secretary

Braithwaite & Co. Limited
Wine and Spirit Merchants since 1877
Food and wine at
THE ULSTER TAVERN
BUTTERY
or
RED LION
ORMEAU ROAD
or a drink and a sandwich at
THE GARRICK LOUNGE
CHICHESTER STREET, BELFAST

by Annesley Harrison. Their powerful pack, coached by Maurice Crabbe and assisted by national coach Syd Millar, all played for Ireland at some stage. Ulster were captained by Willie John McBride. New Zealand made many changes to the side and Joe Karam returned to the full-back berth with a relieved Sid Going reverting to half-back.

The game started at a frantic pace and when Bob Burgess dropped the ball and Jimmy Davidson kicked ahead, wing Joe Myles nearly scored. Shortly afterwards, New Zealand infringed but full-back Brian Marshall missed the penalty attempt. Ulster dominated the game but made critical errors at crucial times. Gibson's absence left the Ulster backs without the organisation and vision to open the All Blacks' defence. It was therefore left to the forwards to do the damage. Ulster had most of the territory and possession in the first half but they couldn't capitalise on their superiority and put points on the board. They targeted Going and managed to subdue him, making the attacking opportunities for Burgess and those outside him scarce. The Irish backs, however, made so many mistakes that New Zealand had many opportunities to attack from turned-over ball. Karam opened the scoring with a penalty and then converted a try from Bob Burgess when the first five-eighth charged down a clearance kick by Harrison to gather and score between the posts. New Zealand led 9-0 at half-time.

In the second half Karam kicked 2 more penalty goals but failed to add the extra points to a try scored by Duncan Hales after Going and Mark Sayers worked a glorious scissors movement. Ulster at last got on the scoreboard when Harry Steele stole the ball at a ruck close to the New Zealand corner flag and drove over the line. McBride was overjoyed. Marshall, who had earlier missed two long-range penalties, converted with a fine kick. Although Ulster were beaten there was a great cheer from the 25,000 crowd for both sides at full time.

NORTH-WEST COUNTIES   1972/73

Wednesday 22 November 1972
Ellis Sports Ground, Workington
Lost 16-14

Rugby history was made at Workington on Wednesday 22 November, when the All Blacks lost to an English regional side for the first time in their history. This was only the second time New Zealand had lost on English soil, the previous time being the defeat against England in 1936. The architect of this famous victory was undoubtedly the North-West coach, John Burgess. Burgess, who had played for North-Western Counties against Wilson Whineray's All Blacks, had coached the England party that toured the Far East in 1971, but was then discarded as his approach was felt to be too intense and professional. This was an era when coaching was still viewed as a dirty word in many English rugby circles, but

NORTH-WEST COUNTIES	NEW ZEALAND
B.J. O'Driscoll (Manchester)	T.J. Morris
A.A. Richards (Fylde)	G.R. Skudder
C.S. Wardlow (Coventry)	D.A. Hales
D.F.K. Roughley (Liverpool)	G.B. Batty
P.S. Maxwell (Richmond)	M. Sayers
A.R. Cowman (Coventry)	R.E. Burgess
S.J. Smith (Sale)	G.L. Colling
Forwards:	Forwards:
F.E. Cotton (Loughborough Colleges, Capt.)	G.J. Whiting
J. Lansbury (Sale)	R.A. Urlich
W.F. Anderson (Orrell)	K.K. Lambert
A.R. Trickey (Sale)	I.A. Eliason
M.M. Leadbetter (Broughton Park)	A.M. Haden
D. Robinson (Gosforth)	I.A. Kirkpatrick (Capt.)
A. Neary (Broughton Park)	B. Holmes
P.J. Dixon (Gosforth)	A.R. Sutherland
	Replacement:
	S.M. Going for Colling

Scorers:
North-West Counties: Tries: Maxwell (2). Con: Cowman.
PG: Cowman. DG: Wardlow.
New Zealand: Tries: Batty, Skudder. PGs: Morris (2).

Referee: T.F.E. Grierson (Scotland).
Attendance: 12,000.

Burgess proved in this game that a properly prepared side could outplay and defeat a major touring team. He got his squad together for six consecutive Sundays, established a game plan aimed at forcing the tourists into errors, planned some attacking ploys and watched films of the All Blacks to pinpoint their weaknesses. In the words of one of the local officials: 'If the officials in England had continued to reject coaching in rugby, the All Blacks would have won this match by 20 or 30 points. John Burgess, not the players, made the difference this time.' The side Burgess selected was certainly a strong one. Barry O'Driscoll was an Irish international, while Chris Wardlow, Alan Cowman, Fran Cotton, Mike Leadbetter, Peter Dixon and Tony Neary had all played for England. Of the remaining players, Dave Roughley, Steve Smith and Frank Anderson were future England caps, Anderson becoming the first capped player from the Orrell club. Steve Smith had played a brief but impressive part in the recent successful England tour to South Africa. In his autobiography, he wrote vividly about the preparations for the clash with New Zealand: 'The

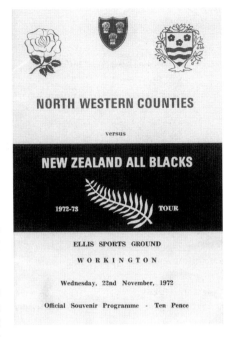

NORTH WESTERN COUNTIES

versus

NEW ZEALAND ALL BLACKS

1972-73 TOUR

ELLIS SPORTS GROUND

WORKINGTON

Wednesday, 22nd November, 1972

Official Souvenir Programme - Ten Pence

build-up to the game was incredible and it was my first experience of a Burgess team talk, although I had heard the Lancashire lads speaking of Burgess as though he were the messiah. We had all had a glass of sherry to calm our stomachs and the glasses were on the table in the room. Burge stripped off his shirt before he even started his talk. There he was in a string vest, kneeling on the floor at the side of the table with his eyes bulging and the veins in his neck pumping blood at a dangerous rate. He looked just like a samurai and the words came flooding out. At one stage he brought his fist down so hard on the table as he pressed home a point that he smashed five sherry glasses into little pieces.' According to Fran Cotton in his autobiography, the Burgess plan for success included the use of short lineouts to disrupt the All Blacks' rhythm. Chris Wardlow was moved to outside half when New Zealand had a lineout throw so that he could tackle any big forward peeling off with the ball, while flanker Dave Robinson was put at the front of the line on the tourists' throw to stop any blind-side moves.

Trevor Morris, playing his first game in Britain after a long injury lay-off, put New Zealand in front with a penalty after five minutes. Within the space of a minute Morris turned from hero to villain, missing a high kick that led to a ruck from which Wardlow dropped the equalising goal. Things got no better for Morris as the game went on; a skilled exponent of the drop goal himself, he was to miss with four such attempts during the game. New Zealand regained the lead after nineteen minutes when Alan Sutherland broke from a scrum near the North-West line. He beat two tacklers and passed to Bob Burgess, who handed on to Grant Batty. Despite the close attentions of Peter Dixon, Batty squeezed over in the corner, but Morris could not add the extra points. The home side took the lead after twenty-seven minutes with a well-worked try. The ball was won from a long lineout and Smith sent it along the backs, where Wardlow was missed out, giving Stuart Maxwell an overlap. Maxwell scored in the corner and a brilliant touchline conversion from Alan Cowman made the score 9-7. However, it was the All Blacks who led at the break, courtesy of another Morris penalty, awarded against Wardlow for encroaching at a lineout.

After seven minutes of the second half, O'Driscoll dropped a cross-kick from Burgess and George Skudder touched down in the corner to make the score 14-9. Then followed a moment of folly from Batty. Lin Colling lost a boot and Batty deliberately delayed a lineout throw while his teammate replaced his errant footwear. Referee Grierson was having none of this and penalised Batty, the resulting Cowman penalty taking the North-West to within 2 points. Thereafter, Kent Lambert had a

North-West Counties players celebrate their victory.

moment of madness, sending punches in all directions after Andy Haden had thumped Robinson. It took several players to calm Lambert down and he was lucky to stay on the field. There was considerable controversy about the winning score. Colling had left the field with a badly cut hand, and with Sid Going poised to replace him, John Burgess intervened, insisting that a doctor check Colling before the substitution was allowed. In the confusion that followed, Going was still running onto the field when the North-West winger Tony Richards took a quick lineout throw. The ball went to Neary at the back of the line and he tapped it down to Cotton who linked with Cowman. Cowman passed it on to Wardlow, whose flick pass gave Maxwell a run to the corner. Many questioned whether the referee should have allowed the lineout to begin in such circumstances, but the try stood and the North-West were in front. Fourteen minutes remained. The rain began to fall and the All Blacks made a desperate attempt to save the game. Mr Grierson missed a late charge on Batty that would have resulted in a kickable penalty, but there was no further score. The final whistle was greeted with scenes of jubilation, Cotton was chaired from the field and a proud New Zealand record came to an end. Despite the controversy surrounding the final try, the better team had won the match, a fact that Ian Kirkpatrick readily accepted after the game. Smith had outshone both Colling and Going at scrum-half, the tackling of Wardlow had been a telling factor, and despite the efforts of Andy Haden and Ian Eliason the New Zealand pack had been vanquished. Bob Burgess had overdone the high kick and the tourists' tackling had been indifferent.

Further trouble followed at the after-match function. Words were exchanged about the final try and some of the All Blacks tried to cause trouble when the highlights of the game were shown on television. Graham Short, the baggage master who had attended to the injured Colling and exchanged words with John Burgess, refused to accept the latter's apology, suggesting he direct it to the tour management. 'I do not want to say any more about your attempt to stop me doing my duty,' were his words. Notwithstanding the acrimonious aftermath, this was a great day for English rugby, a triumph for careful preparation and a sad day for the All Blacks.

Saturday 25 November 1972
Mansfield Park, Hawick
Won 26-6

REST OF SCOTTISH DISTRICTS	NEW ZEALAND
A.R. Brown (Gala)	J.F. Karam
W.C.C. Steele (Bedford)	B.G. Williams
J.N.M. Frame (Gala)	D.A. Hales
J.M. Renwick (Hawick)	G.R. Skudder
L.G. Dick (Loughborough Colleges)	R.M. Parkinson
I.R. McGeechan (Headingley)	I.N. Stevens
I.G. McCrae (Gordonians)	S.M. Going
Forwards:	Forwards:
N. Suddon (Hawick)	J.D. Matheson
F.A.L. Laidlaw (Melrose)	R.W. Norton
R.D.H. Bryce (Bristol)	K. Murdoch
A.F. McHarg (London Scottish)	H.H. McDonald
P.K. Stagg (Sale)	P.J. Whiting
N.A. MacEwan (Gala)	A.I. Scown
W. Lauder (Neath)	I.A. Kirkpatrick (Capt.)
P.C. Brown (Gala, Capt.)	A.J. Wyllie
Replacements:	
J. Henderson (Melrose)	
for McCrae, D. Aitchison (Highland) for A. Brown	

Scorers:
Rest of Scottish Districts: PG: P. Brown (2).
New Zealand: Tries: Skudder, Hales, Going, Parkinson.
Cons: Karam (2). PG: Karam (2).

Referee: J. Kelleher (Wales).
Attendance: 10,000.

In the wake of the defeat at Workington and with the Wales Test looming, the New Zealanders arrived at Mansfield Park needing to raise their confidence. A third defeat at this stage of the tour was unthinkable. Despite several injuries, the tourists fielded a very strong side, including twelve players who would go on to play against Wales the following weekend. Many in Scottish rugby felt that the game should have been awarded to the South of Scotland rather than a composite 'a the airts' side that had little identity or cohesion. The Districts held their only practice together on the morning of the match, but on paper the team had a nice blend of experience and youth. At lock, the gigantic Peter Stagg was chosen to dominate the lineouts, as he had done previously against New Zealand, while stand-off Ian McGeechan, a tidy footballer from Yorkshire, was pushing for his first international cap. The pitch had been protected by straw and a large crowd was present, but as one supporter pointed out it was difficult to shout 'Come away, the Rest of Scottish Districts' with any great enthusiasm. In the event, this turned out to be one of the easiest games of the tour and a fairly dismal one for the Scots. Peter Brown, 'nose-wiping, nonchalant place-kicker, idol of the Borders', opened the scoring with a penalty goal after three minutes. Joe Karam kicked two goals and Brown his second to tie the scores at 6-6. After thirty minutes, the Districts won a scrum near their own line, but full-back Arthur Brown fumbled the kick to touch. Sid Going went blind from the ensuing ruck and sent George Skudder over. The visitors led 10-6 at the interval. In the second half, New Zealand played some good co-ordinated rugby and ran in three further tries. Mike Parkinson scored the pick of the bunch with a fine solo effort through an assembly of tacklers.

New Zealand were the better side by a considerable margin and fully exploited their opponents'

weaknesses. The lop-sided Districts' scrum did not combine together well and Norton managed to take seven strikes against the head. The Scottish forwards were lumbering and slow, and the visitors dominated second and later-phase possession. In the lineout, the Scots paid the price for their own inflexibility and lack of imagination. Stagg almost never left his station at the front and New Zealand countered his presence by simply throwing the ball over his head to Peter Whiting, who was often left unmarked. The New Zealand backs were more willing to run the ball and the Districts stubbornly kept it tight, even when the match was won and lost. David Aitchison, who replaced Arthur Brown for the final fifteen minutes, was one of the few successes for the Districts. He was fearless in defence and pulled off a series of crunching tackles, one on Ian Kirkpatrick that left both players briefly the worse for wear. Peter Brown was praised by the visiting management and scrum-half Ian McCrae struggled heroically with some terrible ball, prompting the comment that he deserved a posthumous VC for his efforts. But in general, the Districts gave a poor display and few reputations were enhanced. A good win for New Zealand, but there was still plenty of room for improvement.

GWENT   1972/73

Tuesday 28 November 1972
Welfare Sports Ground,
Ebbw Vale
Won 16-7

GWENT	NEW ZEALAND
R. Pugh (Pontypool)	T.J. Morris
A. Browning (Newbridge)	G.B. Batty
I. Taylor (Pontypool)	R.M. Parkinson
R. Duggan (Bedwas)	D.A. Hales
R. Parry (Ebbw Vale)	M. Sayers
M. Grindle (Ebbw Vale)	I.N. Stevens
G. Turner (Ebbw Vale)	S.M. Going
Forwards:	Forwards:
A.G. Faulkner (Pontypool)	G.J. Whiting
A. Williams (Newbridge)	R.A. Urlich
G. Howls (Ebbw Vale)	K. Murdoch
S.C. Geary (Newbridge)	A.M. Haden
R. Bendall (Newbridge)	P.J. Whiting
T.J. Cobner (Pontypool)	K.W. Stewart
G. Evans (Ebbw Vale)	I.A. Kirkpatrick (Capt.)
D. Hughes (Newbridge, Capt.)	A.R. Sutherland
Replacement:	Replacement:
A. Tucker (Blaina) for Evans	A.I. Scown for Batty

Scorers:
Try: Turner. PG: Pugh.
New Zealand: Tries: Haden, Stevens. Con: Morris. PG: Morris. DG: Morris.

Referee: K. Pattison (RFU).
Attendance: 20,000.

The All Blacks picked a surprisingly strong side for the midweek game at Ebbw Vale just days before they were to take on Wales in the first international of the tour. The Gwent side was a genuine valleys combination as it was selected from the leading Monmouthshire clubs with the exception of Newport, who had their own fixture with New Zealand. None of the clubs with players included were enjoying great success at the time. They included Tony 'Charlie' Faulkner who was later to become one of the famous 'Pontypool Front Row' and Terry Cobner who had a significant role leading the pack on the 1977 Lions tour. They were captained by Dennis Hughes and had the talented half-back pairing of Mike Grindle and Glyn Turner. All three players had represented Monmouthshire in their 1967 match with New Zealand. Gwent had played London Counties in a preparatory game earlier in the month. The All Blacks had been among the crowd, but how much they saw is unknown as it was played in thick fog. Nevertheless, New Zealand were expected to defeat Gwent by a substantial margin.

New Zealand totally dominated the match, but Gwent tackled ferociously and gave the All Blacks a hard game. The weather was showery, and the pitch slippery which didn't help the tourists' use of the ball, and they kept it tighter than was anticipated. This contributed to a low-scoring game. The

match had been underway only six minutes when Trevor Morris kicked a penalty attempt against the woodwork. The home defence failed to clear it, and the alert Andy Haden dived on the ball to score. Morris made no mistake with the conversion, but the home side worked strenuously to keep the All Blacks out and there was no further score before the break. New Zealand led 6-0.

Morris kicked a penalty and dropped a fine forty-yard goal early in the second half to extend the lead, before Ritchie Pugh eventually managed to kick a penalty for the home side. Then Ian Stevens scored a try from a quickly taken penalty, although there were claims that the ball was not grounded properly. Alan Sutherland had a fine game for the All Blacks but, uncharacteristically, they seemed to ease off. Turner broke down the blind side of a scrum for a late try but there was no further scoring and a subdued New Zealand won without stretching themselves or taking risks. However, they failed to endear themselves to their hosts after the game by leaving after the speeches at the official reception and not going on to a dance organised in their honour. Instead they returned to their base in Porthcawl and announced the Test side to play Wales.

WALES 1972/73

**Saturday 2 December 1972
Cardiff Arms Park, Cardiff
Won 19-16**

WALES	NEW ZEALAND
J.P.R. Williams (London Welsh)	J.F. Karam
T.G.R. Davies (London Welsh)	B.G. Williams
R.T.E. Bergiers (Llanelli)	D.A. Hales
J.L. Shanklin (London Welsh)	G.B. Batty
J.C. Bevan (Cardiff)	R.M. Parkinson
P. Bennett (Llanelli)	R.E. Burgess
G.O. Edwards (Cardiff)	S.M. Going
Forwards:	Forwards:
G. Shaw (Neath)	J.D. Matheson
J. Young (London Welsh)	R.W. Norton
D.B. Llewelyn (Llanelli)	K. Murdoch
D.L. Quinnell (Llanelli)	H.H. Macdonald
W.D. Thomas (Llanelli, Capt.)	P.J. Whiting
W.D. Morris (Neath)	A.J. Wyllie
J. Taylor (London Welsh)	I.A. Kirkpatrick (Capt.)
T.M. Davies (Swansea)	A.R. Sutherland
	Replacement:
	A.I. Scown for Wyllie

Scorers:
Wales: Try: Bevan. PG: Bennett (4).
New Zealand: Try: Murdoch. PG: Karam (5).

Referee: R.F. Johnson (RFU).
Attendance: 50,000.

The All Blacks selected a back row of Alex Wyllie, Alan Sutherland and skipper Ian Kirkpatrick for the international. They had not played together as a unit on tour before but were significantly bigger than the Welsh trio. Wyllie was given the task of suppressing Gareth Edwards. It was the strongest available side and new caps were awarded to Joe Karam, Grant Batty and Hamish MacDonald. Batty had struggled with injury but was eventually passed fit. Bob Burgess, who had not been at his best recently, was preferred to the inexperienced Ian Stevens at first five-eighth. The Wales side had been selected ten days earlier but Arthur Lewis, chosen to captain his country, failed to recover from a hamstring injury and was replaced in the centre by Jim Shanklin, although there were calls to bring back former captain John Dawes as his experience could be vital. Delme Thomas assumed the responsibility of captaincy. Wing John Bevan was also nursing a leg injury. The only new cap in the Wales side was Neath prop Glyn Shaw. With Wales unbeaten at home since 1968 and winning their last 8 games in succession there was genuine confidence that Wales would win.

It was an exciting and tense game that Wales initially struggled to get into and Karam, who had a memorable international debut, kicked two early penalties. Midway into the first half Sid Going kicked ahead and, following the ball, tackled John Bevan. Both packs got to the breakdown quickly but Going worked it back to Keith Murdoch who drove through the Welsh defence and although tackled, his momentum took him over for the try. Karam missed the conversion, but kicked another penalty soon after, followed by one from Phil Bennett, to see the All Blacks ahead 13-3 at half-time.

Early in the second half, a heavy tackle on Sid Going saw the ball emerge on the Welsh side. It was quickly moved to Bevan in space who sprinted forty yards to score in the corner. This gave Wales inspiration. Bennett missed the conversion but kicked a penalty shortly afterwards. Crucially, Karam kicked

Keith Murdoch, who was sent home after the international with Wales.

WALES
v
NEW ZEALAND

his fourth penalty to widen the gap but Bennett pulled back 3 points with another penalty for Wales. Thomas and Barry Llewelyn got in each other's way, were penalised, and Karam kicked another penalty to widen the gap to 6 points. Then controversy arose again. With eleven minutes left, Delme Thomas caught a drop out on the New Zealand 25 and ran towards the New Zealand line. He slipped the ball to John Williams and 'J.P.R.' drove for the corner. He was half tackled but he recovered to score the try. Referee Johnson seemed to award the try, then changed his signal to a penalty to New Zealand. He believed Williams was held and as such was not permitted to make a second movement. Argument then surrounded whether Williams was held or not. It was a remarkably similar movement by the ball carrier to that made by Murdoch when awarded his try. It was a crucial decision. Close to full time Bennett kicked another penalty to narrow the gap to 3 points then, in injury time, Williams was obstructed and Bennett had a wide penalty to draw the match. He kicked well, but not well enough, and New Zealand had won a match that they should have lost. This was recognised by the tourists and Kirkpatrick said: 'We were lucky to hold out.'

Unfortunately the controversy didn't end with the final whistle. Keith Murdoch was sent home in disgrace following a scuffle with a security guard in the kitchen of the team's Cardiff hotel in the early hours of Sunday morning. It was not the first incident of the tour. He had been seen as a rough player on the pitch, scarcely far from trouble, and frequently aggressive and uncontrollable off it. Manager Ernie Todd explained Murdoch had to go 'for the benefit of the player himself and of the team as a whole'. Todd, no doubt acting under severe pressure, was dismayed that much of the publicity his tour party was getting, both in Britain and New Zealand, was for the wrong reasons. He accused the British press of a smear campaign against his team. The New Zealand squad was in turmoil and their focus was scarcely on playing rugby. Lindsay Clark of Otago was called up to replace Murdoch.

MIDLAND COUNTIES (WEST) 1972/73

Wednesday 6 December 1972
The Reddings, Moseley
Lost 16-8

Having lost to an English regional side for the first time at Workington, the All Blacks suffered the same fate in their next English encounter, although the defeat at Moseley was perhaps more predictable. The game was played during the aftermath of the Murdoch affair and team morale was low. Despite his eccentricities, Keith Murdoch was popular with his fellow players, and there was genuine anger that manager Ernie Todd had decided to send him home. The tourists' selectors made the mistake of underestimating the opposition. Even before the tour started, Midland Counties (West) had been tipped as possible conquerors of the All Blacks. The

MIDLAND COUNTIES (WEST)	NEW ZEALAND
S.J. Doble (Moseley)	T.J. Morris
D.J. Duckham (Coventry, Capt.)	G.R. Skudder
P.S. Preece (Coventry)	I.A. Hurst
M.K. Swain (Moseley)	B.G. Williams
M.J. Cooper (Moseley)	M. Sayers
J.F. Finlan (Moseley)	R.E. Burgess
J.G. Webster (Moseley)	G.L. Colling
Forwards:	Forwards:
T.F. Corless (Birmingham)	K.K. Lambert
J.D. Gray (Coventry)	R.A. Urlich
K.E. Fairbrother (Coventry)	G.J. Whiting
N.E. Horton (Moseley)	A.M. Haden
L. Smith (Moseley)	I.A. Eliason
I.N. Pringle (Moseley)	K.W. Stewart
T.M. Cowell (Rugby)	I.A. Kirkpatrick (Capt.)
J.C. White (Moseley)	B. Holmes

Scorers:
Midland Counties (West): Tries: Cooper, Duckham. Con: Doble. PG: Doble. DG: Finlan.
New Zealand: Tries: Sayers, Hurst.

Referee: R. Lewis (Wales).
Attendance: 10,000.

side was particularly strong in the backs, and the game fell straight after the rigours of the Welsh international. The New Zealanders had failed to do their homework. The home side, expertly coached by Loughborough-based 1955 British Lion and Scottish international Jim Greenwood, contained seven internationals. All the backs except Malcolm Swain and Martin Cooper were England caps. Swain later captained Wales B and Cooper received the first of his eleven England caps in 1973. Of the forwards, Keith Fairbrother and Nigel Horton had played for England. In the face of such strong opposition, the tourists unwisely retained only three players – Ian Kirkpatrick, Bryan Williams and Bob Burgess – of the side that defeated Wales. To make matters worse, having won the toss on a heavy pitch, Kirkpatrick elected to play against the elements, thus forcing his side to face a strong breeze, a low sun, plus a slope in the first half. Home captain David Duckham, who had already tasted victory against New Zealand on the 1971 Lions tour, was amazed at the decision. He had intended to claim first use of the wind if he had won the toss himself, claiming: 'We realised they'd be a bit glum, so we wanted to unsettle them early.'

Duckham's plans could hardly have gone better. After just eight minutes the All Blacks trailed 13-0 and hard though they tried, they could not come back from such a deficit. Outside half John Finlan began the scoring after three minutes when he dropped a goal following the second of two Nigel Horton wins in the lineout. Cooper scored the first try after five minutes, evading some poor defence by Trevor Morris and crossing in the corner. The try was initiated by John Gray's heel against the head in a scrum and centre Peter Preece made the break that put Cooper in the clear. Full-back Sam Doble could not convert this try, but three minutes later the Counties scored again. Lin Colling was robbed of the ball at a scrum, and after a forward surge, Mark Sayers's clearing kick was charged down and taken by Horton. Trevor Corless then made ground before the backs created an overlap for Duckham to score out wide. Doble converted to put his side 13-0 in front. New Zealand did manage one score before the break, Sayers touching down after Ian Hurst had tackled Preece close to his own line. Sadly for the tourists, this was not to be Trevor Morris's day with the boot. He missed six kicks, including one in front of the posts and his confidence was badly rattled. Referee Ron Lewis told Ernie Todd after the game that he could tell from the look on the full-back's face that his kicks were going to miss. Eventually, Bryan Williams was called up to attempt one kick, but he fared no better. This was the only game of the tour that contained no All Black points from the boot. After the New Zealand try, there was one further score in the half, a Doble penalty after Ron Urlich was penalised at a scrum. The half-time score was 16-4. The tourists improved in the second half and with the wind at their backs they mounted plenty of attacks, but the home defence was sound and the New Zealand handling was poor. Only one try was scored, by Hurst after Graham Whiting, Bevan Holmes and Kirkpatrick had combined to set the backs in motion. The try came halfway through the second period, but with the crowd chanting 'easy, easy', the home side held on to claim a much-prized scalp. It was a fine team performance, with outstanding contributions from the Moseley half-back pairing of John Finlan and Jan Webster.

This was one of the worst ever performances by an All Black side. The handling was woeful, the wingers rarely saw the ball and the team as a whole paid dearly for its poor preparation. To their credit, the players socialised freely after the game and accepted defeat graciously. In view of what he had seen that day it was hardly surprising that manager Todd predicted that England could defeat his team comfortably.

Saturday 9 December 1972
Lidget Green, Bradford
Won 9-3

NORTH-EAST COUNTIES	NEW ZEALAND
B. Patrick (Gosforth)	J.F. Karam
D.W. Carr (Gosforth)	B.G. Williams
I.R. McGeechan (Headingley, Capt.)	I.A. Hurst
P.S. Warfield (Durham University)	G.B. Batty
A. Cheshire (Harrogate)	R.M. Parkinson
A.G.B. Old (Leicester)	I.N. Stevens
M. Young (Gosforth)	S.M. Going
Forwards:	Forwards:
C. White (Gosforth)	J.D. Matheson
D.F. Madsen (Gosforth)	R.W. Norton
P.M. McLoughlin (Northern)	G.J. Whiting
R.M. Utley (Gosforth)	P.J. Whiting
J. Hall (Cheltenham)	A.M. Haden
R.J. Leathley (Halifax)	A.I. Scown
T. Donovan (Headingley)	I.A. Kirkpatrick (Capt.)
P.G. Nash (Middlesbrough)	A.R. Sutherland
	Replacement:
	G.R. Skudder for Batty

Scorers:
North-East Counties: PG: Old.
New Zealand: Try: Batty. Con: Karam. DG: Going.

Referee: F. Palmade (France).
Attendance: 14,000.

The home side was coached by John Robins, who had been the assistant manager of the 1966 British Lions in New Zealand. Outside half Alan Old was the only international in the team, having won his first England cap earlier in the year, but Peter Warfield, Malcolm Young, Colin White and Roger Utley were all future England players. In fact, the twenty-one-year-old Warfield so impressed with his tackling in this game that he was chosen to face New Zealand again when they met England. His co-centre and captain, Ian McGeechan, made his Scotland debut against the tourists just a week after his appearance at Bradford, although he was selected at outside half rather than centre. Prop forward Phelim McLoughlin, brother of renowned British Lion Ray McLoughlin, received belated Irish international recognition against Australia in 1976. New Zealand chose to field a near Test-strength side with skipper Ian Kirkpatrick playing his seventh consecutive match. The tourists dominated much of the game but failed to turn possession into points, mainly through poor handling. The weather on this bitterly cold day did not help players on either side, particularly the kickers. Both Alan Old and Joe Karam were troubled by the strong wind and only managed one successful kick each. On one occasion Old fell on his backside attempting the simplest of goals.

The North-East enjoyed slightly the better of the early exchanges, particularly in the scrums, where McLoughlin gave Jeff Matheson such a difficult afternoon that Graham Whiting was moved to the Irishman's side of the scrum after half an hour. Two minutes later Whiting was penalised for

punching McLoughlin and Old kicked the home side into the lead. Just before half-time a long, arguably crooked, throw at a lineout was picked up by Sid Going. The tourists' backs started a move in which Ian Stevens missed out Mike Parkinson, before Ian Hurst's long pass gave Grant Batty enough room to outpace home winger David Carr and score in the corner. Karam defied the conditions to land a superb conversion and the half-time score was 6-3.

The only score of the second half came after ten minutes when Kirkpatrick fed Going from a maul and the busy half-back dropped one of his rare goals. Thereafter, despite a constant supply of lineout ball from Peter Whiting, the All Blacks could not add to their lead and 9-3 was the final score. Ian Stevens had endured a particularly frustrating afternoon, dropping numerous passes, and Bryan Williams on the wing received only one pass from a three-quarter move.

Besides the fine tackling of Warfield, there was much to admire in the confident play of eighteen-year-old Gosforth full-back Brian Patrick, but despite their many errors the visitors deserved their victory. John Robins, however, was not impressed. 'They don't compare with previous New Zealand teams since the war,' he said. 'The team is devoid of personalities and this reflects in their play.'

GLASGOW & EDINBURGH   1972/73

Tuesday 12 December 1972
Hughenden, Glasgow
Won 16-10

GLASGOW & EDINBURGH	NEW ZEALAND
B.H. Hay (Boroughmuir FP)	J.F. Karam
R.S.M. Hannah (West of Scotland)	G.R. Skudder
M.D. Hunter (Glasgow HSFP)	B.J. Robertson
I.W. Forsyth (Stewart's FP)	D.A. Hales
S.L. Briggs (Edinburgh Wanderers)	M. Sayers
F.N.F. Dall (Heriot's FP)	R.E. Burgess
D.W. Morgan (Melville FP, Capt.)	G.L. Colling
Forwards:	Forwards:
J. Craig (Ayr)	K.K. Lambert
Q. Dunlop (West of Scotland)	R.A. Urlich
D.S.D. McCallum (Jordanhill)	J.D. Matheson
R.W.T. Wright (Edinburgh Wanderers)	A.M. Haden
R.S. Tolbert (Watsonians)	H.H. McDonald
T. Young (West of Scotland)	A.J. Wyllie (Capt.)
W.S. Watson (Boroughmuir FP)	K.W. Stewart
G.M. Strachan (Jordanhill)	A.R. Sutherland
	Replacement:
	P.J. Whiting for Haden

Scorers:
Glasgow & Edinburgh: Try: Dall. PGs: Morgan (2).
New Zealand: Tries: Sutherland, Urlich. Con: Karam.
PG: Karam (2).

Referee: A. Welsby (Lancashire).
Attendance: 5,000.

The next Test match against Scotland was only four days away, but the New Zealanders fielded a team that was stronger than the usual midweek side with seven of the players who took part in the victory against Wales, and three others of Test status. In contrast, the Combined Cities were understrength, missing several players who had been selected for the forthcoming international. Nevertheless, the cities could boast three former caps in Ronnie Hannah, Quintin Dunlop and Gordon Strachan, and also some promising younger players, such as full-back Bruce Hay and scrum-half Douglas Morgan.

On a soft and muddy pitch, the New Zealand forwards dominated possession, winning the ball in rich and almost unceasing profusion, but the visitors had to work very hard for their win. Living on starvation rations, the Cities played a limited game, lying up in defence, waiting for enemy mistakes and attempting very little on their own initiative. The visitors made many errors in their handling, and there was a lack of confidence in midfield and a shortage of real finishing pace on the wings. The Cities opened the scoring with a typical smash-and-grab try. Bruce Robertson fumbled the ball in midfield and Ian Forsyth hacked on. The New Zealand cover failed to react quickly enough and, as the ball broke to him, Hannah gathered and made ground before passing back inside for Fraser Dall to clinch a fine score. Morgan failed with a difficult conversion. The cities had several chances to extend their lead, Briggs coming close on two occasions. At half-time, the visitors were lucky to be only one point down, Karam having kicked a penalty goal to make the score 4-3.

The second half was still young when the All Blacks forged ahead. Andy Haden breached the defence from a tapped penalty, Lin Colling surged for the line and finally Ron Urlich stole a scrambled try beneath a pile of bodies. Joe Karam, the 'Wellington Boot', converted. Later in the half, Morgan pulled back 3 points with a long-range penalty. With injury time looming, the match was finely balanced at 9-7. Karam kicked another goal, but Morgan replied in kind. In the fifth and final minute of injury time, Mark

Sayers found the home defence sleeping as he raced onto a throw over the top of a lineout. He was tackled just short of the line, but the supporting Alan Sutherland was awarded the try, although many felt that the ball had gone forward and that Hay had beaten Sutherland to the touchdown.

It was another close shave for the midweek team, who once again came up against a side that was stronger than expected. For the Cities, Strachan was the outstanding forward while the back division all tackled extremely well, especially Bruce Hay, who was heroic in defence. Among the All Blacks, Joe Karam continued to show development and Bruce Robertson, although short of match practice, gave hints of being a real thoroughbred.

SCOTLAND   1972/73

Saturday 16 December 1972
Murrayfield, Edinburgh
Won 14-9

SCOTLAND	NEW ZEALAND
A.R. Irvine (Heriot's FP)	J.F. Karam
W.C.C. Steele (Bedford)	B.G. Williams
I.W. Forsyth (Stewart's FP)	B.J. Robertson
J.M. Renwick (Hawick)	G.B. Batty
D. Shedden (West of Scotland)	R.M. Parkinson
I.R. McGeechan (Headingley)	I.N. Stevens
I.G. McCrae (Gordonians)	S.M. Going
Forwards:	Forwards:
J. McLauchlan (Jordanhill)	J.D. Matheson
R.L. Clark (Edinburgh Wanderers)	R.W. Norton
A.B. Carmichael (West of Scotland)	G.J. Whiting
A.F. McHarg (West of Scotland)	P.J. Whiting
G.L. Brown (West of Scotland)	H.H. Macdonald
N.A. MacEwan (Gala)	A.I. Scown
R.J. Arneil (Northampton)	I.A. Kirkpatrick (Capt.)
P.C. Brown (Gala, Capt.)	A.J. Wyllie
	Replacement:
	K.K. Lambert for Matheson

Scorers:
Scotland: PGs: Irvine (2). DG: McGeechan.
New Zealand: Tries: Wyllie, Batty, Going. Con: Karam.

Referee: G. Domercq (France).
Attendance: 50,000.

With a try count of 3-0 in their favour, New Zealand deserved to win the match, but once again they were unable to dominate their opponents and came dangerously close to letting it slip at the end. The tourists were forced to make two changes to their original selection. Alan Sutherland pulled out with flu and was replaced by Alistair Scown with Alex Wyllie falling back to number eight. At stand-off, Bob Burgess dropped out with a leg injury and Ian Stevens was called upon for his first cap. The Scots fielded four new caps, all in the back division: Andy Irvine, Ian Forsyth, David Shedden and Ian McGeechan. In fact, this match is best remembered for the debuts of two players who would go on to have distinguished international careers. At full-back, Andy Irvine, a twenty-one-year-old student at Edinburgh University who played his club rugby for Heriot's FP, was a classic attacking player who could light up a game with his electrifying running. At stand-off, Ian McGeechan, a twenty-six-year-old teacher from Yorkshire, had great cricketer's hands and a shrewd footballer's brain, later becoming one of the most respected coaches in world rugby.

On a mild and windless day, New Zealand suffered a serious blow in the opening five minutes when Jeff Matheson had to leave the field with rib damage. His replacement, Kent Lambert, a twenty-year-old student from Manawatu, came on to win his first cap. Most of the first half was played in Scottish territory with the home side making the occasional breakout. Both sides were rather reluctant to use their backs and the game was largely a series of scrums and lineouts. In the forty-fifth minute of an inexplicably long half, Sid Going slipped round a scrum and fed inside to Wyllie, who bolted through the gap to score. Karam kicked a fine conversion to put the All Blacks 6-0 ahead at the break.

After the interval, Irvine cut the margin with a penalty goal before Robertson made a long weaving run and put in a perfectly placed grubber kick for Batty to score. Scotland roared back and from a lineout McGeechan dropped a brilliant left-footed goal. Irvine reduced the lead to a single point with a massive penalty goal and it was anybody's game going into injury time. As the gloom descended, the Scots made a gallant effort to save the match, but Alastair McHarg lobbed a wild pass inside

that was intercepted by Going, who scampered fifty metres for the clinching score.

It was hard lines on Scotland but justice had been done. New Zealand were the better side and had been able to exert greater pressure on their opponents, who in reply had made too many errors and dropped passes. The visiting forwards were powerful and positive, and Kirkpatrick, the captain, was always in the thick of the action. The New Zealand scrummaging was a huge improvement on previous games and the second-choice front row did wonders against their vastly experienced opponents, especially the novice Lambert, who had a fine match. Behind the scrum, Going was a constant menace, but the biggest failing was the inability to feed Bryan Williams, whose strength and all-round ability ought to have been devastating. For Scotland, Rodger Arneil was very prominent, but props Ian McLauchlan and Sandy Carmichael were unable to repeat their form of the recent Lions' tour. Of the new caps, McGeechan handled well, tackled soundly and had two elusive runs, but some of his kicking was ineffectual. Andy Irvine had an encouraging debut, showing great promise and fielding soundly, although several of his kicks failed to find touch. The New Zealand tour was at last finding its momentum and some of the younger players, such as Karam, Batty and Lambert, were starting to show their true qualities.

SOUTHERN COUNTIES   1972/73

Wednesday 20 December 1972
Iffley Road, Oxford
Won 23-6

The home side, coached by former Saracens and Hertfordshire coach Ken Bartlett, was not expected to challenge the tourists. There were no internationals in the team and several players, including full-back Stuart Crabtree of Bristol and skipper John Vaughan of London Welsh, were not regular members of their club first fifteens. Prop forward Mike Hannell had toured the Far East with England in 1971. Tragically, within two seasons of facing the All Blacks, he died of cancer. Owen Jones later became a respected referee. New Zealand gave a debut to Lindsay Clark, the replacement for Keith Murdoch, and the selected side was very much a 'midweek' one. Despite winning a

SOUTHERN COUNTIES	NEW ZEALAND
S. Crabtree (Bristol)	T.J. Morris
R. Ellis-Jones (London Welsh)	B.G. Williams
R.O.P. Jones (Oxford University)	I.A. Hurst
I. Ray (Oxford)	D.A. Hales
P. Cadle (Saracens)	M. Sayers
D. Llewellyn (London Welsh)	I.N. Stevens
D. Spawforth (Army)	G.L. Colling
Forwards:	Forwards:
M.R. Hannell (Bristol)	G.J. Whiting
H. Malins (Richmond)	R.A. Urlich
K. Richardson (Gloucester)	L. Clark
J.S. Jarrett (Gloucester)	A.M. Haden
J. Harwood (Oxford)	I.M. Eliason
M. Marshall (Richmond)	K.W. Stewart
S. Godfrey (Loughborough Colleges)	I.A. Kirkpatrick (Capt.)
J. Vaughan (London Welsh, Capt.)	B. Holmes

Scorers:
Southern Counties: Try: Cadle. Con: Llewellyn.
New Zealand: Tries: Williams (2), Hales, Haden. Cons: Morris (2). PG: Morris.

Referee: C.G.P. Thomas (Wales).
Attendance: 7,000.

huge amount of possession, poor play by the All Black midfield meant that the final score was not as great as it should have been and much of the good work of the forwards was wasted.

It took New Zealand thirty-three minutes to get points on the board. Bryan Williams latched onto a cross-kick from Ian Stevens and outran Saracens winger Peter Cadle to score. Trevor Morris, who had another unhappy afternoon with his place kicking, even missing a penalty in front of the posts, was

unable to convert. He was, however, successful with a good forty-yard penalty five minutes later, and then just on half-time Duncan Hales scored the second try. Half-back Lin Colling had made a fifty-yard break from a tap penalty, and from the resulting ruck Mark Sayers created the opening for Hales. Morris missed the conversion and the half-time score was 11-0.

After thirteen minutes of the second half a Colling kick bounced off a defender and Williams crossed for his second try, Morris converting beautifully from the touchline. Eight minutes later Colling made a blind-side break, setting up a great charge from Ian Kirkpatrick that resulted in a try under the posts for Andy Haden. Morris had no trouble with the conversion, but there was no further New Zealand scoring. The home try followed shortly afterwards, Cadle intercepting a Colling pass that was intended for Kirkpatrick. The winger touched down under the posts and outside half David Llewellyn converted. Good play in the closing stages, particularly by centre Ian Ray, nearly resulted in further scoring opportunities for Southern Counties, but no points came in the final fifteen minutes.

The All Blacks were never in danger of losing this match, and Andy Haden and Ian Eliason received many plaudits in the press for their domination of the lineouts. Clark and his fellow prop Graham Whiting also performed well, and Clark was delighted to have come through a game successfully, having not played for three months. Much criticism was levelled at Colling, Stevens and Sayers who all made far too many errors. This was a disappointing showing by the All Blacks, and they should have scored in excess of 40 points.

COMBINED SERVICES   1972/73

Tuesday 26 December 1972
Twickenham, London
Won 31-10

The Combined Services had prepared thoroughly for this game, appointing 1966 British Lions captain Mike Campbell-Lamerton as coach and selecting a squad in October. This squad played 2 warm-up games, losing narrowly to Scottish Districts 13-12 and to Bristol 3-0. The side that took the field against the All Blacks contained five internationals – Stephen Turk, Billy Steele and Bobby Clark of Scotland, Peter Larter of England and Jeff Young of Wales. To accommodate two international hookers in the side, Jeff Young was moved to prop and given the captaincy of the team. New Zealand skipper Ian Kirkpatrick rested from the game, having played in nine of the previous ten fixtures.

This was a comfortable victory for the All Blacks against what turned out to be

COMBINED SERVICES	NEW ZEALAND
Tpr A.S. Turk (Army)	T.J. Morris
Cpl W.C.C. Steele (RAF)	G.B. Batty
Capt. D.S. Boyle (Army)	I.A. Hurst
2nd Lieut P.M. Davies (Army)	G.R. Skudder
Sub-Lieut G.P. Phillips (Royal Navy)	R.M. Parkinson
P.O. G. Jones (Royal Navy)	R.E. Burgess
Cpl. D. Spawforth (Army)	G.L. Colling
Forwards:	Forwards:
R.E.A. J.C. Ackerman (Royal Navy)	L.A. Clark
Inst Lieut R.L. Clark (Royal Navy)	R.A. Urlich
Flt Lieut J. Young (RAF, Capt.)	K.K. Lambert
Fg. Off. P.J. Larter (RAF)	P.J. Whiting
Sgt I. Cairns (Army)	I.M. Eliason
Lieut A.J.W. Higginson (Royal Marines)	A.J. Wyllie (Capt.)
Lieut P.J. Bird (Army)	A.I. Scown
Lieut L.C.P. Merrick (Royal Navy)	B. Holmes
Replacement:	
Cpl D.R. Fulford	
(Royal Marines, for Ackerman)	

Scorers:
Combined Services: Try: Davies. PGs: Larter (2).
New Zealand: Tries: Batty, Parkinson, Scown. Cons: Morris (2). PG: Morris (4). DG: Morris.

Referee: N.P. Jones (Gloucestershire).
Attendance: 15,000.

relatively modest opposition, but it was hardly a sparkling performance. Bob Burgess at outside half was reluctant to release his backs, particularly in the first half, and stand-in captain Alex Wyllie was booed and slow-handclapped by the Twickenham crowd when he insisted on giving Trevor Morris shots at goal from penalties when the game was clearly won. At least Morris was successful with the boot. He had not really recovered from his early tour injury, and this was the first time he felt absolutely fit. His personal haul of 19 points was the best individual tally of the tour in one match and his general play was excellent, particularly his mammoth touch-finding kicks. Ironically, in view of what was to come, Morris missed a very easy first shot at goal early in the match, and there was no score for over half an hour. Then Morris kicked two penalties, one following an offside decision against Services scrum-half Dave Spawforth, and the other awarded when Spawforth was penalised for a crooked feed at a scrum. Spawforth, an experienced and popular player, had

an unfortunate afternoon, unintentionally contributing to several New Zealand scores. He was not at fault when Morris added a nicely struck drop goal after thirty-eight minutes – this was the result of a poor clearance from full-back Turk. Spawforth was, however, to blame when Grant Batty caught his weak kick from his own line. Batty cut through three defenders to score the first try of the match. Morris could not add the extras and the half-time score was 13-0 to the visitors.

After just three minutes of the second period, Ian Hurst made an excellent run, handing on to Mike Parkinson for a try under the posts that Morris had no trouble converting. Ten minutes into the half Lin Colling was penalised at a scrum and Larter landed a huge penalty. Morris immediately replied with a further penalty for the All Blacks, thanks once again to a Spawforth scrum infringement, then Larter kicked his second goal following a further offence from Colling. Morris kicked his fourth penalty after twenty minutes. The Services were penalised for handling in a ruck and flanker Andy Higginson argued so much that the kick was moved forwards ten yards. The Combined Services managed a try ten minutes from the end, but it was a bizarre and dubious score. Centre Phil Davies, whose father Mickey had played for Wales in 1939, charged down a George Skudder kick. He then knocked the ball on before kicking ahead to the All Blacks' line, where two New Zealanders appeared to get to the ball before him. Referee Mr Jones, who was not up with the play, awarded a try – 'a very generous gesture indeed' in the words of journalist John Reason. There was one final score, when Alistair Scown finished off a good move by Bevan Holmes and Burgess. Morris converted to seal a happy day for the full-back. Kent Lambert and Ron Urlich also excelled for the visitors, while Peter Whiting and Ian Eliason dominated the lineouts. For the Services, there were sound performances from Higginson, Larter and Peter Bird, but the match in general was disappointing.

Saturday 30 December 1972
Cardiff Arms Park, Cardiff
Won 20-9

EAST GLAMORGAN	NEW ZEALAND
C. Bolderson (Pontypridd)	J.F. Karam
D. Schick (Bridgend)	B.G. Williams
I. Hopkins (Cardiff Coll of Ed.)	B.J. Robertson
I. Hall (South Wales Police & Aberavon)	D.A. Hales
V. Jenkins (Bridgend)	I.A. Hurst
R. Evans (South Wales Police)	I.N. Stevens
G. Evans (South Wales Police)	S.M. Going
Forwards:	Forwards:
D.J. Lloyd (Bridgend, Capt.)	G.J. Whiting
C. Lewis (Bridgend)	R.W. Norton
A. Davies (South Wales Police)	K.K. Lambert
W. Howe (Maesteg)	H.H. Macdonald
P. Williams (Bridgend)	P.J. Whiting
G. Jones (Bridgend)	B. Holmes
D. Brain (Bridgend)	I.A. Kirkpatrick (Capt.)
R. Dudley-Jones (Cardiff Coll of Ed.)	A.R. Sutherland
Replacement:	Replacement:
D. John (Pontypridd) for G. Evans	L.A. Clark for G. Whiting

Scorers:
East Glamorgan: PG: Bolderson, Hopkins. DG: R. Evans.
New Zealand: Tries: Hales (2), Stevens. Con: Karam.
PG: Karam (2).

Referee: K.H. Clark (IRFU).
Attendance: 25,000.

Swansea, one of the traditional 'big four' Welsh clubs, had suffered a few seasons of poor results and consequently were not awarded a match with New Zealand. The WRU refused to change the itinerary even though Swansea were scaling the heights once again in the 1972/73 season. Instead of travelling to the St Helens ground in Swansea, the All Blacks returned to the National Stadium, Cardiff Arms Park, for a game against a club selection consisting of those Welsh clubs, except Swansea, not involved in the other touring games. They were based around the Bridgend side and captained by John Lloyd, their international prop. East Glamorgan included centre Ian Hall, who played for Wales against Lochore's All Blacks, and Ron Evans, who was capped for Wales in 1963. Wing Doug Schick had played for Canada. Peter Williams was a late replacement for the injured Penarth lock Gerry Oram. The All Blacks did not want to risk another embarrassing defeat and picked a strong side and were expected to win by a significant margin. The match was played in extraordinary weather. Dense fog descended on the ground and it seemed likely the game would be called off, but after an inspection at pitch level and a positive weather forecast, the game was given the go-ahead. Spectators were greeted with posters and loudspeaker announcements advising that neither the match, nor the ability to see it, were guaranteed.

Most of the crowd saw the first points of the game when full-back Colin Bolderson gave the home side an early lead with a penalty, which Joe Karam equalled soon afterwards. Then New Zealand won a lineout and Sid Going made a break that led to a try by Duncan Hales. Karam missed the touchline conversion but was more successful with a second penalty goal shortly afterwards. Close to half-time, Going lost control of the ball at a scrum on the New Zealand 25 and it came back to Ron Evans who dropped a goal. New Zealand remained 10-6 ahead at the break.

The home side played with great commitment while New Zealand seemed somewhat uninterested, but they were made to pay attention when Ian Hopkins kicked a penalty for East Glamorgan, shortly after the restart, to reduce the lead to a single point. The superior New Zealand side dominated, without being able to break down the East Glamorgan defence, until Going made another sharp blind-side break for a try for Ian Stevens. Karam converted, and then cross-kicked into space for Hales to score his second try. Karam missed that conversion,

WELSH RUGBY UNION

East Glamorgan
v
New Zealand

NATIONAL STADIUM CARDIFF ARMS PARK

SATURDAY 30 DEC.,1972: KICK-OFF 2.15 p.m. Official Programme 10p indeed the normally reliable full-back had something of a goal-kicking off day. Controversy never seemed far away from the Seventh All Blacks and this game was no exception. Graham Whiting was the victim of foul play and left the field with a badly cut head, but with eight minutes left, the otherwise superb Going obstructed an opponent and after having his offence pointed out by Derek Brain he turned on his opposite number Gareth Evans and punched him so severely that he had to be rushed to hospital where he received a dozen stitches inside his mouth. Going was severely ticked-off and even New Zealand writer Terry McLean felt he should have been sent off. But he wasn't, and the sporting Evans was philosophical about it all: 'you have to take the rough with the smooth in rugby.' It was another incident that the tourists could have done without. Evans was replaced by future Welsh coach Dennis John, whose son Paul later played for Wales.

CORNWALL & DEVON 1972/73

Tuesday 2 January 1973
Recreation Ground, Redruth
Won 30-7

Although this game was officially billed as a South-Western Counties fixture, the match programme called the team Cornwall & Devon. The side contained only one international, Ken Plummer of Bristol, but Neil Bennett and eighteen-year-old John Scott were to play for England in future years and Peter Hendy toured New Zealand with England later in 1973. The captain of the side, Tommy Palmer of Gloucester, had toured South Africa with England in 1972. Experienced prop 'Stack' Stevens was originally selected for the match, but he withdrew as he was due to face the All Blacks in

CORNWALL & DEVON	NEW ZEALAND
R.C. Staddon (Exeter & Devon)	T.J. Morris
K.C. Plummer (Bristol & Cornwall)	D.A. Hales
T. Palmer (Gloucester & Cornwall, Capt.)	I.A. Hurst
R. Friend (Plymouth Albion & Devon)	G.B. Batty
R. Warmington (St Luke's College, Exeter & Devon)	M. Sayers
W.N. Bennett (St Luke's College, Exeter & Devon)	R.E. Burgess
A.F.A. Pearn (Bristol & Devon)	G.L. Colling
Forwards:	Forwards:
D.E.G. Hosking (Hayle & Cornwall)	K.K. Lambert
J. Lockyear (Exeter & Devon)	R.A. Urlich
A.P. Baxter (Exeter & Devon)	L.A. Clark
J.P. Scott (Exeter & Devon)	A.M. Haden
W.J. Baxter (Exeter & Devon)	I.M. Eliason
A.R. Cole (Exeter & Devon)	K.W. Stewart
P.J. Hendy (St Ives & Cornwall)	I.A. Kirkpatrick (Capt.)
A.J. Hollins (Bedford & Devon)	A.J. Wyllie

Scorers:
Cornwall & Devon: Try: Plummer. PG: Pearn.
New Zealand: Tries: Batty (3), Hurst (2), Burgess, Kirkpatrick. Con: Lambert.

Referee: E.M. Lewis (Wales).
Attendance: 16,000.

England colours the following Saturday. His place in the side was taken by Dave Hosking of Hayle. The Cornwall & Devon pack contained a pair of brothers, Paul and John Baxter of Exeter. At scrum-half was Alan Pearn of Bristol, an outstanding player with a fine record as a goal-kicker. The 1972/73 season brought him a personal-best haul of 557 points in all games. He was the first player in the country to pass 100, 200, 300 and 400 points and the only player to pass 500. Sadly for Pearn and his side, the game with the All Blacks was one of his very rare off days as a kicker. A similar fate awaited the kicking of Trevor Morris in this match, thus ensuring that he would not replace Joe Karam in the team to face England in the forthcoming Test. In fact, of the team that faced Cornwall & Devon, only Ian Kirkpatrick, Kent Lambert, Grant Batty and Alex Wyllie played against England, although there was surprise expressed that Ian Hurst did not make the side after his fine display in this game.

The home side had to face a strong wind in the first half, but competed well and reached the interval just a point adrift at 4-3. Morris hooked his first penalty attempt so badly that it almost went into touch, and there was no scoring until, in the twentieth minute, the speedy Batty won the race to the ball after Morris's kick ahead. Pearn was successful with a penalty after twenty-five minutes following a lineout offence, but there was no more scoring in the first half.

CORNWALL AND DEVON
RUGBY FOOTBALL UNIONS

CORNWALL
AND
DEVON
v.
NEW ZEALAND TOURING XV

REDRUTH
TUESDAY, 2nd JANUARY, 1973

OFFICIAL PROGRAMME   **15p**

Facing the strong wind, the All Blacks were relieved to get an early score in the second half, when home full-back Bob Staddon fumbled the ball. From the resulting scrum, Lin Colling fed Bob Burgess who scored under the posts. Morris could not convert. Pearn then missed three penalties in quick succession, any of which could have renewed pressure on the tourists, and after twenty-two minutes the All Blacks scored their third try. The try was made by Hurst, scored by Batty, and rather surprisingly converted by prop forward Kent Lambert, who had not kicked goals regularly since his schooldays. Thereafter, the All Blacks ran riot, scoring 4 tries in the space of eight minutes. First Batty kicked ahead and tackled winger Ralph Warmington. Burgess cross-kicked and Duncan Hales robbed Plummer of the ball and gave a scoring pass to Hurst. Lambert was narrowly wide with the conversion and also missed with his next kick, the attempted conversion of a try by Kirkpatrick. Another Burgess cross-kick had Plummer in difficulties and Colling and Hales sent their skipper away on a twenty-five-yard run to the line. Soon after this, Morris came into the line to give Batty his hat-trick, and Hurst completed the New Zealand scoring with a fine try after an excellent handling move. Morris returned to kicking duties to attempt the final two conversions, but he had no success. In total, Morris missed all six of his goal-kicks, while Pearn missed eight out of nine. There was just time after the final All Black score for the home side to grab a consolation try. Ian Eliason knocked on from the kick-off, Staddon entered the line when the resulting scrum ball was won, and Plummer crossed for the score.

Batty and Hurst were the stars of this New Zealand victory, with Eliason, Kirkpatrick and Lindsay Clark also impressing. Skipper Palmer and his co-centre Richard Friend tackled well for Cornwall & Devon, but this was eventually a comfortable win for the All Blacks.

ENGLAND   1972/73

Saturday 6 January 1973
Twickenham, London
Won 9-0

The England side to face the All Blacks included two new caps. Centre Peter Warfield had already impressed the tourists with his tackling for North-East Counties in the game at Bradford, while Frank Anderson, a member of the victorious North-West Counties team, owed his elevation to injuries sustained by Fran Cotton and his nominated replacement Mike Burton. Alan Old of Leicester was originally chosen to play at outside half, but he aggravated a hamstring injury on the day before the game. His replacement, John Finlan of Moseley, was not among

ENGLAND	NEW ZEALAND
S.A. Doble (Moseley)	J.F. Karam
A.J. Morley (Bristol)	B.G. Williams
P.J. Warfield (Rosslyn Park)	B.J. Robertson
P.S. Preece (Coventry)	G.B. Batty
D.J. Duckham (Coventry)	R.M. Parkinson
J.F. Finlan (Moseley)	I.N. Stevens
J.G. Webster (Moseley)	S.M. Going
Forwards:	Forwards:
C.B. Stevens (Penzance & Newlyn)	K.K. Lambert
J.V. Pullin (Bristol, Capt.)	R.W. Norton
W.F. Anderson (Orrell)	G.J. Whiting
C.W. Ralston (Richmond)	P.J. Whiting
P.J. Larter (Northampton)	H.H. Macdonald
J.A. Watkins (Gloucester)	A.J. Wyllie
A. Neary (Broughton Park)	I.A. Kirkpatrick (Capt.)
A.G. Ripley (Rosslyn Park)	A.R. Sutherland

Scorers:
New Zealand: Try: Kirkpatrick. Con: Karam. DG: Williams.

Referee: J. Young (Scotland).
Attendance: 70,000.

the selected reserves, but he was called into the side to form a Moseley club partnership with Jan Webster. New Zealand selected the same team that had defeated Scotland with two exceptions. Alistair Scown was replaced by Alan Sutherland, and Kent Lambert, who had replaced the injured Jeff Matheson during the Murrayfield game, retained his place now that Matheson was out of the tour.

Two days before the match, Sam Tucker, a Bristol and England hooker of the pre-war era, died. Tucker had played for Wavell Wakefield's England side against the invincible All Blacks in 1925, and it was appropriate that another Bristol man, John Pullin, should be England's hooker and captain for the current game.

The New Zealanders always looked the likely winners of this match, but there was further criticism in the British newspapers about the manner of the victory. Journalist John Reason was particularly hard on the tourists, especially concerning what he saw as a four-man game, involving just scrum-half Sid Going and his back row of Alex Wyllie, Alan Sutherland and Ian Kirkpatrick. 'It is four-man rugby, plain and simple. Very simple, and very, very plain,' was the Reason verdict.

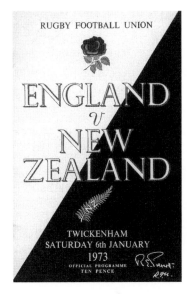

Sid Going was the undoubted star for the All Blacks. He virtually ran the game and was responsible for setting up the only try. After eight minutes of play, Grant Batty threw a long ball over the tail of a lineout, where Going caught it and broke through the first line of defence. The move was carried on by Wyllie, and when a ruck formed near the England line Kirkpatrick collected the ball, sold a dummy and ran through a huge gap to score. It was his eleventh international try, a new record for his country. Joe Karam converted and the score was still 6-0 when half-time arrived.

The only score of the second period came from an unlikely source. Bryan Williams had never dropped a goal before, yet when Finlan, under pressure, failed to find touch, Williams coolly dropped a forty-yard goal to put his side 9-0 ahead. England had their chances, notably in the second half when Peter Preece touched down, only to have the score correctly disallowed by referee Jake Young because Warfield's pass to Preece had been forward. There was also a narrow miss in the first half when Preece was unable to gather David Duckham's pass after a great run from the Coventry winger. Saddest of all for England was the failure of Sam Doble to land any of his four penalty goal attempts. It was, however, generally felt that if England had scored some points, the All Blacks would have done more than sit on their lead and would have created further scores of their own.

New Zealand coach Bob Duff was quick to defend his side's tactics. 'I may be old-fashioned but I've always believed you play to your strength, and that's what we've done so far. It's won us three Tests – and I wouldn't call them dull matches.' Few would have guessed that within months of this game England would defeat the All Blacks in their own back yard.

Wednesday 10 January 1973
Rodney Parade, Newport
Won 20-15

NEWPORT	NEW ZEALAND
R.J. Williams	T.J. Morris
G. Fuller	B.G. Williams
G. Talbot	B.J. Robertson
N. Edwards	G.R. Skudder
P. Ward	M. Sayers
D. Rogers	R.E. Burgess
A. Evans	S.M. Going (Capt.)
Forwards:	Forwards:
I. Barnard	G.J. Whiting
G. Williams	R.A. Urlich
B. Rowland	A.L.R. McNicol
L. Jones	I.M. Eliason
J. Watkins	P.J. Whiting
P. Watts	A.J. Wyllie
G. Evans (Capt.)	A.I. Scown
J.J. Jeffrey	B. Holmes

Scorers:
Newport: Try: Watkins. Con: R. Williams. PG: R. Williams (2).
DG: R. Williams.
New Zealand: Tries: Sayers, Williams. PG: Morris (2), Williams (2).

Referee: G.C. Lamb (RFU).
Attendance: 20,000.

Newport were not the power they had been when they lowered the colours of Wilson Whineray's All Blacks in 1963. They had only won 14 of their 25 games before the visit of New Zealand. They only included one international, John Jeffrey, who won his solitary cap against Lochore's side in 1967, but Lyn Jones and Robin Williams had both played for the Wales B side. Williams was a prodigious goal-kicker who also played for Cardiff and Pontypool. He scored a Welsh club record 517 points for the latter team in 1974/75. Newport were coached by Brian Jones, who had played in their 1954 and 1963 games with the All Blacks, and were captained by Geoff Evans, a popular open-side flank forward. New Zealand introduced Sandy McNichol for his first game since replacing Jeff Matheson, while Ian Kirkpatrick was rested and the captaincy reverted to Sid Going. It was, however, a strong side fielded on a ground where several touring sides had endured difficult games.

Newport started well and, after a few minutes, Robin Williams opened the scoring with a straightforward penalty. Trevor Morris equalised with a penalty, and then eased the All Blacks ahead with a second following a scuffle. Williams equalised with his second goal and the scores were tied 6-6 at half-time.

The second half had been underway only a few minutes when Bryan Williams kicked New Zealand back into the lead, and the tourists went further ahead when a Going break and quick ruck put George Skudder away. He was tackled wide out but was able to pass out of the tackle for Mark Sayers to score an unconverted try. The forward exchanges were now fierce and the referee regularly had to separate the players. Newport scored again when a poor clearing kick went straight to Williams, who dropped a goal. Newport tails were up and they were pressurising New Zealand, but a poor

RODNEY PARADE   JANUARY 10th 1973

NEW ZEALAND

v

NEWPORT

Official Programme   Ten Pence

pass was intercepted by Bruce Robertson who put Bryan Williams in for a try. The conversion was missed but Newport attacked again. Then, following a mix-up between Going and Burgess, Newport intercepted and took play close to the All Blacks' posts. From the ensuing maul, Jeff Watkins drove over for a try that Robin Williams converted. The final whistle went and Newport had given a good account of themselves without ever really threatening to beat New Zealand.

It had been another ill-tempered game which early in the second half erupted into a spectacular fight between Lyn Jones and Peter Whiting. Experienced referee George 'Larry' Lamb told them both to 'grow up!' The New Zealanders also accused Lamb of picking on Going by penalising him for crooked feeds to the scrum. 'I require that every player obeys the laws,' was the Air Commodore's reply.

Saturday 13 January 1973
Welford Road, Leicester
Won 43-12

The home side was coached by Leicester coach 'Chalkie' White. The squad had been well-prepared, with the selectors meeting for the first time in August, and the team was captained by England international David 'Piggy' Powell. The Northampton prop had visited New Zealand as a 1966 British Lion. Peter Larter was the only other England cap in the side, although Peter Wheeler, Garry Adey and Bob Wilkinson would represent their country in the future. Wilkinson had already enjoyed an impressive game against the tourists when playing for Cambridge University.

Despite all the preparations, the Midlands team was no match for the All Blacks, and the visitors recorded a resounding victory to end their games in England on a high note. The final score was the highest All Black total in Britain since the 1924 tourists defeated Durham 43-7. For the first time since the opening fixture at Gloucester, the All Blacks threw the ball around with great confidence and provided the large Welford Road crowd with some carefree and memorable rugby. Lin Colling, the more adventurous of the tourists' half-backs, found the game very much to his liking, and his long spin pass was a feature of the game. The first score came in the sixteenth minute when a high kick from Bob Burgess was allowed to bounce close to the home line. Ken Stewart gained possession and crossed between the posts, leaving Joe Karam the simplest of conversions. Five minutes later, Colling robbed his opposite number John Allen at a scrum. The half-back passed to Stewart who sent Burgess racing in at the corner. Again Karam converted. The Counties came back into the game after half an hour when the All Blacks' midfield lost the ball. Centre Mike Yandle made a good break, and then John Duggan, Larter and Powell carried the move on before Allen touched down. Dave Whibley added the conversion, but New Zealand scored again before half-time. Bruce Robertson caught a weak clearance from Whibley, and a fine move developed, culminating in Burgess drawing the full-back before giving Kirkpatrick a scoring pass. The New Zealand captain touched down near the corner, but Karam struck a brilliant conversion to make the half-time score 18-6.

The home outside half, Bleddyn Jones, was replaced at half-time by Alan Davies, a future coach of Wales. After twelve minutes of the second period, Graham Phillips was penalised for being offside and Karam stretched the lead with a penalty. Robertson then scored a try following a bout of inter-passing with Burgess. Whibley replied with a penalty after twenty-five minutes following obstruction by Stewart, but another All Black try came just three minutes later. Colling collected a poor home throw at a lineout near the Counties' line, touching down near the posts for Karam to convert. A good angled penalty from Whibley brought the home side into double figures, but three further New Zealand tries came in the last ten minutes. Colling made the first with a blind-side break that led to a try for Alan Sutherland. The next score came from Ian Hurst, a memorable effort involving good work from Duncan Hales and

MIDLAND COUNTIES (EAST)	NEW ZEALAND
D.F. Whibley (Leicester)	J.F. Karam
M.J. Duggan (Leicester)	D.F. Hales
M.J. Yandle (Leicester)	B.J. Robertson
G.N. Phillips (Northampton)	G.B. Batty
R.E. Morris (Northampton)	I.A. Hurst
B. Jones (Leicester)	R.E. Burgess
J.A. Allen (Leicester)	G.L. Colling
Forwards:	Forwards:
D.L. Powell (Northampton, Capt.)	G.J. Whiting
P.J. Wheeler (Leicester)	R.W. Norton
P.F. Duffy (Northampton)	L.A. Clark
P.J. Larter (Northampton)	A.M. Haden
R.M. Wilkinson (Cambridge University)	H.H. Macdonald
C.J. Baynes (Leicester)	K.W. Stewart
I. Clayton (Notts)	I.A. Kirkpatrick (Capt.)
G.J. Adey (Leicester)	A.R. Sutherland
Replacement:	
A.B.C. Davies (Notts) for Jones	

Scorers:
Midland Counties (East): Try: Allen. Con: Whibley.
PGs: Whibley (2).
New Zealand: Tries: Stewart, Burgess, Kirkpatrick, Robertson, Colling, Sutherland, Hurst, Batty. Cons: Karam (4). PG: Karam.

Referee: C. Thomas (Wales).
Attendance: 16,000.

Robertson. Finally, Grant Batty sprinted away to score, following a good run from Hurst. Karam missed the final three conversions, but still had the satisfaction of taking his tour points tally past 100.

Everybody played well for the All Blacks. Hurst and Robertson were impressive together in midfield, and Andy Haden definitely came out on top in his rematch at the lineout with Bob Wilkinson. Stewart, Graham Whiting and Hamish Macdonald also had outstanding games. Home scrum-half John Allen endured a difficult afternoon, despite scoring his team's only try. He was guilty of numerous fumbles and bad passes and was constantly under pressure. The day emphatically belonged to the All Blacks, a fact appreciated by the Leicester crowd, which applauded the tourists warmly at end of the match. The All Blacks had produced their best rugby in England in their first and last matches.

MUNSTER 1972/73

Tuesday 16 January 1973
Musgrave Park, Cork
Drawn 3-3

MUNSTER	NEW ZEALAND
T.J. Kiernan (Cork Constitution, Capt.)	T.J. Morris
P. Parfrey (University College, Cork)	B.G. Williams
F.P.K. Bresnihan (London Irish)	D.A. Hales
S. Dennison (Garryowen)	G.R. Skudder
J. Barry (Dolphin)	R.M. Parkinson
B.J. McGann (Cork Constitution)	I.N. Stevens
D.M. Canniffe (Cork Constitution)	G.L. Colling
Forwards:	Forwards:
P. O'Callaghan (Dolphin)	K.K. Lambert
J. Leahy (Cork Constitution)	R.A. Urlich
K. Keyes (Sunday's Well)	A.L.R. McNicol
M.I. Keane (University College, Cork)	I.M. Eliason
J. Madigan (Bohemians)	A.M. Haden
J. Buckley (Sunday's Well)	B. Holmes
S.M. Deering (Garryowen)	A.J. Wyllie (Capt.)
T.A.P. Moore (Highfield)	A.R. Sutherland

Scorers:
Munster: PG: McGann.
New Zealand: PG: Morris.

Referee: D.W. Jones (England).
Attendance: 15,000.

New Zealand went to Cork with confidence after their resounding win in Leicester, but also with some concerns. Munster, although not the leading Irish province at the time, would guarantee a warm welcome and a seriously tough game. Bizarrely, they had been either ahead or drawing nearly all their matches with major touring sides only to be denied in the final minutes of each. Sid Going dropped out of the side three hours before kick off with a thigh injury. Lin Colling stepped up to play and Alex Wyllie was made captain. New Zealand had previously chosen strong sides for midweek games but, with a match with Ireland only a few days away, they only retained a handful of Test match certainties for this game. Coached by Noel Murphy, Munster were led by Tom Kiernan, Ireland's veteran full-back who had captained the 1968 Lions in South Africa. The pack included tough forwards Phil O'Callaghan, Terry Moore, Shay Deering and Moss Keane who all played for Ireland, Keane later touring with the Lions in New Zealand in 1977. The experienced backline included Barry Bresnihan, another Lion from 1968. The match was as tough as expected and the Munster defence was outstanding. They made countless bone-crunching tackles, but were regularly penalised. Unfortunately for the tourists, neither Morris nor Bryan Williams was able to convert these opportunities, missing five straightforward kicks between them. This inability to kick goals nearly cost New Zealand the match.

After a scoreless first half, in which the inspired Keane and Moore were outstanding, the match resumed with similar fare. Then Barry McGann kicked a penalty to put the home side into the lead with half an hour to go. New Zealand attacked constantly but Ian Stevens, who had played provincial rugby as a half-back, seemed unable to catch the ball. He regularly dropped it or passed poorly.

This frustrated New Zealand, particularly as Mike Parkinson looked dangerous whenever he was in possession. Munster played a tighter game. Whenever McGann got the ball, he punted majestically into space and gave Morris and his wings a torrid afternoon. As the match went into injury time, New Zealand were facing their first defeat on Irish soil. Then O'Callaghan was penalised for handling the ball in a ruck and the nervous Trevor Morris stepped up and kicked a penalty to tie the game. The final whistle went and New Zealand had got out of jail and condemned Munster to another last-minute disappointment.

IRELAND 1972/73

Saturday 20 January 1973
Lansdowne Road, Dublin
Drawn 10-10

Irish supporters desperately wanted to see this international, anticipating their first win over the All Blacks, particularly as their side was in good form. They were unbeaten in the previous season's International Championship, one that ended incomplete after political violence in Ireland had forced Scotland and Wales to cancel their games in Dublin. Coach Syd Millar had assisted the Ulster side and attended the match at Leicester to check on the All Blacks. Ireland made four changes from their last international, with wing Tom Grace replacing Alan Duggan, and Kevin Mays coming in to the second row for his first cap. Fergus Slattery was joined in the back row by Terry

IRELAND	NEW ZEALAND
T.J. Kiernan (Cork Constitution, Capt.)	J.F. Karam
T.O. Grace (St Mary's College)	B.G. Williams
C.M.H. Gibson (NIFC)	B.J. Robertson
M.K. Flynn (Wanderers)	G.B. Batty
A.W. McMaster (Ballymena)	I.A. Hurst
B.J. McGann (Cork Constitution)	R.E. Burgess
J.J. Moloney (St Mary's College)	S.M. Going
Forwards:	Forwards:
R.J. McLoughlin (Blackrock College)	K.K. Lambert
K.W. Kennedy (London Irish)	R.W. Norton
J.F. Lynch (St Mary's College)	G.J. Whiting
W.J. McBride (Ballymena)	H.H. Macdonald
K.M.A. Mays (University College, Dublin)	P.J. Whiting
J.F. Slattery (Blackrock College)	A.J. Wyllie
J.C. Davidson (Dungannon)	I.A. Kirkpatrick (Capt.)
T.A.P. Moore (Highfield)	A.R. Sutherland

Scorers:
Ireland: Try: Grace. PGs: McGann (2).
New Zealand: Tries: Going, Wyllie. Con: Karam.

Referee: M. Joseph (Wales).
Attendance: 52,000.

Moore, who won his last cap in 1967, and Jimmy Davidson, who had not donned an Irish jersey since 1969. New Zealand restored Bob Burgess at the expense of Ian Stevens and Ian Hurst replaced Mike Parkinson at second five-eighth to win his first international cap. The All Blacks' pack remained untouched.

With the wind at their backs, Ireland began with fire and passion, taking the game to New Zealand, challenging for every ball and every inch of territory. Barry McGann kicked a penalty and the Irish scrum pushed the All Blacks off the ball. They ran the All Blacks ragged but were unable to score more points and as the minutes ticked by, the New Zealanders began to extinguish the fire and get on with their own game. After half an hour Sid Going used his strength to strip the ball from John Moloney at an Irish scrum and crash over for a try. Joe Karam, who earlier missed a penalty, converted. The All Blacks led 6-3 at half-time.

In the second half Going and Burgess deployed the tactical kick with ruthless efficiency, making Tom Kiernan scamper from touchline to touchline. Midway through the period, the excellent Kent Lambert broke away from a maul, and fed Burgess who passed in turn to Alex Wyllie. He ran through

Kiernan for a try that Karam was unable to convert. New Zealand then appeared to change tactics with only ten minutes to go. They began to kick the ball away rather than retain possession. Ireland suddenly got second wind and inspiration. Going was penalised for a crooked feed and McGann kicked a penalty to bring Ireland within reach. With only seconds to go Moloney broke away from a ruck close to halfway. He drew Grant Batty and passed to Grace, who ran, kicked long over Karam's head, and dived on the ball just ahead of the covering Burgess. The cheers of the crowd were deafening. The sides were level and McGann was given the task of converting the try to win the match for Ireland. The ball soared towards the posts, then veered to one side and missed by inches. The referee then blew for the end of the game. It was the first time Ireland had avoided defeat by New Zealand.

New Zealand were intensely disappointed not to have won the match, although in the end they were lucky to have avoided defeat. Kirkpatrick's All Blacks toured at a time when British and Irish rugby, collectively, was at its height. They suffered more defeats than their predecessors, yet they were closer than most of those who had toured before to achieving the first Grand Slam of wins over the four home unions.

NEATH & ABERAVON   1972/73

Wednesday 24 January 1973
The Gnoll, Neath
Won 43-3

Neath had won the inaugural WRU Challenge Cup the previous April, defeating Llanelli in the final. They were a tough side. Aberavon was also a leading club and the combined might of these clubs was thought likely to give New Zealand another fierce game. In a side of interesting players, Clive Shell was scrum-half. Shell's career coincided with that of Gareth Edwards and, as such, he was limited to only one international appearance, as a replacement for Edwards against Australia later in the year. The forwards included the Aberavon second-row partnership of Billy Mainwaring and Allan Martin, former and future Welsh internationals respectively. The back row also included Wilson Lauder, a Welsh schools international who won eighteen caps for Scotland. Shell's club partner John Bevan,

NEATH & ABERAVON	NEW ZEALAND
W. Davies (Neath)	J.F. Karam
D. Jenkins (Neath)	G.B. Batty
G. Ball (Neath, Capt.)	I.A. Hurst
J. Thomas (Aberavon)	D.A. Hales
K. Collier (Neath)	M. Sayers
D. Parker (Neath)	R.E. Burgess
R.C. Shell (Aberavon)	G.L. Colling
Forwards:	Forwards:
G. Shaw (Neath)	G.J. Whiting
M. Howells (Aberavon)	R.W. Norton
R. Lewis (Neath)	A.L.R. McNicol
W.T. Mainwaring (Aberavon)	H.H. Macdonald
A.J. Martin (Aberavon)	A.M. Haden
W.D. Morris (Neath)	K.W. Stewart
O. Alexander (Aberavon)	I.A. Kirkpatrick (Capt.)
W. Lauder (Neath)	A.J. Wyllie
	Replacement:
	B.G. Williams for Batty

Scorers:
Neath & Aberavon: PG: Martin.
New Zealand: Tries: Burgess (2), Karam, Batty, Hurst, Sayers, Kirkpatrick. Cons: Karam (6). PG: Karam.

Referee: P.E. Hughes (England).
Attendance: 14,800.

later an international and 1977 Lion, dropped out and was replaced by Dai Parker of Neath. Prop Walter Williams withdrew with injury and was replaced by Roy Lewis. The All Blacks changed most of their backs, including the injured Sid Going, but retained most of the forwards who had taken on Ireland.

After a series of games in Wales dominated by forward aggression, it was a relief to see New Zealand play open rugby as they had done regularly in England. Lin Colling wanted to move the ball, and in Bob Burgess the All Blacks had the dynamo that made it all click. Burgess escaped the home defence almost at will and was influential in all that was good from New Zealand. In a close opening phase, Joe Karam and Allan Martin exchanged penalties before the home defence was split open by running movements that ended with tries for Kirkpatrick and Karam. The full-back converted both and the All Blacks led 15-3 at half-time. The home side missed the power and aggression of the injured Brian Thomas, and was no match for New Zealand, except in the lineout.

In the second half the All Blacks put on an exhibition of running rugby. Nine minutes into the half, Grant Batty scored a try, then Burgess set up one for Ian Hurst. Burgess scored 2 tries himself in quick succession and Mark Sayers scored a fine try later in the game following good interplay with Hurst. Karam's conversion saw him end the game with 19 points. At last the All Blacks had shown

what they could do and they were loudly cheered off the field, something of a rarity in their previous matches in Wales.

BARBARIANS   1973

Saturday 27 January 1973
Cardiff Arms Park, Cardiff
Lost 23-11

When the Barbarians selectors sat down to select their side to play New Zealand, the successes of the 1971 Lions was in the forefront of their minds. The captain was John Dawes and he had eleven other Lions with him, along with Phil Bennett, at outside half and uncapped forwards Bob Wilkinson and Tom David. Llanelli prop Barry Llewelyn was originally selected but he had not recovered from a knee injury sustained in his club's cup win at Rhymney. Popular Scot Sandy Carmichael took his place. David came off the bench on the morning of the game to replace 'flu victim Mervyn Davies, and John Bevan replaced Gerald Davies who withdrew with a hamstring injury. Lions coach Carwyn James was asked for his opinions and there was no doubt, this was considered

BARBARIANS	NEW ZEALAND
J.P.R. Williams (London Welsh)	J.F. Karam
D.J. Duckham (Coventry)	B.G. Williams
C.M.H. Gibson (NIFC)	B.J. Robertson
S.J. Dawes (London Welsh, Capt.)	G.B. Batty
J.C. Bevan (Cardiff)	I.A. Hurst
P. Bennett (Llanelli)	R.E. Burgess
G.O. Edwards (Cardiff)	S.M. Going
Forwards:	Forwards:
R.J. McLoughlin (Blackrock College)	G.J. Whiting
J.V. Pullin (Bristol)	R.A. Urlich
A.B. Carmichael (West of Scotland)	K.K. Lambert
W.J. McBride (Ballymena)	H.H. Macdonald
R.M. Wilkinson (Cambridge University)	P.J. Whiting
T. David (Llanelli)	A.I. Scown
J.F. Slattery (Blackrock College)	I.A. Kirkpatrick (Capt.)
D.L. Quinnell (Llanelli)	A.J. Wyllie
	Replacement:
	G.L. Colling for Going

Scorers:
Barbarians: Tries: Edwards, Slattery, Bevan, Williams.
Cons: Bennett (2). PG: Bennett.
New Zealand: Tries: Batty (2). PG: Karam.

Referee: G. Domercq (FFR).
Attendance: 50,000.

the Fifth Lions Test against the All Blacks. New Zealand selected a strong side and took a gamble on the fitness of Sid Going. Alistair Scown replaced Sutherland, who had an eye infection, increasing the mobility of the back row. They took to the field with the intention to win through playing open rugby. There was a great cheer when the All Blacks performed the Haka for the only time on tour.

The excitement was intense and there was expectation that the Barbarians would win and that they would win in style. After four minutes John 'J.P.R.' Williams fielded the ball and ran before kicking

ahead. It was secured by the All Blacks' forwards close to halfway before Kirkpatrick passed the ball to Bryan Williams down the blind side. What happened next was one of the most celebrated scores in the history of rugby, immortalised in Cliff Morgan's famous television commentary: '...to Williams. This is great stuff. Phil Bennett covering. Chased by Alistair Scown. Brilliant, oh, that's brilliant. John Williams, Bryan Williams, Pullin, John Dawes. Great dummy. David, Tom David, the halfway line. Brilliant by Quinnell. This is Gareth Edwards, a dramatic start, what a score!' Edwards, who had felt lethargic before the game through the tension of the occasion, was running the opposite way when John Pullin and John Dawes were charging upfield but hit the line at top speed, taking Derek Quinnell's pass and swerving past Karam to sprint thirty-five yards to the corner. Quinnell may have tried to pass to John Bevan outside him. Had Bennett not decided to sidestep the All Blacks' back row in front of his own posts, the crowd would not have witnessed that remarkable score. Bennett missed the conversion but kicked a penalty shortly after. Both sides attacked with every conceivable opportunity, yet the tackles were hard and the exchanges of Test match intensity. Tom David and David Duckham made spectacular runs, the Llanelli flank forward brushing off New Zealand tackles, the Coventry wing weaving through the defence in a flash. New Zealand struggled to control the ball at a scrum on their line shortly afterwards, and Edwards disrupted Sid Going for Fergus Slattery to pick up and score the second try. Bennett converted, and then the ball was intercepted and moved quickly out to Bevan on the wing who handed off a defender before barging his way over in the corner for the third. The Barbarians were 17-0 ahead at half-time.

The break seemed to disrupt the Barbarians' momentum, or give New Zealand heart, for it was the All Blacks who started the second half stronger. Kirkpatrick was tackled on the Barbarians' line and lost the ball, but Karam kicked a penalty shortly afterwards. Then a few minutes later, Bryan Williams came in from his wing at top speed and created an overlap from which Grant Batty scored a good try. The New Zealand pack was playing well at this point and although the defences cancelled each other out, the All Blacks continued to attack. Eventually the fiery Batty made the most of a half-chance when the ball came to him via a kick, veering outside Dawes and chipping over John Williams's head to re-gather and score again. The conversions were missed but with the score at 17-11 New Zealand were back in the game. The Barbarians stepped up their play and Duckham caught a clearing kick from Lin Colling, who had replaced Going, and counter-attacked. Eventually the ball was moved through several pairs of hands, with forwards and backs involved, to John Williams who scored the decisive try. Bennett converted to complete the scoring. The performance of the Barbarians has been talked about ever since, but the All Blacks played their part in a tremendous game.

New Zealand captain Ian Kirkpatrick was chaired off the field by supporters, Kirkpatrick, a quiet, honourable man, was an outstanding loose forward, a no-nonsense player who possessed great power, pace and vision. He played in 39 internationals, 38 in succession, and scored 16 international tries in his ten-year international career.

The All Blacks then travelled to France to play the final 4 games of their tour. They won their provincial games but went down 13-6 to France. Thus ended a tour that in New Zealand eyes was unsuccessful, featuring, as it did, five defeats. There were lessons to be learned in public relations, and the selection of players and management, but they were popular tourists without, perhaps, the charisma of their predecessors.

1974
NEW ZEALAND TO IRELAND, WALES & ENGLAND

THE MATCHES

Combined Irish Universities	6 November 1974	Cork	won 10-3
Munster	9 November 1974	Limerick	won 14-4
Leinster	13 November 1974	Dublin	won 8-3
Ulster	16 November 1974	Belfast	won 30-15
Connacht	20 November 1974	Galway	won 25-3
IRELAND	23 November 1974	Dublin	won 15-6
Wales XV	27 November 1974	Cardiff	won 12-3
Barbarians	30 November 1974	Twickenham	drew 13-13

Played 8, Won 7, Drew 1, Lost 0. Scored: 127 points, Conceded: 50.

The New Zealand Tour Party:
J.F. Karam (Wellington), K.T. Going (North Auckland), B.G. Williams (Auckland), G.B. Batty (Wellington), T.W. Mitchell (Canterbury), B.J. Robertson (Counties), G.N. Kane (Waikato), I.A. Hurst (Canterbury), J.E. Morgan (North Auckland), D.J. Robertson (Otago), O.D. Bruce (Canterbury), S.M. Going (North Auckland), I.N. Stevens (Wellington), A.R. Leslie (Wellington), L.G. Knight (Auckland), I.A. Kirkpatrick (Poverty Bay), K.A. Everleigh (Manawatu), K.W. Stewart (Southland), P.J. Whiting (Auckland), J.A. Callesen (Manawatu), H.H. Macdonald (Canterbury), W.K.T. Bush (Canterbury), A.J. Gardiner (Taranaki), K.J. Tanner (Canterbury), K.K. Lambert (Manawatu), R.W. Norton (Canterbury), G.M. Crossman (Bay of Plenty).

Captain: A.R. Leslie. Manager: N.H. Stanley. Assistant Manager: J.J. Stewart.

Leading points scorer: J.F. Karam – 48 points.
Leading try-scorer: B.G. Williams – 4 tries.
Most appearances: G.B. Batty, A.R. Leslie, H.H. MacDonald – 7 games.

Wednesday 6 November 1974
The Mardyke, Cork
Won 10-3

COMBINED IRISH UNIVERSITIES	NEW ZEALAND
R.M. Spring (Dublin University, Capt.)	K.T. Going
P. Dee (Dublin University)	T.W. Mitchell
J.F. Crowe (University College, Dublin)	I.A. Hurst
R.G.A. Finn (University College, Dublin)	G.B. Batty
P. Parfrey (University College, Cork)	G.N. Kane
C. Sparks (University College, Dublin)	O.D. Bruce
D. Molloy (University College, Dublin)	I.N. Stevens
Forwards:	Forwards:
P.A. Orr (University College, Dublin)	W.K.TeP. Bush
J.L. Cantrell (University College, Dublin)	G.M. Crossman
M.P. Fitzpatrick (University College, Dublin)	K.K. Lambert
P. Gahan (University College, Dublin)	P.J. Whiting
K.M.A. Mays (University College, Dublin)	J.A. Callesen
C. Cantillon (University College, Cork)	L.G. Knight
J.C. Davidson (Queen's University, Belfast)	K.A. Eveleigh
H.W. Steele (Queen's University, Belfast)	A.R. Leslie (Capt.)

Scorers:
Combined Irish Universities: PG: Spring.
New Zealand: Try: Mitchell. PG: Going (2)

Referee: D.P. D'Arcy (Munster).
Attendance: 8,000.

New Zealand were invited to tour Ireland as part of the centenary celebrations of the Irish Rugby Football Union. The All Blacks were scheduled to play 6 games in Ireland, including an international, plus a non-capped international against Wales midweek and a tour climax against the Barbarians at Twickenham. They had toured Australia and Fiji earlier in the year, winning twelve of their 13 games with a drawn second international against Australia the only blemish to an otherwise impressive record. The first game of that tour featured a 117-6 win over South Australia. The All Blacks then strengthened their squad for the tour of Ireland. Under the leadership of Andy Leslie, the All Blacks took on a scratch student side that included internationals in Kevin Mays and Jimmy Davidson, but also had future internationals Phil Orr, who replaced the injured Tom Feighery from the original selection, Jimmy Crowe, John Cantrell, Mick Fitzpatrick and Pat Parfrey. Their captain was Dick Spring, who won three caps for Ireland in 1979 and entered Irish politics, becoming An Tánaiste, the deputy prime minister of the Republic of Ireland.

Spring opened the scoring early on with a straightforward penalty when Lawrie Knight was offside. New Zealand full-back Ken Going, brother of half-back Sid, missed two early penalty attempts.

Combined Universities of Ireland
v
New Zealand

The Mardyke
Cork
November 6th 1974
3.00 p.m.

Price 10p

After twenty-five minutes, half-back Ian Stevens, who had played as a five-eighth on the 1972/73 tour, broke from a scrum and kicked ahead. The ball deceived Spring, who seemed unsure of its flight, but Kevin Eveleigh got to it first and passed quickly to Terry Mitchell who raced in for the opening try of the tour. Eveleigh had a vigorous afternoon for which he received some criticism. The All Blacks were 4-3 ahead at half-time but appeared very sluggish. The home side had an energetic pack which disrupted the tourists but when New Zealand had the ball they seemed reluctant to move it through their backs.

In the second half, Going kicked two further penalties but they struggled to get any platform or rhythm to their game. They only managed to create one other try-scoring opportunity when Mitchell came off his wing and made a terrific break but the pass to Grant Batty, in space, was dreadful and the chance lost. It was an inauspicious start to the tour.

Saturday 9 November 1974
Thomond Park, Limerick
Won 14-4

MUNSTER	NEW ZEALAND
R.M. Spring (Cork Constitution)	J.F. Karam
P. Parfrey (UCC)	B.G. Williams
L. Moloney (Garryowen)	B.J. Robertson
J. Coleman (Highfield)	G.B. Batty
P. Lavery (London Irish)	J.E. Morgan
B.J. McGann (Cork Constitution, Capt.)	D.J. Robertson
D.M. Canniffe (Cork Constitution)	S.M. Going
Forwards:	Forwards:
O. Waldron (Clontarf)	K.J. Tanner
P.C. Whelan (Garryowen)	R.W. Norton
P. O'Callaghan (Dolphin)	A.J. Gardiner
M.I. Keane (Lansdowne)	H.H. Macdonald
J. Madigan (Bohemians)	P.J. Whiting
C.C. Tucker (Shannon)	I.A. Kirkpatrick
S.M. Deering (Garryowen)	K.W. Stewart
T.A.P. Moore (Highfield)	A.R. Leslie (Capt.)
	Replacement:
	I.N. Stevens for Going

Scorers:
Munster: Try: Moore.
New Zealand: Tries: Williams, Batty. PG: Karam (2).

Referee: K. Clark (Ulster).
Attendance: 10,800.

The All Blacks encountered several familiar faces after they moved to Limerick. Spring and Parfrey had been in the Universities side and several of the pack had been in the Ireland side New Zealand had drawn with eighteen months earlier. There was also Barry McGann, the captain, whose narrow miss in the dying seconds had denied Ireland their first win over New Zealand. Munster were the previous season's leading Irish province. Coached by Tom Kiernan, their side included Colm Tucker, then uncapped but a British Lion in 1980. The All Blacks made wholesale changes with only Grant Batty retaining his place in the backs and Peter Whiting and skipper Leslie in the pack. The New Zealand side was powerful, recognising the long history of tough tour encounters with Munster.

Facing the fiery men in red – and a gale – the All Blacks started well. After early skirmishes, a Karam penalty was held up in the wind. The Munster defence dithered and the All Blacks won the ball, moving it quickly out to Bryan Williams. The ball bounced fortuitously on its way to the Auckland wing but neither Parfrey nor Spring could catch him. The try was scored near the corner flag but the conversion was too difficult for Karam. The home pack then shaded the All Blacks and pressurised New Zealand into conceding penalties. However, McGann was unable to convert the opportunities presented to him. Close to half-time, lock John Madigan was caught offside and Karam kicked the goal that saw New Zealand 7-0 ahead at the break.

As hard as Munster tried to score, and as vociferously as the crowd encouraged them (including actor Richard Harris, a former Young Munster player), the All Blacks retained their composure and their control of the game. Karam kicked another penalty, then midway through the second half Sid Going switched the direction of play and Williams came into the line. He was tackled by several Munster players, but the ball was quickly recycled and moved to Batty in space for the second try. Going damaged his knee shortly afterwards and Ian Stevens came on to replace him. Munster never gave up and their efforts were eventually rewarded when Terry Moore scored a try from a tapped penalty on the stroke of full time. Unfortunately for the Munstermen, it was little more than a consolation.

Munster
V
New Zealand

Thomond Park
Limerick
November 9th 1974
3.00 p.m.

Irish Rugby Football Union
(Munster Branch)

IRFU
1874·1974

Hon. Secretary

Price 10p

Wednesday 13 November 1974
Lansdowne Road, Dublin
Won 8-3

Sid Going was unavailable for New Zealand and although the All Blacks' side was tinkered with, they fielded close to their strongest available. Grant Batty, Peter Whiting and Andy Leslie played their third match in succession. Ken Going was given another run out at full-back. Leinster were expected to provide New Zealand with a serious challenge. Their pack was robust and included Phil Orr, the mobile Old Wesley prop who had impressed the All Blacks in the first match of the tour. Orr later became Ireland's most-capped prop with 58 appearances and played Test match rugby against New Zealand for the British Lions in 1977. Their back row included Denis Hickie, holder of 6 Irish caps. His nephew, also called Denis,

LEINSTER	NEW ZEALAND
A.H. Ensor (Wanderers)	K.T. Going
T.O. Grace (St Mary's College)	B.G. Williams
J.F. Crowe (University College, Dublin)	I.A. Hurst
P. Andrucetti (St Mary's College)	G.B. Batty
V.A. Becker (Lansdowne)	J.E. Morgan
M.A.M. Quinn (Lansdowne)	D.J. Robertson
J.J. Moloney (St Mary's College)	I.N. Stevens
Forwards:	Forwards:
P.A. Orr (Old Wesley)	W.K.TeP. Bush
J.L. Cantrell (University College, Dublin)	R.W. Norton
J.F. Lynch (St Mary's College)	K.K. Lambert
E. O'Rafferty (Wanderers)	H.H. Macdonald
K.M.A. Mays (University College, Dublin)	P.J. Whiting
D.J. Hickie (St Mary's College)	I.A. Kirkpatrick
J.F. Slattery (Blackrock College, Capt.)	K.A. Eveleigh
W.P. Duggan (Blackrock College)	A.R. Leslie (Capt.)
Replacement:	
P. Inglis (Lansdowne) for Mays	

Scorers:
Leinster: DG: Quinn.
New Zealand: Tries: Whiting, Williams.

Referee: P. Beatty (Connacht).
Attendance: 12,000.

later played for Ireland. Leinster were captained by Fergus Slattery, a dynamic flank forward who had recently returned from a successful tour with the 1974 Lions'. A try-scorer for the Barbarians in the famous victory over the All Blacks the previous year, Slattery later captained his country and won sixty-one caps in a remarkable Irish career that stretched from 1970 to 1984.

After fierce, close exchanges early in the match, the Leinster cause was greatly hampered when lock Kevin Mays received a head injury from the boot of Kent Lambert, and had to be replaced by Paul Inglis. Nevertheless, the home pack put up a magnificent battle and was never subdued. Mick Quinn opened the scoring with a drop goal after thirteen minutes and although the Leinster forwards continued to pile on pressure, the New Zealand defence refused to crack. Eventually the visitors began to take control and on the stroke of half-time, a back-row move from a scrum involving Ian

Kirkpatrick and Andy Leslie put the supporting Peter Whiting in for the first try of the match. Going failed to convert, but New Zealand led 4-3 at half-time.

The All Blacks extended this a few minutes after the start of the second period when they launched a back move. Grant Batty came off his wing to make the extra man. Bryan Williams made the most of the chance, shrugged off a tackle and scored in the corner after a fine run. Again, the conversion was missed. The Leinster side then dug deep and launched attack after attack but New Zealand held firm, and although they eventually had the ascendancy it remained a tight, tense contest until the final whistle. There was no further score and New Zealand won a bruising match that lesser sides would have lost. Leinster were magnificent, but with Tony Ensor and Quinn unable to kick several penalty attempts between them they didn't take their chances.

The All Blacks were criticised for over-vigorous play but both sides had wounds to lick after the battle.

Saturday 16 November 1974
Ravenhill, Belfast
Won 30-15

ULSTER	NEW ZEALAND
C.H. McKibbin (Instonians)	J.F. Karam
S.E.F. Blake-Knox (NIFC)	B.G. Williams
R.A. Milliken (Bangor)	B.J. Robertson
H. Adams (CIYMS)	T.W. Mitchell
E.L. Grant (CIYMS)	J.E. Morgan
W.McM. McCombe (Bangor)	O.D. Bruce
W. Postlethwaite (CIYMS)	I.N. Stevens
Forwards:	Forwards:
P.J. Agnew (CIYMS)	K.J. Tanner
I. Kidd (Instonians)	G.M. Crossman
R.J. Clegg (Bangor)	A.J. Gardiner
W.J. McBride (Ballymena, Capt.)	H.H. Macdonald
C.W. Murtagh (Dungannon)	J.A. Callesen
S.A. McKinney (Dungannon)	L.G. Knight
J.C. Davidson (Dungannon)	K.W. Stewart
H.W. Steele (Ballymena)	A.R. Leslie (Capt.)

Scorers:
Ulster: PG: McCombe (5).
New Zealand: Tries: Stevens, Williams, Mitchell, Morgan.
Cons: Karam (4). PG: Karam (2).

Referee: J.R. West (Leinster).
Attendance: 15,000.

Ulster were resigned to being without their outstanding back, Mike Gibson, for their autumn games after he injured his Achilles tendon early in the season. The responsibility as fulcrum in the Ulster backs was left to Billy McCombe, an international in 1968 who made a successful return to the Irish team later in the season. Ulster won the Irish Provincial title under the captaincy of 1974 Lions leader Willie John McBride, and he was one of seven Ulster forwards who had confronted New Zealand the last time the sides met. New Zealand had experienced the nervous atmosphere of Belfast on their previous visit in 1972, and the threat posed by 'the troubles' hung around Ravenhill once again with the Army and police prominent. A week before the international with Ireland, the All Blacks retained a strong side but rested Peter Whiting and Ian Kirkpatrick. Sid Going was still struggling with injury and wasn't risked.

After a strangely tranquil opening quarter of an hour in which little of note happened the scoring began in spectacular fashion. Centre Bruce Robertson made a searing break and, although well tackled, the ball was quickly recycled for Ian Stevens to put Bryan Williams into space. They exchanged passes with the half-back racing over in the corner for a magnificent try. Joe Karam converted. McCombe, who had earlier missed narrowly with two long-range penalties, kicked two easier ones in quick succession to tie the scores before Karam kicked one for the All Blacks. McCombe then kicked two further penalties to see Ulster ahead 12-9 at the interval.

Having recognised the challenge had been made, the All Blacks increased their work-rate in the second half. After the New Zealand pack had tied up the Ulster defence, Stevens passed long to Williams, who this time went for a try himself, fending off the challenge of Eddie Grant on his way to the line. Karam converted and added a penalty before Ulster struck back with McCombe's fifth successful goal. The All Blacks then worked Terry Mitchell in for a try following a simple back-row move before Robertson and Karam combined for a Joe Morgan score. Karam added the extra points.

The match was over and it contrasted greatly with recent games. While the forward exchanges were hard, they were not unduly fierce, and the backs of both sides attempted to score tries. It was a good game and New Zealand played some exhilarating rugby.

Wednesday 20 November 1974
Galway Sportsground, Galway
Won 25-3

CONNACHT	NEW ZEALAND
M.A. Corley (Galwegians)	K.T. Going
J.P. Connolly (Galwegians)	T.W. Mitchell
J.K. Colleran (Corinthians)	B.J. Robertson
N. Jennings (Bective Rangers)	G.B. Batty
D. Lyons (Lansdowne)	G.N. Kane
C.J. Smyth (Corinthians)	D.J. Robertson
R.D. O'Toole (Corinthians)	S.M. Going
Forwards:	Forwards:
R.J. McLoughlin (Blackrock College)	K.J. Tanner
B. Troy (Lansdowne)	R.W. Norton
P.M. McLoughlin (Northern)	K.K. Lambert
M.G. Molloy (London Irish)	H.H. Macdonald
J.B. Glynn (Corinthians)	J.A. Callesen
M.J.A. Sherry (Lansdowne)	I.A. Kirkpatrick (Capt.)
M.N. Casserley (Galwegians, Capt.)	K.A. Eveleigh
D.L. Galvin (Athlone)	L.G. Knight
Replacement:	
N. Hogan (Ballinasloe) for Galvin	

Scorers:
Connacht: PG: Smyth.
New Zealand: Tries: Kirkpatrick (2), Mitchell, Batty, S. Going.
Cons: K. Going. PG: K. Going.

Referee: G. Jamison (Ulster).
Attendance: 6,000.

Connacht, the most junior of the four Irish provinces, had traditionally been able to select stubborn sides that were difficult to overcome. Although they had lost to Argentina the previous year, this was their first match against a 'major' touring side. Connacht were captained by Galwegian flank forward Mick Casserley, an Irish trialist. He was able to call upon experienced international forwards Ray McLoughlin and Mick Molloy. Molloy earned the first of his twenty-seven caps in 1966 when McLoughlin was the Ireland captain. McLoughlin, a Lion in 1966 and 1971, was joined in the front row by his brother Phelim. Flanker Mick Sherry was to play for Ireland before the end of the season. Mick Browne of Blackrock College withdrew with an injury before the game and was replaced by Brendan Troy. The capacity of the small Galway Sportsground was increased when touchline seats were borrowed from Lansdowne Road for the match, but facilities were such that the teams changed at a nearby pub. The Going brothers played for New Zealand, with Sid having a run-out to check his fitness before the international. New Zealand were expected to win comfortably, and there was local concern that if the backs played with the zip of the Ulster game Connacht might be in for a torrid afternoon. There was a minute's silence before the game for Erskine Childers, the President of the Republic of Ireland who had died a few days earlier.

The home side raised their game for the match, with Ray McLoughlin and Molloy inspirational in the pack, and they troubled a seemingly lethargic All Blacks' side. Nevertheless, Ken Going opened

Connacht v New Zealand
SPORTSGROUND, GALWAY
WEDNESDAY, 20th NOVEMBER, 1974
Referee: MR. G. A. JAMISON

DINNER
in honour of the
New Zealand XV
Galwegian Football Club
Glenina

the scoring after ten minutes with a penalty goal but it was late in the half before they scored again when a kick out of defence was run back at the Irish side by Ken Going. He linked with Kirkpatrick who made good ground before being hauled down, and from the ruck, the Going brothers sent Terry Mitchell in for the opening try. Although he missed the conversion, Ken Going joined a back movement in the dying seconds of the half to give Grant Batty a half chance, from which he skilfully scored. The conversion missed but New Zealand led 11-0 at half-time.

In the second half the All Blacks ran back a missed touch kick from which Sid Going scored the tourists' third try. Again the conversion missed. Young Connacht outside half Ciaran Smyth kicked a penalty midway through the half after Niall Hogan had replaced the injured number eight Leo Galvin. New Zealand scored again when a quickly tapped Sid Going penalty was finished off by Kirkpatrick, who had enjoyed several powerful runs during the afternoon. Then the New Zealand backs combined to create space for Kirkpatrick to sprint in from forty yards for a fine try that brought rapturous applause from the crowd. Ken Going, at last, managed to kick a conversion.

It was not a particularly convincing display from the All Blacks, and there was some dismay that Batty was regularly involved in fighting during the game. Nevertheless, Sid Going had come through the match without any adverse reaction and was fit for the international with Ireland.

IRELAND   1974

Saturday 23 November 1974
Lansdowne Road, Dublin
Won 15-6

IRELAND	NEW ZEALAND
A.H. Ensor (Wanderers)	J.F. Karam
T.O. Grace (St Mary's College)	B.G. Williams
J.F. Crowe (University College, Dublin)	B.J. Robertson
R.A. Milliken (Bangor)	G.B. Batty
P. Parfrey (University College, Cork)	J.E. Morgan
M.A.M. Quinn (Lansdowne)	D.J. Robertson
J.J. Moloney (St Mary's College)	S.M. Going
Forwards:	Forwards:
R.J. McLoughlin (Blackrock College)	K.J. Tanner
K.W. Kennedy (London Irish)	R.W. Norton
J.F. Lynch (St Mary's College)	K.K. Lambert
W.J. McBride (Ballymena, Capt.)	H.H. Macdonald
M.I. Keane (Lansdowne)	P.J. Whiting
S.A. McKinney (Dungannon)	I.A. Kirkpatrick
J.F. Slattery (Blackrock College)	K.W. Stewart
T.A.P. Moore (Highfield)	A.R. Leslie (Capt.)

Scorers:
Ireland: PG: Ensor (2).
New Zealand: Tries: Karam. Con: Karam. PG: Karam (3).

Referee: R.F. Johnson (England).
Attendance: 42,000.

The All Blacks increased the intensity of their preparation and their play for the international match, and although it would have been nice for Ireland to win in their centenary season, Leslie and his team had no intention of doing the honourable thing by losing. In fact, Ireland played somewhat below the level expected of them. They were the defending Five Nations Champions and had only lost once at Lansdowne Road since 1967, yet the All Blacks never permitted them to get into the game. Despite typical fire and tenacity up front, they were outplayed in nearly every facet of play. Ireland awarded new caps to Pat Parfrey and Jimmy Crowe, while Mick Quinn was chosen at outside half. There were no new caps in the New Zealand side but they welcomed back Kent Lambert and Hamish MacDonald, who had missed their last international with Australia, and Sid Going who, despite a heavily strapped knee, took the field.

After Ireland put pressure on in the first few minutes, the New Zealand pack took control and dominated proceedings from then on. After ten minutes Tony Ensor failed to deal with a garryowen, the All Blacks piled in and the ball came back to Going who moved it quickly to Joe Karam, who beat two men to score a try, which he converted. Ensor redeemed himself by kicking a penalty shortly afterwards but Karam restored the six point lead with a penalty close to half-time. New Zealand led 9-3 at the break.

Early in the second half, Ensor kicked another penalty to put Ireland within range of New Zealand, but Karam kicked two further penalties to see the All Blacks home 15-6. The score didn't reflect the All Blacks' dominance.

New Zealand played very well and were comfortable winners. Their forwards were outstanding and Karam was superlative at full-back. For Ireland the match had come a year too late as many of their players were now veterans and in the twilight of their international careers. Five of the forwards, including captain Willie John McBride, were to play their last internationals during the 1974/75 season. Bill McBride was a remarkable player. He played 63 times for Ireland, scarcely missed a match after his debut in 1962 and made five Lions tours, played in a record 17 Test matches. Having beaten Ireland, the Five Nations Champions, New Zealand then went to Cardiff to play Wales, arguably the strongest European team, then the Barbarians in London three days later, who were, in effect, the British Lions. It was a busy week.

WALES XV   1974

Wednesday 27 November 1974
Cardiff Arms Park, Cardiff
Won 12-3

WALES XV	NEW ZEALAND
J.P.R. Williams (London Welsh)	J.F. Karam
T.G.R. Davies (Cardiff)	B.G. Williams
R.T.E. Bergiers (Llanelli)	B.J. Robertson
I. Hall (Aberavon)	G.B. Batty
J.J. Williams (Llanelli)	I.A. Hurst
P. Bennett (Llanelli)	D.J. Robertson
G.O. Edwards (Cardiff, Capt.)	S.M. Going
Forwards:	Forwards:
A.G. Faulkner (Pontypool)	K.J. Tanner
R.W. Windsor (Pontypool)	R.W. Norton
D.B. Llewelyn (Llanelli)	K.K. Lambert
G.A.D. Wheel (Swansea)	H.H. Macdonald
D.L. Quinnell (Llanelli)	P.J. Whiting
T.J. Cobner (Pontypool)	I.A. Kirkpatrick
T.P. Evans (Swansea)	K.A. Eveleigh
T.M. Davies (Swansea)	A.R. Leslie (Capt.)
Replacements:	Replacement:
W.R. Blyth (Swansea) for Hall,	L.G. Knight for Eveleigh
J.D. Bevan (Aberavon) for Bergiers	

Scorers:
Wales: PG: Bennett.
New Zealand: Try: Kirkpatrick. Con: Karam. PG: Karam (2).

Referee: D.P. D'Arcy (IRFU).
Attendance: 50,000.

Wales put together as strong a side as they could manage at the time for this midweek match with New Zealand. Several players were unavailable and some of the returning Lions had only just begun playing again. Barry Llewelyn returned to the Welsh XV for the first time since the 1972 international with New Zealand. Trefor Evans and 'Charlie' Faulkner were uncapped. Faulkner joined Pontypool hooker Bobby Windsor in the front row, while the third member of the unit who later achieved fame as the 'Pontypool Front Row', Graham Price, sat on the replacements' bench. Evans, Faulkner and Price were to win their first caps in Paris the following January. The Welsh selectors picked two predominantly front-line jumpers in Derek Quinnell and Geoff Wheel, while Allan Martin, a fine lineout jumper, joined Price on the sidelines. Gareth Edwards was reinstated as captain. The All Blacks brought back Ian Hurst at the expense of Joe Morgan and Kevin Eveleigh for Ken Stewart as the only changes from the international in Dublin. It was not regarded as an official international and caps were not awarded yet it was treated as such by both sides.

New Zealand were immediately on top and Wales seemed sluggish. Nevertheless they defended skilfully as the New Zealand pack began to dominate. The first score was after thirty minutes when Joe Karam kicked a penalty. This was equalised by Phil Bennett and shortly afterwards, Welsh centre Ian Hall, who had made his debut for Wales against New Zealand in 1967, suffered a shocking broken leg and was replaced by Roger Blyth. As Hall was stretchered off so Eveleigh left the field of play with a knee ligament injury to be replaced by Lawrie Knight. The scores were tied at 3-3 at the break.

After half-time Wales had their best spell and attacked incessantly but were repelled by the All Blacks. Then Bryan Williams had a try disallowed following a cross-kick from Karam, referee Paddy

Gareth Edwards with Sid Going at his heels. Throughout the 1970s these two battled for the title of best half-back in the world.

D'Arcy adjudging the winger in front of the kicker, but New Zealand were not to be denied. After a series of rucks and mauls the ball shot out to Ian Kirkpatrick, who ran in from fifteen yards for a try which Karam converted. Wales went back on to the attack but then New Zealand attacked aggressively and Wales infringed for Karam to kick another penalty. It was the final score of the game.

The New Zealand pack played magnificently and the backs ran with pace and purpose. Leslie, Kirkpatrick and Going were outstanding. It was a tribute to the determination of the Welsh defence that the score wasn't more. It was a day Phil Bennett would want to forget. His place kicking wasn't of its usual standard. He missed four penalties in the first half and failed to get the best from his outside backs. The extraordinary outside half who had terrorised the Springboks a few months earlier now looked very ordinary. When Wales next played, Bennett was left out.

BARBARIANS 1974

Saturday 30 November 1974
Twickenham, London
Drawn 13-13

The last game of the All Blacks' eight-match tour saw a rematch of the Barbarians encounter, nearly two years on from the celebrated game in Cardiff. Expectation was high for a repeat of that remarkable match – even the referee, George Domerq, was the same. This time the venue was Twickenham and the focus for the Barbarians' selectors was the successful 1974 British Lions team. Although not all the Lions were available for selection, a strong team was chosen based around the 1974 side. The pack was the Lions' Test eight, but only Andy Irvine and Gareth Edwards of the backs had toured. However, they provided the

BARBARIANS	NEW ZEALAND
A.R. Irvine (Heriot's FP)	J.F. Karam
T.G. R Davies (Cardiff)	B.G. Williams
P.J. Warfield (Cambridge University)	B.J. Robertson
P.S. Preece (Coventry)	G.B. Batty
D.J. Duckham (Coventry)	I.A. Hurst
J.D. Bevan (Aberavon)	D.J. Robertson
G.O. Edwards (Cardiff)	S.M. Going
Forwards:	Forwards:
J. McLaughlan (Jordanhill)	K.J. Tanner
R.W. Windsor (Pontypool)	R.W. Norton
F.E. Cotton (Coventry)	K.K. Lambert
W.J. McBride (Ballymena, Capt.)	P.J. Whiting
G.L. Brown (West of Scotland)	H.H. Macdonald
R.M. Uttley (Gosforth)	I.A. Kirkpatrick
J.F. Slattery (Blackrock College)	K.W. Stewart
T.M. Davies (Swansea)	A.R. Leslie (Capt.)

Scorers:
Barbarians: Try: M. Davies. PG: Irvine (3).
New Zealand: Tries: Leslie, Williams. Con: Karam. PG: Karam.

Referee: G. Domercq (France).
Attendance: 68,000.

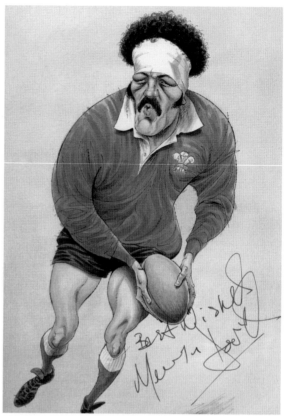

Barbarians try scorer, Welsh number 8 Mervyn Davies who was part of the successful Lions team of 1971. Davies later captained Wales to the Grand Slam in 1976. This excellent caricature is by John Ireland. (John Ireland)

All Blacks with a huge challenge. This time there weren't the opportunities for the silky runners in the Barbarians' backline to light up Twickenham as they had Cardiff Arms Park the previous year. Despite the talents of Gerald Davies and David Duckham there was an air of the scratch team about them. New Zealand made one change to the line-up from the game with Wales, Ken Stewart replacing the injured Eveleigh. Peter Whiting passed a fitness test on his shoulder that morning. The All Blacks were the superior side in a match that never remotely lived up to the heights of excitement seen in Cardiff. Indeed, had the tourists made the most of the opportunities they created and not made errors that the Barbarians capitalised upon, they would have won the match with something to spare.

The Barbarians opened the scoring with a penalty from Irvine following a high tackle. Joe Karam equalised with a penalty before All Blacks skipper Andy Leslie scored a try after a Barbarians attack broke down in their own 25. Karam missed the kick, as he did several others, but the All Blacks led 7-3 at half-time.

Irvine kicked two penalties early in the second half before Bryan Williams collected a fine cross-kick from Grant Batty to score a try for New Zealand that Karam converted. The Barbarians' solitary try came courtesy of an uncharacteristic error by All Blacks full-back Joe Karam. Irvine's high garryowen was misfielded and the ever-present Mervyn Davies gathered the loose ball to crash through Leslie and score. Irvine's conversion, which would have won them the match, went wide.

The Barbarians continued the tradition of selecting an uncapped player and this honour went to Aberavon outside half John Bevan, a late replacement in the Wales XV three days earlier. He subsequently won four caps for Wales and toured New Zealand with the 1977 Lions. He later became Welsh national coach but tragically died of cancer aged thirty-eight in 1986. New Zealand captain Andy Leslie, whose sons Martin and John later played for Scotland, was a rugged number eight who came to prominence late in his career. He was elected captain for his first international and led the side in each of his 10 Test matches. The man who captained New Zealand on an unbeaten tour to celebrate the Centenary of the IRFU later became the Irish Rugby Football Union's Director of Coaching.

1978

NEW ZEALAND TO BRITAIN & IRELAND

THE MATCHES

Cambridge University	18 October 1978	Cambridge	won 32-12
Cardiff	21 October 1978	Cardiff	won 17-7
West Wales	25 October 1978	Swansea	won 23-7
London Counties	28 October 1978	London	won 37-12
Munster	31 October 1978	Limerick	lost 12-0
IRELAND	4 November 1978	Dublin	won 10-6
Ulster	7 November 1978	Belfast	won 23-3
WALES	11 November 1978	Cardiff	won 13-12
South & South-West Counties	15 November 1978	Bristol	won 20-0
Midland Counties	18 November 1978	Leicester	won 20-15
Combined Services	21 November 1978	Sandhurst	won 34-6
ENGLAND	25 November 1978	Twickenham	won 16-6
Monmouthshire	29 November 1978	Newport	won 26-9
North of England	2 December 1978	Birkenhead	won 9-6
North & Midlands of Scotland	5 December 1978	Aberdeen	won 31-3
SCOTLAND	9 December 1978	Edinburgh	won 18-9
Bridgend	13 December 1978	Bridgend	won 17-6
Barbarians	16 December 1978	Cardiff	won 18-16

Played 18, Won 17, Drew 0, Lost 1. Scored: 364 points, Conceded: 147.

The New Zealand Tour Party:
B.J. McKechnie (Southland), C.J. Currie (Canterbury), R.G. Wilson (Canterbury)*, B.G. Williams (Auckland), S.S. Wilson (Wellington), R. Kururangi (Counties), B.R. Ford (Marlborough), B.J. Robertson (Counties), W.M. Osborne (Wanganui), J.L. Jaffray (Otago), N.M. Taylor (Bay of Plenty), O.D. Bruce (Canterbury), E.J. Dunn (North Auckland), D.S. Loveridge (Taranaki), M.W. Donaldson (Manawatu), J.C. Ashworth (Canterbury), W.K.T. Bush (Canterbury), B.R. Johnstone (Auckland), G.A. Knight (Manawatu), J.E. Black (Canterbury), A.G. Dalton (Counties), J.K. Fleming (Wellington), A.M. Haden (Auckland), J.K. Loveday (Manawatu), F.J. Oliver (Otago), B.G. Ashworth (Auckland), W.G. Graham (Otago), G.N.K. Mourie (Taranaki), L.M. Rutledge (Southland), A.A. McGregor (Southland)*, G.A. Seear (Otago). (*replacement on tour)

Captain: G.N.K. Mourie. Manager: R.W. Thomas. Assistant Manager: J. Gleeson.

Leading points scorer: B.J. McKechnie – 89 points.
Leading try-scorer: S.S. Wilson & B.J. Robertson – 5 tries.
Most appearances: G.N.K. Mourie & B.G. Williams – 14 games.

Wednesday 18 October 1978
Grange Road, Cambridge
Won 32-12

New Zealand hosted a tour by Australia during the summer and won the Test series 2-1. The previous year they defeated the 1977 British Lions, largely through the deficiencies of the tourists' back play. They rebuilt their forward unit and Graham Mourie took over from Frank Oliver as captain. Of the Cambridge University team that lined up to face the All Blacks in the first game of the 1978 tour, only scrum-half John Robbie had played international rugby. He had first been capped by Ireland in 1976 and he later emigrated to South Africa, where he came close to gaining a cap for his adopted country. Of the remaining fourteen Cambridge players, only Welshman Eddie Butler was a future international. Centre Matthew Fosh had played first-class cricket

CAMBRIDGE UNIVERSITY	NEW ZEALAND
I.R. Metcalfe (St Catharine's)	B.J. McKechnie
P. Frackleton (Pembroke)	R.R. Kururangi
M.K. Fosh (Magdalene)	B.J. Robertson
A.M. Laycock (Emmanuel)	B.R. Ford
R.H. Tyler (Fitzwilliam)	N.M. Taylor
J.F. Thornton (Magdalene)	O.D. Bruce
J.C. Robbie (Christ's, Capt.)	M.W. Donaldson
Forwards:	Forwards:
R.J. Brooman (Trinity)	J.C. Ashworth
J.J.H. Grant (St Catharine's)	J.E. Black
S.E. Killick (Queens')	W.K. Bush
N.R.M. Heath (Emmanuel)	J.K. Loveday
J.N. Ford (Emmanuel)	J.K. Fleming
C. O'Callaghan (St John's)	B.G. Ashworth
S.J. Glanvil (Pembroke)	G.N.K. Mourie (Capt.)
E.T. Butler (Fitzwilliam)	A.A. McGregor
Replacement:	
M.F. Parr (Trinity Hall) for Frackleton	

Scorers:
Cambridge University: Try: Tyler. Con: Robbie. PGs: Robbie (2).
New Zealand: Tries: Donaldson (2), Taylor, Mourie.
Cons: McKechnie (2). PGs: McKechnie (4).

Referee: K. Rowlands (Wales).
Attendance: 8,500.

for Essex. The students were coached by former Scotland international Ian Robertson, with assistance from forwards coach Murray Meikle, a New Zealander who had played for Otago. Robertson, now a distinguished broadcaster on the game, was entertainingly honest when assessing his side's chances: 'If our tackling improves 1,000 per cent, and our handling 500 per cent, all we need to win is a miracle.'

The match, played in lovely weather, was watched by a record crowd for the ground, with many others gaining free vantage points on the roofs of nearby college buildings. The tourists performed the Haka – a welcome sight following its almost total absence on the 1972 tour – and New Zealand started confidently, Brian McKechnie kicking three penalties within the opening fifteen minutes. The first try of the tour followed soon after the full-back's third goal, half-back Mark Donaldson exchanging passes with Bruce Robertson before touching down in the left-hand corner. McKechnie added the extras with a superb conversion and the tourists stretched their lead to 21-0 when Mark Taylor latched onto a spilled ball after Fosh was tackled, scoring near the posts for McKechnie to covert again. There was no further score in the first half and New Zealand led 21-0 at the break.

Cambridge started the second half with renewed confidence and scored an early try when full-back Ian Metcalfe created an overlap for winger Richard Tyler to touch down. Tyler was stopped on the line by Barry Ashworth, but had enough strength to force his way over. Robbie converted and also kicked a penalty from fifty metres to narrow the gap to 21-9. McKechnie put the All Blacks further ahead with a simple penalty, before another long-range goal from Robbie sent Cambridge into double figures. Things had not gone to plan for the tourists in the second half and they failed to score for half an hour, but they finished strongly with two unconverted tries in the final ten minutes. Donaldson got the first, kicking the ball downfield when Robbie failed to control it from a maul and scoring after running half the length of the pitch. The New Zealand half-back then fed Doug Bruce from a blind-side break. Bruce kicked ahead, the ball was toed on by Brian Ford and skipper Graham Mourie was there to score.

After a promising start, this was not the best of performances by the All Blacks. Many passes had been dropped, and the Cambridge second rows, Nigel Heath and Justin Ford, took a lot of lineout ball from John Loveday and John Fleming. Cambridge actually won the second half 12-11. Mark Donaldson had been the most impressive New Zealand player, with Mourie and McKechnie also enjoying good matches, but the tourists knew they would have to improve if they were to defeat Cardiff in the next game. Cambridge University went on to record a 25-7 victory over their Oxford rivals in the Varsity match. Everybody involved in the New Zealand game played, with the exception of Paul Frackleton, Andy Laycock and Steve Glanvil.

CARDIFF   1978

**Saturday 21 October 1978
Cardiff Arms Park, Cardiff
Won 17-7**

The All Blacks ventured into Wales for the first time on tour to face a confident Cardiff side which had only lost one of its 11 previous games and had dished out some fearful beatings to several sides. They had a substantial pack including young lock Robert Norster, who was a British Lion in 1983 and 1989, and a powerful front row consisting of hooker Mike Watkins, who later captained Wales, and props Mike Knill, who had been capped by Wales, and captain Barry Nelmes, who was to earn his sixth cap for England in the forthcoming international with New Zealand. He would be accompanied in that game by number eight John Scott. The half-backs were Gareth Davies and Terry Holmes. Davies had been groomed to succeed Phil Bennett, who had retired from internationals during the close season, while Holmes had the

CARDIFF	NEW ZEALAND
P. Rees	C.J. Currie
D. Thomas	S.S. Wilson
P.C.T. Daniels	W.M. Osborne
M. Murphy	B.G. Williams
C. Camilleri	J.L. Jaffray
W.G. Davies	E.J. Dunn
T.D. Holmes	D.S. Loveridge
Forwards:	Forwards:
F.M.D. Knill	B.R. Johnstone
M.J. Watkins	A.G. Dalton
B.G. Nelmes (Capt.)	G.A. Knight
H. de Goede	F.J. Oliver
R.L. Norster	A.M. Haden
C. Smith	L.M. Rutledge
R. Dudley-Jones	G.N.K. Mourie (Capt.)
J.P. Scott	G.A. Seear

Scorers:
Cardiff: Try: Smith. DG: Davies.
New Zealand: Tries: Wilson (2), Osborne. Con: Currie. PG: Currie.

Referee: R.C. Quittenton (RFU).
Attendance: 40,000.

unenviable task of succeeding Gareth Edwards at club and international level. Lock Hans de Goede played for Canada and Pat Daniels later played for Wales in the centre. Chris Camilleri, a speedy wing, later played rugby league. They were forced to change their selected side when Stuart Lane dropped out of the back row with injury and was replaced by Carl Smith. New Zealand completely changed their side except Mourie but still fielded a very strong team. They included Bryan Williams, who had played in the violent encounter between the sides of 1972, and who received a silver salver from the Cardiff club before kick-off to commemorate his 100th match for New Zealand.

Cardiff had the best of things early on with their forwards all over the All Blacks. They had the edge in the scrum and Norster was dominant in the lineout. However, rather against the run of play, Clive Currie kicked a penalty to open the scoring. Cardiff returned to the attack but continued to find scoring difficult. Eventually they were awarded a free kick and from this Gareth Davies dropped a goal to equalise. The Cardiff backs had a collective off day. Holmes and Davies were indifferent and Daniels and Mike Murphy in the centre, both fine footballers, were indecisive. It was this midfield unit which was guilty of the mistake which turned the match. While on the attack, some ponderous back play resulted in a misdirected pass from Murphy that was intercepted by Stu Wilson, who raced sixty-five metres and

CARDIFF
v
NEW
ZEALAND

Official Souvenir Programme 20p

scored between the Cardiff posts. Currie converted and with New Zealand 9-3 ahead at the interval the momentum was now with the tourists.

The second half was all New Zealand, as hard as Cardiff battled up front. Bill Osborne scored a glorious try, created by an Eddie Dunn chip over the Cardiff defence that Lyn Jaffray gathered. He drew Paul Rees and passed to Osborne for the Wanganui centre to score. New Zealand were now winning more ball and using their backs to attack. Bryan Williams came into the backline and created an overlap for Wilson to score his second try. Late on Cardiff scored a try when Jaffray was robbed close to his goal line and Carl Smith scored, but by then it was nothing more than a consolation.

Having selected fine forwards and adopted a tight approach on the last few tours, New Zealand suddenly displayed an open style of rugby. It was quite a shock to the home side.

WEST WALES 1978

Wednesday 25 October 1978
St Helen's, Swansea
Won 23-7

The four leading clubs in the west of Wales combined, as they had in 1967, to face the All Blacks. They were expected to provide New Zealand with the biggest challenge outside the Test matches as they had a powerful side. They had eleven internationals in the starting line-up and of the others only hooker Jeff Herdman was never capped. Mysteriously they failed to work together as a team, and despite the cajoling of captain Derek Quinnell and the energy of Ray Gravell, they found it difficult to get into the match for prolonged periods. New Zealand changed most of the side and Wayne Graham started his first game of the tour in the New Zealand back row. Locks Frank Oliver and John Loveday were injured and could not be considered.

The match became a bruising encounter that New Zealand started by pressurising

WEST WALES	NEW ZEALAND
W.R. Blyth (Swansea)	B.J. McKechnie
H.E. Rees (Neath)	S.S. Wilson
R.W.R. Gravell (Llanelli)	W.M. Osborne
R.T.E. Bergiers (Llanelli)	B.G. Williams
J.J. Williams (Llanelli)	N.M. Taylor
D.S. Richards (Swansea)	O.D. Bruce
R.C. Shell (Aberavon)	M.W. Donaldson
Forwards:	Forwards:
S.J. Richardson (Aberavon)	B.R. Johnstone
J. Herdman (Swansea)	J.E. Black
P.D. Llewellyn (Swansea)	G.A. Knight
G.A.D. Wheel (Swansea)	J.K. Fleming
A.J. Martin (Aberavon)	A.M. Haden
G.J. Roberts (Swansea)	W.G. Graham
T.P. Evans (Swansea)	G.N.K. Mourie (Capt.)
D.L. Quinnell (Llanelli, Capt.)	G.A. Seear
Replacements:	Replacement:
D.L. Nicholas (Llanelli) for Williams,	L.M. Rutledge for Seear
R.D. Moriarty (Swansea) for Evans	

Scorers:
West Wales: Try: Bergiers. PG: Blyth.
New Zealand: Tries: Wilson (2), Knight. Con: McKechnie.
PG: McKechnie (2), Williams.

Referee: A. Welsby (RFU).
Attendance: 40,000.

the home side and not allowing them to gain familiarity with their colleagues. There was a major fight between the forwards early on and referee Alan Welsby had to warn both captains as to the conduct of their forwards. After fifteen minutes, during which both packs continued to collide with great force, Roger Blyth was forced off the field with a knee injury. John 'J.J.' Williams moved to full-back while Blyth was receiving treatment and New Zealand attacked the gap out wide. Bryan 'Bee Gee' Williams was brought down by 'J.J.' close to the line but he made a double movement and was penalised. Shortly after Blyth returned, New Zealand turned over West Wales, ball and Donaldson broke down the blind side for Gary Knight to score after a passing rush. The conversion was missed. John Williams was raked by the All Blacks' pack in the process and was stretchered off with deep stud marks to his leg. He was

replaced by David Nicholas, a future international. Within minutes, Nicholas had his nose broken but continued to play, and after some scrappy play by New Zealand, he was put in for a try but dropped the ball with the line at his mercy. The next score was in injury time at the break when Bryan Williams kicked a long-range penalty to see New Zealand ahead 7-0 at half-time.

Trefor Evans injured his knee and was replaced by Richard Moriarty during the interval. West Wales had the best of the opening exchanges of the second half and, when Brian McKechnie failed to clear a ball to touch, Roy Bergiers scored a try. The conversion was missed but Blyth and McKechnie then exchanged penalties to see the All Blacks 10-7 ahead. The All Blacks had struggled in the first half and were a little fortunate to be ahead but they dominated the game from this point, swarming all over the field. They scored a second try when Gary Seear gathered a sliced kick from Blyth, and Donaldson again exploited the blind side to create a try for Stu Wilson, although the home players stopped playing when they spotted a forward pass. The referee didn't and awarded the try, which McKechnie converted. Wilson then scored his second try when Bryan Williams came in off his wing to make the extra man in the backs and the Wellington wing touched down close to the corner. The final minutes were as tough as the first, and Moriarty was escorted from the field, the Swansea forward who captained Wales in the 1987 World Cup being concussed. West Wales offered little in attack other than a few fine runs from Elgan Rees, who had played Test rugby for the Lions the previous year but was still awaiting his first appearance for Wales.

LONDON COUNTIES   1978

Saturday 28 October 1978
Twickenham, London
Won 37-12

The London Counties side included eight internationals. Peter Warfield, Derek Wyatt, Maurice Colclough, Chris Ralston and Bob Mordell were England players, the half-backs Ron Wilson and Alan Lawson were Scotland caps and Keith Hughes had played for Wales. The team was, however, a scratch one which had not trained much together and certainly hadn't played competitively as a unit. New Zealand made one change to the intended starting line-up, John Ashworth coming in when Brad Johnstone withdrew with a muscle injury. John Fleming was tried as a number eight.

The All Blacks scored after just six minutes when Derek Wyatt allowed a high kick from Eddie Dunn to bounce. Robert Kururangi was there to collect the

LONDON COUNTIES	NEW ZEALAND
K.M. Bushell (Harlequins and Kent)	C.J. Currie
R.O. Demming (Bedford and Eastern Counties)	R.R. Kururangi
K. Hughes (London Welsh and Surrey)	B.J. Robertson
P.J. Warfield (Rosslyn Park and Sussex)	B.R. Ford
D.M. Wyatt (Bath and Eastern Counties)	N.M. Taylor
R. Wilson (London Scottish and Middlesex)	E. Dunn
A.J.M. Lawson	D.R. Loveridge
(London Scottish and Middlesex)	
Forwards:	Forwards:
T.C. Claxton (Harlequins and Middlesex)	J.C. Ashworth
P. d'A. Keith-Roach	A.G. Dalton
(Rosslyn Park and Eastern Counties, Capt.)	
A.J. Cutter (Harlequins and Surrey)	W.K. Bush
M.J. Colclough (Angouleme and Sussex)	A.M. Haden
C.W. Ralston (Richmond and Middlesex)	F.J. Oliver (Capt.)
S.R.G. Pratt (London Scottish and Surrey)	L.M. Rutledge
R.J. Mordell (Rosslyn Park and Middlesex)	B.G. Ashworth
A.C. Alexander (Harlequins and Middlesex)	J.K. Fleming
Replacement:	
I.D. Williamson (Blackheath and Kent) for Bushell	

Scorers:
London Counties: PG: Bushell (3), Williamson.
New Zealand: Tries: Kururangi (2), Robertson, Dunn, Oliver, Ford.
Cons: Currie (5). PG: Currie.

Referee: C. Norling (Wales).
Attendance: 17,000.

ball and score, leaving Clive Currie a fairly simple conversion. Outside half Ron Wilson then rashly attempted a quick drop-out from his 22 that was run back by Andy Dalton, and from the resulting maul Mark Taylor fed

Kururangi for the winger to score his second try, Currie again converting. Billy Bushell kicked a penalty for London, but after twenty-eight minutes the tourists scored their third try when Warfield had a clearance kick charged down by Bruce Robertson. It was a soft try for the All Black centre and once again Currie added the conversion points. Bushell kicked a second penalty towards the end of the half, which finished with the visitors leading 18-6.

The second half featured three more tries for the tourists, the first a brilliant solo effort from Dunn, who sold several dummies before touching down. This was the only try that Currie failed to convert, although he had a poor success rate with penalty kicks, goaling just one out of five. Both he and Dunn, who himself made a hash of a long-range penalty, had difficulty kicking out of the exceptionally long Twickenham grass. Bushell kicked his third penalty to bring the score to 22-9, but after fifty minutes Dave Loveridge robbed Lawson at a scrum, sold a dummy and set Barry Ashworth off on a move that led to a try for Frank Oliver. Then two more dummies from Dunn, followed by a kick ahead, created a final try for Brian Ford. Bushell had to leave the field with a badly cut head – he required fourteen stitches in his ear – and his replacement, Ian Williamson, landed a further penalty for London, but Currie had the final say with a lengthy penalty. The unusually small crowd did not approve of the All Blacks electing to kick at goal when the match was already won, and there was much booing, prompting a rebuke over the public address.

For all their forward domination in this match, the All Blacks had not taken full advantage of the weaknesses in the opposition, and the backs had been disappointing as a unit. Eddie Dunn had provided moments of genius, but there was still much that needed improving in the tourists' general play. Rugby writer Wallace Reyburn added an amusing postscript to the match in his book about the tour. When Clive Currie was asked why he did not dig deeper into the Twickenham turf when placing the ball for his goal-kicks, he replied: 'I was afraid of disturbing the wildlife.'

MUNSTER 1978

Tuesday 31 October 1978
Thomond Park, Limerick
Lost 12-0

There had been several close games between the two sides and New Zealand anticipated a fiery welcome, but they were expected to beat Munster. However, in one of the most famous games played in Ireland Munster, coached by Tom Kiernan, were to be victorious over New Zealand. The All Blacks had an eye on the international with Ireland the following weekend but nevertheless chose a strong side for the game. Munster had a side brimming with skill and passion. Their side included nine internationals plus three others who were to be capped by the end of the season. They had the inspirational Moss Keane in the second row and Gerry McLoughlin, then uncapped, at prop. Keane had toured

MUNSTER	NEW ZEALAND
L.A. Moloney (Garryowen)	B.J. McKechnie
M.C. Finn (UC Galway)	S.S. Wilson
S.P. Dennison (Garryowen)	B.J. Robertson
G. Barrett (Cork Constitution)	B.G. Williams
D.St J. Bowen (Cork Constitution)	J.L. Jaffray
A.J.P. Ward (St Mary's College)	E.J. Dunn
D.M. Canniffe (Lansdowne, Capt.)	M.W. Donaldson
Forwards:	Forwards:
G.A.J. McLoughlin (Shannon)	B.R. Johnstone
P.C. Whelan (Garryowen)	J.E. Black
L. White (London Irish)	G.A. Knight
B.O. Foley (Shannon)	F.J. Oliver
M.I. Keane (Lansdowne)	A.M. Haden
C.C. Tucker (Shannon)	W.G. Graham
C. Cantillon (Cork Constitution)	G.N.K. Mourie (Capt.)
D.E. Spring (Dublin University)	A.A. McGregor
	Replacements:
	W.M. Osborne for
	Robertson

Scorers:
Munster: Try: Cantillon. Con: Ward. DG: Ward (2).

Referee: C. Thomas (Wales).
Attendance: 12,000.

New Zealand with the Lions in 1977, while McLoughlin later achieved god-like status after scoring a try for Ireland at Twickenham in 1982. Also in the pack was lock Brendan Foley, whose son Anthony later played for Munster and Ireland. The home side was captained by Donal Canniffe, an intelligent, perceptive scrum-half who had played twice for Ireland. Sadly Canniffe's father collapsed and died while listening to the game on the radio. Immediately outside Canniffe was the mercurial Tony Ward. A prodigious goal-kicker and elusive runner, he was later out of favour with the Irish selectors who preferred the more predictable Ollie Campbell. He was, nonetheless, a British Lion in 1980 and is now a respected rugby journalist.

New Zealand took control and moved the ball confidently, but they were set back when the Munster defence, which was already aggressive, reached new levels. Stu Wilson was brought into the New Zealand backline in an attempt to create space for Bryan Williams. He was spotted by Seamus Dennison who cut the flying wing down with a tackle that brought a gasp then a cheer from the crowd. And so it continued. The All Blacks won the majority of ball but they were knocked back or down, or frequently both, by a series of severe Munster tackles completed without regard for their own safety. The match was eleven minutes old when the scoring opened. Ward, deep in his own half, kicked diagonally for Jimmy Bowen to chase. The wing got to the ball ahead of Wilson, whom he wrong-footed before racing away. He weaved through the New Zealand defence but as he was about to be hauled down he passed to Christy Cantillon in support and the flank forward scored by the posts. The crowd, which had loudly applauded every stride of Bowen's run, erupted into deafening cheers that had barely diminished when Ward converted. Munster harried and disrupted the All Blacks and Graham Mourie battled hard to keep the side together. Ward took a long-range penalty, the only such kick attempted during the game. It fell short but McKechnie knocked it on in front of his posts. From the ensuing scrum Ward dropped a goal. New Zealand raced back up into Munster territory but they were unable to break through, the home side forcing errors and, with Ward in imperious form, the ball was regularly kicked clear long to touch. Munster led 9-0 at half-time.

In the second half the All Blacks won more ball and tried everything in their repertoire to break down the Munster defence but the tackling remained as committed as it had been early on. Bruce Robertson was replaced by Bill Osborne, who was tackled hard by Colm Tucker with his first touch of the ball. The Munster pack played as if all were loose forwards with Keane particularly disruptive. Ward continued to pressurise the All Blacks with his masterful kicking. With ten minutes to go he kicked into the All Blacks' 22 and Wilson, hoping it would roll over the goal line, delayed and had to concede a five-yard scrum. From the scrum Tucker picked up and Ward dropped his second goal to put Munster out of sight. The excitement and tension was extraordinary. There was no further score and Munster won 12-0. It was the first time New Zealand had lost in Ireland and only the second time New Zealand had failed to score outside international matches.

Six years to the day after the All Blacks lost to Llanelli, they were out-thought, out-played and out-scored once again. Munster's victory was complete. After the match coach Jack Gleeson was criticised for describing the Munster tactics as 'defeatist' and for the tacklers 'kamikaze'. Skipper Mourie was more generous stating: 'they played the type of game we tried to play – but played it better.' He recognised that the defeat was comprehensive and that New Zealand had not had the wherewithal to deal with the way Munster played. He was also resolute that this would not happen again to the All Blacks.

**Saturday 4 November 1978
Lansdowne Road, Dublin
Won 10-6**

Anything short of a victory for Ireland would have been an anticlimax following the heroics of Munster four days before. New Zealand licked their wounds and chose a very strong side. Bruce Robertson was still injured so Bill Osborne played at centre and Brian Ford replaced Bryan Williams on the wing. Clive Currie was the only new cap in the New Zealand side. Ireland made several changes to the team they had last fielded against England the previous March and had a new captain in Shay Deering. His selection was something of a surprise as he had previously been an occasional rather than regular member of Ireland's back row. Mike Gibson, who had played on the wing the previous season, returned to the centre

IRELAND	NEW ZEALAND
L.A. Moloney (Garryowen)	C.J. Currie
T.J. Kennedy (St Mary's College)	S.S. Wilson
C.M.H. Gibson (NIFC)	W.M. Osborne
A.R. McKibbin (London Irish)	B.R. Ford
A.C. McLennan (Wanderers)	N.M. Taylor
A.J.P. Ward (Garryowen)	O.D. Bruce
C.S. Patterson (Instonians)	M.W. Donaldson
Forwards:	Forwards:
P.A. Orr (Old Wesley)	B.R. Johnstone
P.C. Whelan (Garryowen)	A.G. Dalton
E.M.J. Byrne (Blackrock College)	W.K.TeP. Bush
M.I. Keane (Lansdowne)	F.J. Oliver
D.E. Spring (Dublin University)	A.M. Haden
J.F. Slattery (Blackrock College)	L.M. Rutledge
S.M. Deering (Garryowen, Capt.)	G.N.K. Mourie (Capt.)
W.P. Duggan (Blackrock College)	G.A. Seear
	Replacement:
	B.G. Williams for Ford

Scorers:
Ireland: PG: Ward (2).
New Zealand: Try: Dalton. DG: Bruce (2).

Referee: C. Norling (Wales).
Attendance: 50,000.

to partner Paul McNaughton, but the Greystones centre withdrew to be replaced by Alistair McKibbin. Terry Kennedy and Colin Patterson won their first caps.

The initial squaring-up phase of the game went on longer than usual and ten minutes passed before either side attempted a back move. Then the game opened up. Doug Bruce dropped a goal to put the All Blacks ahead midway through the half but Tony Ward equalised with a penalty shortly afterwards. Both sets of forwards battled away with the Irish pack challenging everything, but New Zealand were superior in the loose. Andy Haden had a fine game in the lineout. However, the score remained 3-3 at half-time.

Ireland
versus
New Zealand
I.R.F.U. Sat 4th November 1978. Lansdowne Road

Official Twenty Pence

Bruce kicked a second drop goal shortly after the restart and he was joined on the field by Bryan Williams a few minutes later after Ford pulled a leg muscle. The lead was again short-lived when Ward was late tackled by Graham Mourie and kicked a penalty to equalise. Ireland, with four Munster heroes in the team, then applied great pressure on the All Blacks but were unable to score. New Zealand escaped the Irish stranglehold and, with time running out, Mark Donaldson broke from a lineout in the Irish 22 and passed inside to Andy Dalton for the hooker to score an unconverted try.

The game could have gone either way, Ward missed a couple of drop goals and penalties at crucial times and Currie had been wayward with penalty attempts. Gary Seear, who had dominated the tail of the lineout, missed one long-range kick. New Zealand monopolised possession but their backs made too many mistakes under Irish pressure. Dalton's try was too late in the game for Ireland to reply and New Zealand won 10-6.

Tuesday 7 November 1978
Ravenhill, Belfast
Won 23-3

New Zealand rested most of their Test match players a few days before they took on Wales. They were confident their side, captained by Bruce Robertson in Graham Mourie's absence, could account for Ulster, who were not as strong as they had been in the recent past. The side included Colin Patterson, who had made his Irish debut three days before, and Mike Gibson, now a veteran who first took the field against New Zealand for Cambridge University in 1963. Ron Elliott was capped later in the season, and alongside Harry Steele and captain Stewart McKinney in the pack was Willie Anderson, a youthful forward who later captained Ireland. Alistair McKibbin withdrew with injury and was replaced by Chris Gardner.

Ulster played the first half with a gale at their backs, hoping to unsettle the All Blacks early on and score some points when they had the advantage of the weather. Although they attacked they seldom looked like scoring and, after spending the first quarter of the game in defence, the All Blacks took control and eased into Ulster territory. Bryan Williams kicked a fine forty-five-metre penalty into the wind to open the scoring, and then crossed for a try after a clean break by Robertson. The conversion missed but New Zealand led 7-0 at half-time.

In the second half, Brian McKechnie and Adrian Goodrich exchanged penalties before John Black finished off a forward drive from a lineout to score a try. McKechnie converted from the touchline with a splendid kick but he failed to convert a later try from Robert Kururangi. The Counties wing scored when Barry Ashworth and Wayne Graham tied up the Ulster defence with good runs after which a three-quarter move made at pace created the room for him to run in. McKechnie completed the scoring with a late penalty and although New Zealand had won they were unconvincing and frequently kicked away their possession. In the second half they played with the wind but failed to make good use of it. Ulster had battled away but had spent most of the match defending. They had only one clear chance when Gibson, who was otherwise starved of the ball, made a break but the ball went astray.

ULSTER	NEW ZEALAND
W.R.J. Elliot (Bangor)	B.J. McKechnie
J. Myles (Malone)	R. Kururangi
C.M.H. Gibson (NIFC)	B.J. Robertson (Capt.)
A. Irwin (Queen's University, Belfast)	B.G. Williams
C. Gardner (Queen's University, Belfast)	J.L. Jaffray
A. Goodrich (Ballymena)	E.J. Dunn
C.S. Patterson (Instonians)	D.S. Loveridge
Forwards:	Forwards:
B. O'Kane (Ballymena)	J.C. Ashworth
G.G. Beringer (London Irish)	J.E. Black
A. Henry (Malone)	W.K.TeP. Bush
W.A. Anderson (Dungannon)	J.K. Loveday
D. Dalton (Malone)	J.K. Fleming
S.A. McKinney (Dungannon, Capt.)	B.G. Ashworth
A. McLean (Ballymena)	L.M. Rutledge
H.W. Steele (Ballymena)	W.G. Graham
Replacement:	
R. Stewart (Malone) for Patterson	

Scorers:
Ulster: PG: Goodrich.
New Zealand: Tries: Williams, Black, Kururangi. Con: McKechnie. PG: McKechnie (2), Williams.

Referee: P.E. Hughes (England).
Attendance: 17,000.

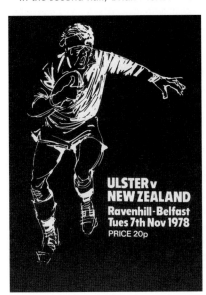

ULSTER v
NEW ZEALAND
Ravenhill - Belfast
Tues 7th Nov 1978
PRICE 20p

Saturday 11 November 1978
Cardiff Arms Park, Cardiff
Won 13-12

WALES	NEW ZEALAND
J.P.R. Williams (Bridgend, Capt.)	C.J. Currie
J.J. Williams (Llanelli)	S.S. Wilson
R.W.R. Gravell (Llanelli)	B.J. Robertson
S.P. Fenwick (Bridgend)	B.G. Williams
C.F.W. Rees (London Welsh)	W.M. Osborne
W.G. Davies (Cardiff)	O.D. Bruce
T.D. Holmes (Cardiff)	D.S. Loveridge
Forwards:	Forwards:
A.G. Faulkner (Pontypool)	B.R. Johnstone
R.W. Windsor (Pontypool)	A.G. Dalton
G. Price (Pontypool)	W.K.TeP. Bush
G.A.D. Wheel (Swansea)	F.J. Oliver
A.J. Martin (Aberavon)	A.M. Haden
J. Squire (Pontypool)	L.M. Rutledge
P. Ringer (Ebbw Vale)	G.N.K. Mourie (Capt.)
D.L. Quinnell (Llanelli)	G.A. Seear
	Replacement:
	B.J. McKechnie for Currie

Scorers:
Wales: PGs: Davies (3), Fenwick.
New Zealand: Try: Wilson. PGs: McKechnie (3).

Referee: R.C. Quittenton (RFU).
Attendance: 50,000.

Wales had won the Grand Slam the previous season, a prize achieved largely through a powerful pack. However, an era had come to an end during the summer. Several players retired from international rugby or from playing altogether and they had been beaten in the Test series on a tour to Australia. Thus they approached their first match without Gareth Edwards, Phil Bennett, Gerald Davies and inspirational forward Terry Cobner. They brought in young half-backs Terry Holmes and Gareth Davies to replace Edwards and Bennett with Clive Rees, a Lion in 1974, replacing Davies. Cobner's place in the back row was taken by the uncapped Paul Ringer. J.P.R. Williams led Wales for the first time but his team was given little chance, particularly after the West Wales defeat. The All Blacks recalled the fit-again Bruce Robertson and moved Bill Osborne to second five-eighth at the expense of Mark Taylor for what was the 200th match New Zealand had played in Britain and Ireland. The forwards were as had played Ireland but Mark Donaldson, who was originally selected, withdrew with an ankle injury and Dave Loveridge replaced him to win his first cap at half-back with Brian McKechnie occupying the vacancy on the bench. Loveridge became one of New Zealand's greatest half-backs. He played 24 Tests for the All Blacks and later captained his country.

Wales kicked off and took the game to New Zealand from the outset. After four minutes Gareth Davies kicked a penalty then Wales surged back into the New Zealand half and the tourists conceded another penalty. Davies kicked the goal again and Clive Currie, injured in a tackle from Steve Fenwick, left the field to be replaced by McKechnie. Currie's broken jaw meant he took no further part in the

tour. With Wales dominating play, Fenwick added a third penalty midway through the half. In danger of the game slipping away from them, New Zealand attacked and the ball went to Bill Osborne. He spotted space behind the Welsh defence and cross-kicked for Stu Wilson to win the race to the ball for a good try. Davies kicked another penalty before McKechnie kicked one for New Zealand. However, Wales went in at the break 12-7 ahead.

The second half was a very close affair with the forwards and backs cancelling each other out. However, after fifteen minutes of th second half Ray Gravell was caught offside in front of his posts and McKechnie kicked an easy penalty. Wales were now only ahead 12-10. With two minutes left Bobby Windsor threw into the lineout. Geoff Wheel leapt high at the front and palmed it back while Andy Haden went careering out of the middle of the lineout. Referee Quittenton penalised Wheel for leaning on Frank Oliver and, under intense pressure, McKechnie calmly kicked the penalty

Far left: *J.P.R. William's Welsh side that narrowly lost to New Zealand.*

Left: *Brian McKechnie celebrates the controversial goal kick that saw New Zealand win with a couple of minutes to go.*

to win the match for New Zealand. They had been fortunate, as Mourie conceded afterwards, but they took their chances, something that Wales had failed to do.

However, there was uproar. Wheel's offence was deemed marginal while Haden's dive out of the lineout was later admitted to be a ploy designed to trick the referee. The argument was ferocious and vitriolic: Wheel leant on Oliver so it rightly was a penalty to New Zealand; Haden cheated at the lineout so it ought to have been a penalty to Wales. Neither side denied their offence, but Quittenton, who was the one that mattered, only saw that of Wheel. The debate between Wales and New Zealand which had raged since the dispute over Bob Deans' try of 1905 now had a new chapter.

SOUTH & SOUTH-WEST 1978

Wednesday 15 November 1978
Memorial Ground, Bristol
Won 20-0

Centre-three-quarter Mike Beese of Bath and Somerset, an England cap in 1972, was due to lead the home side, but withdrew through injury. The captaincy passed to Mike Rafter of Bristol, with Ricky Pellow coming in for Beese. The entire back row of Rafter, John Scott and John Watkins had played for England, as had full-back Peter Butler, winger Alan Morley, scrum-half Peter Kingston and prop Barry Nelmes. John Palmer, Steve Mills and Paul Ackford were future England caps, and prop forward John Doubleday was most unfortunate not to win full international honours. He was to become an England replacement in 1979 and he toured the Far East at the end of that season, playing in Test matches against sides that at that time did not merit capped status. There was much disappointment locally that Bristol's

SOUTH & SOUTH-WEST	NEW ZEALAND
P.E. Butler (Gloucester & Gloucestershire)	N.M. Taylor
A.J. Morley (Bristol & Gloucestershire)	B.G. Williams
S. Donovan (Torquay Athletic & Devon)	B.J. Robertson
R.S. Pellow (Falmouth & Cornwall)	R.R. Kururangi
R. Mogg (Gloucester & Gloucestershire)	J.L. Jaffray
J.A. Palmer (Bath & Somerset)	E.J. Dunn
P.J. Kingston	D.S. Loveridge
(Gloucester & Gloucestershire)	
Forwards:	Forwards:
B.G. Nelmes (Cardiff & Gloucestershire)	J.C. Ashworth
S.G.F. Mills	J.E. Black
(Gloucester & Gloucestershire)	
R.J. Doubleday	G.L. Knight
(Bristol & Gloucestershire)	
R.G. Corin (St Ives & Cornwall)	J.K. Loveday
P.J. Ackford (Rosslyn Park & Devon)	J.K. Fleming
J.A. Watkins	W.G. Graham
(Gloucester & Gloucestershire)	
M. Rafter (Bristol & Gloucestershire)	G.N.K. Mourie (Capt.)
J.P. Scott (Cardiff & Devon)	G.E. Seear
	Replacement:
	S.S. Wilson for Kururangi

Scorers:
New Zealand: Tries: Williams, Dunn, Penalty Try.
Con: Williams. PGs: Williams (2).

Referee: N.R. Sanson (Scotland).
Attendance: 15,000.

exciting young second-row forward, Nigel Pomphrey, did not make the side. Pomphrey, who was a replacement, was in peak form at the time and ended the season in style by creating a new try scoring record for a Bristol forward. Brian McKechnie was originally chosen at full-back for New Zealand, but withdrew through injury. With Clive Currie now out of the tour, Mark Taylor was moved to full-back and Lyn Jaffray came into the side.

The match was played in poor weather, with a strong wind and driving rain making attractive rugby difficult. The Counties had wind advantage in the first half and restricted the visitors to a 4-0 lead at the break. The only score of the half came after thirty-six minutes when Eddie Dunn and Bruce Robertson used long passes to set up a try for Bryan Williams.

Five minutes after the restart Williams added a penalty following a lineout infringement, then New Zealand scored their second try when Dunn and Taylor kicked ahead and capitalised on some failed fly-hacks by the home defence, Dunn eventually getting the touchdown. After twenty-five minutes of the half New Zealand were awarded a penalty try when Gary Seear was prevented from touching down following a break from a 5-metre scrum. The scrum collapsed and there was some confusion when referee Norman Sanson ran towards the posts, many thinking that he had been playing advantage and was going to award a penalty. Penalty tries were still something of a rarity at that time and the general view was that Sanson's decision was a harsh one. Williams converted the penalty try and kicked a further penalty to complete the scoring.

This was a poor game of rugby played in miserable conditions. The All Black scrum had proved too strong for the home outfit, for whom Paul Ackford had shown what a promising player he was with some fine work in the lineout. John Palmer had tended to over-kick and little had been seen of the home backs. Peter Butler, a prolific goal-kicker, had not had a happy afternoon with the boot, missing two penalties when he had wind advantage in the first half. It was not a day for kickers, with Williams missing six out of his nine attempts at goal. Wallace Reyburn, in his tour book, summed up the mood of the day when he wrote: 'When the final whistle went, with the rain still pelting down, everybody oozed out of the park into what I understand is an almost perpetual Bristol traffic jam.'

MIDLAND COUNTIES   1978

Saturday 18 November 1978
Welford Road, Leicester
Won 20-15

The Midlands side contained eight England caps, including the captain, hooker Peter Wheeler. His fellow forwards Robin Cowling, Barry Ninnes, Nigel Horton and Garry Adey were all internationals, as were Paul Dodge, Martin Cooper and 'Dusty' Hare among the backs. New Zealand fielded a near Test-strength side, although Brian McKechnie withdrew again through injury. This meant an earlier than expected tour debut for replacement full-back Richard Wilson. He had been summoned to the tour party when it became clear that Clive Currie would not recover in time to play any more matches, and had arrived halfway through the

MIDLAND COUNTIES	NEW ZEALAND
W.H. Hare	R.G. Wilson
(Leicester and Notts, Lincs and Derbys)	
M.J. Duggan (Leicester and Leicestershire)	S.S. Wilson
P.W. Dodge (Leicester and Leicestershire)	W.M. Osborne
B.P. Hall (Leicester and Notts, Lincs and Derbys)	B.G. Williams
P.F. Knee (Coventry and Warwickshire)	N.M. Taylor
M.J. Cooper (Moseley and Staffordshire)	O.D. Bruce
C.J. Gifford (Moseley and Warwickshire)	M.W. Donaldson
Forwards:	Forwards:
R.J. Cowling (Leicester and Leicestershire)	B.R. Johnstone
P.J. Wheeler (Leicester and Leicestershire, Capt.)	A.G. Dalton
W. Dickinson	G.A. Knight
(Richmond and Notts, Lincs and Derbys)	
B.F. Ninnes (Coventry and Warwickshire)	A.M. Haden
N.E. Horton (Toulouse and North Midlands)	F.J. Oliver
J. Shipsides (Coventry and Warwickshire)	A.A. McGregor
I.R. Smith (Leicester and Leicestershire)	G.N.K. Mourie (Capt.)
G.J. Adey (Leicester and Leicestershire)	J.K. Fleming

Scorers:
Midland Counties: PGs: Hare (4). DG: Hare.
New Zealand: Tries: Williams, Mourie, Taylor. Con: R. Wilson.
PGs: R. Wilson. DG: R. Wilson.

Referee: A.M. Hosie (Scotland).
Attendance: 22,000.

game in Bristol. He had played no rugby at all for seven weeks, so it was quite understandable that he made a cautious start to the Midlands game, although his play improved as the match went on. Scrum-half Mark Donaldson, aware that his Test place was under threat due to the form shown by Dave Loveridge, was most anxious to prove his fitness and he took the field, despite being in obvious pain from his troublesome foot muscle. He, like Wilson, took time to settle and his service to Doug Bruce was wayward at first.

Hare gave the home side an early lead with a penalty after just two minutes, and he soon added a forty-metre drop goal from a tapped penalty. This was the era when, in the early days of the free kick, players were allowed to drop at goal direct from the tap. Wilson, having dropped the first inevitable high testing kick from Cooper, made a dreadful mess of his first penalty attempt, and Bruce did the same with an attempted drop goal. This, however, was so far from the posts that it became a cross-kick from which Bryan Williams scored the first New Zealand try. Hare stretched the home lead to 9-4 after twenty minutes with a monster penalty from fifty-five metres, and a further kick three minutes before half-time took the Midlands up to 12-4. Just before the break, the tourists gained vital points when Wilson took a leaf out of Hare's book and dropped a goal from a tapped penalty. The half-time score was 12-7 to the Midlands.

Rugby Football Union

MIDLANDS

v

NEW ZEALAND

WELFORD ROAD GROUND
LEICESTER

Saturday, 18th
NOVEMBER 1978

Kick-off 2.30 pm.

Official Souvenir
Programme 20p

The Midland flankers were caught offside at a scrum soon after the interval, and Wilson brought his side to within 2 points with a penalty. Winger Paul Knee came close to scoring a try for the Midlands when he kicked the ball over the New Zealand try line, but Williams was there to save the situation. Then the All Blacks took the lead for the first time when Donaldson made a blind-side break from a scrum. His pass found Williams, and he in turn found Graham Mourie who scored a try. After half an hour, the tourists made the game virtually safe when Mark Taylor caught Peter Wheeler's long lineout throw and then finished off the resulting bout of passing from Bill Osborne and Andy Haden to score his side's third try. Wilson converted, and Hare's very late penalty was not enough to prevent a hard-fought but deserved win for the All Blacks. There was an element of controversy about the final try, some commentators questioning whether or not the lineout had been formed – if it had then technically Taylor was offside when he caught the ball.

The All Blacks were happy to complete their fifth consecutive game without conceding a try and received widespread praise for their defensive qualities. Andy Haden had nullified the threat of Nigel Horton in the lineout, thus ensuring that the England selectors decided not to pick Horton for the forthcoming Test. John Fleming had looked good at number eight, and it was only in the front row where the All Blacks had been troubled, losing four tight heads to the Midland unit. Prop forward Will Dickinson gave Brad Johnstone a difficult afternoon, and many felt that he would get into the England side. In the event he was overlooked, although he was selected to play for the Barbarians against the tourists. Sadly for Dickinson, the call from England never came and he remained uncapped.

Tuesday 21 November 1978
Military Stadium, Aldershot
Won 34-6

COMBINED SERVICES	NEW ZEALAND
Lt P.R. Lea (Royal Navy)	B.J. McKechnie
Lt C.R. English (Royal Navy)	R. Kururangi
Cpl S.G. Jackson (Army)	B.J. Robertson
Lt G.H. Fabian (Royal Navy)	B.R. Ford
J. Tech. S. Rogers (Royal Air Force)	J.L. Jaffray
Cpl A. Green (Royal Air Force)	E.J. Dunn
J. Tech. K. Pugh (Royal Air Force)	M.W. Donaldson
Forwards:	Forwards:
Cpl N.J. Gray (Army)	J.C. Ashworth
Cpl R.J. Matthews (Army)	J.E. Black
Lt J.C. Ackerman (Royal Navy)	W.K.TeP. Bush
SAC J. Orwin (Royal Air Force)	J.K. Loveday
F/O N. Gillingham (Royal Air Force, Capt.)	J.K. Fleming
Cpl G.O.W. Williams (Army)	B.G. Ashworth
SAC G. Still (Royal Air Force)	L.M. Rutledge (Capt.)
Lt S. Hughes (Royal Marines)	G.A. Seear
Replacement:	
Cpl G. Davies (British Army On The Rhine and Army) for Pugh	

Scorers:
Combined Services: PG: Fabian. DG: Green.
New Zealand: Tries: Ford, Seear, Jaffray, Robertson, McKechnie.
Cons: McKechnie (4). PGs: McKechnie (2).

Referee: K. Parfitt (England).
Attendance: 6,000.

Gone were the days when the Combined Services could field a side crammed with internationals to play a touring team. This fixture would at one time have been played to a large crowd at Twickenham, often on Boxing Day. Now a small crowd at Aldershot would witness a scratch side of non-internationals take on the might of the All Blacks. Only John Orwin of the RAF was a future England cap, and he would have to wait a further seven years to gain the honour.

Despite the weakness of the opposition, the tourists did not play at all well in the first half, only leading 7-6 at the break. First blood went to the Combined Services when centre Geoff Fabian kicked a penalty after eight minutes. Five minutes later John Black won a tight head, and Gary Seear and the New Zealand backs put Brian Ford in for a try that Brian McKechnie could not convert. A drop goal from a tapped free kick by outside half Tony Green saw the Services regain the lead, but their rhythm was disrupted when scrum-half Ken Pugh left the field with an injury. Green and centre Steve Jackson missed try-scoring opportunities and a McKechnie penalty put New Zealand ahead at the interval.

The All Blacks' play improved markedly in the second half. A wide-angled penalty from McKechnie took the score to 10-6, before Seear scored a pushover try that McKechnie converted from the touchline. Seventeen minutes into the half Bruce Robertson, who looked impressive throughout the game, latched onto a loose ball and Lyn Jaffray scored in the corner. Once again, McKechnie converted brilliantly. Three minutes later, Robertson made a clean break. His pass put Ford clear for a score, but the winger was suffering from a muscle strain and could not outpace the defence. Instead, he lobbed a pass to the supporting Robertson who crossed in the corner, McKechnie adding the now inevitable touchline conversion. The final New Zealand try came from McKechnie himself after Robert Kururangi was held up at a maul. Needless to say, the All Blacks' full-back had no difficulty with the touchline conversion, thus bringing his match total to 18 points. With the England clash so close, it was heartening for the tourists to see their kicker in such fine form.

John Orwin and his skipper Nigel Gillingham won plenty of lineout ball for the home side – the All

Blacks missed Andy Haden – but the best player for the Services was flanker Garston Williams, a speedy forward who brought off some brave, spectacular tackles. Bruce Robertson clearly enjoyed his opportunity to captain New Zealand and looked in superb form for the next Test.

Lineout action from the encounter at Aldershot.

Saturday 25 November 1978
Twickenham, London
Won 16-6

ENGLAND	NEW ZEALAND
W.H. Hare (Leicester)	B.J. McKechnie
P.J. Squires (Harrogate)	S.S. Wilson
A.M. Bond (Sale)	B.J. Robertson
P.W. Dodge (Leicester)	B.G. Williams
M.A.C. Slemen (Liverpool)	W.M. Osborne
J.P. Horton (Bath)	O.D. Bruce
M. Young (Gosforth)	M.W. Donaldson
Forwards:	Forwards:
R.J. Cowling (Leicester)	B.R. Johnstone
P.J. Wheeler (Leicester)	A.G. Dalton
B.G. Nelmes (Cardiff)	G.A. Knight
W.B. Beaumont (Fylde, Capt.)	F.J. Oliver
J.P. Scott (Cardiff)	A.M. Haden
P.J. Dixon (Gosforth)	L.M. Rutledge
M. Rafter (Bristol)	G.N.K. Mourie (Capt.)
R.M. Uttley (Gosforth)	G.A. Seear

Scorers:
England: PG: Hare. DG: Hare.
New Zealand: Tries: Oliver, Johnstone. Con: McKechnie.
PGs: McKechnie (2).

Referee: N.R. Sanson (Scotland).
Attendance: 67,750.

Tony Bond of Sale was the only new cap in the England XV, although there were a couple of unorthodox selections. Barry Nelmes, a loose-head prop, was selected as a tight-head, and Cardiff number eight John Scott was chosen in the second row. Neither selection worked, with Brad Johnstone and Andy Haden comfortably outplaying the two England men. New Zealand kept the same side that defeated Wales, with the exception of Dave Loveridge, who was replaced by the fully fit Mark Donaldson, and Bill Bush who gave way to Gary Knight, now recovered from a skin complaint. Twickenham was packed, stand seats were priced at the then princely sum of £7.50 and much was expected of the game. Sadly for the spectators this was a dull match, and despite the relative closeness of the score the tourists were always in control. The England pack was second-best throughout, with only flanker Mike Rafter of Bristol really standing out, and outside half John Horton relied far too much on the boot, giving his three-quarters few opportunities to shine. Had it not been for some mishandling and bad decision making, the New Zealand victory would have been greater.

England took the lead after six minutes when 'Dusty' Hare dropped a brilliant forty-metre goal from a tap penalty. New Zealand should have scored a try soon afterwards, but Bill Osborne ignored a three-man overlap, cutting inside and getting tackled. Then Brian McKechnie, whose kicking had been outstanding at Aldershot, missed a sitter of a penalty in front of the posts, before Osborne incredibly wasted another three-man overlap, this time electing to kick ahead instead of passing. When a try did eventually come it was a soft one, Frank Oliver touching down after England made a mess of a lineout ten metres from their line. This was Oliver's second try at Twickenham, following his score against London Counties.

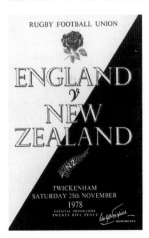

RUGBY FOOTBALL UNION

ENGLAND v NEW ZEALAND

TWICKENHAM
SATURDAY 25th NOVEMBER
1978
OFFICIAL PROGRAMME
TWENTY FIVE PENCE

McKechnie failed to convert the try, and Hare restored England's lead with a penalty when Leicester Rutledge was penalised for killing the ball. Then came another soft lineout try, John Scott tapping Peter Wheeler's throw straight into the arms of an incredulous Brad Johnstone who simply had to flop over the line for a score. This time McKechnie converted from touch and New Zealand led 10-6 at half-time.

The second half was a disappointing affair. McKechnie missed an early penalty, but was successful with kicks in the twelfth and thirty-first minutes of the half. Both kicks were awarded against Rafter, the first for obstruction, the second for hands in the scrum. It was ironic that the best English forward should commit the faults that led to two All Black scores. The nearest England came to further points was when Hare's monster penalty effort bounced back off the crossbar.

This victory gave the All Blacks the opportunity to become the first New Zealand tourists to win all four internationals on a British tour.

Brad Johnstone stood out in a superb forward effort, with Andy Dalton winning the hooking duel against Peter Wheeler. For the seventh game running, the tourists did not concede a try. This unmemorable game was perhaps best summed up by John Hopkins. Writing in the *Sunday Times*, he declared: 'Twickenham was not a very exciting place to be… One was left exhausted by England's ineptitude.'

MONMOUTHSHIRE   1978

Wednesday 29 November 1978
Rodney Parade, Newport
Won 26-9

MONMOUTHSHIRE	NEW ZEALAND
P. Lewis (Pontypool)	R.G. Wilson
A. Browning (Newbridge)	R. Kururangi
D.H. Burcher (Newport)	B.J. Robertson
I. Gosling (Ebbw Vale)	S.S. Wilson
G.H. Davies (Pontypool)	N.M. Taylor
D. Barry (Newport)	E.J. Dunn
D.B. Williams (Newport)	D.S. Loveridge
Forwards:	Forwards:
A.G. Faulkner (Pontypool, Capt.)	B.R. Johnstone
R.W. Windsor (Pontypool)	J.E. Black
G. Price (Pontypool)	W.K.TeP. Bush
S.J. Perkins (Pontypool)	J.K. Loveday
S. Sutton (Pontypool)	A.M. Haden
R.C. Burgess (Ebbw Vale)	W.G. Graham
P. Ringer (Ebbw Vale)	G.N.K. Mourie (Capt.)
J. Squire (Pontypool)	J.K. Fleming
	Replacement:
	J.C. Ashworth for Bush

Scorers:
Monmouthshire: PGs: Lewis (3).
New Zealand: Tries: Dunn, Loveridge, Robertson.
Con: R. Wilson. PGs: Wilson (4).

Referee: J.R. West (IRFU).
Attendance: 22,000.

The 'Pontypool front row' reconvened for Monmouthshire to take on the All Blacks again. Jeff Squire and Paul Ringer from the Wales pack were also there and 'Charlie' Faulkner led the team. The forwards also included tough Ebbw Vale flanker Clive Burgess, known as 'The Claw', who had played for Wales. The Pontypool second-row pair of John Perkins and Steve Sutton later played for Wales. There were six Pontypool forwards in the side. The backs included scrum-half Brynmor Williams, who had toured New Zealand with the Lions and played in 3 Test matches the previous year, a full twelve months before winning his first Welsh cap. He is now a well-respected commentator on Welsh television. Centre David Burcher also toured with the 1977 Lions. The side was coached by 1971 Lion Arthur Lewis. The All Blacks made several changes to the side including the return of Dave Loveridge. Andy Haden was chosen at lock and Graham Mourie played his tenth game of the tour. With five of the Welsh pack that had come so close to beating the tourists playing, New Zealand knew they were in for a tough afternoon. Mysteriously, Monmouthshire failed to raise their game. They had played 4 games in preparation for the match, which included a win over County Championship runners-up Gloucestershire, but were outplayed by the All Blacks.

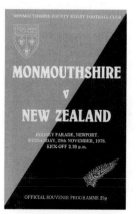

The home pack pressurised the All Blacks from the outset, but Richard Wilson opened the scoring for the visitors with a penalty. He then kicked another, and after Peter Lewis had got one back for Monmouthshire, Wilson kicked his third. Midway through the first half second five-eighth Mark Taylor followed Loveridge down the blind side of a scrum but when confronted he chipped the ball through the Monmouthshire defence and Eddie Dunn followed up to score the first try of the game. Wilson and Lewis then had another bout of penalty exchanging and the All Blacks were 16-9 ahead after half an hour. New Zealand then attacked and Monmouthshire were forced to concede a scrum five metres out. The home pack held the All Blacks and somehow gained possession but Brynmor Williams delayed and the alert Loveridge picked up and dived over Ringer's tackle to score. Wilson converted and at the break New Zealand were ahead 22-9.

Throughout the first half the home forwards had won plenty of ball but the backs played poorly. As if losing confidence in the players outside him, Williams took on more himself but was regularly nullified by Mourie and Graham in particular. Lewis and Tony Browning missed a couple of penalties but Monmouthshire never looked like adding to their score, unlike the All Blacks, who moved the ball quickly through their backs, of whom Taylor was outstanding. Haden nearly scored before Bruce Robertson scored the final try of the game after a kick ahead by Loveridge was chased, and Taylor and Dunn worked space for their centre to score. Prop Bill Bush tore a hamstring and took no further part in the tour. Monmouthshire continued to press but New Zealand were determined not to concede a try and ran out comfortable, if slightly flattering, winners.

NORTH OF ENGLAND 1978

Saturday 2 December 1978
Upper Park, Birkenhead
Won 9-6

NORTH OF ENGLAND	NEW ZEALAND
D. Boyd (West Hartlepool and Durham)	B.J. McKechnie
P.J. Squires (Harrogate and Yorkshire)	S.S. Wilson
R.M. Cardus (Roundhay and Yorkshire)	W.M. Osborne
A.M. Bond (Sale and Lancashire)	B.G. Williams
M.A.C. Slemen (Liverpool and Lancashire)	J.L. Jaffray
J.P. Horton (Bath and Lancashire)	O.D. Bruce
M. Young (Gosforth and Northumberland)	M.W. Donaldson
Forwards:	Forwards:
F. Blackhurst (Waterloo and Lancashire)	G.A. Knight
R. Tabern (Fylde and Lancashire)	A.G. Dalton
J. Bell (Gosforth and Yorkshire)	J.C. Ashworth
W.B. Beaumont (Fylde and Lancashire, Capt.)	F.J. Oliver
J. Butler (Gosforth and Cumbria)	A.M. Haden
P.J. Dixon (Gosforth and Cumbria)	L.M. Rutledge
A. Neary (Broughton Park and Lancashire)	G.N.K. Mourie (Capt.)
R.M. Uttley (Gosforth and Northumberland)	G.A. Seear

Scorers:
North of England: PGs: Young (2).
New Zealand: Try: McKechnie. Con: McKechnie. PG: McKechnie.

Referee: D.I.H. Burnett (Ireland).
Attendance: 12,000.

The North of England coach, Des Seabrook, made it known that his players were determined to prove that they were better than they had looked when playing for England the previous weekend. Eight of the side that took the field at Twickenham encountered the tourists again in this match, and there was a further England cap playing, flanker Tony Neary. The compliment of internationals would have risen to ten if prop forward Fran Cotton had been fit. Of the remainder of the side, centre Richard Cardus was a future England international. The New Zealanders were well aware that a tough challenge awaited them and fielded a strong side. The game nearly fell victim to the snowy weather that had descended on the north of the country. Birkenhead Park had been covered by four inches of snow, but the use of blowers and the hard work of local volunteers ensured that the match went ahead.

North of
England XV
v
New Zealand
At BIRKENHEAD PARK
FOOTBALL CLUB
Park Road North Birkenhead
Saturday Dec 2 1978
Kick off 2·30pm

30p

Scrum-half Malcolm Young scored the first points of the afternoon when he kicked a penalty after three minutes. Thereafter, Bryan Williams and Brian McKechnie both missed penalties for New Zealand – McKechnie was to miss five in all – and the North came close to a try when winger Peter Squires put a foot into touch. Young kicked another penalty after twenty-nine minutes, but New Zealand hit back immediately. The forwards set up a ruck straight from the restart, Mark Donaldson fed his backs and a long pass from Lyn Jaffray put Stu Wilson in the clear. Wilson was bundled into touch just short of the line, but he ensured that he placed the ball in play before he was tackled. McKechnie, following up, picked up the loose ball and scored a try that he converted himself from the touchline. The scores were level at 6-6 at half-time.

The only score of the second period was a McKechnie penalty after eighteen minutes of the half, awarded when Bill Osborne was obstructed.

The North back row played superbly and rarely allowed the tourists' inside backs to settle, but Doug Bruce remained calm under pressure and rescued the All Blacks with his fine tactical kicking. Five minutes from the end, Young had a chance to level the score, but his kick from forty metres shaved an upright.

This match was a very close call for the All Blacks and they had reason to be grateful for the reassuring presence of Bruce. A draw might have been a fairer result, but once again the tourists had kept their line intact. They had now gone 9 games without conceding a try. The North had lost this time, but for Des Seabrook and six of the current side the glory of victory against the All Blacks was less than a year away.

SCOTTISH NORTH & MIDLANDS 1978

Tuesday 5 December 1978
Linksfield Stadium, Aberdeen
Won 31-3

Composed of players from the second, third and even fourth divisions of the Scottish National Leagues, the North and Midlands was the weakest of the four Scottish District teams and was not expected to give the New Zealanders much trouble. At scrum-half, the North included the evergreen Ian McCrae, who had first played District rugby in 1959 and who had played for the North of Scotland against New Zealand in 1964. At number eight, the North also had nineteen-year-old Iain Paxton, who would go on to play four Tests for the British Isles against New Zealand in 1983. New Zealand, meanwhile, fielded an understrength XV, keeping their best in reserve for the international against Scotland.

SCOTTISH NORTH & MIDLANDS	NEW ZEALAND
A. Croll (Gordonians)	R.G. Wilson
S.F. McKenzie (Kirkcaldy)	R. Kururangi
J. Adams (Glenrothes)	B.J. Robertson
S.R. Irvine (Gordonians)	B.G. Williams
P. Robertson (Gordonians)	N.M. Taylor
C.S. High (Highland)	E.J. Dunn
I.G. McCrae (Gordonians)	D.S. Loveridge
Forwards:	Forwards:
A.G.D. Mackenzie (Highland)	B.R. Johnstone
J.A. Hardie (Gordonians)	J.E. Black
G. Brown (Dunfermline)	G.A. Knight
C.W. Snape (Gordonians, Capt.)	F.J. Oliver (Capt.)
A. Dunlop (Highland)	J.K. Loveday
C.F. Watt (Gordonians)	L.M. Rutledge
A.M. Ingle-Finch (Highland)	B.G. Ashworth
I.A.M. Paxton (Glenrothes)	J.K. Fleming

Scorers:
Scottish North & Midlands: DG: High.
New Zealand: Tries: Ashworth (2), Wilson, Rutledge, Robertson, Kururangi. Cons: Wilson (2). DG: Dunn.

Referee: R.C. Quittenton (England).
Attendance: 6,000.

The game was played in a stiffish wind, but the ground was in excellent condition despite torrential rain earlier in the week. To everybody's surprise, the North & Midlands led the tourists for most of the first half. In the opening minute of the match, full-back Richard Wilson fumbled a high kick and from the ensuing scrum McCrae fed Colin High, who dropped a fine goal. A few days earlier, High had become a father for the first time. Watching the game on television from her hospital bed, his wife almost dropped their new baby girl in her excitement at the score. It soon became clear that the North forwards, who were conceding at least a stone a man, were going to have a torrid afternoon, the visitors simply pushing them off the ball in the scrums. New Zealand had most of the play, but handling mistakes and some huge relieving kicks by High and Stewart Irvine kept them at bay. Eddie Dunn struck the bar with a drop goal attempt while High missed two penalty chances to put his side further ahead. Just when it seemed that the North would hold their lead at the interval, the visitors scored a good try. A jinking run by Dave Loveridge set up the move. The ball was swept across the field to Bryan Williams and then to Richard Wilson to score. The All Blacks led 4-3 at the break.

New Zealand took firm control in the second half and ran in 5 tries to see off the plucky North. After forty-five minutes, Leicester Rutledge took a long throw from a lineout to drop over easily. Ten minutes later, the ball was flipped along the line to Williams who cut inside the North defence and then passed out to Bruce Robertson, who had looped his winger. Dunn added three more points with a drop goal before Barry Ashworth barged over after a powerful surge by the All Blacks' pack. Wilson converted. On seventy minutes, Kururangi crossed in the corner after clever switching by Loveridge and Dunn. Shortly before the end, Ashworth scored his second try after Dunn had cut through the defence.

Both sides were reasonably happy with the outcome. After a slow start, New Zealand had produced an impressive performance. Their driving, disciplined forward play had forced the North constantly onto the back foot and given Dunn and Loveridge plenty of time to set the three-quarters moving. The North had covered and tackled like men possessed, especially Alan Croll, Ian McCrae and the back-row trio. But bravery and determination were never going to be enough against the New Zealanders.

NORTH & MIDLANDS OF SCOTLAND

at Linksfield Stadium
Tuesday, 5th December, 1978

V

NEW ZEALAND

SCOTLAND   1978

Saturday 9 December 1978
Murrayfield, Edinburgh
Won 18-9

New Zealand were firm favourites and duly completed their first Grand Slam over the Home Unions, but Scotland made them fight all the way and with a little luck might have snatched a draw. New Zealand kept faith with the same fifteen that had beaten England two weeks earlier. Scotland introduced three new caps in Keith Robertson, Rob Cunningham and Gordon Dickson as well as recalling Alan Lawson at scrum-half and David Leslie at number eight. The kick-off time was advanced by five minutes to compensate for the winter darkness, but the gloom descended and the players were barely visible in the closing stages, the ground having no floodlights.

On a rain-soaked pitch, Scotland sensationally opened the scoring after

SCOTLAND	NEW ZEALAND
A.R. Irvine (Heriot's FP)	B.J. McKechnie
K.W. Robertson (Melrose)	S.S. Wilson
J.M. Renwick (Hawick)	B.J. Robertson
A.G. Cranston (Hawick)	B.G. Williams
B.H. Hay (Boroughmuir)	W.M. Osborne
I.R. McGeechan (Headingley, Capt.)	O.D. Bruce
A.J.M. Lawson (London Scottish)	M.W. Donaldson
Forwards:	Forwards:
J. McLauchlan (Jordanhill)	B.R. Johnstone
C.T. Deans (Hawick)	A.G. Dalton
R.F. Cunningham (Gala)	G.A. Knight
A.J. Tomes (Hawick)	A.M. Haden
A.F. McHarg (London Scottish)	F.J. Oliver
M.A. Biggar (London Scottish)	L.M. Rutledge
G. Dickson (Gala)	G.N.K. Mourie (Capt.)
D.G. Leslie (Gala)	G.A. Seear
Replacement:	
I.K. Lambie (Watsonians) for Leslie	

Scorers:
Scotland: Try: Hay. Con: Irvine. DG: McGeechan.
New Zealand: Tries: Sear, Robertson. Cons: McKechnie (2). PG: McKechnie (2).

Referee: J.R. West (Ireland).
Attendance: 69,000.

nine minutes. Bruce Hay, the chunky Scottish utility back, kicked and chased, and after some quick passing near the line the ball rebounded back into Hay's arms for him to dive over. It was the first try conceded by the tourists since the defeat against Munster, 11 matches earlier, and amazingly Scotland's first try against New Zealand since 1935. Andy Irvine converted with a magnificent kick from near the touchline to put Scotland 6-0 in front. Fourteen minutes later, Brian McKechnie brought the visitors back into the game with a penalty goal. After half an hour, Irvine, who had a disappointing afternoon, fumbled a kick near the Scottish goal line and from the ensuing scrum Gary Seear picked up and drove over for a try. McKechnie converted to put New Zealand 9-6 ahead at the interval.

Both sides missed several chances in the second half, notably Rutledge, who had the ball knocked out of his hands on the point of scoring after a crunching tackle by Mike Biggar. McKechnie kicked a forty-metre penalty goal after sixty-one minutes, but in response Ian McGeechan dropped a goal to set up a dramatic finish. With the match moving into injury time, Scotland pressed furiously near the New Zealand line and looked likely to score. McGeechan, opting for the draw, attempted another drop at goal from fifteen metres out, but the ball was charged down by his opposite number Doug Bruce. Bill Osborne hacked the loose ball down the field and in the ensuing kick-and-chase Bruce Robertson outpaced the defence to score between the posts. McKechnie converted to seal New Zealand's Grand Slam and enhance the tourists' reputation as the 'Last-Gasp All Blacks', once again winning in the dying stages. There was still time for Irvine to hit the post with a penalty attempt and for the Scots to make several brave efforts to save the match. The final score flattered the visitors, but there was no doubt that they deserved their win.

The New Zealand forwards, almost a stone a man heavier than their opponents, had been able to exert more pressure, although the Scots had done well in the lineout thanks to fine jumping by Alastair McHarg and Alan Tomes. In the slippery conditions, Scotland made slightly more mistakes than the New Zealanders, whose efficiency and teamwork had pulled them through. Both sides were warmly applauded as they left the field after an enthralling match. The tourists were rightly proud of their achievement and in the evening prop Billy Bush and centre Bill Osborne ceremoniously shaved off their moustaches and beards to fulfil an early tour promise that they would become clean-shaven if their team achieved the Grand Slam.

BRIDGEND   1978

Wednesday 13 December 1978
The Brewery Field, Bridgend
Won 17-6

Bridgend faced a major touring side for the first time in their history. They had beaten Italy 51-0 in 1971 and had combined with Maesteg to take on Canada and Fiji in the 1960s but the match with New Zealand was the biggest in the club's history and a fine way to celebrate their centenary. They were a good side and had only lost three of their 23 games prior to the match with New Zealand. They were unbeaten at home and captained by J.P.R. Williams, who had fellow British Lion Steve Fenwick in the centre. Scrum-half Gerald Williams later played for Wales, as did prop Ian Stephens and flanker Gareth Williams, the latter two later becoming British Lions.

BRIDGEND	NEW ZEALAND
J.P.R. Williams (Capt.)	R.G. Wilson
I. Davies	R. Kururangi
S.P. Fenwick	W.M. Osborne
L. Thomas	B.G. Williams
V.L. Jenkins	N.M. Taylor
I. Williams	O.D. Bruce
G. Williams	D.S. Loveridge
Forwards:	Forwards:
I. Stephens	J.C. Ashworth
G. Davies	J.E. Black
M. James	G.A. Knight
W. Howe	J.K. Loveday
R. Evans	A.M. Haden
G. Jones	W.G. Graham
G.P. Williams	G.N.K. Mourie (Capt.)
S. Ellis	G.A. Seear

Scorers:
Bridgend: PGs: Fenwick (2).
New Zealand: Tries: Taylor, Mourie. PG: Wilson (3).

Referee: L. Prideaux (RFU).
Attendance: 15,000.

The All Blacks shuffled their side for the penultimate game of the tour and played most of those who would not be involved in the final game. Mark Donaldson and Frank Oliver dropped out late on to be replaced by Dave Loveridge and John Loveday.

On a muddy field, the match started and shortly after the kick-off J.P.R. Williams found himself on the ground underneath a maul. All Black prop John Ashworth then stamped on the full-back's face, twice. Williams was led off the field for treatment to a major gash in his cheek that required several stitches. Bridgend took a gamble not to replace him and they were down to fourteen men for fifteen minutes. The incident caused emotions to rise and both sides were involved in some unsavoury incidents that required referee Laurie Prideaux to warn several players. While Williams was off Richard Wilson kicked a penalty when Bridgend were penalised for punching, then a kick ahead by Ian Williams was fielded by Robert Kururangi who elected to run out of defence. On halfway he passed to Bill Osborne who fed Mark Taylor who cut through and ran the rest of the way to the Bridgend line for a spectacular try. Wilson and Fenwick exchanged penalties, which saw New Zealand ahead 10-6 at half-time.

The second half was played in drizzle and, after a few minutes, Wilson kicked another penalty. The match continued with constant niggle and the shrill whistle of the referee. Both sides missed penalty attempts then, late in the game, Mourie pounced on the ball at a poorly controlled Bridgend lineout to score. Wilson failed to convert but New Zealand won 17-6.

After the game Dr Peter Williams, the Bridgend president and father of J.P.R., spoke at the dinner and criticised the incident that injured his son. Several disgruntled All Blacks got up and walked out.

BARBARIANS 1978

Saturday 16 December 1978
Cardiff Arms Park, Cardiff
Won 18-16

The Barbarians included the remarkable French flank forwards Jean-Pierre Rives and Jean-Claude Skrela for the game, the third time New Zealand had played at the National Stadium, Cardiff Arms Park on the tour. They also included the popular Jim Renwick and Phil Bennett, still playing club rugby for Llanelli. There were three uncapped players in the side: Elgan Rees, Neil Hutchings and Bill Dickinson. Of these only Rees was later capped. The Barbarians were captained by Derek Quinnell. The All Blacks chose Eddie Dunn at first five-eighth and Dave Loveridge at half-back, indicating their intention to also play an open game. John Fleming took over at number eight reflecting his sound contribution on tour.

BARBARIANS	NEW ZEALAND
A.R. Irvine (Heriot's FP)	B.J. McKechnie
H.E. Rees (Neath)	S.S. Wilson
R.N. Hutchings (Aberavon)	B.J. Robertson
J.M. Renwick (Hawick)	B.G. Williams
M.A.C. Slemen (Liverpool)	W.M. Osborne
P. Bennett (Llanelli)	E.J. Dunn
D.B. Williams (Newport)	D.S. Loveridge
Forwards:	Forwards:
P.A. Orr (Old Wesley)	B.R. Johnstone
P.J. Wheeler (Leicester)	A.G. Dalton
W. Dickinson (Richmond)	G.A. Knight
W.B. Beaumont (Fylde)	F.J. Oliver
A.J. Martin (Aberavon)	A.M. Haden
J-C. Skrela (Toulouse)	L.M. Rutledge
J-P. Rives (Toulouse)	G.N.K. Mourie (Capt.)
D.L. Quinnell (Llanelli, Capt.)	J.K. Fleming
	Replacement:
	J.C. Ashworth for Johnstone

Scorers:
Barbarians: Tries: Slemen (2). Con: Bennett. PG: Bennett (2).
New Zealand: Tries: Johnstone, Rutledge, Williams.
PG: McKechnie. DG: Dunn.

Referee: N.R. Sanson (SRU).
Attendance: 50,000.

The entire New Zealand party took to the field before the game and waved to the crowd, a gesture that was well received. Then the game kicked off and both sides immediately demonstrated a willingness to run the ball. Renwick made a break from which Elgan Rees should have scored had Hutchings not

Barbarian Football Club

BARBARIANS
v
NEW ZEALAND

THE CARDIFF ARMS PARK
SATURDAY, 16th DECEMBER
1978

Official Programme: Twenty Five Pence

Brian McKechnie attempts to fend off Jean-Pierre Rives. All Black Bruce Robertson and Barbarian Neil Hutchings are in support.

delayed his pass. Soon afterwards, the All Blacks raced fifty metres on a threatening run. This approach eventually led to the first try of the match. From deep in New Zealand territory, Dunn and Bill Osborne opened up the Barbarians' defence and raced upfield. They had men in support and, after some quick passing, the ball went to Brad Johnstone who drove through the tackles of Mike Slemen and Andy Irvine to score an unconverted try. The Barbarians were then close to scoring when Rees was tackled after a fine break by Bennett, then the All Blacks nearly scored when first Bryan Williams and then Brian McKechnie were tackled just short of the goal line. It was mesmerising rugby that the crowd loved. The Barbarians equalised when the ball was deftly chipped through the New Zealand defence and Slemen got to it first. He kicked ahead past McKechnie and won the race to the ball for the try but Bennett missed the conversion. On the stroke of half-time New Zealand were awarded an easy penalty and McKechnie kicked it to give New Zealand a 7-4 interval lead.

Bennett equalised with a penalty early in the second half then Johnstone, who later became the national coach of Italy, went off injured. He was replaced by John Ashworth, and with this being a few days after the incident in Bridgend it was unfortunate that it was he who came on. He was welcomed with a loud chorus of booing, to which he raised a clenched fist. Leicester Rutledge, who had enjoyed an outstanding tour, then put New Zealand back into the lead with a try after a break by Loveridge was taken on by Fleming. Bryan Williams scored a try from a scrum close to the Barbarians' line, the veteran winger making his final appearance for New Zealand. 'Bee Gee' had scored 66 tries in his 113 matches in the black shirt of New Zealand. McKechnie added the extra points. The exciting Renwick then made a break but just as he looked certain to score, he was tackled and the ball dislodged from his arms inches from the New Zealand line. New Zealand were penalised at the scrum and Brynmor Williams took a quick penalty, threw long to Skrela who passed out to Slemen who caught the ball at top speed and scored wide out. Bennett converted with a fine kick. Irvine then hit the crossbar with a long-range penalty before Bennett successfully kicked a closer one which put the Barbarians into the lead with ten minutes remaining. McKechnie then missed two simple penalties, forcing rueful smiles from the Welsh crowd, but from the last miss the Barbarians failed to clear the ball properly and conceded scrum five metres out. The New Zealand heel was quick and Loveridge passed to Dunn who dropped the goal that won the match. The All Blacks escaped defeat again, much to the dismay of the partisan crowd.

Skipper Graham Mourie led the side with great skill and inspiration. He was a fine loose forward in the best traditions of New Zealand rugby and as the captain of the first New Zealand team to win a 'Grand Slam' of victories over the home unions he attained a record that can never be surpassed. Unlike the sombre Seventh All Blacks, Mourie's men were very popular and fine ambassadors for the sport and their country.

NEW ZEALAND TO EUROPE

THE MATCHES

London Division	24 October 1979	Twickenham	won 21-18
South of Scotland	27 October 1979	Hawick	won 19-3
Edinburgh	31 October 1979	Edinburgh	won 16-4
Midland Division	3 November 1979	Leicester	won 33-7
Glasgow	6 November 1979	Glasgow	won 12-6
SCOTLAND	10 November 1979	Murrayfield	won 20-6
Anglo Scots	14 November 1979	Dundee	won 18-9
Northern Division	17 November 1979	Otley	lost 21-9
South & South-West Counties	20 November 1979	Exeter	won 16-0
ENGLAND	24 November 1979	Twickenham	won 10-9
Italy	28 November 1979	Rovigo	won 18-12

Played 11, Won 10, Drew 0, Lost 1. Scored: 192 points, Conceded: 95.
In Britain & Ireland: Played 10, Won 9, Drew 0, Lost 1. Scored: 174 points, Conceded: 83.

The New Zealand Tour Party:
A.R. Hewson (Wellington), R.G. Wilson (Canterbury), G.R. Cunningham (Auckland), B.R. Ford (Marlborough), B.G. Fraser (Wellington), T.M. Twigden (Auckland), S.S. Wilson (Wellington), E.J. Dunn (North Auckland), K.J. Keane (Canterbury), M.B. Taylor (Waikato), M.W. Donaldson (Manawatu), D.S. Loveridge (Taranaki), R.C. Ketels (Counties), B.R. Johnstone (Auckland), J.E. Spiers (Counties), B.A. Thompson (Canterbury), A.G. Dalton (Counties), P.H. Sloane (North Auckland), J.K. Fleming (Wellington), A.M. Haden (Auckland), V.E. Stewart (Canterbury), M.M. Burgoyne (North Auckland), K.W. Stewart (Southland), G.N.K. Mourie (Taranaki), M.G. Mexted (Wellington).

Captain: G.N.K. Mourie. Manager: R.W. Thomas. Assistant Manager: E.A. Watson.

Leading points scorer: R.G. Wilson – 56 points (53 in Britain).
Leading try-scorer: B.G. Fraser – 5 tries (4 in Britain).
Most appearances: G.N.K. Mourie, A.M. Haden and J.K. Fleming – 10 games (9 in Britain).

Wednesday 24 October 1979
Twickenham, London
Won 21-18

LONDON DIVISION	NEW ZEALAND
K.M. Bushell (Harlequins and Kent)	R.G. Wilson
R.O. Demming (Bedford and Eastern Counties)	S.S. Wilson
N.J. Preston (Richmond and Surrey)	T.M. Twigden
M.K. Fosh	B.R. Ford
(Cambridge University and Eastern Counties)	
D.M. Wyatt (Bath and Eastern Counties)	K.J. Keane
T.A. Bryan (Metropolitan Police and Middlesex)	E.J. Dunn
B. Murphy (London Irish and Surrey)	M.W. Donaldson
Forwards:	Forwards:
T.C. Claxton (Harlequins and Middlesex)	R.C. Ketels
A.V. Boddy (Metropolitan Police and Middlesex)	P.H. Sloane
C.M. McGregor (Saracens and Middlesex)	B.A. Thompson
N.O. Martin (Bedford)	J.K. Fleming
C.W. Ralston (Richmond and Middlesex, Capt.)	A.M. Haden
A.C. Alexander (Harlequins and Middlesex)	M.M. Burgoyne
R.J. Mordell (Rosslyn Park and Middlesex)	G.N.K. Mourie
A.G. Ripley (Rosslyn Park and Middlesex)	M.G. Mexted
Replacement:	Replacement:
J.F. Thornton (Rosslyn Park) for Bryan	K. Stewart for Burgoyne

Scorers:
London Division: Tries: Martin, Ralston. Cons: Bushell (2).
PGs: Bushell (2).
New Zealand: Try: Mexted. Con: R.G. Wilson. PGs: R.G. Wilson (5).

Referee: J.W. Dinsmore (Scotland).
Attendance: 21,000.

New Zealand had played 2 games in Australia the previous July, but had been defeated by Australia in the solitary Test match. They played two internationals against France earlier in the year, winning in Christchurch but being defeated in the second international, staged on Bastille day, in Auckland. They also played a Test series against Argentina in the September that proved to be a tough game that New Zealand struggled to win. With some players unavailable and Bruce Robertson injured, the New Zealand selectors viewed the tour to England and Scotland as a chance to experiment and rebuild. London's captain, veteran England international Chris Ralston, felt that his side was well prepared and capable of challenging the All Blacks in the opening game of their 1979 tour. However, there was disappointment for the home team when England second row Maurice Colclough withdrew from the side with a rib injury, and London also lost future England scrum-half Nick Youngs. Besides Ralston, forwards Andy Ripley, Bob Mordell and Nick Martin were England players, along with winger Derek Wyatt, while centre Nick Preston would gain his first England cap against the All Blacks later in the tour. Flanker Mordell had actually taken part in a secret rugby league trial and he turned professional not long after the match. Seven of the side had played in the corresponding fixture against New Zealand in 1978, while Ralston, Ripley and hooker Tony Boddy had all played in 1972.

Richard Wilson kicked New Zealand into an early lead with a simple penalty, but London full-back Billy Bushell soon equalised with a fine penalty from the halfway line. Then home outside half Tim

Bryan failed to control a kick near his own line and Murray Mexted touched down for the first try of the tour, Wilson converting. Soon afterwards, Bryan departed with a hamstring injury – his replacement was James Thornton of Rosslyn Park. A new law had recently been introduced allowing touch judges to inform the referee of incidents of foul play, and when touch judge Tony Trigg spotted a late tackle by Brian Ford, he alerted the referee who gave London a penalty, which Bushell goaled. The referee, Jim Dinsmore of Scotland, then incurred the wrath of Ralston by not penalising Ford for a head-high tackle on Wyatt. However, London scored soon after this incident when a run by Adrian Alexander from a tap penalty allowed Martin to crash through some rather weak defence for a try that Bushell converted. London led 12-9 at the interval.

Just before the break Mike Burgoyne left the field with torn a calf muscle, Ken Stewart coming on to replace him for the second half. Wilson kicked an equalising penalty shortly after the restart when Bushell was penalised for failing to roll away from the ball, and he was successful with three more penalties during the half, giving New Zealand a lead of 21-12. Seven minutes from the end of the game the home side rallied and Alexander again burst from a tap penalty to put Ralston over near the posts. Bushell converted, and had a chance to tie the scores in the final minute, but his fifty-metre penalty fell well short of the target. London at least had the consolation of scoring 2 tries to the All Blacks' one.

Richard Wilson was the match winner for New Zealand, kicking six goals from nine attempts. The London forwards played well, although Andy Haden, John Fleming and Murray Mexted dominated the lineouts. Captain Graham Mourie also stood out for the tourists. After the match, Chris Ralston was highly critical of the referee, accusing him of inconsistency. He was particularly incensed about the Wyatt incident and also claimed that Mr Dinsmore had missed a perfectly good try by scrum-half Barry Murphy. 'The referee was inconsistent, I have never seen him before and I never want to see him again' were the angry words of the London skipper.

SOUTH OF SCOTLAND   1979

Saturday 27 October 1979
Mansfield Park, Hawick
Won 19-3

SOUTH OF SCOTLAND	NEW ZEALAND
P.W. Dods (Gala)	A.R. Hewson
K.W. Robertson (Melrose)	S.S. Wilson
J.M. Renwick (Hawick)	G.R. Cunningham
A.G. Cranston (Hawick, Capt.)	B.G. Fraser
D.J. Ledingham (Gala)	K.J. Keane
J.Y. Rutherford (Selkirk)	M.B. Taylor
R.J. Laidlaw (Jed-Forest)	D.S. Loveridge
Forwards:	Forwards:
J. Aitken (Gala)	B.R. Johnstone
C.T. Deans (Hawick)	A.G. Dalton
N.E.K. Pender (Hawick)	J.E. Speirs
A.J. Tomes (Hawick)	A.M. Haden
T.J. Smith (Gala)	V.E. Stewart
J.M. Berthinussen (Gala)	K.W. Stewart
C.B. Hegarty (Hawick)	G.N.K. Mourie (Capt.)
G. Dickson (Gala)	M.G. Mexted

Scorers:
South of Scotland: PG: Dods.
New Zealand: Tries: Fraser (2), Wilson. Cons: Hewson (2). PG: Hewson.

Referee: L. Prideaux (England).
Attendance: 10,000.

Many in Scottish rugby felt that the South of Scotland, then the strongest of the District sides, could 'do a Munster' and become the first Scottish side to defeat New Zealand, just as Munster had done for Ireland the previous year. On paper, the South looked a good side with four international players in the backs and another six in the forwards. The South had prepared with special training sessions and were confidently expected to trouble the visitors. New Zealand fielded a strong line-up, making ten changes from the side that had defeated London Counties the previous Wednesday. Making his debut in the famous black jersey was Allan Hewson, a talented and controversial full-back from Wellington who would go on to make nineteen appearances at Test level despite his rather frail build.

A tremendous match was anticipated but sadly not realised. On a fine autumn afternoon, New Zealand effectively killed the game with a quick score in the opening minute. A towering up-and-under by Murray Taylor was spilled in front of the posts by the South full-back Peter Dods. The visiting forwards won the ensuing ruck, Dave Loveridge went blind and sent Stu Wilson in for the easiest of tries. Hewson converted. The South seemed to lose confidence after this early setback, the visitors scoring two further tries from South mistakes. After twenty-four minutes, Hewson came into the line and slipped an inside pass to Bernie Fraser, who battered his way through several weak tackles to score. Dods kicked a penalty to make the half-time score 10-3.

Fifteen minutes into the second half, Fraser scored his second try. There seemed no danger as Keith Robertson and Peter Dods moved to cover a clearing kick by Hewson, but the ball was fumbled straight into the arms of Fraser, who ran fifty metres to score near the posts. Hewson converted and three minutes

later landed a penalty goal via a post. The closing stages were the best part of the match when the South and the crowd finally came alive. Both sides had good runs and the South came close, but the New Zealand tackling was firm and they managed to hold out to the final whistle.

The New Zealanders had given an impressive performance and they were pleased with their win. The fact that they had missed three further try-scoring opportunities and six penalty kicks showed how much they were on top. Fraser and Wilson proved themselves in the tradition of powerful New Zealand wingers and Hewson was always ready to join in the attack. Taylor and Loveridge had used the ball more intelligently than their South counterparts. At forward, Andy Haden had given the visitors a big advantage in the lineout and the back-row trio of Ken Stewart, Murray Mexted and Graham Mourie had been very prominent. For the South, the match was a great anticlimax, one or two of the side seeming to find the occasion too much. Constant pressure by the visitors had forced uncharacteristic errors and the experienced players had achieved little.

EDINBURGH 1979

Wednesday 31 October 1979
Myreside, Edinburgh
Won 16-4

Unlike the South of Scotland, Edinburgh took a rather low-key approach, having not played together since their tour of the South of France in late August. With six of the team from Heriot's FP, the reigning Scottish champions, the capital side produced an excellent display and could have taken more from the match if they had taken their chances.

Playing into a strong breeze, Edinburgh made a good start and immediately Andy Irvine showed their intentions by opting to run a penalty rather than kicking for touch. After six minutes, the Edinburgh forwards wheeled a scrum in their own 25, but the ball was kicked through to Eddie Dunn who slipped the cover and passed to Mourie who crashed over. The rest of the half was almost constant New Zealand pressure and

EDINBURGH	NEW ZEALAND
A.R. Irvine (Heriot's FP, Capt.)	R.G. Wilson
R.S. Page (Heriot's FP)	S.S. Wilson
E.A. Kennedy (Watsonians)	T.M. Twigden
D.I. Johnston (Watsonians)	B.R. Ford
B.H. Hay (Boroughmuir)	M.B. Taylor
K.D.M. Wilson (Boroughmuir)	E.J. Dunn
A.J.M. Lawson (Heriot's FP)	M.W. Donaldson
Forwards:	Forwards:
J.N. Burnett (Heriot's FP)	B.R. Johnstone
J.C. Munro (Heriot's FP)	P.H. Sloane
I.G. Milne (Heriot's FP)	B.A. Thompson
I.K. Lambie (Watsonians)	A.M. Haden
D.G. Armstrong (Leith Acads)	V.E. Stewart
J.H. Calder (Stewart's-Melville FP)	K.W. Stewart
A.K. Brewster (Stewart's-Melville FP)	G.N.K. Mourie (Capt.)
W.S. Watson (Boroughmuir)	J.K. Fleming
Replacement:	
J.A. Stewart (Watsonians) for Watson	

Scorers:
Edinburgh: Try: Wilson.
New Zealand: Tries: Mourie, Twigden. Con: R. Wilson. PG: R. Wilson (2).

Referee: A. Welsby (England).
Attendance: 8,000.

stout Edinburgh defence, the centres Euan Kennedy and David Johnston and stand-off Duncan Wilson making some crunching tackles. For New Zealand, Richard Wilson missed two penalties and Dunn sent a drop goal attempt wide. Shortly before half-time, Irvine missed a penalty and Jim Stewart replaced Bill Watson, who had to have six stitches in a deep cut above his left eye. The bulky Stewart went to lock and Iain Lambie dropped back to number eight. New Zealand led 4-0 at half-time.

Edinburgh enjoyed most of the play in the second half, but crucially the New Zealanders managed to score on their infrequent visits to their opponents' half. Richard Wilson put the visitors further ahead with a penalty goal before Edinburgh hit back with a great try. Taking quick ruck ball inside the

New Zealand 22, Alan Lawson went blind and fed Duncan Wilson, who dived over in the corner. Edinburgh kept up the pressure, but in the fifty-third minute New Zealand delivered the killer blow. The three-quarters moved the ball right and sucked in the Edinburgh backs. The ball was then whipped back across the pitch and Tim Twigden raced thirty metres through the splintered defence for a try. Wilson converted to put the visitors 13-4 in front. Undaunted, Edinburgh continued to press. Irvine sent Bruce Hay away with a long pass but Johnston dropped the ball with the line at his mercy. Wilson landed his second penalty after Iain Milne was judged to have gone over the top at a ruck. Minutes from the end, Edinburgh almost scored a second try, but Lambie was unable to hold a popped pass after a great run from Lawson.

In an entertaining encounter, the final score did little credit to Edinburgh, especially the forwards who had out-performed the visitors at the rucks and scrums. The two Heriot's props, Jimmy Burnett and Iain Milne, had put in a hard afternoon and caused the New Zealand front row plenty of trouble. Alan Lawson had a superb game at scrum-half, especially with his kicking, and his partner Duncan Wilson was always penetrative. Edinburgh's downfall was their lack of finishing. Time and again the defence was breached only for the final pass to go astray or be blocked. New Zealand dominated in the lineouts thanks to the experienced Andy Haden, but the forwards had been lacklustre and the backs had made too many mistakes.

MIDLAND DIVISION 1979

Saturday 3 November 1979
Welford Road, Leicester
Won 33-7

The Midland Division included six England players in skipper Peter Wheeler, 'Dusty' Hare, Robin Cowling, Garry Adey, Nigel Horton and Paul Dodge. Outside half Les Cusworth would win his first England cap in the forthcoming Test against the All Blacks, while Steve Redfern and Clive Woodward were also future England players. Seven of the team had appeared in the previous season's encounter. Wheeler and Adey had also played against the 1972 tourists for Midland Counties East, while Horton was a member of the Midland Counties West side that defeated the 1972 visitors. New Zealand fielded a strong side for the game, with Dave Loveridge now established as the first-choice scrum-half. Ken Stewart should not really have started the game as he had a hamstring problem, and had to be replaced by Mike Burgoyne.

MIDLAND DIVISION	NEW ZEALAND
W.H. Hare (Leicester and Notts, Lincs and Derbys)	R.G. Wilson
M.H. Perry (Liverpool and North Midlands)	S.S. Wilson
P.W. Dodge (Leicester and Leicestershire)	G.R. Cunningham
C.R. Woodward (Leicester and Leicestershire)	B.G. Fraser
P.F. Knee (Coventry and Warwickshire)	M.B. Taylor
L. Cusworth (Leicester and North Midlands)	E.J. Dunn
I.G. Peck (Cambridge University and East Midlands)	D.S. Loveridge
Forwards:	Forwards:
R.J. Cowling (Leicester and Leicestershire)	B.R. Johnstone
P.J. Wheeler (Leicester and Leicestershire, Capt.)	A.G. Dalton
S.P. Redfern (Leicester and Leicestershire)	J.E. Spiers
N.E. Horton (Toulouse and North Midlands)	J.K. Fleming
R. Field (Moseley and Staffordshire)	A.M. Haden
G.N. Phillips (Bedford and East Midlands)	K.W. Stewart
D.J. Forfar (Leicester and Leicestershire)	G.N.K. Mourie (Capt.)
G.J. Adey (Leicester and Leicestershire)	M.G. Mexted
	Replacement:
	M.M. Burgoyne for K. Stewart

Scorers:
Midland Division: Try: Knee. PG: Hare.
New Zealand: Tries: Fraser (2), Burgoyne, Mexted, Fleming.
Cons: R. Wilson (2). PGs: R. Wilson (3).

Referee: J.A. Short (Scotland).
Attendance: 14,000.

The afternoon started in sombre fashion. News had reached the squad the previous evening that Jack Gleeson, coach of the 1978 side, had died of cancer, and a silence was kept before the kick-off. The tourists were desperate to play an attacking game in his memory, but the Midland pack competed well in the first half, restricting the All Blacks to three Richard Wilson penalties. Hare missed a straightforward penalty for the home side and was also wide with two attempted drop goals. Both Woodward and young winger Mike Perry threatened the New Zealand line, but the visitors' defence was secure and the score was 9-0 at half-time.

Soon after the break, the All Blacks scored their first try when the backs started a move from inside their own half. The ball eventually reached Bernie Fraser, who chipped it over Hare before winning the race to the touchdown. Ten minutes later, Loveridge dummied a pass to Stu Wilson, broke down the touchline and sent a high pass infield to Burgoyne for the replacement forward to score. Neither try was converted, but the lead had been stretched to 17-0. The next try followed almost immediately, numerous players handling before Murray Mexted crossed for an excellent score that Richard Wilson converted. Hare finally kicked a goal for the Midlands when Gary Cunningham was caught offside, and ten minutes from the end the home side scored a consolation try, a tap penalty from Cusworth leading to a score for winger Paul Knee. There was still time for two further New Zealand tries, a second for Fraser after good work from Cunningham, and a final try right on full time when the two Wilsons interpassed before John Fleming crossed under the posts. Richard Wilson's conversion sealed a comfortable win of the visitors and the second half display, with the tourists willing to attack from anywhere, had been a fitting memorial to the coaching of Jack Gleeson. Mexted, Burgoyne, and captain Graham Mourie had all looked good in open play, while Stu Wilson, Cunningham, Loveridge and Fraser had all enjoyed impressive games. At this stage of the tour, the All Blacks were looking difficult to beat.

GLASGOW 1979

Tuesday 6 November 1979
Hughenden, Glasgow
Won 12-6

Cheered on by a vociferous crowd, Glasgow put up an extremely brave display against a strangely out-of-sorts New Zealand. Playing sometimes on the edge of the law, the home side pressurised the visitors and did not allow them to settle into their normal rhythm, which in turn led to frustrations and frayed tempers. In the fiftieth minute, Mark Donaldson floored the Glasgow flank forward Gavin Angus, who had come through illegally. Donaldson was given a strong lecture by referee Roger Quittenton and was judged by many to be lucky to stay on the field. New Zealand opened the scoring after twelve minutes. Winning a ruck in front of the Glasgow posts, the pack passed the ball to Brian Ford who ran over

GLASGOW	NEW ZEALAND
C.D.R. Mair (West of Scotland)	A.R. Hewson
S. Munro (Ayr)	S.S. Wilson
A.G. Dougall (Jordanhill)	T.M. Twigden
J.S. Gossman (West of Scotland)	B.R. Ford
A.D. Armstrong (Jordanhill)	K.J. Keane
B.M. Gossman (West of Scotland)	M.B. Taylor
A.M. Service (West of Scotland)	M.W. Donaldson
Forwards:	Forwards:
G.M. McGuinness (West of Scotland)	R.C. Ketels
D.R. Livingstone (West of Scotland)	P.H. Sloane
H. Campbell (Jordanhill)	B.A. Thompson
W. Cuthbertson (Kilmarnock)	J.K. Fleming
W. Wyroslawski (Jordanhill)	V.E. Stewart
J.R. Dixon (Jordanhill, Capt.)	M.M. Burgoyne
G.M. Angus (Kilmarnock)	G.N.K. Mourie (Capt.)
J.R. Beattie (Glasgow Acads)	M.G. Mexted
Replacement:	Replacement:
H. Hamilton (Kilmarnock) for Dixon	A.M. Haden for Mexted

Scorers:
Glasgow: PG: B. Gossman (2).
New Zealand: Tries: Ford (2), Hewson.

Referee: R.C. Quittenton (England).
Attendance: 6,000.

unopposed on the left. Murray Mexted had to leave the field after twenty minutes with rib damage and was replaced by Andy Haden. Later in the half, Glasgow applied some pressure. A good break by scrum-half Sandy Service failed through lack of support and Colin Mair missed a penalty kick. Glasgow captain and talisman Richie Dixon, playing in his fiftieth District game, also went off with a rib injury and was later replaced by Kilmarnock's Hugh Hamilton. In the thirty-fifth minute, the visitors had a piece of good fortune, turning 3 points into four. Allan Hewson hooked a penalty attempt but Mike Burgoyne was quickly onto the ball. From the ensuing ruck, the ball was whipped out to the left where Hewson appeared in the line to score a try. Just before the interval, Mair broke through the centre but was brought back by the referee because of a scuffle between props Barry Thompson and Gerry McGuinness. It was hard lines on Glasgow as Mair missed the ensuing penalty kick. The visitors led 8-0 at half-time.

Glasgow made an encouraging start to the second half and Brian Gossman kicked a penalty after the visitors had been caught offside. After the Donaldson-Angus incident, the visiting forwards made a powerful rush, Peter Sloane and Barry Thompson leading the charge. The ball was quickly transferred across the field and Ford scored his second try in the corner. After sixty minutes, Gossman kicked his second penalty. Glasgow fought hard to save the game. A good break up the touchline by John Beattie was spoiled by a forward pass and another Glasgow move ended with Steve Munro dropping the ball. In a hard and uncompromising game, both teams had made many mistakes. The New Zealand backs had kicked poorly and Hewson had missed four penalty attempts. The visitors were unhappy about Glasgow's spoiling tactics and claimed that they had been victims of provocation. Not the best of build-ups to Saturday's international at Murrayfield.

SCOTLAND   1979

Saturday 10 November 1979
Murrayfield, Edinburgh
Won 20-6

After their good showing the previous year against the Grand Slam All Blacks, the Scots went into the match optimistic that they could record their first ever win over New Zealand. Captained by Ian McLauchlan, Scotland introduced one new cap in David Johnston, a smooth-running centre from Watsonians who had once signed as part-time football player with Heart of Midlothian. The New Zealanders were unbeaten on their tour, but by their own high standards their form had been unconvincing. The visitors introduced six new caps, including Bernie Fraser, a tough winger from Wellington, and Murray Mexted, a brilliantly athletic number eight. Both players would become major stars of New Zealand rugby in the 1980s, causing the British Lions all sorts of problems in 1983.

SCOTLAND	NEW ZEALAND
A.R. Irvine (Heriot's FP)	R.G. Wilson
K.W. Robertson (Melrose)	S.S. Wilson
J.M. Renwick (Hawick)	G.R. Cunningham
D.I. Johnston (Watsonians)	B.G. Fraser
B.H. Hay (Boroughmuir)	M.B. Taylor
J.Y. Rutherford (Selkirk)	E.J. Dunn
A.J.M. Lawson (Heriot's FP)	D.S. Loveridge
Forwards:	Forwards:
J. McLauchlan (Jordanhill, Capt.)	B.R. Johnstone
C.T. Deans (Hawick)	A.G. Dalton
I.G. Milne (Heriot's FP)	J.E. Speirs
A.J. Tomes (Hawick)	A.M. Haden
D. Gray (West of Scotland)	J.K. Fleming
M.A. Biggar (London Scottish)	K.W. Stewart
G. Dickson (Gala)	G.N.K. Mourie (Capt.)
I.K. Lambie (Watsonians)	M.G. Mexted
	Replacement:
	M.W. Donaldson for Loveridge

Scorers:
Scotland: PGs: Irvine (2).
New Zealand: Tries: Loveridge, Mexted, S. Wilson, Dunn.
Conversions: R. Wilson (2).

Referee: R.C. Quittenton (England).
Attendance: 70,000.

Touted as the best-ever prepared Scotland XV, the home players were their own worst enemies. The Scottish pack held its own at the set-pieces, but the backs made too many errors. Kicks regularly failed

to find touch, the handling was erratic and the tackling was far below international standard. The game started off at a tremendous pace and after seventeen minutes New Zealand opened the scoring. Dave Loveridge broke blind from a scrum and grubber-kicked through. Andy Irvine took too long to collect and was tackled by Stu Wilson as he kicked. Gathering the loose ball, Graham Mourie drove to the line and Loveridge sent four defenders the wrong way with an outrageous dummy to score. Both sides came close to scoring later in the half and Irvine sliced a drop goal attempt in front of the posts, but the All Blacks led 4-0 at the break.

After the interval, Mexted scored a memorable solo try, which summed-up the difference between the sides. Taking the ball at a two-man lineout – a tactic that New Zealand used to great effect – he stormed thirty metres through some weak tackling to score. Richard Wilson converted. Scotland came back with two penalties by Irvine, but New Zealand never really looked like losing. Mark Donaldson replaced the injured Loveridge before Stu Wilson sealed the match with a superbly executed try after another shortened lineout. Towards the end, a Scottish movement broke down and the visitors rushed to the home 25. Dunn went blind and linked with Donaldson and Mourie before taking an inside pass to score. Richard Wilson converted with a magnificent kick.

New Zealand had given the Scots a real lesson in how to play purposeful and efficient rugby. Their kicking had been tactically superior, any mistakes had been quickly covered up and the tackling was safe and secure. Mourie led by example and played an important part in two of the tries. Wilson was solid at full-back and the half-backs Loveridge and Dunn were a constant danger. Few of the Scots enhanced their reputation and for Ian McLauchlan, one of Scotland's great rugby servants, the match was a sad ending to a long international career.

ANGLO SCOTS 1979

Wednesday 14 November 1979
Mayfield, Dundee
Won 18-9

New Zealand successfully completed the Scottish leg of their tour with a match against the Anglo Scots, a scratch selection of players with Scottish connections who played their rugby outside the country. Captained by the experienced Mike Biggar, the Anglos included six international players, five of whom had played against New Zealand in Scotland's test in Auckland in 1975. Their pack included Jeremy Campbell-Lamerton, whose father Mike captained the 1966 Lions in New Zealand. New Zealand fielded a weakened side, but were confidently expected to win. The match was in some doubt because of a very hard frost, but members of Dundee High School FP, the

ANGLO SCOTS	NEW ZEALAND
A.R. Grant (Coventry)	A.R. Hewson
G.A. Birkett (Harlequins)	G.R. Cunningham
A.P. Friell (London Scottish)	T.M. Twigden
J.C.S. Gibson (Sale)	B.R. Ford
L.G. Dick (Gloucester)	K.J. Keane
R. Wilson (London Scottish)	E.J. Dunn
G.J.M. Irvine (Harrogate)	M.W. Donaldson
Forwards:	Forwards:
F. Melvin (Coventry)	R.C. Ketels
C.D. Fisher (Waterloo)	P.H. Sloane
J.A. Fraser (London Scottish)	B.A. Thompson
J.A. Stewart (Watsonians and Ebbw Vale)	A.M. Haden (Capt.)
J.R.E. Campbell-Lamerton	J.K. Fleming
(Army and London Scottish)	
M.A. Biggar (London Scottish, Capt.)	K.W. Stewart
W. Lauder (Neath)	M.M. Burgoyne
I.D. McKie (Sale)	V.E. Stewart

Scorers:
Anglo Scots: PGs: Grant, Gibson (2).
New Zealand: Try: Hewson. Con: Hewson. PGs: Hewson (4).

Referee: B. Head-Rapson (England).
Attendance: 5,000.

host club, worked through the night to ensure that the pitch was playable. Conditions were very difficult with heavy rain and mud, and a greasy ball. The light also faded badly during the second half.

The Anglos made a real game of it and pushed the tourists all the way. The man of the match was the New Zealand full-back Allan Hewson, who scored all of his side's points and kept the Anglos at bay with his long raking touch-kicks and safety under the high ball. In the first half, Hewson landed two penalties before Roddy Grant kicked a penalty after a stirring rush by the Anglo forwards. On twenty-three minutes, Hewson kicked his third penalty and just before half-time the tourists got an important score. Kieran Keane kicked through and the ball bounced into the hands of centre Tim Twigden. After quick passing, Hewson raced over in the left corner. The same player converted with a great kick to put New Zealand 15-3 ahead at the break.

Three minutes into the second half, John Gibson, the Sale centre, kicked a huge penalty almost from the halfway line. Encouraged by this success, the Anglos continued to press. At stand-off, Ron Wilson kept his side going forward with some fine high kicks and two good runs by Ian McKie, the Sale number eight, stretched the New Zealand defence. Wilson and Alan Friell combined well and the former almost made it after a good scissors move. The closing stages of the match degenerated into kick and rush, although both sides managed to land a penalty goal each.

It was another victory for New Zealand, but the Anglos won many plaudits. They had pressurised the visitors and tackled courageously, several players revelling in the difficult conditions. New Zealand were well served by their captain Andy Haden in the lineouts and Ken Stewart in the loose. Behind the scrum, only Keane, Gary Cunningham and Hewson showed any urgency about their play.

NORTHERN DIVISION   1979

Saturday 17 November 1979
Cross Green, Otley
Lost 21-9

The Northern Division team for this historic encounter contained eight England players, and several others who would go on to feature at international level. Of the pack, skipper Bill Beaumont, the entire back row of Peter Dixon, Roger Uttley and Tony Neary plus prop Fran Cotton were all caps, while Jim Syddall and Colin White were England players of the future. Only hooker Andy Simpson remained uncapped, and he was a regular on the England bench for many years. Both the half-backs, Steve Smith and Alan Old, had played for England, as had Mike Slemen and Tony Bond. John Carleton was to win his first cap the following Saturday, while

NORTHERN DIVISION	NEW ZEALAND
K.A. O'Brien (Broughton Park and Lancashire)	R.G. Wilson
J. Carleton (Orrell and Lancashire)	S.S. Wilson
A. Wright (Sale and Lancashire)	G.R. Cunningham
A.M. Bond (Sale and Lancashire)	B.G. Fraser
M.A.C. Slemen (Liverpool and Lancashire)	M.B. Taylor
A.G.B. Old (Sheffield and Yorkshire)	E.J. Dunn
S.J. Smith (Sale and Lancashire)	M.W. Donaldson
Forwards:	Forwards:
C. White (Gosforth and Northumberland)	B.R. Johnstone
A.W. Simpson (Sale)	A.G. Dalton
F.E. Cotton (Sale and Lancashire)	J.E. Spiers
W.B. Beaumont (Fylde and Lancashire, Capt.)	J.K. Fleming
J.P. Sydall (Waterloo and Lancashire)	A.M. Haden
R.M. Uttley (Wasps and Northumberland)	K.W. Stewart
A. Neary (Broughton Park and Lancashire)	G.N.K. Mourie (Capt.)
P.J. Dixon (Gosforth and Cumbria)	M.G. Mexted
	Replacement:
	P.H. Sloane for Dalton

Scorers:
Northern Division: Tries: Bond (2), Smith, Old. Con: Old. PG: Old.
New Zealand: Try: S. Wilson. Con: R. Wilson. PG: R. Wilson.

Referee: A.M. Hosie (Scotland).
Attendance: 10,000.

Kevin O'Brien was a future Ireland full-back. Only centre Tony Wright of the backs was never to play international rugby. Four of the side – Smith, Cotton, Neary and Dixon – had tasted victory against New Zealand when playing for North-West Counties in 1972. The strength of the side was built around

Every vantage point was taken at the small Cross Green ground to witness the North's famous win.
(Yorkshire Post)

the successful Lancashire team of the period. Lancashire had won the County Championship in 1977 and would do so again in 1980. Lancashire's coach, Des Seabrook, was also the coach for the Northern Division, and he began his preparations for the match by inviting some non-Lancashire players to take part in the county's tour of South Africa. Thereafter, he prepared the side thoroughly and received full backing from his selectors. There had been pressure from the England selectors for the side not to include Dixon, Old and Smith and there was a feeling in some quarters that the side was rather over the hill. Old in particular had been in the representative wilderness for some time, but Seabrook and his selectors knew exactly what they were doing and Old, the only Yorkshire player in the team, was crucial to the victory. Chairman of selectors, ex-England captain Mike Weston, later claimed that the final selection meeting took just fifteen minutes.

In an astonishingly daring, yet as it happened totally justified, pre-match report, Bill Bridge, writing in the local press on the morning of the game, stated: 'Today's thundering clash of the unbeaten All Blacks and the supremely confident North at Otley will be the match when a twenty-match winning run for the tourists will come to an end.' The confidence of Mr Bridge was shared by the local populace, and the picturesque Cross Green ground was full to bursting, with many people obtaining vantage points in the surrounding poplar trees. New Zealand entered the game with a near full-strength side. Dave Loveridge had an ankle injury, so Mark Donaldson took his place at scrum-half, but Andy Haden declared himself fit, despite having an injured neck muscle. The weather was overcast and the wind blustery as the sides took the field, and New Zealand full-back Richard Wilson had great difficulty managing the elements, missing the target with four first-half penalties and hitting the post with a drop kick. In contrast, Old kicked a simple goal for the home side, despite the fact that the ball had to be held, and the North scored a try after Stu Wilson dropped a pass in his own 22. Slemen kicked on, picked up the loose ball and put Smith in for the score, giving the home side a 7-0 advantage at the break.

Richard Wilson finally found the target for New Zealand with a penalty after three minutes of the second half, but following a chip kick from Old, Smith ran the ball from a ruck and Bond scored in the corner. The conversion was missed, but the All Blacks now trailed 11-3. Halfway through the second period, the game was put out of New Zealand's reach when Beaumont led a forward drive from a lineout. The backs carried the move on and Bond crashed through the defence for his second try, Old converting. 'Easy, easy', chanted the home crowd happily. The All Blacks did manage a try of their own when, after a rare mistake from O'Brien who failed to gather a high kick, Stu Wilson crossed near the posts, for his namesake to convert. However, the North had the last word when the mighty home pack shoved the All Blacks at a scrum on their own line. Smith picked up the ball and Old scored the final try, and although O'Brien missed the conversion, a famous victory had been achieved.

Many factors contributed to this remarkable result. The North pack played superbly, the tackling of the centres was awesome, and Alan Old's tactical kicking and general reading of the game was brilliant. Bill Beaumont later claimed that this was the best match he ever played in, and the recent twenty-fifth anniversary of the occasion was commemorated by the publication of a special brochure, an anniversary dinner and the issuing of a video and DVD of the game. The match remains one of the finest achievements in English regional rugby and is rightly celebrated to this day.

Tuesday 20 November 1979
County Ground, Exeter
Won 16-0

SOUTH & SOUTH-WEST COUNTIES	NEW ZEALAND
N. Thomson (Plymouth Albion and Devon)	A.R. Hewson
A. Swift (Swansea)	T.M. Twigden
M.C. Beese (Bath, Capt.)	G.R. Cunningham
J.A. Palmer (Bath and Somerset)	B.R. Ford
R.R. Mogg (Gloucester and Gloucestershire)	M.B. Taylor
J.P. Horton (Bath)	E.J. Dunn
D. Murphy (Bath and Somerset)	D.S. Loveridge
Forwards:	Forwards:
M. Fry (Bristol & Somerset)	B.R. Johnstone
S.G.B. Mills (Gloucester and Gloucestershire)	P.H. Sloane
A. Sheppard (Bristol and Gloucestershire)	B.A. Thompson
N.J.C. Pomphrey (Bristol and Gloucestershire)	J.K. Fleming
P.J. Ackford	V.E. Stewart
(Cambridge University and Plymouth Albion)	
P. Hendy (St Ives and Cornwall)	K.W. Stewart
S. Jones (Bath and Somerset)	G.N.K. Mourie
S. Hughes (Exeter and Devon)	M.G. Mexted
Replacement:	
A.J. Morley (Bristol and Gloucestershire)	
for Beese	

Scorers:
New Zealand: Tries: Cunningham, Loveridge. Con: Hewson.
PGs: Hewson (2).

Referee: N.R. Sanson (Scotland).
Attendance: 9,000.

Mike Beese, who had withdrawn from the previous season's South & South-West team to play New Zealand, finally got a chance to lead his side against the tourists in this encounter at Exeter. However, he was unfortunate with injury again, and after a second-half tackle on Murray Mexted he had to be replaced by Alan Morley, an England winger. A number of prominent local players were unable to take part in the game. Full-back Alistair Hignell and prop Barry Nelmes, both England caps, pulled out through injury, while back-row forwards Mike Rafter and John Scott withdrew when they were selected for the England match on the following Saturday. Hignell's replacement, Neil Thomson of Plymouth Albion, was actually an outside half – this was to be only his second senior match as a full-back. The withdrawal of Nelmes at least gave a belated representative call-up to Mike Fry, a much-respected prop from Bristol. Fry, the Bristol captain, was in the course of a run of 102 consecutive appearances in the Bristol front row, and in his two-year stint as Bristol skipper he featured in all 95 first-team games. Arguably the Bristol club's greatest ever prop, he was unjustly ignored at the top level of the game for many years, but was given the job of pack leader for this match. Of the remainder of the side, outside half John Horton had played for England, while Tony Swift, John Palmer, Paul Ackford, Austin Sheppard and Steve Mills were future England caps. New Zealand's team originally featured Andy Haden, but the second row had a neck injury and Graham Mourie insisted that he be rested ahead of the England test. Mike Burgoyne was another original selection for the game, but he was troubled by a leg injury and replaced by Ken Stewart. Eddie Dunn was partnered with Dave Loveridge, in what was seen as a last chance for the first five-eighth to fight off the challenge of Murray Taylor for the Test number ten shirt. Tim Twigden was chosen on the wing and Gary Cunningham in the centre – the reverse of their normal positions in the Auckland side.

The game was staged at the venue of the first ever All Black game in Britain, but in this case the match was a disappointment, being referred to in various reports as 'forgettable'. New Zealand led 6-0 at half-time, courtesy of two Allan Hewson penalties, although the full-back missed a further five goals during the half. After thirteen minutes of the second half, Eddie Dunn took a quick drop out from his own 22, the ball was kicked on by Cunningham and Brian Ford, Thomson and Swift failed to cover the loose ball and Cunningham

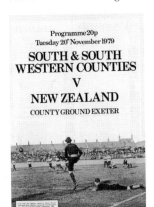

Programme 20p
Tuesday 20 November 1979

SOUTH & SOUTH WESTERN COUNTIES

V

NEW ZEALAND

COUNTY GROUND EXETER

The teams are pictured together before the game at the County Ground.

eventually hacked on to score the first try of the match. In the sixty-fourth minute Murray Mexted made good ground from a tap penalty. He linked with Mourie and the ball travelled via Ken Stewart and Cunningham to Loveridge who scored in the corner. Hewson kicked a fine conversion and a poor match had been settled in favour of the visitors.

For the South & South-West, lineout forwards Paul Ackford and Nigel Pomphrey had performed well. Pomphrey, whose bruised hip made him a doubtful starter for the game – Roger Corin of St Ives was put on standby – almost scored a try following a trademark charge. Skipper Beese was taken to hospital following his brave tackle on Mexted, but he recovered quickly enough to attend the post-match function. Vance Stewart had battled well against the home locks, despite suffering from a knee injury, but Dunn and Loveridge did not combine well together, and Dunn's chance of a place in the side to face England vanished. As for pack leader Mike Fry, he later claimed that he had played harder games in Wales, a country where his considerable skills were always feared and admired.

ENGLAND 1979

Saturday 24 November, 1979
Twickenham, London
Won 10-9

Much to the relief of the All Blacks, just seven of the victorious Northern Division side were chosen for England. Only Tony Neary of the highly effective North back row was selected, and the selectors failed to appreciate the potency of the half-back partnership of Alan Old and Steve Smith, preferring to pick Les Cusworth of Leicester as Smith's partner. It was Cusworth's first cap and there were also debuts for centre Nick Preston and winger John Carleton. The New Zealand side had a rather lop-sided look, with four wingers picked in the back division. Stu Wilson, Gary Cunningham, Bernie Fraser

ENGLAND	NEW ZEALAND
W.H. Hare (Leicester)	R.G. Wilson
J. Carleton (Orrell)	B.R. Ford
A.M. Bond (Sale)	S.S. Wilson
N.J. Preston (Richmond)	B.G. Fraser
M.A.C. Slemen (Liverpool)	G.R. Cunningham
L. Cusworth(Leicester)	M.B. Taylor
S.J. Smith (Sale)	D.S. Loveridge
Forwards:	Forwards:
C.E. Smart (Newport)	B.R. Johnstone
P.J. Wheeler (Leicester)	P.H. Sloane
F.E. Cotton (Sale)	J.E. Spiers
W.B. Beaumont (Fylde, Capt.)	J.K. Fleming
M.J. Colclough (Angouleme)	A.M. Haden
A. Neary (Broughton Park)	K.W. Stewart
M. Rafter (Bristol)	G.N.K. Mourie (Capt.)
J.P. Scott (Cardiff)	M.G. Mexted

Scorers:
England: PGs: Hare (3).
New Zealand: Try: Fleming. PGs: R.G. Wilson (2).

Referee: N.R. Sanson (Scotland).
Attendance: 60,000.

270

Above left: Graham Mourie, captain of the 1978, 1979 and 1980 New Zealand tourists. A Taranaki farmer, Mourie is regarded as one of the greatest of all New Zealand captains. His place in New Zealand rugby history was secured when he led the 1978 side to the first 'Grand Slam' of victories over the four Home Unions. (Rugby Museum of New Zealand)

and Brian Ford were all principally wingers, and as expected there was no place for Eddie Dunn. The sole new cap was hooker Peter Sloane who had replaced Andy Dalton at Otley. It was to be the North Auckland hooker's only cap. In the words of English rugby historian John Griffiths, this game was 'one of the poorest seen at Twickenham for many years.' New Zealand, well marshalled as usual by Graham Mourie, played a sound defensive game, while England seemed short of a tactical plan, never certain whether to play a tight or an open game. In the event, when chances presented themselves in the second half Cusworth kicked too much and, despite starting the match as favourites in the eyes of many, England were unable to record their first Twickenham victory over New Zealand since 1936.

Richard Wilson kicked an early penalty for New Zealand, but was soon off-target with two other attempts. In all, he managed two penalties out of six, while his opposite number 'Dusty' Hare kicked three out of six. Hare was wide with two attempted drop goals in the first half, and Bernie Fraser missed a certain try for the All Blacks when he knocked on having won the race to his own kick ahead. However, New Zealand did manage the game's only try after twenty-seven minutes, when John Fleming crossed the line following a high kick from Dave Loveridge. Wilson could not convert, and the lead was soon reduced to 7-3 when Hare kicked a penalty after Ken Stewart was caught offside. A Wilson penalty, this time for offside against Mike Rafter, brought the half-time score to 10-3 in New Zealand's favour.

Hare reduced the deficit to 4 points with a penalty in the first minute of the second half, and Preston and Carleton launched a promising attack for England that was eventually squeezed into touch by the astute defence of Fraser. A further Hare penalty, awarded after Fleming had pushed England captain Bill Beaumont at a lineout, brought England to within a point with ten minutes remaining, but the full-back was wide of the mark with a final attempt from forty metres late in the game.

New Zealand were deserved winners of this dull encounter, if only because they scored the game's only try. The pack had looked secure, and Loveridge had directed operations well at scrum-half. England would have to wait another four years for a day of Twickenham glory against the All Blacks. New Zealand went on from London to play Italy in Rovigo, where they struggled to overcome a spirited Italian side 18-12. England built on the promising performances of their regional sides and moulded a strong side that went on to win a Five Nations Grand Slam later in the season.

1980

NEW ZEALAND TO
NORTH AMERICA & WALES

THE MATCHES

USA	8 October 1980	San Diego	won 53-6
Canada	11 October 1980	Vancouver	won 43-10
Cardiff	18 October 1980	Cardiff	won 16-9
Llanelli	21 October 1980	Llanelli	won 16-10
Swansea	25 October 1980	Swansea	won 32-0
Newport	28 October 1980	Newport	won 14-3
WALES	1 November 1980	Cardiff	won 23-3

Played 7, Won 7, Drew 0, Lost 0. Scored: 197 points, Conceded: 41.
In Britain: Played 5, Won 5, Drew 0, Lost 0. Scored: 101 points, Conceded: 25.

The New Zealand Tour Party:
B.W. Codlin (Counties), D.L. Rollerson (Manawatu), S.S. Wilson (Wellington), B.G. Fraser (Wellington), F.A. Woodman (North Auckland), B.J. Robertson (Counties), W.M. Osborne (Wanganui), M.B. Taylor (Waikato), N.H. Allen (Counties), M.W. Donaldson (Manawatu), D.S. Loveridge (Taranaki), A.G. Dalton (Counties), H.R. Reid (Bay of Plenty), J.C. Ashworth (Canterbury), R.C. Ketels (Counties),G.A. Knight (Manawatu), J.E. Spiers (Counties), A.M. Haden (Auckland), G. Higginson (Canterbury), F.J. Oliver (Manawatu), G.R. Hines (Waikato), G.N.K. Mourie (Taranaki), M.W. Shaw (Manawatu), M.G. Mexted (Wellington), G.H. Old (Manawatu).

Captain: G.N.K. Mourie. Manager: R.W. Thomas. Assistant Manager: E.A. Watson.

Leading points scorer: D.L. Rollerson – 35 points (24 in Britain).
Leading try-scorer: S.S. Wilson – 5 tries (3 in Britain).
Most appearances: W.M. Osborne – 7 games (5 in Britain).

Saturday 18 October 1980
Cardiff Arms Park, Cardiff
Won 16-9

CARDIFF	NEW ZEALAND
G. Davies	B.W. Codlin
D. Preece	B.G. Fraser
D.H. Burcher	B.J. Robertson
R.N. Hutchings	F. Woodman
P.C.T. Daniels	W.M. Osborne
W.G. Davies	N.H. Allen
T.D. Holmes	D.S. Loveridge
Forwards:	Forwards:
J. Whitefoot	J.C. Ashworth
M.J. Watkins	A.G. Dalton
I.H. Eidman	G.A. Knight
A. Mogridge	G. Higginson
R.L. Norster	A.M. Haden
O. Golding	M.W. Shaw
J.R. Lewis	G.N.K. Mourie (Capt.)
J.P. Scott (Capt.)	M.G. Mexted
Replacement:	
P. Souto for Norster	

Scorers:
Cardiff: PG: W.G. Davies. DG: W.G. Davies (2).
New Zealand: Tries: Fraser, Woodman. Con: Codlin. PG: Codlin.
DG: Allen.

Referee: F. Palmade (France).
Attendance: 33,000.

New Zealand were invited to tour Wales to celebrate the centenary of the Welsh Rugby Union. Their itinerary was tough, as they were scheduled to play the four clubs that, historically, had been the leading teams of the previous 100 years. They were also four sides who had previously defeated New Zealand, although they were not necessarily the four strongest clubs in Wales at this time as Bridgend, Pontypridd and Pontypool were also difficult to beat. The tour was to end with an international with Wales. During the previous summer the British Lions had toured South Africa and had ten Welsh players in the party. The remaining leading Welsh players had toured North America. The All Blacks had embarked on a sixteen-match tour of Australia and Fiji, on which they had lost twice to Australia and been defeated by Queensland. Captain Graham Mourie had been unavailable and, as well as his deputy Dave Loveridge had played, the omission of some experienced players and the drop in form of others had resulted in a disappointing tour. After much soul-searching and an examination of Australian tactics, a twenty-five-man squad, which looked stronger than that which had travelled across the Tasman Sea, was chosen for the autumn tour. Only eleven of the players seen in Britain the previous year were included but Mourie returned to lead the team. On the way over, New Zealand played 2 games in North America, defeating the United States under floodlights in San Diego, and Canada in Vancouver. They then flew to Britain where manager Ray Harper stated the aim of the tour was to reinforce the strong and friendly relations between New Zealand and Wales. The opening match in Wales was against Cardiff, who were in the process of rebuilding. They had not lost at home before this game, but had only won once away from home and been thrashed by Bristol. They had a substantial pack that included props Jeff Whitefoot and Ian Eidman, plus flanker Rhodri Lewis, who were all later to play for Wales. Robert Norster had played for Wales in an uncapped international with Romania the previous season and was on the verge of full international honours. 1977 Lion David Burcher had joined from Newport and the half-backs Terry Holmes and Gareth Davies had only just recovered from serious injuries that had forced their early exit from the Lions tour. Stuart Lane, Cardiff's open-side flanker, had not regained full fitness from the injury he sustained in the first few seconds of the opening Lions game. The side was captained by England number eight John Scott. The All Blacks selected a side on form that neatly mixed youth and experience, and they were strong favourites to win. Centre Bruce Robertson had been in the All Blacks' team that had beaten Cardiff in 1972.

Cardiff started well and Gareth Davies dropped an early goal but the lead was brief. Dave Loveridge raced around the front of a lineout in the Cardiff 22 and fed the ball to Bernie Fraser who scored in the corner. Brett Codlin missed the conversion but he and Davies later exchanged penalties. Then Loveridge ran down the blind side of another lineout and kicked ahead. Mark Shaw regained the ball and when it came back to Loveridge, the half-back passed to Nicky Allen who moved it on to Fred

Woodman to score the second try. Codlin converted from wide out and Allen drop a goal by the stroke of half-time. New Zealand led 16-6 at the break.

New Zealand, rusty in the first half, failed to build on their position in the second and were disappointing. Cardiff raised their game and proved spirited and awkward to break down. The only score of the half was a second dropped goal to Gareth Davies, who evaded Shaw to score. Davies had kicked superbly, pressurising the All Blacks but rarely running at them. At the end Cardiff were relieved not to have suffered a bigger defeat while the All Blacks knew they had not played well.

LLANELLI   1980

Tuesday 21 October 1980
Stradey Park, Llanelli
Won 16-10

New Zealand changed most of their pack for the game with only Graham Mourie and Graeme Higginson retained from the Cardiff game. The forwards were quite inexperienced although there was a more familiar feel about the backs. It was similar for Llanelli. Most of their side was young, although Phil Bennett, Derek Quinnell and J.J. Williams joined skipper Ray Gravell as survivors of the 1972 triumph over the All Blacks. Williams had been on the verge of retirement but had been encouraged to continue playing. The passionate Gravell, who had played Test rugby for the Lions the previous summer, imbued his side with the spirit and heroism needed to win again. Paul Ringer had returned to rugby after suspension imposed following his sending off for Wales at Twickenham the previous season, a sentence that cost him a

LLANELLI	NEW ZEALAND
M. Gravelle	D.L. Rollerson
M. Jones	S.S. Wilson
P.J. Morgan	B.J. Robertson
R.W.R. Gravell (Capt.)	F. Woodman
J.J. Williams	W.M. Osborne
P. Bennett	M.B. Taylor
M.H.J. Douglas	M.W. Donaldson
Forwards:	Forwards:
C. Thomas	R.C. Ketels
H. Thomas	H.R. Reid
L. Delaney	J.E. Spiers
D.L. Quinnell	F.J. Oliver
R. Cornelius	G. Higginson
P. Ringer	G.R. Hines
D.F. Pickering	G.N.K. Mourie (Capt.)
A.E. Davies	G.H. Old
Replacement:	
P.S. May for Davies	

Scorers:
Llanelli: Try: M. Jones. PG: Bennett. DG: Gravelle.
New Zealand: Tries: Rollerson, Robertson. Con: Rollerson.
PG: Rollerson. DG: Taylor.

Referee: A.M. Hosie (Scotland).
Attendance: 20,000.

place on the Lions tour. Peter Morgan was an international and Mark Douglas, Alun Davies, who passed a late fitness test to play, and Laurence Delaney were later capped, as was David Pickering who, as a schoolboy, had played in the curtain-raiser to the 1972 thriller.

The match was tough and tense, with the atmosphere electric. It became a tremendous game of rugby in which Llanelli raised their performance and gave the All Blacks a thorough examination. Bennett kicked Llanelli into the lead with a penalty early in the game before Doug Rollerson equalised with a penalty for the All Blacks. Twenty minutes later Llanelli had an attacking scrum. Bennett made a break that was carried on by full-back Martin Gravelle who drew the New Zealand defence and put Mark Jones in for a try in the corner. The crowd erupted with joy, and when Gravelle dropped a goal later in the half memories of 1972 came flooding back. Both Bennett and Gravelle missed kicks at goal but the home pack was dominant and Llanelli led 10-3 at half-time.

The second half was seconds old when rain began to fall, which made the pitch slippery, and muddy patches appeared. The All Blacks started the period at top speed. A high garryowen pressurised the home defence and the All Blacks' forwards got to the breakdown quicker. The ball came back to Mark Donaldson who moved down the blind side and fed Rollerson who drove through the home defence for a try. The conversion hit the post and shortly afterwards, Murray Taylor dropped a fine goal to tie the scores. The second half had only been in play six minutes and from staring defeat in the face New Zealand were in the ascendancy. Llanelli regained some of their first-half composure but New Zealand were the more dominant side. The exchanges were hard and the atmosphere electric. Then, with fifteen minutes to go, New Zealand had a scrum on the Llanelli 22. The ball emerged untidily and a hurried pass meant for Rollerson was gathered by Bruce Robertson. He was tackled by Ringer, who had been receiving medical attention for much of the second half. However, the flank forward was suffering from concussion and double-vision and he failed to hold on to the centre, who escaped and raced in to score under the posts. Rollerson converted. Ringer was distraught but had his colleagues kicked the penalties they were awarded in the first half, the result may have been different. There was no further score.

It was a ferocious battle played in good spirit but it regularly threatened to spill over. Gravell and Mourie were warned as to the future conduct of their players. The dazed Ringer was cautioned; the fiery Reid was cautioned. As the game came to its close a move went to ground. Higginson joined in and was seen to stamp into the ruck. The movement of his leg did not look like the act of someone heeling the ball out and referee Hosie blew his whistle. He took Higginson and Mourie to one side and after a substantial lecture he pointed to the stand. Mourie visibly sagged, the crowd roared and then Bennett jumped in, pleading for clemency. Gravell and Quinnell joined too. They argued it had been a good game and this was the WRU centenary and nobody wanted it blemished with even more controversy between Wales and New Zealand. Weighed down by the protests and the ticking of the clock, Hosie blew his whistle for the end of the match. Was Higginson sent off? No. The referee later said he hadn't sent the player off but was merely threatening to do so. Everybody else in the ground was convinced he had.

Stradey Park — Parc-y-Strade
Llanelli

LLANELLI

NEW ZEALAND

Tuesday, 21st October, 1980
Kick-off 2.30 p.m.

Official Programme 40p

SWANSEA 1980

Saturday 25 October 1980
St Helen's, Swansea
Won 32-0

Mark Shaw scores for the All Blacks, to the approval of Murray Mexted. (Dave Fox)

SWANSEA	NEW ZEALAND
W.R. Blyth	D.L. Rollerson
A.H. Swift	S.S. Wilson
G. Jenkins	B.J. Robertson
M. Dacey	B.G. Fraser
A. Meredith	W.M. Osborne
D.S. Richards	N.H. Allen
D.B. Williams	D.S. Loveridge
Forwards:	Forwards:
C. Williams	R.C. Ketels
J. Herdman	H.R. Reid
G. John	G.A. Knight
G.A.D. Wheel (Capt.)	G. Higginson
B.G. Clegg	A.M. Haden
M. Keyworth	M.W. Shaw
M. Davies	G.N.K. Mourie (Capt.)
R.D. Moriarty	M.G. Mexted
Replacement:	
T. Cheeseman for Keyworth	

Scorers:
New Zealand: Tries: Wilson (2), Higginson, Shaw, Loveridge, Fraser. Con: Rollerson. PG: Rollerson (2).

Referee: J.R. West (IRFU).
Attendance: 25,000.

Swansea were the strongest club side in Britain and many felt their challenge could exceed that of Wales. In the 1979/80 season they were runners-up in the Welsh Cup and until the match with New Zealand had only lost one of

their 12 games. Their captain was Geoff Wheel, who had been the first Welsh player to be sent off in an international in 1977. At the end of that season he was selected to tour with the Lions but a heart condition, which later proved insignificant, forced his withdrawal. Elsewhere in the pack were Barry Clegg, who had previously been capped, and double-Lions prop Clive Williams. Future international flanker Mark Davies was selected along with England international Mark Keyworth. David Richards was at outside half, although a centre for Wales, and at centre was Malcolm Dacey, a future international outside half. Winger Tony Swift later played for England. Swansea were forecast to give New Zealand a hard match and the All Blacks picked as strong a side as possible.

The opening quarter of the game was close but the All Blacks took the lead when Doug Rollerson kicked an early penalty, then after twenty-five minutes, a lineout on the Swansea line was won by Graeme Higginson, who dived over for the try. The conversion was missed but almost immediately New Zealand attacked and won a scrum close to the Swansea line. Murray Mexted picked up and fed Mark Shaw who drove over. Just before half-time, Swansea took a twenty-two drop out that Shaw caught and drove forward. He released the ball and first Mexted then Stu Wilson and Hika Reid drove on in a move that Dave Loveridge finished off. Rollerson missed the conversion but New Zealand were 15-0 up at the break.

An early second half penalty was followed by another try. A Swansea attack broke down and Graham Mourie started a counter-attack that ended with Bernie Fraser scoring. Rollerson converted and then was involved in another attack. Swansea stood off him and he fed Mourie, who passed to Wilson for another score. Playing terrific rugby, the All Blacks back row burst away in a passing rush. The ball was moved to Rollerson, whose pass to Wilson was low, but the wing kicked it on and was first to the ball for the final try.

Wheel stated afterwards that 'our biggest mistake was that we turned up'. Swansea had been run ragged and few players had improved their chances of playing for Wales the following Saturday.

NEWPORT 1980

Tuesday 28 October 1980
Rodney Parade, Newport
Won 14-3

Newport, theoretically the weakest of the Welsh clubs to face New Zealand, were further weakened when they lost British Lions centre Gareth Evans and England prop Colin Smart with injury. Wing Robert Ackerman had to stand down following his selection to play for Wales the following weekend. Newport had won only 7 of their 13 matches so far that season, losing heavily to Pontypool, Newbridge and Swansea. However, they had enjoyed a 38-6 win over Gloucester. Another young side, Newport possessed a strong forward unit in which prop Rhys Morgan and lock David Waters later became internationals. Their captain was Geoff Evans, who had performed the same duties in the 1973 encounter between

NEWPORT	NEW ZEALAND
A. Watkins	B.W. Codlin
J. Churchill	S.S. Wilson
P. Waters	W.M. Osborne
P. Bolland	F. Woodman
N. Webb	D.L. Rollerson
J. Robinson	M.B. Taylor
A. Billinghurst	M.W. Donaldson (Capt.)
Forwards:	Forwards:
J. Dale	J.C. Ashworth
S. O'Donoghue	A.G. Dalton
G.R. Morgan	J.E. Spiers
G. Fynn	F.J. Oliver
D.R. Waters	A.M. Haden
R. Powell	M.W. Shaw
G. Evans (Capt.)	G.R. Hines
K. Williams	G.H. Old
	Replacement:
	M.G. Mexted for Shaw

Scorers:
Newport: PG: Bolland.
New Zealand: Tries: Shaw, Wilson. PG: Codlin (2).

Referee: A. Welsby (RFU).
Attendance: 20,000.

the sides. The All Blacks changed two-thirds of their team for the game but there was competition for places in the Test side in several positions. Half-back Mark Donaldson captained the side. Light rain had made the pitch greasy which didn't help handling, but Newport, in particular scrum-half Alun Billinghurst and his pack, harassed and pressurised New Zealand throughout the game in an heroic performance.

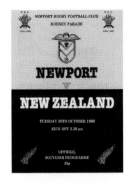

The opening score came after ten minutes when the Newport backs were caught offside. Codlin kicked the penalty and then kicked another after Newport centre Peter Bolland had missed two kickable goals. Bolland missed a third just before half-time and New Zealand went into the break 6-0 up.

Having contested everything in the first half, the Newport pack were even more difficult to handle in the second. However, after five minutes a New Zealand rolling maul made good ground. The Newport forwards managed to strip the ball from them in their own 22 and worked it back to outside half Justin Robinson. Donaldson was on top of him quickly and charged down his kick. Mark Shaw followed up and dived on the ball just before it reached the dead-ball line for the opening try. The conversion missed. Newport surged into New Zealand territory but Bolland missed his fourth penalty. Murray Mexted replaced the injured Shaw before Bolland at last hit the target with a penalty from twenty-seven metres. In the dying minutes Donaldson broke down the blind side from a scrum in the Newport 22 and passed to Codlin, who received and delivered the ball in one movement to Stu Wilson who raced in for the try. Codlin missed the conversion and shortly afterwards, the referee blew for time. It had been an exciting game with a winning margin that, again, failed to reflect the contribution of Newport.

The spirit and promise of the Newport performance failed to blossom. 3 matches later they lost 4-0 to Village side Penclawdd in the Welsh Cup.

WALES   1980

Saturday 1 November 1980
Cardiff Arms Park, Cardiff
Won 23-3

Wales had won their 2 home matches in the previous season's Five Nations Championship but had been pilloried after a rough game at Twickenham and lost both away games. They had played a match against an Overseas XV earlier in the season and were unconvincing in a 32-25 win. With the All Blacks in exhilarating form there was an air of gloom and a justifiable belief that for Wales this tour had come a season or so too late. The second golden era of Welsh rugby was over. The Welsh were able to select a strong side but there were concerns over a number of players. Several of the backs who had returned from South Africa had lost form and new caps were awarded to Gareth Williams, a tall number eight who

WALES	NEW ZEALAND
J.P.R. Williams (Bridgend)	D.L. Rollerson
H.E. Rees (Neath)	S.S. Wilson
D.S. Richards (Swansea)	B.J. Robertson
S.P. Fenwick (Bridgend, Capt.)	B.G. Fraser
R.A. Ackerman (Newport)	W.M. Osborne
W.G. Davies (Cardiff)	N.H. Allen
T.D. Holmes (Cardiff)	D.S. Loveridge
Forwards:	Forwards:
C. Williams (Swansea)	R.C. Ketels
A.J. Phillips (Cardiff)	H.R. Reid
G. Price (Pontypool)	G.A. Knight
D.L. Quinnell (Llanelli)	G. Higginson
A.J. Martin (Aberavon)	A.M. Haden
J. Squire (Pontypool)	M.W. Shaw
P. Ringer (Llanelli)	G.N.K. Mourie (Capt.)
G.P. Williams (Bridgend)	M.G. Mexted
Replacements:	
E.T. Butler (Pontypool) for Squire,	
P.J. Morgan (Llanelli) for Rees	

Scorers:
Wales: PG: Fenwick.
New Zealand: Tries: Mourie, Allen, Fraser, Reid. Cons: Rollerson (2). PG: Rollerson.

Referee: J.R. West (IRFU).
Attendance: 53,000.

Steve Fenwick's team for the WRU's centenary international.

had been a Lion, and Robert Ackerman, a nineteen-year-old student who had scored 6 tries for his club against Gloucester earlier in the season. Ackerman's father, Doug, had played for Newport against New Zealand in 1954. Geoff Wheel was forced to withdraw with injury and Allan Martin took over in the second row. J.P.R. Williams was duly reinstated at full-back having retired the previous year and Alan Phillips, first-choice hooker for Wales and a 1980 Lion but second choice at his club, formed a decent front row with Graham Price and Clive Williams. Steve Fenwick captained the team. New Zealand selected the same XV that had demolished Swansea. Rod Ketels, Graeme Higginson and Doug Rollerson made their international debuts.

New Zealand immediately began moving the ball at pace in the backs and the forwards took on Wales and quickly achieved dominance. However, the first score came midway through the first half when Rollerson kicked a penalty. Then after half an hour, a New Zealand attack was intercepted by David Richards, who raced upfield. He appeared short of fitness and looked for support on halfway. A mix-up ensued and New Zealand regained possession. Bruce Robertson raced back into Welsh territory and fed captain Graham Mourie, who worked a dummy scissors with Stu Wilson and dived in the corner to score the opening try. Nicky Allen scored a second try close to half-time although he appeared to lose the ball when tackled on the goal line. New Zealand turned around 11-0 ahead.

Fenwick scored a penalty for Wales some way into the second half but the last twenty-five minutes were all New Zealand, and Bernie Fraser scored the next try, coming in close to a scrum deep in the Welsh 22 and using great determination and power to ride three tacklers to score. With the match won and a few minutes left New Zealand scored a fine try. The All Blacks won a lineout on their 22 and Dave Loveridge broke away with Mourie in support. Then Loveridge cleverly switched direction with a long pass into midfield that was taken by Bill Osborne, who fed Bruce Robertson in his 100th game for New Zealand, who in turn passed to Wilson. The winger went flat out for the corner but was brought down by a magnificent tackle from Ackerman. Wilson flipped the ball up to the supporting Hika Reid for the hooker to score. With Reid and Wilson's tries converted by Rollerson, New Zealand ran out comfortable winners. It was the biggest home defeat for Wales in ninety-eight years.

New Zealand received a standing ovation from a partisan crowd for a fine performance. All the New Zealanders returned with their reputations enhanced, but for Wales only Robert Ackerman excelled, and that in defence.

NEW ZEALAND TO ENGLAND & SCOTLAND

THE MATCHES

Edinburgh	26 October 1983	Edinburgh	won 22-6
South of Scotland	29 October 1983	Galashiels	won 30-9
Northern Division	2 November 1983	Gateshead	won 27-21
London Division	5 November 1983	Twickenham	won 18-15
Midland Division	8 November 1983	Leicester	lost 19-13
SCOTLAND	12 November 1983	Murrayfield	drawn 25-25
South & South-West England	15 November 1983	Bristol	won 18-6
ENGLAND	19 November 1983	Twickenham	lost 15-9

Played 8, Won 5, Drew 1, Lost 2. Scored: 162 points, Conceded: 116.

The New Zealand Tour Party:
B.W. Codlin (Counties), D.L. Rollerson (Manawatu), S.S. Wilson (Wellington), B.G. Fraser (Wellington), F.A. Woodman (North Auckland), B.J. Robertson (Counties), W.M. Osborne (Wanganui), M.B. Taylor (Waikato), N.H. Allen (Counties), M.W. Donaldson (Manawatu), D.S. Loveridge (Taranaki), A.G. Dalton (Counties), H.R. Reid (Bay of Plenty), J.C. Ashworth (Canterbury), R.C. Ketels (Counties), G.A. Knight (Manawatu), J.E. Spiers (Counties), A.M. Haden (Auckland), G. Higginson (Canterbury), F.J. Oliver (Manawatu), G.R. Hines (Waikato), G.N.K. Mourie (Taranaki), M.W. Shaw (Manawatu), M.G. Mexted (Wellington), G.H. Old (Manawatu).

Captain: S.S. Wilson. Manager: P.W. Mitchell. Assistant Manager: D.B. Rope.

Leading points scorer: R.M. Deans – 52 points.
Leading try-scorer: S.S. Wilson & B.G. Fraser – 3 tries.
Most appearances: S.S. Wilson – 8 games.

Wednesday 26 October 1983
Myreside, Edinburgh
Won 22-6

EDINBURGH	NEW ZEALAND
A.G. Hastings (Watsonians)	R.M. Deans
P.D. Steven (Heriot's FP)	S.S. Wilson (Capt.)
A.E. Kennedy (Watsonians, Capt.)	S.T. Pokere
D.I. Johnston (Watsonians)	B.W. Smith
J.C.W. Beazley (Edinburgh Wanderers)	C.I. Green
D.S. Wylie (Stewart's-Melville FP)	W.R. Smith
D. Macdonald (Musselburgh)	D.E. Kirk
Forwards:	Forwards:
A.K. Brewster (Stewart's-Melville FP)	K.G. Boroevitch
J.C. Munro (Heriot's FP)	H.B. Wilson
I.G. Milne (Heriot's FP)	S. Crichton
G.P. Millar (Heriot's FP)	A. Anderson
A.L. Dunlop (Heriot's FP)	G.J. Braid
J.H. Calder (Stewart's-Melville FP)	F.N.K. Shelford
P.M. Drennan (Edinburgh Acads)	M.W. Shaw
F. Calder (Stewart's-Melville FP)	G.H. Old

Scorers:
Edinburgh: PGs: Steven, Hastings.
New Zealand: Tries: Shelford, H.B. Wilson, Green.
Cons: Deans (2). PG: Deans (2).

Referee: L.M. Prideaux (England).
Attendance: 7,000.

New Zealand had enjoyed a significant 4-0 series win over the British Lions earlier in the year, the final Test of which had seen a 38-6 victory for the All Blacks. They followed that with a Bledisloe Cup win in Sydney, and planned to tour Argentina in the autumn. However, they failed to get the green light from the South Americans and the tour was called off. Following the cancellation, the New Zealanders undertook an impromptu 8-match visit to Scotland and England. Captained for the first time in Britain by a back, Stu Wilson, the tourists were forced to leave behind several of the best players from the recent Test series against the British Lions, including the captain Andy Dalton, Andy Haden and the man of the series, half-back Dave Loveridge. The squad of twenty-six included a dozen new to the All Blacks. The New Zealanders faced a potentially difficult opening to their tour with a fixture against Edinburgh. The tourists fielded nine new All Blacks. Among these was the Canterbury full-back Robbie Deans, a distant relative of Bob Deans who played for New Zealand against Wales in 1905. Another newcomer was Otago half-back David Kirk, who four years later would become the first man to raise the Rugby World Cup as a winning captain. Edinburgh fielded a strong side with several Scottish international players, including the British Lions prop Iain Milne. Both sides were fairly evenly matched at forward, the two back rows were adept in support play and the back divisions had some very fast runners, including Steve Pokere for the All Blacks and David Johnston for the home side.

On a blustery day, the New Zealanders got their tour off to a winning start, showing themselves adept at the traditional virtues of powerful driving in the loose and speed to the ball on the ground. However, the tourists displayed an uncharacteristic lack of discipline and conceded a large number of penalties, which was to prove their undoing as the tour progressed. Edinburgh would have fared

a lot better if Peter Steven had not had such a dismal day with his goal-kicking. The Heriot's winger missed six out of seven kicks at goal, four of them in the first twenty minutes when Edinburgh were trying to capitalise on their wind advantage. In a scrappy opening, Steven's one successful kick was matched by one from Robbie Deans, following which the New Zealanders began to find their rhythm and exert some control. Frank Shelford scored the opening try of the tour after a majestic run by Pokere. Deans, a polished performer at full-back, converted and kicked another penalty after the Edinburgh backs had crept offside. Before the interval, Steven handed the kicking duties over to Gavin Hastings, who landed a penalty to make the score 12-6 at the break.

The visitors had most of the pressure in the second period, but the Edinburgh defence was admirably solid. After sixty-six minutes, the visitors put the result beyond doubt when Brett Wilson, helped by the rest of his forwards, was swept over the line. New Zealand sealed the match in injury time when Craig Green crossed after an incisive scissors movement with Wayne Smith. Deans converted to complete a satisfactory, but not entirely convincing, win for the All Blacks.

SOUTH OF SCOTLAND   1983

Saturday 29 October 1983
Netherdale, Galashiels
Won 30-9

After New Zealand's less than impressive display at Myreside, it was felt the South of Scotland, the reigning Scottish district champions, had an outside chance of a win. The home side could boast almost 200 caps between them, including the British Lions pairing of John Rutherford and Roy Laidlaw at half-back and an all-international forward pack, which was expected to exploit weaknesses in the visitors' scrum. Unfortunately, on the eve of the match, the South's inspirational captain Jim Aitken was forced to withdraw because of flu, the uncapped Jed-Forest prop Keith Sudlow taking his place. This was a bad omen for the South as New Zealand, showing eleven changes from the midweek side, turned on a blistering five-try demolition of the Scots. In retrospect, it was the best performance of the tour.

SOUTH OF SCOTLAND	NEW ZEALAND
P.W. Dods (Gala)	K.J. Crowley
A. Thomson (Kelso)	S.S. Wilson (Capt.)
G.R.T. Baird (Kelso)	S.T. Pokere
K.W. Robertson (Melrose)	B.G. Fraser
I. Tukalo (Selkirk)	W.T. Taylor
J.Y. Rutherford (Selkirk)	I.T.W. Dunn
R.J. Laidlaw (Jed-Forest, Capt.)	A.J. Donald
Forwards:	Forwards:
K. Sudlow (Jed-Forest)	B. McGrattan
C.T. Deans (Hawick)	H.R. Reid
R.F. Cunningham (Gala)	M.G. Davie
A.J. Tomes (Hawick)	G.J. Braid
T.J. Smith (Gala)	A. Anderson
D.B. White (Gala)	M.W. Shaw
D.G. Leslie (Gala)	M.J.B. Hobbs
I.A.M. Paxton (Selkirk)	M.G. Mexted
Replacement:	
A.J. Campbell (Hawick) for Paxton	

Scorers:
South of Scotland: PGs: Dods (2). DG: Rutherford.
New Zealand: Tries: Wilson (2), Fraser, Hobbs, Crowley.
Cons: Crowley (2). PGs: Crowley (2).

Referee: F. Howard (England).
Attendance: 10,000.

The South led three times and were ahead 9-8 early in the second half, but that was as good as it got for the home side. Peter Dods kicked two penalties in the first half, both of which were answered by New Zealand tries. Bernie Fraser scored the first, running onto Steve Pokere's chip after the South backs had been caught flat by a miss move and a decoy run. In injury time, Stu Wilson completed the Wellington

double act after his forwards had poached a loose South scrummage heel. Full-back Kieran Crowley, who had a shaky half, missed both conversions but the tourists held a slender 8-6 lead at the interval.

The second period was increasingly one-way traffic as the New Zealand pack began to function together as a unit. Time and again, Murray Mexted or Hika Reid, the firey hooker, would surge into the merest hint of a gap, their colleagues would support in tight formation, and when the movement came to a halt the ball was spun wide. It was textbook rugby of the highest order, exemplified by the fourth try. Mexted drove down the left, his forwards carried on and crossfield passing found Crowley, who looped Wilson to score. Finding his form, the New Zealand full-back ended the match with a personal tally of 14 points from his try, two penalties and conversions of tries by Wilson and Jock Hobbs. By the finish, the South looked a thoroughly well-beaten side.

The New Zealanders had made great strides since their previous game. Their teamwork was much improved, Pokere showed his class and awareness in the centre while the back row of Mexted, Hobbs and Mark Shaw was immense. By contrast, the South's lineout play was very loose and the scrum was under more pressure than expected. Some of the players seemed to lose heart too easily, although back-row men Derek White and David Leslie fought hard to stem the tide, despite the latter having sustained a nasty leg gash in the first half.

NORTHERN DIVISION   1983

Wednesday 2 November 1983
International Stadium,
Gateshead
Won 27-21

Seven of the home side had played in the famous Northern Division victory over New Zealand in 1979. Of these, John Carleton, Tony Bond, Mike Slemen, Alan Old, Steve Smith and Jim Syddall were England internationals, while Colin White would win his first cap against the All Blacks later in the tour. Of the remaining eight players, Steve Bainbridge and Peter Winterbottom had played for their country, while Paul Simpson would join White as a new cap when New Zealand met England. Following the two comfortable victories in Scotland, there were first starts of the tour in the New Zealand side for Warwick Taylor and Alastair Robinson.

The capacity crowd witnessed a fiery

NORTHERN DIVISION	NEW ZEALAND
D.M. Norton (Headingley)	R.M. Deans
J. Carleton (Orrell)	S.S. Wilson (Capt.)
S. Townend (Wakefield)	C.I. Green
A.M. Bond (Sale)	B.G. Fraser
M.A.C. Slemen (Liverpool)	W.T. Taylor
A.G.B. Old (Sheffield)	W.R. Smith
S.J. Smith (Sale, Capt.)	A.J. Donald
Forwards:	Forwards:
C. White (Gosforth)	B. McGrattan
A.W. Simpson (Sale)	H.R. Reid
J. Curry (Gosforth)	M.G. Davie
J.P. Syddall (Waterloo)	A. Anderson
S.J. Bainbridge (Gosforth)	A.G. Robinson
S. Hodgson (Vale of Lune)	M.W. Shaw
P.J. Winterbottom (Headingley)	M.J.B. Hobbs
P.D. Simpson (Bath)	M.G. Mexted

Scorers:
Northern Division: Tries: A. Simpson, P. Simpson. Cons: Old (2). PGs: Old (2). DG: Old.
New Zealand: Tries: Donald, Shaw, McGrattan. Cons: Deans (3). PGs: Deans (3).

Referee: J.M. Fleming (Scotland).
Attendance: 15,000.

first-half performance from the home pack, and when Alan Old put the North 9-3 ahead with two penalties and a drop goal, it seemed as if there might be a repeat of the Otley triumph of four years ago. As the game approached half-time, all the tourists had to show for their efforts was a solitary Robbie Deans penalty, but just before the break scrum-half Andy Donald crossed for a try that Deans converted to leave the sides level at 9-9 at the interval. Such was the concern among the tourists' ranks at this point in the match that coach Bryce Rope and physio Peter Stokes complained to the watching RFU

secretary, Bob Weighill, that the Northern Division coach, Dave Robinson, was coaching from the touchline during play. This was frowned upon at the time, and Robinson was spoken to. He subsequently moved away from the pitch, although he later claimed that he had merely been enquiring about the state of Jim Syddall's gashed knee.

The second half was totally different, with the All Blacks dominating the third quarter. Bernie Fraser missed two scoring chances, and one brilliant break from Craig Green saw Deans lose possession when he was tackled over the line by Carleton. There were, however, two penalties from Deans, plus a try from Mark Shaw, which Deans converted to put his side comfortably ahead at 21-9. To their credit, the North did not throw in the towel, choosing instead to take the attack to their opponents by tapping penalties instead of kicking them. One of these taps led to a try by hooker Andy Simpson, the first try conceded by the All Blacks on the tour. Old converted, but New Zealand stretched their lead when Brian McGrattan scored a try, Deans again adding the extras. Another tap penalty brought a further North try, this time by Paul Simpson, and Old's conversion once again reduced the deficit to 6 points. Despite this late rally, the game finished with the visitors deservedly claiming revenge for the Otley defeat.

North skipper Steve Smith was disappointed that his side had lost, but felt that the game had proved that the tourists were beatable. 'At least they are not invincible,' he claimed. 'They can be beaten provided you select good footballers with plenty of spirit. That was the Northern policy.'

LONDON DIVISION   1983

Saturday 5 November 1983
Twickenham, London
Won 18-15

LONDON DIVISION	NEW ZEALAND
N.C. Stringer (Wasps)	K.J. Crowley
R.M. Cardus (Wasps)	B.W. Smith
N.J. Preston (Richmond)	S.S. Wilson (Capt.)
M.A. Williams (Wasps)	B.G. Fraser
M.D. Bailey (Cambridge University)	C.I. Green
G.H. Davies (Wasps)	I.T.W. Dunn
I.K. George (London Welsh)	D.E. Kirk
Forwards:	Forwards:
P.A.G. Rendall (Wasps)	K.G. Boroevich
A. Simmons (Wasps)	H.B. Wilson
M.F. Claxton (Harlequins)	S. Crichton
M.C.F. Pinnegar (Wasps)	G.J. Braid
M.J. Colclough (Wasps, Capt.)	A.G. Robinson
F. Emeruwa (Wasps)	M.W. Shaw
D.H. Cooke (Harlequins)	F.N.K. Shelford
C.J.S. Butcher (Harlequins)	G.H. Old

Scorers:
London Division: PGs: Stringer (5).
New Zealand: Try: Shelford. Con: Crowley. PGs: Crowley (4).

Referee: T.E. Allan (Scotland).
Attendance: 15,000.

Four of the London backs, Huw Davies, Nick Stringer, Richard Cardus and Nick Preston had appeared for England, as had forwards David Cooke and skipper Maurice Colclough. Paul Rendall, Chris Butcher and Mark Bailey would all be capped during the following year. In contrast to the numerous survivors from the Northern Division's previous encounter with the All Blacks, only Preston survived from the 1979 London side. The All Blacks chose to rest most of their first-choice players. This game was another close call for the tourists, and it was felt that had London been a little more positive in their approach they could have won. The home pack had the satisfaction of pushing their opponents backwards on several occasions, and the tackling of Cooke, Butcher and Francis Emeruwa in the back row did much to contain the opposition. Unfortunately, outside half Huw Davies only got the ball in his hands twice outside his own twenty-five, and this statistic perhaps best sums up London's lack of adventure.

The game was full of niggle, with strict referee Eric Allan awarding a total of thirty-seven penalties, twenty-one of them against New Zealand. Many of the offences were avoidable misdemeanours such as shirt-pulling, and skipper Stu Wilson was critical of his team's lack of discipline after the match. There were no tries in the first half, which ended level at 9-9, Stringer kicking three penalties for London and Kieran Crowley replying with three for the All Blacks. There was, however, a crucial miss by Stringer at a time when his side led 9-6. A penalty was awarded in front of the posts, but the full-back pulled it wide.

The second half began in more positive fashion, both sides looking more willing to attack. The only try of the match came early in the half, when Geoff Old picked up from a scrum on halfway as the London forwards were wheeling it. Bruce Smith worked the blind side, finding David Kirk in support before the impressive Mark Shaw put Frank Shelford in for the score. There was some doubt about whether Stringer had prevented Shelford from touching down cleanly, but the score stood and Crowley's conversion gave the visitors a six-point advantage. A further Crowley penalty stretched the lead to 18-9, but London were not finished, and came back into the game with two more Stringer penalties, although New Zealand did not really look in much trouble during the closing stages.

Despite struggling on occasions in the scrum, the All Black eight had done enough wheeling to give London scrum-half Ian George a difficult afternoon. Shaw had been the outstanding New Zealand forward, while Shelford belied his position as one of the 'dirtracker' players of the tour party. Overall, though, with challenging matches ahead, the All Blacks knew that they would have to improve considerably if they were to remain unbeaten on tour.

MIDLAND DIVISION 1983

Tuesday 8 November 1983
Welford Road, Leicester
Lost 19-13

The Midland Division included nine England players in the team to face New Zealand in what would be the first All Black game in Britain to be played under lights. Of the Midland backs, only the wingers were uncapped, while in the pack Bob Wilkinson, Peter Wheeler, Gary Pearce and Nick Jeavons had all appeared for their country. Of the remaining forwards, Gary Rees and Graham Robbins were future England players, as was Dean Richards, who replaced Robbins in the final minute of the game. Wheeler was the only remaining member of the Midland Division pack that had lost to New Zealand in 1979, while in the backs his Leicester teammates 'Dusty' Hare, Paul Dodge, Clive Woodward and Les Cusworth survived from that match. Second-row forward Wilkinson had first faced the All Blacks as long ago as the opening game of the 1972/73 tour, when he was a student at Cambridge University. Recognising the strength of the home challenge, the New Zealand management chose a strong side containing the bulk of the first-choice players.

MIDLAND DIVISION	NEW ZEALAND
W.H. Hare (Leicester)	R.M. Deans
S. Holdstock (Nottingham)	S.S. Wilson (Capt.)
P.W. Dodge (Leicester)	S.T. Pokere
C.R. Woodward (Leicester)	B.W. Smith
J. Goodwin (Moseley)	W.T. Taylor
L. Cusworth (Leicester)	W.R. Smith
N.G. Youngs (Leicester)	A.J. Donald
Forwards:	Forwards:
S. Redfern (Leicester)	B. McGrattan
P.J. Wheeler (Leicester, Capt.)	H.R. Reid
G.S. Pearce (Northampton)	M.G. Davie
R. Wilkinson (Bedford)	G.H. Old
V. Cannon (Northampton)	A. Anderson
N.C. Jeavons (Moseley)	M.W. Shaw
G. Rees (Nottingham)	M.J.B. Hobbs
G.L. Robbins (Coventry)	M.G. Mexted
Replacement:	
D. Richards (Leicester) for Robbins	

Scorers:
Midland Division: Tries: Robbins, Holdstock. Con: Hare. PGs: Hare (2). DG: Hare.
New Zealand: Try: Pokere. PGs: Deans (3).

Referee: W.D. Bevan (Wales).
Attendance: 18,000.

New Zealand opened the scoring when Robbie Deans kicked an early penalty, but the Midlands hit back after eight minutes with a try from Robbins. The home pack had taken play up to the New Zealand line, and after scrum-half Nick Youngs was held up as he attempted to touch down himself, the ball was recycled for Robbins to score. Hare could not convert – in contrast to his later heroics his first-half kicking was poor – and the All Blacks had regained the lead by the break thanks to a further Deans penalty.

The 6-4 half-time advantage soon became 9-4 when Deans was successful with another penalty. The home side missed a clear chance of a try when Woodward failed to create enough space for winger John Goodwin after a good break from Youngs, but in the fiftieth minute Hare found the target with a forty-yard penalty awarded for offside to cut the deficit to just 2 points. As the game neared its final quarter, the New Zealand lead was stretched once again when Steve Pokere juggled a fine diagonal kick from Wayne Smith before touching down for a try. Deans missed the conversion, but New Zealand looked to be in control with a

13-7 advantage. Then the drama began. Immediately from the restart the Midland forwards rucked the ball, Youngs released his backs and winger Simon Holdstock just had enough strength to squeeze over for a corner try. Hare's superb touchline conversion brought the scores level at 13-13 with twenty minutes left. Then the full-back was handed a simple penalty opportunity to put his side back into the lead, but to the horror of the home supporters the kick failed. Hare was disgusted with himself and, when a further penalty was awarded, he angrily attempted another goal-kick, although the distance for this one was all of sixty-five yards. Frustration turned to elation as the ball sailed between the posts. Twelve minutes remained and the Midlands were back in front. A couple of minutes later, Hare caught a wayward clearance kick and thumped over an incredible drop goal from over fifty yards out. The Midlands now had a six-point advantage, but could they survive the inevitable final All Black onslaught? The final minutes of the game were full of drama as the tourists did everything in their power to preserve their unbeaten record. They mounted some thrilling attacks, but Midland players defended bravely, determined to secure a famous victory. On one occasion Stu Wilson beat five men before he was collared, and another move saw Hika Reid stopped just yards from the try line. At last, the final whistle signalled only the fourth ever victory by an English provincial side over the All Blacks.

While Hare was ultimately the hero of this Midlands victory, much of the credit for the win deservedly went to the home pack. Wilkinson, Jeavons and Vince Cannon secured some crucial lineout ball and the entire pack never gave second best to its opponents. The tackling of Youngs was another telling feature. The New Zealanders had played some good rugby and made a thrilling attempt to rescue the match in the dying stages, but the Midlands outscored the tourists 2-1 in tries and the players deserved their night of glory. Bryce Rope and Stu Wilson were gracious in defeat, acknowledging the quality and of the opposition, while local hero Dusty Hare had this to say about his evening's work: 'I called myself a very obscene name when I missed that sitter. But I felt elated when I landed those goals. At such a stage you have to take a whack almost from anywhere and in the end it was my night and the team's.'

SCOTLAND 1983

**Saturday 12 November 1983
Murrayfield, Edinburgh
Drawn 25-25**

The New Zealanders moved back north of the Border for the Test match against Scotland. The result at Leicester had shaken their confidence, but they were still expected to defeat Scotland after their stunning demolition of the South two weeks earlier. The tourists fielded six new caps against a fairly experienced Scottish side, although seven of the Scots had also played in the South debacle. The match had an extra edge to it as many of the home side, including the coach Jim Telfer, had taken part in the hugely disappointing British Lions tour in the summer. This was an early opportunity for them to gain revenge and to show what they were capable of. For once, the New Zealanders let an important match slip through their

SCOTLAND	NEW ZEALAND
P.W. Dods (Gala)	K.J. Crowley
J.A. Pollock (Gosforth)	S.S. Wilson (Capt.)
A.E. Kennedy (Watsonians)	S.T. Pokere
D.I. Johnston (Watsonians)	B.G. Fraser
G.R.T. Baird (Kelso)	W.T. Taylor
J.Y. Rutherford (Selkirk)	W.R. Smith
R.J. Laidlaw (Jed-Forest)	A.J. Donald
Forwards:	Forwards:
J. Aitken (Gala, Capt.)	B. McGrattan
C.T. Deans (Hawick)	H.R. Reid
I.G. Milne (Heriot's FP)	S. Crichton
W. Cuthbertson (Harlequins)	G.J. Braid
T.J. Smith (Gala)	A. Anderson
J.H. Calder (Stewart's Melville FP)	M.W. Shaw
J.R. Beattie (Glasgow Acads)	M.J.B. Hobbs
I.A.M. Paxton (Selkirk)	M.G. Mexted
	Replacement:
	C.I. Green for Taylor

Scorers:
Scotland: Try: Pollock. PGs: Dods (5). DG: Rutherford (2).
New Zealand: Tries: Fraser (2), Hobbs. Cons: Deans (2).
PGs: Deans (3).

Referee: R. Hourquet (France).
Attendance: 50,500.

285

Robbie Deans kicks a penalty to make the score 3-3 against Scotland in 1983. (Scottish Rugby Union/Ray Davidson)

fingers. They outscored Scotland by 3 tries to one and had a greater share of the game, but their constant indiscretions and the accurate goal-kicking of Peter Dods meant that they could never shake Scotland off. In the closing minutes the Scots almost snatched their first ever win over New Zealand and the match ended with the tourists thoroughly frustrated.

Scotland opened the scoring with a well-taken drop goal by John Rutherford, but this was quickly cancelled out by a penalty from Robbie Deans. Rutherford dropped his second goal after some terrific driving play by the Scottish forwards, but then the visitors began to take control. Typically opportunist play by Murray Mexted from a quick lineout resulted in the opening try for Jock Hobbs. Soon afterwards, Andrew Donald and Mark Shaw created space for Bernie Fraser down the touchline and his carefully placed chip ahead gave him the fraction of a second he needed to beat Dods to the touch down. Robbie Deans converted and later kicked a penalty. Meanwhile, Dods, having a superb day with his boot, kicked three penalties for the Scots and the New Zealanders were only ahead 16-15 at the interval.

Canterbury's Craig Green replaced Warwick Taylor during the break to win his first cap. In the second half, Fraser scored his second try, almost a carbon copy of his first as he kicked ahead and beat the covering defence. Deans converted, but successive penalties by Dods brought the plucky Scots back to within striking distance. Deans stretched the lead with another penalty, but then there was a dramatic finale. From a fortunate lineout ricochet, the ball sped down the line to David Johnston, who sent a perfectly judged kick over the line for his winger Jim Pollock to race onto for a try. Peter Dods, who later claimed that he had no idea of the score, attempted the conversion close to the touchline, but the ball missed by the width of an upright. In a controversial finish, there was still time for New Zealand to launch a last assault on the Scottish line. It seemed that Shaw had scored the winning try, but they were brought back for a penalty award, which looked eminently kickable. However, after consulting with his touch judge, referee Hourquet reversed the decision for a New Zealand infringement, allowing the Scots to clear their lines and hang on for an historic draw.

In an exciting and well-contested game, the New Zealanders never quite found their rhythm and lacked finishing power at the crucial moments. By contrast, much of the Scottish play was a revelation, especially the wholehearted commitment of the forwards, whose driving and ruck play was of the highest order. At full-back, Peter Dods gave a near-faultless display while Jim Aitken showed himself an inspiring captain. It was a memorable game that set the scene for Scotland's successful campaign in the 1984 Five Nations where they won the Grand Slam for the first time since 1925.

Tuesday 15 November 1983
Memorial Ground, Bristol
Won 18-6

SOUTH & SOUTH-WEST ENGLAND	NEW ZEALAND
C.R. Martin (Bath)	K.J. Crowley
D.M. Trick (Bath)	S.S. Wilson (Capt.)
J.A. Palmer (Bath)	S.T. Pokere
S. Barnes (Oxford University)	B.W. Smith
R.R. Mogg (Gloucester)	C.I. Green
J.P. Horton (Bath)	I.T.W. Dunn
R.M. Harding (Bristol)	D.E. Kirk
Forwards:	Forwards:
M. Preedy (Gloucester)	K.G. Boroevich
S.G.F. Mills (Gloucester)	H.B. Wilson
P.J. Blakeway (Gloucester, Capt.)	M.G. Davie
J. Orwin (Gloucester)	A. Anderson
S.B. Boyle (Gloucester)	A.G. Robinson
J. Gadd (Gloucester)	G.H. Old
J.P. Hall (Bath)	F.N.K. Shelford
M.C. Teague (Gloucester)	M.G. Mexted
Replacements:	
A.J. Morley (Bristol) for Martin,	
A. Sheppard (Bristol) for Preedy	

Scorers:
South & South-West England: PGs: Barnes (2).
New Zealand: Tries: S. Wilson, Smith. Cons: Crowley (2).
PGs: Crowley (2).

Referee: D.I.H. Burnett (Ireland).
Attendance: 17,000.

The South & South-West had not enjoyed the best of build-ups to their clash with the All Blacks. A warm-up game was arranged at the Memorial Ground against Welsh club side Newbridge, the regular Boxing Day opponents of the Bristol club and a side which had a notoriously poor record on the ground, not having won there since 1969. However, on this occasion Newbridge really turned on the style, perhaps benefiting from the vocal backing given them by a home crowd that felt that there were insufficient Bristol players in the divisional starting lineup to merit the team's support. The Welsh club ran the home side ragged, winning plenty of possession and mounting attacks from all parts of the field. The final scoreline, much to the amusement of the Bristol faithful, was 21-6 to Newbridge. Despite this setback, a strong-looking side took the field against the All Blacks. David Trick, John Horton, Steve Boyle, Steve Mills and skipper Phil Blakeway had all played for England, while the remainder of the side, with the exception of Richard Mogg and John Gadd, were all future caps. Both the used replacements had also represented their country. Stuart Barnes, normally the club half-back partner of Richard Harding, was selected to play at centre when Simon Halliday of Bath withdrew through injury. Seven of the forwards were from the Gloucester club, the only exception being twenty-year-old John Hall of Bath. Of the New Zealand side that had drawn with Scotland the previous Saturday, only Stu Wilson, Steve Pokere, Murray Mexted and Albert Anderson were selected to appear at Bristol.

The match was a huge disappointment to the capacity crowd, mainly because the home side refused to play any adventurous rugby until the dying stages. The South & South-West forwards won a sizable amount of ball from set pieces and in the loose but Horton, clearly acting under instructions, seemed intent on bombing Kieran Crowley with high kicks, and Trick and Mogg, both talented wingers, were ignored. No attempt was made to create anything interesting in attack, but even so the home side could have led at the break if John Palmer, selected to kick the goals ahead of Barnes, had not missed three penalties in eight minutes. Crowley was no more successful with three kicks of his own, and with Horton, normally an expert at such things, missing a drop goal attempt, there was no score in the first half.

The one sublime moment of the game came from New Zealand after six minutes of the second period. Bruce Smith robbed Trick of the ball, and from a ruck inside their own half the tourists worked the ball, via three long passes, to Wilson. The All Black skipper had forty yards to run, but he raced round to score under the posts, Crowley adding the conversion. Home full-back Chris Martin had been struggling with a dead leg and he lost his footing as he attempted to cut Wilson off, but even taking into account this element of good fortune for the visitors, the try was a memorable one. The home pack continued to battle after this setback and Barnes, who had moved to full-back when Martin finally limped off, leaving replacement Alan

Stu Wilson races clear to score for New Zealand. (Dave Fox)

Morley to play in the centre, kicked two penalties out of three attempts to bring his side level at 6-6 after an hour. Thereafter though, with star forward Murray Mexted increasingly dominant, the tourists took control of the game, Crowley adding two penalties to the scoreline to give his team a 12-6 lead. When it was all far too late, the South & South-West finally began to run the ball, but the attacks were mounted from far too deep, and in injury time Bruce Smith intercepted a Boyle pass intended for Morley near the home line and ran in for a soft try. Crowley converted to give the final margin of victory a flattering look.

Despite the defeat, Phil Blakeway was pleased with the performance of his forwards, famously claiming that he would happily make the impressive Hall an honorary Gloucester player. The Gloucester skipper had himself played superbly, but he did not do enough to impress the watching England selectors, only gaining a place on the replacements' bench for the forthcoming England game. Barnes was the pick of the home backs, but the player of the day was undoubtedly Mexted, who produced a performance of great power at number eight. The match as a whole was perhaps best summed up by Bryce Rope when he described it as 'a slow motion game.' Incidentally, Newbridge, returning to the Memorial Ground for the annual Boxing Day clash with Bristol, reverted to type, losing 22-13 to their hosts.

ENGLAND   1983

Saturday 19 November 1983
Twickenham, London
Lost 15-9

England entered this game with a new chairman of selectors, a new coach and a new captain. The chairman of selectors, Derek Morgan, and the coach, Dick Greenwood, were both former England internationals, while the new skipper was the highly experienced Peter Wheeler. Seven of the Midland Division side that had defeated the All Blacks were selected for the game, while there were two new caps in Paul Simpson and thirty-four-year-old Colin White. Mike Slemen was recalled on the wing after a year away from international rugby. The New Zealand side was the same one that finished the Scotland game, with Craig Green retaining his place instead of the injured Warwick Taylor.

ENGLAND	NEW ZEALAND
W.H. Hare (Leicester)	R.M. Deans
J. Carleton (Orrell)	S.S. Wilson (Capt.)
C.R. Woodward (Leicester)	S.T. Pokere
P.W. Dodge (Leicester)	B.G. Fraser
M.A.C. Slemen (Liverpool)	C.I. Green
L. Cusworth (Leicester)	W.R. Smith
N.G. Youngs (Leicester)	A.J. Donald
Forwards:	Forwards:
C. White (Gosforth)	B. McGrattan
P.J. Wheeler (Leicester, Capt.)	H.R. Reid
G.S. Pearce (Northampton)	S. Crichton
M.J. Colclough (Wasps)	G.J. Braid
S. Bainbridge (Gosforth)	A. Anderson
P.D. Simpson (Bath)	M.W. Shaw
P.J. Winterbottom (Headingley)	M.J.B. Hobbs
J.P. Scott (Cardiff)	M.G. Mexted
Replacement:	Replacement:
N.C. Stringer (Wasps) for Carleton	M.G. Davie for Crichton

Scorers:
England: Try: Colclough. Con: Hare. PGs: Hare (3).
New Zealand: Try: Davie. Con: Deans. PG: Deans.

Referee: A.M. Hosie (Scotland).
Attendance: 60,000.

The game began with the only sustained period of All Black pressure, resulting in an early penalty for Robbie Deans. Thereafter, the England forwards took control of the match, and with the home backs tormenting the tourists with high kicks, two Dusty Hare penalties out of three attempts put the home side ahead 6-3 after eighteen minutes, a lead they still held at the break. The discipline of the tourists had not been good in the first half, and there was a particularly unsavoury incident in the thirty-eighth minute when a cynical late charge from Bernie Fraser led to John Carleton leaving the field.

The second half was a triumph for the England pack, and began with a sustained assault on the All Blacks' line. Ten minutes into the half, Nick Youngs surged towards the line after England had won a lineout, and the forwards piled in to drive Maurice Colclough over for a try. Hare converted to give his side a 12-3 lead, but the All Blacks hit back almost immediately when Murray Davie, who had come on as a replacement for Scott Crichton after just fifteen minutes of the first half, was driven over from a wheeled scrum. This was Davie's sole appearance in an international, and his try was converted by Deans to reduce the England lead to 3 points. However, any thoughts of a New Zealand revival soon vanished as the England forwards once again dominated the game. Both Slemen and Carleton's replacement Nick Stringer came close to scoring tries, but the only other score came from a simple Hare penalty, awarded when the All Black forwards were caught offside. The final whistle heralded an historic moment in the history of rugby. This was England's first home victory over New Zealand since 1936, the first New Zealand defeat in an international in Britain since 1953, and the first time ever that an All Black team would return home without a Test victory.

There was universal praise for the efforts of the England forwards in subduing the threat of the visitors. Peter Winterbottom and Paul Simpson were outstanding, as was Youngs, who acted like a ninth forward and was generally regarded as man of the match. The game itself was rarely spectacular, but this fact was largely forgotten as a rare England victory over New Zealand was celebrated. The visitors themselves could claim little credit from the match. Discipline had been bad and, apart from Carleton's injury, Simpson, Gary Pearce and John Scott all required stitches, while Slemen's back was raked. The England triumph of 1936 is generally referred to as Obolensky's match – a tribute to the try-scoring genius of the Russian Prince Alexander Obolensky. After the England triumph of 1983, skipper Peter Wheeler, aware that England's try-scorer had played much of his recent rugby in France, suggested the England now had a new hero, the Marquis de Colclough!

NEW ZEALAND TO CANADA, BRITAIN & IRELAND

THE MATCHES

British Columbia	8 October 1989	Vancouver	won 48-3
Cardiff	14 October 1989	Cardiff	won 25-15
Pontypool	18 October 1989	Pontypool	won 47-6
Swansea	21 October 1989	Swansea	won 37-22
Neath	25 October 1989	Neath	won 26-15
Llanelli	28 October 1989	Llanelli	won 11-0
Newport	31 October 1989	Newport	won 54-9
WALES	4 November 1989	Cardiff	won 34-9
Leinster	8 November 1989	Dublin	won 36-9
Munster	11 November 1989	Cork	won 31-9
Connacht	14 November 1989	Galway	won 40-6
IRELAND	18 November 1989	Dublin	won 23-6
Ulster	21 November 1989	Belfast	won 21-3
Barbarians	25 November 1989	Twickenham	won 21-10
Oxbridge XV	28 November 1989	Oxford	won 80-20 (Unofficial match)

Played 14, Won 14, Drew 0, Lost 0. Scored: 454 points, Conceded: 122 (excludes Oxbridge game). In Britain & Ireland: Played 13, Won 13, Drew 0, Lost 0. Scored: 406 points, Conceded: 119.

The New Zealand Tour Party:
J.A. Gallagher (Wellington), M.J. Ridge (Auckland), C.R. Innes (Auckland), J.J. Kirwan (Auckland), B.J. McCahill (Auckland), J.T. Stanley (Auckland), J.K.R. Timu (Otago)*, V.L. Tuigamala (Auckland), T.J. Wright (Auckland), F.M. Botica (North Harbour), G.J. Fox (Auckland), W.K. Little (North Harbour), N.J. Schuster (Wellington), G.T.M. Bachop (Canterbury), I.B. Deans (Canterbury), R.W. Loe (Waikato), S.C. McDowell (Bay of Plenty), G.H. Purvis (Auckland), R.O. Williams (North Harbour), S.B.T. Fitzpatrick (Auckland), W.D. Gatland (Waikato), S.B. Gordon (Waikato), I.D. Jones (North Auckland), M.J. Pierce (Wellington), G.W. Whetton (Auckland), M.R. Brewer (Otago), A.T. Earl (Canterbury), P.W. Henderson (Otago), K.J. Schuler (Manawatu)*, A.J. Whetton (Auckland), Z.V. Brooke (Auckland), W.T. Shelford (North Harbour). (*replacement on tour)

Captain: W.T. Shelford. Manager: J.A. Sturgeon. Coach: A.J. Wyllie.

Leading points scorer: G.J. Fox – 83 points (83 in Britain & Ireland).
Leading try-scorer: C.R. Innes – 8 tries (8 in Britain & Ireland).
Most appearances: S.C. McDowell – 10 games (9 in Britain & Ireland).

Saturday 14 October 1989
Cardiff Arms Park, Cardiff
Won 25-15

CARDIFF	NEW ZEALAND
M.A. Rayer	M.J. Ridge
C. Thomas	J.J. Kirwan
M.G. Ring	C.R. Innes
G. John	T.J. Wright
S.P. Ford	N.J. Schuster
D.W. Evans	G.J. Fox
A. Booth	G.T.M. Bachop
Forwards:	Forwards:
J. Whitefoot	R.O. Williams
I.J. Watkins	S.B.T. Fitzpatrick
D. Young	R.W. Loe
M. Rowley	M.J. Pierce
H. Stone	I.D. Jones
T. Crothers (Capt.)	A.J. Whetton
R.G. Collins	M.R. Brewer
M. Edwards	W.T. Shelford (Capt.)

Scorers:
Cardiff: Try: Edwards. Con: Rayer. PG: Evans (2), Rayer.
New Zealand: Tries: Loe, Whetton, Brewer. Cons: Fox (2).
PGs: Fox (3).

Referee: R.J. Megson (Scotland).
Attendance: 28,000.

Having won the inaugural World Cup in 1987 and crushed a Welsh side who had won the Triple Crown the following year, Wayne Shelford's All Blacks were eagerly awaited. Since the World Cup they were unbeaten and had enjoyed substantial international victories over Australia in 1988, and twice against Argentina the previous July. During the summer, the British Lions had toured Australia and won the three-Test series 2-1. New Zealand played against British Columbia on the way over, a game in which they scored 7 tries. They selected a strong squad, but left behind injured loose forward Michael Jones. They included a handful of players new to the All Blacks, including wing Va'aiga Tuigamala. Lock Ian Jones, full-back Matthew Ridge and three-quarter Craig Innes all made their first appearances for New Zealand against Cardiff. They were captained by Wayne 'Buck' Shelford. Cardiff had won only six of their 9 games to date, had enjoyed good wins over Moseley and Newport but been well beaten by Neath and Pontypridd. Lions prop David Young had recovered from a hamstring injury to play, but they were missing lock Robert Norster, who had received a serious shoulder injury on the controversial South African Rugby Board centenary tour, which effectively ended his senior rugby career. Norster was replaced by Howard Stone and Cardiff were captained by Tim Crothers.

New Zealand had problems in the scrum early on and the front row was penalised for scrummaging misdemeanours. Cardiff's defence was aggressive and quick to move up on the All Blacks. Mike Rayer kicked a penalty and converted a fine try from number eight Mark Edwards who, with help from Ritchie Collins and Mark Ring, drove over the New Zealand line. Otherwise, the defensively excellent Cardiff full-back had an off day with the boot and eventually handed goal-kicking responsibilities to David Evans. Although Grant Fox kicked a penalty for New Zealand, Cardiff were dynamic in attack and resilient in defence. At the end of an heroic first half Cardiff led 9-3. It should have been more.

In the second half, the New Zealand forwards monopolised possession but rarely used their backs, who seemed out of sorts. Even Fox missed a few kicks. Then the All Blacks' forwards started a rolling maul. Shelford and Allan Whetton burst out and fed Richard Loe for the All Blacks' first try. Loe had been a slight doubt before the game but was in the thick of things. Shortly afterwards, powerful wing John Kirwan made a run and linked with his forwards for Whetton to drive over the line for New Zealand's second try. They tried to sap the energy from the Cardiff side with rolling mauls, but Evans kicked two penalties and Cardiff were back to within 3 points. Then a fine run by Ridge was taken on by the forwards, who rolled and mauled over the line and Mike Brewer was awarded the decisive try. Fox converted two of the tries and added two more penalties for a rather unconvincing win.

PONTYPOOL 1989

Wednesday 18 October 1989
Pontypool Park, Pontypool
Won 47-6

PONTYPOOL	NEW ZEALAND
G. Davies	J.A. Gallagher
M. Egan	J.J. Kirwan
R.A. Bidgood	J.T. Stanley
K. Orrell	V.L. Tuigamala
S. White	W.K. Little
M. Silva	F.M. Botica
D. Wright	G.T.M. Bachop
Forwards:	Forwards:
S.T. Jones	S.C. McDowell
G.R. Jenkins	S.B.T. Fitzpatrick
G. Price	G.H. Purvis
D. Churchill	I.D. Jones
K. Moseley (Capt.)	G.W. Whetton (Capt.)
C. Huish	A.T. Earl
R. Goodey	P.W. Henderson
D.J. Oswald	Z.V. Brooke
Replacement:	Replacement:
A.J. Carter for Oswald	B.J. McCahill for Kirwan

Scorers:
Pontypool: PG: Silva (2).
New Zealand: Tries: Little, Gallagher, Kirwan, Fitzpatrick, Tuigamala, Bachop, Botica, Jones. Cons: Gallagher (3). PGs: Gallagher (3).

Referee: B. Stirling (Ireland).
Attendance: 20,000.

Pontypool had built a fearsome reputation through a succession of aggressive but skilful forwards who terrorised visitors to Pontypool Park with their physical approach to the game. They were successful and won several titles in the unofficial leagues of the time. 'Pooler' were a consistently good side ideally suited for the attrition of league campaigns but had struggled in the one-off game, only winning the Welsh Cup once and losing to Australia twice. By the time New Zealand played them they were some way past their best, although they had not lost to a Welsh club so far during the season. Of the great players who had become household names only thirty-seven-year-old Graham Price was still there, and he had come out of retirement to assist an horrendous injury crisis. Fellow prop 'Staff' Jones toured with the British Lions in 1983, while Roger Bidgood and Garin Jenkins later went on to play for Wales. They also included number eight Dean Oswald, a New Zealander from Bay of Plenty. He was a highly respected forward who was greatly admired in Pontypool. The home side were captained by Kevin Moseley, a second row who played nine times for Wales and also played some rugby in Poverty Bay. New Zealand brought experienced campaigners Joe Stanley and Gary Whetton into the side which showed eleven changes from the Cardiff game. Frano Botica had missed the match in Canada for family reasons so took the field for the first time on tour. Prop Steve McDowell had the rare privilege of playing against his childhood hero when he packed down opposite Price. Va'aiga Tuigamala made his first appearance for New Zealand on British soil. Gary Whetton captained the team.

New Zealand started this game with such determination and skill, with the forwards and backs linking together with smooth efficiency, that after ten minutes the home crowd, resigned to a heavy defeat,

watched, marvelled and applauded the All Blacks' every move. The British press described the first thirty minutes of the game as 'perfect rugby'. At this point the only blemish on New Zealand's day occurred. John Kirwan ruptured his Achilles tendon and took no further part on the tour. He was replaced in the match by Bernie McCahill, and in the squad by John Timu. In the first twenty minutes, with Joe Stanley outstanding New Zealand scored tries from, in sequence, Walter Little, John Gallagher, Kirwan and Sean Fitzpatrick. Gallagher kicked a conversion and a penalty and New Zealand were scoring at a point a minute. Then Matthew Silva kicked a penalty for the home side to interrupt the flow, which was only temporary as Tuigamala powered over for the fifth try shortly afterwards. The loss of Kirwan disrupted the All Blacks' momentum and at half-time the score was 31-3.

Although the second half was played almost exclusively in Pontypool territory, New Zealand didn't make their supremacy tell on the scoreboard even though tries were added by Graeme Bachop, Frano Botica and Ian Jones. Gallagher's goal-kicking was inconsistent. For Pontypool there was grit and determination, but aside from Chris Huish, Oswald and Bidgood, there were few who threatened the All Blacks. Graham Price, in his 561st appearance for Pontypool, led a forward rush that took Pontypool close late in the game but it was a match to forget for the home team.

SWANSEA   1989

Saturday 21 October 1989
St Helen's, Swansea
Won 37-22

The result at Pontypool sent shock-waves throughout Wales and those at Swansea were deeply concerned as they had lost 34-6 to Pontypool a fortnight earlier. The 'All Whites' had been badly beaten by the All Blacks the last time the sides had met and there seemed little chance of obtaining revenge, or avoiding a similar defeat. They were led by future Welsh captain Robert Jones, and the side included former Welsh captain Billy James. They had a tough back row of Ian Davies, Stuart Davies and Alan Reynolds, the latter two later being capped. In an otherwise youthful side, several other players went on to play for Wales. Locks Richard Moriarty and Mark Langley couldn't be considered so future international Steve Williams, in his first season of rugby out of school, was chosen in the second row. The All Blacks changed the entire team from the Pontypool game and forwards Warren Gatland and Steve Gordon made their first appearances in Britain. Also making his UK debut was half-back Bruce Deans, whose great uncle was Bob Deans, an 'Original' All Black who caused something of a stir in Wales in 1905. Bernie McCahill, John Schuster and Murray Pierce all recovered from injuries to play, but a training ground injury to Grant Fox brought Frano Botica back into the side.

SWANSEA	NEW ZEALAND
M.A. Wyatt	M.J. Ridge
M.H. Titley	C.R. Innes
K. Hopkins	B.J. McCahill
S.A. Parfitt	T.J. Wright
A. Emyr	N.J. Schuster
A. Clement	F.M. Botica
R.N. Jones (Capt.)	I.B. Deans
Forwards:	Forwards:
I.M. Buckett	R.O. Williams
W.J. James	W.D. Gatland
M. Morgan	R.W. Loe
S.M. Williams	M.J. Pierce
P. Arnold	S.B. Gordon
I. Davies	A.J. Whetton
A.D. Reynolds	M.R. Brewer
S. Davies	W.T. Shelford (Capt.)
Replacement:	Replacements:
L. Rutherford for Reynolds	A.T. Earl for Whetton,
	W.K. Little for Schuster

Scorers:
Swansea: Tries: I. Davies, Arnold, Hopkins. Cons: Wyatt (2). PG: Wyatt (2).
New Zealand: Tries: Innes (2), Brewer (2), Gatland, Deans. Cons: Botica (5). PG: Botica.

Referee: R. Hourquet (France).
Attendance: 16,000.

St. Helen's Ground
Swansea

Swansea

Versus

New Zealand

Saturday, 21st October, 1989
Kick-Off 2.30 p.m.

Souvenir Programme · £1.00 · Donation to Club

Defying form, Swansea began the match in determined mood and, playing into the wind, caused New Zealand problems. They ran at the All Blacks and harried them into mistakes, but crucially the biggest errors came from the Swansea defence and, despite the hard work of their forwards, New Zealand scored tries with relative ease. Craig Innes scored the first after a back-row move, and Warren Gatland supported a back move to cross for the second. Botica converted both and added a penalty. After twenty minutes, Alan Whetton suffered a serious hamstring injury and was replaced by Andy Earl. Mike Brewer scored a try close to half-time when the home defence hesitated under a garryowen from Botica, and he gathered the ball while they decided who should go for it. New Zealand capitalised upon Swansea's errors to lead 21-3 at half-time.

With the wind at their backs in the second half, Swansea played with pride and passion and took the game to New Zealand. They forced the All Blacks into making further errors, and Mike Morgan and Paul Arnold were constant threats with their driving runs. Anthony Clement ran and kicked well and the tourists had to deal with some powerful runs from Arthur Emyr. However, the All Blacks seemed to score on every occasion they went into the Swansea 22. Brewer scored his second try from a scrum before Swansea's Ian Davies scored a fine try from a back-row move involving Jones and Stuart Davies. The All Blacks' fifth try came from a drive by Shelford and Brewer into the Swansea midfield, which was followed by the swift movement of the ball through the backs for Matthew Ridge to put Innes in for his second try of the game. Losing 33-10, Swansea struck back. Arnold scored after James was held up on the line and almost immediately after, Kevin Hopkins went over for a third try after a fine run by Emyr. Former Wales full-back Mark Wyatt kicked 10 points. Swansea played good rugby but their defence let them down again when Deans scored supporting a forward drive. The All Blacks' sixth try ended Swansea's chances of victory. Swansea were left to ponder what might have been, although their 22 points against New Zealand was a total only exceeded by the Barbarians in 1973 and Scotland in 1983.

NEATH   1989

Wednesday 25 October 1989
The Gnoll, Neath
Won 26-15

Neath were Wales' leading club, holders of the Welsh Cup and a fiercely supported side who successfully adopted a fast-moving, aggressive style that was based on fitness and purpose. With the New Zealand All Blacks playing the Welsh All Blacks. the home side changed their shirts and wore white, with a crest incorporating the Maltese Cross of Neath and the Silver Fern of New Zealand. Martyn Morris was preferred at open-side flanker to former Wales captain David Pickering, while lock Mike Whitson, whose father Geoff had played for Wales, surprisingly played ahead of Andrew Kembery. Their side included future Lions centre Allan Bateman, who also enjoyed a successful career in rugby league, and prop Brian Williams, who made up for his small stature with extraordinary strength and

NEATH	NEW ZEALAND
P.H. Thorburn	J.A. Gallagher
C. Higgs	V.L. Tuigamala
C. Laity	J.T. Stanley
A.G. Bateman	T.J. Wright
D.A. Edmunds	W.K. Little
P. Williams	F.M. Botica
C.J. Bridges	G.T.M. Bachop
Forwards:	Forwards:
B.R. Williams	S.C. McDowell
K.H. Phillips (Capt.)	S.B.T. Fitzpatrick
J.D. Pugh	G.H. Purvis
M. Whitson	I.D. Jones
G.O. Llewellyn	G.W. Whetton (Capt.)
P. Pugh	A.T. Earl
M.S. Morris	P.W. Henderson
M.A. Jones	Z.V. Brooke
	Replacements:
	C.R. Innes for Tuigamala,
	M.R. Brewer for Henderson

Scorers:
Neath: Try: Edmunds. Con: Thorburn. PG: Thorburn (3).
New Zealand: Tries: Gallagher (2), Innes, Brooke. Cons: Botica (2). PG: Botica (2).

Referee: F.A. Howard (RFU).
Attendance: 12,000.

power. He later played for Wales along with several of his teammates. Full-back was Paul Thorburn, a prodigious points scorer who kicked a sixty-four-metre penalty for Wales against Scotland in 1984. They were captained by hooker Kevin Phillips. The All Blacks changed most of the side again and fielded a mobile pack under the captaincy of Gary Whetton. Frano Botica played his third match in succession.

It proved to be a magnificent contest between two good teams. After ten minutes New Zealand scored a fine try when Zinzan Brooke picked up from a scrum in midfield and passed out to Graeme Bachop. He ran and fed John Gallagher in space for the English-born full-back to score. Botica converted, and then Thorburn opened Neath's account with a penalty. New Zealand scored a similar try shortly afterwards but this time Gallagher passed to Craig Innes in space to score. Botica missed the conversion but kicked a penalty and New Zealand led 13-3 at the interval.

The second half started in sensational fashion. Mark Jones made a powerful surge through four All Blacks before the ball was moved to the left into midfield where Bateman made a break and sent Alan Edmunds in for a glorious try that Thorburn converted. The cheers from the crowd, which had bayed out 'Neath, Neath' incessantly, were deafening. Gareth Llewellyn, the twenty-year-old lock, dominated the lineout, and Neath met fire with fire and stretched the All Blacks almost to the point of breaking. Neath tails were up and when they attacked again they made space for their captain Phillips, but he dropped the ball when a try seemed a certainty. New Zealand were on the rack but Whetton gathered the team together during a break in play and urged his men to dig deep. Thorburn kicked a penalty and after an hour's play the gap was a single point, but the All Blacks eased away in the dying minutes as Neath continued to dominate but couldn't get the score that would take them into the lead. They lacked composure and made crucial, mistakes at critical times while the New Zealand defence was well organised. With time running out, Gallagher scored a second try to ease New Zealand worries. Botica and Thorburn exchanged penalties before a Brooke push-over try made the game safe for the All Blacks.

When Neath were at their best, New Zealand adopted disruptive tactics that infuriated the home crowd but failed to concern referee Fred Howard. Disgracefully, Howard was jostled by a disgruntled supporter as he left the field at the end of the match. Paul Henderson was injured in the game and played no further part on tour. Kevin Schuler from Manawatu was sent out to replace him. Neath went on to win the *Western Mail* Championship and the Whitbread Merit Table for the 1989/90 season, and retained the Welsh Cup. In 1990/91 they won the inaugural Welsh National League title.

LLANELLI 1989

Saturday 28 October 1989
Stradey Park, Llanelli
Won 11-0

The All Blacks' next stop was Stradey Park. The conditions were appalling. Heavy rain was accompanied by a storm-force wind so strong the rain was almost horizontal. A temporary stand erected at the back of the Tanner Bank terrace that stretched the length of the pitch opposite the main stand, could not be used as it was impossible to guarantee the spectators' safety. Instead, the 2,300 ticket holders had to wedge themselves into the ground wherever they could. The club said that had the All Blacks not been playing the following Tuesday, the match would have been put back a day. Llanelli were

LLANELLI	NEW ZEALAND
J. Bird	M.J. Ridge
S. Bowling	C.R. Innes
N.G. Davies	J.T. Stanley
S. Davies	T.J. Wright
C. Davies	W.K. Little
C.J. Stephens	G.J. Fox
M. Griffiths	I.B. Deans
Forwards:	Forwards:
D.A. Buchanan	S.C. McDowell
A.E.H. Lamerton	S.B.T. Fitzpatrick
L. Delaney	R.W. Loe
P.S. May	M.J. Pierce
P.T. Davies (Capt.)	G.W. Whetton
G. Jones	A.T. Earl
I. Jones	M.R. Brewer
J. Williams	W.T. Shelford (Capt.)

Scorers:
New Zealand: Tries: Deans, Earl. PG: Fox.

Referee: K. McCartney (Scotland).
Attendance: 18,000.

coached by Gareth Jenkins, a member of the side that had beaten New Zealand in 1972. However, the club had lost the services of half-backs Jonathan Davies and Jonathan Griffiths to rugby league, and Lions wing Ieuan Evans was injured. The young team included nineteen-year olds Colin Stephens at outside half and Andrew Lamerton at hooker, with Phil Davies as captain. New Zealand welcomed back Grant Fox from a mouth injury and fielded their strongest pack. Bruce Deans had a chance to impress and Craig Innes was again on the wing. The game revolved around who could make the best use of the wind. When Llanelli had the wind at their backs the All Blacks' forwards denied them possession. When New Zealand played with the elements they kicked long into the corners and pinned the home side in their own 22.

With the gale at their back, New Zealand attacked in the first half but found the wind almost too strong to play with, let alone against. Llanelli, on the other hand, contrived some close passing rushes that eased them up field, only to lose possession and see Fox kick the ball back down to their line. Nevertheless, Phil Davies and Phil May were both denied close to the New Zealand line, and Gary Jones had an outstanding game. Fox kicked a penalty when the home centres were caught offside but failed to convert a try from a rolling maul that Deans joined to touch down after thirty-three minutes. The All Blacks led 7-0 at half-time.

In the second half, the tourists kept the ball tight and rumbled up the pitch, never passing more than a few feet. Fifteen minutes in, Andy Earl scored from a slow rolling maul. Stephens regularly kicked too long and enabled Fox to utilise a clever drop-out-and-gather system. Kicking into the gale, he aimed his kick so when the ball was blown back it came directly to his pack. They kept the ball alive and avoided kicking for touch. Again, the referee's view of New Zealand's practices at rucks and mauls incurred the displeasure of the crowd. They appeared to obstruct the home forwards from challenging for the ball, but it was not seen that way by Ken McCartney. At the end of the game he was assaulted in another shameful incident.

When the final whistle was blown there was a collective cheer of relief. There was also loud applause, a tribute to both teams that they had attempted to play rugby in such absurd conditions.

NEWPORT   1989

Tuesday 31 October 1989
Rodney Parade, Newport
Won 54-9

On a bright, sunny afternoon, the All Blacks took the field for a game with Newport. The once-great Welsh side had fallen from the pinnacle of club rugby and many felt they did not deserve a fixture against the All Blacks. Having only won 3 games so far in the season and been recently defeated 48-0 at home by Newbridge, their coaches Jim McCreedy and Keith James had resigned. However, they agreed to help prepare the team for this game. Their captain was Glen George, who later played for Wales and was still playing league rugby in his forties. The All Blacks chose John Timu and Kevin Schuler, the replacements for seriously injured All Blacks John Kirwan and Paul Henderson, for their first games. Injured Va'aiga Tuigamala withdrew and Terry

NEWPORT	NEW ZEALAND
G. Hardacre	J.A. Gallagher
D. Griffiths	J.K.R. Timu
A. Evans	B.J. McCahill
L. Jones	T.J. Wright
J. Thomas	N.J. Schuster
G. Abraham	G.J. Fox
N. Callard	G.T.M. Bachop
Forwards:	Forwards:
F. Hillman	R.O. Williams
K. Gregory	W.D. Gatland
A. Williams	G.H. Purvis
A. Perry	M.J. Pierce
D.R. Waters	S.B. Gordon
G.M. George (Capt.)	K.J. Schuler
A. Pocock	Z.V. Brooke
I. McKim	W.T. Shelford (Capt.)
Replacements:	
C. Scott for Pocock, G. Stockwell for	
Gregory, M. Davis for Hillman	

Scorers:
Newport: Try: Gregory. Con: Abraham. DG: Abraham.
New Zealand: Tries: Wright (3), Gallagher (2), Bachop, Timu, Brooke, Schuster, McCahill. Cons: Fox (7).

Referee: O.E. Doyle (Ireland).
Attendance: 13,000.

Wright took the winger's place, but another doubt, John Schuster, was passed fit. 'Buck' Shelford led the side and was incensed when Newport decided not to face the challenge offered by the Haka and stood as a group by their posts. The All Blacks' captain, a fearsome sight at the best of times, moved the Haka down to where they huddled and added even more aggression to the challenge.

The All Blacks were too strong for Newport, whose defence was not up to the task and leaked tries regularly. The New Zealanders took control from kick-off and continued to dominate until the final whistle. The first score came after seven minutes when Timu came off the right wing to create a try for Wright on the left. Graeme Bachop scored a second shortly afterwards. Gary Abraham dropped a goal for Newport before the John Gallagher ran in 2 tries before the break. Grant Fox converted three and New Zealand were 22-3 ahead at half-time.

In the second half the All Blacks' pack was allowed to do what it wanted and further tries followed. Schuster was cutting holes in the defence and Timu scored a try, followed by one from Brooke, then Schuler scored. The New Zealand forwards were regularly penalised for obstruction at the breakdown and maul, and Shelford had a severe ticking off after punching Andy Pocock, knocking out three of the Newport forward's teeth. Later in the game Wright ran in two more tries for New Zealand. In the closing stages, Newport were awarded a penalty close to the New Zealand line after a good run by Gareth Hardacre. Hooker Kieran Gregory took it quickly to himself and dived over for a try that Abraham converted. Then the unselfish Wright created a try for Bernie McCahill, although the Auckland winger could easily have scored his fourth try of the match. The All Blacks had scored 10 tries and totally destroyed Newport. Sadly for the home supporters, it was not a surprise.

WALES   1989

Saturday 4 November 1989
Cardiff Arms Park, Cardiff
Won 34-9

Earlier in 1989, Wales had escaped a Five Nations whitewash with a fortunate win over England, then toured North America in the summer. Worried about the impending match with the All Blacks, they undertook a short internal tour, defeating Newbridge 25-4 but then embarrassingly losing to Bridgend 24-17. Bridgend centre John Devereux, who scored against New Zealand in the World Cup, had switched to rugby league, wing Ieuan Evans was injured and confidence was at a low ebb. New caps were awarded to Gareth Llewellyn and Phil Pugh, the lineout master and his minder from Neath. Robert Jones became the 101st captain of Wales. The All Blacks chose their strongest side, with Andy Earl taking the place of the injured Alan Whetton. Graeme Bachop was selected ahead of Bruce Deans after several good performances at half-back, and won his first cap. Craig Innes also made his international debut.

WALES	NEW ZEALAND
P.H. Thorburn (Neath)	J.A. Gallagher
M.R. Hall (Bridgend)	C.R. Innes
D.W. Evans (Cardiff)	J.T. Stanley
M.G. Ring (Cardiff)	T.J. Wright
A. Emyr (Swansea)	N.J. Schuster
A. Clement (Swansea)	G.J. Fox
R.N. Jones (Swansea, Capt.)	G.T.M. Bachop
Forwards:	Forwards:
M. Griffiths (Bridgend)	S.C. McDowell
K.H. Phillips (Neath)	S.B.T. Fitzpatrick
D. Young (Cardiff)	R.W. Loe
P.T. Davies (Llanelli)	M.J. Pierce
G.O. Llewellyn (Neath)	G.W. Whetton
P. Pugh (Neath)	A.T. Earl
G. Jones (Llanelli)	M.R. Brewer
M.A. Jones (Neath)	W.T. Shelford (Capt.)

Scorers:
Wales: PGs: Thorburn (3).
New Zealand: Tries: Innes (2), Wright, Bachop. Cons: Fox (3). PGs: Fox (4).

Referee: A.R. MacNeil (Australia).
Attendance: 55,000.

place of the injured Alan Whetton. Graeme Bachop was selected ahead of Bruce Deans after several good performances at half-back, and won his first cap. Craig Innes also made his international debut.

New Zealand dominated the game through a powerful display by their pack. They deployed the rolling maul with ruthless efficiency and Wales had no answer to it. Once the tackler had failed to bring the ball-carrier down the New Zealand forwards joined and moved as a unit, sometimes at alarming speed. Llewellyn was totally eclipsed by Murray Pierce, and the bulky Welsh back row of Pugh, Gary Jones and Mark Jones was regularly beaten to the loose ball by the faster New Zealand trio of Wayne Shelford, Mike Brewer and Earl. The tourists opened the scoring after two minutes when the All Blacks worked a back-row move from a scrum close to the Welsh line. Innes joined the move and scored, as he had on previous occasions. Grant Fox converted and added two penalties in a half in which Wales did well to keep the All Blacks out. Paul Thorburn kicked two penalties which made the half-time score of 12-6 look closer that the rugby had indicated.

However, it was all New Zealand in the second half. Fox kicked two more penalties and the New Zealand backs ran amok. Joe Stanley and John Gallagher tore holes in the first line of defence, and they combined to make a try for Bachop. Thorburn kicked a penalty before Innes scored his second try. Then Arthur Emyr was robbed in the Welsh 22 and a good pass from Fox put Terry Wright in for the final try. In the dying minutes, Fox kicked another penalty and scored 18 points in total.

New Zealand played sublime rugby in the second half. Although Thorburn was accurate with his goal-kicking, Wales offered little other than some dangerous runs from Emyr. Their defence was effective and committed, and Jones had a fine game leading his country. It was this pride that kept the score to 34-9. It was, however, the biggest home defeat Wales had suffered. Later in the season, Wales suffered the ignominy of losing all four Five Nations matches for the first time. Welsh rugby was at a considerable low.

LEINSTER

1989

Wednesday 8 November 1989
Lansdowne Road, Dublin
Won 36-9

Leinster had competed well in the Inter Provincial Championship but had only managed a close home win over Connacht. They had a young side that included the Lions centre Brendan Mullin and future Lions prop Nick Popplewell. Several other players were to become internationals and Fergus Aherne and Neil Francis were current Ireland players. Outside half Brian Smith had played international rugby for Australia. Smith, Mullin and Aherne were to play for Ireland later in the tour. For the tourists only Gary Whetton and Steve McDowell remained in the side from the Welsh international. New Zealand got the Irish leg of their tour underway with a victory after a first half in which they were distinctly off-colour. Leinster ripped into

LEINSTER	NEW ZEALAND
F.J. Dunlea (Lansdowne)	M.J. Ridge
J.F. Sexton (Lansdowne)	V.L. Tuigamala
P. Clinch (Lansdowne, Capt.)	B.J. McCahill
B.J. Mullin (London Irish)	J.K.R. Timu
P. Purcell (Lansdowne)	W.K. Little
B.A. Smith (Oxford University)	F.M. Botica
L.F.P. Aherne (Lansdowne)	I.B. Deans
Forwards:	Forwards:
N.J. Popplewell (Greystones)	S.C. McDowell
N. Kearney (Old Wesley)	W.D. Gatland
D.C. Fitzgerald (Lansdowne)	G.H. Purvis
B.J. Rigney (Greystones)	I.D. Jones
N.P.T. Francis (Blackrock College)	G.W. Whetton (Capt.)
K. Leahy (Wanderers)	A.J. Whetton
A. Blair (Old Wesley)	K.J. Schuler
P. Kenny (Wanderers)	Z.V. Brooke
Replacements:	Replacements:
N. Farren (Old Wesley) for Dunlea,	A.T. Earl for A. Whetton,
V.J.G. Cunningham (St Mary's College)	C.R. Innes for Tuigamala
for Sexton, C. Pim (Old Wesley) for Blair	

Scorers:
Leinster: Tries: Sexton. Con: Smith. PG: Smith.
New Zealand: Tries: Timu (2), Brooke, Innes, Jones, McCahill, G. Whetton. Cons: Botica (4).

Referee: G. Maurette (France).
Attendance: 18,000.

the All Blacks from the kick-off with typical Irish tenacity and aggression. Eventually the All Blacks managed to subdue them and take control. Playing into the strong breeze in the first half, New Zealand kept the game tight. Zinzan Brooke opened the scoring with a pushover try after three minutes that Frano Botica failed to convert. The Leinster pack rallied, and after twenty minutes Aherne chipped into the corner for John Sexton to gather and score. Smith converted and Leinster held the lead until John Timu scored a try seconds before half-time. Botica missed that conversion too but New Zealand led 8-6 at the interval.

Shortly after half-time, Andy Earl replaced the injured Alan Whetton. A few minutes later Fergus Dunlea and Tuigamala collided with such force that both had to leave the field, Dunlea unconscious. New Zealand extended their lead twelve minutes into the half when Bernie McCahill scored a try and with this the floodgates opened. With the New Zealand pack dominant, Bruce Deans had a steady supply of ball with which to feed the backs and they ran with pace and confidence. A kick from Botica was caught by Timu for the wing's second try. There were further scores from Gary Whetton and Ian Jones, and a fine try from Craig Innes who had replaced the injured Tuigamala. Botica converted four. Smith added a late penalty for Leinster when the All Blacks were penalised for obstruction. It had been a contest for an hour but New Zealand were too good for the home side.

New Zealand hooker Warren Gatland suffered from being around at the same time as Sean Fitzpatrick, and consequently never played in a Test match, despite making four All Blacks' tours. He began to bring creative coaching ideas into the New Zealand squad when he was a player. He later coached Ireland out of the doldrums and guided London Wasps to the European Cup in 2004.

MUNSTER   1989

Saturday 11 November 1989
Musgrave Park, Cork
Won 31-9

There was great expectation in Ireland that Munster would repeat their great win over New Zealand of 1978. They had been a tough side in the Inter Provincial Championship where their captain, Paul Collins, had been outstanding. Coached by Pat Whelan, hooker in their famous win over the All Blacks, Munster included several international players, including fine lock Donal Lenihan and fiery flanker Pat O'Hara. The side also included Peter Clohessy and Mick Galwey, who would have lengthy careers for province and country. Having visited the Blarney Stone to make their desires for a win come true, New Zealand selected a strong side including the entire back division that had played Wales. Va'aiga Tuigamala dropped out with an injury and Craig Innes stepped

MUNSTER	NEW ZEALAND
K.J. Murphy (Cork Constitution)	J.A. Gallagher
J. Galvin (Old Crescent)	C.R. Innes
M.J. Kiernan (Dolphin)	J.T. Stanley
C. Murphy (Cork Constitution)	T.J. Wright
P.V. Murray (Shannon)	N.J. Schuster
R.P. Keyes (Cork Constitution)	G.J. Fox
M.T. Bradley (Cork Constitution)	G.T.M. Bachop
Forwards:	Forwards:
P.M. Clohessy (Young Munster)	R.O. Williams
T.J. Kingston (Dolphin)	S.B.T. Fitzpatrick
J.J. Fitzgerald (Young Munster)	R.W. Loe
M.J. Galwey (Shannon)	M.J. Pierce
D.G. Lenihan (Cork Constitution)	S.B. Gordon
K. O'Connell (Cork Constitution)	Z.V. Brooke
P.T.J. O'Hara (Sunday's Well)	M.R. Brewer
P.C. Collins (London Irish, Capt.)	W.T. Shelford (Capt.)
Replacements:	Replacements:
P. Hogan (Garryowen) for O'Connell,	B.J. McCahill for
D. Larkin (Garryowen) for Kiernan	Stanley, K.J. Schuler
	for Brooke

Scorers:
Munster: PGs: Keyes (3).
New Zealand: Tries: Schuster, Pierce, Bachop, Innes.
Cons: Fox (3). PGs: Fox (3).

Referee: D. Leslie (Scotland).
Attendance: 18,000.

in at the eleventh hour. Zinzan Brooke was tried out again on the side of the scrum.

Munster started well and put great pressure on New Zealand as the excited crowd revived memories of 1978. They had the greater share of territory in the first half but struggled to score, while New Zealand always looked dangerous. Grant Fox kicked two penalties for New Zealand and Ralph Keyes one for Munster during the early exchanges. Shortly before half-time, Michael Kiernan, nephew of the great Tom, received a blow to the head and left the field to be replaced by Dan Larkin. Almost immediately after this, a back-row move from a scrum five metres from the Munster line saw Bachop and Shelford put John Schuster into a gap. He ran at, and through Larkin for a try. Virtually from the restart, Murray Pierce scored after Munster failed to control a lineout and Michael Bradley was pressurised into a mistake. Fox converted both tries and suddenly New Zealand were ahead, and led 18-3 at half-time.

New Zealand continued with their use of powerful driving mauls and fast support play, although Munster worked out ways of dealing with the rolling mauls which were not entirely legal. They were only occasionally penalised for it and continued to frustrate the All Blacks. New Zealand went further ahead early in the second half with a try from Innes when he joined a move that Graeme Bachop directed down the blind side of a maul. Bachop scored the final try when driven over the Munster line by his pack. Fox converted one and kicked a penalty. Keyes kicked two more penalties but they were little more than consolations.

The All Blacks lost Joe Stanley with a neck injury. He was replaced by Bernie McCahill, and Kevin Schuler replaced Brooke who had damaged ribs. It was a comfortable win for New Zealand who firmly dealt with Munster and made sure there was no repetition of the 1978 defeat, nor the drawn game of 1973 in which current coach Alex Wyllie had been the New Zealand captain.

CONNACHT   1989

Tuesday 14 November 1989
Galway Showground, Galway
Won 40-6

Connacht, the weakest of the four Irish provinces, had improved their performance during the Inter Provincial Championship. Although they had lost all 3 games, they had only been defeated by a few points in two, including the match at Leinster. They had former internationals Tom Clancy and Mick Moylett in the pack together with current Irish number eight Noel Mannion. The side was captained by Noel McCarthy but was given little hope of doing more than avoiding a defeat. Although the New Zealand side had a midweek feel about it, the crowd was pleased to see Wayne Shelford, Steve McDowell and Gary Whetton play. Zinzan Brooke's rib injury prevented him from playing and Andy Earl came in.

CONNACHT	NEW ZEALAND
J.E. Staples (London Irish)	M.J. Ridge
D. Holland (Corinthians)	V.L. Tuigamala
M. Cosgrove (Wanderers)	B.J. McCahill
M. Feely (Old Belvedere)	J.K.R. Timu
E. Guerin (Galwegians)	W.K. Little
E.P. Elwood (Galwegians)	F.M. Botica
S. O'Beirne (St Mary's College)	I.B. Deans
Forwards:	Forwards:
D. Henshaw (Athlone)	S.C. McDowell
J. O'Riordian (Cork Constitution)	W.D. Gatland
T.P.J. Clancy (Lansdowne)	G.H. Purvis
A. Higgins (London Irish)	I.D. Jones
M.M.F. Moylett (Shannon)	G.W. Whetton
N. McCarthy (St Mary's College, Capt.)	A.T. Earl
M.J.J. Fitzgibbon (Shannon)	K.J. Schuler
N.P. Mannion (Corinthians)	W.T. Shelford (Capt.)
Replacement:	
J. Healy (Galwegians) for Mannion	

Scorers:
Connacht: PGs: O'Beirne (2).
New Zealand: Tries: Botica (3), Earl (2), Deans, Ridge, Tuigamala.
Cons: Botica. PGs: Botica (2).

Referee: L.J. Peard (WRU).
Attendance: 8,000.

On a misty afternoon in Galway, Connacht had no answer to the dazzling running of Frano Botica, who curiously had an off day with the boot, missing ten of his thirteen attempts on goal. However, he ran in three spectacular tries and opened up the home defence for two others. Sean O'Beirne made life difficult for Bruce Deans by pressurising him throughout, and Connacht never gave up but New Zealand, playing within themselves at times, were never in any danger. Referee Les Peard made sure the players adhered to the laws and respected his authority. He had a fine game but stood no nonsense. Even Shelford was penalised for arguing. The All Blacks' pack was totally dominant, and three of their tries came directly from attacking scrums close to the home side's line. Earl twice, and Deans scored with Buck Shelford having a hand in each. When they needed to the All Blacks were able to increase the intensity of their play. One attacking scrum on the All Blacks' line looked dangerous for the tourists but the New Zealand pack focussed and took the ball against the head and cleared. Connacht attacked when they could but the New Zealand defence dealt with them with organisation and calmness.

The All Blacks led 13-6 at half-time and attacked constantly throughout the second half, running in 6 tries. Botica made a break that was taken on by Shelford and Warren Gatland, and finished off by Matthew Ridge in a move that began midway in the New Zealand half for the best try of the game. Had Botica had his kicking boots on the All Blacks would have roared past 50 points.

Franco Botica was New Zealand's first five-eighth immediately before Grant Fox arrived on the international scene but from that point he tended to play second fiddle to the Aucklander. A highly talented runner, as Connacht found out, he was more of an individual than Fox and as such was considered something of a risk. He turned to rugby league after this tour, but when rugby union became professional he returned to the union code and played club rugby for Llanelli for two seasons before returning to New Zealand.

IRELAND   1989

Saturday 18 November 1989
Lansdowne Road, Dublin
Won 23-6

Ireland experienced an indifferent 1989 Five Nations, losing heavily to Scotland but winning in Cardiff. They also lost to England and France in Dublin. Coached by former Ireland forward Jimmy Davidson, the Irish included eight Ulstermen in the side. For the New Zealand match Ken Hooks replaced Michael Kiernan, who had been concussed playing for Munster against the All Blacks. New caps were awarded to Phil Rainey, future Lion Nick Popplewell and Australian Brian Smith, who replaced the injured Paul Dean. They were captained by Willie Anderson, who had played for Ulster against New Zealand in 1978. An injury to Alan Whetton prevented his selection so the combative Andy Earl continued to deputise. Concerns over Joe Stanley's

IRELAND	NEW ZEALAND
P.I. Rainey (Ballymena)	J.A. Gallagher
K.J. Hooks (Ards)	C.R. Innes
D.G. Irwin (Instonians)	J.T. Stanley
B.J. Mullin (London Irish)	T.J. Wright
K.D. Crossan (Instonians)	N.J. Schuster
B.A. Smith (Oxford University)	G.J. Fox
L.F.P. Aherne (Lansdowne)	G.T.M. Bachop
Forwards:	Forwards:
N.J. Popplewell (Greystones)	S.C. McDowell
S.J. Smith (Ballymena)	S.B.T. Fitzpatrick
J.J. McCoy (Bangor)	R.W. Loe
D.G. Lenihan (Cork Constitution)	M.J. Pierce
W.A. Anderson (Dungannon, Capt.)	G.W. Whetton
P.M. Matthews (Wanderers)	A.T. Earl
P.T.J. O'Hara (Sunday's Well)	M.R. Brewer
N.P. Mannion (Corinthians)	W.T. Shelford (Capt.)

Replacements:
D.C. Fitzgerald (Lansdowne) for Popplewell,
P.P.A. Danaher (Garryowen) for Hooks

Scorers:
Ireland: PGs: B. Smith (2).
New Zealand: Tries: Gallagher, Shelford, Wright. Con: Fox.
PGs: Fox (3).

Referee: A.R. MacNeil (Australia).
Attendance: 55,000.

fitness lifted and he played. Craig Innes remained on the wing. Thus the team was the same as had played Wales.

Anderson led the response to the All Blacks' Haka. As Wayne Shelford led the challenge, Anderson and his team advanced arm-in-arm in 'V' formation towards the All Blacks until Anderson and Shelford stood nose to nose. The challenge was thus accepted in disrespectful fashion, which made New Zealand yet more determined to win. The opening phases were very physical. Shelford was trampled by the Irish pack after he dived at the feet of a foot-rush, and there were many bruising challenges. Referee Sandy MacNeill struggled to officiate. Brian Smith and Grant Fox exchanged penalties, then from a scrum on their own ten-metre line, New Zealand ran the ball. A long pass to Joe Stanley was followed by another to Terry Wright, who created a gap through which John Gallagher raced, ending with a full-length dive for the line. Fox missed the conversion but New Zealand were 13-6 ahead at half-time.

New Zealand threw everything at Ireland but the Irish defence just held out. Twice Graeme Bachop was inches from the Ireland line only to be denied by Pat O'Hara, and a despairing tackle by Hooks on Innes saved a certain try. The winger received concussion and had to be replaced by Philip Danaher. Fox later went over for a try but it was called back for an infringement. Playing into the wind in the second half, Ireland were heroic in defence. Nevertheless, New Zealand were not to be denied. The All Blacks' forwards controlled a rolling maul and as it approached the line, the ball was released and moved quickly for Gallaher to create room for Wright to run in for the second try. Going into injury time, Shelford crossed for the final New Zealand try. Fox converted and New Zealand had secured their biggest win over Ireland.

It was the nineteenth international in a row that New Zealand had avoided defeat, a run extending back to the 'Battle of Nantes' when they lost to France in 1986, and including the 1987 World Cup victories.

ULSTER 1989

Tuesday 21 November 1989
Ravenhill, Belfast
Won 21-3

Ulster was Ireland's leading province, having recently won the Inter Provincial Title for a sixth successive year. They had scored many tries in the process and had enjoyed a 38-3 win over Connacht in Galway, in which they scored 8 tries a few weeks previously. They provided the backbone of the Ireland side and Steve Smith, Jimmy McCoy, Willie Anderson, Phil Matthews from the pack and Philip Rainey, David Irwin and Keith Crossan from outside played against the All Blacks three days before. Only three of the team, Porter, Blair and Reynolds, were never capped by Ireland at some stage. They were a strong side and under the captaincy of Lions centre, Doctor David Irwin, they offered a stern challenge to the All Blacks. The All Blacks recognised

ULSTER	NEW ZEALAND
P.I. Rainey (Ballymena)	M.J. Ridge
S. Porter (Malone)	V.L. Tuigamala
J.A. Hewitt (London Irish)	B.J. McCahill
D.G. Irwin (Instonians, Capt.)	J.K.R. Timu
K.D. Crossan (Instonians)	W.K. Little
P. Russell (Instonians)	F.M. Botica
A.G. Blair (Dungannon)	I.B. Deans
Forwards:	Forwards:
M.E. Reynolds (Malone)	S.C. McDowell
S.J. Smith (Ballymena)	S.B.T. Fitzpatrick
J.J. McCoy (Bangor)	G.H. Purvis
P.S.C. Johns (Dublin University)	I.D. Jones
W.A. Anderson (Dungannon)	G.W. Whetton (Capt.)
P.M. Matthews (Wanderers)	A.J. Whetton
W.D. McBride (Malone)	K.J. Schuler
B.F. Robinson (Ballymena)	Z.V. Brooke
Replacement:	
B.M. McKibbin (Instonians) for Reynolds	

Scorers:
Ulster: PG: Russell.
New Zealand: Tries: Brooke, Tuigamala. Cons: Botica (2).
PGs: Botica (3).

Referee: I.M. Bullerwell (England).
Attendance: 20,000.

the challenge, and McDowell and Fitzpatrick were retained in the side, as was Gary Whetton, who was in charge. Alan Whetton had sufficiently recovered from his hamstring injury to join his brother in the team, although he was not completely fit.

The match was played under floodlights and kick-off was delayed as there was congestion getting the crowd into the ground. In a dour first half, in which the Ulster pack fought like terriers with their New Zealand counterparts, the All Blacks failed to make the most of the wind. Frano Botica kicked two long-range penalties, but New Zealand conceded many when they had established good attacking positions. Peter Russell missed a drop goal attempt and the tourists led 6-0 at half-time.

Russell opened the Ulster scoring with a penalty five minutes into the second half and with the strong wind at their backs, Ulster looked confident and a shock was on the cards. Hope was short-lived. Botica kicked a penalty and then Zinzan Brooke drove over from close to the line for a try after Kevin Schuler had made a telling run deep into the Ulster 22. Botica converted, and then added the extra points to a fine try from Tuigamala. Ulster lost the ball in attack and it was gathered by Bernie McCahill close to halfway. He passed out to the Samoan who beat one despairing tackle and then raced in to score. New Zealand had scored 15 points in a seven-minute burst and put themselves out of sight. There was no further score and although New Zealand had won, they were not convincing.

BARBARIANS 1989

Saturday 25 November 1989
Twickenham, London
Won 21-10

BARBARIANS	NEW ZEALAND
A.G. Hastings (London Scottish)	J.A. Gallagher
T. Underwood (Leicester)	C.R. Innes
S. Hastings (Watsonians)	N.J. Schuster
J.C. Guscott (Bath)	T.J. Wright
R. Underwood (Leicester)	W.K. Little
A. Clement (Swansea)	G.J. Fox
N.C. Farr-Jones (Sydney University)	G.T.M. Bachop
Forwards:	Forwards:
D.M.B. Sole	S.C. McDowell
(Edinburgh Acads, Capt.)	
B.C. Moore (Nottingham)	S.B.T. Fitzpatrick
D. Young (Cardiff)	R.W. Loe
W.A. Dooley (Preston Grasshoppers)	M.J. Pierce
P.J. Ackford (Harlequins)	G.W. Whetton
P.M. Matthews (Wanderers)	A.T. Earl
G.W. Rees (Nottingham)	M.R. Brewer
P.T. Davies (Llanelli)	W.T. Shelford (Capt.)
Replacement:	Replacement:
B.J. Mullin (London Irish) for Guscott	Z.V. Brooke for Shelford

Scorers:
Barbarians: Try: Matthews. PGs: G Hastings (2).
New Zealand: Tries: Brooke, Innes, Loe. Cons: Fox (3). PG: Fox.

Referee: C. Norling (Wales).
Attendance: 60,000.

The Barbarians selected the successful Lions front five from their Australian tour, and Nick Farr-Jones at scrum-half. Although on the losing side against the Lions, he captained the Australian team that won the World Cup two years later. Wing Tony Underwood was the traditional uncapped player and

was joined by his older brother, Rory, on the other wing. The younger Underwood had only played 26 matches for Leicester, but possessed blistering pace and later played for England and the British Lions. Rory Underwood came into the side late after David Campese withdrew with injury. A knee injury to Craig Chalmers also meant a late change with Tony Clement replacing the Melrose outside half. Joe Stanley dropped out with a recurrence of a neck injury and was replaced by Walter Little, the youngest player in the tour party. Little fitted in at second five-eighth with John Schuster moving to centre. This was the only change to the side that had won the 2 international games.

The outstanding Philip Matthews faced the All Blacks for the third time in eight days and it was he who opened the scoring with a try after three minutes, crashing over after the equally influential Paul Ackford had won good lineout ball. The conversion missed, and then David Young was desperately close to scoring following a spectacular run from Tony Underwood. However, after twenty-two minutes, All Black Craig Innes scored from a scrum move that had been deployed regularly

Wayne Shelford, the fearsome New Zealand captain who later played for Northampton and coached Saracens.

on tour. It was the young wing's eighth tour try. Innes later played in his natural position of centre for New Zealand before turning to rugby league when only twenty-two. Grant Fox converted the try but the Barbarians hit back, and Gavin Hastings kicked two penalties after the home forwards pressurised the All Blacks and their backs were caught offside. The Barbarians led 10-6 at half-time.

Twelve minutes into the second half, Zinzan Brooke, who had replaced the injured 'Buck' Shelford at half-time, scored after Bachop and Little had worked a scissors move close to a scrum, for Fox to convert. The first five-eighth added a penalty and a few minutes later, Richard Loe barged over the line for a converted try following a scrum back-row move to make the game safe for the tourists.

For the first hour of the game the Barbarians forwards had dominated but they were unable to make their supremacy show as the half-backs failed to 'click', the midfield regularly took wrong options and Gavin Hastings mishandled at key times. They had ample opportunity to win the match but they failed to take their chances. It may have been a different story had they had more time to prepare. While the New Zealand tight five had a torrid afternoon, their loose forwards and backs played with pace, vision and almost telepathic understanding to dominate open play, particularly in the final quarter of the game. New Zealand finished the tour with an unblemished record of 13 wins from 13 games in Britain and Ireland, 14 from 14 in all. After the match Shelford was critical of the home team: 'We don't waste possession in New Zealand' he said. The matter-of-fact Shelford was a magnificent leader, not the biggest number eight and not a lineout forward like his predecessor Murray Mexted, but a hard, pugnacious individual with a rare presence on the field. Everything was done with 100 per cent focus, and he restored the Haka from being an interesting precursor to the game to a passionate prefix and a fearsome, intimidating war dance. He was able to impart his mental strength to the rest of his team. Wayne 'Buck' Shelford was one of the greatest of all New Zealand captains.

Tuesday 28 November 1989
Iffley Road, Oxford
Won 80-20

This was not an official fixture in the All Blacks' tour. The game was staged to celebrate the 150th anniversary of the Treaty of Waitangi. Although played a year before the actual anniversary, this was an opportunity to commemorate the Treaty, which was an agreement to protect Maori interests, including land, between the Maori and British settlers. The home side was made up of players who had donned the jerseys of Oxford or Cambridge University, and included England internationals Simon Halliday and Simon Smith, plus Victor Ubogu, who later played for England. Stuart Barnes of Bath and David Evans of Cardiff both dropped out of the home team. They were captained by Simon Griffin, formerly of Oxford and now of Pontypridd. New Zealand included guest players Iain Wood, who replaced Matthew Ridge when the full-back withdrew, David van Praagh, Mike Speight, who played for New Zealand in 1986, Dean Oswald of Pontypool and David Kirk, New Zealand's 1987 World Cup-winning captain who had studied at Oxford immediately after that triumph. John Gallagher was originally chosen at centre before moving to full-back when Ridge withdrew, and Oswald was drafted in when fellow Wales-based Kiwi Hemi Taylor dropped out. Kirk himself had chosen this New Zealand side.

OXBRIDGE PAST XV	NEW ZEALAND
A.P. Kennedy (Saracens)	J.A. Gallagher (Wellington)
C. Wigeratna (Oxford University)	C.R. Innes (Auckland)
R.A. Rydon (Oxford University)	I.D. Wood (North Harbour)
S.R.J. Vessey (Northampton)	J.K.R. Timu (Otago)
S.T. Smith (Wasps)	W.K. Little (North Harbour)
S.J. Halliday (Bath)	F.M. Botica (North Harbour)
M.E. Hancock (Richmond)	D.E. Kirk (Auckland, Capt.)
Forwards:	Forwards:
V.E. Ubogu (Bath)	R.O. Williams (North Harbour)
P.A. Green (Wasps)	W.D. Gatland (Waikato)
T.G. Willis (Narbonne)	D.B. van Praagh (North Harbour)
C.M. Crane (Waterloo)	I.D. Jones (North Auckland)
S.T. O'Leary (Wasps)	M.W. Speight (North Harbour)
S.J.M. Griffin (Pontypridd, Capt.)	D.J. Oswald (Bay of Plenty)
S.R. Kelly (Wasps)	K.J. Schuler (Manawatu)
C.B. Vyvyan (Richmond)	M.R. Brewer (Otago)
Replacement:	Replacement:
G.E.C. Fell (Oxford University)	B. Mather (Waikato)
for Hancock	for Wood

Scorers:
Oxbridge Past XV: Tries: Fell, Green, Vessey. Con: Kennedy. PG: Kennedy (2).
New Zealand: Tries: Gallagher (2), Little (2), Wood, Timu, Gatland, Botica, Innes, Wood, Kirk, Mather, Oswald, Schuler. Cons: Botica (9), Little (2), Gallagher.

Referee: W.D. Bevan (Wales).
Attendance: 4,100.

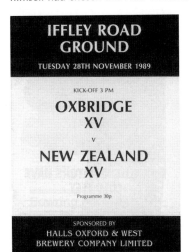

IFFLEY ROAD GROUND

TUESDAY 28TH NOVEMBER 1989

KICK-OFF 3 PM

OXBRIDGE XV

v

NEW ZEALAND XV

Programme 30p

SPONSORED BY
HALLS OXFORD & WEST
BREWERY COMPANY LIMITED

New Zealand declined the option of using their forwards to win the game and threw the ball around with an exuberance common in charity games. They scored 14 tries, eleven from their backs. It was demonstration, celebration rugby in which John Gallagher had a wonderful match, scoring 2 tries himself and creating opportunities from which his colleagues helped themselves to further scores. The running lines of the backs, and outstanding support play, were fine illustrations of the beauty of the sport. Despite the dash of the New Zealanders, the Oxbridge team played with determination and grit, and never gave up. These traits were personified in Ubogu who had an extraordinary game, primarily in defence, but also making powerful runs with the ball in hand.

New Zealand were far too strong but the Treaty, which meant so much to native New Zealanders, was soundly celebrated on the field and long into the night.

1993
NEW ZEALAND TO BRITAIN & IRELAND

THE MATCHES

London & South-East Division	23 October 1993	Twickenham	won 39-12
Midland Division	26 October 1993	Leicester	won 12-6
South-West Division	30 October 1993	Redruth	won 19-15
Northern Division	2 November 1993	Liverpool	won 27-21
England A	7 November 1993	Gateshead	won 26-12
South of Scotland	10 November 1993	Galashiels	won 84-5
Scotland A	13 November 1993	Glasgow	won 20-9
Scottish Development XV	16 November 1993	Edinburgh	won 31-12
SCOTLAND	20 November 1993	Murrayfield	won 51-15
England Emerging Players	23 November 1993	Gloucester	won 30-19
ENGLAND	27 November 1993	Twickenham	lost 15-9
Combined Services	30 November 1993	Devonport	won 13-3
Barbarians	4 December 1993	Cardiff	won 25-12

Played 13, Won 12, Drew 0, Lost 1. Scored: 386 points, Conceded: 156.

The New Zealand Tour Party:

S.P. Howarth (Auckland), J.K.R. Timu (Otago), F.E. Bunce (North Harbour), E. Clarke (Auckland), M.J.A. Cooper (Waikato), E.J. Rush (North Harbour), V.L. Tuigamala (Auckland), J.W. Wilson (Otago), S.J. Bachop (Otago), M.J. Berry (Wellington), M.C.G. Ellis (Otago), L. Stensness (Auckland), J.P. Preston (Wellington), S.T. Forster (Otago), M.R. Allen (Taranaki), O.M. Brown (Auckland), C.W. Dowd (Auckland), G.H. Purvis (Waikato), S.B.T. Fitzpatrick (Auckland), N.J. Hewitt (Hawke's Bay), R.M. Brooke (Auckland), R.T. Fromont (Auckland), S.B. Gordon (Waikato), I.D. Jones (North Auckland), L.J.P. Barry (North Harbour), M.R. Brewer (Otago)*, P.W. Henderson (Southland), J.W. Joseph (Otago), B.P. Larsen (North Harbour)*, J.E.P. Mitchell (Waikato), Z.V. Brooke (Auckland), A.R.B. Pene (Otago). (*replacement on tour)

Captain: S.B.T. Fitzpatrick. Manager: N. Gray. Coach: L.W. Mains. Assistant Coach: E.W. Kirton.

Leading points scorer: S.P. Howarth – 81 points. Leading try-scorer: J.W. Wilson & M.C.G. Ellis – 6 tries. Most appearances: J.W. Wilson – 9 games. ZV Brooke also played in 9 matches, two as a replacement.

Saturday 23 October 1993
Twickenham, London
Won 39-12

New Zealand were buoyant following a 2-1 series win over the British Lions earlier in the summer, and had trounced Western Samoa in a one-off Test match. While the Lions were battling their way around New Zealand, England's other players had toured Canada and Scotland's completed a bruising tour of the South Seas. The All Blacks took the opportunity to introduce some new players on the tour, and had an eye on developing them for the 1995 World Cup. London fielded a strong side for the opening match of the tour. The team looked particularly potent behind the scrum, where only centre Damian Hopley, a future international, had not played for England. The pack contained a further four England players, with Chris Sheasby a future cap. Of the entire fifteen, only forwards Rory Jenkins, Alex Snow and Matt Greenwood would never play international

LONDON & SOUTH-EAST COUNTIES	NEW ZEALAND
G.H. Davies (Wasps)	M.J.A. Cooper
T. Underwood (Leicester)	J.W. Wilson
W.D.C. Carling (Harlequins)	F.E. Bunce
D.P. Hopley (Wasps)	V.L. Tuigamala
C.C. Oti (Wasps)	M.J. Berry
C.R. Andrew (Wasps, Capt.)	S.J. Bachop
S.M. Bates (Wasps)	S. Forster
Forwards:	Forwards:
J. Leonard (Harlequins)	C.W. Dowd
B.C. Moore (Harlequins)	S.B.T. Fitzpatrick (Capt.)
J.A. Probyn (Wasps)	O.M. Brown
A.C. Snow (Harlequins)	I.D. Jones
D. Ryan (Wasps)	S.B. Gordon
M.J. Greenwood (Wasps)	J.W. Joseph
C.M.A. Sheasby (Harlequins)	P.W. Henderson
R.H.J. Jenkins (London Irish)	A.R.B. Pene
	Replacement:
	Z.V. Brooke for
	Henderson (temp)

Scorers:
London & South-East Division: Tries: Jenkins, Oti. Con: Andrew.
New Zealand: Tries: Bachop (2), Wilson (2), Berry.
Cons: Cooper (4), PGs: Cooper (2).

Referee: P. Thomas (France).
Attendance: 56,400.

rugby. New Zealand were touring without some of their big names from recent years, including flanker Michael Jones, winger John Kirwan and star goal-kicker and outside half Grant Fox. Many observers in Britain felt that the absence of Fox in particular would be a handicap for the tourists. On the evidence of this game, those observers were proved very wrong. Jason Leonard, Brian Moore, Rob Andrew, Tony Underwood and Will Carling had faced the All Blacks in the red shirt of the Lions a few months earlier.

Steve Bachop, the replacement for Fox at outside half, enjoyed an impressive start to the tour as the All Blacks ran in 5 tries, two of them going to Bachop himself. The number ten varied his play throughout, showing plenty of willingness to run the ball, but also seeming to choose exactly the right moment to kick. He scored his side's first try after fifteen minutes when powerhouse winger Va'aiga Tuigamala brushed aside the attempted tackles of Carling and Dean Ryan, and he directed operations efficiently

throughout. His performance was contrasted by a disappointing display from his opposite number Rob Andrew. Andrew's tactical kicking was poor and he rarely got his backline moving. In addition to this, he suffered a rare off day with his goal-kicking, missing three first-half penalties. The first of these, awarded early in the game when All Black skipper Sean Fitzpatrick high-tackled Jenkins, was a simple one by his standards. The second All Black try was made by another of their stars of the day, centre Frank Bunce. He had already charged straight through Hopley in the early stages of the match, and when he did so again he drew full-back Huw Davies, before giving a scoring pass to Jeff Wilson. This was actually Wilson's twentieth birthday in New Zealand, although he was still nineteen in Britain when the game kicked off. New Zealand led 15-0 at the break, their other points coming from a penalty and conversion by full-back Matt Cooper.

Eight minutes after the restart London scored their first points when, following a run from Davies, Chris Oti and Hopley manufactured a try for Jenkins that Andrew converted. However, a third New Zealand try killed off any hope of a London recovery. Bachop was again the scorer, this time running in untouched after taking Arran Pene's pass from a 5-metre scrum. Another great run from Bunce resulted in flanker Paul Henderson giving a scoring pass to Marty Berry, and the final New Zealand try went to Wilson following a Bachop break. The young winger should have had a hat-trick, but Fitzpatrick ignored him when he was unmarked, choosing instead to attempt a dummy that was not bought. Cooper converted all 3 tries and added a further penalty, but London had the last word when Oti scored after good work from Ryan and Carling.

This was an excellent start to the tour for New Zealand. In addition to Bunce and Bachop, both the wingers had enjoyed fine games, as had Pene and scrum-half Stu Forster. Tony Underwood, Moore, Davies and Sheasby, as well as veteran prop Jeff Probyn, had all defended well for London, but already there was talk of an undefeated tour following this impressive opener. Only the lineout remained an area of concern following the efforts of Snow, Ryan and Sheasby for the home side.

MIDLAND DIVISION 1993

Tuesday 26 October 1993
Welford Road, Leicester
Won 12-6

Ten days before this fixture the Midlands had been thrashed 31-3 by the South & South-West in the Divisional Championship. They went on to lose their remaining 2 divisional games as well, yet before this they battled gallantly against the All Blacks, coming close to claiming at least a draw. The side, coached by former Coventry and England full-back Peter Rossborough, contained only four current internationals in England players Martin Johnson, Dean Richards, Gary Pearce and John Olver, although Neil Back, Stuart Potter, Graham Rowntree and Matt Dawson were future England caps. A further England player, full-back Simon Hodgkinson, withdrew from the

MIDLAND DIVISION	NEW ZEALAND
J. Steele (Northampton)	S.P. Howarth
S.T. Hackney (Leicester)	J.K.R. Timu
S. Potter (Leicester)	E. Clarke
I. Bates (Leicester)	E.J. Rush
H.S. Thorneycroft (Northampton)	L. Stensness
A.P. Challinor (Harlequins)	M.C.G. Ellis
M.J.S. Dawson (Northampton)	J.P. Preston
Forwards:	Forwards:
G.C. Rowntree (Leicester)	M.R. Allen
C.J. Olver (Northampton)	N.J. Hewitt
G.S. Pearce (Northampton)	G.H. Purvis
M.O. Johnson (Leicester)	I.D. Jones
S.J. Lloyd (Moseley)	R.T. Fromont
J.M. Wells (Leicester)	Z.V. Brooke (Capt.)
N.A. Back (Leicester)	L.J.P. Barry
D. Richards (Leicester, Capt.)	J.E.P. Mitchell
	Replacement:
	M.J.A. Cooper for Stensness

Scorers:
Midland Division: PGs: Steele (2).
New Zealand: PGs: Howarth (2), Cooper (2).

Referee: B.W. Stirling (Ireland).
Attendance: 15,000.

side with a thigh strain on the day before the match, his place going to John Steele. British Lions and England forward Martin Bayfield was also unavailable through injury, and his place in the second row went to Steve Lloyd of Moseley. Lloyd had dual English and Welsh international qualification, although he was destined never to play international rugby. There was some surprise that the veteran prop Gary Pearce had been selected ahead of Leicester's Darren Garforth, while many felt that flanker Neil Back had the perfect opportunity in this game to prove to the sceptics that his lack of height should not preclude him from playing for England. Well though he played, he did not get into the England side to face New Zealand, although he gained his first cap later in the season. Midlands skipper Dean Richards had appeared as a late replacement in the victorious Midland XV against New Zealand in 1983 and Pearce had also played in this game. Martin Johnson was well known to the tourists, having played in New

Zealand where he won a New Zealand Colts cap. New Zealand gave a first start in an All Black jersey to Richard Fromont, while the captaincy went to Zinzan Brooke. His brother, Robin, was ruled out of the tour for the next two weeks, and the tour management sent for Blair Larsen as a temporary replacement. In the event, Robin Brooke played no further part in the tour and Larsen remained with the team.

During the first half of the match there were two penalties apiece for Steele and his opposite number Shane Howarth. There was a controversial moment ten minutes before the break when the Midlands pushed the All Blacks off the ball at a defensive scrum. It appeared that the home side had scored a try from the push, but the referee, Irishman Brian Stirling, was unsighted and could not award the score. The sides remained level at half-time.

Early in the second half Howarth, who was later to switch international allegiance and play for Wales, missed two penalty chances to put New Zealand ahead. Shortly after this, Lee Stensness left the field with an injury, and it was his replacement, Matthew Cooper, who attempted the next penalty, striking an upright from fifty metres. Mr Stirling made his second controversial decision of the game when he stopped an All Black maul when it appeared certain that a try would result, and then Steele, who had already missed a second-half penalty, had a chance to clinch the game with a kick six minutes from time. Sadly for the home fans he missed, and two minutes later New Zealand were ahead, replacement Cooper goaling from forty-five metres after Richards was offside at a ruck. His second penalty, just before full-time, sealed an unconvincing New Zealand victory. Only Norm Hewitt and Ian Jones had impressed in the tourists' pack, while Richards, Back and Lloyd had all excelled for the Midlands. The home side's tackling had been excellent throughout, particularly from Stuart Potter and Ian Bates in the centre, but little had been seen of the backs in attack, partly because the half-backs Dawson and Paul Challinor over kicked. Matthew Cooper had certainly been New Zealand's saviour. Not only had he kicked the winning points, but he had also brought off a superb tackle on Back when a Midlands try looked possible.

SOUTH-WEST DIVISION 1993

Saturday 30 October 1993
Recreation Ground, Redruth
Won 19-15

England internationals and British Lions Stuart Barnes and Jeremy Guscott were injured and therefore unavailable for the South-West Division, while Bath winger Adedayo Adebayo, an original selection for the game, also withdrew, his place going to fellow Bath player Audley Lumsden. Bath was the leading English club at the time, and the starting line-up included eleven Bath players. Steve Ojomoh, one of the replacements used in the match, was also from Bath. Number eight forward Ben Clarke had been suffering from a sternum injury, but declared himself fit to play. Only Chris Clark and Andy Blackmore of the forwards had not played for England, but there was only one capped player

SOUTH-WEST DIVISION	NEW ZEALAND
J.E.B. Callard (Bath)	J.K.R. Timu
P.A. Hull (Bristol)	J.W. Wilson
P.R. de Glanville (Bath)	F.E. Bunce
N.D. Beal (Northampton)	V.L. Tuigamala
A.E. Lumsden (Bath)	M.J.A. Cooper
M.J. Catt (Bath)	S.J. Bachop
K.P.P. Bracken (Bristol)	J.P. Preston
Forwards:	Forwards:
C.J. Clark (Oxford University and Bath)	C.W. Dowd
R.G.R. Dawe (Bath)	S.B.T. Fitzpatrick (Capt.)
V.E. Ubogu (Bath)	O.M. Brown
N.C. Redman (Bath)	I.D. Jones
A.G. Blackmore (Bristol)	S.D. Gordon
J.P. Hall (Bath, Capt.)	J.W. Joseph
R.A. Robinson (Bath)	P.W. Henderson
B.B. Clarke (Bath)	A.R.B. Pene
Replacements:	Replacement:
P. Holford (Gloucester) for de Glanville,	Z.V. Brooke for Joseph
S.O. Ojomoh (Bath) for Robinson,	
D. Sims (Gloucester) for Blackmore	

Scorers:
South-West Division: PGs: Callard (4). DG: Hull.
New Zealand: Try: Joseph. Con: Cooper. PGs: Cooper (4).

Referee: Clayton Thomas (Wales).
Attendance: 15,000.

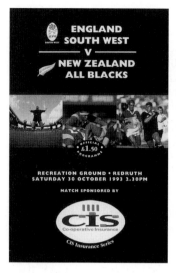

The South-West squad which faced New Zealand at Redruth.

in the backs – centre Phil de Glanville. Of the remaining backs, Nick Beal, Mike Catt and Paul Hull were future England players, while Jon Callard and Kyran Bracken made their England debuts against New Zealand later in the tour. New Zealand fielded a strong side and a close game was anticipated.

This was a passionate, physical match that left many of its participants bruised and battered, and in some cases in need of hospital treatment. The support at Redruth, a place very much at the heart of Cornish rugby, was equally passionate and the game was played in a highly charged atmosphere. The South-West, playing up the Redruth slope in the first half, led 9-6 at the break. Callard kicked two penalties, one after a high tackle and one after Olo Brown had collapsed a scrum. Crucially, he missed three other penalties during the half and ended the day with success from only half of his eight kicks at goal. In contrast, Matthew Cooper kicked five out of five. He scored from two penalties in the first half, while the other South-West points came from a Paul Hull drop goal. Fifteen minutes after the start of play, Phil de Glanville left the field with an eye injury and was replaced by Paul Holford.

The home side held the lead until six minutes into the second half, when Arran Pene picked up at the base of a scrum and began a move which saw Va'aiga Tuigamala and Paul Henderson handle before Jamie Joseph crossed for the only try of the game. Cooper converted, but a further Callard penalty fifteen minutes later, following obstruction by Steve Bachop, cut the tourists' lead to just a point. Ojomoh joined the action as a replacement for Andy Robinson, but the future England cap had barely been on the field when he conceded a penalty that Cooper goaled. Once again, Callard reduced the arrears to a point, but Cooper's final late penalty sealed a hard-fought but deserved New Zealand victory.

There had been fine home performances from skipper John Hall, Victor Ubogu and in particular Nigel Redman, but New Zealand had dominated the lineouts, where Andy Blackmore had failed to make much of an impression for the home side. Blackmore was concussed late in the game and was replaced by another England cap of the future, Dave Sims of Gloucester. The Bristol second row shared an ambulance journey with Jamie Joseph, who had suffered a rib injury. The main talking point after the game concerned the injury to Phil de Glanville. He required fifteen stitches in his eye wound and there seemed little doubt that the injury had been caused by an All Black boot, but despite protests from the RFU the New Zealand management insisted that the incident was accidental and refused to discipline anybody. De Glanville, who also suffered concussion, came close to losing an eye and the whole affair soured the New Zealand victory. Many other players from both sides bore the marks of battle on their bodies. Hooker Graham Dawe's back, for example, was covered in grazes. In the words of journalist John Mason, this was 'a mighty match that had a bruising impact in every sense'.

Tuesday 2 November 1993
Anfield, Liverpool
Won 27-21

Liverpool Football Club was the unusual venue for the Northern Division's clash with the 1993 All Blacks. The North had not been enjoying the best of seasons in the Divisional Championship, having already lost to London and the South & South-West, and the side to face New Zealand contained only four England caps. Of these, Tim Rodber was the sole capped forward, and none of his fellow pack members was destined to win a cap in the future. In the backs, Ian Hunter, Kevin Simms and Rory Underwood had played for their country, although Underwood was badly short of match practice, having played just one friendly game so far in the season. Of the remaining backs, Jim Mallinder and Paul Grayson were England caps of the future, while scrum-half Dave Scully had been a member, along with Rodber, of the winning England seven in the World Cup Sevens earlier in the year. The divisional side was coached by former England captain and coach Dick Greenwood, who courted controversy in the build-up to the game by claiming that the All Blacks were boring.

Greenwood must have regretted his rash statement long before half-time as the tourists ran in three brilliant first-half tries in an electrifying ten-minute spell. The North had started well with two early penalties from Grayson – he was to kick seven of his ten attempts during the game. Jeff Wilson replied with a penalty for the All Blacks, but the North's 6-3 advantage disappeared in the try glut that followed. First the front row set up Mark Ellis for a run to the line in which he outpaced the home defence. Ellis scored again when he cleverly wrongfooted the defence, chipped ahead and won the race to touch down. The third try went to hooker Norm Hewitt, who barged his way over in unstoppable

NORTHERN DIVISION	NEW ZEALAND
I.G. Hunter (Northampton)	S.P. Howarth
D.J. Mallinder (Sale)	J.W. Wilson
M.R. Fielden (Northampton)	E. Clarke
K.G. Simms (Liverpool St Helens, Capt.)	E.J. Rush
R. Underwood (Leicester and RAF)	M.J. Berry
P.J. Grayson (Northampton)	M.C.G. Ellis
D. Scully (Wakefield)	S. Forster
Forwards:	Forwards:
M.P. Hynes (Orrell)	M.R. Allen
G.J. French (Orrell)	N.J. Hewitt
S. McMain (Sheffield)	G.H. Purvis
J. Dixon (West Hartlepool)	B.P. Larsen
D.N. Baldwin (Sale)	R.T. Fromont
T.A.K. Rodber (Northampton)	Z.V. Brooke (Capt.)
N. Ashurst (Orrell)	L.J.P. Barry
A. MacFarlane (Sale)	J.E.P. Mitchell
Replacement:	
C Cusani (Orrell) for Baldwin	

Scorers:
Northern Division: PGs: Grayson (7).
New Zealand: Tries: Ellis (2), Hewitt, Rush. Cons: Wilson (2).
PG: Wilson.

Referee: J.M. Fleming (Scotland).
Attendance: 24,636.

fashion. Wilson converted two of the tries and New Zealand looked comfortably in control with a lead of 22-6 as half-time approached. However, Grayson landed two more kicks before the break, and the 22-12 half-time score gave the home side some hope.

That hope was increased shortly after the restart when Grayson landed a monster goal to reduce the arrears to 7 points. After that came the fourth New Zealand try, scored in the corner by Eric Rush after Eroni Clarke had broken through two tackles. Wilson failed to convert, and the stage was set for a late home rally. Rodber and his fellow forwards pressurised the All Blacks into handling errors, while Scully and centre Mike Fielden put in some dangerous runs. Grayson landed two more huge kicks, and the tourists certainly looked out of sorts in the closing stages of the game. Sadly for the home supporters, there was no further scoring, and with a try count of 4-0 in their favour there was no doubt that New Zealand deserved to win.

Before the game, members of the victorious 1979 North team that had defeated the All Blacks were presented to the crowd. There was to be no repeat of the 1979 heroics in 1993, but the North had not been disgraced. Confidence was high the following Saturday when the North played their final Divisional Championship game against the Midlands, and Kevin Simms's side ran away with the game, recording a 31-9 victory.

ENGLAND A   1993

Sunday 7 November 1993
International Stadium,
Gateshead
Won 26-12

ENGLAND A	NEW ZEALAND
J.E.B. Callard (Bath)	J.K.R. Timu
I.G. Hunter (Northampton)	J.W. Wilson
D.P. Hopley (Wasps)	F.E. Bunce
M.J. Catt (Bath)	V.L. Tuigamala
P.A. Hull (Bristol)	M.J.A. Cooper
S. Barnes (Bath)	M.C.G. Ellis
K.P.P. Bracken (Bristol)	S. Forster
Forwards:	Forwards:
G.C. Rowntree (Leicester)	C.W. Dowd
R.G.R. Dawe (Bath)	S.B.T. Fitzpatrick (Capt.)
A.R. Mullins (Harlequins)	O.M. Brown
N.C. Redman (Bath)	I.D. Jones
D. Sims (Gloucester)	S.B. Gordon
J.P. Hall (Bath, Capt.)	B.P. Larsen
N.A. Back (Leicester)	Z.V. Brooke
T.A.K. Rodber (Northampton)	A.R.B. Pene
Replacement:	
S.O. Ojomoh (Bath) for Redman (temp.)	

Scorers:
England A: PGs: Callard (4).
New Zealand: Tries: Wilson, Timu. Cons: Cooper (2). PGs: Cooper (3). DG: Ellis.

Referee: R.J. Megson (Scotland).
Attendance: 19,000.

The England A side, managed by Jack Rowell, who had enjoyed huge success as coach of Bath, contained seven full internationals. Ian Hunter and Stuart Barnes were the only capped backs, while the five England players in the forwards were Andy Mullins, Graham Dawe, Nigel Redman, John Hall and Tim Rodber. Barnes, who had been suffering from injury, was playing at his own request as he was anxious to prove his fitness. The remainder of the side all went on to full England honours in the future. For New Zealand, original selection Eroni Clarke withdrew with illness and his place was taken by Jeff Wilson. The game was a sell-out.

For the fourth consecutive match the All Blacks kept their line intact and the home side had to rely on the boot of Jon Callard to keep them in contention. Callard certainly enjoyed a better afternoon with the boot than he did for the South & South-West at Redruth, kicking four of the eight penalty

chances he was offered. Unfortunately, he blotted his copybook by sending out a long telegraphed pass inside his own half after twenty-six minutes that was gratefully intercepted by Wilson who touched down under the posts for the first All Black try. This score, easily converted by Matthew Cooper – he missed only one of his six goal attempts in the game – gave the tourists a 13-0 lead, and England A's woes were increased two minutes later when Marc Ellis dropped a goal from a free kick. This goal should not have been allowed to stand as the ball had not touched an opposition player after the award of the free kick, but despite this setback England heads did not drop and Callard redeemed himself with three penalties to make the half-time score 16-9 to New Zealand. The tourists' earlier scores had come from Cooper penalties – one awarded for offside and one for killing the ball at a ruck.

England A began the second half in positive fashion and enjoyed a period of prolonged pressure. However, the All Black defence remained firm, and when the siege was raised Stu Forster made a blind-side break to start a move that was carried on by Arran Pene before full-back John Timu appeared in the line to take the try-scoring pass. Cooper converted, and added a further penalty from forty metres to complete his side's scoring. The only home points of the second half came from another Callard penalty.

Several players had impressed in a losing cause for England A. Kyran Bracken and Stuart Barnes had combined well at half-back, Barnes showing great courage in daring to tackle the mighty Va'aiga Tuigamala, while John Hall and Neil Back had shown up well in the forwards. Tuigamala himself had tackled with his usual vigour for New Zealand, as had Frank Bunce. Timu and Forster also starred for the visitors and the All Blacks left for Scotland in good heart, doubtless intrigued by the words of their coach Laurie Mains: 'We haven't come up anywhere near peak performance. We are arriving at the stage now where we have to start cranking up a bit.'

SOUTH OF SCOTLAND   1993

Wednesday 10 November 1993
Netherdale, Galashiels
Won 84-5

The day was fair, the sky was clear
No breath came o'er the lea.
When I went owre to Gala town
The All Blacks for to see.
I hoped the South would match them well,
Might even win the day,
I was a sadder, wiser man
By the time I came away.

Ian Landles

A truly black day for Scottish rugby! Fearing a midweek ambush and upping their commitment from previous matches, the New Zealanders turned on an astonishing display of power rugby in a twelve-try demolition of the reigning Scottish District champions, a side that contained five

SOUTH OF SCOTLAND	NEW ZEALAND
M. Dods (Gala)	S.P. Howarth
A.G. Stanger (Hawick)	E. Clarke
S.A. Nichol (Selkirk)	M.J. Berry
A.G. Shiel (Melrose)	E.J. Rush
G.A. Parker (Melrose)	L. Stensness
C.M. Chalmers (Melrose)	S.J. Bachop
B.W. Redpath (Melrose)	J.P. Preston
Forwards:	Forwards:
G.R. Isaac (Gala)	M.R. Allen
J.A. Hay (Hawick)	N.J. Hewitt
H.A. Hunter (Gala)	G.H. Purvis
R.R. Brown (Melrose, Capt.)	S.B. Gordon
G.W. Weir (Melrose)	R.T. Fromont
D.J. Turnbull (Hawick)	B.P. Larsen
J.P. Amos (Gala)	Z.V. Brooke (Capt.)
B.L. Renwick (Hawick)	J.E.P. Mitchell
Replacement:	Replacement:
S. McColm (Selkirk) for Hunter	M.C.G. Ellis for Berry

Scorers:
South of Scotland: Try: Parker.
New Zealand: Tries: Brooke (4), Hewitt (2), Howarth (2), Ellis, Bachop, Preston, Mitchell. Cons: Howarth (9). PGs: Howarth (2).

Referee: D.W. Matthews (England).
Attendance: 5,000.

internationals. Conceding around two stones per man in the pack, the South of Scotland had no answer to the New Zealanders' irresistible forward drives, their brilliant support play and all-round urgency to get to the second phase. In a superbly efficient display, the visitors made only five unforced errors and never allowed their opponents any respite, even when the scores were piling up. Outclassed from the start, the South did themselves no favours with some atrociously weak first-time tackling.

Full-back Shane Howarth's personal tally was 34 points through 2 tries, two penalties and nine conversions. Captain Zinzan Brooke, who many rated as the best forward in the world, scored 4 tries, but perhaps the man of the match was the massive hooker Norm Hewitt. The 17-stone Hawke's Bay Maori scored 2 tries and created havoc every time he had the ball. There were few bright spots for the home side, although in the thirty-fifth minute they did manage to score a fine try. Craig Chalmers sent a miss-pass to Scott Nichol; Michael Dods made a blistering intrusion from full-back, enabling the diminutive Melrose wing Gary Parker to score the South's first try against New Zealand since

1935. Doddie Weir competed well in the lineout and Derek Turnbull never shirked the hard work, but these were mere crumbs of comfort. At one point, it looked like New Zealand would break the 100-point mark. Leading 46-5 at half-time, they later led 77-5 after fifty-four minutes. To their credit, the South managed to find some resolve and even mounted some fruitless attacks of their own. But by the final whistle, the Scottish players, coaching staff and many of the spectators were thoroughly shell-shocked.

For the record, this was, and remains, New Zealand's highest score in the British Isles and Ireland. This calamitous defeat had important consequences for Scottish rugby. It confirmed fears that the Scottish game was falling behind the rest of the world and encouraged the development of district rather than club rugby, a controversial policy that some felt was misdirected. It was clear to everybody that hastily assembled scratch sides were no match for the supermen of New Zealand rugby.

SCOTLAND A 1993

Saturday 13 November 1993
Old Anniesland, Glasgow
Won 20-9

New Zealand never looked like losing the match, but Scotland A, essentially the Scottish second XV, fought hard to restore some credibility into Scottish rugby after the South of Scotland debacle earlier in the week. The visitors retained only Marc Ellis and Steve Gordon from the previous match. Scotland A had some very big forwards and presented a stronger challenge than the South, although it was expected that the New Zealanders would have greater dynamism and mobility. The Scots included three players from Stirling County, the new kids on the block of Scottish club rugby. The match was played in front of a sell-out crowd of 8,000 people, a tribute to a successful marketing campaign in a city largely devoted to soccer. The visitors won their seventh

SCOTLAND A	NEW ZEALAND
M. Dods (Gala)	J.K.R. Timu
K.M. Logan (Stirling County)	J.W. Wilson
S.A. Nichol (Selkirk)	F.E. Bunce
I.C. Jardine (Stirling County)	V.L. Tuigamala
G.A. Parker (Melrose)	M.J.A. Cooper
D.S. Wyllie (Stewart's Melville FP, Capt.)	M.C.G. Ellis
B.W. Redpath (Melrose)	S. Forster
Forwards:	Forwards:
A.G.J. Watt (GHK)	C.W. Dowd
K.D. McKenzie (Stirling County)	S.B.T. Fitzpatrick (Capt.)
D.J. Herrington (Dundee HSFP)	O.M. Brown
D.S. Munro (GHK)	I.D. Jones
A.E.D. Macdonald (Heriot's FP)	S.B. Gordon
D.J. McIvor (Edinburgh Acads)	J.W. Joseph
R.I. Wainwright (Edinburgh Acads)	P.W. Henderson
C.D. Hogg (Melrose)	A.R.B. Pene
	Replacements:
	M.R. Allen for Dowd,
	B.P. Larsen for Gordon

Scorers:
Scotland A: PG: Dods. PGs: Wyllie (2).
New Zealand: Try: Ellis. PGs: Cooper (5).

Referee: A.J. Spreadbury (England).
Attendance: 8,500.

consecutive victory of the tour, but they failed to exert the pressure of their previous outings, largely thanks to the sustained efforts of the home players, who gave a spirited performance that ruffled a few feathers. Indeed, the result might have been much closer if the normally reliable Gary Parker had not missed three penalty attempts. The Scottish backs, perhaps lacking some confidence, also tended to kick too much when it might have been more profitable to have kept the ball in hand.

In ideal conditions, New Zealand led 11-3 at the interval. Matthew Cooper kicked two penalties and Marc Ellis scored the game's only try, latching onto to Tuigamala's powerful burst through some fragile defence. In response, the veteran stand-off Douglas Wyllie kicked the first of his brace of drop goals. The Scottish forwards raised their momentum in the second half, producing some forceful driving play that put their opponents onto the back foot. In one of the best moments of play, Rob Wainwright won a lineout and, after a series of quick rucks, Wyllie dropped his second goal. Cooper kicked his fifth penalty in the dying minutes to put an undeserved gloss on New Zealand's victory.

In a stirring performance, many of the Scots worked hard to enhance their reputations, none more so than centre Ian Jardine, who had an immense game. He made numerous important tackles, including one on Ellis running on the outside arc that saved a certain try. The Scots, as predicted, did well in the lineouts and managed to steal eight of their opponents' throw-ins. Andy Macdonald ruled in the middle while Wainwright and Carl Hogg were equally authoritative towards the tail. At hooker, the pocket battleship Kevin McKenzie exploded the myth that he was too small for international rugby, while Dave McIvor excelled in his powerful drives. By contrast, many of the New Zealanders looked rather ordinary, although Ellis played well in midfield. As the game went on, the visitors lost much of their traditional discipline and control in the face of concerted heroics by opponents who refused to be subdued.

SCOTLAND DEVELOPMENT XV   1993

Tuesday 16 November 1993
Myreside, Edinburgh
Won 31-12

This was a rather uninspiring game, essentially little more than a trial match for both camps. A scratch side with little sense of identity or cohesion, the Scotland Development XV was mainly composed of up-and-coming individuals who were on the fringes of international recognition. The side contained three capped players in Derek Stark, a smooth-running winger from Boroughmuir, Northampton's Neil Edwards and Gloucester's Ian Smith, who handed over the captaincy of the side to Hawick's Jim Hay just before the start. It said much about the standard of Scottish rugby that six of the side played outside Scotland. Their cause was not helped by an eleventh-hour reshuffle after the talented Ally Donaldson withdrew with food poisoning. The Australian Scot Kent Bray moved to stand-

SCOTLAND DEVELOPMENT XV	NEW ZEALAND
I.C. Glasgow (Heriot's FP)	S.P. Howarth
D.A. Stark (Boroughmuir)	J.W. Wilson
F.J. Harrold (London Scottish)	E. Clarke
R.C. MacNaughton (Northampton)	E.J. Rush
C.S. Dalgleish (Gala)	L. Stensness
K.A. Bray (Harlequins)	S.J. Bachop
D.W. Patterson (Edinburgh Acads)	J.P. Preston
Forwards:	Forwards:
J.J. Manson (Dundee HSFP)	M.R. Allen
J.A. Hay (Hawick, Capt.)	N.J. Hewitt
D.J. Herrington (Dundee HSFP)	G.H. Purvis
N.G.B. Edwards (Northampton)	B.P. Larsen
S.J. Campbell (Dundee HSFP)	R.T. Fromont
P. Walton (Northampton)	J.W. Joseph
I.R. Smith (Gloucester)	L.J.P. Barry
F.D. Wallace (GHK)	J.E.P. Mitchell (Capt.)
Replacement:	
S. McIntosh (West of Scotland) for Stark	

Scorers:
Scotland Development XV: PGs: Bray (4).
New Zealand: Tries: Rush, Barry, Mitchell. Cons: Howarth (2). PGs: Howarth (4).

Referee: G. Black (Ireland).
Attendance: 4,500.

off and Cameron Glasgow came in at full-back. The New Zealanders fielded their second-string side captained from the number eight berth by future All Blacks' coach John Mitchell.

In a game that lacked any real passion, and arguably much meaning, the visitors played well below their best but still did enough to win comfortably. To their credit, there was much to admire in the performance of the Development XV, in particular their courageous tackling. The spirit of the side was epitomised in the thirty-sixth minute, when number eight Fergus Wallace pulled off a crunching tackle on the fearsome All Black hooker Norm Hewitt, who was in full cry. Similarly, in the second half, the London Scot Fraser Harrold, who was just back from injury and awaiting shoulder surgery, magnificently downed Eric Rush when a try looked certain. Captain Jim Hay led by example, the Scottish forwards produced some unceremonious driving and makeshift stand-off Bray made some assiduous tackles

and kicked well, although his drop-outs gave his pack little chance. However, there was never any doubt that the New Zealanders would win. Richard Fromont dominated the lineout with a commanding performance, although the Scots did better in the second half thanks to Stewart Campbell. For the neutral, the most disappointing feature was the visitors' failure to unleash the simmering Eric Rush, who got the ball in open space only sporadically. Rush did manage to score New Zealand's first try after ruck provision from Eroni Clarke and Shane Howarth's intrusion. Liam Barry, whose father Kevin toured in 1963, got the second, albeit with a pass from Jamie Joseph that looked forward. Mitchell scored the third after a series of advancing mauls. Howarth bagged 16 points with four penalties and two conversions, although he missed three other goal-kicks. On a sour note, Mitchell was guilty of a high tackle on Stark early in the second half, which resulted in the Scottish wing being taken to hospital with concussion. Several of the Development XV went on to win caps for Scotland in the future, perhaps proving that the game was a worthwhile exercise.

SCOTLAND 1993

Saturday 20 November 1993
Murrayfield, Edinburgh
Won 51-15

A nation winced as the Scots conceded over 50 points for the first time in their 122-year history. The match was as one-sided as the score suggests, New Zealand running in 7 tries and giving Scotland a near-perfect lesson in the art of rugby football. Both sides fielded new caps. Making their debuts for Scotland were hard-tackling Stirling County centre Ian Jardine and 6ft 8in Heriot's lock Andy Macdonald, who had played for Cambridge in the 1989 Varsity match. Five players involved in the previous weekend's match for Scotland A won promotion to the senior side, but the main talking point was the bizarre selection of Scott Hastings, one of the game's most experienced centres, on the left wing. New Zealand fielded a new half-back partnership of Marc Ellis and Stu Forster, both of Otago, and at lock Waikato's Steven Gordon, a front jumper and a great ball-winner. Also making his

SCOTLAND	NEW ZEALAND
A.G. Hastings (Watsonians, Capt.)	J.K.R. Timu
A.G. Stanger (Hawick)	J.W. Wilson
I.C. Jardine (Stirling County)	F.E. Bunce
A.G. Shiel (Melrose)	V.L. Tuigamala
S. Hastings (Watsonians)	M.J.A. Cooper
C.M. Chalmers (Melrose)	M.C.G. Ellis
A.D. Nicol (Dundee HSFP)	S. Forster
Forwards:	Forwards:
A.G.J. Watt (GHK)	C.W. Dowd
K.S. Milne (Heriot's FP)	S.B.T. Fitzpatrick (Capt.)
A.P. Burnell (London Scottish)	O.M. Brown
D.F. Cronin (London Scottish)	I.D. Jones
A.E.D. Macdonald (Heriot's FP)	S.B. Gordon
D.J. McIvor (Edinburgh Acads)	J.W. Joseph
R.I. Wainwright (Edinburgh Acads)	Z.V. Brooke
G.W. Weir (Melrose)	A.R.B. Pene
Replacements:	Replacement:
D.S. Wyllie (Stewart's-Melville FP)	E. Clarke for Cooper
for Chalmers, C.D. Hogg (Melrose)	
for Cronin, B.W. Redpath (Melrose)	
for Nicol (temp.), K.M. Logan (Stirling County)	
for G. Hastings (temp.)	

Scorers:
Scotland: PGs: G. Hastings (4), Chalmers.
New Zealand: Tries: Wilson (3), Ellis (2), Brooke, Bunce.
Cons: Cooper (4), Wilson. PGs: Cooper (2).

Referee: F. Burger (South Africa).
Attendance: 37,000.

debut was the multi-talented twenty-year-old Jeff Wilson, the new golden boy of New Zealand rugby who had already represented his country at cricket.

The main stand at Murrayfield was being redeveloped so both sides were forced to change in temporary accommodation. New Zealand went ahead in the opening minute with a penalty goal by Matthew

Cooper and never relinquished their iron grip on the game. They led 22-9 at the interval, Ellis, Wilson and Zinzan Brooke scoring tries, Cooper converting two against 3 penalty goals for the Scots. In the second half, there were further tries for Frank Bunce and Ellis while Wilson completed his hat-trick. The young New Zealand winger enjoyed a dream debut and showed that his tour selection above the seasoned John Kirwan was completely justified. Always dangerous and full of running, he took any chances that came his way and gave his opponents a most uncomfortable afternoon. Wilson completed the scoring by banging over the difficult conversion of his third try, taking his personal tally to 17 points. At the final whistle, Scotland looked a thoroughly dispirited side.

Motivated by fear of failure, this was an awe-inspiring performance by the visitors, who brushed aside the Scottish challenge with the contemptuous ease of a training session. Captain Sean Fitzpatrick described it as: 'the most satisfying performance in which I have been involved in terms of commitment, total aggression and mental hardness'. Scotland had no answer to New Zealand's cerebral brutality, which produced some fine rugby with the accent on power and pace rather than anything spectacular. Ian Jones was prominent in the lineout, where he outshone Scotland's sentinel Doddie Weir, while the rampaging Olo Brown proved himself in the tradition of fearsome All Black forwards. Some of the Scottish players did not look fully fit, while the experiment of playing Scott Hastings on the wing backfired horribly, his defensive angles being exposed in two of Wilson's tries. As so often in the past, the New Zealanders had found an extra gear when it mattered most.

ENGLAND EMERGING PLAYERS 1993

Tuesday 23 November 1993
Kingsholm, Gloucester
Won 30-19

The Emerging England side was hit by two late withdrawals when both second rows, Andy Blackmore of Bristol and Alex Snow of Harlequins pulled out through injury. To the delight of the home crowd, both of the replacements, Dave Sims and Richard West, were Gloucester players. The team was captained by a full international, Dean Ryan, who had won three caps, while Sims, along with Damien Hopley, Paul Hull, Mike Catt and Steve Ojomoh had already played for England A against the All Blacks. With the exception of Paul Challinor, Paul Holford, Chris Clark and Kevin Dunn, all the uncapped players went on to play for England. There were two strange features in the selection of the team – the back row consisted entirely of number eight forwards, while Challinor, normally an outside half, was selected to play at full-back in a meaningful game for the first time since his schooldays.

ENGLAND EMERGING PLAYERS	NEW ZEALAND
A.P. Challinor (Harlequins)	S.P. Howarth
P. Holford (Gloucester)	E. Clarke
N.D. Beal (Northampton)	M.J. Berry
D.P. Hopley (Wasps)	E.J. Rush
P.A. Hull (Bristol)	L. Stensness
M.J. Catt (Bath)	S.J. Bachop
M.J.S. Dawson (Northampton)	J.P. Preston
Forwards:	Forwards:
C.J. Clark (Oxford University and Bath)	M.R. Allen
K.A. Dunn (Wasps)	N.J. Hewitt
J.A.H. Mallett (Bath)	G.H. Purvis
D. Sims (Gloucester)	B.P. Larsen
R.J. West (Gloucester)	R.T. Fromont
D. Ryan (Wasps, Capt.)	L.J.P. Barry
C.M.A. Sheasby (Harlequins)	P.W. Henderson
S.O. Ojomoh (Bath)	J.E.P. Mitchell (Capt.)

Scorers:
England Emerging Players: Tries: Sims, Challinor. PGs: Challinor (3).
New Zealand: Tries: Rush, Clarke, Howarth. Cons: Howarth (3).
PGs: Howarth (2). DG: Bachop.

Referee: D. Mene (France).
Attendance: 13,000.

In near-freezing conditions the All Blacks gained another deserved victory, although they conceded 2 tries for the first and only time on tour. Prior to this game the tourists' line had been crossed just three times, and the 2 tries scored at Kingsholm were the final ones scored against the visitors. The Emerging Players enjoyed much of the early play against a rather sluggish New Zealand team, but Challinor missed two penalties and it was the tourists who took the lead when Shane Howarth kicked a penalty awarded for an offside offence. The first All Black try came from a Challinor error – he caught a high kick from Steve Bachop, but kicked the ball straight into the arms of Eric Rush, who sprinted thirty metres down the touchline to score in the corner. Howarth converted, and although Challinor found the target with two penalties, New Zealand surged further ahead when Eroni Clarke scored a brilliant solo try after a dodging run. Once again Howarth added the extra points, but there was great local rejoicing when Sims caught a five-metre lineout and was driven over the line by his fellow forwards. Challinor could not convert, so the score at half-time was 17-11.

At the start of the second half, Ojomoh excited the crowd with a charge into All Black territory. Challinor cut the deficit to 3 points with a further penalty and the pressure was now on New Zealand. However, the All Blacks were next to score when John Mitchell and Jon Preston mounted a blind-side attack that resulted in a corner try for Howarth which he converted himself from the touchline. The lead was extended further by another Howarth penalty and a Bachop drop goal, but the home side had the final word when Hopley ran through three tackles before giving a scoring pass to Challinor.

New Zealand had certainly been challenged by the Emerging Players, and the steadying influence of Bachop had been a major factor in the tourists' victory. The home side had failed to take early chances, and this ultimately ruined any chance of victory, although the grandstand finish provided by Hopley's run brought deserved respectability to the final scoreline.

ENGLAND 1993

Saturday 27 November 1993
Twickenham, London
Lost 15-9

Jon Callard, the Bath full-back, was due to be the only new cap in the England side to face New Zealand, but the selected scrum-half, Dewi Morris, was suffering from a tracheal virus, and withdrew from the team on the day before the game. His replacement, Kyran Bracken of Bristol, was called up to win his first cap just four days after his twenty-second birthday. Lock forward Martin Bayfield and centre Jeremy Guscott were both unavailable through injury, yet England were still able to field a strong side containing seven players who had played in the Second Test of the British Lions' tour of New Zealand earlier in the

ENGLAND	NEW ZEALAND
J.E.B. Callard (Bath)	J.K.R. Timu
T. Underwood (Leicester)	J.W. Wilson
W.D.C. Carling (Harlequins, Capt.)	F.E. Bunce
P.R. de Glanville (Bath)	V.L. Tuigamala
R. Underwood (Leicester and RAF)	E. Clarke
C.R. Andrew (Wasps)	M.C.G. Ellis
K.P.P. Bracken (Bristol)	S. Forster
Forwards:	Forwards:
J. Leonard (Harlequins)	C.W. Dowd
B.C. Moore (Harlequins)	S.B.T. Fitzpatrick (Capt.)
V.E. Ubogu (Bath)	O.M. Brown
M.O. Johnson (Leicester)	I.D. Jones
N.C. Redman (Bath)	S.B. Gordon
T.A.K. Rodber (Northampton)	J.W. Joseph
B.B. Clarke (Bath)	Z.V. Brooke
D. Richards (Leicester)	A.R.B. Pene

Scorers:
England: PGs: Callard (4). DG: Andrew.
New Zealand: PGs: Wilson (3).

Referee: F. Burger (South Africa).
Attendance: 68,000.

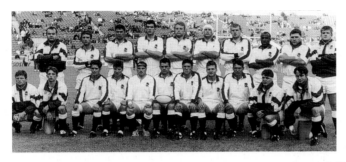

From left, back row: J. Hall (replacement), P. de Glanville, B. Clarke, M. Johnson, T. Rodber, N. Redman, D. Richards, V. Uboga, J. Leonard, G. Rowntree (replacements). Front row: G. Dawe (replacements), M. Dawson (replacement), K Bracken, R. Andrew, B. Moore, W. Carling (Capt.), T. Underwood, J. Callard, R. Underwood, S. Barnes (replacement), I. Hunter (replacement).

year, a match the Lions won 20-7. Four weeks after his serious eye injury in the South & South-West v. New Zealand game, centre Phil de Glanville received his first England start, having played twice as a replacement. New Zealand announced the same side that started the Scotland Test, but Matthew Cooper had not recovered from his groin injury, and Eroni Clarke, who had replaced Cooper at the end of the game at Murrayfield, was promoted to the starting lineup just before kick-off. Mike Brewer, who had joined the tour on the previous day, sat on the bench because Paul Henderson was unfit.

The game opened with an unsavoury incident when Jamie Joseph deliberately stamped on Bracken's ankle. The young debutant had to have the ankle strapped, but bravely stayed on the field and played a full part in England's victory. Callard opened the scoring after sixteen minutes when Eroni Clarke was penalised for a high tackle on England skipper Will Carling, and added a second goal twelve minutes later when Arran Pene was penalised for a bit of offside gamesmanship. He had 'accidentally' got in the way when retreating after a tackle, but South African referee Freek Burger, unlike others who had officiated at the tourists' games, was quick to penalise the offence. Callard missed a third goal later in the half, but he enjoyed far more success than young Jeff Wilson who was given the All Black kicking duties when Cooper pulled out of the game. Wilson missed three first-half kicks, and five out of eight in total. England led 6-0 at half-time and thoroughly deserved to do so. The forwards had played New Zealand at their own game, and rattled the tourists with their driving play and tight marking. Victor Ubogu had disrupted Pene's game with the strength of his charges, while the tackling of Rob Andrew and the gallant Bracken was too much even for the mighty Va'aiga Tuigamala. In truth, England should have had a greater lead at the break, having squandered three try-scoring opportunities. First, Tony Underwood was put clear by Ben Clarke only to be downed by John Timu when a try looked more than likely. Then Clarke lost control of the ball as an England maul was being driven towards the line, and finally Tony Underwood again failed to make the most of a break, this time being caught by Eroni Clarke.

Wilson managed two early second-half penalties for the All Blacks, but in between these Callard scored a third for England. A double drive by the home pack set up Andrew for a drop goal after an hour of play, and England entered the final quarter of the game leading 12-6. Wilson soon replied with a fifty-metre penalty, but another Callard kick ten minutes from the end stretched the lead again. New Zealand made frantic efforts to save the game in the final stages, but Wilson missed two more penalties, and Timu was just nudged into touch by the covering Ubogu when it seemed that he had scored. The final whistle heralded scenes of wild celebration at Twickenham. The tourists had lost their unbeaten record to a side that was not afraid to take the game to its opponents, and in Bracken and Callard, two new England stars were born. There were many other stars in this England triumph, notably Nigel Redman with his excellent work in the lineout and the back row of Tim Rodber, Dean Richards and Ben Clarke, who outshone their opposite numbers and defended brilliantly.

This was England's first victory over New Zealand for ten years, and captain Will Carling could now claim an England victory under his leadership against the seven other major rugby nations. The match was a triumph both for the players for and their coach Geoff Cooke whose game plan engineered a famous day in English rugby.

COMBINED SERVICES 1993

Tuesday 30 November 1993
The Rectory Field, Devonport
Won 13-3

COMBINED SERVICES	NEW ZEALAND
Cpl P.A. Hull (Royal Air Force)	S.P. Howarth
Cpl S. Bartliff (Army)	E. Clarke
SAC G. Sharpe (Royal Air Force)	M.J. Berry
AB D. Sibson (Royal Navy)	E.J. Rush
Ft Lt R. Underwood (Royal Air Force)	L. Stensness
Ft Lt A. Johnson (Royal Air Force)	S.J. Bachop
Sgt S. Worrall (Royal Air Force, Capt.)	J.P. Preston
Forwards:	Forwards:
Cpl A. Billett (Royal Air Force)	M.R. Allen
Capt. J. Brammer (Army)	N.J. Hewitt
Sgt J. Fowers (Army)	G.H. Purvis
Cpl R. Armstrong (Royal Marines)	B.P. Larsen
Sgt B. Richardson (Royal Air Force)	R.T. Fromont
Ft Lt C. Moore (Royal Air Force)	L.J.P. Barry
Capt. R.I. Wainwright (Army)	P.W. Henderson
L Cpl M. Watson (Army)	J.E.P. Mitchell (Capt.)
Replacements:	
L Sgt S. Berryman (Army) for Watson	

Scorers:
Combined Services: PG: Worrall.
New Zealand: Try: Hewitt. Con: Howarth. PGs: Howarth (2).

Referee: D.R. Davies (Wales).
Attendance: 5,700.

Few gave the Combined Services even the slightest chance of winning this match. The general view was that services rugby was so weak compared to that of a major touring side, that fixtures between the two were now an anachronism and should be discontinued. Certainly the home side did not look particularly strong on paper, and it looked even less so when England cap Tim Rodber withdrew, his place in the side going to Chris Moore. Of the side that took the field, only Rory Underwood of England and Rob Wainwright of Scotland were internationals, although full-back Paul Hull would win his first cap the following year. This was Hull's fourth game against the 1993 tourists – he had previously featured for the South-West, England A and Emerging England. Three of the Services players, Hull, Moore and Bob Armstrong had played for the Bristol club, while Gavin Sharp would do so in the future. New Zealand fielded their regular midweek side under the captaincy of John Mitchell. The Combined Services shocked New Zealand with a brave and determined performance, restricting their illustrious opponents to just one try and tackling heroically throughout. Hull's defence was particularly impressive, as was the tackling of centre Sharp, at the time a Henley player under the guidance of fledgling coach Clive Woodward. Moore proved a thoroughly capable deputy for Rodber and was probably the best of the home forwards.

Shane Howarth missed three first-half penalties for the All Blacks before the Services took the lead when their captain, Steve Worrall, kicked a penalty from fifty-five metres. The home side strove to build on this success, but the team suffered a blow when number eight Mike Watson was caught at the bottom of a ruck and had to leave the field. His replacement, Steve Berryman of the Army, did well in Watson's place, but Howarth finally found the target with a penalty when the Services were penalised for a late tackle on Jon Preston. A second successful kick gave the tourists a narrow 6-3 lead at the interval.

Thereafter, Howarth's kicking form deserted him again, and with the Services still competing vigorously, there was no further score until the final quarter. At this stage  a highly unlikely home victory was a real possibility. The tourists were rescued from possible embarrassment by Steve Bachop, who made a powerful run to set up a corner try for Norm Hewitt which Howarth converted from the touchline. Even then the home side refused to lie down and die, and there was a further bold attack by Hull before the final whistle.

This was a remarkable performance from the Combined Services, which did much to boost the standing of services rugby within the game. The All Blacks had not played especially well, but this fact should not detract from the fine fighting effort of the gallant underdogs.

Saturday 4 December 1993
Cardiff Arms Park, Cardiff
Won 25-12

The Barbarians were not permitted to base their team on the previous summer's Lions squad. The English clubs were unhappy to release players for the game as they had league fixtures to fulfil on the same day. However, they did select some Lions, including the captain, Gavin Hastings. Unfortunately, he was forced to withdraw and was replaced by Tony Clement, who played in the 1989 match between the sides when Craig Chalmers dropped out. Tony Stanger replaced Tony Underwood from the original selection and Neil Back was the only uncapped player in the side. Back went on to play in 66 internationals, including the 2003 World Cup final.

The Barbarians' number eight was Scott Quinnell, who possessed one cap for Wales. His father, Derek, had played

BARBARIANS	NEW ZEALAND
A. Clement (Swansea)	J.K.R. Timu
A.G. Stanger (Hawick)	J.W. Wilson
S. Hastings (Watsonians, Capt.)	F.E. Bunce
I.S. Gibbs (Swansea)	V.L. Tuigamala
N.K. Walker (Cardiff)	L. Stensness
E.P. Elwood (Lansdowne)	M.C.G. Ellis
G. Armstrong (Jed-Forest)	S.T. Forster
Forwards:	Forwards:
N.J. Popplewell (Greystones)	C.W. Dowd
T.J. Kingston (Dolphin)	S.B.T. Fitzpatrick (Capt.)
E.J.A. McKenzie (Paris University)	O.M. Brown
P.S.C. Johns (Dungannon)	I.D. Jones
O. Roumat (Dax)	S.B. Gordon
R.L. Wainwright (Edinburgh Acads)	B.P. Larsen
N.A. Back (Leicester)	Z.V. Brooke
L.S. Quinnell (Llanelli)	A.R.B. Pene
Replacements:	Replacement:
R. Howley (Cardiff) for Armstrong,	M.R. Brewer for Larsen
C.P. Scholtz (Western Province) for Gibbs	

Scorers:
Barbarians: PG: Elwood (4).
New Zealand: Tries: Dowd, Tuigamala, Jones. Cons: Wilson (2).
PGs: Wilson (2).

Referee: P. Robin (France).
Attendance: 51,000.

in the 1973 match between the sides. Similarly, the father of All Blacks' captain Sean Fitzpatrick, Brian, played for New Zealand in the 1954 game. The All Blacks changed their Test line-up and brought Lee Stensness into the side at the expense of Eroni Clarke, but the headlines went to the inclusion of Blair Larsen instead of Jamie Joseph, villain at Twickenham the previous weekend.

Jeff Wilson kicked an early penalty for the All Blacks, then six minutes later French international Olivier Roumat rose high in a lineout close to the Barbarians' line but misdirected his palm back. It was gathered by Craig Dowd who scored the opening try, which Wilson converted. Then Va'aiga Tuigamala scored a try where his determination exceeded that of Scott Hastings and Stanger combined, to blast between the Scots and through the cover defence, Wilson again converting. The All Blacks were 17-0 ahead and the Barbarians were facing a serious defeat with less than a quarter of the game gone. The Barbarians' teamwork started to improve and Eric Elwood kicked three penalties to keep them in the game. Wilson then kicked his second penalty and, on the stroke of half-time, Elwood kicked his fourth. The All Blacks led 20-12 at half-time.

New Zealand piled on the pressure in the early stages of the second half but good Barbarians' defence stopped the New Zealanders from scoring on several occasions. The tourists dominated the forward exchanges and Arran Pene had a profitable afternoon in the lineout jumping against Back. Gary Armstrong left the field with a rib injury and the uncapped Rob Howley replaced him. Elwood missed two penalty kicks and the final score came after a fine run out of defence from full-back John Timu. When tackled, he found Larsen in support who in turn passed to Ian Jones for the lock to crash over. Wilson missed the conversion but New Zealand were out of sight and comfortable winners. Late in the game, Scott Gibbs was tackled when charging for the All Blacks' line and suffered a serious knee injury. He was replaced by Christian Scholtz and required an operation which kept him out of the 1994 Five Nations Championship.

The Barbarians had been able to stretch the tourists on several occasions, mainly through the counter-attacking of Clement and the outstanding pace of Nigel Walker, but the New Zealand defence had been too well organised to concede any tries. Remarkably, the All Blacks' line was only crossed on five occasions during the tour. This was the last match New Zealand played at the old Cardiff Arms Park. The scene of arguably their most famous defeat back in 1905, it staged 26 tour games involving New Zealand, who managed 20 wins, 5 defeats and a draw. They also won their only World Cup game played there.

On the way home, many of the tourists played for a New Zealand Invitation XV against a LEGA XV in Padova, Italy. The homes side included former All Black captain Wayne Shelford.

1997
NEW ZEALAND TO BRITAIN & IRELAND

THE MATCHES

Llanelli	8 November 1997	Llanelli	won 81-3
Wales A	11 November 1997	Pontypridd	won 51-8
IRELAND	15 November 1997	Dublin	won 63-15
Emerging England	18 November 1997	Huddersfield	won 59-22
ENGLAND	22 November 1997	Manchester	won 25-8
English Rugby Partnership XV	25 November 1997	Bristol	won 18-11
WALES	29 November 1997	Wembley	won 42-7
England A	2 December 1997	Leicester	won 30-19
ENGLAND	6 December 1997	Twickenham	drawn 26-26

Played 9, Won 8, Drew 1, Lost 0. Scored: 395 points, Conceded: 119.

The New Zealand Tour Party:
C.M. Cullen (Central Vikings), T.J. Miller (Waikato), F.E. Bunce (North Harbour), J.T. Lomu (Counties), G.M. Osborne (North Harbour), J.C. Stanley (Auckland), J.F. Umaga (Wellington), J.W. Wilson (Otago), A. Ieremia (Wellington), W.K. Little (North Harbour), S.J. McLeod (Waikato), A.P. Mehrtens (Canterbury), C.J. Spencer (Auckland), J.W. Marshall (Canterbury), J.P. Preston (Wellington),

M.D. Robinson (North Harbour), M.R. Allen (Manawatu), C.K. Barrell (Canterbury), O.M. Brown (Auckland), C.W. Dowd (Auckland), G.L. Slater (Taranaki), S.B.T. Fitzpatrick (Auckland), N.J. Hewitt (Southland), A.D. Oliver (Otago), R.M. Brooke (Auckland), M.S.B. Cooksley (Waikato), I.D. Jones (North Harbour), C.C. Riechelmann (Auckland), A.R. Hopa (Waikato), T.J. Blackadder (Canterbury), A.F. Blowers (Auckland), Z.V. Brooke (Auckland), M.P. Carter (Auckland), J.A. Kronfeld (Otago), T.C. Randell (Otago), S.D. Surridge (Canterbury).

Captain: S.B.T. Fitzpatrick. Manager: M. Banks. Coach: J. Hart.

Leading points scorer: A.P. Mehrtens – 88 points.
Leading try-scorer: C.M. Cullen – 7 tries.
Most appearances: Several players started 5 games, including Kronfeld and Allen, who also appeared once as a replacement. McLeod started 4 and was a replacement in 3 games.

LLANELLI   1997

Saturday 8 November 1997
Stradey Park, Llanelli
Won 81-3

The All Blacks had won the Tri-Nations Championship by winning all 4 matches and had enjoyed wins over Argentina and Fiji, plus a one-off Bledisloe Cup victory over Australia in Christchurch. Coach John Hart chose a powerful squad to tour Britain and Ireland under the captaincy of Sean Fitzpatrick, who sadly was injured and unable to take part in much of the tour. They welcomed back iconic Tongan wing Jonah Lomu to the squad after a debilitating kidney condition which had kept him out of rugby for some time. It was New Zealand's first tour to the northern hemisphere since the sport had become professional. British rugby was on a considerable high following a series-winning Lions tour to South Africa. However, the

LLANELLI	NEW ZEALAND
D.J. Williams	C.M. Cullen
W.T. Proctor	J.W. Wilson
N. Boobyer	F.E. Bunce
S.M. Jones	G.M. Osborne
W. Leach	A.I. Ieremia
C. Warlow	A.P. Mehrtens
R.H.StJ.B. Moon	J.W. Marshall (Capt.)
Forwards:	Forwards:
R. Jones	C.W. Dowd
R.C. McBryde (Capt.)	N.J. Hewitt
S. Gale	O.M. Brown
S. Ford	I.D. Jones
M.J. Voyle	R.M. Brooke
C.P. Wyatt	A.F. Blowers
I. Jones	J.A. Kronfeld
H. Jenkins	T.C. Randell
Replacements:	Replacements:
P. Morris for Jenkins, H. Williams-Jones	Z.V. Brooke for Kronfeld,
for R. Jones, A. Thomas for Moon,	J.C. Stanley for Wilson,
A. Gibbs for I. Jones	J.P. Preston for Mehrtens

Scorers:
Llanelli: PG: Warlow.
New Zealand: Tries: Cullen (4), Wilson (2), Jones, Kronfeld, Marshall, Ieremia, Z Brooke. Cons: Mehrtens (2), Wilson (2), Preston. PG: Mehrtens (2).

Referee: B. Campsall (RFU).
Attendance: 13,800.

Lions were dominated by England with the Celtic nations having little more than bit parts in the tour. New Zealand viewed the English part of their autumn tour as their real challenge, although coach John Hart criticised the itinerary, which included 3 games against an England A selection, as being 'totally contrary to the spirit of the tour.' Twenty-five years and a week or so since Llanelli had defeated New Zealand, the All Blacks returned to Stradey Park for a match played under floodlights. Whereas in 1972 they met a well-established side with a tough core of experience running through it and a coach who previously guided a side to defeat over New Zealand, the 1997 Llanelli side was very young team decimated by injuries and struggling for form. Llanelli outside half Frano Botica, who had sat on the bench for New Zealand the last time the sides had met, had an injured shoulder and could not be considered. The 1997/98 season so far had been forgettable, Llanelli having won only seven of their 13 games before facing New Zealand. Robin McBryde captained Llanelli and their coach was Gareth Jenkins, flank forward in the 1972 match. Having trained at Stradey Park earlier in the week the sides were reminded of the score of the 1972 game – 'Llanelli 9 Seland Newydd 3' appearing on the scoreboard. New Zealand picked a strong team for the match and were determined to win to silence those who kept reminding them of that defeat. Justin Marshall captained the side when Fitzpatrick withdrew with a knee injury.

Full-back Christian Cullen opened the scoring with an early try that was followed after fourteen minutes by a Craig Warlow penalty for the home side. From that point it was all New Zealand and their backs ran in tries almost at will. Llanelli were unable to compete and were totally destroyed. Andrew Mehrtens kicked two penalties before Jeff Wilson scored the second New Zealand try. This was followed by tries from Ian Jones, Josh Kronfeld and a second from Wilson. The conversions were missed but New Zealand led 31-3 at half-time.

The second half was embarrassingly one-sided and New Zealand scored 50 points without reply. Their tries were scored by, in sequence, Marshall, Cullen, Cullen again, and then Cullen scored his fourth try. Norm Hewitt scored next, then Alama Ieremia, Hewitt again and finally Zinzan Brooke, who had replaced Kronfeld. New Zealand scored 13 tries but, remarkably, only converted five. The rugby they displayed was outstanding, particularly as the wet conditions were not ideal for running rugby.

The match was, by some margin, the biggest defeat Llanelli had experienced. New Zealand felt the Scarlets had been put firmly in their place but it also raised serious doubts about whether an individual rugby club would ever be strong enough to take on a major rugby nation in the professional era.

WALES A   1997

Tuesday 11 November 1997
Sardis Road, Pontypridd
Won 51-8

The All Blacks ventured to the foot of the Rhondda Valley to play a second-string Welsh team at Pontypridd Rugby Club, again under floodlights. The Wales A side had an experimental feel about it with only a handful of capped players on show, although all except local players Jason Lewis and Mark Spiller of the team that started the match were to be capped at some time. New Zealand changed their complete team and Jonah Lomu returned to the All Blacks' side after more than a year out of action with a kidney complaint. Todd Blackadder captained the side.

There was a huge cheer from the crowd when Carlos Spencer led the Haka. Then Wales A attacked from the kick-off and within two minutes pressurised New Zealand into conceding a penalty, but Byron Hayward missed the kick at goal. Shortly after this, Wales A were twice caught offside but Spencer missed both penalty attempts. The home side showed resilience in defence and was equal to the attacks of the New Zealanders. Sixteen minutes into the match, the Welsh side took a quick

WALES A	NEW ZEALAND
M.J. Back (Bridgend)	T.J. Miller
G. Thomas (Bridgend)	J.F. Umaga
N. Boobyer (Llanelli)	S.J. McLeod
J.L. Lewis (Pontypridd)	J.T. Lomu
D.R. James (Pontypridd)	W.K. Little
B.I. Hayward (Ebbw Vale)	C.J. Spencer
A.P. Moore (Richmond)	M.D. Robinson
Forwards:	Forwards:
I.M. Buckett (Swansea)	M.R. Allen
G.R. Jenkins (Swansea)	A.D. Oliver
C.T. Anthony (Swansea)	C.K. Barrell
C. Stephens (Bridgend)	C.C. Riechelmann
G.O. Llewellyn (Harlequins, Capt.)	M.S.B. Cooksley
M. Spiller (Pontypridd)	T.J. Blackadder (Capt.)
M.E. Williams (Pontypridd)	M.P. Carter
C.P. Wyatt (Llanelli)	S.D. Surridge
Replacements:	Replacements:
L. Jarvis (Cardiff) from Thomas, N. Eynon (Pontypridd) for Buckett, D. Thomas (Swansea) for Wyatt, W.S. Roy (Pontypridd) for Stephens, H.J. Harries (Harlequins) for Hayward	A.R. Hopa for Riechelmann, G. Slater for Barrell

Scorers:
Wales A: Try: James. PG: Hayward.
New Zealand: Tries: McLeod (2), Carter, Lomu, Miller, Oliver, Robinson. Cons: Spencer (5). PG: Spencer (2).

Referee: J. Pearson (England).
Attendance: 8,000.

throw-in deep in their own half and Gareth Thomas dummied the All Blacks and raced upfield. The ball was quickly moved out to Dafydd James and the wing sprinted forty metres for a fine try. Byron Hayward missed the conversion. Then Spencer got the All Blacks' score going with a penalty before Todd Miller scored a soft try after a Spencer kick into the corner caused confusion, and the full-back picked up the loose ball to score. Spencer converted, then kicked a second penalty and New Zealand led 13-5 at half-time.

Byron Hayward kicked a penalty to put Wales A back in touch. The Welsh defence had been dogged, with the back row and Hayward in particular having fine games. However, having troubled the tourists for the first hour, during which Martyn Williams was outstanding, they began to suffer from fatigue and New Zealand took total control midway through the second half.

An Anton Oliver try eased New Zealand two scores ahead then the All Blacks ran in tries regularly from, in order, Mark Robinson, Jonah Lomu, Scott McLeod, McLeod again then finally Mark Carter. Spencer converted four of them for a comfortable win.

The All Blacks had played efficiently and Lomu had come through his test unscathed. Blackadder had led his side well and with 6 tries in the final twenty minutes there seemed to be no issues with their fitness. Gareth Llewellyn and Gareth Thomas played for the full Welsh side against the All Blacks later in the tour.

IRELAND   1997

Saturday 15 November 1997
Lansdowne Road, Dublin
Won 63-15

Ireland selected five new caps in Kevin Nowlan, John McWeeney, Conor McGuinness, Kieran Dawson and Malcolm O'Kelly. There was some criticism in the local press of the constitution of the pack, and the loss of the injured Jeremy Davidson, who had enjoyed a fine tour with the Lions the previous summer, was sorely felt. Later in the game Kevin Maggs and Dave Erskine came off the replacements' bench to also make their international debuts. Zinzan Brooke came into the New Zealand side ahead of Josh Kronfeld in the only change to the Saturday team. It was an experienced side and they were full of confidence.

Traditionally, Ireland start with a furious onslaught and this match was no exception. With a strong breeze behind them they dominated the game for the first half-hour. They refused to allow New Zealand to settle, pressurising them into

IRELAND	NEW ZEALAND
K.W. Nowlan (St Mary's College)	C.M. Cullen
J.P.J. McWeeney (St Mary's College)	J.W. Wilson
R.A.J. Henderson (Wasps)	F.E. Bunce
M.C. McCall (London Irish)	G.M. Osborne
D.A. Hickie (St Mary's College)	A.I. Ieremia
E.P. Elwood (Galwegians)	A.P. Mehrtens
C.D. McGuinness (St Mary's College)	J.W. Marshall (Capt.)
Forwards:	Forwards:
N.J. Popplewell (Newcastle)	C.W. Dowd
K.G.M. Wood (Harlequins, Capt.)	N.J. Hewitt
P.S. Wallace (Saracens)	O.M. Brown
P.S.C. Johns (Saracens)	I.D. Jones
M.E. O'Kelly (London Irish)	R.M. Brooke
E.O. Halvey (Shannon)	T.C. Randell
K. Dawson (London Irish)	A.F. Blowers
E.R.P. Miller (Leicester)	Z.V. Brooke
Replacements:	Replacements:
R.P. Nesdale (Newcastle) for Wood,	C.C. Riechelmann for
D.J. Erskine (Sale) for Halvey,	R. Brooke, J.A. Kronfeld
K.M. Maggs (Bristol) for McWeeney,	for Blowers, J.P.
B.T. O'Meara (Cork Constitution)	Preston for Mehrtens,
for McGuinness	S.J. McLeod for Bunce

Scorers:
Ireland: Tries: Wood (2). Cons: Elwood. PG: Elwood.
New Zealand: Tries: Osborne (2), Wilson (2), Ieremia, Marshall, Mehrtens. Cons: Mehrtens (5). PGs: Mehrtens (6).

Referee: A.J. Spreadbury (England).
Attendance: 52,000.

making mistakes. Despite this, New Zealand scored first through an Andrew Mehrtens penalty. Then Eric Elwood and Mehrtens exchanged penalties before Keith Wood scored the first try of the match, from a

lineout after seventeen minutes. Elwood converted but New Zealand counter-attacked, and when Mehrtens skipped outside Rob Henderson the ball went to Jeff Wilson to score the first All Blacks' try and put New Zealand back into the lead. Wood scored again close to the half hour after Frank Bunce lost the ball in a heavy tackle and Eric Miller kicked ahead. Wood showed remarkable speed in beating Wilson to the ball. The conversion was missed but three penalties in quick succession from Mehrtens and a conversion of a try from Justin Marshall from a ruck close to half-time saw the All Blacks 27-15 ahead at half-time.

Wood suffered an injury early in the game and was replaced by Ross Nesdale, a New Zealander, at half-time. The second half was all about New Zealand. Shortly after the restart, Glen Osborne scored a try, then Wilson crossed for his second, before Mehrtens scored the fourth New Zealand try. He converted all three and kicked a penalty in the third quarter of the game where the All Blacks scored 24 points and Ireland were not allowed the ball. Playing simple, patient but dynamic rugby, New Zealand scored further tries from Alama Ieremia and a second from Osborne. The All Blacks had scored 7 tries and Mehrtens had contributed thirty-three points in a thrashing.

It was the biggest defeat in Ireland's history and their coach, Brian Ashton, considered these All Blacks the best side he had ever seen.

EMERGING ENGLAND 1997

Tuesday 18 November 1997
Alfred McAlpine Stadium,
Huddersfield
Won 59-22

Emerging England seemed a foolish title to give to the team that lined up at the McAlpine Stadium. Most of the players in the squad had well and truly emerged, many were already England internationals and seven had toured with the British Lions a few months before. In all, twelve had played international rugby, and only Matt Allen and Rory Jenkins would never play in a full international. The decision to field such a strong XV lay with new England coach Clive Woodward who felt that an experienced choice was essential in view of the quality of the opposition. The New Zealanders were not impressed by what they saw as an unscheduled change to the tour itinerary. Coach John Hart claimed that the selection went against touring protocol, but still felt that his fringe players would rise to the challenge.

EMERGING ENGLAND	NEW ZEALAND
D.J. Mallinder (Sale)	T.J. Miller
J. Bentley (Newcastle)	J.F. Umaga
N.J.J. Greenstock (Wasps)	S.J. McLeod
M.C. Allen (Northampton)	J.T. Lomu
T.D. Beim (Sale)	W.K. Little
P.J. Grayson (Northampton)	C.J. Spencer
A.S. Healey (Leicester)	M.D. Robinson
Forwards:	Forwards:
G.C. Rowntree (Leicester)	M.R. Allen
M.P. Regan (Bath)	N.J. Hewitt
D.J. Garforth (Leicester)	G. Slater
S.D. Shaw (Wasps)	C.C. Riechelmann
D.J. Grewcock (Saracens)	M.S.B. Cooksley
R.H.J. Jenkins (Harlequins)	T.J. Blackadder (Capt.)
N.A. Back (Leicester, Capt.)	J.A. Kronfeld
C.M.A. Sheasby (Wasps)	S.D. Surridge
Replacements:	Replacements:
M.J. Corry (Leicester) for Jenkins,	A.R. Hopa for Surridge,
K.P. Yates (Bath) for Garforth, N. McCarthy	J.C. Stanley for Umaga
(Gloucester) for Regan, D. Sims (Gloucester)	
for Shaw	

Scorers:
Emerging England: Try: Greenstock. Con: Grayson. PGs: Grayson (5).
New Zealand: Tries: Miller (3), Lomu (2), Kronfeld, Surridge, Riechelmann. Cons: Spencer (5). PGs: Spencer (3).

Referee: P. Deluca (Argentina).
Attendance: 12,000.

Three Paul Grayson penalties in the first seven minutes gave Emerging England an excellent start. However, the All Blacks soon hit their stride and the first try came when Steve Surridge and Mark

Robinson worked the blind side from a 5-metre scrum to set up a score for Josh Kronfeld. Carlos Spencer missed the conversion, but he was successful following the next score, a Jonah Lomu try. A long Emerging England throw was off target, Walter Little collected the ball, and Kronfeld and Scott McLeod put Lomu in the clear with no-one to beat on his run to the line. Just before this, Grayson had missed a kick, but Spencer added two penalties to take New Zealand's lead up to 18-9. Shortly before half-time Austin Healey hesitated to clear a kick-ahead by Todd Miller, the ball was pinched and Surridge scored the third try. Spencer converted and New Zealand led 25-9 at the break.

Early in the second half Grayson kicked two more penalties to leave his team just 10 points behind. Then New Zealand took over, Miller scoring a try in the fifty-second minute, Spencer kicking a penalty soon after and then converting a Charles Riechelmann try. Miller's second try, converted by Spencer, took the score to 47-15, and he completed his hat-trick from a Jeremy Stanley pass. Spencer's conversion made it 54-15. There was a further try from Lomu before Nick Greenstock gained an injury-time consolation, Grayson's conversion completing the scoring.

This was an excellent performance from the midweek New Zealand XV. For the home side Darren Garforth impressed sufficiently to be put straight into the England line-up for the game at Manchester the following Saturday, a game which was also to feature replacement appearances from Back and Healey.

ENGLAND 1997

Saturday 22 November 1997
Old Trafford, Manchester
Won 25-8

There were two changes to the England side that had drawn with Australia at Twickenham the previous Saturday, Cockerill replacing Long at hooker and Garforth coming in for Green. The All Blacks changed two of the team that had defeated Ireland, bringing in Kronfeld for Blowers and Lomu for Osborne. Lomu's call-up was a surprise as he was considered to be on the tour as a rehabilitation exercise after a long spell out of the game with a kidney disease. The venue demonstrated the RFU's willingness to take internationals to grounds other than Twickenham. It was the first time England played two tests against the same touring side.

There was an element of controversy before the game when the England players faced up to the Haka, hookers Cockerill and Hewitt standing so close together that

ENGLAND	NEW ZEALAND
M.B. Perry (Bath)	C.M. Cullen
D.L. Rees (Sale)	J.W. Wilson
W.J.H. Greenwood (Leicester)	F.E. Bunce
P.R. de Glanville (Bath)	J.T. Lomu
A.A. Adebayo (Bath)	A. Ieremia
M.J. Catt (Bath)	A.P. Mehrtens
K.P.P. Bracken (Saracens)	J.W. Marshall (Capt.)
Forwards:	Forwards:
J. Leonard (Harlequins)	C.W. Dowd
R. Cockerill (Leicester)	N.J. Hewitt
D.J. Garforth (Leicester)	O.M. Brown
M.O. Johnson (Leicester)	I.D. Jones
G.S. Archer (Newcastle)	R.M. Brooke
L.B.N. Dallaglio (Wasps, Capt.)	T.C. Randell
R.A. Hill (Saaracens)	J.A. Kronfeld
A.J. Diprose (Saracens)	Z.V. Brooke
Replacements:	Replacements:
N.A. Back (Leicester) for Diprose,	A.F. Blowers for
A.S. Healey (Leicester) for Adebayo	Z.V. Brooke, S.J. McLeod
	for Ieremia, J.P. Preston
	for Wilson

Scorers:
England: Try: de Glanville. PG: Catt.
New Zealand: Tries: Jones, Wilson, Randell. Cons: Mehrtens (2).
PGs: Mehrtens (2).

Referee: P.L. Marshall (Australia).
Attendance: 55,243.

the referee, Peter Marshall, had to speak to them. All Black coach John Hart described England's attitude as 'disrespectful'. Once the match began, New Zealand soon established an advantage, and two quick scores did much to settle the result early on. First, a diagonal kick from Catt was plucked out of the air by Lomu. The ball was recycled following a ruck for Wilson and Brooke to engineer a try for Jones. Five minutes later Brooke put Wilson in for the second try, and with Mehrtens converting the first score, New Zealand led 12-0. Before either try was scored however, there was another controversial moment when Martin Johnson punched Justin Marshall, the New Zealand half-back and captain. The incident was to earn the Leicester player a one-match ban, keeping him out of the England team to face South Africa the following weekend. Five minutes from half-time, Catt scored England's first points with a penalty, but he missed three simple attempts during the course of the game. There was time after the penalty for Mehrtens to reply with one for the visitors, and at half-time the score was 15-3 to the All Blacks. England restricted the visitors to just one try in the second half, scored by Taine Randell from a 5-metre scrum. Mehrtens converted this and also kicked a penalty, but England managed a good try of their own, Catt's diagonal kick being caught by Healy who put de Glanville in. Unfortunately, Catt had no luck with the conversion.

This was a fine effort against the odds by England, there was plenty of passion in the England play, the tackling was of a high standard, and Cockerill and Garforth provided the home side with a steady scrum and good protection for scrum-half Kieran Bracken. Young David Rees did not shirk from the challenge of marking Jonah Lomu, and the All Blacks were often forced into uncharacteristic errors. England captain Lawrence Dallaglio had an immense game, making tackle after tackle, and earning the comment from coach Clive Woodward that he would not be out of place in the All Black XV.

ENGLAND RUGBY PARTNERSHIP XV   1997

Tuesday 25 November 1997
Ashton Gate, Bristol
Won 18-11

The All Blacks' next game was at Ashton Gate, home of Bristol City Football Club. Rugby has been occasionally played at the stadium over the years. Bristol Rugby Club played intermittently there, before making a permanent home at the Memorial Ground in 1921, but later played floodlit rugby there in the 1950s. The last England 'home' international fixture against Wales before the opening of Twickenham was staged there in 1908, Wales enjoying a 28-18 win in dense fog. The 1998 Welsh Cup final was played there while the Millennium Stadium was being built and New Zealand were to face Tonga there in the 1999 Rugby World Cup. The England Rugby Partnership XV included five players who started the match for Emerging England, and Kevin Yates and Dave

ENGLAND RUGBY PARTNERSHIP XV	NEW ZEALAND
T.R.G. Stimpson (Newcastle)	T.J. Miller
J. Bentley (Newcastle)	J.F. Umaga
N.J.J. Greenstock (Wasps)	J.C. Stanley
M.C. Allen (Northampton)	G.M. Osborne
S.P. Brown (Richmond)	S.J. McLeod
R.de V. Butland (Bath)	C.J. Spencer
M.B. Wood (Wasps)	J.P. Preston
Forwards:	Forwards:
K.P. Yates (Bath)	M.R. Allen
M.P. Regan (Bath)	A.D. Oliver
P.J. Vickery (Gloucester)	C.K. Barrell
D. Sims (Gloucester)	C.C. Riechelmann
R.J. Fidler (Gloucester)	M.S.B. Cooksley
P.H. Sanderson (Sale)	T.J. Blackadder (Capt.)
T.A.K. Rodber (Northampton, Capt.)	M.P. Carter
C.M.A. Sheasby (Wasps)	A.R. Hopa
Replacements:	Replacements:
A.E. Long (Bath) for Regan, R. Winters (Bedford) for Sims, J.P.R. Worsley (Wasps) for Sanderson, S. Benton (Gloucester) for Wood, P.J. Grayson (Northampton) for Butland	W.K. Little for Stanley, S.B.T. Fitzpatrick for Oliver

Scorers:
England Rugby Partnership XV: Tries: Wood. PG: Stimpson (2).
New Zealand: Tries: Hopa, Spencer. Con: Spencer. PG: Spencer (2).

Referee: R. Davies (Wales).
Attendance: 18,120.

Sims retained the replacement berths they had occupied at Huddersfield. When Paul Grayson replaced Richard Butland during the game, the RFU's plan to give their National and A squads as much exposure as possible was confirmed. Newcastle wing John Bentley had a fine game in attack and defence. The team was coached by former England scrum-half Richard Hill. The All Blacks passed the captaincy to Todd Blackadder in the continued absence of Sean Fitzpatrick, although the tour captain did find a place on the replacements' bench and joined the fray late on to make his tour debut.

The home side took the game to New Zealand. Tim Stimpson missed a penalty in the first minute and the game was ten minutes old before New Zealand ventured into their opponents' territory. Phil Vickery had a fine game in the tight and loose, but it was the All Blacks who opened the scoring, when Tana Umaga was tackled in the home 22 and the ball was moved to Glen Osborne who beat one man and crossed for Carlos Spencer to convert. All Blacks' prop Mark Allen caused problems with some powerful runs, but Stimpson kicked two penalties midway through the half and New Zealand led 7-6 at half-time.

The English selection took the lead nine minutes into the second half when Martyn Wood scored a try. The forwards secured the ball and drove through the New Zealand pack before releasing Spencer Brown. The Richmond wing made good ground, then, after a series of rucks, the scrum-half scored. Carlos Spencer kicked two penalties before a push-over try by Aaron Hopa made it safe for the tourists.

Blackadder praised the home side: 'We made too many mistakes but they took the game to us,' he said.

WALES   1997

<table>
<tr><td>Saturday 29 November 1997
Wembley Stadium, London
Won 42-7</td><td>WALES
K.A. Morgan (Pontypridd)
G. Thomas (Bridgend)
A.G. Bateman (Richmond)
I.S. Gibbs (Swansea)
N.K. Walker (Cardiff)
N.R. Jenkins (Pontypridd)
R. Howley (Cardiff)
Forwards:
C.D. Loader (Swansea)
B.H. Williams (Richmond)
D. Young (Cardiff)
M.J. Voyle (Llanelli)
G.O. Llewellyn (Harlequins)
R.C. Appleyard (Swansea)
R.G. Jones (Cardiff, Capt.)
N. Thomas (Bath)
Replacements:
L.B. Davies (Cardiff) for Gibbs,
S.M. Williams (Cardiff) for N. Thomas,
A.C. Thomas (Swansea) for Bateman
(temp.), J.M. Humphreys (Cardiff) for
B. Williams, S.C. John (Cardiff) for Loader</td><td>NEW ZEALAND
C.M. Cullen
J.W. Wilson
F.E. Bunce
J.T. Lomu
W.K. Little
A.P. Mehrtens
J.W. Marshall (Capt.)
Forwards:
C.W. Dowd
N.J. Hewitt
O.M. Brown
I.D. Jones
R.M. Brooke
T.C. Randell
J.A. Kronfeld
Z.V. Brooke
Replacements:
S.B.T. Fitzpatrick for Hewitt,
M.R. Allen for Brown,
A.F. Blowers for Randell,
S.J. McLeod for Little
(temp.)</td></tr>
</table>

Cardiff Arms Park was demolished at the end of the 1996/97 season to make way for the Millennium Stadium. The project meant Wales had to play their 'home' matches elsewhere for two full seasons. Major games were staged at Wembley Stadium and minor internationals at club grounds in Wales. The first of these visits to north London was for a match with the All Blacks. While the Lions were touring South Africa, Wales toured North America and introduced several new players to international rugby. Then they played two matches before the New Zealand game, defeating Romania and Tonga. Robert Howley recovered from injury sustained on the Lions tour but Scott Quinnell, the Richmond number eight, was injured and could not be considered. They

Scorers:
Wales: Try: Walker. Con: Jenkins.
New Zealand: Tries: Cullen (3), Randell, Marshall. Cons: Mehrtens (4).
PGs: Mehrtens (2). DG: Z. Brooke.

Referee: W.J. Erickson (Australia).
Attendance: 78,000.

were captained by Gwyn Jones, a medical student and fine open-side flank forward who suffered severe spinal injuries in a club match against Swansea two weeks later and never played again. The All Blacks made one change to the test side, bringing Walter Little back in place of Alama Ieremia. Captain Sean Fitzpatrick, although not fit enough to start the game, took a place on the replacements' bench. Justin Marshall continued to captain the All Blacks.

Taine Randell opened the scoring after five minutes with an unconverted try, and then Andrew Mehrtens kicked a penalty. With New Zealand dominant, Christian Cullen scored a try after he gathered a clearing kick to touch and ran it back. Mehrtens converted, then added the extra points to Cullen's second try after a Kevin Morgan pass was intercepted and Robin Brooke created space for the full-back to race through. The All Blacks played powerful, dynamic rugby yet Wales tackled heroically. On the stroke of half-time Mehrtens kicked another penalty to give his team a 25-0 lead at half-time.

Cullen scored his third try five minutes after the restart after a fine passing movement. Mehrtens converted and Marshall scored the All Blacks' fifth try after Zinzan Brooke flipped the ball deftly through his legs. At 39-0 after an hour's rugby the match was over as a contest. However, the Welsh defence was gritty and several attacks were stifled by good tackles. Nigel Walker twice caught Jeff Wilson in full flight and Neil Jenkins stopped Josh Kronfeld in his tracks. Gareth Thomas subdued Jonah Lomu but Mehrtens kicked superbly and stretched the Welsh defence with probing kicks to the corner. After twenty-three minutes of the second half, Wales won the ball and attacked. Gareth Llewellyn made a good run and passed to Walker, who raced in to score by the posts. Neil Jenkins converted. Jenkins nearly scored himself but the impact of a tackle dislodged the ball and New Zealand cleared. As the game went into injury time Zinzan Brooke dropped a goal. The All Blacks played magnificently yet Wales contributed fully to a memorable match.

Sean Fitzpatrick replaced Norm Hewitt during the second half to make his 128th and last appearance for New Zealand. He won ninety-two caps and captained his country in 51 internationals.

ENGLAND A   1997

Tuesday 2 December 1997
Welford Road, Leicester
Won 30-19

Five of the England A players were full internationals, with a further seven destined to win caps. Only Matt Allen, Rory Jenkins and Rich Butland, would never play for England. Of the replacements used during the game, three were England caps, two were future internationals and only Roy Winters of Bedford remained uncapped. This was the final fixture for New Zealand's non-Test XV, and they were anxious to go out on a high. The visitors had to work hard for victory, and were still going for goal from penalties well into the second half.

A capacity Welford Road crowd watched in horror as Butland sliced the kick-off, but the home side soon settled into the game, with

ENGLAND A	NEW ZEALAND
T.R.G. Stimpson (Newcastle)	T.J. Miller
S.P. Brown (Richmond)	J.F. Umaga
S. Potter (Leicester)	S.J. McLeod
M.C. Allen (Northampton)	G.M. Osborne
A.A. Adebayo (Bath)	A. Ieremia
R.de V. Butland (Bath)	C.J. Spencer
S. Benton (Gloucester)	M.D. Robinson
Forwards:	Forwards:
G.C. Rowntree (Leicester)	M.R. Allen
M.P. Regan (Bath)	A.D. Oliver
P.J. Vickery (Gloucester)	G. Slater
D. Sims (Gloucester)	C.C. Riechelmann
R.J Fidler (Gloucester)	M.S.B. Cooksley
R.H.J. Jenkins (Harlequins)	T.J. Blackadder (Capt.)
P.H. Sanderson (Sale)	M.P. Carter
B.B. Clarke (Richmond, Capt.)	S.D. Surridge
Replacements:	Replacements:
V.E. Ubogu (Bath) for Vickery, R. Winters (Bedford) for Jenkins, M.S. Mapletoft (Gloucester) for Butland, N. McCarthy (Gloucester) for Regan	J.P. Preston for Robinson, A.F. Blowers for Carter, A.R. Hopa for Cooksley

Scorers:
England A: Try: Benton. Con: Stimpson. PGs: Stimpson (4).
New Zealand: Tries: McLeod, Oliver, Riechelmann, Umaga.
Cons: Spencer (2). PGs: Spencer, Preston.

Referee: A. Lewis (Ireland).
Attendance: 16,048.

Rob Fidler pinching some lineout ball from All Black throws and Jenkins putting in some good runs. However, it was New Zealand who scored the opening try in the ninth minute, when Scott McLeod found a gap in the defence after play had been moved both right and left. Then, eight minutes later, after Carlos Spencer had kicked the tourists to within a few metres of the home line, Mark Cooksley won the ensuing lineout and the pack drove over the line for Anton Oliver to claim the touchdown. Spencer converted one of the tries, but England A full-back Tim Stimpson kept his side in the game, kicking four penalties from six attempts to tie the scores at 12-12 at half-time.

The home side continued to battle well during the second half, with hooker Mark Regan making an outstanding contribution. Again though, it was New Zealand who scored early, manufacturing a brilliant try after just two minutes of the half. Again the England defence was stretched, first by a surge up the middle and then by Todd Miller's run to the left. Eventually, the ball reached Tana Umaga who was held up short of the line, but had sufficient time to pass to Charles Riechelmann for a try. Spencer converted and added a penalty, leaving New Zealand 22-12 ahead going into the final quarter. A further Spencer penalty followed, plus a brilliant Umaga try after a prolonged bout of New Zealand possession. Finally, Scott Benton grabbed a last-ditch consolation try for England A, which Stimpson converted.

The late score was the least England A deserved for a gutsy performance against a strong New Zealand second string. Many felt that Regan's display would be sufficient to propel him into the starting lineup for Saturday's international, but he had to be content with a place on the bench, although he replaced Richard Cockerill later in the match. Stimpson too was to come off the bench during the game. Of the New Zealanders involved in the match, only 'Bull' Allen was called upon to face England from the start, with Riechelmann, Spencer and McLeod appearing as replacements.

ENGLAND   1997

Saturday 6 December 1997
Twickenham, London
Drawn 26-26

England changed three players from the team that had lost at Old Trafford a fortnight before. Austin Healey replaced Adedayo Adebayo, Paul Grayson replaced Mike Catt and Neil Back replaced Tony Diprose. In between the two meetings with New Zealand, England had lost 29-11 to South Africa and ten of the starting lineup were retained from that game. Catt was concussed against the Springboks, and not considered for selection. The chief selection debates for England concerned the rival claims of Kyran Bracken and Matt Dawson for the scrum-half position and Richard Cockerill and Mark Regan for the hooking berth. Surprise was expressed at the inclusion of Healey, a scrum-half,

ENGLAND

M.B. Perry (Bath)
D.L. Rees (Sale)
W.J.H. Greenwood (Leicester)
P.R. de Glanville (Bath)
A.S. Healey (Leicester)
P.J. Grayson (Northampton)
K.P.P. Bracken (Saracens)
Forwards:
J. Leonard (Harlequins)
R. Cockerill (Leicester)
D.J. Garforth (Leicester)
M.O. Johnson (Leicester)
G.S. Archer (Newcastle)
L.B.N. Dallaglio (Wasps, Capt.)
N.A. Back (Leicester)
R.A. Hill (Saracens)
Replacements:
T.R.G. Stimpson (Newcastle)
for Rees (temp.) and for de Glanville,
C.M.A. Sheasby (Wasps) for Back (temp.),
M.J.S. Dawson (Northampton)
for Bracken, M.P. Regan (Bath) for Cockerill

NEW ZEALAND

C.M. Cullen
J.W. Wilson
F.E. Bunce
J.T. Lomu
W.K. Little
A.P. Mehrtens
J.W. Marshall (Capt.)
Forwards:
M.R. Allen
N.J. Hewitt
O.M. Brown
I.D. Jones
R.M. Brooke
T.C. Randell
J.A. Kronfeld
Z.V. Brooke
Replacements:
C.C. Riechelmann for
Kronfeld (temp.), C.J. Spencer
for Little, S.J. McLeod
for Bunce

Scorers:
England: Tries: Rees, Hill, Dallaglio. Con: Grayson. PGs: Grayson (3).
New Zealand: Tries: Mehrtens, Little. Cons: Mehrtens (2).
PGs: Mehrtens (4).

Referee: J.M. Fleming (Scotland).
Attendance: 75,000.

The Royal & SunAlliance International

ENGLAND
v
NEW ZEALAND

TWICKENHAM 6th December 1997
Kick-off 2.00pm

Royal & SunAlliance
COLTS COUNTY CHAMPIONSHIP FINAL
NORTH MIDLANDS v GLOUCESTERSHIRE
Kick-off 11.45 am

OFFICIAL PROGRAMME £3.00
(including contribution to the Wooden Spoon/Wakefield Youth Trust)

on the wing. Craig Dowd was the only face missing from the New Zealand team that had beaten Wales, his place going to 'Bull' Allen. The match was Zinzan Brooke's 100th in an All Black shirt.

This was an outstanding game of rugby, one of the finest matches ever staged at Twickenham and the highest-scoring draw in the history of international rugby. Few had given England the slightest chance of winning, yet they led 20-3 after the first quarter and 23-9 at half-time. Ultimately, they had to be content with a draw and the players even felt disappointed that they had not won. The match was exciting throughout, and both teams attacked when the scores were level in the final ten minutes in an effort to claim the winning score.

England scored 3 tries in an incredible burst of attacking in the opening quarter of the game. David Rees opened the scoring with a superb individual try after five minutes, chipping the ball over Jonah Lomu, brushing past the tackle of Zinzan Brooke and just making it to the line in the corner despite the attentions of Frank Bunce and Josh Kronfeld. Rees cut his face in the act of scoring, but returned to the field after treatment, receiving a hero's welcome for his pains. Grayson could not convert the try, but England's lead was increased in the ninth minute when a long Grayson pass released Healey down the left wing. Healey's inside pass found Will Greenwood, who beat two defenders before giving a scoring pass to Richard Hill. Once again, the conversion was missed, but after Andrew Mehrtens reduced the deficit with a fourteenth-minute penalty, England scored a third try. An All Black move broke down, allowing England captain Lawrence Dallaglio (who along with Hill and Neil Back formed an outstanding back-row unit) the chance to hack the ball to the line where he touched down under the posts, Grayson converting. At the end of the first quarter Grayson stretched the lead to 20-3 with a penalty, but two penalties from Mehrtens brought New Zealand to within 11 points, before an injury-time penalty from Grayson gave England their unbelievable 23-9 half-time lead. The team left the field to a standing ovation and was similarly greeted on its return.

It was inevitable that New Zealand should hit back strongly after the break, and after a series of tap-penalty moves Zinzan Brooke and Justin Marshall produced a fourth-minute try for Mehrtens, which he also converted. Ten minutes later the gap was narrowed to just 4 points when Mehrtens kicked a penalty and then, after England had knocked on in a promising attacking position, New Zealand took the lead when Walter Little burst through for a try that Mehrtens converted. To the delight of the crowd, England immediately went back on the attack and after some thrilling phases of play New Zealand were caught offside, Grayson levelling the scores with the subsequent penalty. Eight minutes of normal time remained, and with both teams attacking there was much thrilling rugby to come. Mehrtens failed with a drop goal for the All Blacks, and the final whistle was the signal for the crowd to acclaim a fantastic England performance against a top-quality New Zealand side.

Both Justin Marshall and John Hart were lavish in their praise of England's efforts. Marshall said 'we were lucky today', while Hart commented 'England should be very proud after the way they played. That was probably the best I've ever seen them play.' The reaction in the England camp revealed their desire for success. 'There was no real celebrating in the England dressing room because we feel we should have won', was the verdict of skipper Lawrence Dallaglio. In view of the contribution of both sides to a thrilling encounter, it was perhaps fitting that such a wonderful match should end with the spoils shared.

NEW ZEALAND TO SCOTLAND, IRELAND & ARGENTINA

THE MATCHES

Ireland A	13 November 2001	Belfast	won 43-30
IRELAND	17 November 2001	Dublin	won 40-29
Scotland A	20 November 2001	Perth	won 35-13
SCOTLAND	24 November 2001	Murrayfield	won 37-6
ARGENTINA	1 December 2001	Buenos Aires	won 24-20

Played 5, Won 5, Drew 0, Lost 0. Scored: 179 points, Conceded: 98.
In Britain & Ireland: Played 4, Won 4, Drew 0, Lost 0. Scored: 155 points, Conceded: 78.

The New Zealand Tour Party:
B.A. Blair (Canterbury), L.R. MacDonald (Canterbury), D.C. Howlett (Auckland), J.T. Lomu (Wellington), N.K. Mauger (Canterbury), C.S. Ralph (Canterbury), R.Q. Randle (Waikato), J.F. Umaga (Wellington), P.F. Alatini (Otago), D.W. Hill (Waikato), A.J.D. Mauger (Canterbury), A.P. Mehrtens (Canterbury), B.T. Kelleher (Otago), M.D. Robinson (North Harbour), G.E. Feek (Canterbury), D.N. Hewett (Canterbury), K.J. Meeuws (Otago), G.M. Somerville (Canterbury), J.E. Spice (Wellington), A.D. Oliver (Otago), T.E. Willis (Otago), C.R. Jack (Canterbury), T.S. Maling (Otago), N.M.C. Maxwell (Canterbury), D.A.G. Waller (Wellington), M.R. Holah (Waikato), R.H. McCaw (Canterbury), P.C. Miller (Otago), R.D. Thorne (Canterbury), J. Collins (Wellington), S.M. Robertson (Canterbury).

Captain: A.D. Oliver. Manager: A.J. Martin. Coach: J.E.P. Mitchell. Assistant Coach: R.M. Deans.

Leading points scorer: B.A. Blair – 58 points (58 in Britain & Ireland).
Leading try-scorer: B.A. Blair – 4 tries (4 in Britain & Ireland).
Most appearances: D.N. Hewett – 5 games (4 in Britain & Ireland), 2 of these as a replacement.

Tuesday 13 November 2001
Ravenhill, Belfast
Won 43-30

The All Blacks opened a short tour of Ireland and Scotland at Ravenhill. After a Tri-Nations Championship in which New Zealand had lost both games to Australia, New Zealand took the opportunity to introduce new players and a new coach, John Mitchell. At home, Mitchell was criticised for his squad selection as established players like Christian Cullen, Jeff Wilson and Taine Randell were not required. Consequently, the New Zealand side included nine new All Blacks and was led by one of them, hooker Tom Willis. Successful Munster coach Declan Kidney took charge of an experimental Ireland A side that had a mix of youth and experience. They were captained by scrum-half Brian O'Meara, who had represented Ireland in the 1999 World Cup.

The All Blacks, desperate to get the game underway, started at a furious pace.

IRELAND A	NEW ZEALAND
G.W. Duffy (Connacht)	B.A. Blair
A.P. Horgan (Munster)	R.Q. Randle
J. Holland (Munster)	N.K. Mauger
J.P. Bishop (London Irish)	C.S. Ralph
J.A. Topping (Ulster)	P.F. Alatini
P.R. Wallace (Ulster)	D.W. Hill
B.T. O'Meara (Leinster, Capt.)	M.D. Robinson
Forwards:	Forwards:
R. Corrigan (Leinster)	D.N. Hewett
J.S. Byrne (Leinster)	T.E. Willis (Capt.)
S.J. Best (Ulster)	K.J. Meeuws
L.F.M. Cullen (Leinster)	D.A.G. Waller
M. O'Driscoll (Munster)	T.S. Maling
K.D. Gleeson (Leinster)	J. Collins
A. Quinlan (Munster)	M.R. Holah
V.C.P. Costello (Leinster)	P.C. Miller

Replacements:
P.J. O'Connell (Munster) for Cullen,
A.J. Ward (Ulster) for Cullen, J.M. Fitzpatrick (Ulster) for Corrigan, B.J. Willis (Leinster) for O'Meara

Scorers:
Ireland A: Tries: Horgan (2). Con: Wallace. PGs: Wallace (6).
New Zealand: Tries: Blair (3), Miller. Cons: Blair (4). PGs: Blair (5).

Referee: R. Dickson (Scotland).
Attendance: 10,500.

The Irish kept them out and Ben Blair and Paddy Wallace exchanged early penalties. The All Blacks impressed with the speed of their attack and it was only good defence that kept the score down. They also tackled well and when Justin Bishop lost the ball in contact, crisp passing from half-back Mark Robinson to David Hill and out to Roger Randle sent the Waikato wing on a run deep into the Irish 22. He was tackled but first himself then Hill tried to drive over the line before it came to Paul Miller who crashed through for the first try. Blair converted, then added a penalty before scoring his first try of the game after he entered the three-quarter line at pace and rounded opposite number Gavin Duffy close to halfway, and raced in for a score he also converted. An Irish attack close to half-time was ended when Jerry Collins stiff-arm tackled Shane Byrne and earned himself ten minutes in the sin bin to cool off. Two further penalties saw New Zealand ahead 23-6 at half-time.

Ireland A played a tighter game in the second half as they became more familiar with each other. They pressurised New Zealand into making mistakes and Wallace was able to reduce the lead with a series of penalties. Then New Zealand struck back when Caleb Ralph took a quick throw-in and the ball was moved through Blair and Pita Alatini to Marty Holah who made good ground down the opposite touchline. Play then changed direction and a scissors between Nathan Mauger and Blair saw the full-back run in for another try. Two minutes later, turn-over ball was run back and Hill, Ralph and Mauger swept upfield before, Blair received the ball and scored his third try of the match. However, New Zealand were regularly penalised by the referee and Wallace kept Ireland A in the game with a series of successful penalty kicks. They hit back with a try after a good run by Duffy was finished off by Anthony Horgan, and after Blair had kicked two more penalties to increase his contribution to 38 points, Horgan scored again. Wallace converted one of Horgan's tries and a late penalty to conclude the scoring.

It was an acceptable start for New Zealand, who showed tremendous form in attack and outstanding support play on times. They were unhappy about being out-scored in the second half and incurring the wrath of the referee.

Saturday 17 November 2001
Lansdowne Road, Dublin
Won 40-29

Ireland shared the 2001 Six Nations Championship with England after the tournament was interrupted by a serious outbreak of foot-and-mouth. Irish authorities restricted movement to and from the Republic and games were put back from the spring to the autumn. Ireland were soundly beaten by Scotland but recovered to register good wins over Wales and England, the latter depriving the English of a Grand Slam, four weeks before taking on the All Blacks. Humphreys recovered from injury and was chosen ahead of O'Gara at outside half. Doubts over the fitness of all three Irish back-row players and the influential O'Driscoll were dispelled but his fellow Lions centre, Henderson, was not considered through injury. Nevertheless Ireland were confident and fielded the same

IRELAND	NEW ZEALAND
G.T. Dempsey (Terenure College)	L.R. MacDonald
S.P. Horgan (Lansdowne)	D.C. Howlett
B.G. O'Driscoll (Blackrock College)	J.F. Umaga
K.M. Maggs (Bath)	J.T. Lomu
D.A. Hickie (St Mary's College)	A.J.D. Mauger
D.G. Humphreys (Dungannon)	A.P. Mehrtens
P.A. Stringer (Shannon)	B.T. Kelleher
Forwards:	Forwards:
P.M. Clohessy (Young Munster)	G.E. Feek
K.G.M. Wood (Harlequins, Capt.)	A.D. Oliver (Capt.)
J.J. Hayes (Shannon)	G.M. Somerville
M.J. Galwey (Shannon)	C.R. Jack
M.E. O'Kelly (St Mary's College)	N.M.C. Maxwell
E.R.P. Miller (Terenure College)	R.D. Thorne
D.P. Wallace (Garryowen)	R.H. McCaw
A.G. Foley (Shannon)	S.M. Robertson
Replacements:	Replacement:
E. Byrne (Blackrock College) for Hayes,	D.N. Hewett for Feek
M.J. Mullins (Young Munster) for Horgan,	
G.W. Longwell (Ballymena) for Galwey	

Scorers:
Ireland: Tries: Maggs, Hickie, Miller. Con: Humphreys.
PGs: Humphreys (2). DGs: Humphreys (2).
New Zealand: Tries: Jack, Lomu, Mauger, Thorne, Howlett, Hewett.
Cons: Mehrtens (5).

Referee: A.J. Watson (South Africa).
Attendance: 52,000.

starting XV that had beaten England. New Zealand introduced a new back-row unit in which McCaw made his international debut. Second five-eighth Mauger also played in his first test match. The two coaches, Warren Gatland of Ireland and John Mitchell were both former All Blacks and both had represented the Waikato province.

Ireland started at pace and put New Zealand immediately on the back foot. The Irish forwards ripped into the All Blacks and denied them the possession and time to mount sustained attacks. Lomu was made to look ordinary in defence, and Irish captain Wood charged around the field. Brian O'Driscoll made a break and beat two All Blacks before linking with Humphreys for Maggs to score the opening try. Humphreys converted, kicked six further points, and Ireland were in control. Then Jack scored for New Zealand on a rare excursion to the Ireland 22. Mehrtens converted before another kick from Humphreys

put Ireland ahead 16-7 at half-time. The home side totally dominated the first half but failed to capitalise on several scoring opportunities.

A few minutes into the second half, O'Driscoll made a break from which Hickie scored a try. The conversion missed but at 21-7 ahead Ireland were looking favourites to record their first win over New Zealand. However, the All Blacks were resilient and patient and with ruthless efficiency and power, clawed back the deficit and stretched ahead. Thorne and Howlett scored tries early in the second half before the All Blacks introduced Lomu into the attack after his marker, Horgan, had been replaced, and he quickly created a try for Mauger. The favour was returned later when Lomu blasted through the Ireland defence to score after a break by Mauger. With Mehrtens controlling the match and McCaw stealing Irish ball in the tackle, the tourists completely dominated the half and relentlessly pressurised the Irish.

The final try came from Hewett, who had replaced Feek to win his first cap. A late try by Miller was scant reward for the disconsolate Irish who had had the game in their grasp. Wood was disappointed: 'We didn't touch the ball for twenty minutes and our defence let us down.' It had, however, been a fine encounter.

SCOTLAND A   2001

Tuesday 20 November 2001
McDiarmid Park, Perth
Won 35-13

SCOTLAND A	NEW ZEALAND
B.J. Laney (Edinburgh Rugby)	B.A. Blair
A.J. Bulloch (Glasgow Rugby)	R.Q. Randle
M.P. Di Rollo (Edinburgh Rugby)	N.K. Mauger
K.N. Utterson (Edinburgh Rugby)	C.S. Ralph
R.C. Kerr (Glasgow Rugby)	P.F. Alatini
D.W. Hodge (Edinburgh Rugby, Capt.)	D.W. Hill
G. Beveridge (Glasgow Rugby)	M.D. Robinson
Forwards:	Forwards:
A.F. Jacobsen (Edinburgh Rugby)	D.N. Hewett
S.J. Brotherstone (Northampton)	T.E. Wills (Capt.)
G.R. McIlwham (Glasgow Rugby)	K.J. Meeuws
N.J. Hines (Edinburgh Rugby)	D.A.G. Waller
N. Ross (Glasgow Rugby)	T.S. Maling
A.K. Dall (Edinburgh Rugby)	M.R. Holah
G. Flockhart (Glasgow Rugby)	J. Collins
G.F. Dall (Edinburgh Rugby)	P.C. Miller

Replacements:
G. Scott (Glasgow Rugby) for Brotherstone,
T. Walker (Gala) for Flockhart, G. Kerr (Leeds Tykes)
for McIllwham, S. Griffith (Glasgow Rugby)
for Ross, M.R.L. Blair (Boroughmuir) for Beveridge

Scorers:
Scotland A: Try: Hodge. Con: Hodge. PGs: Hodge (2).
New Zealand: Tries: Ralph, Robinson, Blair, Alatini. Cons: Blair (3).
PGs: Blair (3).

Referee: D. Courtney (IRFU).
Attendance: 3,600.

With one eye on the World Cup in 2003, both sides gave their second strings and younger players a chance gain some valuable experience at the top level. For Scotland, the main talking point was the controversial inclusion of Laney at full-back. Born in Invercargill and a successful player with Otago Highlanders, Laney had been fast-tracked into the Scottish set-up, despite having only arrived in the country the previous week and without having played for his new club Edinburgh Rugby. In the event, Laney had few chances to show his paces because of New Zealand's ability to keep him out of the game. The visitors fielded eight uncapped players, but still managed to deliver an education in clinical rugby. Playing with pace, the New Zealanders showed skill and purpose, attacking through the phases without loss of shape or conviction. The Scots, to their credit, always maintained their discipline in defence and produced some thumping tackles, making sure that there was no humiliation in defeat. At times, the home side made some promising breaks, but these were largely wasted because of poor support play or the New Zealanders' ability to control the post-tackle situations. Holah dominated at the breakdown, despite having received four stitches in a head wound.

The visitors were ahead 20-3 at the interval. The opening try, after just twelve minutes, showed their

readiness to think on the move. Marcus Di Rollo pulled off two crunching tackles that left him temporarily on the ground. Roger Randle exploded through the space to create the opportunity for Robinson to score. The visitors then soaked up some Scottish pressure and hit back with a try by Caleb Ralph. Blair converted both tries and kicked two penalties to leave the visitors cruising at half-time, Hodge having kicked a penalty for the Scots. Blair's try within two minutes of the restart killed any hopes of a Scottish comeback. The sides then exchanged penalties before Hodge gained some reward for Scottish determination. Good lineout work by Hines and Nathan Ross set up an attacking platform and the Scottish captain powered through a gap to score. New Zealand managed a fourth try after winning turnover ball and Ralph's sublime pass out of the tackle sent Pita Alatini racing away to score.

Saturday 24 November 2001
Murrayfield, Edinburgh
Won 37-6

SCOTLAND	NEW ZEALAND
B.J. Laney (Edinburgh Rugby)	L.R. MacDonald
J.F. Steel (Glasgow Rugby)	D.C. Howlett
J.G. McLaren (Glasgow Rugby)	J.F. Umaga
J.A. Leslie (Northampton Saints)	J.T. Lomu
C.D. Paterson (Edinburgh Rugby)	A.J.D. Mauger
G.P.J. Townsend (Castres)	A.P. Mehrtens
A.D. Nicol (Glasgow Rugby)	B.T. Kelleher
Forwards:	Forwards:
T.J. Smith (Northampton Saints, Capt.)	G.E. Feek
G.C. Bulloch (Glasgow Rugby)	A.D. Oliver (Capt.)
M.J. Stewart (Northampton Saints)	G.M. Somerville
S. Murray (Saracens)	C.R. Jack
S.B. Grimes (Newcastle Falcons)	N.M.C. Maxwell
J.P.R. White (Glasgow Rugby)	R.D. Thorne
A.L. Mower (Newcastle Falcons)	R.H. McCaw
G.L. Simpson (Glasgow Rugby)	S.M. Robertson
Replacements:	Replacements:
S.M. Taylor (Edinburgh Rugby) for Simpson,	M.D. Robinson for Kelleher,
G. Graham (Newcastle Falcons)	B.A. Blair for MacDonald,
for Stewart, G.G. Burns (Edinburgh Rugby)	D.N. Hewett for Feek
for Nicol, A.R. Henderson (Glasgow Rugby)	
for Leslie, S. Scott (Edinburgh Rugby)	
for Bulloch, I.A. Fullarton (Sale Sharks) for Murray	

Scorers:
Scotland: PGs: Paterson (2).
New Zealand: Tries: Umaga, Robinson, Lomu. Cons: Mehrtens (2).
PGs: Mehrtens (6).

Referee: P.C. Deluca (Argentina).
Attendance: 67,456.

This was the twenty-fourth meeting between the two sides with Scotland still seeking a first win. Three of the Scottish starting line-up had been born in New Zealand, including Laney, who was controversially parachuted into the side after playing only one game in Scotland.

The unerring boot of Andrew Mehrtens put paid to a spirited home side, landing 22 points to go with tries from Umaga, Robinson and, inevitably, Lomu. In a joyless game that sometimes resembled a war of attrition, Scotland were only 9 points adrift with fifteen minutes remaining, but then the visitors stretched away with a blitz of late scores. The result flattered New Zealand, although there was an air of inevitability about the outcome. The Scots had several good chances, especially in the first half, but their skills and composure let them down when it mattered most. Crucially, Paterson missed several penalty attempts.

New Zealand led 9-6 at the interval after a fairly even first half. Scotland had launched several enterprising attacks, but none had enough momentum or speed to penetrate the black wall. The difference between the sides was the Scottish failure to keep the scoreboard ticking over while Mehrtens snapped up anything that came his way. However, it was only in the final fifteen minutes that the visitors picked up the pace, exploiting space as the Scots began to tire. Mehrtens made a quick lineout throw on his own 22, which was the spark for Umaga to break the defence and run half the length of the pitch to score. In the final three minutes, substitute half-back Robinson slipped a weak tackle for the second try. The mighty Lomu finished the show in injury-time after a great break by McCaw.

In a match that was less than memorable, the New Zealanders played well within themselves, but still came away with a comfortable win. It was a harsh lesson for the Scots, who had given everything with precious little to show for their efforts. Flank forward Andrew Mower and centre James McLaren had tackled like men possessed, and locks Scott Murray and Stuart Grimes had caused the visitors plenty of problems in the lineout. But at this level a side had to grab every opportunity that came its way to stand a chance of beating the All Blacks. Scotland was incapable of doing that. The All Blacks left Scotland and played Argentina on their way home. The international, staged at the River Plate Stadium in Buenos Aires, saw New Zealand just scrape home. Their 24-20 win came courtesy of a last-minute try from Scott Robertson that saved the All Blacks' blushes.

NEW ZEALAND TO EUROPE

THE MATCHES

ENGLAND	9 November 2002	Twickenham	lost 31-28
FRANCE	16 November 2002	Paris	drawn 20-20
WALES	23 November 2002	Cardiff	won 43-17

Played 3, Won 1, Drew 1, Lost 1. Scored: 91 points, Conceded: 68.
In Britain & Ireland: Played 2, Won 1, Drew 0, Lost 1. Scored: 71 points, Conceded: 48.

The New Zealand Tour Party:
B.A. Blair (Canterbury), C.M. Cullen (Wellington), D.C. Howlett (Auckland), R.M. King (Waikato), K.R. Lowen (Waikato), J.T. Lomu (Wellington), M.P. Robinson (Canterbury), J.F. Umaga (Wellington), A.P. Mehrtens (Canterbury), C.J. Spencer (Auckland), P.C. Steinmetz (Wellington), S.J. Devine (Auckland), D.D. Lee (Otago), C.J. Hayman (Otago), K.J. Meeuws (Auckland), J.M. McDonnell (Otago), T.D. Woodcock (North Harbour), A.K. Hore (Taranaki), K.F. Mealamu (Auckland), B.M. Mika (Auckland), K.J. Robinson (Waikato), A.J. Williams (Auckland), D.J. Braid (Auckland), M.R. Holah (Waikato), T.C. Randell (Otago), S.R. Broomhall (Canterbury), R. So'oialo (Wellington).

Captain: T.C. Randell. Manager: T. Thorpe. Coach: J.E.P. Mitchell. Assistant Coach: R.M. Deans.

Leading points scorer: A.P. Mehrtens – 37 points (27 in Britain & Ireland).
Leading try-scorer: D.C. Howlett – 3 tries (3 in Britain & Ireland).
Most appearances: 3 games for Randell, Lomu, Howlett, Williams and Umaga. Many players played in both games in Britain.

ENGLAND   2002

Saturday 9 November 2002
Twickenham, London
Lost 28-31

The All Blacks arrived on the back of a successful Tri-Nations campaign. Coach John Mitchell had one eye on the 2003 World Cup, and his selection was one of youth and experience. Significant players, including back-row forwards Reuben Thorne and Richie McCaw plus half-back Justin Marshall were left at home. Although there was some risk, Mitchell took a longer-term view and Lowen, Devine, Hore, and second-row forwards Robinson and Williams made their international debuts at Twickenham. When Mika later replaced Robinson, a third second row won his first cap for New Zealand. England awarded a first cap to wing James Simpson-Daniel of Gloucester and coach Clive Woodward promoted Lewis Moody to the back row in place of his Leicester teammate Neil Back. It was, however, a very experienced side, twelve of which were to win the World Cup final a year later. Both sides contributed to a superb game of rugby football played at pace with a willingness to run at ever opportunity.

After a rousing Haka, the match began with New Zealand immediately on the attack. There were some early exchanges between the packs and tight forwards Robinson and Meeuws were conspicuous in tight and loose play. Then England ran loose ball, with Greenwood prominent. The New Zealand defence infringed and Wilkinson kicked two penalties in quick succession to give England an early 6-0 lead. The All Blacks ventured deep into English territory and the back row of Broomhall, Holah and Randell led a forward drive that

ENGLAND	NEW ZEALAND
J.T. Robinson (Sale)	B.A. Blair
J.D. Simpson-Daniel (Gloucester)	D.C. Howlett
W.J.H. Greenwood (Harlequins)	J.F. Umaga
M.J. Tindall (Bath)	J.T. Lomu
B.C. Cohen (Northampton)	K.R. Lowen
J.P. Wilkinson (Newcastle)	C.J. Spencer
M.J.S. Dawson (Northampton)	S.J. Devine
Forwards:	Forwards:
T.J. Woodman (Gloucester)	J.M. McDonnell
S.G. Thompson (Northampton)	A.K. Hore
P.J. Vickery (Gloucester)	K.J. Meeuws
M.O. Johnson (Leicester, Capt.)	K.J. Robinson
D.J. Grewcock (Saracens)	A.J. Williams
L.W. Moody (Leicester)	T.C. Randell (Capt.)
R.A. Hill (Saracens)	M.R. Holah
L.B.N. Dallaglio (Wasps)	S.R. Broomhall
Replacements:	Replacements:
B.J. Kay (Leicester) for Grewcock,	B.M. Mika for K. Robinson,
N.A. Back (Leicester) for Dallaglio,	D.D. Lee for Devine,
A.S. Healey (Leicester) for Simpson-Daniel,	A.P. Mehrtens for Spencer,
J.B. Johnston (Saracens) for Greenwood	M.P. Robinson for Lowen

Scorers:
England: Tries: Cohen, Moody, Wilkinson. Cons: Wilkinson (2).
PGs: Wilkinson (3). DG: Wilkinson.
New Zealand: Tries: Lomu (2), Howlett, Lee. Cons: Blair (2), Mehrtens (2).

Referee: J.I. Kaplan (SARFU).
Attendance: 73,000.

England halted illegally. The confident Randell instructed Spencer to kick for the corner rather than the posts. Robinson won the lineout and the ball was quickly moved to the left. A miss-pass gave Lomu space to run at and through Robinson and Tindall to score in the corner. Referee Jonathan Kaplan referred the decision to the video referee, who awarded the score. Full-back Blair converted majestically from the touchline and New Zealand were ahead. As the half progressed so the England pack became more dominant. They were able to disrupt the New Zealand lineout and had the edge in the scrum. Prop Trevor Woodman was also prominent in loose play and showed fine running skills to open the New Zealand defence on two occasions. Mid-way through the first half Wilkinson found the space to drop a goal, which eased England back into the lead. Later they attacked but the ball was intercepted by Tana Umaga on halfway who moved it quickly to Doug Howlett. The Auckland winger, who as a schoolboy had been a champion sprinter, outstripped Robinson and the rest of the England defence to run around and touch down between the posts. Blair converted quickly and the All Blacks were in front again. Play see-sawed from end to end before New Zealand infringed again and Wilkinson kicked a long-range penalty to keep England in touch. The Newcastle outside half then combined with Simpson-Daniel to create enough space for Moody to crash over in the corner shortly before the break. Wilkinson narrowly missed the conversion but England had regained the lead and went in 17-14 ahead at the interval.

The teams reappeared with a change on each side. Spencer had a shoulder injury and was replaced by Mehrtens, and Johnson took the place of Greenwood, who was suffering from a dead leg. The second half started in spectacular style. England established a good position deep in the New Zealand 22 and pressurised the defenders into an infringement. Kaplan signalled a penalty but the sharp-eyed Wilkinson made the most of the advantage, disguised to drop a goal then chipped over the flat-footed defence to score a try. He converted to complete a full-house of scoring. Mehrtens restarted but, almost immediately after, mis-handled close to halfway. Cohen snapped up the loose ball and raced away to score England's third try. Wilkinson converted and the All Blacks looked in danger of being humbled. 17 points adrift, Randell and Umaga showed great leadership. The All Blacks' pack rumbled up field, their rolling maul moving at pace before releasing the ball and quickly moving it to Umaga. The Wellington back, now a regular at centre,

created space for Lomu to receive the ball in midfield. His pace and power dumped Tindall on his back again on his way to his second try. Mehrtens converted and the initiative was now with New Zealand. Desperate to score, the All Blacks moved the ball at every opportunity and produced some breathtaking rugby. Lomu was well tackled by Simpson-Daniel, and Blair and Howlett were constant threats. Then Broomhall made a powerful run that tied up the English defence. Half-back Danny Lee spotted a gap and wrong-footed the defence to score a try on his debut, which Mehrtens converted. A furious Martin Johnson saw his side fritter away a lead that once looked unassailable. With 3 points between the sides, the end of the match was exciting and tense. A miss-move involving Howlett in the All Blacks' half presented the ball to Blair who sprinted down the touchline towards the corner but Cohen raced across from his wing and produced a magnificent cover-tackle on the full-back. The All Blacks continued to pressurise but time was running out. However, they remained confident and were awarded an attacking lineout close to the England line as the match went into injury time. The throw was intercepted by Kay, who had replaced Grewcock during the second half, and cleared to touch. England's last-ditch defence had held out and a famous victory had been earned.

The All Blacks' selection had raised some eyebrows and caused some to reflect on the game being England's first fifteen against New Zealand's second fifteen. This failed to recognise the skills of the All Blacks, who so nearly won, nor the strenuous efforts of Wilkinson and the rest of the victorious England team.

WALES   2002

Saturday 23 November 2002
Millennium Stadium, Cardiff
Won 43-17

The All Blacks arrived in Cardiff following a 20-20 draw with France the previous weekend. New Zealand were facing the extraordinary prospect of returning home from a tour without a victory, but they were opposing a Wales team in seemingly endless turmoil, battered by off-field politics and on-field selection and form problems that had seen them win only 3 games against other 'big eight' rugby nations since the 1999 World Cup. They had toured South Africa in the summer and although demonstrating some improvement, were beaten by the Springboks. New Zealand were overwhelming favourites. New Zealander Graham Henry resigned as Welsh coach earlier in the year and was succeeded by former Canterbury centre Steve

WALES	NEW ZEALAND
G.R. Williams (Cardiff)	B.A. Blair
G. Thomas (Bridgend)	D.C. Howlett
J.P. Robinson (Cardiff)	J.F. Umaga
S.T. Parker (Pontypridd)	J.T. Lomu
M.A. Jones (Llanelli)	R.M. King
S.M. Jones (Llanelli)	A.P. Mehrtens
D.J. Peel (Llanelli)	S.J. Devine
Forwards:	Forwards:
I.D. Thomas (Llanelli)	T.D. Woodcock
M. Davies (Pontypridd)	K.F. Mealamu
B.R. Evans (Cardiff)	C.J. Hayman
R.A. Sidoli (Pontypridd)	K.J. Robinson
G.O. Llewellyn (Neath)	A.J. Williams
D.R. Jones (Llanelli)	T.C. Randell (Capt.)
M.E. Williams (Cardiff)	D.J. Braid
C.L. Charvis (Swansea, Capt.)	R. So'oialo
Replacements:	Replacements:
I.R. Harris (Cardiff) for S. Jones,	M.R. Holah for Randell,
G.D. Jenkins (Pontypridd) for	M.P. Robinson for Blair,
I. Thomas, M.J. Owen (Pontypridd)	K.J. Meeuws for Hayman,
for Llewellyn, D.R. James (Bridgend)	P.C. Steinmetz for M. Robinson,
for M. Jones	B.M. Mika for Williams

Scorers:
Wales: Tries: Robinson, Penalty try. Cons: S. Jones, Harris.
PG: S. Jones. New Zealand: Tries: Howlett (2), Meeuws, King.
Cons: Mehrtens (4). PGs: Mehrtens (5).

Referee: W.T.S. Henning (South Africa).
Attendance: 74,000.

Hansen, who had previously been his assistant. All Blacks' coach John Mitchell continued with his pledge to play all his players on tour and gave international debuts to second five-eighth Regan King, and forwards Keven Mealamu, Tony Woodcock, Rodney So'oialo and Daniel Braid. Paul Steinmetz also made his debut when replacing Mark Robinson late in the game.

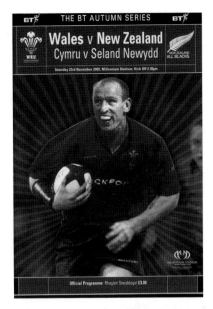

New Zealand started well on a greasy Millennium Stadium pitch and were immediately on the attack. They caught Wales unaware and Braid was driven over by the rest of the pack but failed to ground the ball. Wales regathered their composure and attacked and Stephen Jones kicked a penalty when the All Blacks infringed at a ruck. Andrew Mehrtens equalised with a penalty soon after. Wales regained the lead on thirteen minutes when an All Blacks' attack broke down and possession was lost. Stephen Jones kicked the ball behind the New Zealand defence and centre Jamie Robinson chased it and dived on the ball as it went over the goal line. Jones converted from the touchline with a fine kick. Mehrtens kicked two more penalties but Wales were 10-9 ahead at half-time.

The New Zealand tight five monopolised possession and the tourists attacked incessantly, but the Welsh defence held out with defiance and determination. However, New Zealand took the lead from another Mehrtens penalty and the match then went into a tense but scrappy phase in which the All Blacks made many mistakes and Wales tackled feverishly. An injury to Ben Blair forced a reshuffle in the backs with Doug Howlett moving to full-back and King to the wing with replacement Mark Robinson at second five-eighth. A Welsh kick to touch was fielded by King. The ball went to Mehrtens and then on to Howlett who came in from full-back, beat a man then exchanged passes with Tana Umaga and scored the first New Zealand try. The referee missed a forward pass but with Mehrtens converting, New Zealand moved further ahead. Wales surged back into New Zealand territory and pressurised the try line. After a series of 5-metre scrums that the All Blacks struggled to hold, the referee awarded a penalty try that Iestyn Harris, who had replaced Jones, converted. It was 22-17 to the All Blacks with five minutes to go, but New Zealand went straight back into attack and a grubber kick from Mehrtens was well taken by Howlett for his second try. Minutes later, a powerful forward drive ended with a Kees Meeuws try in injury time. Almost immediately after, Regan King finished off a back move for the fourth try. With kicks from Mehrtens, the All Blacks scored 21 points in the last nine minutes to win by a margin that failed to reflect the contribution of the Welsh.

Whether Mitchell obtained answers to his questions is unclear. His side subsequently looked dominant during the early stages of the following year's World Cup but failure to reach the final cost him his job. He was replaced by Graham Henry who then appointed Steve Hansen as his assistant.

NEW ZEALAND TO EUROPE

THE MATCHES

ITALY	13 November 2004	Rome	won 59-10
WALES	20 November 2004	Cardiff	won 26-25
FRANCE	27 November 2004	Paris	won 45-6
BARBARIANS	4 December 2004	Twickenham	won 47-19

Played 4, Won 4, Drew 0, Lost 0. Scored: 177 points, Conceded: 60.
In Britain & Ireland: Played 2, Won 2, Drew 0, Lost 0. Scored: 73 points, Conceded: 44.

The New Zealand Tour Party:
J.M. Muliaina (Auckland Blues), D.C. Howlett (Auckland Blues), J.T. Rokocoko (Auckland Blues), R.L. Gear (Auckland Blues), J.F. Umaga (Wellington Hurricanes), C.D.E. Laulala (Canterbury Crusaders), C.G. Smith (Wellington Hurricanes), M.A. Nonu (Wellington Hurricanes), A.J.D. Mauger (Canterbury Crusaders), D.W. Carter (Canterbury Crusaders), P.A.T. Weepu (Wellington Hurricanes), B.T. Kelleher (Waikato Chiefs), Q.J. Cowan (Otago Highlanders), T.D. Woodcock. (Auckland Blues), G.M. Somerville (Canterbury Crusaders), C.J. Hayman (Otago Highlanders), S. Taumoepeau (Auckland Blues), C.R. Flynn (Canterbury Crusaders), A.D. Oliver (Otago Highlanders), K.F. Mealamu (Auckland Blues), A.J. Williams (Auckland Blues), C.R. Jack (Canterbury Crusaders), N.M.C. Maxwell (Canterbury Crusaders), R.D. Thorne (Canterbury Crusaders), R.H. McCaw (Canterbury Crusaders), R. So'oialo (Wellington Hurricanes), S.P. Bates (Waikato Chiefs), J. Collins (Wellington Hurricanes), J. Kaino (Auckland Blues), M.R. Holah (Waikato Chiefs), M. Tuiali'i (Canterbury Crusaders).

Captain: J.F. Umaga. Manager: D. Shand. Coach: G. Henry. Assistant Coach: S. Hansen.

Leading points scorer: D.W. Carter – 55 points (11 in Britain & Ireland).
Leading try-scorer: Several scored 2 on tour. J.T. Rokocoko & R.L. Gear scored 2 each in Britain & Ireland.
Most appearances: J.M. Muliaina – 4 games (2 in Britain & Ireland). Others played in 4 games but Muliaina was the only player to start every game.

WALES   2004

Saturday 20 November 2004
Millennium Stadium, Cardiff
Won 26-25

Following a disappointing Tri-Nations tournament in which New Zealand promised much but delivered little, new coach Graham Henry and assistant Steve Hansen began rebuilding with a short European tour. Following a satisfying 59-10 win over Italy, Henry rested tour captain Tana Umaga and gave the captaincy to Richie McCaw for the match with Wales. He awarded debuts to half-back Piri

Weepu and centre Casey Laulala. Wales had recently enjoyed a 66-7 win over Romania but had narrowly lost to Tri-Nations champions South Africa. Henry and Hansen, who had both coached Wales before taking up their current positions, anticipated a difficult encounter in a rematch of the best game of the previous year's World Cup. Injuries affected the Welsh team selection and Gareth Llewellyn was chosen in the second row for his ninety-second international appearance. There was genuine belief that the run of defeats by New Zealand going back to 1963 could at last be halted.

Wales began the match at a furious pace and were soon on the attack. After ten minutes Stephen Jones kicked a penalty before Daniel Carter equalised with a penalty of his own. Then Colin Charvis turned over New Zealand ball in midfield and Wales launched a quick counter-attack. Jones deftly kicked ahead for Tom Shanklin

WALES	NEW ZEALAND
G. Thomas (Toulouse, Capt.)	J.M. Muliaina
T.G.L. Shanklin (Cardiff Blues)	D.C. Howlett
S.T. Parker (Ospreys)	C.D.E. Laulala
G.L. Henson (Ospreys)	J.T. Rokocoko
S.M. Williams (Ospreys)	A.J.D. Mauger
S.M. Jones (Clermont Auvergne)	D.W. Carter
D.J. Peel (Llanelli Scarlets)	P.A.T. Weepu
Forwards:	Forwards:
G.D. Jenkins (Cardiff Blues)	T.D. Woodcock.
M. Davies (Ospreys)	K.F. Mealamu
A.R. Jones (Ospreys)	G.M. Somerville
B.J. Cockbain (Ospreys)	C.R. Jack
G.O. Llewellyn (Narbonne)	A.J. Williams
D.R. Jones (Llanelli Scarlets)	R. So'oialo
C.L. Charvis (Newcastle)	R.H. McCaw (Capt.)
M.J. Owen (Gwent Dragons)	M. Tuiali'i
Replacements:	Replacements:
S. Jones (Gwent Dragons) for Davies,	C.J. Hayman for Woodcock,
D.J. Jones (Ospreys) for Jenkins (later	B.T. Kelleher for Weepu,
Jenkins for A. Jones), R.P. Jones (Ospreys)	M.A. Nonu for Mauger
for Llewellyn, M.E. Williams (Cardiff Blues)	
for Charvis, G.J. Cooper (Gwent Dragons) for Peel	

Scorers:
Wales: Tries: Shanklin, Davies. PG: Jones (3), Henson (2).
New Zealand: Tries: Rokocoko (2), Muliaina. Con: Carter. PGs: Carter (3).

Referee: A.J. Spreadbury (England).
Attendance: 74,500.

to collect the ball and beat Laulala and Mils Muliaina for the opening try. Shanklin, whose father Jim had played in the 1972 encounter between the sides, had scored 4 tries against Romania the previous weekend. Jones missed the conversion and a straightforward penalty before extending the Welsh lead with a successful goal. Then New Zealand scored their first try. Excellent support and passing at pace down the blind side saw Joe Rokocoko score. Carter converted and kicked a penalty to put New Zealand ahead before Jones restored the Welsh lead with another penalty just before half-time. At 14-13, Wales deserved their lead.

That lead was extended three minutes after the restart. Hooker Mefin Davies drove over after the Welsh pack had pressurised the All Blacks on their line. Jones missed the conversion but New Zealand struck back shortly after with a try from Muliaina after good play from McCaw. Then came the try of the match. New Zealand stole Welsh ball on their own 22 and Doug Howlett moved play to the blind side. The move swept upfield to Rokocoko who sped away then dummied to kick over Shanklin. It left the Cardiff Blues player flat-footed and the Auckland Blues wing raced past him for a glorious

try. Carter failed to convert either try but the All Blacks were now back in the lead. Replacement Ma'a Nonu was then yellow-carded for a dangerous tackle on Gavin Henson. Henson took a long-range penalty that hit a post, but then kicked a penalty before the All Blacks became dominant. Wales defended heroically but Carter kicked another goal. With time running out Wales pressed and were awarded a penalty. Believing the stadium clock was recording elapsed time, as it had previously, rather than match time Henson successfully kicked the goal. Had they realised time was short Wales may have gone for position. Four minutes later the game was over and a terrific encounter had, again, been won by New Zealand. Although there was disappointment in defeat for Wales, they went on to win the Grand Slam in the 2005 Six Nations championship.

Saturday 4 December 2004
Twickenham, London
Won 47-19

New Zealand selected a second-string side for the last match of the tour. Mauger was chosen as captain and former skipper Thorne was selected in the second row. Flynn dropped out and Mealamu was promoted to play. Kaino made his All Blacks' debut. Despite criticism from British supporters, the Barbarians side took the field without a single UK-based player in the squad. Their side was coached by Australian Bob Dwyer and captained by Canterbury half-back Justin Marshall, a player rested for the All Blacks' tour.

The Barbarians kicked-off poorly and New Zealand immediately attacked. After four minutes Holah crashed over from a lineout despite a fine tackle by Matt Giteau, Mauger converted. The ball was moved from end to end by both sides who spurned opportunities to kick penalties. Then the Barbarians drove from a lineout, and the New Zealander Xavier Rush

BARBARIANS	NEW ZEALAND
M.S. Rogers (NSW & Australia)	J.M. Muliaina
C.E. Latham (Queensland & Australia)	D.C. Howlett
L. Tuqiri (NSW & Australia)	C.D.E. Laulala
M. Turinui (NSW & Australia)	R.L. Gear
S. Bobo (Wellington & Fiji)	M.A. Nonu
M.J. Giteau (ACT & Australia)	A.J.D. Mauger (Capt.)
J.W. Marshall	O.J. Cowan
(Canterbury & New Zealand, Capt.)	
Forwards:	Forwards:
W.K. Young (ACT & Australia)	G.M. Somerville
B.J. Cannon (NSW & Australia)	K.F. Mealamu
S.J. Rautenbach	S. Taumoepeau
(Western Province & South Africa)	
D.J. Vickerman (ACT & Australia)	R.D. Thorne
P.A. Van Den Bergh (Natal & South Africa)	A.J. Williams
S.W.P. Burger	J. Kaino
(Western Province & South Africa)	
P.R. Waugh (NSW & Australia)	M.R. Holah
X.J. Rush (Auckland & New Zealand)	S.P. Bates
Replacements:	Replacements:
A. Lo Cicero (L'Aquila & Italy) for Young,	A.D. Oliver for Mealamu,
G. Botha (Blue Bulls) for Cannon,	C.J. Hayman for Taumoepeau,
A.J. Venter (Natal & South Africa) for	C.R. Jack for Thorne,
Van Den Bergh, R. Samo (ACT & Australia)	M. Tuiali'i for Bates,
for Waugh, W.W. Greef (Western Province	P.A.T. Weepu for Cowan
& South Africa) for S. Bobo, G. Bobo	
(Lions & South Africa) for Turinui, A. Tuilevo	
(Otago & Fiji) for Latham	

Scorers:
Barbarians: Tries: Rush, Lo Cicero, Van Den Bergh. Cons: Giteau, Rogers.
New Zealand: Tries: Gear (2), Holah, Kaino, Laulala, Nonu, Weepu.
Cons: Mauger (5), Weepu.

Referee: D.A. Turner (South Africa).
Attendance: 55,000.

was driven over for a try. Giteau converted to tie the scores. Rico Gear scored a try shortly after the restart. After a scrappy period in which Kaino was prominent in defence, the wing-forward, was tackled just short of the line. On the stroke of half-time Ma'a Nonu cut between two Barbarians forwards to score a try that Mauger converted to end the first half with New Zealand ahead 19-7.

Two minutes after half-time Gear scored his second try after good play by Mils Muliaina. Gear narrowly failed to score again shortly afterwards. Barbarians replacement Andrea Lo Cicero, drove through a maul in the New Zealand 22 to score a try. The next try came from Casey Laulala, who scored from a move begun from turned-over ball following a late and dangerously high tackle by Cowan on Rogers, which everybody except the officials saw. Mauger's conversion was accompanied by a loud chorus of booing. Midway through the second half, Kaino scored a spectacular try with a thirty-metre run to the line. Then an interception by Albert Van Den Bergh deep in Barbarians territory saw the Natal Sharks lock sprint two-thirds of the field to score. Rogers converted and in the dying minutes Weepu scored a try from a ruck close to the line. He successfully converted and at the final whistle New Zealand had won 47-19.

THE CENTENARY TOUR
NEW ZEALAND TO BRITAIN & IRELAND

THE MATCHES

WALES	5 November 2005	Cardiff	Won 41-3
IRELAND	12 November 2005	Dublin	Won 45-7
ENGLAND	19 November 2005	Twickenham	Won 23-19
SCOTLAND	26 November 2005	Murrayfield	Won 29-10

Played 4, won 4, drew 0, lost 0. Scored: 138 points, Conceded: 39.

The New Zealand Tour Party:
L.R. MacDonald (Crusaders), J.M. Muliaina (Blues), I. Toeava (Blues), R.L. Gear (Crusaders), D.C. Howlett (Blues), J.T. Rokocoko (Blues), S.W. Sivivatu (Chiefs), M.A. Nonu (Hurricanes), C.G. Smith (Hurricanes), J.F. Umaga (Hurricanes), A.J.D. Mauger (Crusaders), D.W. Carter (Crusaders), N.J. Evans (Highlanders), Q.J. Cowan (Highlanders), B.T. Kelleher (Chiefs), P.A.T. Weepu (Hurricanes), I.F. Afoa (Blues), C.J. Hayman (Highlanders), S. Taumoepeau (Blues), N.S. Tialata (Hurricanes), T.D. Woodcock (Blues), A.K. Hore (Hurricanes), K.F. Mealamu (Blues), A.D. Oliver (Highlanders), J.J. Eaton (Taranaki), C.R. Jack (Crusaders), A.J. Williams (Blues), J.A.C. Ryan (Highlanders), J. Collins (Hurricanes), S. Lauaki (Chiefs), A.J. MacDonald (Blues), M.C. Masoe (Hurricanes), R.H. McCaw (Crusaders), R. So'oialo (Hurricanes), M.M. Tuiali'i (Crusaders).

Captain: J.F. Umaga, Manager: D. Shand. Coach: G. Henry. Assistant Coaches: S. Hansen, W.R. Smith.

Leading points scorer: D.W. Carter – 39 points.
Leading try scorer: R.L. Gear – 5 tries.
Most appearances: L.R. MacDonald – 4 games.

WALES   2005

Saturday 5 November 2005
Millennium Stadium, Cardiff
Won 41-3

New Zealand hosted the British Lions during the summer and cruised to a comfortable 3-0 series whitewash. They then won the Tri-Nations tournament before embarking on a four-match tour of Britain and Ireland. It was the first tour encompassing these nations undertaken by the All Blacks since the 'Grand Slam' tour of 1978. The tour marked the centenary of Dave Gallaher's 'Original' All Blacks. Wales had won their first Six Nations Grand Slam the previous season, their first International Championship clean-sweep since 1978, and had enjoyed a successful tour of North America. However, several of their key players from the previous season's success were recovering from injuries.

Led by Gareth Thomas, who had captained the Lions in the last two internationals, Wales chose combative scrum-half Mike Phillips ahead of Lions scrum-half Gareth Cooper. New Zealand chose a strong side led by Umaga, and awarded debuts to forwards Tialata and Chris Masoe, whose elder brother Maselino is the World middleweight boxing champion. The match was played with the Millennium Stadium roof closed.

Hopes were high that Wales would triumph at last over New Zealand, but they were dashed by a display of power and pace from the tourists. Although under pressure, Wales initially held their own before Daniel Carter kicked two penalties to Stephen Jones's

WALES	NEW ZEALAND
G. Thomas (Toulouse, Capt.)	J.M. Muliaina
K.A. Morgan (Newport-Gwent Dragons)	R.L. Gear
M. Taylor (Sale)	C.G. Smith
C. Sweeney (Newport-Gwent Dragons)	J.T. Rokocoko
S.M. Williams (Ospreys)	J.F. Umaga (Capt.)
S.M. Jones (Clermont Auvergne)	D.W. Carter
M. Phillips (Cardiff Blues)	B.T. Kelleher
D.J. Jones (Ospreys)	N.S. Tialata
M. Davies (Gloucester)	A.D. Oliver
A.R. Jones (Ospreys)	C.J. Hayman
B.J. Cockbain (Ospreys)	C.R. Jack
R.A. Sidoli (Cardiff Blues)	J.A.C. Ryan
J. Thomas (Ospreys)	J. Collins
C.L. Charvis (Newcastle)	M.C. Masoe
M.J. Owen (Newport-Gwent Dragons)	R. So'oialo
Replacements:	Replacements:
T.R. Thomas (Cardiff Blues) for Davies,	A.K. Hore (for Oliver),
C.L. Horsman (Worcester) for A Jones,	T.D. Woodcock (for Tialata),
L.C. Charteris (Newport-Gwent Dragons)	A.J. Macdonald (for Ryan),
for Cockbain, R. Sowden-Taylor	R.H. McCaw (for Masoe),
(Cardiff Blues) for Charvis, G.J. Cooper	Q.J. Cowan (for Kelleher),
(Newport-Gwent Dragons) for Phillips,	M.A. Nonu (for Gear),
N.J. Robinson (Cardiff Blues) for Sweeney,	L.R. MacDonald (for Muliaina)
L. Byrne (Llanelli Scarlets) for G Thomas	

Scorers:
Wales: PG: S. Jones.
New Zealand: Tries: Gear (3), Carter (2). Cons: Carter (5). PGs: Carter (2)

Referee: C.R. White (RFU)
Attendance: 74,402

one. Close to half an hour had gone before New Zealand scored the first try, Rico Gear crossing from a lineout in the corner. Carter converted and New Zealand turned around 13-3 ahead.

The second half was all New Zealand. Three minutes after the restart, Gear scored his second try and then his third six minutes later. Carter converted both, then a fine break saw James Ryan sprint clear. Magnificent defensive work by Thomas prevented a try, but the Welsh captain was injured and replaced by Lee Byrne, who made his debut, as had Worcester prop Chris Horsman five minutes earlier. Angus MacDonald also joined the fray, the Auckland Blues forward making his debut – his father Hamish had been a leading All Black lock in the 1970s. Despite their efforts, Wales rarely threatened and two further tries, both from Carter, saw New Zealand comfortable winners. Wales were poor shadows of the side who ran the All Blacks close the previous season, whilst the All Blacks erased memories of their defeat one hundred years earlier.

IRELAND   2005

Saturday 12 November 2005
Lansdowne Road, Dublin
Won 45-7

Ireland had toured Japan during the summer but were forced to play the All Blacks without their inspirational captain Brian O'Driscoll, who was still recovering from his serious shoulder injury sustained on the Lions tour. A strong and experienced Ireland side was captained by Simon Easterby. The All Blacks chose a largely second-string side, led by Richie McCaw, who was regarded by many as the world's leading rugby player. Forwards John Afoa and Jason Eaton made their international debuts for New Zealand. The Lansdowne Road ground was damaged by a fire in the week leading to the game forcing the IRFU to turn away 7,000 disappointed spectators, who were not allowed to take their places for safety reasons.

New Zealand demonstrated their remarkable strength in depth with an impressive demolition of Ireland. The first score came after eleven minutes when Sitiveni Sivivatu was on the end of a great pass from Piri Weepu from a scrum deep in Ireland territory. Nick Evans converted, but failed with his second after a try from Weepu ten minutes later, the half-back ending a fine move involving McCaw and Ma'a Nonu. Evans kicked two penalties shortly afterwards then converted Sivivatu's second try late in the half. 25-0 ahead at half-time, New Zealand had the game won.

In the second period Evans slotted over two quick penalties before Doug Howlett scored the fourth All Black try. Then Nonu was penalised for a heavy tackle on Gordon D'Arcy before he and Howlett had tries disallowed by the video referee. Howlett was not to be denied, however, and raced in for his second try late in the game before Marcus Horan scored a consolation try for the Irish, converted by David Humphreys, close to full time. Ireland had the unusual sight of three players with the surname Best on the bench, brothers Simon and Rory with unrelated namesake Neil, who all took the field in the second half. Ireland were disappointing but New Zealand had played some scintillating rugby with an unfamiliar line-up.

IRELAND	NEW ZEALAND
G.E.A. Murphy (Leicester)	L.R. MacDonald
T. Bowe (Ulster)	D.C. Howlett
G.W. D'Arcy (Leinster)	M.A. Nonu
S.P. Horgan (Leinster)	S.W. Sivivatu
A. Horgan (Munster)	A.J.D. Mauger
R.J.R. O'Gara (Munster)	N.J. Evans
P.A. Stringer (Munster)	P.A.T. Weepu
M.J. Horan (Munster)	T.D. Woodcock
J.S. Byrne (Leinster)	K.F. Mealamu
J.J. Hayes (Munster)	I.F. Afoa
D.F. O'Callaghan (Munster)	J.J. Eaton
M.E. O'Kelly (Leinster)	A.J. Williams
S.H. Easterby (Llanelli Scarlets, Capt.)	S. Lauak
J. O'Connor (Wasps)	R.H. McCaw (Capt.)
D. Leamy (Munster)	M.M. Tuiali'i
Replacements:	Replacements:
R. Best (Ulster) for Byrne,	A.K. Hore for Mealamu,
S.J. Best (Ulster) for Hayes,	S. Taumoepeau
M.T. McCullough (Ulster) for O'Kelly,	for Woodcock,
N. Best (Ulster) for Easterby,	R. So'oialo for McCaw,
D.G. Humphreys (Ulster) for O'Gara,	Q.J. Cowan for Weepu
G.T. Dempsey (Leinster) for Murphy	

Scorers:
Ireland: Try: Horan. Con: Humphreys.
New Zealand: Tries: Howlett (2), Sivivatu (2), Weepu.
Cons: Evans (4). PGs: Evans (4)

Referee: J.I. Kaplan (SARFU)
Attendance: 42,000

ENGLAND   2005

Saturday 19 November 2005
Twickenham, London
Won 23-19

Richie McCaw, who had sustained a head injury against Ireland, ruled himself out of the New Zealand side on the eve of the game, his place going to Chris Masoe. Doug Howlett and Sitiveni Sivivatu held off the strong challenge of Rico Gear and Joe Rokocoko to claim the wing positions. England retained the side which had defeated Australia 26-16 on the previous Saturday.

This was a thrilling encounter, in which the power of English forwards just failed to overcome the stubborn defence of the All Blacks. The visitors were very much on the back foot in the closing stages of the match, but a lack of creativity in the English backs proved crucial, and New Zealand survived to keep their grand slam dreams alive.

Martin Corry gave the home side a dream start after just three minutes, driving over from a lineout for the opening score of the afternoon. Charlie Hodgson converted the try, but New Zealand hit back after seventeen minutes when Tana Umaga touched down, following a break by the ever-impressive Dan Carter. Carter ghosted past Corry to set up the try, but there was a suspicion that his pass to Umaga was forward. Hodgson restored England's lead two minutes later with a penalty, but a brace of penalties from Carter, and a miss from Hodgson, gave the All Blacks a 13-10 advantage at half-time.

Carter missed a similar penalty at the start of the second half, but a further break from the number ten led to New Zealand's second try, scored on forty-five minutes by Keven Mealamu. Carter converted this score to stretch New Zealand's lead to 20-10. Hodgson and Carter then exchanged penalties, but Carter's was his side's final score of the afternoon. As the England pack gained control and put increased pressure on the visitors, first Tony Woodcock (pulling down a maul), then Neemia Tialata (killing the ball) and finally Chris Masoe (handling on the ground) were sent to the sin-bin. The All Blacks played the last twenty-three minutes with fourteen men, and were briefly down to thirteen, but apart from two more Hodgson penalties, England were unable to benefit from this advantage.

Andy Robinson, the England coach, felt that the game was 'an opportunity missed' for his side, while his opposite number, Graham Henry, rightly commended the high quality of rugby on show in this memorable game.

ENGLAND	NEW ZEALAND
O.J. Lewsey (Wasps)	J.M. Muliaina
M.J. Cueto (Sale)	D.C. Howlett
J.D. Noon (Newcastle)	J.F. Umaga (Capt.)
M.J. Tindall (Gloucester)	S.W. Sivivatu
B.C. Cohen (Northampton)	A.J.D. Mauger
C.C. Hodgson (Sale)	D.W. Carter
M.J.S. Dawson (Wasps)	B.T. Kelleher
A.J. Sheridan (Sale)	T.D. Woodcock
S.G. Thompson (Northampton)	K.F. Mealamu
P.J. Vickery (Gloucester)	C.J. Hayman
S.W. Borthwick (Bath)	C.R. Jack
D.J. Grewcock (Bath)	A.J. Williams
P.H. Sanderson (Worcester)	J. Collins
L.W. Moody (Leicester)	M.C. Masoe
M.E. Corry (Leicester, Capt.)	R. So'oialo
Replacement:	Replacements:
M. Stevens (Bath) for Sheridan	N.S. Tialata for Masoe,
	J.J. Eaton for Williams,
	M.M. Tuiali'i for So'oialo,
	P.A.T. Weepu for Kelleher,
	J.T. Rokocoko for Sivivatu,
	L.R. MacDonald for Mauger

Scorers:
England: Try: Corry. Con: Hodgson. PGs: Hodgson (4)
New Zealand: Tries: Umaga, Muliaina.
Cons: Carter (2). PGs: Carter (3)

Referee: D.A. Lewis (IRFU)
Attendance: 62,000

SCOTLAND 2005

Saturday 16 November 2005
Murrayfield, Edinburgh
Won 29-10

New Zealand made thirteen changes from the side that had defeated England with only captain Tana Umaga and Chris Jack retaining their places. At full-back, the Samoan-born Isaia Toeava was awarded his first cap, despite having played only one match in New Zealand's National Provincial Championship. Scotland made four changes from the side that had edged past Samoa 18-11 the previous weekend. In the twenty-fifth meeting between the two sides, New Zealand were firm favourites to retain their unbeaten record against the Scots.

It was a thrilling match. New Zealand thoroughly deserved their victory and their second Grand Slam in the British Isles. To their credit, the Scots competed well and made New Zealand fight all the way, but they could not match the superior speed, continuity and support play of the visitors and made too many basic errors.

Played in drizzling rain, the match had an explosive start with both New Zealand wingers testing the defence. However, Scotland opened the scoring with a penalty goal by Chris Paterson after five minutes. The visitors hit back immediately. From a scrum, Weepu made a simple ahead for Gear to score, although there were suspicions that he had not grounded the ball properly. Scotland were unlucky not to be awarded a try soon afterwards when Lawson was driven over the line. A quick attack by New Zealand created an overlap for Evans to score under the posts. Evans converted and later added a penalty goal. Shortly before half-time, New Zealand scored their third try. Evans kicked across the field to Toeava, who popped the wet ball inside to Ryan. The lock juggled with it before flicking it back to Lauaki, who stretched for the line. Evans converted to put his side 22-3 ahead at the interval.

SCOTLAND	NEW ZEALAND
H.F.G. Southwell (Edinburgh Gnrs)	I. Toeava
C.D. Paterson (Edinburgh Gnrs)	R. Gear
M. Di Rollo (Edinburgh Gnrs)	C. Smith
A.R. Henderson (Glasgow Warriors)	T. Umaga (Capt.)
S.F. Lamont (Northampton Saints)	J. Rokocoko
D.A. Parks (Glasgow Warriors)	N. Evans
C.P. Cusiter (Border Reivers)	P. Weepu
G. Kerr (Leeds Tykes)	S. Taumoepeau
S. Lawson (Glasgow Warriors)	A. Oliver
B.A.F. Douglas (Border Reivers)	J. Afoa
C.P. Hamilton (Glasgow Warriors)	C. Jack
S. Murray (Edinburgh Gnrs)	J. Ryan
J.P.R. White (Sale Sharks) Capt.	A. MacDonald
A. Hogg (Edinburgh Gnrs)	S. Lauaki
S.M. Taylor (Edinburgh Gnrs)	R. McCaw
Replacements:	Replacements:
D.W.H. Hall (Edinburgh Gnrs) for Lawson,	A. Hore for Oliver,
C.J. Smith (Edinburgh Gnrs) for Douglas,	N. Tialata for Taumoepeau,
A.D. Kellock (Edinburgh Gnrs) for Hamilton,	J. Eaton for Ryan,
K.D.R. Brown (Border Reivers) for Hogg,	M. Tuiali'i for McCaw;
M.R.L. Blair (Edinburgh Gnrs) for Cusiter,	J. Cowan for Weepu,
P.J. Godman (Edinburgh Gnrs) for Parks,	L. MacDonald for Evans,
S. Webster (Edinburgh Gnrs) for Di Rollo	M. Nonu for Smith

Scorers:
Scotland: Try: Webster, Con: Paterson, PG: Paterson.
New Zealand: Tries: Gear, Evans, Lauaki, Gear, Cons: Evans (2) MacDonald, PG: Evans

Referee: N Whitehouse (Wales)
Attendance: 47,678

A big score looked likely, but the floodgates failed to open. Cheered on by a vociferous crowd, the Scots raised their game and dominated territorially. On several occasions, they laid siege to the New Zealand line, but could not penetrate the Black wall. Sean Lamont made a dramatic 60-metre run from his own 22, but opted to look for support when he should have kept running. On the sixty-eighth minute, the New Zealanders made a typical breakout and great support play created a try for Gear. Evans' replacement Leon MacDonald converted to go 29-3 and seal the match. In the final minute, the Scots scored a good consolation try. From a lineout, Blair passed to Godman, who chipped through for Webster to race on and score. Paterson converted to end the scoring. The New Zealanders were delighted at their achievement, which confirmed their status at the pinnacle of world rugby.

THE RUGBY WORLD CUP

There have been two World Cup tournaments held in Britain and Ireland. New Zealand have competed in both but lost in the semi-finals.

1991   England   3 October at Twickenham, London   Won 18-12

New Zealand: T.J. Wright, J.J. Kirwan, C.R. Innes, J.K.R. Timu, B.J. McCahill, G.J. Fox, G.T.M. Bachop; S.C. McDowell, S.B.T. Fitzpatrick, R.W. Loe, I.D. Jones, G.W. Whetton (Capt.), A.J. Whetton, M.N. Jones, Z.V. Brooke. Replacement: A.T. Earl for Brooke.
England: J.M. Webb, R. Underwood, W.D.C. Carling (Capt.), J.C. Guscott, C. Oti, C.R. Andrew, R.J. Hill; J. Leonard, B.C. Moore, J.A. Probyn, P.J. Ackford, W.A. Dooley, M.C. Teague, P.J. Winterbottom, D. Richards.

Scorers: New Zealand: Try: M. Jones. Cons: Fox. PGs: Fox (4). England: PGs: Webb (3). DG: Andrew.
Referee: J.M. Fleming (Scotland).

1991   USA   8 October at Kingsholm, Gloucester   Won 46-6

New Zealand: T.J. Wright, J.K.R. Timu, C.R. Innes, V.L. Tuigamala, B.J. McCahill, J.P. Preston, G.T.M. Bachop; S.C. McDowell, S.B.T. Fitzpatrick, G.H. Purvis, I.D. Jones, G.W. Whetton (Capt.), A.J. Whetton, M.N. Jones, A.T. Earl.
USA: P. Sheehy, G.M. Hein, M.A. Williams, J.R. Burke, EA Whitaker, C.P. O'Brien, M.D. Pidnock; C. Lippert, P.W. Johnston, N. Mottram, C.E. Tunnacliffe, K.R. Swords, M.H. Sawicki, S. Lipman, A.M. Ridnell. Replacement: L. Manga for Lippert.

Scorers: New Zealand: Tries: Wright (3), Earl, Innes, Purvis, Timu, Tuigamala. Cons: Preston (4). PGs: Preston (2).
USA: PGs: Williams (2).
Referee: E.J. Sklar (Argentina).

1991   Italy   13 October at Welford Road, Leicester   Won 31-21

New Zealand: T.J. Wright, J.J. Kirwan, C.R. Innes, V.L. Tuigamala, W.K. Little, G.J. Fox, J.A. Hewett; S.C. McDowell, S.B.T. Fitzpatrick, R.W. Loe, I.D. Jones, G.W. Whetton (Capt.), A.J. Whetton, M.P. Carter, Z.V. Brooke. Replacement: S. Philpott for Wright.
Italy: P. Vaccari, E. Venturi, F. Gaetaniello, D. Dominguez, M. Cuttitta, M. Bonomi, I. Francescato; F. Properzi Curti, C. Pivetta (Capt.), M. Cuttitta, G. Croci, R. Favaro, M. Giovanelli, A. Bottachiari, C. Checchinato. Replacement: G. Grespan for Properzi.
Scorers: New Zealand: Tries: Brooke, Hewett, Innes, Tuigamala. Cons: Fox (3). PGs: Fox (3). Italy: Tries: Bonomi, M. Cuttitta. Cons: Dominguez (2). PGs: Dominguez (3).
Referee: K.V.J. Fitzgerald (Australia).

Quarter-Final. Having qualified as pool winners, New Zealand then defeated Canada 29-13 on 20 October at the Stade Du Nord in Lille, France.

1991   Semi-Final   Australia   27 October at Lansdowne Road, Dublin   Lost 16-6

New Zealand: K.J. Crowley, J.J. Kirwan, C.R. Innes, J.K.R. Timu, B.J. McCahill, G.J. Fox, G.T.M. Bachop; S.C. McDowell, S.B.T. Fitzpatrick, R.W. Loe, I.D. Jones, G.W. Whetton (Capt.), A.J. Whetton, M.P. Carter, Z.V. Brooke.
Australia: M.C. Roebuck, R.H. Egerton, J.S. Little, T.J. Horan, D.I. Campese, M.P. Lynagh, N.C. Farr-Jones (Capt.); A.J. Daly, P.N. Kearns, E.J.A. McKenzie, R.J. McCall, J.A. Eales, S.P. Poidevin, V. Ofahengaue, T. Coker.

Scorers: New Zealand: PGs: Fox (2). Australia: Tries: Campese, Horan. Con: Lynagh. PGs: Lynagh (2).
Referee: J.M. Fleming (Scotland).

1991   Third-Fourth-Place Play-Off   Scotland   30 October at Cardiff Arms Park   Won 13-6

New Zealand: T.J. Wright, J.J. Kirwan, C.R. Innes, V.L. Tuigamala, W.K. Little, J.P. Preston, G.T.M. Bachop; S.C. McDowell, S.B.T. Fitzpatrick, R.W. Loe, I.D. Jones, G.W. Whetton (Capt.), A.T. Earl, M.N. Jones, Z.V. Brooke. Replacements: S. Philpott for Tuigamala.
Scotland: A.G. Hastings, A.G. Stanger, S. Hastings, S.R.P. Lineen, I. Tukalo, C.M. Chalmers, G. Armstrong; D.M.B. Sole (Capt.), J. Allan, A.P. Burnell, G.W. Weir, C.A. Gray, J. Jeffrey, F.C. Calder, D.B. White. Replacements: P.W. Dods for Stanger.

Scorers: New Zealand: Try: Little. PGs: Preston (3). Scotland: PGs: G. Hastings (2).
Referee: S.R. Hilditch (Ireland).

1999   Tonga   3 October at Ashton Gate, Bristol   Won 45-9

New Zealand: J.W. Wilson, J.F. Umaga, C.M. Cullen, J.T. Lomu, A. Ieremia, A.P. Mehrtens, J.W. Marshall; C.H. Hoeft, A.D. Oliver, K.J. Meeuws, N.M.C. Maxwell, R.M. Brooke, R.D. Thorne, J.A. Kronfeld, T.C. Randell (Capt.). Replacements: C.W. Dowd (for Meeuws), R.K. Willis (for Willis), B.T. Kelleher (for Marshall), D.P.E. Gibson (for Ieremia).
Tonga: S. Taumalolo, S. Taupeaafe, T. Tiueti, F. Tatafu, T. Taufahema, E. Vunipola (Capt.), S. Martens; T. Fainga'anuku, F. Vunipola, T. Taumoepeau, I. Fatani, B. Kivalu, V. Fakatau, S. Koloi, V. Toloke. Replacements: N Ta'ufe'ou for Fainga'anuku, D. Edwards for Koloi, F. Mafi for Kivalu, M. Te Pou for Toloke, L. Maka for Martens, I. Tapueluelu for Tiueti, S.M. Tu'ipulotu for Tapueluelu.

Scorers: New Zealand: Tries: Lomu (2), Kelleher, Kronfeld, Maxwell. Cons: Mehrtens (4). PGs: Mehrtens (4). Tonga: PGs: Taumalolo (3).
Referee: W.D. Bevan (Wales).

1999   England   9 October at Twickenham, London   Won 30-16

New Zealand: J.W. Wilson, J.F. Umaga, C.M. Cullen, J.T. Lomu, A. Ieremia, A.P. Mehrtens, J.W. Marshall; C.H. Hoeft, A.D. Oliver, C.W. Dowd, N.M.C. Maxwell, R.M. Brooke, R.D. Thorne, J.A. Kronfeld, T.C. Randell (Capt.). Replacements: G.E. Feek (temp. sub. for Dowd), R.K. Willis (for Brooke), B.T. Kelleher (for Marshall), T.E. Brown (for Mehrtens), D.P.E. Gibson (for Ieremia).
England: M.B. Perry, D.D. Luger, J.C. Guscott, P.R. de Glanville, A.S. Healey, J.P. Wilkinson, M.J.S. Dawson; J. Leonard, R. Cockerill, P.J. Vickery, M.O. Johnson (Capt.), D.J. Grewcock, N.A. Back, R.A. Hill, L.B.N. Dallaglio. Replacements: P.B.T. Greening (for Cockerill), D.J. Garforth (Vickery), T.A.K. Rodber (for Grewcock), M.J. Corry (temp. sub. for Hill and Back), P.J. Grayson (for Wilkinson).

Scorers: New Zealand: Tries: Kelleher, Lomu, Wilson. Cons: Mehrtens (3). PGs: Mehrtens (3). England: Try: de Glanville. Con: Wilkinson. PGs: Wilkinson (3).
Referee: P.L. Marshall (Australia).

1999   Italy   14 October at McAlpine Stadium, Huddersfield   Won 101-3

New Zealand: J.W. Wilson, G.M. Osborne, P.F. Alatini, J.T. Lomu, D.P.E. Gibson, T.E. Brown, B.T. Kelleher; G.E. Feek, M.G. Hammett, C.W. Dowd, I.D. Jones, R.K. Willis, D.G. Mika, A.F. Blowers, T.C. Randell (Capt.). Replacements: K.J. Meeuws (for Feek), R.M. Brooke (for Willis), S.M. Robertson (for Blowers), R.J.L. Duggan (for Kelleher), C.M. Cullen (for Randell).
Italy: M.J. Pini, N. Zisti, C. Stoica, S. Ceppolino, P. Vaccari, D. Dominguez, A. Troncon; A. Moreno, A. Moretti, A. Castellani, C. Checchinato, M. Giacheri, S. Saviozzi, M. Giovanelli (Capt.), C. Caione. Replacements: A. Moscardi (for Moretti), F. Properzi Curti (for Castellani), V. Cristofoletto (for Checchinato), O. Orancio (Caione), N. Mazzucato (temp. sub. for Vaccari)

Scorers: New Zealand: Tries: Wilson (3), Lomu (2), Osborne (2), Brown, Cullen, Gibson, Hammett, Mika, Randell, Robertson. Cons: Brown (11). PGs: Brown (3). Italy: PGs: Dominguez.
Referee: J.M. Fleming (Scotland).

1999   Quarter-Final   Scotland   24 October at Murrayfield, Edinburgh   Won 30-18

New Zealand: J.W. Wilson, J.F. Umaga, C.M. Cullen, J.T. Lomu, A. Ieremia, A.P. Mehrtens, J.W. Marshall; C.W. Dowd, A.D. Oliver, C.H. Hoeft, N.M.C. Maxwell, R.M. Brooke, R.D. Thorne, J.A. Kronfeld, T.C. Randell (Capt.). Replacements: M.G. Hammett (for Oliver), K.J. Meeuws (for Hoeft), I.D. Jones (for Maxwell), T.E. Brown (for Mehrtens), D.P.E. Gibson (for Umaga).
Scotland: G.H. Metcalfe, K.M. Logan, A.V. Tait, M.J.M. Mayer, C.A. Murray, G.P.J. Townsend, G. Armstrong (Capt.); T.J. Smith, G.C. Bulloch, A.P. Burnell, G.W. Weir, S. Murray, M.D. Leslie, A.C. Poutney, G.L. Simpson. Replacements: R. Russell (for Bulloch), G. Graham (for Burnell), S.B. Grimes (for Weir).

Scorers: New Zealand: Tries: Umaga (2), Wilson, Lomu. Cons: Mehrtens (2). PGs: Mehrtens (2). Scotland: Tries: Murray, Poutney. Con: Logan. PG: Logan. DG: Townsend.
Referee: E.F. Morrison (England).

1999   Semi-Final   France   31 October at Twickenham, London| Lost 43-31

New Zealand: J.W. Wilson, J.F. Umaga, C.M. Cullen, J.T. Lomu, A. Ieremia, A.P. Mehrtens, B.T. Kelleher; C.W. Dowd, A.D. Oliver, C.H. Hoeft, N.M.C. Maxwell, R.M. Brooke, R.D. Thorne, J.A. Kronfeld, T.C. Randell (Capt.). Replacements: K.J. Meeuws (for Dowd), R.K Willis (for Brooke), J.W. Marshall (for Kelleher), D.P.E. Gibson (for Ieremia).
France: X. Garbajosa, P. Bernat-Salles, R. Dourthe, E. Ntamack, C. Dominici, C. Lamaison, F. Galthie; C. Soulette, R. Ibanez (Capt.), F. Tournaire, F. Pelous, A. Benazzi, M. Lievremont, O. Magne, C. Juillet. Replacements: P. de Villiers (for Soulette), O. Brouzet (for Juillet), A. Costes (for Lievremont), S. Castaignede (for Galthie), S. Glas (for Ntamack), U. Mola (for Dominici).

Scorers: New Zealand: Tries: Lomu (2), Wilson. Cons: Mehrtens (2). PGs: Mehrtens (4). France: Tries: Bernat-Salles, Dominici, Dourthe, C. Lamaison. Cons: Lamaison (4). PGs: Lamaison (3). DGs: Lamaison (2).
Referee: J.M. Fleming (Scotland)

1999   Third-Fourth-Place Play-Off   South Africa   4 November at the Millennium Stadium, Cardiff   Lost 22-18

New Zealand: J.W. Wilson, J.F. Umaga, C.M. Cullen, J.T. Lomu, A. Ieremia, A.P. Mehrtens, J.W. Marshall; C.W. Dowd, M.G. Hammett, K.J. Meeuws, R.K. Willis, N.M.C. Maxwell, R.D. Thorne, J.A. Kronfeld, T.C. Randell (Capt.). Replacements: A.D. Oliver (for Hammett) C.H. Hoeft (for Dowd), D.G. Mika (for Thorne), P.F. Alatini (for Umaga).
South Africa: P.C. Montgomery, B.J. Paulse, R.F. Fleck, P.G. Muller, S.C. Terblanche, H.W. Honiball, J.H. van der Westhuizen (Capt.); J.P. du Randt, A.E. Drotske, I.J. Visagie, M.G. Andrews, K. Otto, A.G. Venter, R.B. Erasmus, A.N. Vos. Replacements: C.leC. Rossouw (for Drotske), A.H. le Roux (for du Randt), P.A. van den Berg (for Andrews), R.J. Kruger (for Vos), W. Swanepoel (temp. sub. for van der Westhuizen).

Scorers: New Zealand: PGs: Mehrtens (6). South Africa: Tries: Paulse. Cons: Honiball. PGs: Honiball (3). DGs: Montgomery (2).
Referee: P.L. Marshall (Australia).

BIBLIOGRAPHY

International Histories
Billot, John, *History of Welsh International Rugby*
Chester, Rod, & McMillan, Neville, *Centenary: 100 Years of All Black Rugby*
Chester, Rod, & McMillan, Neville, *Men in Black*
Chester, Rod, Palenski, Ron, & McMillan, Neville, *The Encyclopedia of New Zealand Rugby*
Davidson, John McI., *International Rugby Union: A Compendium of Scotland's Matches*
Griffiths, John, *The Book of English International Rugby 1871-1982*
Griffiths, John, *British Lions*
Griffiths, John, *The Phoenix Book of International Rugby Records*
Guiney, David, *100 Years of Rugby Football: Ireland v New Zealand*
McLean, Terry, *Great Days in New Zealand Rugby*
Palenski, Ron, *Century in Black*
Parry-Jones, David, *Prince Gwyn: Gwyn Nicholls and the First Golden Era of Welsh Rugby*
Smith, David, & Williams, Gareth, *Fields of Praise*
Thorburn, A.M.C., *The History of Scottish Rugby*
Thorburn, A.M.C., *The Scottish Rugby Union – Official History*
Titley, U.A., & McWhirter, Ross, *Centenary History of the Rugby Football Union*
van Esbeck, Edmund, *One Hundred Years of Irish Rugby*

Tours
Ackford, Paul, *125 Years of the RFU*
Daily Mail, The, Why the All Blacks Triumphed
Dixon, George H., *The Triumphant Tour of the New Zealand Footballers*
Evans, Richard, *Whineray's All Blacks*

Hayhurst, John, *The Fourth All Blacks 1953-54*
Howitt, Bob, & Reason, John, (Eds), *Rugby News Tour Books 1 to 4 (1972-73 Tour)*
Masters, Read, *With the All Blacks in Great Britain, France Canada & Australia 1924-25*
McCarthy, Winston, *All Blacks on Trek Again*
McCarthy, Winston, *Broadcasting with the Kiwis*
McCarthy, Winston, *Round the World with the All Blacks*
McLean, Terry, *All Blacks Come Back*
McLean, Terry, *Bob Stuart's All Blacks*
McLean, Terry, *Mourie's All Blacks*
McLean, Terry, *They Missed the Bus – Kirkpatrick's All Blacks of 1972-73*
McLean, Terry, *Willie Away*
Mulligan, Andrew, *All Blacks Tour 1963-64*
Oliver, C.J., & Tindill, E.W., *The Tour of the All Blacks 1935*
Quinn, Keith, *Grand Slam All Blacks*
Quinn, Keith, *Tour of the Century – the All Blacks in Wales 1980*
Reilly, P., *Guesswork and Gumption*
Reyburn, Wallace, *Mourie's Men*
Reyburn, Wallace, *The Winter Men*
Thomas, J.B.G., *The Avenging All Blacks*
Thomas, J.B.G., *Rugby in Focus*
Thomas, J.B.G., *The Lions on Trek*
Thomas, J.B.G., *The Fifth All-Blacks*
Watkins, L.T., *The All Blacks of Jubilee Year 1935*
Watkins, L.T., *The Triumphant Tour of the All Blacks 1924-25*
Wooller & Owen, *Fifty Years of the All Blacks*

Club/County Histories
Allaby, David, *Wilmslow Centenary 1884-1984*
Alston, Rex, (Ed.), *One Hundred Years of Rugby Football: A*

History of Rosslyn Park Football Club 1879-1979

Auty, T.W.J., *Headingley Football Club Centenary Souvenir Brochure 1878-1978*

Barak, Monty, *A Century of Rugby at Sale*

Barker-Davies, J.R., *Coventry Football Club (RU) 1874-1974*

Barron, Brian, *Oh When the Saints... The Official History of Northampton Football Club*

Batten, Raymond C., *A Torquay Athletic RFC History*

Berkeley Cowell, C., & Watts Moses, E., *Durham County Rugby Union: Sixty Years Records of the County Fifteen 1876-1936*

Bogle, Ken, & Smith, Ron, *The Green Machine: 125 Years of Hawick Rugby*

Bowker, Barry, *North Midlands Rugby 1920-1970*

Bywater, C.L., *Old Merchant Taylors RFC Centenary 1882-1982*

Cogley, Fred, *St Mary's College RFC 1900-2000*

Collard, Bob, Squibbs, Mike, & Watkins, David, *Bridgwater & Albion Centenary Handbook 1875-1975*

Coughlan, Hall & Gale, *Before the Lemons. A History of Bath Football Club RFU 1865-1965*

Cox, Jack, *The Centenary of Wasps Football Club 1867-1967*

Croxford, W.B., *Rugby Union in Lancashire & Cheshire*

Daglish, J.R.A., *Red, Black & Blue: The First 125 years of Liverpool Football Club*

Dargavel, Trevor, *Neath RFC Centenary Year 1871-1971*

Davey, F.A., *The Story of the Devon Rugby Football Union*

Davies, D.E., *Cardiff Rugby Club History & Statistics 1876-1975: 'The Greatest'*

Davis, Jack, *Newport Rugby Football Club 1875-1960*

Davis, Jack, *One Hundred Years of Newport Rugby*

Dunbar, T.F., *A History of Devonport Services Rugby Football Club 1912-1981*

Eggleshaw, Maurice, *New Brighton FC 1875-1975*

Evans, Alan, *Taming the Tourists*

Farmer, David, *The All Whites: The Life and Times of Swansea RFC*

Farmer, Stuart, & Hands, David, *The Tigers Tale: The Official History of Leicester Football Club 1880-1993*

Fox, Dave, & Hoskins, Mark, *Bristol Football Club 100 Greats*

Gaunt, Phillip, (Ed.), *Yorkshire Rugby Union Centenary Year 1869-1969*

Hamilton Fazey, Ian, *Waterloo FC 1882-1982*

Hammond, Dave, *The Club: Life and Times of Blackheath FC*

Hands, David, *Leicester Football Club 1880-1980*

Harley, Andrew, (Ed.), *Gloucester RFC: 125 Glorious Years*

Harris, C.R.G., *The Statistical History of Cardiff RFC 1876-1984*

Harris, Gareth, *Pontypridd RFC: Three Seasons at the House of Pain*

Hayle Rugby Football Club Centenary Magazine 1877-1977

Hoskins, Mark, & Fox, Dave, *Bristol Football Club: 1888-1945*

Hughes, Gareth, *One Hundred Years of Scarlet*

Hughes, Gareth, *The Scarlets: A History of Llanelli Rugby Club*

Hutt, Horace, *Gloucestershire Rugby Football Union Centenary Year Book 1878-1978*

Ingall, David, *Wakefield Rugby Football Club: A Centenary History*

Keen, Dennis, *The Rugby Lions – A History of the Rugby Football Club 1873-1991*

Lancashire County Rugby Football Union Centenary 1881-1981

Lewis, Steve, *Newport Rugby Football Club 1874-1950*

Mace, John, *The History of Royal Air Force Rugby 1919-1999*

Matthews, Brinley E., *The Swansea Story*

McLaren, John, *The History of Army Rugby*

McWhirter, Ross, & Noble, Sir Andrew, *Centenary History of Oxford University Rugby Football Club 1869-1969*

Methven, John, *Midlands First and Latest: A Centenary Year History of Rugby in the Scottish Midlands*

Middlesex County Rugby Football Union 1879-1979

Middleton, Douglas, *Heriots! A Centenary History of George Heriot's School Former Pupils' Rugby Club*

Morris, Frank, *The First 100: History of the London Scottish Football Club*

Mulqueen, Charles, *The Carling Story of Munster Rugby*

Murrish, Peter, *Alright in the end! The St Ives Rugby Football Club 1887-1987*

Northern FC 1876-1976

O'Reilly, Mike, *United Services Portsmouth RFC Centenary Year Handbook 1982-83*

Pelmear, Kenneth, *Rugby in the Duchy (Rugby Heritage) 1884-1956*

Phillips, Dr C.V., *The First Hundred Years of the Camborne School of Mines 1896-1996*

Powell, Terry, *An Illustrated History of Newbridge RFC*

Reed, John, *Surrey Rugby: 100 Years*

Reid, D.A., *Northampton Football Club 'The Saints' 1880-1948*

Reid, Peter, & Jeavons-Fellows, Robert, (Eds), *Hampshire RFU: County History & Centenary Year Programme 1983-84*

Roderick, Alan, *Newport Rugby Greats*

Roy, Neil, (Ed.), *100 Years of the Blues: Bedford RUFC 1886-1986*

Ruddick, Ray, *Pontypool Rugby Football Club*

Rule, P., & Thomas, A., *Camborne Rugby Football Club 1878-1978*

Russell, Arthur, *One Hundred Cherry & White Years – The Gloucester RFC 1873-1973*

Sale Football Club: 125 Years 1861-1996

Salmon, Tom, *The First Hundred Years: The Story of Rugby Football in Cornwall*

Scott, W.J.R., *Durham County Rugby Union 1936-1976*

Shaw, K.T., *Huddersfield Rugby Union Football Club: The First 75 years (1909-1985)*

The Centenary of Moseley Football Club 1873-1973

Thomas, David, *A View from the Garth: One Hundred Years of Taffs Well Rugby*

Wakelam, H.B.T., *Harlequin Story*

Walters, Glyn, *Scarlet Fever*

Warner, Phillip, *The Harlequins: 125 years of Rugby Football*

Watson, Roy, *Plymouth Albion RFC Centenary Season 1876-1976*

Wemyss, A., *The Barbarians: The Official History of the Barbarian Football Club – 1890-1955*

West, Trevor, *150 Years of Trinity Rugby*

Westren, Phil, Thomas, Johnny, & Matthews, Harry, *50 Golden Years: An Illustrated History of the Penzance & Newlyn Rugby Football Club 1945-1995*

Woodward, J., *Cheltenham Rugby Football Club 1889-1989*

Yorkshire Rugby Football Union – In Memoriam 1914-18

Biographies

Auty, Timothy, Jenkins, John, & Pierce, Duncan, *Who's Who of Welsh International Rugby Players*

Boobbyer, Brian, *Like a Cork out of a Bottle*

Clarke, Don, & Booth, Pat, *The Boot: Don Clarke's Story*

Cotton, Fran, *An Autobiography*

Fitzpatrick, Sean, & Johnstone, Duncan, *Turning Point: The Making of a Captain*

Godwin, Terry, *The Complete Who's Who of International Rugby*

Hearn, Danny, *Crash Tackle*

Maule, Raymond, *The Complete Who's Who of England Rugby Union Internationals*

McCarthy, Winston, *Rugby in My Time*

Morgan, Cliff, *The Autobiography: Beyond the Fields of Praise*

Mourie, Graham, & Palenski, Ron, *Graham Mourie: Captain*

Scally, John, *The Good the Bad and the Rugby: The Official Biography of Tony Ward*

Smith, Steve, *The Scrum Half of my Life*

Quinn, Keith, *A Century of Rugby Greats*

Walmsley, David, *Lions of Ireland*

Verdon, Paul, *Born to Lead*

Annuals

Forsyth's Rugby Record

IRB International Rugby Yearbook

John Wisden's Rugby Almanack 1923/24, 1924/25, 1925/26

Playfair Rugby Union Yearbooks

Rothman's Rugby Yearbooks

Rugby Football Annuals

The Rugby Almanack of New Zealand

Welsh Brewer's Rugby Annual for Wales

Others

Barrett, Norman, (Ed.), *The Daily Telegraph Chronicle of Rugby*

Bush, Peter, *Pride, Power and Pain 1987-1991*

Gallaher, David, & Stead, W.J., *The Complete Rugby Footballer*

Grierson, Henry, *The Ramblings of a Rabbit*

Jenkins, John M., *A Rugby Compendium*

Kilburn, J.M., *In Search of Rugby Football*

Miller, Geoff, *The Reed Book of All Black Records 1883-2003*

Moorhouse, Geoffrey, *The Official History of Rugby League: A People's Game*

Pallant, Anne, *A Sporting Century: 1863-1963*

Pelmear, Kenneth, *Rugby Football: An Anthology*

Williams, Gareth, *1905 And All That*